WINDOWS 3
POWER TOOLS

WINDOWS 3 POWER TOOLS

The LeBlond Group

Geoffrey T. LeBlond
William B. LeBlond
Jennifer L. Palonus

BANTAM BOOKS
NEW YORK • TORONTO • LONDON • SYDNEY • AUCKLAND

WINDOWS 3 POWER TOOLS
A Bantam Book / March 1991

Interior design by Nancy Sugihara
Produced by MicroText Productions
Composed by Context Publishing Services, San Diego, CA

All rights reserved.
Copyright © 1991 by The LeBlond Group

No part of this book may be reproduced or transmitted
in any form or by any means, electronic or mechanical,
including photocopying, recording, or by any information
storage and retrieval system, without permission in writing from
the publisher.
For information address: Bantam Books.

Throughout this book, tradenames and trademarks of some
companies and products have been used, and no such uses
are intended to convey endorsements of or other affiliations with the book.

BANTAM AND THE AUTHORS SPECIFICALLY DISCLAIM ALL
OTHER WARRANTIES, EXPRESS OR IMPLIED, INCLUDING
BUT NOT LIMITED TO IMPLIED WARRANTIES OF MERCHANTABILITY
AND FITNESS FOR A PARTICULAR PURPOSE WITH RESPECT
TO THE DISKETTES, THE PROGRAMS THEREIN CONTAINED,
THE PROGRAM LISTINGS IN THE BOOK, AND/OR THE TECHNIQUES
DESCRIBED IN THE BOOK, AND IN NO EVENT SHALL
BANTAM AND OR THE AUTHORS BE LIABLE FOR ANY LOSS OF PROFIT
OR ANY OTHER COMMERCIAL DAMAGE, INCLUDING BUT NOT LIMITED
TO SPECIAL, INCIDENTAL, CONSEQUENTIAL, OR OTHER DAMAGES.

ISBN 0-553-35298-9

Published simultaneously in the United States and Canada

Bantam Books are published by Bantam Books, a division of Bantam Doubleday Dell Publishing Group, Inc. Its trademark, consisting of the words "Bantam Books" and the portrayal of a rooster, is Registered in U.S. Patent and Trademark Office and in other countries. Marca Registrada, Bantam Books, 666 Fifth Avenue, New York, New York 10103.

PRINTED IN THE UNITED STATES OF AMERICA

0   9   8   7   6   5   4   3

*To our uncle, Richard E. LeBlond, Jr.,
the most rugged individualist we know.*
  — *Geoff and Bill*

Preface

In June 1990, Tracy Kidder, author of the 1981 computer cult-classic, "The Soul of a New Machine," was on a local Silicon Valley talk show discussing his most recent book. During that interview, he gave a brief but candid assessment of the current state of computer software. "Too often," he said, "using computer software is like being stuck in line at the Bureau of Motor Vehicles."

It's a long way from a Silicon Valley talk show to a book about Windows 3. But if there is a single line that encapsulates how it felt to use early copies of Microsoft Windows, it would be that line from Tracy Kidder. Too often using Windows was bureaucratically frustrating. For example, navigating between directories to locate a program in the MS-DOS Executive could be excruciating.

Windows 3, on the other hand, is a different story. Its Graphical User Interface (GUI) has been completely redesigned, making it more powerful and easier to use than any previous version of Windows. Nevertheless, it, too, can be frustrating if you don't know your way around it. In addition, the more seasoned computer user may find the Windows 3 GUI somewhat confining, even restrictive.

Windows 3 Power Tools is aimed squarely at those users who want to customize and fine-tune the Windows environment for optimal performance. This book is not about the applications that come with Windows. Rather, it is about Windows itself. You won't learn how to use Write or Paintbrush. Instead, this book deals with issues that affect all your applications—both Windows and non-Windows applications alike. For example, you'll find discussions on memory management, sharing data between applications, using soft fonts, and much more. You'll also find an extensive collection of Windows tips, techniques, and operating secrets, many of which are or only hinted at in the documentation or not mentioned at all.

THE SOFTWARE

In addition to showing you how to improve the performance of Windows, *Windows 3 Power Tools* comes with a collection of software that lets you further customize the operation of Windows. The software features *Oriel for Windows*, a graphics-based batch language that lets you build your own Windows applications. In addition, you'll find three shareware products: *Command Post*, a character-based program that is capable of serving as an alternate shell or substitute for File Manager; *Aporia*, a completely graphical object-oriented shell for Windows; and *Icondraw*, an icon-drawing program that lets you design your own custom icons for use with your applications.

THE BOOK

This book is organized into seventeen chapters and one appendix. The first thirteen chapters deal with different aspects of customizing Windows, and the last four chapters are devoted to showing you how to use the software that is included with *Windows 3 Power Tools*. A brief overview of each chapter follows.

Chapter 1: Introduction

This chapter begins with a brief history of Windows. This historical account focuses on the changes from Windows 1.X to 2.X, and, most importantly, from Windows 2.X to Windows 3. It also provides an extensive overview of the significant features in Windows 3. For example, you'll learn about the various operating modes of Windows and why the program runs in different modes on different machines. You'll also learn how Windows accomplishes its multitasking magic.

Chapter 2: Program Manager Techniques

Most Windows users, including power users, simply accept the default arrangement of icons in Program Manager. However, this chapter shows you how to change the organization of Program Manager to better suit the way you work. You'll learn how to define and customize icons for both DOS and Windows applications. You'll also find valuable techniques for running Windows and DOS applications, and using multiple applications at the same time.

Chapter 3: File Manager Techniques

Many power users have criticized File Manager as slow and unwieldy and have refused to use it. However, once you explore its full potential, you'll find that File Manager brings a new level of power to Windows. This chapter explores not only the design philosophy behind File Manager, but also shows you how you can use File Manager to do such things as create customized directory listings, modify file attributes, create associations to link data files with their programs, and create or change disk or diskette volume labels.

Chapter 4: Of Fonts and Printing

This chapter provides extensive coverage of font and printer-related topics. It shows you how to install and configure multiple printers and how to select a printer for use with the current application. This chapter also discusses such topics as generating .EPS files for printing on PostScript printers, installing and using third-party soft font packages, and using Print Manager to manage your printed output.

Chapter 5: Recorder Techniques

Many experienced Windows users have tried their hand at using the Recorder to create a macro, experienced difficulties, and have concluded that the technology is still not there. This chapter takes an in-depth look at the Recorder and its very real limitations. It also shows the kinds of situations in which the Recorder can be valuable, and shows you some workarounds that you can use to overcome many of Recorder's deficiencies.

Chapter 6: Sharing Data between Applications

This chapter discusses the various data-sharing tools that Windows offers. For example, you'll learn how to use the Windows Clipboard to cut and paste information between DOS and Windows applications, share data between applications running in different modes, and capture Windows screens for display or output. This chapter also explores Dynamic Data Exchange (DDE) and shows you how you can use it to create live links between your applications.

Chapter 7: Windows Memory Management

This chapter discusses Windows memory management in each of the three operating modes. It features discussions of Windows extended and expanded memory managers and shows you how to configure your system to make the best use of available memory and, at the same time, optimize the performance of Windows. This chapter also provides tips on how you can free up memory when you need to and how you can configure your copy of Windows so that you are least likely to encounter the dreaded "Insufficient memory to perform this operation" error message.

Chapter 8: Control Panel

This chapter shows you how to use the various options on the Control Panel to customize the appearance and operation of Windows. For example, you'll learn how you can modify the default color scheme used by Windows, display distinctive wallpaper, configure the operation of your mouse, and adjust the priority of foreground versus background processes in 386 enhanced mode.

Chapter 9: Changing Your Setup

This chapter shows you how to set up new device drivers for the keyboard, the video display, and the mouse. For example, if you have a third-party video display driver, this chapter shows you how to install that driver for use with Windows.

Chapter 10: Using Non-Windows Applications

This chapter provides you with the information you'll need to effectively run your DOS applications in Windows. The primary focus of this chapter is on PIFs (Program Information Files) and how you can use them to make your DOS applications run more reliably and effectively in Windows. This chapter also covers a broad range of other topics including running TSRs with Windows and managing memory needed by DOS applications.

Chapter 11: Improving Windows Performance

Although the entirety of *Windows 3 Power Tools* is devoted to showing you how to optimize the performance of Windows, this chapter deals with topics not discussed elsewhere in the book. For example, you'll find discussions on modifying your CONFIG.SYS and AUTOEXEC.BAT files to provide an optimal environment for Windows, improving the performance of your hard disk by changing its interleave, and boosting Windows' performance by creating a permanent swap file.

Chapter 12: Customizing Your .INI Files

Two major system-configuration files—WIN.INI and SYSTEM.INI—have a direct bearing on the operation of Windows. This chapter discusses how Windows uses these files and how you can modify them to fine-tune the operation of Windows.

Chapter 13: Networking Windows

This chapter shows you how to use Windows with your network. Each of Windows' "hooks" into your network—through File Manager, Control Panel, and Print Manager—are explored in detail. Particular attention is paid to Novell and 3Com networks.

Chapter 14: Oriel for Windows

This chapter covers *Oriel for Windows*, the featured product in the *Windows 3 Power Tools* software. *Oriel for Windows* is a graphics-based batch language for Windows that is composed of 33 Englishlike commands that give you direct access to the Graphics Device Interface (GDI)—the same tool used by Windows programmers. By placing these commands in an ASCII text file, you can create your own custom Windows applications.

Chapter 15: Command Post

Command Post, developed by Wilson Windoware, is a shareware product that is included with *Windows 3 Power Tools*. *Command Post* is a character-based shell for Windows that features an extensive menu system that you can modify through a sophisticated batch language. It is often used as either a replacement for File Manager or as an alternate shell replacing Program Manager. This chapter provides documentation on how to use *Command Post* as well as how to use its batch language to create your own custom menus.

Chapter 16: Aporia

Aporia, developed by NewTools, is also a shareware product that has been included with *Windows 3 Power Tools*. Like *Command Post*, *Aporia* serves as an alternate shell for Windows; it can replace both File Manager and Program Manager. However, unlike *Command Post*, or Windows 3, for that matter, *Aporia* offers a more consistently graphical, object-oriented user interface. This chapter systematically documents how you can create a customized Windows environment with Aporia.

Chapter 17: Icondraw

Icondraw, written by Philip B. Eskelin, Jr., is the last of the shareware products bundled with *Windows 3 Power Tools*. It is, quite literally, an icon drawing program that lets you create custom icons for use with your applications. This chapter documents Icondraw's features and covers the process of defining a custom icon.

Appendix A: The Windows 3 Power Tools Software

This appendix tells you how to install the Windows 3 Power Tools software on your system.

Acknowledgments

There are many people to whom we owe special thanks for helping us to produce this book.

To 3COM corporation for the use of their 3+ Share network, and especially to Karen Fredrickson and Genie Pichulo for their excellent help.

To the many members of the Microsoft Product Support Team who spent untold hours answering our questions, thanks for your gracious efforts. In many ways, this is your book. Special thanks to Tania Van Dam of Microsoft for making sure we got everything we needed.

To Tom Mann for the use of the Novell Network and HP scanner, and to Suzanne Mann for a terrific dinner.

To the many people who let us evaluate their products, including: Gibson Research Corporation for a copy of Spinrite II and to David Kaye for being so helpful in answering our questions; Therese Meyers of Quarterdeck Office Systems for copies of QEMM-386 and Manifest, and to the product support team for helping us to understand how Windows and QEMM-386 work together; Halcyon Software for a copy of DoDOT; Adobe Systems for a copy of the Adobe Type Manager; Bitstream for a copy of Facelift and for their kind assistance; Zsoft for a copy of SoftType; and Asymetrix for ToolBook.

To Laura Mann and Charles J. LeBlond, Jr., for holding down the fort while we were writing this book.

To Paul Yao for a great technical edit and for that long data-transfer session from Seattle during the December snowstorm.

To Steve Davis for letting us use the images of "Irene" in Oriel.

To Dave Edson for an elegant installation program and to Morrie Wilson for his hours of labor in preparing the Windows 3 Power Tools master diskette.

To the many people at Bantam Electronic who helped to produce the book, including: Kenzi Sugihara, whose quiet and thoughtful leadership was apparent throughout the entire project; May K. Chapman for copy editing; Maureen Drexel and Tom Szalkiewicz for production; and last but not least to our editor, Ron Petrusha, for the knowledge and foresight to put this whole project together.

Contents

Preface vii
Acknowledgments xiii

1   An Introduction to Windows 3   1

The Development Of Windows: A Brief History   1

*Windows 1 2   Windows 2 4   Windows/286 and Windows/386 5
Windows 3 6*

Windows 3 Features   7

*Advanced Memory Management 7   Optimizing Performance 13
Multitasking 14   Refinement of the Graphical User Interface 15
Compatibility with DOS Applications 17   Enhancements to
Applications 20   Device Independence 20   Font and Printer
Support 21   Control Panel 23   Data Sharing 25   The Windows Setup
Program 26   More .INI Files 26   Network Support 27   Getting
Help 28*

Summary   30

2 Program Manager Techniques 31

Program Manager's Default Layout 32

Managing Icons 34

Copying Icons 34   Moving Icons 36   Deleting Icons 37   Setting Up New Icons 37   Changing Icon Properties 42   Borrowing Icons 42   Setting Up Icons with File Manager 44   Starting an Application in a Specific Directory 45   Linking Data Files to Icons 47   Launching Applications by Association 48   Arranging Application Icons in Group Windows 49

Managing Group Windows 51

Creating New Group Windows 52   Changing Group Window Properties 52   Deleting Old Group Windows 53   Arranging Group Windows 53

Saving Your Setup 57

Customizing Program Manager 59

The Category Approach 59   The Specific Application Approach 60   The Project Approach 61   Problems with the Smorgasbord Approach 61   Stacking and Tiling Desktop Windows 62   The Minimize on Use Option 64

Power User Techniques 65

Using the File Run Command 65   Running a DOS Application in a Window 66   Techniques for Switching between Applications 66   Keyboard and Mouse Shortcuts 69   Auto-loading Programs on Windows Startup 73   Tips on Using Multiple Applications 74   Using the MS-DOS Executive 79   Tips On Running DOS 79

Summary 82

3 File Manager Techniques 83

File Manager Basics 84

Managing the Directory Tree 86   Managing Directory Windows 86

Changing the Display of Directory Windows 88

Choosing a Sort Order 88   Limiting Directory Window Contents 89   Getting Information about Files and Directories 90   Saving Your Settings 92

Managing Files and Directories   92

Creating Directories 92   Selecting Files 93   Copying Files and Directories 95   Moving Files and Directories 99   Renaming Files and Directories 101   Deleting Files and Directories 101   Searching for Files and Directories 102

Creating Associations   104

Running Applications   105

Dragging with the Mouse 105   Using Commands 106   The Minimize on Use Option 107

Changing File Attributes   107

Printing ASCII Files   108

Using the Options Menu   109

Turning Off Confirmation Messages 109   Displaying File and Directory Names in Lower Case 110   Turning Off the Status Bar 110

Working with Disks   111

Formatting Disks 111   Creating a Boot Disk 111   Copying Data between Disks 111   Changing the Volume Label 112

Summary   112

4   Of Fonts and Printing   115

Installing Printers   116

Configuring a Port 117   Installing the LaserJet II Printer: An Example 119   Activating a Printer 125   Choosing a Default Printer 125   Changing the Default Printer from Within an Application 126   Removing an Installed Printer Driver 126   Printing to a File 127   Installing PostScript Printers 128   Installing a Dot-Matrix Printer 133   When Your Printer Model Isn't Listed 135

Fonts   136

About Windows Screen Fonts 136   Installing Screen Fonts 139   Font Terms 139   Font Technology 141   Installing Printer Fonts 142   Formatting with Installed Fonts 148   Using Fonts with Dot-Matrix Printers 148   Printing ANSI Characters 148   Third-Party Soft-Font Packages 149   TrueType and TrueImage 156

The Role of Print Manager   156

Viewing the Print Queue 156   Rescheduling Print Jobs 157   Pausing and Resuming a Print Job 158   Removing a Print Job 158   When Your Applications Get Sluggish 158   Controlling Print Manager Messages 159   Simplifying the Display 159   Disabling Print Manager 160

Printing from DOS Applications   160

Summary   160

5   Recorder Techniques   163

Recorder Basics   164

Starting the Recorder   165

Recording a Simple Text-Input Macro   165

Setting Up the Macro 165   Recording the Macro 166   Running the Macro 168   If You Make a Mistake 169   Saving the Macro 169

Manipulating Command Menus: An Example   170

Setting Up the Macro 170   Recording the Macro 170   Testing and Saving the Macro 171

Loading An Application: An Example   172

Setting Up the Macro 172   Recording the Macro 172

About Shortcut Keys   173

Using Other Non-Alphanumeric Shortcut Keys 174   Conflicts with Other Windows Applications 175   Conflicts with DOS Applications 175

Assigning Names and Descriptions   176

Dealing with Errors   177

Deleting Macros 177   Changing the Playback Speed 177

Managing Your Macros   178

Organizing Recorder Files 178   Merging Recorder Files 178

Problems with Recording Mouse Actions   179

Deciding What Mouse Actions to Record 180   Deciding Where Mouse Actions Are Recorded 181

Stopping a Macro   182

Pausing and Resuming Recording 183

Deciding Where a Macro Plays Back 183

Application-Specific Macros 183   Any-Application Macros 184

Combining Macros 188

Setting Up for Combining Macros 189   Changing Combined Macros 189   Creating a Macro That Cannot Combine Other Macros 189

Modifying Macro Properties 189

Even More Options 191

Disabling Recorder Temporarily 191   The Minimize On Use Option 191   Setting Recorder Defaults 191

Starting an Application in a Specific Directory 192

Continuous-Loop Macros 193

A Continuous-Loop Example 194   Running a Nonstop Demo 195

Running a Macro on Start-Up 195

Start-up Macro Considerations 195   Entering the Command Line 195

Loading Your Macros on Start-Up 196

Assigning an Icon to a Macro 197

Closing the Recorder with a Macro 198

Supplementing the Recorder with DOS .BAT Files 200

Summary 202

6 Sharing Data between Applications 203

An Overview of Using the Clipboard 204

Working with Windows Applications 205

Selecting Data to Copy to the Clipboard 205   Checking What Is on the Clipboard 206   Pasting Data to Other Windows Applications 207   Saving Clipboard Data to Disk 208   Deleting the Contents of the Clipboard 210

Capturing Screens 210

Capturing the Whole Screen 210   Capturing Just a Window 211   Memory Considerations 211

Working with DOS Applications 212

> *Capturing Data in Standard or Real Mode 212   Pasting to DOS Applications in Standard or Real Mode 213   Capturing Data in 386 Enhanced Mode 214   Pasting Data in 386 Enhanced Mode 216*

Clipboard File Formats 218

Dynamic Data Exchange 220

Object Linking and Embedding 224

Summary 224

7 Windows Memory Management 227

Conventional and Reserved I/O Memory 228

Expanded Memory and EMS 229

> *EMS Emulators 235*

Extended Memory 236

> *The eXtended Memory Specification (XMS) 237   The High Memory Area (HMA) 237   The HIMEM.SYS Extended Memory Manager 239   DOS Extenders 239*

Windows Memory Configurations 242

Real Mode 242

> *How Windows Manages Segments and Memory Blocks 243   How Windows Uses Extended Memory in Real Mode 245*

Real Mode with EMS 4.0 Memory 245

> *Small- Versus Large-Frame EMS Mode 245   Adjusting the EMS Line: The /L Switch 247   Adjusting the Large-Frame EMS Point: The /E Switch 248   Disabling Windows' Use of Expanded Memory: The /N Switch 248*

Standard Mode 248

386 Enhanced Mode 250

> *How Virtual Memory Works in 386 Enhanced Mode 251*

DOS Applications in Windows 254

> *DOS Applications in Windows/286 254   DOS Applications in Real and Standard Modes 255   DOS Applications in 386 Enhanced Mode 259*

Free Memory and Free System Resources 261

Managing Memory with QEMM-386 262

    Installing QEMM-386 263 Fine-Tuning Your System with QEMM-386 266 Special Considerations for Windows 266

MS-DOS 5.0 268

Summary 268

8 Using the Control Panel 269

Control Panel Basics 269

Changing Desktop Colors 272

    Choosing a Predefined Color Scheme 273 Changing a Predefined Color Scheme 273 Creating Your Own Custom Colors 274

Configuring a Communications Port 276

Configuring Your Mouse 279

Setting Options for the Desktop 280

    Displaying a Pattern on the Desktop 281 Hanging Wallpaper 282 Setting the Distance between Icons 285 Activating the Invisible Grid 285 Setting the Width of Window Borders 286 Changing the Cursor Blink Rate 286

Changing International Settings 286

Setting the Keyboard Repeat Rate 288

Changing the Date and Time 288

Suppressing the Beep 289

386 Enhanced Settings 290

    Device Contention 290 Setting Multitasking Options 294

Summary 295

9 Changing Your Setup 297

Running Setup from within Windows 297

    Changing Hardware Drivers 298 Adding Applications 302

Running Setup from DOS   303

An Example 304

Changing Your Display Fonts Manually   306

Changing Your DOS Application Font 307   Changing Your System Fonts 308   Changes to Your Raster Fonts 309

Summary   310

10 Using Non-Windows Applications   311

Using Memory-Resident Utilities   312

Starting Memory-Resident Utilities Before You Start Windows 312   Starting Memory-Resident Utilities Within Windows 313

What is a PIF?   314

Using Predefined PIFs 314

The PIF Editor   317

Changing the PIF Mode   318

Using DOS Batch Files   318

Standard and Real Mode PIF Options   320

Program Filename 320   Window Title 320   Optional Parameters 320   Start-up Directory 321   Video Mode 323   Memory Requirements 324   XMS Memory 325   Directly Modifies 326   No Screen Exchange 328   Prevent Program Switch 329   Close Window on Exit 330   Reserve Shortcut Keys 330

386 Enhanced Mode PIF Options   330

Duplicated Options 332   Memory Requirements 332   Display Usage 335   Execution 336

Advanced 386 Enhanced Mode PIF Options   337

Multitasking Options 338   Memory Options 340   Display Options 346   Other Options 349

Changing a Running Application   352

Display Options 352   Tasking Options 353   Priority Options 353   Terminate Option 353

Using the Mouse with DOS Applications   353

> *MOUSE.COM 354   MOUSE.SYS 354   Special Considerations for the Logitech Mouse 355   Special Considerations for the Microsoft Mouse 355*

What To Do When Things Go Wrong   357

> *When You Run Out of Memory 357   When You Cannot Switch Away 361   When You Cannot Switch to Full Screen Display 362   When the Application's Display Is Lost 363   A Common VGA Error 363   When Applications Are Running Too Slowly 365   Communications Errors 367   When a Key Doesn't Produce the Desired Effect 367   When PRINTSCREEN or ALT+PRINTSCREEN Do Not Work 368   When You Cannot Paste Information 368   When an Application Stays Around After You've Closed It 369   When an Application Won't Let You Exit 369   When Your System Hangs 369*

Summary   369

11   Improving Windows' Performance   371

Swap Files   372

> *Using a Permanent Swap File 373   Using a Temporary Swap File 378   Improving Windows' Use of Application Swap Files 380*

Configuring Your PC's Memory   382

> *80386- and 80486-Based Systems 382   80286-Based Systems 384   8086- or 8088-Based Systems 385   Slimming Down Your CONFIG.SYS and AUTOEXEC.BAT Files 386*

Improving Your Hard Disk's Performance   388

> *Hard Disk Fundamentals 388   Deleting Unnecessary Files 392   Running CHKDSK with the /F Switch 393   Compacting Your Hard Disk 394   Optimizing Your Disk Drive's Interleave 395*

Adjusting the HIMEM.SYS Extended Memory Manager   397

Using the SMARTDrive Disk-Caching Program   399

> *How SMARTDrive Works 400   How to Set SMARTDrive 401   Improving SMARTDrive's Performance 403*

Setting Up a RAM Disk with RAMDrive   404

Using the Temp Environment Variable   406

Using the EMM386 Expanded Memory Emulator 407

Installing EMM386 408   Command-Line Options 409

The EGA.SYS Device Driver 409

386 Enhanced Mode Performance Check List 409

Summary 410

12 Customizing Your .INI Files 411

Editing WIN.INI and SYSTEM.INI 412

The Structure of WIN.INI and SYSTEM.INI 412

WIN.INI 413

The [Windows] Section 414   The [Desktop] Section 420   The [Extensions] Section 422   The [Intl] Section 423   The [Ports] Section 423   The [Fonts] Section 424   The [PrinterPorts] Section 424   The [Devices] Section 425   The [Colors] Section 425

SYSTEM.INI 427

The [Boot] Section 427   The [Boot.description] Section 430   The [Keyboard] Section 430   The [NonWindowsApp] Section 430   The [Standard] Section 430   The [386Enh] Section 431

Summary 435

13 Networking Windows 437

Supported Networks 438

Installing Windows on a Workstation 438

Setting Up a Local Copy of Windows 439   Installing a Shared Copy of Windows on a Workstation 439

Network Basics 440

Running a Shared Copy of Windows Versus a Local Copy 440   Connecting to Network Resources 441   3Com 3+Share 442   Novell NetWare 445

Connecting to Network Drives 447

Printing on a Network 450

   Connecting to the Network Printer 451 Printing from Windows 453 Viewing Network Print Queues 453

Accessing Network Features from Windows 456

   Logging On and Off the Server 457 Changing Your Password 459 Sending and Receiving Messages 460

Running Network Applications 460

   Using File Manager 461 Using Program Manager 461

Network Administration 462

   Installing Windows on the Server 462 Configuring Windows 464 Configuring User Workstations 465 Getting Information about Your Network 467

Summary 467

14 Oriel for Windows 469

How Oriel for Windows Works 470

Memory Requirements 471

Basic Rules and Syntax 471

   Commands 471 Variables 472 Tokens 473 Labels 473 Comments 473 White Space 474

Starting a Program 474

Stopping a Program 476

The Oriel Coordinate System 477

Selecting Drawing Tools 477

   Using Pens 478 Using Brushes 478 Using Fonts 479

Drawing and Writing 479

   Drawing Text 479 Drawing Lines and Shapes 480 Drawing Bitmaps 480

Flow of Control Commands 481

Message Boxes 481

Controlling the Window Size 482

Pausing a Program 482

Pausing a Specified Number of Seconds 482   Pausing Indefinitely 482

Building Menus 483

Getting Mouse Input 483

Getting Keyboard Input 485

Running Other Programs 486

Command Reference 487

Quick Reference 543

15 Command Post 547

It's a File Manager 548

It's a Custom Workstation Builder 548

Using Command Post as a File Manager 549

Selecting Files 549   The Menus 550   The System Menu 561

Command Post Accessory Programs 562

Browser 562   The Command Post Clock 567

Using Command Post as Your Shell 568

Your Own Menus 569

Setting Up a Menu File 569   The Initialization Section 586   Linking Menu Files Together 587   WIN.INI Support 588   Password-Protecting Your Windows Environment 588   Debugging Statements 590

Pushing CPML'S Limits 591

Building Statements with Substitution 591   Faking Arrays 592   The Execute Statement 593   Running a Macro from a Menu 594

Table of CPML Statements 595

Summary 605

16 Aporia 607

Aporia Basics 608

The Default Tools 608   The Aporia Menu 610   Moving Tools 610   Running Tools 611   Getting Help 611

Using Tools 612

Creating User Tools 612   Creating Directory Tools 614   Copying Tools 615   Creating Desk Tools 615   Customizing Tools 617   Creating Aporia Image Files 619   Getting Information about a Tool 621   Hiding Tools 621   Keeping Notes 621   Removing Tools 622   Using the Size Tool 623

Managing Files and Directories 623

Managing Directories with the Tree Tool 623   Managing Files with Directory Windows 625

Summary 629

17 Icondraw 631

Using an .ICO File in Program Manager 632

The Drawing Tools 632

The Color Palette 633

Using the Clipboard 634

Notes On IconDraw 634

Appendix A: The Windows Power Tools Software 637
Index 647

1

An Introduction to Windows 3

Microsoft shipped its first version of Windows in November of 1985. However, it was not until 1990, almost 5 years later, with the introduction of Windows 3, that it began to receive mainstream acceptance. Why? What makes Windows 3 more special than any previous version of Windows? Perhaps the answer lies in the fact that Windows 3 offers the most extensive feature set of any version of Windows so far.

This chapter introduces you to the significant features in Windows 3. You'll learn about such things as the advanced memory management features in Windows, how it interacts with DOS applications, how it multitasks, and so on. However, on the lighter side, this chapter begins with an historical account of Windows. This account will give you some background on where Windows has been and where it stands now. Along the way, you might develop your own opinion, if you haven't already, as to why Windows 3 is the best selling IBM-PC software application since Lotus 1-2-3.

THE DEVELOPMENT OF WINDOWS: A BRIEF HISTORY

The first version of Windows was a long time in coming. Microsoft first announced its plans for the product in November of 1983. However, it was not until two years later, in November of 1985, that Microsoft actually shipped the first version of Windows, Windows 1.01.

From the beginning, Microsoft has staunchly supported the concept of a graphical user interface (GUI), and Windows is their expression of that vision. The historical account that follows traces the evolution of that interface from the first version of Windows up to Windows 3. However, as you'll soon see, there is a great deal more to Windows than just a graphical interface. In fact, each version of Windows represents a significant stride in the evolution of software for the IBM PC.

Windows 1

When Version 1.01 of Windows shipped in November of 1985, it made quite a splash. Part of this was due to the anticipation of Microsoft's finally shipping this long-awaited product. Another aspect was the competition that was going on between Windows and GEM, Digital Research's GUI environment. However, most of the attention centered around Windows features.

Windows 1.01 offered a unique form of graphical user interface. It represented something of a marriage between the graphics and character-based worlds. The main shell for Windows was the MS-DOS Executive, prevalent in all versions of Windows up until Version 3.0. The MS-DOS Executive window was composed of a menu bar with pull-down menus along the top and disk drive icons below, which you could use to quickly switch to the different drives on your system. Beneath this, all the files in the current directory were listed. You could start any Windows application by simply double-clicking on its executable filename. Windows also came with multiple applications (Write, Paint, Notepad, and so on) which you could run (multitask) at the same time, each in its own window. Figure 1-1 shows an example of what Windows 1.01 looks like.

You could also run DOS applications in Windows 1.01, though you couldn't multitask them. Each DOS application required a PIF (Program Information File), a special file that provided Windows the information it needed to run a DOS application.

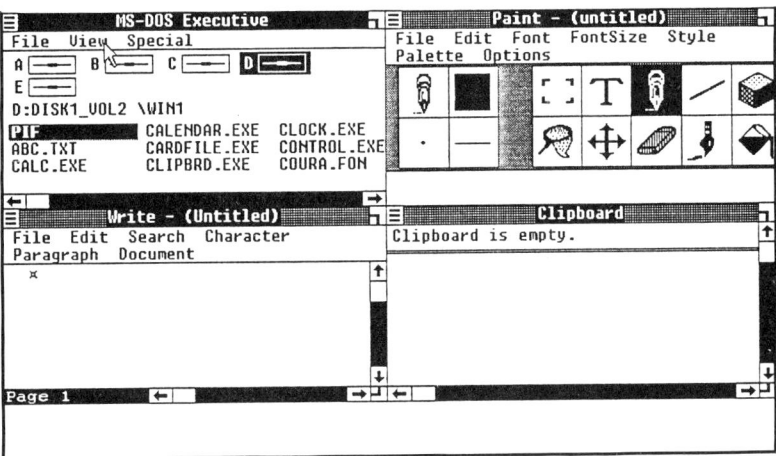

Figure 1-1 An example of Windows 1.01

Thus, Windows 1.01 (as well as other versions of Windows since that time) relied on the user for a basic working knowledge of DOS drives, paths, and file-naming conventions. Unlike some GUI products, Windows never has (and hopefully never will) completely insulate the user from the underlying DOS platform.

Windows 1.01 also had a unique approach to memory management. Although it was limited to running in real mode beneath the 640K barrier, it was also capable of consolidating free memory that was fragmented by starting and quitting multiple applications.

Windows 1.01 was also capable of discarding program code when memory became tight. That is, if a Windows program was too large to fit in memory, Windows 1.01 could discard code from other Windows programs and read that code back into memory again from the programs' .EXE files when needed. Windows 1.01 was also capable of running more than one instance (copy) of the same Windows program, and both instances would share segments of the same code.

The architecture of Windows 1.01, like all versions of Windows, was based on a messaging system. Each Windows application was responsible for receiving and responding to messages sent to it by Windows' central messaging system. Through this messaging system, Windows is capable of communicating with, and controlling, multiple applications at the same time.

The Windows messaging system was, and is, event driven. That is, when an event of interest occurs, such as a mouse click or a keyboard entry, Windows generates a message to that effect and sends it through its central message queue. So how does Windows know which application to pass that message to? Actually, Windows doesn't make this decision, you do. When you focus your attention on an application by giving it mouse or keyboard input, you also focus the attention of Windows on that application. That application is then responsible for checking the Windows central message queue and acting on any messages that may be there. In fact, while a Windows application is active, it is constantly checking the message queue and reacting to messages, until you activate another application.

Windows 1.01 also offered something else that was new at the time for the IBM PC—device independence for applications. Most DOS applications came, and still come, with a disk that includes device drivers for the support of different displays, printers, plotters, keyboards, mice, and so forth. Windows, however, came, and still comes, with these device drivers already provided. To do this, Microsoft developed a device-independent graphics interface—the Graphics Device Interface or GDI—that allows application developers to display graphics and formatted text within their applications. Through the GDI, Windows itself is responsible for passing this information on to the system hardware. Therefore, if you purchased an application designed for Windows, you didn't, and still don't, have to worry about what hardware that application supports. It automatically supports all the hardware supported by Windows.

Windows 1.01 had its share of limitations, though. For one thing, the windows in which its applications ran were always in tiled configuration, similar to Figure 1-1. This "automatic tiling" feature was built into the product based on studies that had been done which indicated that it reduced the amount of work required of the user when first opening an application. However, because of this feature, you could not overlap application windows, nor could you easily resize or move them about the screen.

Windows 1.01 suffered from something else that has plagued the Windows project since its inception—the disparity between the capabilities of software and the slow evolution of hardware required to run that software. At the time Windows 1.01 was first introduced, many users were still running systems with two floppy-disk drives. There were more than a few XTs out there with hard disks, of course, and the occasional AT, but most users just didn't have the RAM or the disk space needed to make Windows really perform as it should.

Windows 2

Believe it or not, Windows got its first real boost in 1987 when Microsoft and IBM jointly announced OS/2 and Presentation Manager. Development of this operating system and its associated graphical user interface actually led to the development and introduction of Windows 2.01.

Part of the significance of Windows 2.01 was that it conformed to the Systems Application Architecture (SAA) standard developed by IBM for the Presentation Manager portion of OS/2. This standard proposed a uniform system of windows, menus, and dialog boxes for managing an application. To this day, a copy of the SAA literature ships with every copy of the Windows Software Development Kit (SDK). This kit includes software tools that developers can use to develop Windows applications. Further, Microsoft itself adheres to the SAA standard, where appropriate, both for Windows itself and for applications developed by Microsoft for Windows.

Conforming to the SAA standard allows users to transfer their skills from one application to the next. For example, most Windows applications have a File Open command. Selecting this command results in the display of a dialog box that lets you open a data file for an application. Although the content of this dialog box may vary slightly from one application to the next, it performs basically the same function and operates in largely the same way. Therefore, a user need not learn a new command, nor a different interface style, when using the File Open command in different Windows applications.

Version 2 also represented an improvement in the Windows graphical user interface. For one thing, it supported overlapping windows. (Figure 1-2 shows an example of Windows 2.) Notice in that figure that the Notepad window overlaps the Cardfile window. To create this figure, the Notepad window was sized and then moved on top of the Cardfile window, a significant enhancement indeed. Version 2 also included a number of other enhancements to the keyboard and mouse interface for menus and dialog boxes.

Windows 2 also marked the first version of Windows that included Dynamic Data Exchange (DDE). DDE allowed Windows applications to communicate with one another, via the messaging system, for the purpose of exchanging blocks of data.

Windows 2, however, was not without its problems. As always, there was the hardware problem. You needed the equivalent of an AT-class machine with 640K to run it. You could run it on a lesser machine, but it was doggedly slow. Also, Windows 2 had difficulty

An Introduction to Windows 3   5

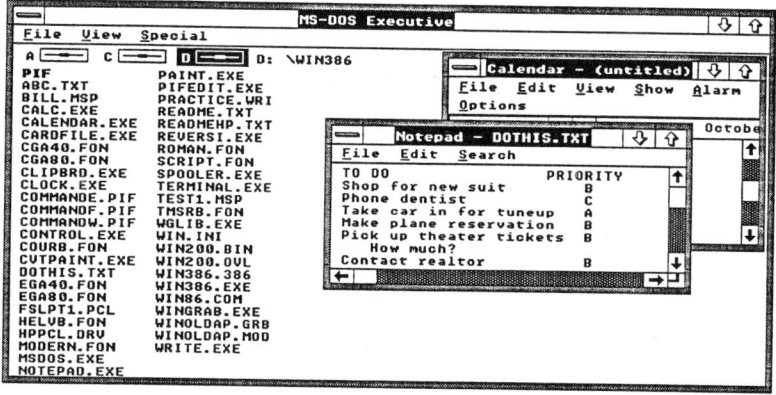

Figure 1-2   An example of Windows 2

running many of the popular DOS applications of the day. In general, those applications that wrote directly to the screen, used graphics, or controlled the keyboard could not be run in a window. In addition, some of these applications even had difficulty running full screen.

Windows/286 and Windows/386

Another big boost for Windows came with mainstream acceptance of the 386 PC. Windows/386, introduced in 1987, took advantage of the "virtual 8086" mode of the 80386 processor, at a time when few other applications did. This meant that DOS applications and Windows applications could now be multitasked, each DOS application in its own 640K virtual machine. Thus, for the first time, you could multitask DOS applications along with your Windows applications. (See "Multitasking," later, for a further discussion of how Windows muititasks.)

In that same year (1987), Microsoft re-introduced Windows 2 and re-christened it Windows/286. In this version, Windows could access 64K of extended memory above the 640K available through DOS and still run in real mode. Thus, the power of the 80286 machine was further exploited and the operation of Windows further enhanced.

However, despite these dramatic improvements, enthusiasm for Windows was on the wane in the late 1980s. Frankly, there just weren't that many "killer" applications available for it. In fact, Windows was relegated to something of a *niche phenomenon* and wasn't given serious consideration by many of the big software houses. However, some companies, including Aldus and Micrografx as well as Microsoft, continued to develop aggressively for Windows. Further, Windows kept showing up underneath major applications. Many people were surprised to learn that their copy of Microsoft Excel or Aldus Pagemaker was actually running on top of a run-time version of Windows. In short, they had been running Windows all along and didn't know it.

Windows 3

Windows 3, introduced in May of 1990, represents the culmination of years of hard work at Microsoft. It implements all the best features from previous versions of Windows as well as a host of new features. Perhaps this version of Windows marks the beginning of what Microsoft really had in mind all along.

The features in Windows 3 address most of the problems that have plagued Windows in the past. Perhaps the most exciting of these features, though, is the new memory management scheme.

Windows 3 unlocks the power of your 80286 or 80386 computer by accessing the protected-mode capabilities of these processors. Thus, if extended memory above the 640K of conventional memory is available, Windows 3 is capable of accessing that memory directly. Further, you don't have to purchase a specific version of Windows for your particular machine. Instead, Windows 3 is capable of running in one of three different modes (real, standard, or 386 enhanced), depending on the type of processor in your machine and the amount of memory you have. When you install Windows, it figures out what processor you have, as well as your available memory, and configures itself accordingly. When you start Windows, it automatically comes up in the mode that is best suited to your particular system.

The graphical user interface in Windows has also been further refined. In fact, Windows has a whole new look, as shown in Figure 1-3. Instead of the old MS-DOS Executive, so prevalent in previous versions, Windows 3 uses Program Manager, an entirely new shell that presents your applications as icons. You can run any application by simply double-clicking on its icon. However, true to the tradition of Windows,

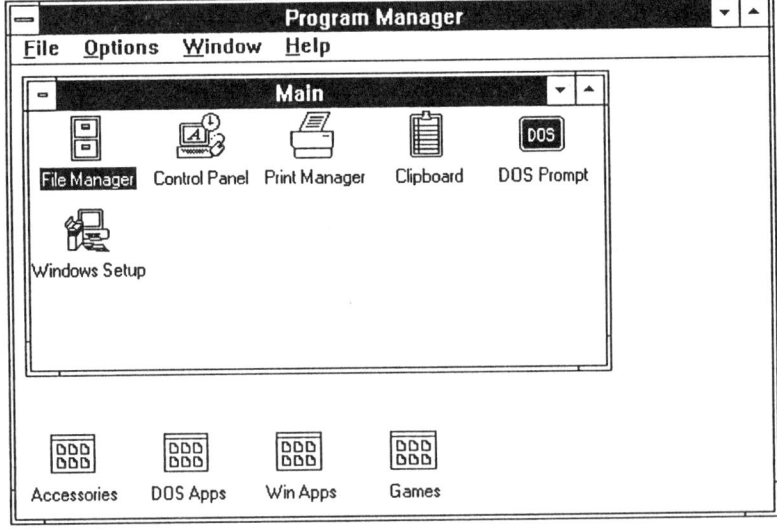

Figure 1-3 The Windows 3 Program Manager

Program Manager does not completely insulate you from the DOS. In fact, the purpose of each of the icons in Program Manager is to initiate a specific DOS command.

You can also run a mixture of Windows and DOS applications at the same time with Windows 3. If Windows is running in 386 enhanced mode, you can run multiple DOS applications at the same time, each in its own window, and switch back and forth between them.

Windows 3 also includes a whole host of other powerful new features. However, to give you a complete rundown of all the new features in Windows 3 would be to steal thunder from the rest of this chapter, as well as the rest of this book. Suffice it to say that although Windows 3 is a powerful product, it is also a very complex one. The purpose of this book is to give you the insight you will need to deal with that complexity.

In concluding the history of Windows, one final point should be made. For the first time in the history of the Windows project, the timing is right. The average user has evolved to the point where he or she is capable of appreciating the benefits of running multiple applications at the same time. Further, the hardware and software are finally in sync. Now, 286 and 386 computers with one or more megabytes of memory and larger hard disks have become the norm instead of the exception. In addition, powerful Windows applications exist in abundance, with more becoming available all the time. At last, Windows is ready to receive the mainstream acceptance that it so richly deserves.

WINDOWS 3 FEATURES

The sections that follow discuss many of the more salient features in Windows 3. Most of these features will be discussed on an introductory level, and you will be pointed to other chapters in this book for additional detail. Practically every feature discussed here will affect you as a Windows user at one time or another.

Before delving into the major features of Windows 3, though, it is important that you have at least a passing understanding of the extent of the relationship between Windows and your system. As you know, you start Windows as you would any other DOS application. However, once it's up and running, it takes over many of the functions that are normally attributable to a full-blown operating system. For example, it is responsible for handling the video display, the keyboard, the mouse, printers, I/O ports, and memory management. It also controls the execution and scheduling of all programs that you run from within Windows. In short, a great deal happens when you type **WIN** and press ENTER.

Advanced Memory Management

As mentioned, one of the most exciting aspects of Windows 3 is its advanced memory management capabilities. Windows 3 is capable of running in one of three different modes: real, standard, or 386 enhanced. The mode in which Windows runs depends on the type of processor in your machine and its available memory. When you install Windows, it checks your system resources and configures itself to run in a particular mode by default. That way, when you start Windows, it automatically comes up in the mode that is best suited to the capabilities, or limitations, of your machine.

The sections that follow explain the various processor configurations associated with each Windows' operating mode. In addition, these sections will tell you what kind of performance you can expect from Windows in each of the three modes.

Note: You can determine the mode in which Windows is running by selecting the About command from the Help menu in either Program Manager or File Manager. When you select this command, Windows displays a dialog box that shows you the mode in which Windows is currently running. As an added bonus, this box also shows you the free memory that is available to Windows.

If you are already familiar with Windows basic operating modes, you may want to skip this section and read Chapter 7, "Memory Management." It provides the most comprehensive overview you'll find anywhere of Windows memory management.

Real Mode

Real mode is automatically selected for those computers with less than one megabyte of memory. For example, if you have a 286 machine with 640K of conventional memory, Windows defaults to running in real mode. Real mode is also the default for those machines with 8086 and 8088 based processors. So, if you are running the equivalent of an XT or earlier, Windows will automatically default to running in real mode on that machine.

Real mode is also intended to assure backward compatibility with older Windows 2.X applications that have not been updated for Windows 3. In fact, to run those applications without risking data loss or a possible system crash, you must run them in real mode. If you attempt to run an older Windows application in standard or 386 enhanced mode, Windows will display a message box similar to the one in Figure 1-4. You can select OK twice from this message box to run the application in standard or 386 enhanced mode, but you do so at your own risk.

If you are capable of running Windows in standard or 386 enhanced mode, but you need to run an older Windows application, you can easily start Windows in real mode and run the application. To do this, start Windows with the /R switch. For example, you might type the following at the DOS prompt:

```
WIN /R
```

Initially, you won't notice much difference between real mode and standard or 386 enhanced mode, as far as Windows applications are concerned. You can, of course, run multiple Windows applications simultaneously and switch back and forth between them. However, you will notice quite a difference where DOS applications are concerned. In real mode, Windows will only let you actively run one DOS application at a time. Further, that application will run as a full-screen display, completely covering the Windows desktop.

An Introduction to Windows 3 9

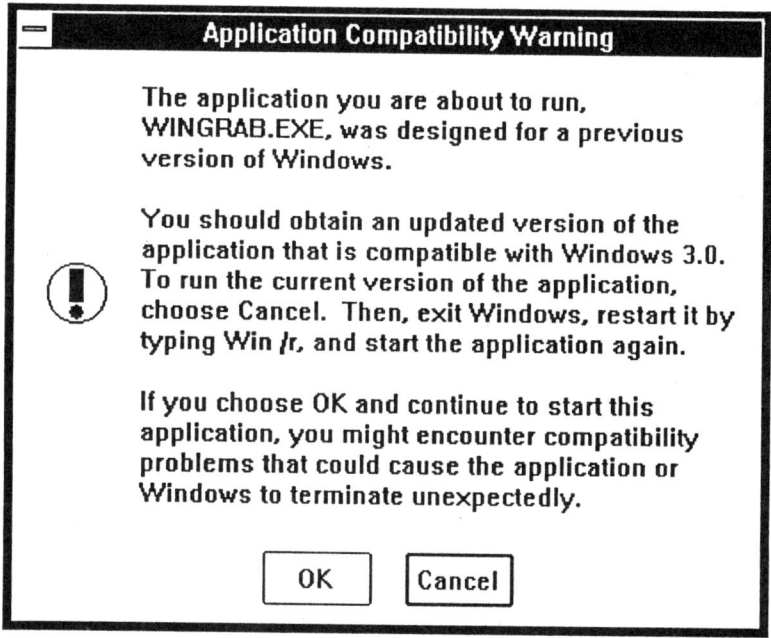

Figure 1-4 Windows 3 displays an error message when you attempt to run an older Windows application in standard or 386 enhanced mode

You can, however, "launch" more than one DOS application and switch between them. Windows accomplishes this through a process known as *task switching*. When you switch from one DOS application to another in real mode, Windows copies the first one to a temporary application swap file on disk. It then loads the second DOS application into memory and runs it as a full-screen display.

Another characteristic of real mode is that you cannot switch between two DOS applications without first returning to Windows. Further, all activity in the first DOS application will be suspended while the second is running. For example, imagine you are currently running WordPerfect in real mode as a full screen display and you decide to switch to Lotus 1-2-3. To do this, you must first switch from WordPerfect back to Windows. When you do, Windows copies WordPerfect to a temporary application swap file, suspending all further activity in that application. Therefore, when you start 1-2-3, it comes into memory as the only active DOS application. If you then switch back to WordPerfect from 1-2-3 (via Windows, of course), Windows stores 1-2-3 in an application swap file. It then resumes the suspended WordPerfect session by copying it back into memory as the only active DOS application.

Switching between DOS applications in real mode can be a little frustrating at times. For one thing, it can be time-consuming. How much time is consumed depends on the size of the application you are switching from and the size of the application you are switching to. Also, the I/O speed of your hard disk can play a major role here. For another, problems may result when activity in an application is suspended. For example, imagine you are running a communications program in real mode and that you are in the process of transferring a file from a remote source. When you switch away from the communications program to go to another DOS application, communication may time out, causing you to lose all or part of the file you are attempting to transfer.

Note: As mentioned, Windows only uses 640K of conventional memory in real mode. However, if you have expanded memory available, Windows can make extensive use of that memory. If you have a 80386- or 80486-based system with sufficient extended memory, you can convert some of that extended memory to expanded using EMM386.SYS, an installable device driver that comes with Windows 3.0. See Chapter 11, "Improving Windows Performance," for a discussion of how to install EMM386.SYS in your system.

Standard Mode

Standard mode, sometimes called 286 standard mode, is the default mode used for those machines with the following processor and memory configurations:

- An 80286 processor with one full megabyte of memory or more.
- An 80386 processor with one full megabyte of memory but less than two.

In standard mode, Windows is capable of exploiting the protected-mode capabilities of the Intel 80286 or 80386 chip. This, theoretically, gives Windows access to up to 16 megabytes of memory. If only a single megabyte of memory is available, though, Windows will use the first 640K of conventional memory as well as the additional 384K of memory above the one megabyte line. If additional extended memory is available, Windows can use that memory directly, up to 15 megabytes. Thus, in most cases, you can run more and larger Windows applications in standard mode than you can in real mode.

Where DOS applications are concerned, however, standard mode works basically the same as real mode. That is, although you can launch more than one DOS application, only one of those applications can be active in memory at any one time. Further, that application will run as a full-screen display. To switch to another DOS application, you must return to Windows. Moreover, when you switch away from a DOS application, Windows copies it to a temporary application swap file and suspends all further activity in that application. When you subsequently switch back to the application, Windows restores it to memory from the temporary swap file and processing in that application is resumed.

Generally speaking, standard mode is considered to be the fastest of the three modes. Therefore, if raw speed is an issue for running your Windows applications, and you are not switching between DOS applications frequently, you may want to run Windows in standard mode. If your machine runs in 386 enhanced mode by default, you can force it to run in standard mode by starting Windows with the /S or /2 switch (both are the same). For example, you might type the following at the DOS prompt:

```
WIN /2
```

386 Enhanced Mode

The full power of Windows 3 becomes apparent in 386 enhanced mode. This mode, sometimes called 386 protected mode, is the default for those machines with an 80386 or 80486 processor and two or more megabytes of memory.

In 386 enhanced mode, the 80386 processor operates in protected mode, which, in theory, allows it to address up to four gigabytes of memory. Moreover, 386 enhanced mode allows Windows to take advantage of the inherent capability of the 386 chip to use virtual (disk-based) memory, up to 64 megabytes. Therefore, when Windows runs out of physical memory, it can create and use a swap file on your hard disk to make up the difference. Therefore, the amount of memory available to your Windows applications can often be several times more than the amount of physical memory that is actually available on your machine. The end result is that you can run more and larger Windows applications in 386 enhanced mode than you can in standard or real mode.

Although Windows may not run as fast in 386 enhanced mode as it does in standard mode, its capabilities are dramatically enhanced, especially where DOS applications are concerned. For example, in 386 enhanced mode you can run multiple concurrent DOS applications, each in its own window, and you can switch back and forth between them with a click of the mouse. The end result is true multitasking of DOS applications. For example, Figure 1-5 shows an example of WordPerfect and Lotus 1-2-3 running side-by-side under Windows 3 in 386 enhanced mode.

There are some other advantages to running your DOS applications in 386 enhanced mode. For example, as you'll learn in Chapter 6, you can use the Clipboard to transfer information between DOS applications, regardless of the mode in which you are running Windows. However, in standard or real mode you must copy an entire screenful of data (rather than a selected portion) from a DOS application to the Clipboard. Further, you cannot copy graphics from a DOS application to the Clipboard in either of these modes. However, in 386 enhanced mode, you can copy a selected portion of a DOS screen to the Clipboard and you can also copy graphics images.

Windows also offers advanced PIF (Program Information File) settings for DOS applications running in 386 enhanced mode (over those available in standard or real mode). For example, you can specify whether you want a DOS application to run in a window or as a full-screen display. You can also specify a shortcut key for a DOS application that lets you instantly switch to that application from whatever application you happen to be running at the time. There are many other advanced options for 386 enhanced mode PIFs. All of these are covered in Chapter 10, "Using Non-Windows Applications."

Many people will say that you need four megabytes of memory to effectively run Windows in 386 enhanced Mode. Where Windows applications are concerned, their

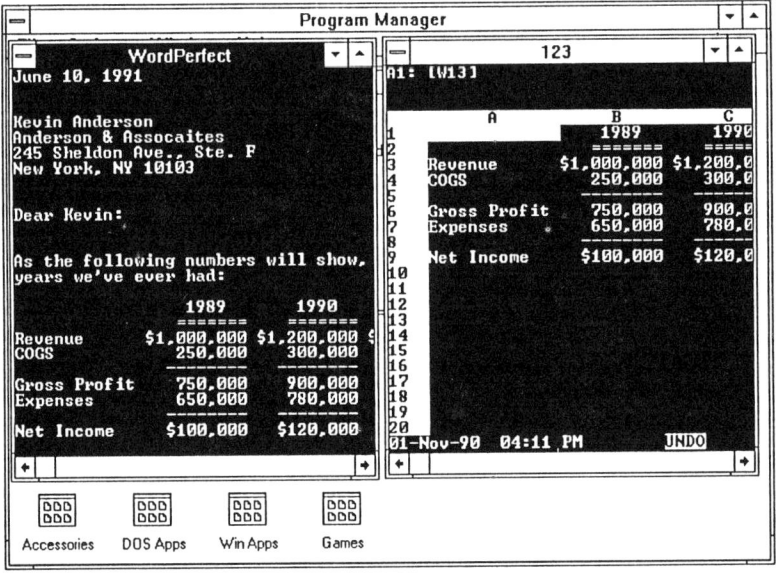

Figure 1-5 Two DOS applications running side-by-side in 386 enhanced mode

argument is only partially supported. As you'll learn in Chapter 7, when memory gets tight, Windows is capable of discarding segments of Windows applications and reloading them from the applications' .EXE files when it needs them. As a further hedge, Windows can use a swap file to access virtual (disk-based) memory as needed. Therefore, additional memory over two megabytes is, of course, desirable but not absolutely critical, provided you have sufficient disk space.

Where DOS applications are concerned, these nay sayers have something of a point. As you'll learn in Chapter 7, Windows is capable, through a process called *paging*, of copying active DOS applications to and from disk in 386 enhanced mode. However, a DOS application must be present in memory when you use it. Further, this process of copying DOS applications between disk and physical memory noticeably detracts from Windows' performance. Therefore, a strong argument can be made for the additional memory above two megabytes, if you intend to multitask large DOS applications in Windows.

Note: You can force Windows to run in 386 enhanced mode by using the /3 switch on Windows startup. However, you must have between 580 and 624K of memory available. To do this, you would type the following at the DOS prompt:

```
WIN /3
```

> **Tip: Configure expanded memory as extended memory**
>
> In 386 enhanced mode, Windows makes use of extended memory, as opposed to expanded memory, for running Windows applications. However, it is also capable of emulating expanded memory for those DOS applications that ask for it. Often, an expanded memory board will allow you to configure all or part of its available memory for extended memory, possibly allowing you to run in 386 enhanced mode to begin with, and enhancing the operation of your Windows applications in the bargain. Therefore, if you configure your expanded memory board for extended memory, Windows can use it to run in 386 enhanced mode and still provide expanded memory for those applications that need it. See Chapter 7, "Memory Management," for further details on how Windows 3 emulates expanded memory in 386 enhanced mode.

Optimizing Performance

Operating modes are only a part of the Windows memory management story. There are other significant factors as well. For example, three features of Windows you should know about are HIMEM.SYS, SMARTDrive, and Swapfile. These have a definite impact on how Windows uses the resources of your system. Generally, these features are transparent to the average user. However, as a power user, you should be aware of what these features are, what they do, and how you can use them to enhance the performance of Windows. A brief introduction to these topics follows.

HIMEM.SYS

HIMEM.SYS is an installable extended memory device driver that was brought forward from Windows/286. It is intended for those computers that are capable of running Windows in standard and in 386 enhanced mode.

HIMEM.SYS controls the use of extended memory according to the eXtended Memory Specification (XMS). It is directly responsible for the allocation of extended memory to those applications, including Windows, that ask for it. If you don't use HIMEM.SYS, Windows won't be able to run in standard or 386 enhanced mode. Normally, when you install Windows, a DEVICE=C:\HIMEM.SYS statement is inserted into your CONFIG.SYS file so that this XMS driver is loaded automatically when you boot your system. For a detailed description of HIMEM.SYS and its function in Windows, see Chapter 7, "Memory Management." Also, see Chapter 11, "Improving Windows Performance," for a description of how to set HIMEM.SYS to make sure Windows is using extended memory properly.

SMARTDrive

SMARTDrive is a disk-caching program that comes with Windows and can make it run much faster. It is intended for use on computers that have extended or expanded memory. Its purpose is to reduce the amount of time your computer spends reading data from its hard disk. It does this by taking information previously read from your hard disk and storing it in extended or expanded memory. That way, when an application, like Windows, calls for that information, it can get it directly from memory, rather than from disk. The result is a dramatic improvement in the performance of Windows. This feature of Windows is discussed at length in Chapter 11, "Improving Windows Performance."

Note: Windows also comes with RAMDrive, a RAM disk capable of operating in expanded or extended memory. See Chapter 11, "Improving Windows Performance," for information on how to install RAMDrive on your system.

Swapfile

Windows makes extensive use of swap files in 386 enhanced mode. When memory gets tight, Windows can compensate by "swapping" (copying) part of the contents of physical memory to a hidden file on your hard disk. It can then draw on that information when it needs to. Thus, swap files are used to extend the capability of Windows beyond the limitations of physical memory.

By default, Windows uses a temporary swap file. This file is removed from your hard disk when you leave Windows. When reading and writing to a temporary swap file, though, Windows must use whatever disk space may be available at the time. Often, available space is fragmented, causing Windows to have to skip around to various areas on your hard disk to find the space it needs. This skipping around can be time-consuming and can impede Windows' performance.

However, you can specify that Windows use a permanent rather than a temporary swap file. To do this, you use the Swapfile utility that comes with Windows. When you set up a permanent swap file, Windows reserves a set of empty and consecutive tracks on your hard disk that it can use for its swapping operations. You can, of course, control the amount of space that is reserved. Nevertheless, when you set up a permanent swap file, Windows always knows where to go when it needs disk space. Further, it can write to and read from a contiguous set of tracks. The result is a healthy improvement in performance.

For additional information about swap files, see Chapter 11, "Improving Windows Performance." This chapter also tells you how to go about using the Swapfile utility to set up a permanent swap file.

Multitasking

As you know, Windows provides a multitasking environment in which you can run several applications at the same time and switch back and forth between them. Yet all of this magic is performed on top of a single-tasking operating system, DOS. This section gives you some insight into how Windows performs its multitasking.

Windows actually employs two forms of multitasking, one for Windows applications—called nonpreemptive multitasking—and a second form for DOS applications—called preemptive multitasking.

To understand how nonpreemptive multitasking works for Windows applications, you have to understand a little about Windows applications themselves. When you run a Windows application, it's periodically given control of the machine by Windows. This act is often referred to as giving an application the *focus*. However, after the application has finished performing its work, it's responsible for immediately giving control back to Windows. That way, Windows can give it to another application that needs it. However, an application does not necessarily have to give control back to Windows. In fact, if it's ill-behaved, it can keep control indefinitely. Windows cannot preempt in this case and take control away—hence the term "nonpreemptive" multitasking.

To understand how preemptive multitasking works for DOS applications, you have to know a little about how Windows interacts with DOS applications. In real and standard mode, there is no multitasking of DOS applications, strictly speaking. In these modes, Windows is only capable of running one DOS application at a time. However, in 386 enhanced mode Windows is capable of truly multitasking DOS applications. To do this, Windows takes advantage of the 386 processor's "virtual 8086" mode, allowing each DOS application to run in its own virtual machine. In effect, a series of 8086 sessions are running simultaneously in memory, each separate from the other.

When you start multiple DOS applications in 386 enhanced mode, Windows is still responsible for doling out the resources of a single processor to all the applications that need it. Therefore, Windows must "preempt" and provide each DOS application an equal amount of processing time. To do this, Windows uses the hardware clock on your machine. It devotes an equal amount of time (a time slice) to each DOS application in turn. When an application's time is up, Windows takes the processor away from that application and gives it to the next DOS application that is waiting in line. In this way, Windows works its way around to all the DOS applications you are running and evenly distributes processor time among all of them. Thus, in 386 enhanced mode, Windows performs true preemptive multitasking, similar to that in OS/2.

However, as a power user, you can do a little preempting of your own where DOS applications are concerned. As you'll learn in Chapter 10, "Using Non-Windows Applications," you can control the amount of processor time that Windows devotes to one DOS application versus another. To do this, you must specify the settings you want in the PIF (Program Information File) for each DOS application. In addition, you can use the Control Panel to set multitasking options for DOS applications. See Chapter 8, "Using the Control Panel," for more details on this.

Refinement of the Graphical User Interface

In Windows 3, the Graphical User Interface is more refined and intuitive than ever. As mentioned, Windows' new shell is Program Manager, which is composed entirely of graphic elements. (Figure 1-3, shown earlier in this chapter, shows an example of the Windows 3 Program Manager.) In Program Manager, applications are now represented by icons. To start an application, you need only double-click on its icon.

16 *Windows 3 Power Tools*

Like all Windows applications, Program Manager runs in a window. However, the Program Manager window is always present. That is, although you can minimize the Program Manager to an icon, you can't close it. Therefore, it's always there whenever you need to start another application or access one of the system management applications that come with Windows, like Control Panel, Print Manager, or Windows Setup.

Program Manager itself is composed of a series of internal windows, known as group windows. Group windows let you organize related application icons into, well, groups. A group window can remain open, or you can minimize it to an icon. This scheme allows you to assemble only the applications you need to perform a specific job. You can then put your other applications away until you need them. Thus, you can simplify the appearance of the Windows desktop and streamline your use of Windows. See Chapter 2 for a complete discussion of how you can set up Program Manager to meet your specific needs.

Windows 3 also includes File Manager, a new application that in some ways replaces the old MS-DOS Executive so prevalent in previous versions of Windows. (A view of File Manager's window appears in Figure 1-6.) However, File Manager's capabilities far exceed those of the old MS-DOS Executive. Its extensive menu system gives you most, if not all, of the tools you need to perform your daily file management chores. In addition, File Manager supports extensive use of the mouse in copying and moving files and directories by dragging their icons from one location to another. File Manager is such an

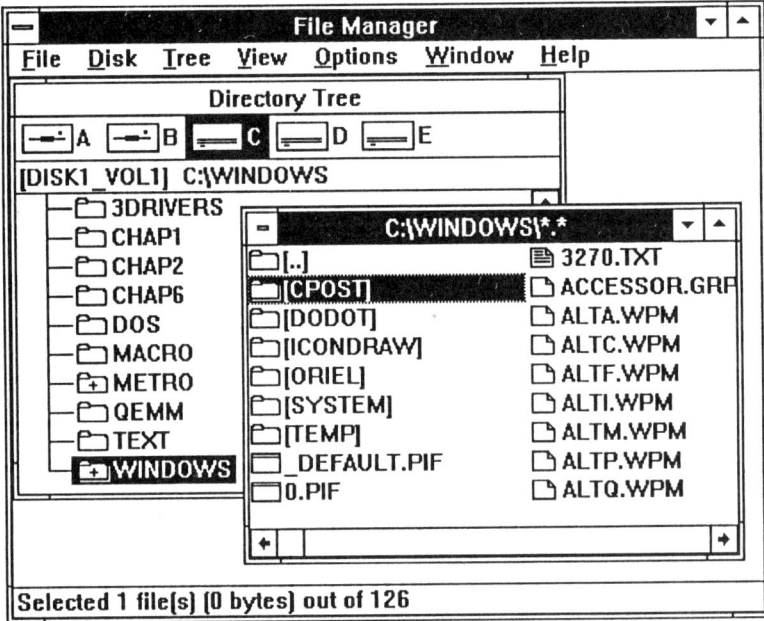

Figure 1-6 The File Manager window

integral part of Windows that an entire chapter of this book, Chapter 3, "File Manager Techniques," is devoted to providing you with tips and techniques for using it.

Compatibility with DOS Applications

As mentioned, one of the things that discouraged users from embracing Windows for so many years was its problems running popular DOS applications. In Windows 3, however, these problems have been largely rectified.

> *Note:* What follows is only a brief introduction to some of the issues associated with running DOS applications under Windows. It is intended only to give you a basic overview. For a detailed discussion of running DOS application under Windows, see Chapter 10, "Using Non-Windows Applications."

Like Windows 3, older versions of Windows were also capable of running DOS applications. If a DOS application was a character-mode application, Windows would run the application within a window. On the other hand, if a DOS application made use of graphics or directly accessed the machine's hardware (the screen or keyboard), Windows would run the application full screen, all the while continuing to run with the DOS application.

Windows 3, on the other hand, represents something of a compromise as well as a technological advance where DOS applications are concerned. Each mode of Windows has its own way of dealing with DOS applications, allowing them to run under Windows.

For example, in real and standard mode, no attempt is made to run a DOS application within a window or to multitask DOS applications. Instead, only one DOS application is allowed to be active in memory at any one time. Further, all DOS applications are run as a full-screen display. In effect, when you start a DOS application, Windows copies the application into memory and copies itself out to disk, out of harm's way. And, although Windows constantly monitors the activities of the DOS application, it does not interfere with that application's use of your system resources. However, if you return to Windows without first quitting the DOS application, Windows copies that application to a temporary application swap file on disk and suspends all further activity within that application until you return to it.

Operating in 386 enhanced mode is another matter. As mentioned, in 386 enhanced mode, Windows takes advantage of the inherent capability of the 386 processor to run in virtual 8086 mode. Therefore, each DOS application is confined within its own independent virtual machine. Under these conditions, Windows is capable of preemptive multitasking of DOS applications. That is, it can choose to devote full system resources to each of your various DOS applications. Although each application is only given access to system resources for a limited period of time, based on the tick of the hardware clock, each is attended to in turn.

In 386 enhanced mode, you are given the option of running a DOS application either as a full-screen display or in a window. While the application is running as a full-screen display, very few, if any, limitations are placed on the application. However, when a DOS application is running as a windowed display, Windows 3 may, of necessity, place limitations on the operation of that application. In virtually all cases, so long as the application is running in text mode, no limitations will be imposed. However, under certain circumstances, when a DOS application switches to graphics mode, Windows may need to impose limitations on its operation, perhaps even suspending it, until you return to a full-screen display.

Most commonly, problems with windowed DOS applications occur only when the application uses high resolution graphics. For example, imagine you are running Borland's Quattro Pro 2.0 in 386 enhanced mode as a full-screen display in text mode on a VGA screen. You then switch that application to a windowed display. Windows is now displayed in the background, and the application appears in a window. However, you now enter some numbers in the spreadsheet followed by commands to display a graph, causing the application to switch to high resolution graphics mode. At this point, Windows displays an error message box informing you that the application is suspended until you return to a full-screen display. Once you return to a full-screen display, operation of the suspended application is resumed and the graph is displayed.

Many problems with DOS applications can be rectified through modification of the application itself or by modifying its PIF (Program Information File). A complete discussion of this important, and often complex, topic appears in Chapter 10, "Using Non-Windows Applications." For example, you can solve the problem mentioned in the previous paragraph by simply using a lower-resolution graphics driver for the application.

Advanced PIF Settings

To make your DOS applications compatible with the Windows environment, you can create a custom PIF (Program Information File) for each DOS application that you run. PIFs supply parameters to Windows that tell it how to best allocate resources to a given DOS application. Once you create a custom PIF for an application, it is automatically loaded whenever you start that application. Otherwise, Windows uses the default PIF settings which may, or may not, be the correct settings for the application. Creating custom PIFs for DOS applications is discussed at length in Chapter 10, "Using Non-Windows Applications."

If you are an experienced Windows user, you know that PIFs have been around for a long time in Windows. So has the PIF Editor, which allows you to streamline the creation of custom PIFs. However, in Windows 3, the PIF Editor application has been further refined. Figure 1-7 shows an example of the Windows 3 PIF Editor available for applications running in standard or real mode.

Among other things, the PIF Editor window lets you specify optional command-line parameters that will be used automatically when you start an application. You can also specify a directory to make current when an application is started. In addition, if running in 386 enhanced mode, Windows offers a whole new set of advanced PIF options for configuring DOS applications. An example of the advanced PIF options window appears in Figure 1-8. Using the Windows 3 PIF Editor is also discussed in Chapter 10, "Using Non-Windows Applications."

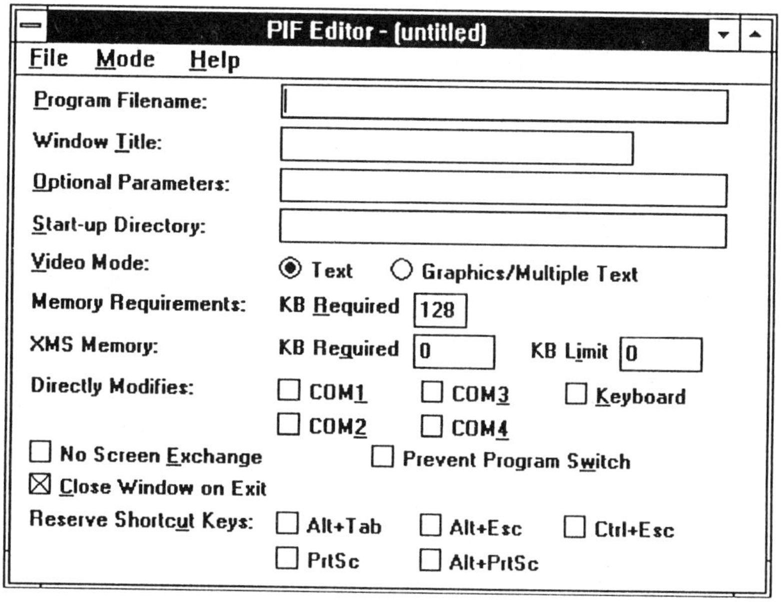

Figure 1-7   The Windows PIF Editor

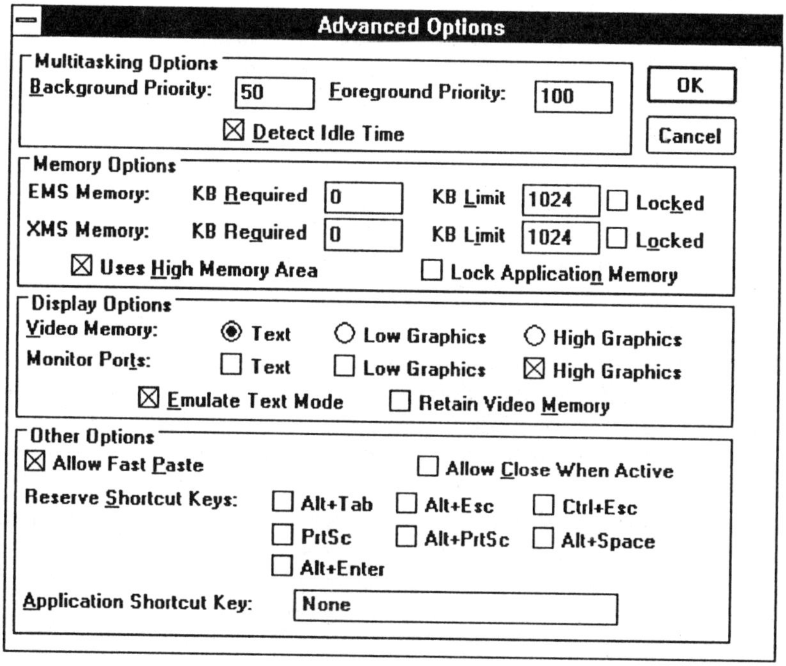

Figure 1-8   Advanced PIF options for DOS applications in 386 enhanced mode

Enhancements to Applications

Many of the same accessory applications included with prior versions of Windows have been updated and enhanced for Windows 3 and new applications have been added. Perhaps the most notable addition to the Windows suite is the Recorder.

The Recorder lets you record keystrokes and mouse actions within Windows and store them in the form of a macro. Each macro can be assigned a shortcut key, like ALT+F. Once a macro has been recorded, you can play back the actions associated with that macro by simply pressing the shortcut key you've assigned. Windows will then execute the keystrokes and mouse actions for that macro exactly as they were recorded. Thus, the Recorder allows you to automate many of your routine Windows tasks (as well as some that are not so routine).

On the surface, using the Recorder seems easy. All you do is turn on the record feature and start entering keystrokes and mouse actions. When you're done, turn off the record feature and save the macro to disk. However, often when you play the macro back, you don't get the results you expect. In fact, after a few frustrating experiments, many people put the Recorder aside, dismissing it as great idea that just doesn't happen to work. However, the Recorder does work, if you know how to use it. In the right hands, it can be a useful tool for automating your Windows sessions. In light of this, an entire chapter of this book, Chapter 5, has been devoted to the Recorder.

Device Independence

Since Version 1.1, a device independent graphics interface has been a hallmark of Windows. Applications written for Windows do not need to directly access hardware devices such as video displays or printers. Instead, Windows takes care of this by providing an on-board complement of hardware device drivers. Programmers need only rely on a library of graphics display routines provided by the GDI that lets them draw text and graphics on the screen from within their applications. Through its device drivers, Windows is responsible for displaying or printing that output. Therefore, any program specifically written for Windows will automatically support all the hardware for which Windows itself has drivers.

Windows 3, however, takes device independence a step further. Windows 3 marks the introduction of device-independent color bitmaps. The operative word here is *color*.

Windows often uses bitmaps to display graphics images, such as icons, pictures you create in Paintbrush, and so on. However, in older versions of Windows, the bitmap file format used was very closely tied to the device (video adapter) on which the bitmap was to be displayed. Bitmaps are basically rectangular arrays of bits in which one or more bits corresponds to the pixels in a graphics image. However, the number of bits required to represent a pixel is different for a monochrome screen than it is for a color screen. Therefore, in order to be able to display bitmaps in older versions of Windows, it was necessary to render them in black and white. This assured that they would be successfully displayed on a variety of video displays.

However, in Windows 3, the bitmap file format has been changed, allowing the display of color while still maintaining device independence. In addition, tools have been added to the GDI that allow the programmer to write color bitmaps to the screen. Windows itself provides the device drivers necessary to display those bitmaps on the currently installed video display.

What all this means for the user is a raging color display. Practically everywhere you go in Windows, you are bombarded with graphics images that are loaded with color. What's more, you can create your own richly colored bitmaps from within Paintbrush. The importance of this technical enhancement cannot be overemphasized. Beyond lending a whole new look to Windows, it makes it a serious contender in the graphical user interface market.

Font and Printer Support

In keeping with its heritage of hardware device independence, Windows 3 allows you to install a single printer for use by all applications. In addition, it allows you to install various fonts for use with that printer. However, installing and using printers and fonts from within Windows can be a bit complex at times. Therefore, an entire chapter of this book, Chapter 4, "Of Fonts and Printing," is devoted to the topic.

Actually, when you install a printer, you are in reality installing a printer driver. Printer drivers are special software files that tell Windows how to interact with a particular type and model of printer. It should be noted that Windows 3 offers more printer drivers than any previous version of Windows.

You can also install more than one printer for Windows, each on a separate port. In Windows 3, printers are either active or inactive. To choose a particular printer for all your applications, all you need do is activate that printer (or more accurately, its printer driver). Installing and configuring multiple printers for Windows is discussed in Chapter 4.

As mentioned, Windows also allows you to install printer fonts for use with all your applications. Many printers have resident fonts that are "burned in" to the printer's ROM. In other cases, fonts are provided by one or more cartridges that plug into the printer. When you install a particular printer for use with Windows, the resident fonts associated with that printer are also installed, provided they are supported by the Windows printer driver (which they usually are). Further, as a general rule, Windows allows you to install fonts associated with a particular cartridge for those printers that use cartridges.

In addition to resident or cartridge-based fonts, Windows allows you to install soft (downloadable) fonts and associate them with a particular printer driver. You can install these fonts permanently or temporarily. If you install a font permanently, it is automatically downloaded to your printer when you boot your system. On the other hand, if you install a font temporarily, it is only downloaded when you print from a Windows application. Installing fonts temporarily allows you to reserve valuable printer memory for printing graphics images.

The ability to install soft fonts for Windows printer drivers is especially important in light of the growing number of third-party font packages that are becoming available. For example, in Chapter 4 you'll learn about several third-party font packages that you can use with Windows.

In Windows, screen fonts are differentiated from printer fonts. Therefore, on occasion, what you see is not what you get—that is, your printed output may not match what appears on your screen. For on-screen display, Windows provides a basic set of screen fonts, many of which are device dependent. When you install Windows for a particular type of display, the screen fonts associated with that display are also installed. If a screen font is not available to match a printer font you've selected, Windows will substitute the closest font it has available. In virtually all cases, the substitute screen font generates the same line lengths, page breaks, and so on as the printer font, but not always. Nevertheless, you can usually rest assured that the layout shown on your screen will closely match the output from your printer.

Windows also allows you to install additional fonts for screen display. This is done through the Control Panel discussed later in this chapter. This may allow you to have a matching screen-display font for each of your installed printer fonts. In fact, most of the third-party font packages discussed in Chapter 4 have a matching screen font for each printer font they provide.

Note: Windows 3 has a new system font that is proportional. This font is far more attractive than the system font in prior versions of Windows, which had fixed characters and spacing.

Windows 3 also includes a print spooler called Print Manager. Print Manager lets you print in the background while continuing to work in an application. In fact, you can send several print jobs from different applications and still keep working. Figure 1-9 shows an example of the Print Manager window.

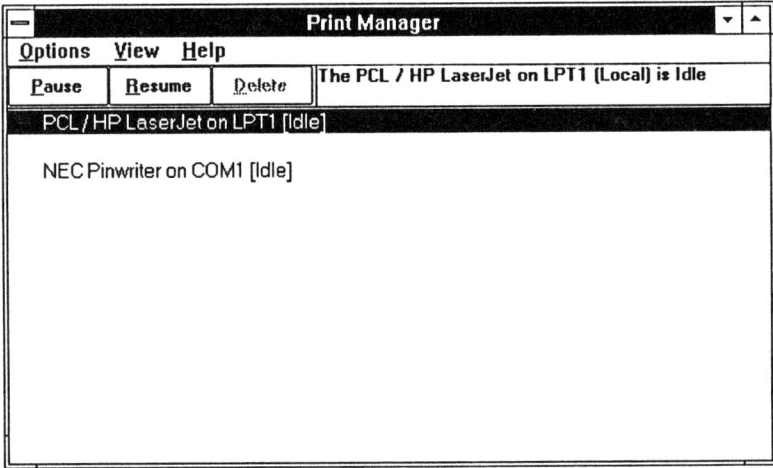

Figure 1-9 The Print Manager window

An Introduction to Windows 3   23

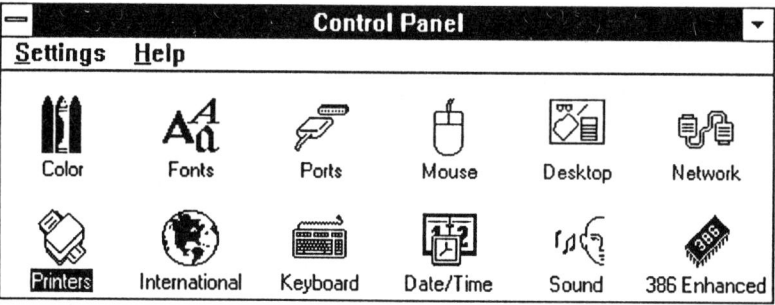

Figure 1-10 The Control Panel window

Print Manager performs its magic by organizing print jobs in a print queue (an area of your computer's memory) and sending them to the printer in the order in which they were received. Print Manager also allows you to look at the contents of the print queue, cancel a print job, or change the order in which print jobs are sent to the printer. In addition, if you are connected to a network, Print Manager may give you access to the network print queue. Using Print Manager to manage your print jobs is discussed in Chapter 4, "Of Fonts and Printing."

Control Panel

The Control Panel has been improved for Windows 3. It now allows you to change many of Windows' hardware and software configuration settings without leaving Windows or running the Setup program. Figure 1-10 shows the Control Panel window. You can open the Control Panel by double-clicking on its icon located in Program Manager's Main group window. The Control Panel is discussed in Chapter 8, "Using the Control Panel."

The Control Panel gives you access to a series of icons that represent different settings you can change for Windows. The following icons are available.

Color

Lets you set colors for the various elements of the Windows desktop. You can set colors for the active window title bar, active window border, scroll bars, and so on. You can choose from the Windows default color set or you can make up custom colors of your own. In addition, you can choose from various predesigned desktop color schemes.

Fonts

Lets you install screen fonts beyond those already installed for Windows. Often, third-party fonts packages provide matching screen and printer fonts, to assure that your printed output matches what appears on your screen.

24   *Windows 3 Power Tools*

Ports

Lets you configure communication parameters for the serial ports on your system.

Mouse

Lets you control the settings for your mouse. For example, you can set mouse speed—the rate at which the mouse pointer moves across the screen. You can also change the speed for double-clicking and swap the left and right mouse buttons.

Desktop

Lets you select from various predesigned wallpaper (bitmap) patterns to adorn the Windows desktop. In addition, you can change the spacing between icons in Program Manager and activate an invisible grid that controls the positioning of application windows on the desktop.

Network

Lets you control your connection to a network. The options available here will vary, depending on the type of network you are connected to. In general, though, you might be able to use this icon to do such things as sign on and off the network.

Printers

Lets you install and configure printers for Windows. More accurately, this option lets you configure Windows to recognize one or more printer drivers and specify settings for those drivers.

International

Lets you set international options for Windows. For example, you can specify a different country and language or change the number, currency, and date/time formats used by Windows.

Keyboard

Lets you adjust the keyboard repeat rate.

Date/Time

Lets you change the date and time for Windows.

Sound

Lets you turn off the warning beep that Windows sounds to inform you of a specific error or condition.

386 Enhanced

Lets you set options for multitasking DOS applications in 386 enhanced mode. For example, you can arbitrate device contention. If two applications are trying to use the same printer port at the same time, you can have Windows warn you of this. You can also specify a percentage of Windows' resources that will be devoted to an application running in the foreground versus those in the background.

Data Sharing

Windows 3 provides a comprehensive set of tools for sharing data between applications. These are discussed in Chapter 6, "Sharing Data Between Applications."

The primary means for sharing data between applications in Windows is the Clipboard. The Clipboard is actually an area of your computer's memory to which you can copy or cut text or graphics from an application. Once information is placed on the Clipboard, you can then paste that information into another application.

In Windows 3, use of the Clipboard is markedly enhanced. For example, you can now place objects on the Clipboard that are larger than 64K. Windows 3 also provides a Clipboard Viewer application, appropriately entitled Clipboard. This application allows you to view the contents of the Clipboard in a window. (Figure 1-11 shows the Clipboard Viewer window.) You also can use the Clipboard Viewer to save the contents of the Clipboard to a file on disk or to delete the contents of the Clipboard to reclaim valuable memory.

The Windows 3 Clipboard also lets you transfer information to and from DOS applications. However, use of the Clipboard for this purpose is often limited by the mode in which you are running Windows. Chapter 6 brings you up to date on what you can and can't do in each of the respective operating modes.

In addition to the Clipboard, Windows also provides Dynamic Data Exchange (DDE). DDE is a data-sharing protocol that allows you to link one application's data file to another application's data file for the purpose of exchanging data between those applications. For example, you might link a Word for Windows document file to a graph file in Microsoft Excel. That way, the Excel graph is displayed in the Word document. Moreover, when you change the underlying spreadsheet numbers for the Excel graph, the Word for Windows document is automatically updated for the change. Implementing DDE between applications is also discussed in Chapter 6.

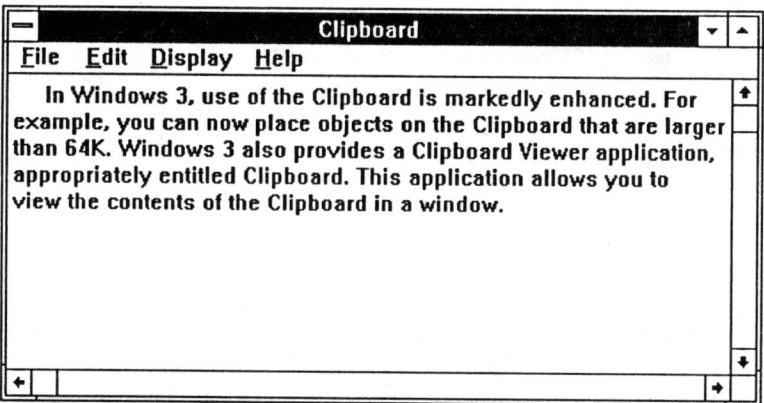

Figure 1-11 The Clipboard Viewer window

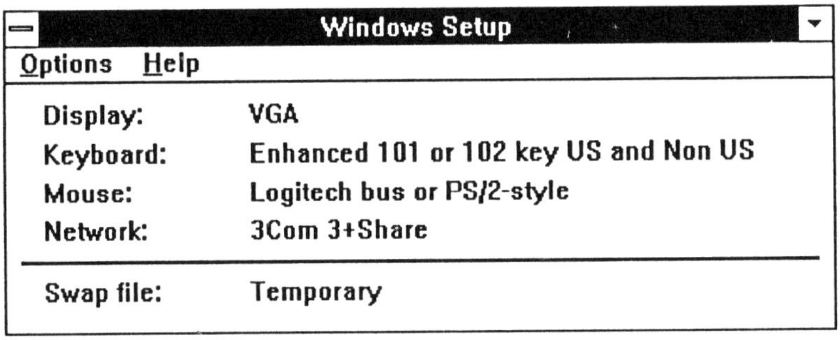

```
┌─────────────────────────────────────────────────────────┐
│ ─            Windows Setup                          ▼   │
│ Options  Help                                           │
│   Display:     VGA                                      │
│   Keyboard:    Enhanced 101 or 102 key US and Non US    │
│   Mouse:       Logitech bus or PS/2-style               │
│   Network:     3Com 3+Share                             │
│   ─────────────────────────────────────────────────     │
│   Swap file:   Temporary                                │
└─────────────────────────────────────────────────────────┘
```

Figure 1-12 Windows Setup

The Windows Setup Program

In Windows 3, you can run the Setup program without exiting Windows. To run Windows Setup, simply double-click on its icon, located in Program Manager's Main group window. The Change System Settings window shown in Figure 1-12 then appears on your screen.

Windows Setup lets you change the software drivers you selected when you originally installed Windows. For example, suppose you upgrade to a new monitor or you buy a different mouse. You can use Windows Setup to install drivers for these devices. In addition, if your machine is connected to a supported network, you can use Setup to install a driver that allows Windows to access that network.

You can also use Windows Setup to install groups of applications. If you only have one application to install, however, it is easier to install that application through Program Manager. (See Chapter 2, "Program Manager Techniques," for details on how to do this.) Nevertheless, if you have multiple Windows or DOS applications that you want to install simultaneously, Windows Setup is the way to do it. Also, when you install DOS applications in this way, Windows automatically creates a PIF (Program Information File) for those applications it recognizes. As you'll learn in Chapter 10, "Using Non-Windows Applications," Windows comes with PIF settings for a variety of popular DOS applications.

More .INI Files

Older versions of Windows use a single initialization file, WIN.INI, to specify the default settings for Windows. WIN.INI is actually an ASCII text file that Windows reads each time you start the program. Often, when you modify a default setting from within Windows, the WIN.INI file is updated to reflect that change. However, you can also manually edit the WIN.INI file yourself by using any editor capable of reading and writing ASCII files, such as Notepad.

Along with the added power of Windows 3, however, comes added complexity. Windows 3 uses five different .INI files to control its default settings. These are as follows:

- WIN.INI—Lets you specify startup defaults for Windows itself. For example, you can use the run= or load= statements in this file to automatically run or load an application on Windows startup.
- SYSTEM.INI—Lets you control Windows hardware-related settings. For example, you can use the settings in this file to disable expanded memory support or specify the maximum size of the temporary swap file.
- PROGMAN.INI—Program Manager's configuration file.
- WINFILE.INI—File Manager's configuration file.
- CONTROL.INI—Control Panel's configuration file.

You won't need to edit PROGMAN.INI, WINFILE.INI, or CONTROL.INI. In fact, you should avoid doing so. Windows maintains these configuration files for you. However, you may develop a need to edit either WIN.INI or SYSTEM.INI. In fact, having a basic understanding of what is in these files can help you to customize the operation of Windows. To aid you in editing these files, Chapter 12 of this book, "Customizing Your .INI Files," discusses some of the more common settings you can change through SYSTEM.INI and WIN.INI.

Note: To help you in editing your system configuration files, Windows 3 includes the System Configuration Editor (SysEdit for short). Its filename is SYSEDIT.EXE and it resides on the \WINDOWS\SYSTEM directory. When you start this handy application, it displays all your pertinent system files (CONFIG.SYS, AUTOEXEC.BAT, WIN.INI, and SYSTEM.INI) in a window, similar to Figure 1-13. Although the use of this application is not documented in the *Windows User's Guide*, it's basically an ASCII text editor that works just like Notepad. You'll find it to be a convenient tool in helping you to configure your system.

Network Support

Windows 3 includes features that make it much easier to use in a network environment than previous versions of Windows. Briefly, some of these features are

- Using File Manager, you can connect your computer to network drives. You can also delete this connection when you want to.
- Using Control Panel, you can add or delete connections to network printers.
- Windows' new Print Manager (called Spooler in previous releases) is capable of recognizing both local and network printers. It lets you display the contents and status of the network print queues.

28 *Windows 3 Power Tools*

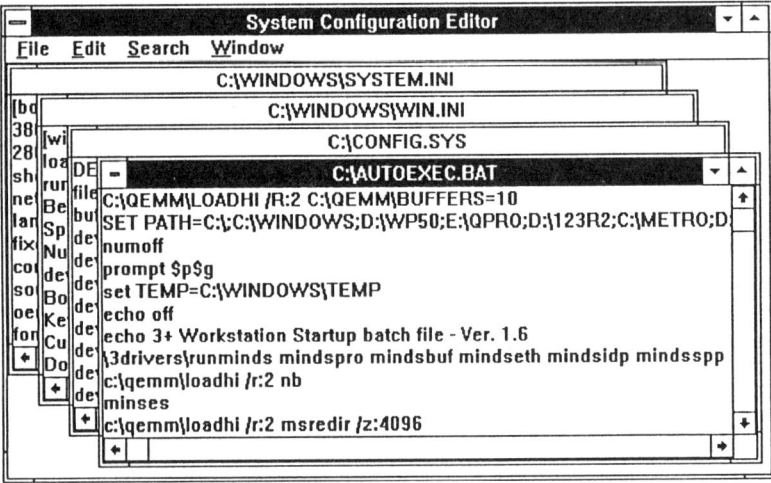

Figure 1-13 SysEdit, the Windows System Configuration Editor

- Using Control Panel, you may be able access a network-specific dialog box that lets you access selected network features. For example, you might be able to log on and off the network from within Windows.
- Multiple users can share a single copy of Windows that is located on the network server. Windows 3 has a new network architecture that allows for the different hardware configurations on each workstation.

Getting Help

Windows 3 includes a new standardized Help application (WINHELP.EXE) that is available for use by all Windows applications. To get to this application, you can select the Help command from the menu of a Windows application, or you can press F1. The Help command is available in all the applications that come with Windows, except Clock. When you select the Help command, Windows displays a pull-down menu of sub-options that let you access a specific category of Help for the current application. When you select an option, Windows displays the Help window in Figure 1-14.

The information displayed on the Help window will, of course, vary depending upon the application that you are currently using and the option that you select from the Help menu. Selecting an option from the Help menu not only opens the Help window but takes you to a specific section of the Help text for the current application.

Although the options on the Help pull-down menu will vary slightly from one application to the next, you'll generally find the Index, Keyboard, Commands, Procedures, and About... options are available. The Index option opens the Help window and displays a master list of Help topics for your selection. You can tell which topics are selectable because the names of the topics appear in a different color from the rest of the

An Introduction to Windows 3 29

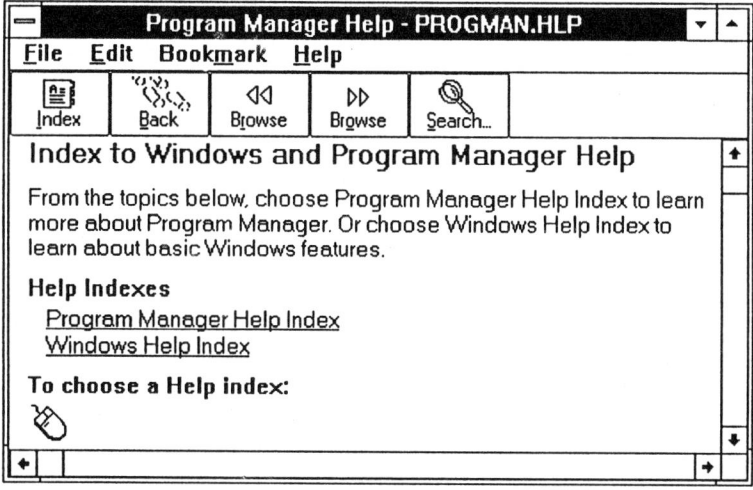

Figure 1-14 The Help window

text in the Help window (usually green on a color screen). You can select a topic either by clicking on it or by pressing TAB to move to it and pressing ENTER to select it. The remainder of the options in the Help menu simply allow you to jump directly to specific category of the Help text for the current application. You can then select from topics for that particular category.

Note: If you press F1 to open the Help window for an application, you are taken directly to the index section of the Help text for that application. You can then select a specific topic on which you want more information.

   The Help window also features a series of buttons that make it easier to navigate within the Help window. For example, the Index button returns you to the main index for the current application. The Back button takes you back to the previous screen or topic, thereby allowing you to backtrack your way through the Help window. The Browse buttons allow you to jump quickly to major categories in the Help text for the current application. For example, imagine the Index section is currently displayed. If you press the right-hand Browse button, Help jumps to the Keys section. If you press this button again, Help jumps to the Commands section, and if you press it again, Help jumps to the Procedures section. To jump backward by major category, select the left-hand Browse button. Finally, the Search button lets you search for a specific topic, keyword, or phrase in the Help text. When you select this button, a dialog box is displayed that lets you select from existing Help topics or type a specific word or phrase you want to find in the Help text.
   The Help window also comes with its own menu. The File menu option lets you open Help files for applications other than the current one. Help files have a .HLP extension.

This extension is preceded by a name that usually allows you to easily identify the application to which that help file belongs. For example, the help file for Program Manager is PROGMAN.HLP, and the help file for Paintbrush is PBRUSH.HLP. You can also use the File menu to send the text for a specific Help topic to your printer.

The Edit menu allows you to copy a specific help topic onto the Windows Clipboard. Once that information is on the Clipboard, you can transfer it to other applications. You can also use the Edit menu option to annotate (add) to the Help text for a specific topic. For example, if you have something helpful to add to a procedure or description, you can access a dialog box that lets you add a paragraph or two to the Help text for the current topic.

The Bookmark menu option lets you mark your place within the current Help file so that you can quickly return to it in future. In effect, the Bookmark menu lets you define a short cut to specific Help topics that you use frequently. This allows you to avoid paging though two or three levels of topics to get to the one you want. Once a bookmark is defined, you can use the Bookmark menu to jump directly to that bookmark whenever you want.

SUMMARY

This chapter discusses the salient features in Windows 3. Most topics are dealt with in an introductory fashion, and you are pointed to other chapters in this book for additional detail. Nevertheless, you now have a base to work from.

You now know a little about advanced memory management in Windows, and you know what you can expect from Windows in each of its various operating modes. You're also aware of what you'll need in terms of a processor and available memory to get Windows to run in a particular mode.

You also know how Windows goes about the business of multitasking. The next time somebody uses the buzzwords "preemptive" or "nonpreemptive" when referring to Windows multitasking, you'll be able tell in an instant if they really know their stuff or if they're just blowing smoke.

You're also aware of the history of Windows. You know where it has been and where it is now. In fact, you know that by simply owning a copy of Windows 3, you are part of one of the most significant strides in the history of the personal computing industry.

2
Program Manager Techniques

As you know, Program Manager is the central program management facility for Windows 3.0. It is prevalent in almost everything you do. For example, when you start Windows, the Program Manager is the first thing you see. Further, it remains active throughout your entire Windows session. Finally, when you want to leave Windows, you close the Program Manager.

Because Program Manager is such an integral part of Windows, a thorough understanding of how to manage it is imperative if you intend to become a Windows power user. In fact, the more effectively you can manage Program Manager, the more productive your Windows sessions will ultimately become.

This chapter assumes you already know a little about running Windows. You won't find information here about how to minimize a window or scroll window contents, for example. Instead, this chapter will focus on providing you with tips and techniques that will help you customize Program Manager to better suit the way you actually work. For example, you'll find the following topics discussed in this chapter:

- Various ways you can manipulate and manage your icons, including borrowing icons from other programs.

- Techniques you can use to change Program Manager's layout and improve on its organization.

32   *Windows 3 Power Tools*

- How to control the order in which windows are stacked or tiled.
- Techniques and considerations for running multiple applications at the same time.

These are but a few of the topics discussed in this chapter. However, they serve to give you a general feel for what lies ahead.

To establish some common ground for discussion, the next section takes a look at Program Manager's default layout. This introductory material will be used as a jumping off point for the rest of the topics discussed in this chapter. If you are already familiar with Program Manager's default layout, you may want to skip the next section and jump directly to "Managing Icons."

PROGRAM MANAGER'S DEFAULT LAYOUT

The first time you start Windows, the Program Manager window appears on your screen as shown in Figure 2-1. Within Program Manager itself are a series of internal windows, called *group windows*. Only the Main group window is open at first, however. The other group windows appear as icons located along the bottom edge of Program Manager's window. The only way to tell these group-window icons apart is by the description that appears beneath each one. You can open any one of these iconized group windows by double-clicking on it. Alternatively you can press CLTR+F6 or CTRL+TAB to move to a group window and press ENTER, or you can choose the Window command from Program Manager's menu and select the name of the group window from the list that appears.

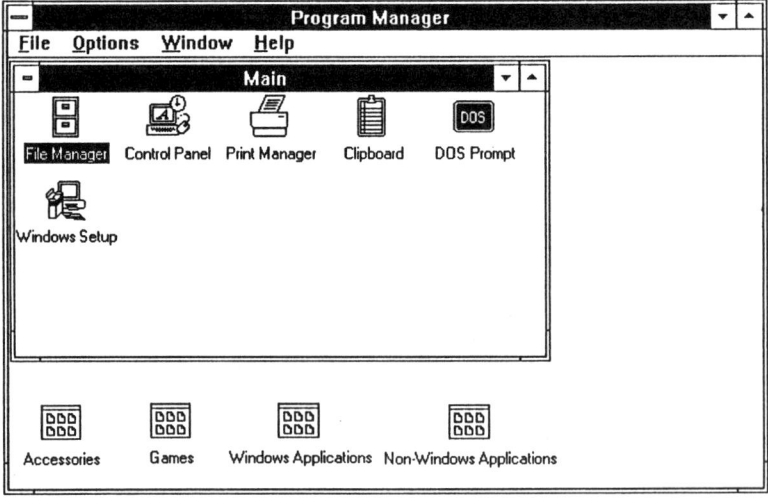

Figure 2-1 Program Manager's default layout

Within each group window are icons that represent the applications included in each group. You can run any application in a group by simply double-clicking on its icon. What's more, you can run multiple applications at the same time and switch back and forth between them.

Note: Throughout the *Windows User's Guide*, the term "program item" is often used when referring to icons for both group windows and for applications. However, in the interest of simplicity, the term "icon" will be used throughout this chapter.

By default, you start out with Main, Accessories, and Games group windows. Two additional group windows are added if you asked Windows Setup to search your hard disk(s) for existing applications during installation. These two windows are entitled Windows Applications and Non-Windows Applications, respectively. As you might imagine, Setup installs your Windows applications in the Windows group and installs your DOS applications in the Non-Windows group. The applications included within each of the default group windows are as follows:

- Main: File Manager, Control Panel, Print Manager, Clipboard, DOS Prompt, and Windows Setup
- Accessories: Write, Paintbrush, Terminal, Notepad, Recorder, Cardfile, Calendar, Calculator, Clock, and PIF Editor
- Games: Solitaire and Reversi
- Windows Applications: Applications, such as Microsoft Excel or Microsoft Word for Windows, that are specifically designed for the Windows environment
- Non-Windows Applications: Applications, such as Lotus 1-2-3 Release 2.2, or WordPerfect 5.1, that are not designed for Windows

Although Microsoft believes that this default layout is suitable for a large segment of the population, it may not be suitable for you. In fact, after you use Windows for a while, you may well become frustrated with Microsoft's forced dichotomy between Windows and non-Windows applications and decide to make up a few organizational rules of your own.

Fortunately, Program Manager is completely customizable. You can create as many group windows as you want and you can locate the icon for a given application in one or all them. And, as you might imagine, you can include both Windows and non-Windows applications in the same group.

Before you begin adding new group windows to Program Manager, though, you should have a good basic understanding of how to copy and move application icons between group windows as well as how to set up new application icons. These topics are discussed in the next section. Once you've mastered these skills, you can move on to "Managing Group Windows," which shows you how to create new group windows, delete old ones, and arrange group windows. The section after that, "Customizing Program Manager," shows you various techniques for organizing group windows to better suit the way you work.

MANAGING ICONS

This section shows you how to manipulate and manage application icons within Program Manager group windows. Some of the topics discussed here include

- Copying and moving existing icons between group windows
- Deleting icons
- Setting up new icons
- Borrowing icons from other Windows programs for use with your DOS applications
- Setting up icons that start an application in a specific directory
- Linking application data files to icons
- Arranging application icons both within Program Manager group windows and on the Windows desktop

Copying Icons

The easiest way to copy an icon from one group window to another is to use a combination of the CTRL key and your mouse. To do this, press the CTRL key and hold it down. Then click on the icon you want to copy and drag it to the desired location in another group window. (As you drag, Windows shows a faded black and white image of the icon that moves along with your mouse pointer.) When you get to the new group window, release both the CTRL key and your mouse button. Windows copies the icon to the new group window and places it in the location you specified.

For example, imagine you have the default Program Manager configuration shown earlier in Figure 2-1, and that you want to copy the Notepad icon from the Accessories group window to your Windows Applications group window. Before copying this icon, you'll probably want to open both the source and destination group windows, as shown in Figure 2-2. That way, you can choose a precise position for the icon in the destination group window. Once you have your source and destination group windows properly displayed, you can use the combination of the CTRL key and your mouse to copy the Notepad icon from the Accessories group window to your Windows Applications group window.

Each time you copy an icon from one group window to another, you'll hear Windows hitting your hard disk. It is saving the new configuration for future reference. That way, the next time you start Windows, your newly copied icons will continue to appear in the appropriate group windows.

Note: You can locate the icon for an application in as many group windows as you want. However, avoid overkill on this. You should only place the icon for a given application in those group windows where you are most likely to need it.

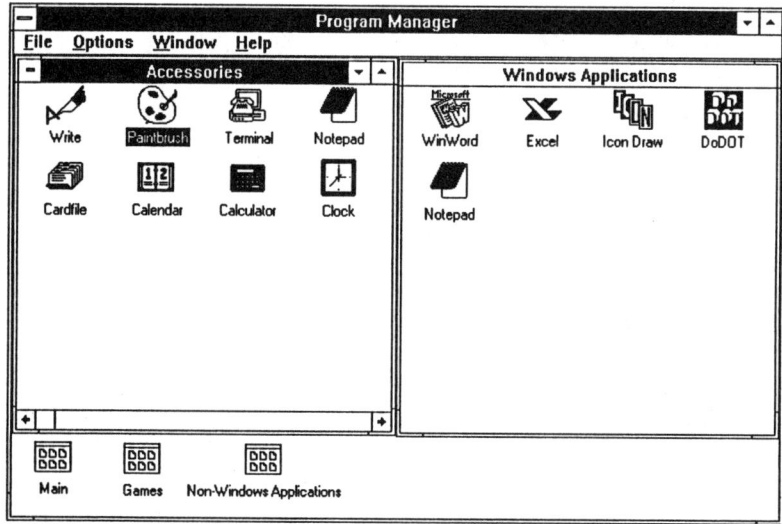

Figure 2-2 Use the CTRL key in combination with your mouse to copy an icon between open group windows

---

Tip: You can leave the destination group window minimized when copying icons

If you don't care about the positioning of an icon in a group window after you copy it, you can open the source group window (the window containing the icon you want to copy) but leave the destination group window (the window you want to copy the icon to) closed. When you copy the icon, Windows will place it in the first available spot in the destination group window.

You can also copy icons by using your keyboard. However, it involves a few extra steps in comparison to using the mouse to copy an icon. In addition, the keyboard method doesn't allow you choose the precise location of the icon in the destination group window.

To copy an icon with the keyboard, first use Program Manager's Window command to open the group window that contains the icon (if it isn't already open). Then, use the arrow keys to move to the icon itself. When you're ready, select the File Copy command from Program Manager's menu. Windows displays the Copy Program Item dialog box. At the top of this box, Windows displays information about the program item (the icon) you've selected as well as its group window. Below this is a drop-down list box entitled

To Group, which lists the names of the Program Manager's current group windows. Press ALT+↓ or F4 to open this list box and highlight the name of the group window you want to copy the icon to. Press ENTER to confirm your choice. Windows copies the icon to the group window you selected, placing it in the first available spot.

Tip: Icons consume relatively little memory

Don't worry too much about the memory issues associated with copying the same icon to multiple group windows. Frankly, the memory "hit" is negligible. Generally, group-window icons consume between 32 and 64 bytes each. The size of application icons, varies depending on your display device. For example, on a VGA screen, icons consume 640 bytes. On an EGA screen 512 bytes are consumed, and on a CGA screen 128 bytes are consumed. However, if memory is tight, Windows can discard (copy to disk) those icons that are not presently displayed, and reload them back from disk when it needs them. For more information on memory issues related to Windows, see Chapter 7, "Memory Management."

Moving Icons

Moving an icon from one group window to another is very similar to copying one. All you do is click on the icon, drag it to another group window, and release your mouse button. Windows moves the icon from the old group window to the new one.

For example, imagine you have the group windows in Figure 2-2 displayed and you want to move the Cardfile icon from the Accessories Group window to your Windows Applications group window. To do this, click on the Cardfile icon in the Accessories window and drag it to the appropriate spot in the Windows Applications window. (As you drag, Windows displays a faded black and white image that follows the motion of your mouse pointer.) When you're ready, release your mouse button. Windows moves the icon to the new location.

Similar to copying icons, it's always best to have both your source and destination group windows open when you move an icon. That way, you can choose exactly where the icon will be positioned in the destination group window. Otherwise, if the destination group window is iconized, Windows will simply place the icon in the first available spot.

You can also move icons by using your keyboard. To do this, begin by opening the group window containing the icon (if it isn't already open) and then activate the icon itself. When you're ready, select the File Move command from Program Manager menu. Windows displays the Move Program Item dialog box. At the top of this box, Windows displays information about the program item (the icon) you've selected as well as its group window. Below this is a drop-down list box entitled To Group which lists the names of other group windows. Open this list box and highlight the name of the group window you want to move the icon to. Select OK or press ENTER to confirm your choice. Windows moves the icon to the group window you've selected and places it in the first available spot.

Deleting Icons

To delete an icon, simply click on it and press the DEL key. Windows displays a Yes/No message box asking you if you really want to delete the icon. As you might imagine, you can select Yes to delete the icon or No to cancel the delete operation.

When you delete the icon for an application, the program files related to that icon are not affected in any way. Therefore, don't be afraid to delete old icons that you no longer need. In fact, deleting old and unneeded icons is one of the best ways to keep your Program Manager group windows neat and organized. In addition, If you later change your mind, you can always use the techniques described in the next section to set the icon up again.

Setting Up New Icons

To create a new icon, begin by activating the group window in which you want to locate the new icon. Then, select the File New command from Program Manager's menu. When you select this command, Windows displays the New Program Object dialog box shown in Figure 2-3.

To create a new application icon, select the Program Item radio button, then select OK to begin defining the properties of the icon. Windows displays the Program Item Properties dialog box shown in Figure 2-4.

In the Description dialog box, type the capsule description you want to appear beneath the icon and in the title bar of the window in which it will run. (This description also appears in the Task List window when you activate it.) You can type up to 40 characters here. However, it's always best to keep these descriptions short. Otherwise, the labels from two adjacent icons may overlap. For example, rather than *1-2-3 Release 3.1* or *Word for Windows*, you may be able to get by with *1-2-3 R3* or *WinWord*.

In the Command Line text box, enter the executable filename that will be used to run the application. It's always best to include the full drive, path, and filename. For example,

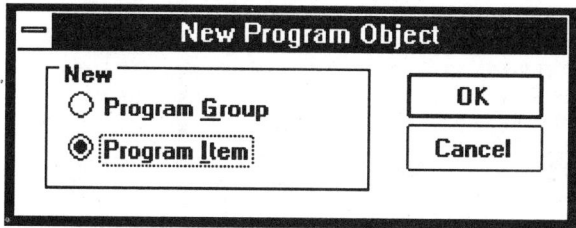

Figure 2-3 The New Program Object dialog box

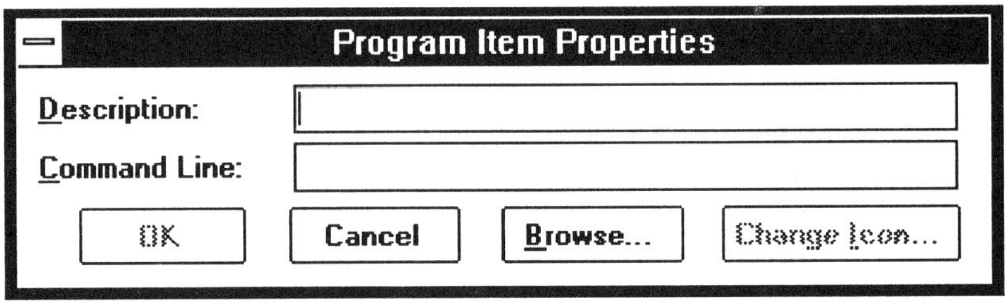

Figure 2-4 The Program Item Properties dialog box

if you are creating a new icon for Microsoft Excel, located in your C:\EXCEL directory, you would type **C:\EXCEL\EXCEL.EXE**. If you can't remember the executable filename, select the Browse button to have Windows display the Browse dialog box in Figure 2-5.

The Browse dialog box allows you to select the filename that will be used to run the application. Ultimately, the file you select will appear in the File Name text box. Initially, however, Windows displays *.exe in this box, causing all the .EXE executable files in your Windows directory to appear in the Files list box below. Table 2-1 shows a list of applications these file names represent. (To see a list of files in another directory, use the Directory list box to select the directory you want.) To select a particular file from the Files List box, double-click on it. Windows returns you to the Program Item Properties dialog box and displays the full drive, path, and name for the file you selected in the Command Line text box.

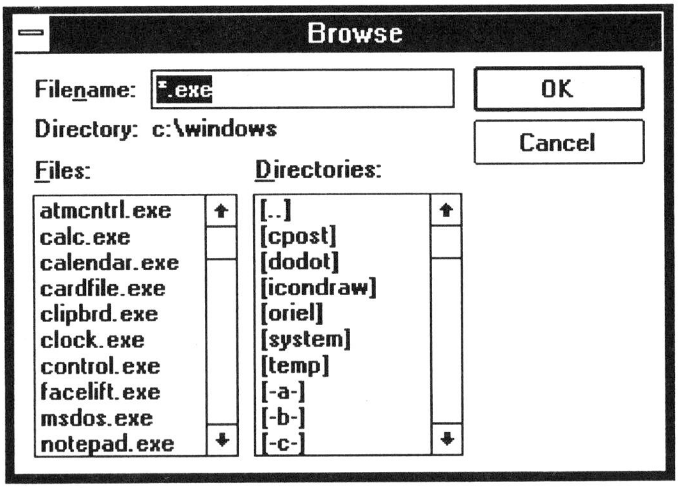

Figure 2-5 The Browse dialog box

> **Tip: Specify a directory before you select Browse**

You can also enter the path to the directory in the Command Line text box before you select Browse. For example, suppose you know that Word for Windows is located in your C:\WINWORD directory, but you can't remember its executable file name. You can type the name of this directory in the Command Line text box (for example **C:\WINWORD**) and then select the Browse button. When the Browse dialog box is displayed, it will list the executable files in your C:\WINWORD directory, and you can select the one you want.

Filename	*Application*
CALC.EXE	Calculator
CALENDAR.EXE	Calendar
CARDFILE.EXE	Cardfile
CLIPBRD.EXE	Clipboard
CLOCK.EXE	Clock
CONTROL.EXE	Control Panel
MSDOS.EXE	MS DOS Executive
NOTEPAD.EXE	Notepad
PBRUSH.EXE	Paint Brush
PIFEDIT.EXE	PIF Editor
PRINTMAN.EXE	Print Manager
PROGMAN.EXE	Program Manager
RECORDER.EXE	Recorder
REVERSI.EXE	Reversi
SETUP.EXE	Setup
SOL.EXE	Solitaire
SYSEDIT.EXE	System Configuration Editor (On \WINDOWS\SYSTEM)
SWAPFILE.EXE	Swapfile (On \WINDOWS\SYSTEM)
TERMINAL.EXE	Terminal
TASKMAN.EXE	Task List
WINFILE.EXE	File Manager
WINHELP.EXE	Windows Help
WINVER.EXE	Windows Version and Mode information
WRITE.EXE	Write

Table 2-1 Common Windows Executable Files

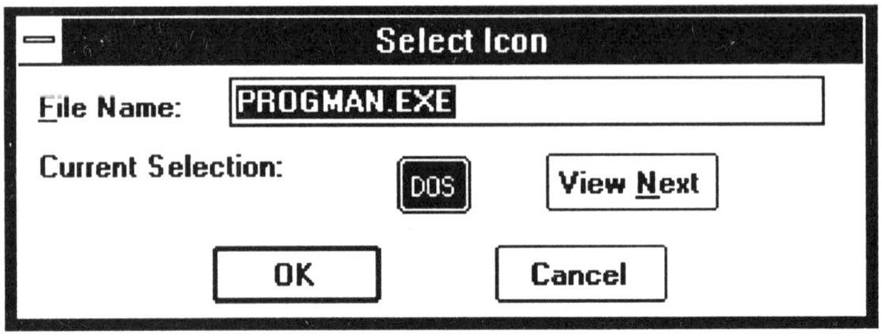

Figure 2-6 The Select Icon dialog box

Before you select OK to create the icon, select the Change Icon button to see the different icons that are available for the application you've selected. When you select this button, Windows displays the Select Icon dialog box shown in Figure 2-6. To see what icons are available, select the View Next button.

Each time you select the View Next button, Windows displays the next available icon for the current application. If you are setting up a Windows application, generally only one or perhaps two icons are available. On the other hand, if you are setting up a DOS application, Windows offers the selection of icons shown in Figure 2-7 (more about these icons in a moment). To return to the Program Item Properties dialog box, select OK. Then select OK again to have Windows display the icon in the next available spot in the currently active group window. If the position chosen by Windows is not to your liking, you can, of course, drag the icon to a more desirable location.

As mentioned, if you are setting up a DOS application icon, Windows provides the icons shown in Figure 2-7. Windows gets all of these icons from PROGMAN.EXE, Program Manager's executable file. In fact, if you take a look at Figure 2-6, you'll notice that PROGMAN.EXE appears in the File Name text box. Additional details on these icons are as follows:

- DOS Generic—This is the default assigned to a non-Windows application unless you specify otherwise.

- Document—You can use this icon to represent a text-based wordprocessing application like WordPerfect.

- Spreadsheet—You can use this icon to represent spreadsheet applications like Lotus 1-2-3 or Borland's Quattro Pro.

- Database—The blocks in this icon look like the fields in a database. Therefore, you might want to use this icon to represent a database product like dBASE or Paradox.

- Communications—The telephone in this icon makes it best suited for use with communications packages like Procomm or CrossTalk.

- Generic—Use this application when none of the other non-Windows icons seem appropriate.

- Group—This is Program Manager's group window icon. There are relatively few instances where you would want to use this icon.

Program Manager Techniques 41

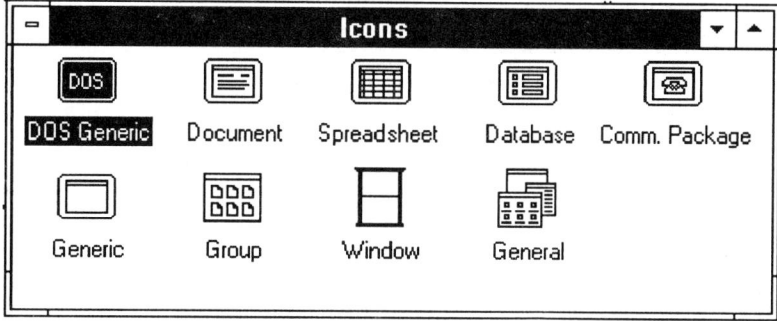

Figure 2-7 The icons associated with PROGRAM.EXE

- Window—When you set up a PIF (Program Information File) for a DOS application, you can specify that the application run in a window (much like a standard Windows application) rather than in full-screen mode. You can use this icon to remind you of that setting. See Chapter 10, "Using Non-Windows Applications," for additional information about setting up PIFs for DOS applications.
- General—This is the icon you see when you minimize Program Manager. This icon has a little of everything in it. Use it when you're setting up a multipurpose application like Lotus Symphony or Symantec's Q&A.

Icon properties are not cast in stone. That is, you can always change the properties of an icon at a later time. For example, you can change its description or command line, and you can even select a new icon to be displayed in place of the old one. To do this, you use the File Properties command. See the next section for details on how to use this command.

Tip: **You can use Windows Setup to create icons for applications**

When you installed Windows, the SETUP.EXE program asked you whether it should scan your hard disk for applications. You were then given the opportunity to install all (or some) of those applications for use with Windows. This same facility is still available to you through the Windows Setup application located in the Main group window. One the advantages to setting up DOS applications in this way is that Windows will automatically create PIFs (Program Information Files) for many popular DOS applications. See Chapter 9, "Changing Your Setup," for additional details on using the Windows Setup program and Chapter 10, "Using Non-Windows Applications," for more information about PIFs.

Note: Some newer releases of DOS applications come with both a PIF and an icon. For example, 1-2-3 Release 3.1 includes both of these—the PIF is 123.PIF and the icon is 123.ICO. See Chapter 10, "Using Non-Windows Applications," for details on how PIF files are used. See "Borrowing Icons" later in this chapter for details on how you can use an .ICO file to display an icon for an application.

Changing Icon Properties

You can easily change the current properties of an application icon. For example, you can change both its description and its command line. You can even select an entirely new icon that will be displayed in place of the old one.

To change the properties of an icon, first select the icon whose properties you want to change by clicking on it. When you're ready, select the File Properties command from Program Manager's menu. When you select this command, Windows displays the Program Item Properties dialog box shown in Figure 2-8, which shows the current properties of the icon you've selected. As you may recall, this same dialog box was shown earlier in Figure 2-4 in association with the File New command for setting up new icons, and you use it in the same way. However, in this case, the Program Item Properties dialog box allows you to change the properties of the icon you've selected.

The Description text box shows the current description for the icon, which you can accept or change. In addition, the Command Line text box shows you the current command line for the icon you've selected. You can type a new command line or you can select the Browse button and use the Browse dialog (shown in Figure 2-5) to select an application filename. At this point, you can select OK to save the changes you've made thus far, or you can select the Change Icon button to display the Select Icon dialog box (see Figure 2-6) and change the icon for the application as well.

Borrowing Icons

Icons are a special form of bitmap that are 32-by-32 pixels. (The one exception is icons designed for the CGA, which are 32-by-16 pixels.) Icons are typically created by programmers using SDKPaint in the Windows 3 SDK (Software Development Kit) and

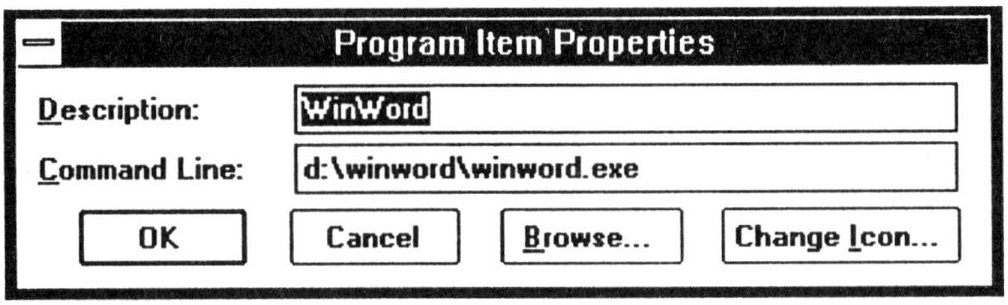

Figure 2-8 Using the File Properties command to change the properties of an application icon

saved as .ICO files. These .ICO files are then compiled and linked with other files to create a single executable (.EXE) file that represents the finished Windows application. In this case, the icon actually becomes a part of the finished application. On the other hand, .ICO files can also exist independently. As mentioned, some newer releases of DOS applications come with .ICO files that contain icons.

You can easily borrow an icon from either a Windows application or an .ICO file. Further, you can use that icon in association with either another Windows application or with a DOS application.

To borrow an icon, you need only reference the appropriate filename in the File Name text box of the Select Icon dialog box. As you may recall, this dialog box was shown earlier in Figure 2-6. (See "Setting Up New Icons" or "Changing Icon Properties" earlier in this chapter for details on how to access this dialog box.)

Once the Select Icon dialog box is displayed, type the filename of any Windows application, or the name of an .ICO file, in the File Name text box. You'll have to type this name in place of the one that is already there (typically PROGMAN.EXE or the Windows application name). The icon associated with that filename will then be displayed below when you select the View Next button. To see if there is more than one icon available (Windows applications only), select View Next again to review those icons and select the one you want. When you select OK to leave the Select Icon dialog box, Windows will use the icon you specified for the application you are currently setting up. In this way, you can borrow icons either from Windows applications or from .ICO files and use them with your other applications.

For your information, the following applications that come with Windows have multiple icons that you can borrow for use with other applications:

PROGMAN.EXE—Program Manager offers the nine icons shown earlier in Figure 2-7.

CONTROL.EXE—Control Panel has the twelve icons shown in Figure 2-9, plus one more that is not shown.

WINFILE.EXE—File Manager has two icons.

SETUP.EXE—Windows Setup also has two icons.

SYSEDIT.EXE—Windows System Editor also has two icons that you can use. This application file is located in the \WINDOWS\SYSTEM directory.

Tip: Creating your own icons

Icondraw is a Windows application included with this book that lets you design your own icons. The icons you design are saved as standard Windows .ICO files. Therefore, you can use these icons with both Windows and DOS applications. See Chapter 17 for details on installing and using Icondraw.

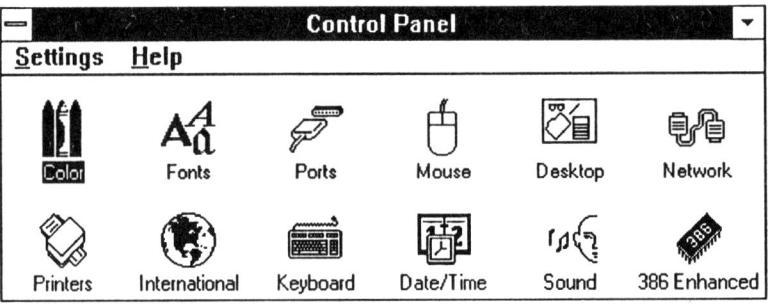

Figure 2-9 Icons associated with CONTROL.EXE

Setting Up Icons with File Manager

You can also set up new icons with the aid of File Manager. Frankly, this method is a bit unwieldy, though. It involves using your mouse to drag an application filename from a File Manager directory window to an open group window in Program Manager. When you release your mouse button, Windows will create an icon for that application. Obviously, you cannot perform this operation with your keyboard.

To perform this operation, it's best to display the Program Manager and File Manager windows side by side, as shown in Figure 2-10. You can do this by starting File Manager and then double-clicking on the desktop, or pressing CTRL+ESC, to display the Task List window. Once the Task List window is dislayed, select the Tile button, or press ALT+T. Once the windows are displayed side by side, activate the File Manager window by clicking on it or pressing ALT+ESC to move to it. Once you are in the File Manager window, open a directory window that contains the executable file for the application you want to setup. Next, activate Program Manager and open the group window in which you want to create the icon.

To create the new icon, click on the icon of any .EXE, .COM, or .BAT filename in the File Manager directory window, and drag that icon from File Manager to the open group window in Program Manager. As you drag, Windows displays a small black and white icon that follows the movement of your mouse pointer. When you get to the group window in Program Manager, position the icon and release your mouse button. Windows creates the new icon. If you are setting up this icon for a DOS application, Windows uses the generic DOS icon from PROGMAN.EXE by default. However, if you are setting up a Windows application, Windows uses the icon that is associated with that application's executable file. In either case, the description assigned to the icon is the application's filename, less its extension.

By now, you've no doubt surmised that this procedure represents a great deal of work to create only a single icon. In addition, you have no control over which icon is used; nor do you have any control over the description assigned to that icon. However, once you have the File Manager and Program Manager windows properly set up, you can quickly create multiple icons with a minimum of effort. Further, if you don't like the displayed

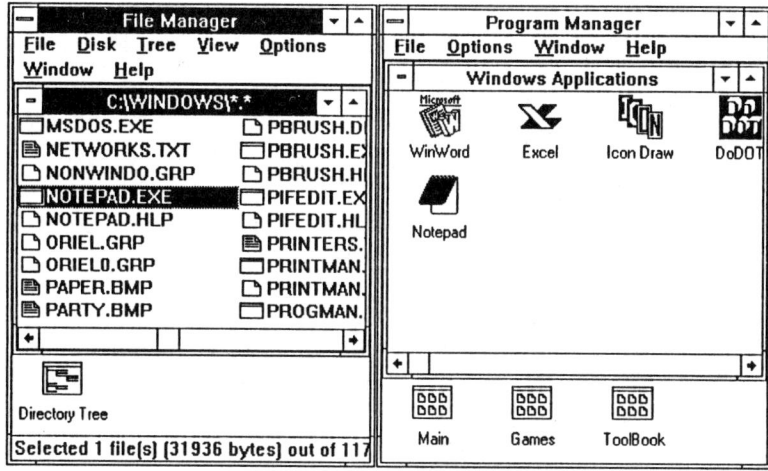

Figure 2-10 Using File Manager to set up new icons

icon or its description, you can always change these later by using Program Manager's File Properties command. See "Changing Icon Properties" earlier in this chapter for details on how to use this command.

Starting an Application in a Specific Directory

One of the most frustrating things about previous versions of Windows was the lack of an easy way to make a specific directory current when starting an application. Thus, when you selected the File Open or File Save command from within an application, you always had to look at the files in your Windows directory first. Since very few people locate their application data files in the same directory as Windows, you always had to make a concerted effort to reference the appropriate directory for a File Save or Open command.

Now, however, Windows 3.0 offers an easy way to make a specific directory current when you start an application. To do this, you must specify the appropriate command line for the application's icon. You can accomplish this in one of two ways. On the one hand, you can use the File Properties command to change the command line for the current icon. A better way, though, is to set up an entirely new icon by using the File New command. That way, you can choose a different group window for the new icon, and you can supply a custom description that better describes what the icon actually does.

For example, imagine you want to start Word for Windows and automatically make your C:\LETTERS directory the current directory for that application. To do this, open the group window in which you want to create the new icon and select the File New command from Program Manager's menu. Select OK to display the Program Item Properties dialog box. In the Description text box, enter a description for the icon, for example, **WinWord\LETTERS**. In the Command Line text box, enter the following command line:

```
C:\LETTERS\WINWORD.EXE
```

where C:\LETTERS refers to your \LETTERS directory and WINWORD.EXE starts Word for Windows. Select the Change icon button to display the Select Icon dialog box. Windows displays C:\LETTERS\WINWORD.EXE in the File Name text box and the generic DOS application icon below. Type the drive, path, and name of the Word for Windows executable file—for example, C:\WINWORD\WINWORD.EXE. Then, select the View Next button to display the appropriate icon. Finally, select OK to return to the Program Item Properties dialog box.

When you select OK, to create the icon, Windows displays an "Invalid Path" error message box. Ignore this error message box and select OK to clear it. Windows creates the new icon. When you start Word for Windows by using this icon, it will come up with your C:\LETTERS directory as the current directory.

There is a catch to all this. For it to work, the directory containing Word for Windows must be included in the PATH statement in your AUTOEXEC.BAT file. Otherwise, Windows won't be able to find the directory and will issue an error message when you attempt to use the icon. However, if the directory containing the application is not included in your PATH statement, the next tip will show you how you can easily fix this.

Note: If you want to make a specific directory current when you start a DOS application, you can use the Startup Directory text box in the application's PIF (Program Information File). See Chapter 10, "Using Non-Windows Applications," for more information on creating and using PIFs with your DOS applications.

Tip: Use SysEdit to update AUTOEXEC.BAT

A little-known application that comes with Windows 3.0 lets you edit your system configuration files. This application is called the System Configuration Editor, or SysEdit for short. Its filename is SYSEDIT.EXE, and it resides in the \WINDOWS\SYSTEM directory. When you run this file, the window in Figure 2-11 appears on your screen. The SysEdit window is composed of four internal windows, each containing a different system configuration file: AUTOEXEC.BAT, CONFIG.SYS, WIN.INI, and SYSTEM.INI. SysEdit is basically an ASCII editor that works just like Notepad. To edit a particular file, activate its window by clicking on it and then click on the document within the window. You can then make any additions or changes you need. To save your changes, select the File Save command. If you change AUTOEXEC.BAT or CONFIG.SYS, you'll need to reboot your computer to have those changes take effect. On the other hand, if you change WIN.INI or SYSTEM.INI, you must restart Windows to have those changes take effect.

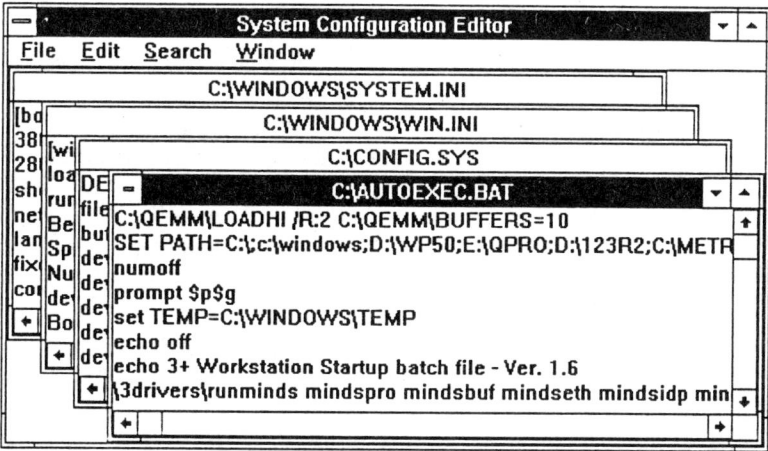

Figure 2-11 The System Configuration Editor (SysEdit) window

Linking Data Files to Icons

You can also set up an icon that starts a given Windows application and then loads a specific data file for that application's use. For example, imagine you are working on a rather large report in Word for Windows that will take you several weeks to complete. In conjunction with that report, you are building a supporting spreadsheet in Microsoft Excel to which you will need to refer periodically. In this case, you might want to create two new icons. The first one would start Word and load your document. The second would start Excel and load your spreadsheet. That way, you could set up your work session quickly with only a couple of double-clicks of the mouse.

Linking data files to icons is easier than you think. All you do is use the File New command and then select OK to display the Program Item Properties dialog box. In the Command Line text box, type the path and filename for the application you want to start, followed by a space and the path and name of the data file. For instance, following up on the example in the previous paragraph, suppose you have Word for Windows located in your D:\WINWORD directory. Imagine further that you have the file PROJECT5.DOC located in your C:\DOCUMENT directory. With this configuration, you would enter the following command line:

```
D:\WINWORD\WINWORD.EXE C:\DOCUMENT\PROJECT5.DOC
```

If the data file is located in the same directory as the application (which is, of course, extremely rare), you do not need to provide the drive and directory for the data file. Instead, you could get by with just the following:

```
D:\WINWORD\WINWORD.EXE PROJECT5.DOC
```

Launching Applications by Association

You can also create an association between a data file with a specific extension and its application program. Once an association exists, you can set up an icon that starts the application and loads that data file. However, in the Command Line text box for the icon, you can simply enter the path and name for the data file. Because an assocation exists, a reference to the path and name of the executable file is not necessary. When you double-click on the icon, Windows will automatically start the appropriate application by association and load the data file referenced in the Command Line text box.

The easiest way to create an association between a data file and its application is to use the File Assocation command from within File Manager. To do this, start File Manager by double-clicking on its icon in Program Manager's Main group window. The File Manager window appears on your screen and the Directory Tree window is displayed. Double-click on the name of a directory in the directory tree. For example, you might double-click on the name of the directory that contains your Word for Windows document files. Once you make a selection, File Manager opens a directory window displaying the names of files in that directory.

Click on the name of a document file that has an extension you commonly use for your Word for Windows files. For example, if you usually assign a .DOC extension, click on any file that has that extension. Finally, select the File Association command. Windows displays the Associate dialog box in Figure 2-12. Type the name of an executable file for Word for Windows, for example **WINWORD.EXE**, and press ENTER to complete the command. Windows creates an association between files with a .DOC extension and Word for Windows.

Once an association exists, you can take advantage of it when setting up an icon in Program Manager. For example, imagine you want to create an icon that starts Word for

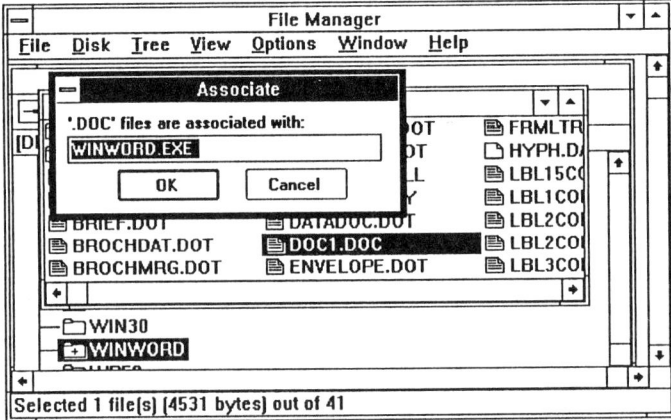

Figure 2-12 The Associate dialog box lets you link a data file extension to an application

Windows and loads the file PROJECT5.DOC located in your C:\LETTERS directory. To do this, select the File New command to display the New Program Object dialog box. Select the Program Item radio button and then select OK to display the Program Item Properties dialog box. In the Command Line text box, type the following command line:

```
C:\DOCUMENT\PROJECT5.DOC.
```

Select OK to create the icon and return to Program Manager. When you double-click on this new icon, Windows starts Word for Windows by association and loads the PROJECT5.DOC file.

When you create an association with File Manager, Windows records that association in the [Extensions] section of the WIN.INI file. That way, the association is available for your next Windows session. For example, you might find an entry like **doc=winword.exe ^.doc** referencing the association between Word for Windows and files with a .DOC extension. In addition, you'll find similar entries for all of the standard applications that come with your copy of Windows.

You can, of course, manually edit the [Extensions] section of the WIN.INI file by using the SysEdit application mentioned in the last tip. However, it is just as easy to update this file by using the File Association command explained above. Nevertheless, when you acquire a new Windows application, you should make a point of creating an association between that application and its data files. Many Windows applications will update your WIN.INI file for you when you install the product. However, you cannot always count on this.

Note: For a more detailed discussion of how you can use WIN.INI to customize your Windows environment, see Chapter 12, "Customizing Your .INI Files." For more about using File Manager, see Chapter 3, "File Manager Techniques."

Keep in mind that certain DOS applications have their own command-line conventions for loading a specific data file on start-up. You must observe these same conventions when setting up the command line for a Windows icon. For example, if you're a 1-2-3 user, you know that you must use the -w switch if you want to start 1-2-3 and automatically load a specific worksheet file. For instance, if 1-2-3 is located in your C:\LOTUS directory and the worksheet file you want to load is SALES_92.WK1 in your C:\BUDGETS directory, you would use the following command line at the DOS prompt:

```
C:\LOTUS\123.EXE -wC:\BUDGETS\SALES_92.WK1
```

Use this same entry in the Command Line text box when you set up your Windows icon.

Arranging Application Icons in Group Windows

As you copy and move icons from one group window to another and set up new icons, you may begin to notice that your icons are getting a little out of hand. That is, the placement of icons within some of your group windows may appear uneven and disorganized (perhaps even downright sloppy). However, you can tidy up a group window in a real hurry by using the Window Arrange Icons command from Program Manager's menu. This command lets you restore the icons in a group window into neat, evenly spaced rows again.

To use the Window Arrange Icons command, first select any icon in the group window whose icons you want to arrange. When you are ready, select the Window Arrange Icons command. Windows arranges your icons into evenly spaced rows within the group window, working from its upper-left corner. During this process, some of your icons may be moved up to the previous row or down to the next, depending on the size of the window. However, the order of your icons is not affected.

Note: You can also use the Window Arrange Icons command to restore the arrangement of group-window icons. See "Arranging Group Window Icons" later in this chapter for details on how to do this.

Tip: Changing the spacing between icons

You can increase or decrease the spacing between application icons in group windows. To do this, select the Desktop icon in the Control Panel to display the Desktop dialog box. To increase the spacing between icons, increase the number in the box labeled Icon Spacing. The next time you use the Window Arrange Icons command, Windows will use the value you specify here as a guide for arranging your icons. Increasing the spacing between icons is helpful when the description labels for several of the icons in a group window are overlapping. Conversely, if you want to fit more icons in less space, you can decrease the spacing. See Chapter 8, "Using the Control Panel," for more on using the Control Panel to customize Windows.

Arranging Icons Automatically

You can have your application icons arranged automatically within a group window by selecting the Options Auto Arrange command from the Program Manager menu. This little-known command makes your group windows somewhat dynamic. That is, when you change the size of a group window, your icons are automatically arranged to fit the new size. Normally, the Auto Arrange feature is turned off. To turn it on, select Options Auto Arrange. To turn it off again, select Options Auto Arrange a second time.

Arranging Icons for Running Applications

In addition to arranging application icons within group windows, you can also arrange icons for running applications. As you know, when you minimize a running application (Write, Paint, Program Manager, and so on) its icon appears along the bottom edge of the Windows desktop (the gray area). Normally, Windows maintains these icons in a neat, evenly spaced row. However, as you're also aware, you can move these icons about yourself either by clicking on an icon and dragging it elsewhere or by using the Move command from the icon's window Control menu.

Nevertheless, when you move the icon for a running application, you are, in effect, overriding Windows' default icon arrangement scheme. However, you can easily restore this default arrangement. To do this, you use the Arrange Icons button from Task List. (As you know, you can access the Task List window either by double-clicking on any unused portion of the desktop (the gray area) or by pressing CTRL+ESC. In either case, Windows displays the Task List window.) When you select this button, Windows restores all the icons for running applications to a neat evenly spaced row at the bottom of the Windows desktop.

Tip: When you move an icon for a running application, it stays put

When you move an icon for a running application, Windows remembers where you put it. For example, imagine you move an icon for a running application and then double-click on it to restore its window to the desktop. A short time later, you minimize that application again. Windows will put the icon for that application back in the same spot it last occupied, not in the location you originally moved it from.

MANAGING GROUP WINDOWS

If you use Windows a lot, it won't take long before you become frustrated with how its group windows are laid out. There are certain tell-tale signs for determining when your frustration level is reaching a critical peak. Some of these are as follows:

- You can't remember where things are. You're always having to think about which application is in which group window. Or worse, you find yourself opening and closing group windows, searching for a specific icon.

- You can't see what you're doing. You've got so many group windows open that your screen reminds you more of a three-ring circus than it does a work surface.

- There are certain applications that you just don't use that much. Frankly, you would rather not have these icons displayed in a particular group window anymore.

If any of these thoughts sound familiar to you (or maybe you've come up with a few of your own), you can solve them with a little organization.

The key to organizing Program Manager lies with its group windows. Group windows allow you to arrange your application icons into logical working categories. The more closely you can tailor the contents of your group windows to the way you actually work, the more effective your Windows sessions will become.

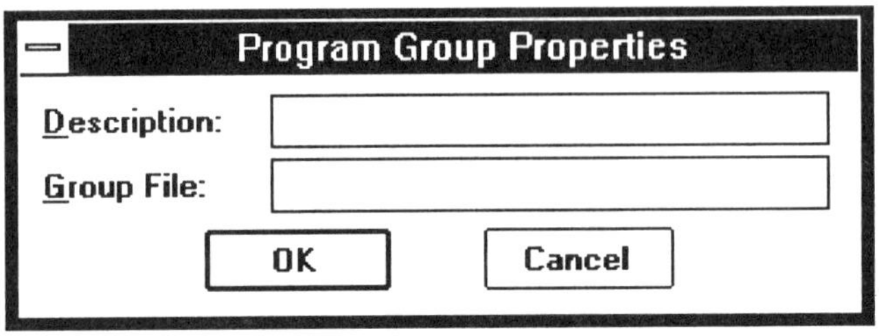

Figure 2-13 The Program Group Properties dialog box

Creating New Group Windows

As you decide on what group windows you will ultimately have and what their contents will be, you'll undoubtedly develop the need to create new group windows. To create a new group window, begin by selecting the File New command from Program Manager's menu. Windows displays the New Program Object dialog box shown earlier in Figure 2-3. Select the Program Group option and then select OK. This causes Windows to display the Program Group Properties dialog box shown in Figure 2-13.

In the Description text box, enter the description you want to appear in the title bar for the group window as well as beneath its icon. You do not need to type a filename in the Group File text box unless you want to (Windows will automatically use the first eight letters of your description as a filename and add the .GRP extension to it). At this point, you select OK or press ENTER to create the new group window. After a moment's hesitation and a little disk grinding, an empty group window will appear on your screen. Once the new group window is displayed, you can begin adding application icons to that window by using the techniques described earlier in the chapter under "Managing Icons."

Changing Group Window Properties

Much like icon properties, group window properties are not cast in stone. In fact, you can change them quite easily. To do this though, you must minimize the group window to an icon. Once the Group window has been minimized, make sure it is selected and then select the File Properties command from Program Manager's menu. Windows displays the Program Group Properties dialog box shown earlier in Figure 2-13. In the Description and Group File text boxes, Windows displays the current description and group filename assigned to the group window. You can, of course, change either of these. To have the new properties take effect, select OK or press ENTER. From that point on, the group window will take on the properties you've specified.

Note: Changing the filename in the Group File text box serves no purpose. If you type the name of another existing group file, for example MAIN.GRP, Windows will not use that group file. Instead, it renames the original group file to a file called

MAIN0.GRP, which contains all the icons from the original group window. If you try it again, Windows renames the file to MAIN1.GRP. The point here is that the only property you can meaningfully change for a group window is its description, and you can do that without creating a new .GRP file.

The most common group window property you'll find yourself changing is the description for a group window. Often, when you have several group windows iconized at the bottom of Program Manager's window, their descriptions overlap. If this bothers you, simply shorten these descriptions. For example, you might change "Non-Windows Applications" to "DOS Apps."

In addition, as you copy and move application icons to and from a group window, its character may begin to change. For example, imagine you have a group window named "Excel," which is devoted entirely to Microsoft Excel. However, as time goes on, you add Lotus 1-2-3 and Borland's Quattro Pro to this group. At that point, you might consider changing the name of the group window to "Spreadsheets."

Note: When you use Windows Setup to install new applications, their icons are added to either the Windows Applications or Non-Windows Applications group windows, depending on which is appropriate. However, if you change the description for either of these group windows, and then use Windows Setup to create a new icon, Windows will create either a new Windows or Non-Windows Applications group, because it can't find the old one.

Deleting Old Group Windows

You can also delete unneeded group windows by using the File Delete command from Program Manager's menu. To use this command to delete a group window, though, that group window must be minimized to an icon. Further, that icon must be active. When you're ready, select the File Delete command. Windows displays a Yes/No message box asking if you are sure you want to delete the group window. Respond as appropriate.

When you delete a group window, you also delete the application icons in that window. Of course, the program files on disk that are associated with those icons are not affected in any way. Nevertheless, it is always a good idea to move or copy all one-of-a-kind icons to other group windows before deleting the original group window. That way, you can save yourself the time and effort of having to set those icons up again from scratch.

Arranging Group Windows

You should always minimize group windows that you don't presently need. This gets them out of the way temporarily and helps you to maintain an orderly display. However, it's not always possible (or convenient) to do this. Therefore, Windows offers several techniques and commands that you can use to arrange open group windows in an orderly way.

Tiling and Stacking Group Windows

Program Manager's menu includes two commands, Window Cascade and Window Tile, that let you stack and tile your group windows. A stacked window configuration appears as shown in Figure 2-14. You can achieve this effect by using the Window Cascade command (or by pressing SHIFT+F5). Notice the windows appear stacked one behind the other, sloping upward to the left, with the title bar of each window exposed. The currently active group window appears at the front of the stack. With this configuration, you can click on the title bar for a particular window and quickly bring it to the foreground for use. Alternatively, you can press CTRL+F6 to move one group window at a time until you get to the one you want or you can use the Window command from Program Manager's menu and select a window.

Note: When Program Manager stacks group windows, it adjusts the size of each open group to occupy the same amount of display space. The windows are then stacked working from the upper-left corner of the Program Manager window. However, if the Program Manager window is too small to display all of the open group windows in a single stack, it starts layering a second stack of group windows on top of the first one.

A tiled window arrangement, on the other hand, appears as shown in Figure 2-15. You can achieve this effect by using the Window Tile command or by pressing SHIFT+F4. Notice the group windows appear side by side and that roughly the same amount of display space is devoted to each group window. The currently active group window appears in the upper-left corner. Once again, you can move to a particular group window

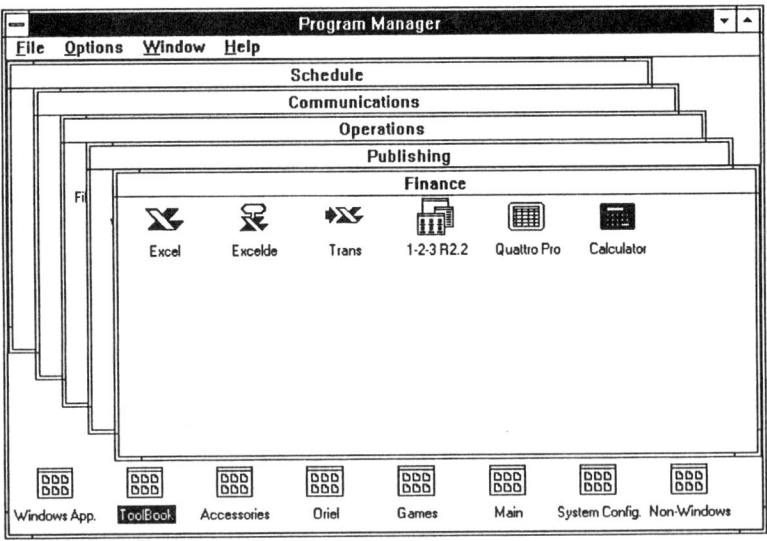

Figure 2-14 Stacked group windows

Program Manager Techniques 55

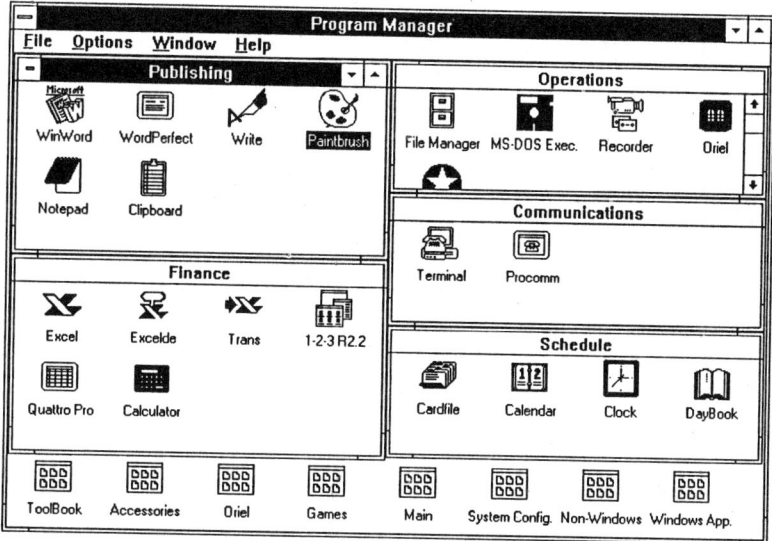

Figure 2-15 Tiled group windows

by clicking on it, by pressing CTRL+F6 to move to it, or by using the Window command from Program Manager's menu to select a window.

Unfortunately there is no easy way to undo tiled or stacked group windows and to restore them to their original sizes and positions. You can, however, exit Windows without saving your setup and restart it again. When you start Windows again, it will display your group windows in their orginal sizes and positions. See "Saving Your Setup" later in this chapter for details on how you can exit Windows and choose to save, or not save, your setup.

Controlling How Group Windows Are Stacked or Tiled

The order in which group windows are stacked and tiled is not indiscriminate. Windows are stacked or tiled in the order in which you activate them. Therefore, you can control the order in which windows are stacked or tiled, if you so desire.

Figure 2-16 shows the various configurations that Windows will use when tiling from two to eight open group windows. Notice that each group window frame is numbered. These numbers represent the order in which each of the respective group windows was activated. To control this order yourself, simply click once on each group window in the order in which you want them to appear stacked or tiled. When you're ready, use the Window Stack or Window Tile command to stack or tile the windows.

For example, imagine you have four open group windows named Finance, Publishing, Schedule, and Operations respectively. You want these windows to appear tiled, as shown in Figure 2-17. Notice that the Finance group window appears in the upper-left corner as

56 *Windows 3 Power Tools*

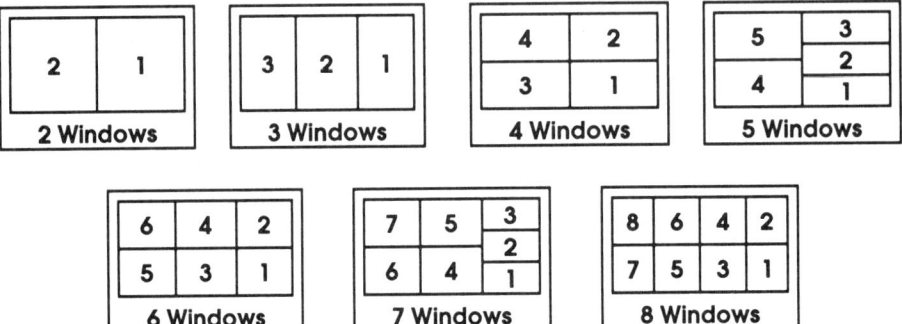

Figure 2-16 Tiling configurations for up to eight windows

the active group window. To do this, you would click on these windows in the following order:

1. Communications
2. Publishing
3. Schedule
4. Finance

Now, when you use the Window Tile command, the windows will be tiled as shown in Figure 2-17.

Arranging Group Window Icons

As you know, when you minimize a group window, its icon appears along the bottom edge of Program Manager's window. If the first row is already filled with group window icons, Program Manager starts a second row above the first, and so on. You can, of course, click on any group window icon and drag it to another location in Program Manager.

As you move group window icons from one spot to another, they tend to get out of alignment with the other icons at the bottom of Program Manager's window. In addition, if you decrease the size of Program Manager's window, some or all of your group window icons may disappear from view. Further, if you either decrease or increase the size of Program Manager's window and then minimize a group window, its icon may appear out of alignment with other group window icons.

You can easily restore the alignment of your group window icons, however. To do this, begin by activating any group window icon by clicking on it, pressing CTRL+F6 to move to it. When you're ready, select the Window Arrange Icons command from Program Manager's menu. When you complete this command, Windows arranges your group icons in neat evenly spaced rows at the bottom of Program Manager's window. (This includes any group window icons that are not presently in view.)

Program Manager Techniques 57

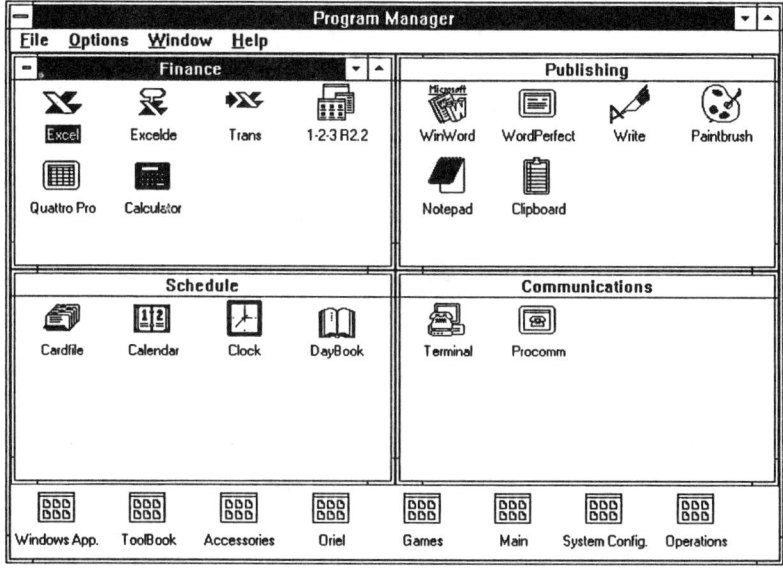

Figure 2-17 You can choose the order in which group windows are tiled

---

Tip: Windows recalls the size and location of group windows

Windows recalls the location and size of open group windows as well as group window icons. For example, imagine you close a group window (minimize it to an icon). Then, you click on that icon and drag it to another place in Program Manager. A short time later, you double-click on that icon to restore it to an open group window. Windows restores that group window to the same size and location it previously occupied. If you now minimize the group window again, Windows will display the icon for that group window in the same spot you moved it to just a short time ago.

SAVING YOUR SETUP

You can save the appearance of the desktop when you exit Windows. That way, the same arrangement of group windows (and group window icons) will be displayed the next time you start Windows. As you know, you exit Windows by simply closing Program Manager. When you do, the Exit Windows dialog box in Figure 2-18 appears on your

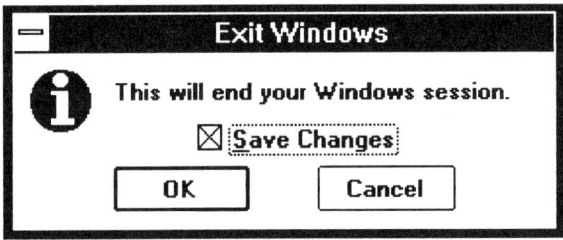

Figure 2-18 Use the Save Changes check box to save the current Program Manager group window configuration

screen. This dialog box contains a check box entitled Save Changes. If you select this check box and then select OK to leave Windows, the current group window configuration will be saved before quitting. (In fact, you'll notice some disk grinding taking place as the current configuration is saved.)

When you save the current Program Manager configuration, the following information is saved:

- The size and location of open group windows.
- The last application used in each group window.
- The relative positioning and activation order of group window icons. The next time you start Windows, the current activation order will be used to position the group window icons at the bottom of Program Manager's window.
- Whether Program Manager's minimize on use feature is active or inactive. See "The Minimize On Use Option" later in this chapter for details on this feature.
- Whether the Auto-Arrange feature for application icons is active or not. See "Arranging Application Icons in Group Windows" earlier for details on this feature.

When you save the current Program Manager configuration, much of the information is recorded in the PROGMAN.INI file in your Windows directory. Windows reads this file each time it loads Program Manager (PROGMAN.EXE) at the start of a session. You can view this file yourself by using Notepad.

Note: You do not need to save Program Manager's configuration when you've changed the properties of an application icon, moved or copied an application icon, or created a new application icon. These changes are automatically saved when you make them.

> **Tip: Exiting Windows when DOS applications are active**
>
> If you attempt to exit Windows when a DOS application is active, Windows will display a message box informing you that you must close the DOS application before you will be allowed to exit. However, if you want to leave Windows without exiting each of your DOS applications individually, you can turn on the Allow Close When Active check box in the DOS application's PIF. See Chapter 10, "Using Non-Windows Applications," for more on this subject.

CUSTOMIZING PROGRAM MANAGER

This section shows you various ways that you can organize your applications within group windows to better suit the way you work. It will not tell you which application to put in which group window. Instead, this section simply discusses some of the more prevalent schools of thought on the subject.

The sections that follow discuss organizing group windows by application category, by specific application, and by project. In practice, though, most people end up using a combination of all three.

Unfortunately, Windows will not let you create subgroups within group windows. Many people view this as one of the few shortcomings in the product (especially if they're familiar with the Macintosh world where you can, in effect, create subgroups). In some cases, this shortcoming forces you to create a large number of group windows in order to get the organization you ultimately want within Windows. Hopefully, however, the previous section on managing group windows will give you the tools you need to keep your group windows under control.

The Category Approach

One school of thought for organizing group windows is to organize them by application category. Figure 2-19 shows a series of group windows that are organized in this way. For example, notice that all spreadsheet-related applications are stored in a group window entitled Finance. Word processing and presentation graphics applications are stored in a group window entitled Publishing, and so on. You can set up similar group windows yourself by using the techniques described earlier in this chapter under "Managing Icons" and "Managing Group Windows."

Many people like the category approach because it makes it easy to remember where your applications are. Just look for a group window title that roughly describes how you use the application, and your chances of being right are relatively high. In addition, the category approach lets you consolidate those applications that you just don't use that often into a single group. For example, notice toward the bottom of Figure 2-19 that there is a group window entitled System Config. This window contains applications like Windows Setup, SysEdit, and PIF Editor that you probably won't need on a daily basis.

60 Windows 3 Power Tools

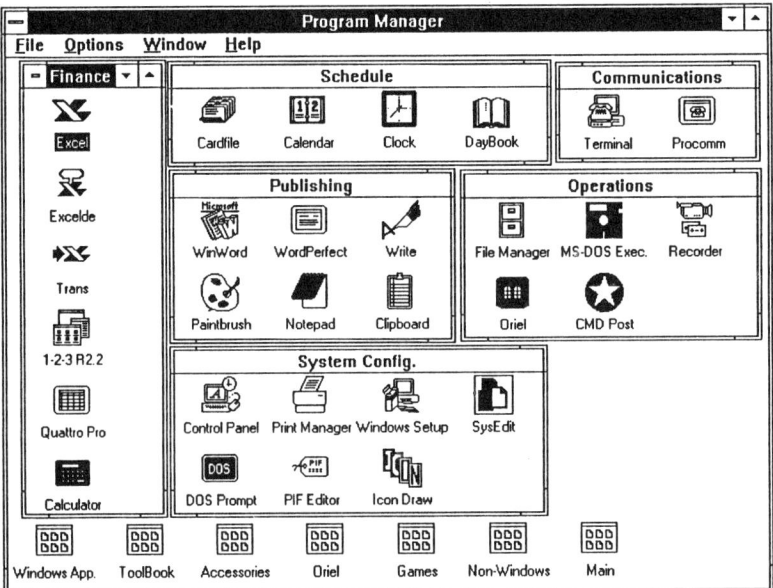

Figure 2-19 Applications organized in group windows by category

You can keep a group window like this one minimized most of the time, thereby saving valuable display space for your other group windows.

One problem with the application category approach, though, is that it is not geared toward applications using a particular data file. For example, it can be very convenient to be able to double-click on an icon that starts a given application and loads a specific data file associated with that application. However, if you create such icons in a multiple application window (for example, the Finance window in Figure 2-19), the situation soon gets out of hand. As the number of icons increases, the window grows to the point where you begin to lose track of what it contains.

The Specific Application Approach

In some cases, you may want to devote an entire group window to a specific application. This is often appropriate when you use the application a great deal. For example, Figure 2-20 shows a series of open group windows, each of which is devoted to a specific application.

Notice that in most of the group windows in Figure 2-20, an icon appears for the master application itself followed by other icons that access various data files for that application. Keeping a master icon in a group window offers two advantages. On the one hand, you can start the application without automatically loading a data file. On the other, you always have a template handy that you can copy when you want to create another data-file icon.

Program Manager Techniques 61

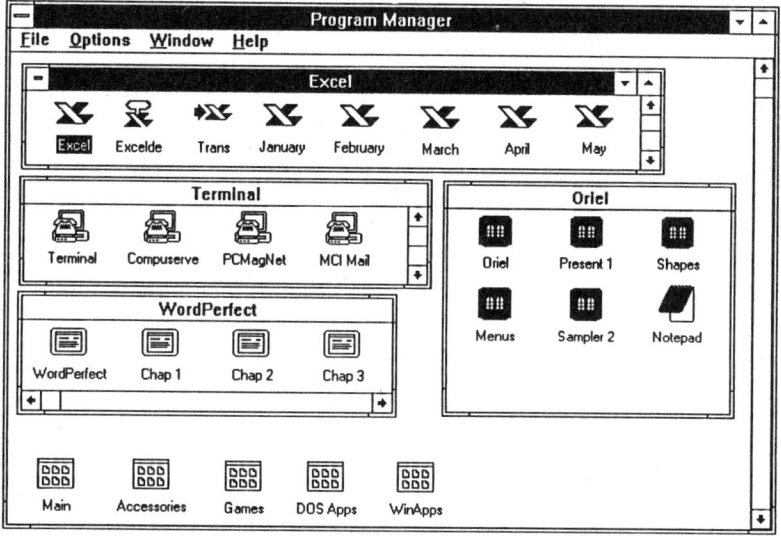

Figure 2-20 Group windows devoted to specific applications

The Project Approach

Another popular way of organizing group windows is by project. For example, imagine you are working on a project that will take you several weeks to complete. It involves a large word-processed document, a supporting spreadsheet, and several graphic images. Rather than selecting these applications from Program Manager's default group windows, you can set up a new group window that contains just the application icons you need. Further, you can link data files to icons where appropriate. That way, when you double-click on a particular icon, its data file is automatically loaded. When you eventually complete the project, you can, of course, delete the group window. Figure 2-21 shows an example of such a group window.

Problems with the Smorgasbord Approach

One configuration you want to avoid when organizing Program Manager is the "smorgasbord" approach. This approach involves displaying every application you own, and some you don't, in an open group window. (New Windows users often succumb to this temptation.) With this approach, your desktop ends up looking like Figure 2-19, wherein practically every square inch of Program Manager is consumed by a group window.

One problem you often encounter with the smorgasbord approach is that the Program Manager window gets too big. For example, notice in Figure 2-19 that the bottom of Program Manager's window extends all the way to the bottom of the desktop. Therefore, when you minimize a running application, its icon is automatically hidden behind Program Manager. Thus, you find yourself grabbing Program Manager's bottom border

62   *Windows 3 Power Tools*

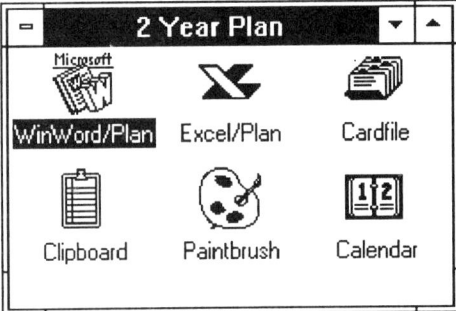

Figure 2-21   A project-oriented group window

periodically and lifting it up to peek underneath. Or you end up minimizing Program Manager, just so you can see what is going on behind it. If you're not constantly on the ball, you might even open a second copy of an application by accident.

Instead of creating the impressive display of the smorgasbord, try keeping only a few group windows open at a time. Populate these with applications you use frequently and minimize your other group windows. You'll thank yourself in the long run.

Stacking and Tiling Desktop Windows

When you run multiple applications in Windows, you're constantly faced with the challenge of arranging your display so that you can easily access the windows in which those applications are running. Microsoft provides at least a partial solution to this problem by allowing you to stack and tile application windows. An example of a stacked window configuration appears in Figure 2-22 and a tiled configuration in Figure 2-23.

To stack or tile open application windows, you use Task List. (An image of the Task List window appears in Figure 2-22, overlaying the stacked windows in that figure.) As you may recall, you can access the Task List window either by double-clicking on any unused portion of the desktop (the gray area) or by pressing CTRL+ESC. Once the Task List window is displayed, you can stack open application windows, by selecting the Cascade button, or Tile them by selecting the Tile button. (You can select either of these buttons by clicking on them or by pressing ALT+C or ALT+T, respectively.) As soon as you select one of these buttons, the open application windows are either stacked or tiled and the Task List window disappears from your screen.

Although Program Manager performs some rather specialized tasks, it is nevertherless a Windows application. Its window is subject to many of the same rules that govern any other application window. Therefore, when you stack or tile the windows for open applications, the Program Manager window is stacked or tiled along with them.

Once windows are either stacked or tiled, you can easily move among them. For example, notice in Figure 2-22 that the stacked windows appear in a cascading pattern sloping downward from left to right. Because of this arrangement, the title bar of each

Program Manager Techniques 63

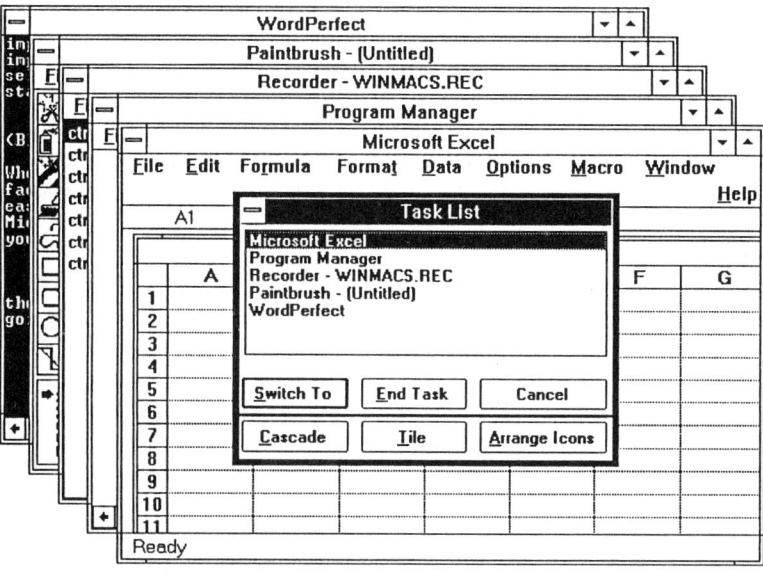

Figure 2-22 Stacked application windows

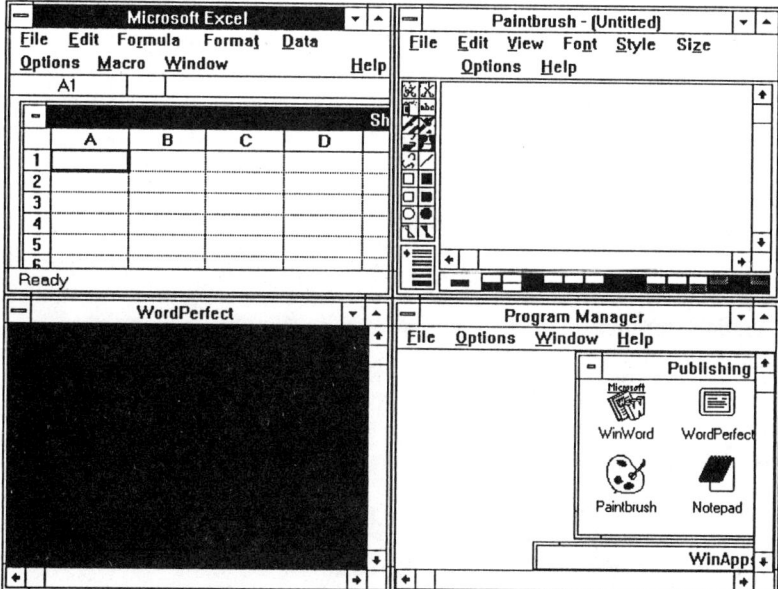

Figure 2-23 Tiled application windows

application window remains exposed. Thus, you can easily activate a particular window by clicking on its title bar, causing it to pop up in the foreground as the active window. As an alternative to clicking on the title bar for a window, you can press ALT+ESC to move sequentially through windows until you reach the window you want.

Moving among tiled windows is equally easy. As you can see in Figure 2-23, roughly equal portions of each open application window are exposed. The currently active application window appears in the upper-left corner. You can move to an application by clicking anywhere on its window or by pressing ALT+ESC to sequentially move to it.

Note: Generally speaking, when you tile application windows, an equal amount of display space is devoted to each window. However, there are exceptions to this. To get an idea of how your application windows will be tiled, see Figure 2-16 shown earlier in this chapter. This figure shows tiling configurations for up to eight open group windows—the same configurations are used to tile application windows.

As is the case with group windows in Program Manager, Windows does not stack or tile application windows indiscriminately. Instead, the order in which application windows are either stacked or tiled is based on the order in which you activated or opened them. For example, notice in Figure 2-22 that the Task List window shows the names of the applications that are currently open. The currently active application (Excel) appears at the top of the list, the next most recently activated application appears second, and so on. Notice as well that the order of the window's names in the Task List window matches the order in which the windows are stacked in Figure 2-22. This same activation order is used when application windows are tiled.

Because you control the order in which applications are activated, you can also control the order in which windows are stacked or tiled. To select a specific order for stacking or tiling, click once on each group window, using a reverse order, before you stack or tile them. The window you select first will appear last in the stacked or tiled configuration, and the window you select last will be the active window, or first in the stacked or tiled configuration.

Note: Figure 2-16, shown earlier in this chapter, shows the order in which your application windows will be tiled. As mentioned, this figure shows tiling configurations for up to eight open group windows, but the same conventions are also used for application windows.

The Minimize on Use Option

You can also have Program Manager shrink to an icon whenever you start an application. This has the effect of getting Program Manager out of the way while your application is running, creating a less complicated display. To do this, select the Options Minimize on Use command from Program Manager's menu before you start an application. The next time you start an application, Program Manager will automatically shrink to an icon.

Further, when you leave that application, Program Manager will remain iconized. However, you can easily restore the Program Manager window by simply double-clicking on its icon. To return Program Manager to the default setting of remaining open when you start an application, select the Options Minimize on Use command a second time.

POWER USER TECHNIQUES

This section discusses a series of techniques that you can use to improve your efficiency within Windows. Most of these techniques relate to running applications, navigating and making selections, improving the layout of your display, and auto-loading programs on Windows startup.

Using the File Run Command

You can use the File Run command from either Program Manager's menu or File Manager's menu to run an application. When you select this command, Windows displays the Run dialog box shown in Figure 2-24. In the Command Line text box, type the executable filename for the application. If the directory containing that application is not in your path, make sure to include the appropriate drive and directory information as well. For example, if you want to run Microsoft Excel located in your C:\EXCEL directory, type:

```
C:\EXCEL\EXCEL.EXE
```

To start the application, select OK or press ENTER.

Note: If you also want the application to shrink to an icon as soon as it starts running, select the Minimize check box before selecting OK or pressing ENTER to complete the File Run command.

You can use the same command-line conventions for the File Run command as you would when setting up an icon for an application. For example, you can start an application and make a specific directory current, or you can start an application and load a specific data file for that application. For instance, imagine you want to start Word for

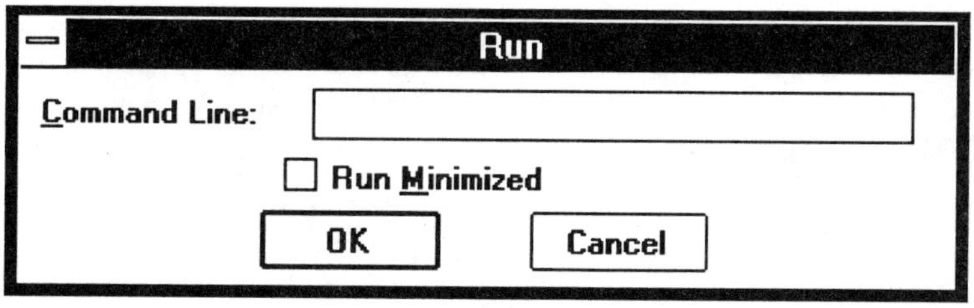

Figure 2-24 The File Run dialog box

Windows and make your C:\LETTERS directory current. To do this you would use the following command line:

```
C:\LETTERS\WINWORD.EXE
```

Of course, for this to work, the directory containing your Word for Windows program files must be included in the PATH statement in your AUTOEXEC.BAT file.

On the other hand, suppose you want to start Word for Windows and load a file called REP12_91.DOC in your C:\LETTERS directory. You could do this with the following command line:

```
WINWORD.EXE C:\LETTERS\REP12_89.DOC
```

Running a DOS Application in a Window

As you know, when you run a DOS application for the first time, it will typically occupy your entire screen. If you're running Windows in 386 enhanced mode, though, you can easily switch a DOS application to a windowed display. To do this, press ALT+ENTER. Windows displays the DOS application in a window, complete with a window Control menu, scroll bars, and so on. To get back to a full-screen display again, press ALT+ENTER a second time.

Note: If you want your DOS application to run in a window by default, you can set up a PIF (Program Information File) for the application. In this PIF, you can specify a windowed, as opposed to a full-screen, display. See Chapter 10, "Using Non-Windows Applications," for additional details on this.

If you are running Windows in real or standard mode, though, your DOS applications cannot run in a window. To determine what mode you are running in, press ALT+ESC to return to Program Manager and then use the About Program Manager command from the Help menu. A message box is displayed that tells you the current mode setting. For more information about modes and memory, see Chapter 7, "Memory Management."

Tip: If you have trouble running a DOS application in a window

If you have a VGA monitor and you're having trouble running a DOS application in a window in 386 enhanced mode, it may be because that application is operating in high graphics mode. See Chapter 10, "Using Non-Windows Applications," for further details.

Techniques for Switching between Applications

As you know, the simplest way to switch to an application is to click on the title bar of its window. This activates the window, bringing it to the foreground, and gives it the *focus*. This means that Windows will now pass keyboard input to that application. (Mouse input is passed to the application only when the mouse pointer is located on the window.) However, besides clicking on a window to switch to an open application, there are a number of other techniques you can use. These techniques are discussed in the balance of this section.

Note: Having the focus can mean other things as well. For example, if the currently active application is a Windows application, having the focus means that the application will have priority where processing time is concerned. Only when there is idle time in this application will processing time be allocated to ongoing processes in other application windows. As you learned in Chapter 1, this is referred to as "nonpreemptive multitasking." For DOS applications, on the other hand, Windows allocates processing time based on the tick of the hardware clock. This is referred to as "preemptive multitasking." See Chapter 1 for additional details on these two terms.

Using Task List

Another way to switch between applications is to use the Task List window, shown in Figure 2-25. To get to Task list, you can use any one of the following methods:

- Press CTRL+ESC. This method will work from anywhere, including when you're in a DOS application that is running as a full-screen display.
- Double-click on any unused portion of the desktop (the gray area).
- If you are in an application window, you can open its window Control menu and select the Switch To... command.

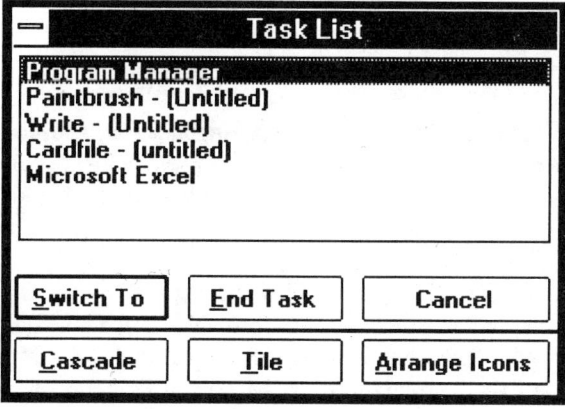

Figure 2-25 The Task List window

The Task List window lists the names of all open applications. The order of the names in this list reflects the order in which the applications were either opened or most recently activated. For example, the currently active application appears at the top of the list. The application that was opened or activated before that appears second in the list, and so on. Understanding how Windows stacks your application windows can give you some insight into its operation. For example, earlier in this chapter, under "Stacking and Tiling Windows," you learned how to control the order in which windows are tiled or stacked by changing their activation order.

To select an application to switch to, you can use any one of several techniques. The easiest method is to simply double-click on the name of an application in the Task List window. The application you select is activated and its window will come to the foreground. If the application is currently iconized (open but minimized to an icon), this action restores it to a window.

Alternatively, you can highlight the name of an application in the Task List window and press ENTER. Or, once an application name is highlighted, you can select the Switch To button. You can do this either by clicking on the button or by typing ALT+S to select it. To highlight a window name in the first place, you can either click on it, use the arrow keys to move to it, or type the first letter of its name.

Note: In addition to the Switch To button, the other buttons at the bottom of the Task List window let you perform a number of routine Windows operations. Each of these buttons, with the exception of End Task, is discussed at various points throughout this chapter. For example, the Cascade button rearranges open application windows in a cascaded stack. The Tile button, on the other hand, rearranges application windows so that each gets roughly an equal amount of display space. Both of these options are discussed earlier in this chapter under "Stacking and Tiling Desktop Windows." The Arrange Icons button lets you arrange group-window icons at the bottom of Program Manager's window in neat evenly spaced rows. This option is discussed earlier under "Arranging Group Windows." The End Task button simply allows you close the application that is currently selected in the Task List window.

Using ALT+ESC

Rather than using the Task list to go directly to an open application, you can press ALT+ESC to activate the next application. This works even when the next application happens to be an icon. In fact, pressing ALT+ESC repeatedly lets you cycle though all the open applications on the desktop. The order of activation is based on the order in which you opened or activated each application.

The ALT+ESC key sequence is particularly handy when you only have one or two applications open. For example, imagine you have Microsoft Excel open in addition to Program Manager. Pressing ALT+ESC lets you conveniently switch back and forth between the two. Or, suppose Excel is minimized to an icon and Program Manager is maximized. This causes the Excel icon to be hidden behind Program Manager. However, you can bring the Excel icon to the foreground by pressing ALT+ESC. You can then double-click on the icon to open Excel's window.

Note: You can also hold down the ALT key and press TAB to cycle through the applications on the desktop. In fact this key sequence seems to perform the function just a little faster than ALT+ESC. However, if the last application you activate happens to be iconized, Windows will restore that application's window to the desktop when you release the ALT key.

Tip: A quick way to switch between DOS applications

As you'll learn in Chapter 10, you can assign a short cut key to a DOS application when you set up its PIF (Program Information File). Once this shortcut key is assigned, you can quickly switch to that DOS application from either another DOS Application or from Windows by pressing the shortcut key. (Of course, the DOS application must already be open for this to work.)

However, if you have two DOS applications open, you can quickly switch back and forth between them without returning to Windows by using a combination of the PIF-assigned shortcut key and ALT+ESC. For example, imagine you're in one DOS application and you press a PIF-assigned shortcut key to jump to the other one. At that point, if you press ALT+ESC, you are taken directly back to the first DOS application, not to Windows. To get back to the original DOS application, simply press the PIF-assigned shortcut key again. The upshot here is that you can quickly switch back and forth between two DOS applications by assigning a shortcut key to only one of them.

Keyboard and Mouse Shortcuts

This section discusses different keyboard and mouse shortcuts that are available to you when you are using Windows. Some you're bound to know, but others you may not.

Clicking and Dragging Menus

Rather than clicking on a menu item to open the menu, and then clicking again to select a submenu option, you can click only once and drag to select a submenu option. For example, imagine you want to select the File Run command from Program Manager's menu. To do this, click once on the File command and hold your mouse button down. Windows opens the File menu. Now, drag downward until you reach the Run option and release your mouse button. Windows displays the File Run dialog box. You can then complete the command in the usual way.

The Amazing ALT Key

The ALT key has myriad uses in Windows for selecting menu and dialog box options. For example, imagine you want to select the File command from Program Manager's menu. To do this press ALT plus the first letter of the command name, in this case ALT+F. To cancel the menu and close it, press ALT again. (If you press ESC, Windows leaves the menu open so that you can make another selection.)

When working in dialog boxes, you know that you can press TAB to move forward and SHIFT+TAB to move backward between options. However, if the option has an underlined letter, you can also press ALT plus that letter to jump directly to that option.

ALT works for push buttons, check boxes, and radio buttons. Be aware, however, that this action will have the effect of selecting the push button. Radio buttons or check boxes, on the other hand, are simply filled or cleared.

List Box Shortcuts

The following table shows a list of keyboard and mouse shortcuts that you may find helpful when working in list boxes. Obviously, not all of these shortcuts will work in every Windows application. In fact, you'll have to experiment a bit (or perhaps even stoop to actually reading the manual) to determine if they work in your particular application.

Action	*Result*
ALT+↑, or F4	Opens a drop-down list box.
ALT+↓	Selects an item in a drop-down list box.
ALT+↑, or F4	
PGUP and PGDN	Scrolls up or down a list-box full at a time.
HOME	Moves to the first item in a list box.
END	Moves to the last item in a list box.
SPACEBAR	Selects an item in a list box or cancels a selected item. With commands that allow you to select several items, you can use the arrow keys to move to each item, pressing the SPACEBAR to select them as you go.
CTRL+/ (slash)	Selects all the items in a list box.
CTRL+\ (backslash)	Cancels all selections except the current selection in a list box.
SHIFT+↑ or SHIFT+↓	Extends the current list-box selection in the direction of the arrow.
Double-clicking	Selects an item and completes a command. For example, if you select the File Open command for a given application, a dialog box is displayed that contains a list box of filenames. When you double-click on a filename, that file is selected and the File Open command is executed.

Text Box Shortcuts

Often, when you activate a text box that contains an entry, that entry is automatically selected (highlighted). As soon as you start typing, however, the text box is cleared to accommodate your new entry. Occasionally, you might want to simply edit the entry in a text box, without deleting the entire entry. For example, you might be using the File Properties command to change the description or command line for an icon. For editing the contents of a text box, there are a few techniques you should know about that might make the editing process more efficient.

Rather than starting to type a new entry in a text box, causing a selected (highlighted) entry to be cleared, simply press → or ←. This has the effect of removing the highlight, allowing you to edit the text entry as you like.

To move quickly from one word to the next while editing the contents of a text box, you can press CTRL+→ to move one word to the right or CTRL+← to move one word to the left. You can also press HOME to get to the beginning of an entry in a text box or END to get to the end of the entry.

If you make a mistake while typing a new text entry or editing an old one, you can highlight the errant text (see below) and press DEL to delete it. Alternatively, you can press ALT+BACKSPACE to undo the previous edit.

You can also use the Clipboard to assist in the editing process. For example, you can copy or cut text to the Clipboard and use it elsewhere in the text box. To do this, begin by highlighting a section of text (see below). Then, press CTRL+INS to copy the text to the Clipboard, or press SHIFT+DEL to cut the text to the Clipboard. To insert the text elsewhere, move to where you want the text inserted by clicking on the appropriate spot or by using the arrow keys to move to it. When you're ready, press SHIFT+INS to paste the entry from the Clipboard into the text box.

Note: Using the Clipboard to cut and paste text and graphics between both Windows and DOS applications is discussed in Chapter 6, "Sharing Data Between Applications."

To highlight text with the mouse, you have two options. In many applications, if you double-click on a single word, only that word is selected. Alternatively, you can click anywhere you want within a text-box entry and drag to the left or right to select a portion of that entry. To cancel a selection of this kind, simply click your mouse again.

To highlight text with the keyboard, use the ← or → keys to move the blinking cursor to where you want the highlight to begin. Then, press SHIFT+→ to highlight text to the right or SHIFT+← to highlight text to the left. In addition, you can press SHIFT+END to highlight from the current position the end of an entry or SHIFT+HOME to highlight from the current position to the beginning of an entry. Finally, you can press CTRL+SHIFT+→ to highlight only the next word to the right or CTRL+SHIFT+← to highlight only the next word to the left. To cancel any of these selections, simply press an arrow key.

Extending a Selection

As you know, many Windows applications allow you to select (highlight) a section of text, or a series of filenames, for a particular command. You can, of course, make a selection (or change one) by clicking and dragging with your mouse. However, the following table shows some keyboard shortcuts that let you extend the current selection to include additional text or additional filenames. In some cases, these keyboard sequences are more convenient and more precise than using the mouse.

Action	Result
SHIFT+→	Extends the current selection to the right.
SHIFT+←	Extends the current selection to the left.
SHIFT+↓	Extends selection to the next line. Or, if the next line is already selected, cancels the selection.
SHIFT+↑	Extends the current selection to the previous line. Or, if the previous line is already selected, cancels the selection.
SHIFT+END	Extends the current selection to the end of a line.
SHIFT+HOME	Extends the current selection to the beginning of a line.
SHIFT+PGDN	Extends the current selection down to include the next windowfull. Or, if the next windowfull is already selected, cancels the selection.
SHIFT+PGUP	Extends the current selection up to include the previous windowfull. Or, if the previous windowfull is already selected, cancels the selection.
CTRL+SHIFT+→	Extends a selection to include the next word. Or, if the next word is already selected, cancels the selection.
CTRL+SHIFT+←	Extends a selection to include the previous word. Or, if the previous word is already selected, cancels the selection.
CTRL+SHIFT+END	Extends the current selection to the end of a document.
CTRL+SHIFT+HOME	Extends the current selection to the beginning of a document.

Maximizing and Restoring Windows

As you know, you can open the window Control menu for a window and select Maximize to have the window occupy the entire screen. Or, you can click on the Maximize box located in the window's upper-right corner. However, what you may not know is that you can also maximize a window by simply double-clicking anywhere on its title bar. The title bar of a window is usually a much larger target and can be far more convenient, especially if you're in a hurry.

You can also restore a maximized window to its former size and location by double-clicking on its title bar. Once again, this method can be far more convenient than using the Restore command from the window Control menu or clicking on the Restore box in the window's upper-right corner.

Closing Windows

You can always close a window by opening the window Control menu and selecting the Close command. However, this method can be rather cumbersome when you have multiple windows to close. There are much easier and less time-consuming methods. For example, you can simply double-click on the window Control menu box. Alternatively, you can press ALT+F4. Either of these methods will have the effect of closing the currently active window. They also work with dialog boxes.

Displaying the Control Menu for Full-Screen DOS Applications

As you know, you can press ALT+SPACEBAR when running a windowed application to display the window Control menu. However, what you may not know is that you can also press ALT+SPACEBAR when running a DOS application as a full-screen display. Windows will automatically display the DOS application in a window and open the window control menu. You can then select a command from that menu. Of course, this will only work when Windows is running in 386 enhanced mode.

Auto-loading Programs on Windows Startup

When you start Windows, you can also specify an application that you want to start as well. In fact, there are two ways you can do this. On the one hand, you can enter a special command line at the DOS prompt when you start Windows. This method will be discussed here. On the other hand, you can also modify the run= or load= statements in the WIN.INI file. This method is discussed in Chapter 12, "Customizing Your .INI Files."

To start windows from the DOS prompt and automatically start a specific application as well, follow the WIN statement with the filename for that application and an optional data-file name. (Table 2.1, earlier in this chapter, shows a list of standard Windows application filenames.) Thus, your DOS command line would take the following form:

```
WIN [Application-Name] [Data-File-Name]
```

where *Application-Name* is the filename for the application you want to run, and *Data-File-Name* is the filename for a data file that is associated with that application. As mentioned, the Data-File-Name argument is optional.

For example, imagine you want to start Windows and load Write as well. To do this, you can use the following command line at the DOS prompt:

```
WIN WRITE
```

where WIN runs WIN.COM to start Windows and WRITE runs WRITE.EXE to start Write.

You can also add the name of a Write document file that will be opened in Write. For example, to load the file REP12_91.WRI, you can use the following command line:

```
WIN WRITE REP12_91.WRI
```

You can also abbreviate this command line to simply:

```
WIN REP12_91.WRI
```

In this case, Windows will run Write and load the REP12_91.WRI file, because it associates all files with a .WRI extension with Write. See "Launching Applications by Association" earlier in this chapter for a brief description of how Windows associates data files with their corresponding applications.

If the application you want to run is not located in your Windows program directory, make sure to include the appropriate drive and path identifiers. For example, if you want to run Microsoft Excel, located in your C:\EXCEL directory, and load the file BUDGET.XLS, located in your C:\ACCTG directory, you might use the following command line:

```
WIN C:\EXCEL\EXCEL.EXE C:\ACCTG\BUDGET.XLS
```

You can also start Windows in a specific mode and load a specific application. For example, suppose you have an older copy of Microsoft Excel in your C:\EXCEL directory that you must run in Real Mode. Imagine further that you also want to load a spreadsheet file named REP12_91.XLS located in the same directory. To do this, you might use the following command line:

```
WIN/R C:\EXCEL\EXCEL.EXE REP12_91.XLS
```

Note: When you use the command-line method to run an application on Windows startup, the Program Manager window is automatically minimized to an icon. In addition, Program Manager remains iconized when you leave the application.

Tips on Using Multiple Applications

This section discusses some of the issues associated with running multiple applications in Windows. Among these are running out of memory, what happens when you switch away from an application, and running multiple instances of the same program.

Running Out of Memory

At some point, you may be running several applications, or attempting to start an additional one, when Windows displays an out-of-memory error message. This message indicates that Windows does not have access to enough memory to complete the current operation.

The amount of memory available to Windows depends on a number of factors, including the amount and type of memory in your machine and the mode in which you are running Windows. You can find out roughly how much and what type of memory

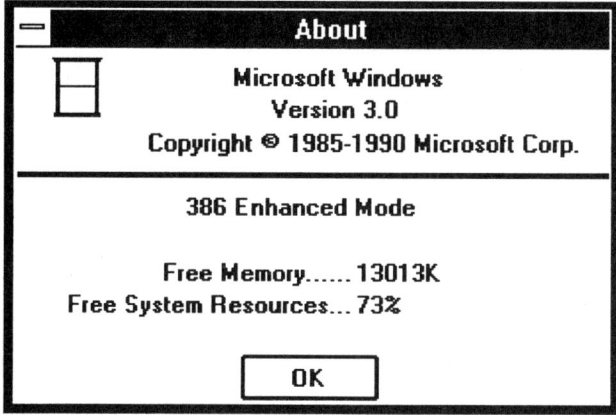

Figure 2-26 Selecting About Program Manager from the Help menu tells you how much memory is available on your system

you have, as well as the mode in which Windows is currently running, by selecting the About command from the Help menu in either Program Manager or File Manager. When you select this command, Windows displays a dialog box like the one in Figure 2-26.

Immediately below the title and copyright information in the About box appears the mode in which Windows is currently running. For example, Figure 2-26 indicates that Windows is currently running in 386 enhanced mode. (If you are running in real mode, and you have installed an expanded memory driver, Windows will note whether you are running in large- or small-frame EMS mode here as well.) Below this, Windows displays information about the amount of memory available on your system. This information may vary, depending on the mode in which you are running Windows. Briefly, however, the following information is available:

Free Memory: If you are running in Windows in Real mode, this number shows the amount of conventional memory in kilobytes (K) that is available for running new applications. (If you have installed an expanded memory driver, Windows also shows the amount of EMS memory that falls within conventional memory here. See Chapter 7 for details.) If you are running Windows in Standard mode, this number also includes extended memory. If you are running Windows in 386 Enhanced mode, this number also includes virtual (disk-based) memory, possibly causing this number to appear larger than the actual amount of memory you know you have in your machine. In general, if this number is less than 30K, you'll need to close some applications.

(continued)

76   *Windows 3 Power Tools*

Free Expanded Memory: If you are running windows in Real mode, and you've installed an expanded memory driver, Windows shows the amount of expanded memory you have available. However, having a large amount of expanded memory available may not allow you to start another application. It is possible to show a large amount of expanded memory and be completely out of the conventional memory required to load the application.

SMARTDrive: If you are running windows in Real mode and have installed SMARTdrive to run in expanded memory (using the /a switch), Windows shows the amount of expanded memory claimed by SMARTDrive. Windows will allocate memory from SMARTDrive as it is needed.

Free System Resources: Shows the total percentage of system resources that are available. This number will never reach 100%, because Windows itself requires system resources. In general, if this number is around 15% or less, you won't be able to run another application, even though you may have sufficient free memory. Instead, you'll need to close some applications to free up system resources.

As mentioned, the amount of memory available to Windows depends on a multiplicity of factors. Some of these are the amount and type of memory in your machine, the mode in which Windows is currently running, and the amount of free disk space you have available. However, these are only some of the factors involved; there are others as well. See Chapter 7, "Memory Management," for a complete discussion of these factors.

Switching Away From Applications

As mentioned, when you switch to an open application, the window containing that application becomes the active window. This means the window is brought to the foreground, and it receives the focus. When an application has the focus, Windows will pass keyboard input to that application, and mouse input when the pointer is on the application's window. Any other windows you may have open remain open, of course; but they are shifted into the background. However, what happens if there is an ongoing process taking place in one of these windows? For example, imagine you have a spreadsheet that is recalculating.

What happens to ongoing processes in background windows depends on whether the window contains a DOS application or a Windows application. If it contains a Windows application, the process just keeps going. It will simply run to completion as a background operation. Windows will devote as much processing time to this background operation as it can. That is, when idle time is detected in the currently active application, Windows will take that time to work on the background operation. (In some cases, this may cause the application in the currently active window to appear somewhat sluggish.)

If a background window contains a DOS application, though, Windows will suspend all ongoing processes when you switch away from that window. Further, processing will not resume until you return to the window. However, if you are running Windows in 386 enhanced mode, you can change this in one of two ways.

On the one hand, you can use the Settings option from the window Control menu for the DOS application. When you select this option, a dialog box is displayed. Select Background from the Tasking Options section and then select OK. Windows will now devote processing time to the application when you switch away from it.

The second way to allow background processing to occur in an inactive DOS application is to modify the PIF (Program Information File) for the DOS application. That way, the DOS application will run in the background by default. See Chapter 10, "Using Non-Windows Applications," for further details both on using the Settings option in the window Control menu and on setting up PIFs for DOS applications.

Getting Messages from Background Applications

Occasionally, you may get an error or status message box from a Windows application that is running in the background. When this happens, the error or status message box will appear right in the middle of whatever window you happen to be working in at the time. As a result, the currently active window will lose the focus (its title bar will go white) and Windows will give the focus to the intervening application.

Whether you must respond to the message box depends on the severity of the error. In some cases, you must respond to the message box. For example, Windows might be experiencing an internal system error and will freeze all further processing until you respond to the message box. However, in most cases, you can simply click on the window in which you were working and continue what you were doing. When you switch back to the application that generated the status or error message, though, the message box will again be displayed. You must then respond to the message box to continue working in that application.

In some cases, Windows, or an application, will display one of the four icons in Figure 2-27 in a message box to help you identify the severity of an error message. There are no hard and fast rules here; but in general, a red stop sign indicates the message is critical, a yellow circle with an exclamation mark indicates a warning, a green circle with a question mark is simply a request for user verification, and a purple circle with a small *i* in it indicates the message box contains information.

Occasionally, you may get an alternative form of messaging from a background application. In this case, the border or icon for a background application will begin flashing when an error or status message is available from that application. (This is very

Figure 2-27 Icons displayed in Windows message boxes

rare, but it can happen.) When you subsequently click on the window or icon, a message box will be displayed that identifies the nature of the error or message. This form of messaging usually only takes place when one application is dependent on another application for its data.

For example, in Chapter 6, you'll learn about Dynamic Data Exchange (DDE), which allows two Windows applications to communicate with one another in order to exchange information between their data files. If you open a data file for an application that contains a DDE link, and the application and data file to which that link refers is not open, the first application will often attempt to open the second application along with its associated data file. If this operation is only partially successful—that is, the second application is opened but the proper data file cannot be found—you may get the alternative form of messaging mentioned here.

Using Multiple Instances of the Same Program

As you know, Windows lets you run multiple instances (more than one copy) of the same application at the same time. Each instance runs in its own window. For example, you might run two copies of Write at the same time, each with a different document file. That way, you can work on multiple documents at the same time, allowing you to compare documents as well as copy data back and forth between them. (See Chapter 6, "Sharing Data Between Applications," for information on using the Clipboard to copy data between open applications.)

Note: When you run a second instance of a Windows application, it always uses less memory than the first instance. This is because it shares certain segments of program code with the first instance. For additional information on this, see Chapter 7, "Memory Management."

A number of applications come with Windows for which you cannot open a second instance. In these cases, when you attempt to open a second instance of that application, Windows will simply activate the first instance. Some examples are File Manager, Control Panel, and Windows Setup, as well as most of the other applications in the Main group window. On the other hand, you can run a second instance of most of the applications in the Accessories and Games group windows, with the notable exception of Recorder.

As you know, Windows also allows you to run multiple instances of the same DOS application. For example, you can run multiple instances of Lotus 1-2-3 or Borland's Quattro Pro. If you're running in 386 enhanced mode, you can have each instance run in its own window, allowing you to quickly switch back and forth between them. To identify the second instance of a DOS application, Windows displays a dot (.) following the description in the title bar of the window in which the application is running. An additional dot is added for each additional instance you run.

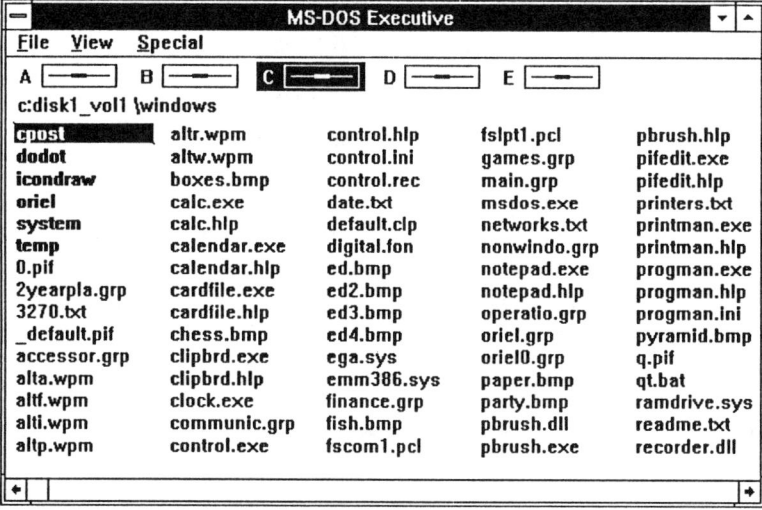

Figure 2-28 The MS-DOS Executive window

Using the MS-DOS Executive

If you're an experienced Windows user, you know that Program Manager's group windows and icons are new to Windows 3.0. In previous versions of Windows, the primary shell for Windows is called the MS-DOS Executive. If you liked some of the aspects of using the MS-DOS Executive, you should be aware that it has also been included in Windows 3.0. In fact, a screen shot of the MS-DOS Executive window appears in Figure 2-28. (Notice the resemblance to File Manager.)

The MS-DOS Executive is pretty much the same as in prior versions of Windows. In fact, the similarities are so striking that they do not bear further discussion here. However, the beauty of the Windows 3.0 version of the MS-DOS Executive is that you can use it if you want to, and ignore it if you don't. This was not possible in previous versions of Windows.

The file name associated with the MS-DOS executive is MSDOS.EXE. This file is automatically copied to your Windows directory when you install the product. Typical of all Windows programs, MSDOS.EXE comes with its own icon, which you can install in one of Program Manager's group windows. (See "Creating New Icons" earlier in this chapter for details on how to do this.)

Tips On Running DOS

As you know, you can exit to DOS by selecting the DOS Prompt icon from Program Manager's Main group window. You can then enter as many DOS commands as you like. To return to Windows, simply type **EXIT** at the DOS prompt.

When you select the DOS Prompt icon, you are actually running a second copy of COMMAND.COM. In fact, if you use the File Properties command to check the properties for this icon, you'll see that the Command Line text box contains COMMAND.COM.

You can also use the COMMAND.COM command line with the /C switch to execute resident DOS commands. For example, imagine you have a file named C:\EXCEL\SALES.XLS that you back up several times a day to a floppy disk in drive A. You can, of course, use File Manager to do this. However, you have to go through the tedious cycle of starting File Manager, selecting the file, and dragging it to the Drive A icon or using the File Copy command. On the other hand, you can set up a new icon that uses the following command line:

```
COMMAND.COM /C COPY C:\EXCEL\SALES.XLS A:
```

Once you have this icon set up, all you need to do is double-click on it to run the command. Your screen will go blank for a for a moment as the command executes. You are then returned to Windows.

Note: Do not attempt to run DOS commands such as CHKDSK with the /F switch or other DOS commands that change the FAT (File Allocation Table) while running Windows. This command will remove any Windows' swap files from your hard disk, causing Windows to crash. Also, you should avoid using undelete utilities, disk compaction utilities, or disk optimization utilities such as Norton's SD.EXE from within Windows.

Tip: **When the DOS icon won't work**

The first time you try the DOS Prompt icon, it may not work. Normally the COMMAND.COM file is located in your root directory on drive C, C:\, which is often the first entry in the PATH statement in your AUTOEXEC.BAT file. However, if this directory is not included in your path statement, Windows will not be able to find the COMMAND.COM file. A simple fix for this is to use the File Properties command to modify the command line for the icon to read C:\COMMAND.COM. Once this is done, Windows should be able to find COMMAND.COM and your DOS Prompt icon should work just fine.

When you use the DOS Prompt icon to exit temporarily to DOS from Windows, the copyright information for your current DOS version appears followed by a DOS prompt. Otherwise, there is no direct evidence that Windows is "resident" in your machine's memory. If you leave your computer for a while and then return, you may not be able to remember whether Windows is up or not. In fact, you may fall into the trap of typing **WIN** to start Windows, rather than **EXIT** to return to it. This causes DOS to load a second copy of Windows. Even if you have the memory required to support the second copy of Windows, there is a significant chance that it will eventually crash.

There is a technique you can use that may help you to avoid starting a second copy of Windows. It involves changing the appearance of the DOS prompt to remind you that Windows is present. To do this, you must create a small batch file and run that file though the use of a PIF (Program Information File). This PIF file is in turn started through the use of a DOS icon that you can locate in any one of Program Manager's group windows. To Begin, open Notepad and type the following lines:

```
@ECHO OFF
PROMPT Exit Returns to Windows$_ %PROMPT%
%COMSPEC%
```

The @ECHO OFF prevents the commands in the batch file from being displayed on your screen as they are executed. The PROMPT command serves to display the string "Exit Returns to Windows". However, you can use any string you want. The $_ simply provides a carriage return after this string so that is displayed on one line and the DOS prompt is displayed on the next. The %PROMPT% is a reference to the %PROMPT% environment variable and causes your current DOS prompt to be displayed. Finally, %COMSPEC% is a reference to the %COMPSPEC% environment variable which contains the path and name of COMMAND.COM. When this line of the batch file executes, DOS will load a second copy of COMMAND.COM that will come up with the prompt you defined. Save this file as CMD.BAT in the directory where you normally save your .BAT files, for example C:\BAT.

Open the PIF Editor window and make the following entries in the text boxes provided:

Program Filename:	C:\COMMAND.COM
Window Title:	DOS Prompt
Optional Parameters:	/E:200 /C C:\BAT\CMD.BAT

Accept the remainder of the parameter settings as they are and use the File Save As command to save this file as CMD.PIF in your Windows program directory. Briefly, the C:\COMMAND.COM entry in the Program File Name box serves to start the first copy of COMMAND.COM. The DOS Prompt entry in the Window Title box is optional, because it is never displayed. In the Optional Parameters box, the /E:200 serves to increase the size of the environment space above the default of 160. This is necessary to accommodate the new longer prompt. The /C switch in conjunction with C:\BAT\CMD.BAT serves to run the .BAT file you created above.

To set up your new DOS icon, return to Program Manager and use the File New command to set up an icon in the group window of your choice. For a description, specify a name of your choosing, (for example, DOS Prompt) and for a command line, specify simply CMD.PIF. When you double-click on this icon, Windows will exit to DOS and display the string "Exit Returns to Windows" followed by a traditional DOS prompt on the next line.

SUMMARY

This chapter discusses various techniques that you can use to get the most out of Program Manager. The first part of the chapter shows you how to manage application icons. For example, you now know how to copy and move existing icons between group windows and how to set up new icons. You also know how to borrow icons from other applications when you need to.

From reading this chapter, you also know how to manage group windows. For example, you know how to create new group windows and delete old ones you no longer need. You also know how to stack and tile group windows and how to control the order in which group windows are stacked or tiled.

Finally, you know how to customize Program Manager—that is, you know how to organize its group windows to better suit the way you work. In fact, with the skills you've acquired from reading this chapter, you are no longer dependent on Microsoft's view of the world. Instead, you're ready to make up your own.

3

File Manager Techniques

When Windows 3 was first released, File Manager received some bad reviews from the press. The primary complaint was the so-called "clumsy interface." However, what many of these reviewers failed to point out is the extensive functionality that File Manager brings to Windows. In some cases, File Manager is capable of performing tasks that go beyond the abilities of conventional DOS file management commands. In addition, although the default settings for File Manager's display can make navigation a little slow at times, you can change the defaults to have File Manager conform more closely to your work habits.

File Manager allows you to perform many of your routine file management chores without having to leave Windows. For example, you can do such things as copy, move, rename, and delete files and directories. You can also use File Manager to create directories, search for files and directories, change file attributes, and format floppy disks. In addition, you can use File Manager as a shell for launching both DOS and Windows applications. Finally, if you are connected to a network, File Manager lets you connect your PC to directories on the network and manage files in those directories. Using File Manager in a network context, however, is discussed in Chapter 13, "Networking Windows."

Note: As you'll soon see, the File Manager user interface is largely icon driven. This style of interface will appeal to many Windows users. However, if the File Manager style of interface is not to your liking, you might want to take a look at a product that comes with this book called Command Post, a shareware product from Wilson WindowWare. Command Post offers a more DOS-like, text-based style of user interface for managing files and launching programs. And, although Command Post comes with an extensive set of predefined commands and features, it also provides a programming language that lets you define your own custom file management shell and menu system.

FILE MANAGER BASICS

To use File Manager, you must open its window. To do this, you can double-click on its icon, located in Program Manager's Main group window. Alternatively, you can use Program Manager's File Run command to run the file WINFILE.EXE. Whichever method you choose, the File Manager window appears on your screen as shown in Figure 3-1.

File Manager lets you access directories and view files in those directories through two objects, directory trees and directory windows. When you first open File Manager, the directory tree for the current drive appears in File Manager's window, as shown in Figure 3-1. The window containing this tree is called the Directory Tree window. The disk drives that are available on your system are defined by the disk-drive icons positioned along the top of the Directory Tree window. The icon for the currently active drive appears highlighted.

To see the directory tree for a different drive, simply select the appropriate drive by clicking on its drive icon. Alternatively, you can press TAB to move to the drive icon

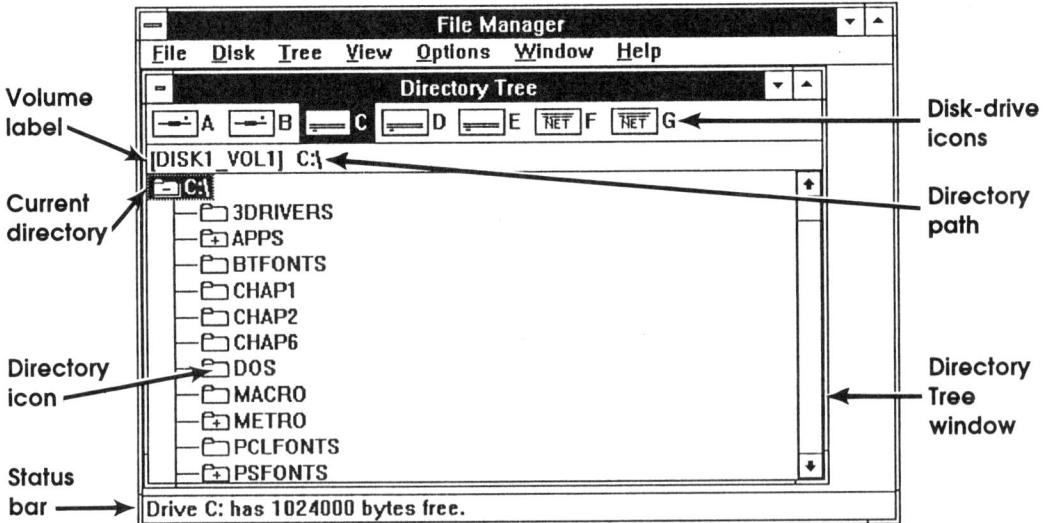

Figure 3-1 The File Manager Window

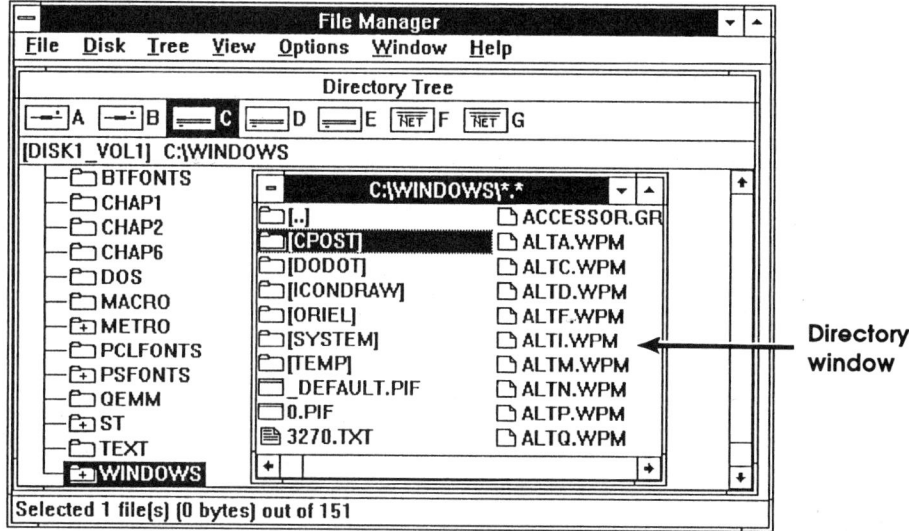

Figure 3-2 A directory window displayed on the File Manager work surface

section, use the arrow keys to highlight the drive you want, and press ENTER. (You can also hold down the CTRL key and press the letter of the drive you want.) Whichever method you choose, Windows displays a directory tree for the drive you've selected. Windows also shows you the amount of free space on that drive (in bytes) in the status line at the bottom of the Directory Tree window.

To see the files in a particular directory, double-click on the icon for that directory in the directory tree. Windows opens a directory window, as shown on the right side of Figure 3-2, showing you the names of files located in the directory you've selected. Alternatively, you can use the arrow keys to highlight the icon for a directory in the directory tree and press ENTER to open a directory window for that directory. Once the directory window is displayed, you can copy, move, and rename files in that directory as well as perform other file management chores. To explore the contents of the directory window, you can use the scroll bars at the bottom and right edges of the window, or you can use the arrow keys to move among file and subdirectory names. You can also highlight the name of an executable file for a DOS or Windows application and press ENTER (or double-click on the file name) to start the application.

Note: By default, Program Manager is the primary shell for Windows. Therefore, Program Manager is the first thing you see when you start the program. However, if you would like to use File Manager as your primary shell, you can change the SHELL= statement in your SYSTEM.INI file. When you first install Windows this statement reads SHELL=PROGMAN.EXE. However, you can use Notepad to change this statement to SHELL=WINFILE.EXE, thereby defining File Manager as the primary shell when you start Windows. See Chapter 12, "Customizing Your .INI Files," for more details on modifying the SYSTEM.INI file.

Managing the Directory Tree

When you start File Manager, the directory tree shows only the first-level directories on the current drive. Those directories that contain subdirectories are marked by a plus (+) sign that appears in the icon for the directory. However, you can view the subdirectories for a first-level directory by expanding the directory tree. You can expand the directory tree for a single directory in the directory tree, an entire branch in the tree, or all branches in the tree. When a directory has been expanded, a minus sign (-) appears in the icon for the directory.

To expand a specific directory in the directory tree, click on the plus sign in that directory's icon. Windows expands the directory tree for that specific directory. Alternatively, you can use the arrow keys to move the icon for a directory and press the + key. Or, once the directory is selected, you can use the Tree Expand One Level command from File Manager's menu to expand the directory by one level. To see all the directory levels beneath the selected directory, select the Tree Expand Branch command from File Manager's Menu or press the asterisk (*) key.

To expand all directories in the directory tree at once, select the Tree Expand All command from File Manager's menu, or press CTRL+* (CTRL+ASTERISK). Windows expands all the directories in the directory tree.

Tip: Expanding the directory tree with your mouse

As an alternative to the Tree Expand All command or the CTRL+* key sequence, you can expand the directory tree to show all the directories on a given drive by using your mouse. To do this, hold down the SHIFT key and click on a drive icon. File Manager expands the directory tree to show all the directories on the drive you've selected.

As you might imagine, you can also collapse specific directories in the directory tree. To do this, click your mouse on the minus sign (-) in the icon for an expanded directory in the directory tree. Alternatively, once the directory is selected, you can press the minus key (-) or use the Tree Collapse Directory command from File Manager's menu to collapse the directory.

Managing Directory Windows

As mentioned, when you double-click on a directory icon in the directory tree, File Manager opens a directory window showing a list of files and subdirectories in the directory you've selected. The name of each file and subdirectory in the list is preceded by an icon, which you can use to access the file or sub-directory. An example of a directory window was shown earlier in Figure 3-2. Directory windows conform to the same conventions as any other window. Therefore, they can be moved, resized, minimized, maximized, and so on.

Each file and directory in a directory window is represented by an icon. As you'll soon see, these icons are used to manipulate files and directories. The following four types of icons are available:

📁   Directories

▭   Executable program files with .EXE, .COM, .BAT, and .PIF extensions.

📄   Document (data) files associated with applications.

▢   All other files that are not included in the first three categories.

The files and directories in a directory window are listed in alphabetical order by name. Any subdirectories of the current directory appear first in the list enclosed in square brackets and are followed by the names of the files in the directory.

Note: You can change the order in which files are listed in a directory window. For example, you can have them sorted alphabetically by extension rather than name. You can also get additional information about files, like date and time of creation and their sizes in bytes. See "Viewing Files" later for more information on how you can sort the files in a directory window and get information about files.

You can easily view the files in a subdirectory displayed in a directory window by double-clicking on the icon for the subdirectory. Alternatively, you can highlight the name of the directory and press ENTER. Either of these actions causes File Manager to open a separate directory window showing the files in the subdirectory you've selected.

To move between open directory windows, you have several choices. The easiest way to move to a directory window is to click on it with your mouse. To move sequentially from one directory window to the next by using the keyboard, you can press CTRL+TAB or CTRL+F6 or press ALT+- (ALT+HYPHEN) to open the window Control menu and select the Next option. You can also jump to a specific directory window by using the Window command from File Manager's menu and selecting the name of the window you want from the pull-down menu that appears.

If you open multiple directory windows, the File Manager screen can become quite crowded, and navigating among directory windows can become awkward. To cut down on some of the crowding, you can, of course, close or minimize directory windows that are not in use. On the other hand, if you want to leave more than one directory window open at the same time, you can use the Window Stack command (or press SHIFT+F5) to neatly stack directory windows, or you can use the Window Tile command (or press SHIFT+F4) to create a tiled arrangement of directory windows.

Perhaps the best solution, though, to overcrowding of the File Manager window is to have one directory window replaced by the next. That way, when you open a new directory window, it replaces the current directory window. To do this, select the View Replace On Open command from File Manager's menu. From then on, each time you open a new directory window, it replaces the current one.

CHANGING THE DISPLAY OF DIRECTORY WINDOWS

Later in this chapter you'll learn how to select files from directory windows and perform operations on them. For example, you'll learn how to copy a group of files from one directory to another. However, to make this process just that much easier, you can sort the displayed files and directories in different ways, allowing you to quickly find a particular file or a group of files. You can also choose categories of files to be displayed, rather than looking at all the files in a particular directory. In addition, you can get information about the size of selected files and directories, allowing you to determine whether the copy or move operation you are about to perform is feasible.

Choosing a Sort Order

When you open a directory window, File Manager displays the name of files and directories in alphabetical order. Directories are listed first enclosed in square brackets, followed by filenames. Because of this organization, finding a particular file in a large directory can become rather cumbersome. However, you can make the process more efficient by sorting the files in the directory in different ways. For example, you can sort the files by extension, size, or date of last modification.

To sort the files in a directory by file extension, select the By Type option from the View menu. File Manager sorts the files in the current directory window by extension, and then by filename, in alphabetical order. With this type of sort, all of the files with a given extension are grouped together. For example, all of the files with an .EXE extension now appear together. That way, you can easily locate a particular executable file and double-click on it to start an application. To return the list of files to the default alphabetical sort by filename, select the Name option from File Manager's View menu.

You can also sort the files in a directory window by size and date they were last modified. To do this, select the Sort by... option from the View menu. File Manager displays the Sort By dialog box in Figure 3-3. This dialog box contains four radio buttons including Name, Type, Size, and Last Modification Date. The Name and Type options correspond to the Name and Type options on the View menu. The Size option sorts the files and directories in the current directory window by size, working from largest to smallest. The Date Last Modified option sorts files and directories by the date they were

File Manager Techniques 89

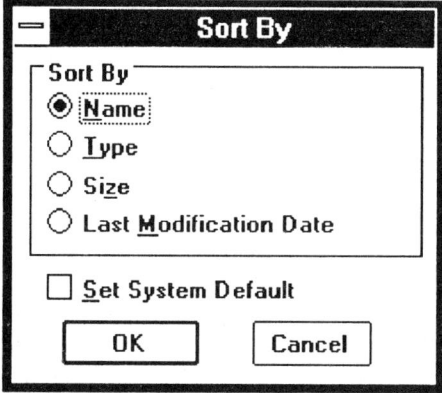

Figure 3-3 The Sort By dialog box

last modified (or created), working from newest to oldest. To have the sort option you select apply to all the directory windows you open, select the Set System Default check box. To return to the current directory window and have the sort sequence you've selected implemented, select OK.

Limiting Directory Window Contents

File Manager also provides command options that let you limit the contents of a directory window. This option can be very handy when you only want to look at a specific set of files in a large directory.

To control the display of directory and files in a directory window, select the Include... option from the View menu. When you select this option, File Manager displays the Include dialog box in Figure 3-4. The Name text box allows you to limit the files displayed in a directory window to those that fit a specific file specification that you define. Initially, File Manager displays *.* in this box, causing all the files in the current directory to be displayed. However, you can use the standard DOS wild-card characters (* and ?) to build any wild-card pattern you want. For example, to display only those files that begin with the letter T and have a .WP extension, type **t*.WP**. To return to the current directory window and implement your selection, choose OK.

The check boxes in the File Type section of the Include dialog box in Figure 3-4 let you further limit the directories and files that are displayed in directory windows. As you can see, these check boxes correspond to the display of directories, program files, document files, and other files. By default all of these check boxes are selected (contain an X). To remove a particular category from the current directory window display, simply clear the appropriate check box. To return to the current directory window and implement your selection, choose OK.

The second to last check box in the Include dialog box, labeled Show Hidden/System Files, allows you to view files that are normally hidden (have a hidden attribute). If you are familiar with DOS, you know that it does not provide a means for you to view hidden

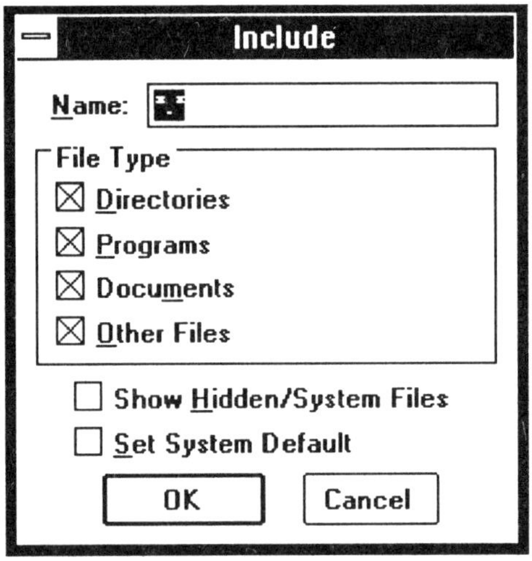

Figure 3-4 The Include dialog box

files. Instead, you must turn to special utility programs. The Show Hidden/System Files selection does not change the attribute for the file, but it does allow you to display information about hidden files in the current directory window. (See "Changing Attributes" later for details on how to change the attribute for a file.)

For example, imagine you want to take a look at the hidden system files for your particular version of DOS. To do this, open a directory window that shows the contents of the root directory on your primary drive (usually C:\). Once this directory window is open, select the View Include command to display the Include dialog box in Figure 3-4. Select the Show/Hidden System Files check box and then select OK to return to File Manager. The hidden system files for your version of DOS are now displayed in the current directory window. To make the names of these files easier to find, select the View By Type command to sort the files in the current directory window by extension. Then, scroll the current directory window until the group of .COM files is displayed. If you are running PC DOS, you should see the files IBMBIO.COM and IBMDOS.COM in the list. On the other hand, if you are running a clone, take a look in the group of files with a .SYS extension for the files MSDOS.SYS and IO.SYS.

The last check box in the Include dialog box, Save System Default, lets you save the settings you've made for use during the current Windows session. When you select this box, Windows will use the settings you've specified in the Include dialog box for any directory windows you subsequently open.

Getting Information about Files and Directories

You can also change the information for files and directories that is displayed in a directory window. Normally, File Manager displays only the names of files and directo-

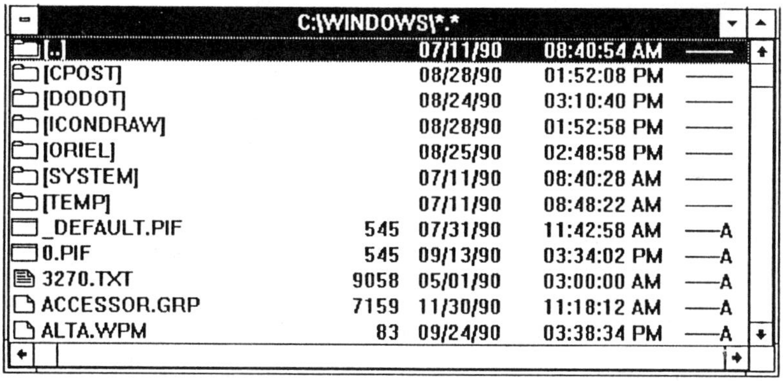

```
┌─────────────────────────────────────────────────┬───┐
│ ─          C:\WINDOWS\*.*                    ▼  │ ▲ │
├─────────────────────────────────────────────────┤   │
│ ▭ [..]                  07/11/90  08:40:54 AM ──│ ↑ │
│ 🗁 [CPOST]                08/28/90  01:52:08 PM ──│   │
│ 🗁 [DODOT]                08/24/90  03:10:40 PM ──│   │
│ 🗁 [ICONDRAW]             08/28/90  01:52:58 PM ──│   │
│ 🗁 [ORIEL]                08/25/90  02:48:58 PM ──│   │
│ 🗁 [SYSTEM]               07/11/90  08:40:28 AM ──│   │
│ 🗁 [TEMP]                 07/11/90  08:48:22 AM ──│   │
│ ▭ _DEFAULT.PIF     545  07/31/90  11:42:58 AM ──A│   │
│ ▭ 0.PIF            545  09/13/90  03:34:02 PM ──A│   │
│ ▤ 3270.TXT        9058  05/01/90  03:00:00 AM ──A│   │
│ ▭ ACCESSOR.GRP    7159  11/30/90  11:18:12 AM ──A│   │
│ ▭ ALTA.WPM          83  09/24/90  03:38:34 PM ──A│ ↓ │
│ ←                                              → │   │
└─────────────────────────────────────────────────┴───┘
```

Figure 3-5 Using the File Details command to get information about files

ries. However, you can also get information about the size of a file, the date and time of last modification, and the attributes that are currently assigned to the file.

To display additional information about the files and directories in a directory window, select the File Details command from the View menu. When you select this option, File Manager changes the display of the current directory window to appear as shown in Figure 3-5. A separate line is displayed for each directory and file. Each line includes the following information: name, size in bytes (files only), date last modified, time last modified, and the current attribute(s) for a file. Possible file attributes include A (archive), H (hidden), R (read-only), or S (system). See "Changing Attributes" later in this chapter for a description of what these attributes are and how they are used.

To control which file-detail information is displayed in the current directory window, select the Other... option from the View menu. When you select this option, File Manager displays the View Other dialog box shown in Figure 3-6. As you can see, the check boxes

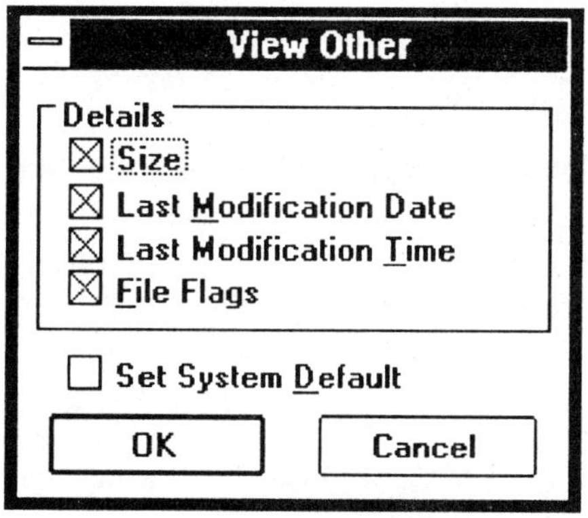

```
┌──────────────────────────────────┐
│ ─           View Other           │
├──────────────────────────────────┤
│ ┌─Details─────────────────────┐  │
│ │ ☒ Size                      │  │
│ │ ☒ Last Modification Date    │  │
│ │ ☒ Last Modification Time    │  │
│ │ ☒ File Flags                │  │
│ └─────────────────────────────┘  │
│                                  │
│    ☐ Set System Default          │
│                                  │
│    ┌────────┐    ┌────────┐      │
│    │   OK   │    │ Cancel │      │
│    └────────┘    └────────┘      │
└──────────────────────────────────┘
```

Figure 3-6 The View Other dialog box

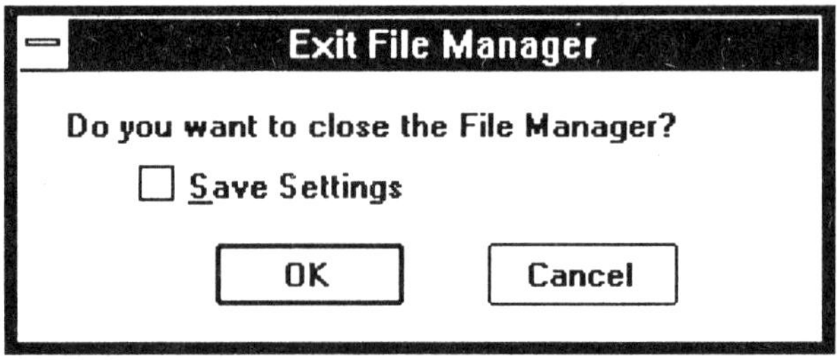

Figure 3-7 The Exit File Manager dialog box

in this dialog box correspond to the display of size, date, time, and attribute (file flags) information for files that are displayed in a directory window. By default, all four check boxes are selected, causing all the information available on each file to be displayed. To remove an option, simply clear the appropriate check box. To have the settings you make apply to other directory windows you may open during the current File Manager session, select the Save System Default check box. To return to the current directory window and implement your changes, select OK.

Saving Your Settings

When you make a settings change by using the View menu, those changes apply only to the current File Manager session. To make those settings available for use in future sessions, you must save them. To do this, you must close the File Manager window. You can do this by using the File Exit command, by selecting Close from the window Control menu, or by pressing ALT+F4. Any of these commands causes Windows to display the Exit File Manager dialog box shown in Figure 3-7. You'll notice that this dialog box contains a Save Settings check box. Select this box and then select OK to leave File Manager. The settings changes you've made will be saved and used in your next File Manager session.

MANAGING FILES AND DIRECTORIES

As mentioned, File Manager lets you perform many of your routine file management chores without having to leave Windows. For example, you can create new directories. You can also copy, move, rename, and delete files and directories. This section shows you how to go about using File Manager to perform these operations.

Creating Directories

To create a new directory with File Manager, you use the File Create Directory command. In preparation for this command, select a directory from the directory tree or an appropriate directory window. The directory you subsequently create will be a subdirec-

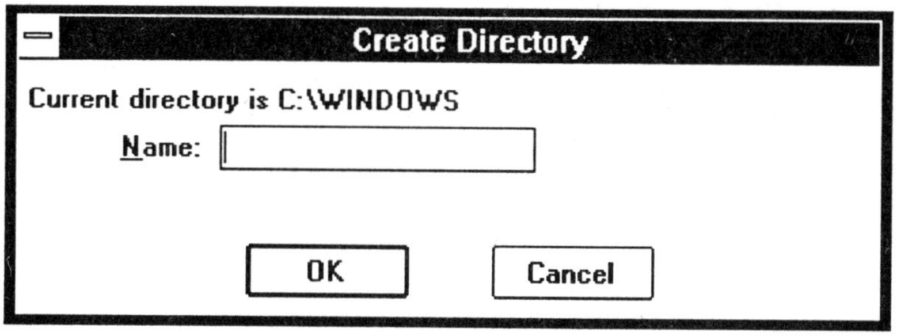

Figure 3-8 The Create Directory dialog box

tory of the directory you select. When you've made your selection, choose the File Create Directory command. File Manager displays the dialog box shown in Figure 3-8. The name of the current directory appears at the top of this box. To create a subdirectory of that directory, type an appropriate name in the Name text box and select OK. File Manager creates the new directory under the name you specified. You can now create files in that directory as well as copy and move files to or from that directory.

Selecting Files

Before you can perform an operation on a file or directory (for example, copy it or move it), you must select it from an open directory window. You can select a single file or directory, multiple files or directories scattered throughout the current directory window, or all the files in the directory window. Once files and/or directories are selected, you can use the commands in File Manager's menu to perform operations on them.

Selecting a Single File

The easiest way to select a single file or directory is to simply click on its icon. File Manager moves the highlight to that file. Alternatively, you can use the arrow keys to move the highlight to the name of the file. To move up or down one windowful at a time, press PGUP and PGDN. To move to the first or last file or directory in a directory window, press HOME or END.

Selecting Multiple Files

You can also select multiple files and subdirectories scattered throughout a directory window. This is done by selecting an initial file or subdirectory and then adding additional files or subdirectories to that selection. This is sometimes referred to as *extending a selection*.

You can create a multiple-file selection by using either your mouse or your keyboard. To do this with your mouse, hold down the CTRL key and click on each of the icons for the files or subdirectories you want to include in the selection. As you click on each entry,

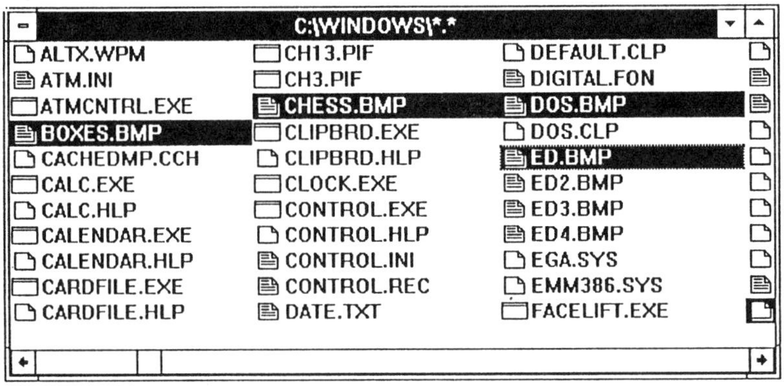

```
┌─────────────────────────────────────────────────────────┐ ▼ ▲
│  -                    C:\WINDOWS\*.*                    │
├─────────────────────────────────────────────────────────┤
│ 🗋ALTX.WPM         ☐CH13.PIF          🗋DEFAULT.CLP   🗋 │
│ 🖹ATM.INI          ☐CH3.PIF           🖹DIGITAL.FON    🖹│
│ ☐ATMCNTRL.EXE     🖹CHESS.BMP         🖹DOS.BMP       🖹 │
│ 🖹BOXES.BMP        ☐CLIPBRD.EXE       🗋DOS.CLP       🗋 │
│ 🗋CACHEDMP.CCH     🗋CLIPBRD.HLP       🖹ED.BMP        🗋 │
│ ☐CALC.EXE         ☐CLOCK.EXE         🖹ED2.BMP       🗋 │
│ 🗋CALC.HLP         ☐CONTROL.EXE       🖹ED3.BMP       🗋 │
│ ☐CALENDAR.EXE     🗋CONTROL.HLP       🖹ED4.BMP       🗋 │
│ 🗋CALENDAR.HLP     🖹CONTROL.INI       🗋EGA.SYS       🗋 │
│ ☐CARDFILE.EXE     🖹CONTROL.REC       🗋EMM386.SYS    🖹 │
│ 🗋CARDFILE.HLP     🖹DATE.TXT          ☐FACELIFT.EXE  🗋 │
├─────────────────────────────────────────────────────────┤
│ ←                                                     → │
└─────────────────────────────────────────────────────────┘
```

Figure 3-9 Selecting multiple files from a directory window

File Manager highlights it, indicating that it is included in the current selection. Figure 3-9 shows a selection of this kind. To cancel this selection, simply click on any file or subdirectory icon. To cancel only part of the selection, hold down the CTRL key and click on the items you don't want included.

To perform this same operation with the keyboard, move the highlight to the first entry in the selection and press SHIFT+F8. The highlight begins to blink. Use the arrow keys to move to the next file in the selection and press the spacebar to select it. Use the SPACEBAR to select any additional files you may want to include. When you are done, press SHIFT+F8 again to end the selection process. To cancel the selection, press any arrow key. To cancel only part of the selection, press SHIFT+F8. The cursor begins to blink. Use the arrow keys to move to the item you don't want included and press the SPACEBAR. Do this for each item you do not want included. When you are done, press SHIFT+F8 again.

Tip: Calculating the size of a group of files

When you select multiple files in a directory window, File Manager displays the total size in bytes of all the files in the selection in the status line at the bottom of File Manager's window. This information can be invaluable. For example, if you want to copy or move the files in the current selection to another directory, this information can tell you how much free disk space will be required to complete the copy or move operation.

You can also extend a selection to include a consecutive group of files. To do this with your mouse, begin by clicking on the first item in a group. Then, hold the SHIFT key and click on the last item in the group. File Manager extends the selection to include those files in between the first and last items you've selected. You can cancel this selection by clicking on any filename.

Selecting a consecutive group of files with your keyboard is equally easy. To do this, hold down the SHIFT key and use the arrow keys to extend the selection to include the files you want. To cancel the selection, press any arrow key.

To select more than one group of consecutive files, you must be a little ambidextrous. To do this with your mouse, highlight the first group of consecutive files by clicking on the first item in the group and holding down SHIFT and clicking on the last item. To highlight the next group, hold down CTRL and click on the first item in the group, then hold down CTRL+SHIFT and click on last item in the group. Repeat this operation for each individual group you want to include in the selection. To cancel the selection, click on any filename.

Selecting more than one group of consecutive files with your keyboard is a bit harder. To begin, hold down the SHIFT key and use the arrow keys to highlight the first group of files. Then, press and release SHIFT+F8. The cursor begins to blink. Now, use the arrow keys to move to the first item in the next consecutive group of files and press the SPACEBAR to select the first item in that group. Then, hold down the SHIFT key and use the arrow keys to extend the selection to include the group of files you want. Finally, press SHIFT+F8 to complete the selection of the second group of files. You can extend the selection to include additional groups by pressing SHIFT+F8 before and after highlighting files with the SHIFT+arrow-key combination. To cancel the selection, press any arrow key.

Selecting All the Files in a Directory Window

You can also select all the files and subdirectories in the current directory window. This feature can be convenient when you want to copy or move all the files in one directory to another. To do this, select the File Select All command from File Manager's menu, or press CTRL+/ (CTRL+SLASH). File Manager selects all the files in the current directory window. To cancel this selection, choose the File Deselect All command from File Manager's menu or press CTRL+\ (CTRL+BACKSLASH).

Copying Files and Directories

You can copy a directory or file by using either your mouse or your keyboard. The mouse method is more flexible, however. With the mouse, you can simply press the ALT key and drag the icon for a file or directory from its present location on the directory tree or in an open directory window to a new location. The new location can be either another open directory window, a minimized directory window, a directory icon on the directory tree, or a drive icon. The keyboard method, on the other hand, is dialog box-driven. Both methods are explained in the sections that follow.

Copying with the Mouse

Perhaps the easiest copy operation with the mouse is copying a file from one open directory window to another. To do this, open the *source* directory window (the window you want to copy the file from) as well as the *destination* window (the window you want to copy the file to). Once the source and destination directory windows are displayed, press the **CTRL** key and hold it down. Then, click on the icon for the file you want to copy and drag it to the other group window. Position the icon anywhere in the directory window except on top of a directory icon. (If you position the file icon on top of a directory icon, File Manager will copy the file to that directory.) When you are ready, release your mouse button and then release the CTRL key. Windows displays the dialog box shown in Figure 3-10. Select OK to complete the copy operation.

Note: If File Manager detects that you are about to overwrite a file of the same name in the destination directory, it displays a message box informing you of this. This message box gives you the option of canceling the copy operation or proceeding.

The same rules apply for copying a directory. However, copying a directory has the effect of creating a new subdirectory under the same name in the destination directory. In addition, all of the files in the source directory are copied to the new directory. To copy a directory, simply hold down the CTRL key and drag the icon for the directory from one directory window to another. If you locate the icon for the directory on top of a directory icon in the destination directory window, File Manager will create the new directory as a subdirectory of that directory. On the other hand, if you locate the directory icon anywhere else in the destination directory window, File Manager will simply add the directory to those already displayed in the destination directory window.

You can also copy files and directories from an open directory window to a minimized directory window. To do this, simply use the procedures described in the previous paragraphs. However, your destination window will be the minimized directory window.

You can also copy multiple files and directories in a single operation. To do this, though, you must first select the files and directories you want to copy from an open directory window by using the techniques described earlier under "Selecting Files and

Figure 3-10 File Manager asks you to confirm a copy operation initiated with the mouse

Directories." Once the appropriate files and directories are selected, hold down CTRL and click your mouse on any part of the highlighted selection; then drag the selection to its new destination. As you drag, File Manager displays an icon that looks like three stacked cards. When you release your mouse button in the destination directory window, File Manager copies all the directories and files in the current selection to the destination.

You can also use the CTRL key and your mouse to copy a file or directory from an open directory window to a directory icon on the directory tree or to a drive icon. Simply hold down CTRL and drag the appropriate file or directory icon from the open directory window and place it on top of the directory icon in the directory tree, or on top of a drive icon. When you are ready, release your mouse button and then release the CTRL key. However, if you decide to drag an icon to a drive button, be aware that File Manager will copy the source file or directory to the directory that was last used on that drive.

Note: If you are copying files or directories to a different disk drive, you can simply drag the current selection to a disk-drive icon. Pressing the CTRL key at the same time is not necessary.

You can also copy between directories displayed on the directory tree. Simply press CTRL and drag the icon for one directory on top of another. File Manager copies the directory itself, any files in the directory, and any subdirectories to the destination directory.

In case this all seems a bit confusing, Figure 3-11 provides an overview of potential sources and destinations for copying files and directories in File Manager.

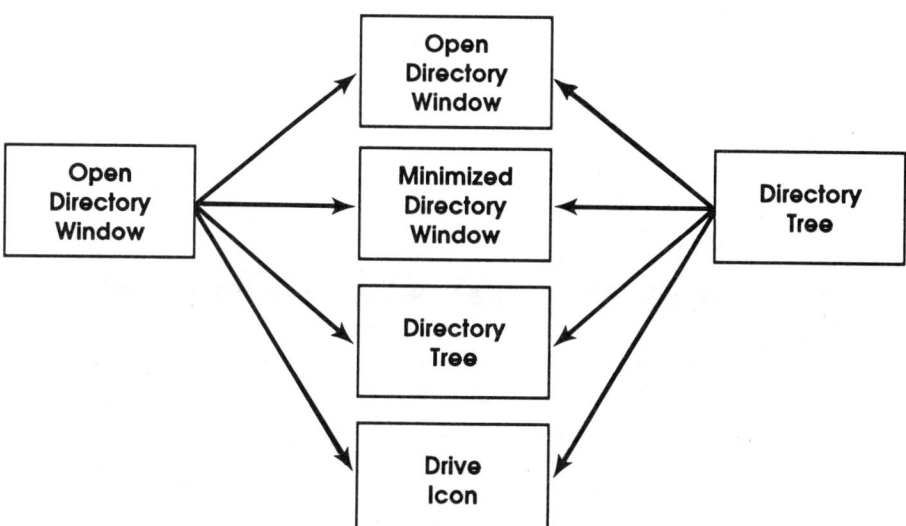

Figure 3-11 Potential sources and destinations for copying with the mouse in File Manager

Note: If you minimize a directory window and then copy to the directory tree icon for that directory, the minimized directory is not updated. In fact, when you restore the minimized directory window, it will not show any evidence that the copy has taken place. To have the new files and/or directories displayed in the restored directory window, select the Window Refresh command from File Manager's menu or press F5. Either of these selections causes File Manager to read the directory again and update the current directory window for any changes.

Copying with the Keyboard

As mentioned, you can also copy files and directories by using the keyboard. To do this, first select the files and/or directories you want to copy from either an open directory window or, in the case of directories, from the directory tree. When you are ready, select the File Copy command from File Manager's menu, or press F8. File Manager displays the Copy dialog box shown in Figure 3-12. In the From text box, File Manager shows the names of all the files and directories you have previously selected. In the To text box, type the path and name of the directory you want to copy the data to. To perform the copy operation, select the Copy button.

If the files you want to copy from a given directory have something in common—for example, the same file extension—you don't need to select them beforehand. Instead, you can use the standard DOS wild-card characters to build a template for the files you want to copy. For example, imagine you want to copy all the files with a .WK1 extension in the C:\ACCOUNTI directory to the directory C:\BACK. To do this, select the File Copy command to display the Copy dialog box. In the From box, type **C:\ACCOUNTI*.WK1**. Press TAB to move to the To text box and type **C:\BACK**. Press ENTER to select the Copy button. File Manager copies all the files with a .WK1 extension in the C:\ACCOUNTI directory to the C:\BACK directory under the same names.

You can also use the File Copy command to copy and rename a file. To do this, select the file you want to copy from a directory window, and select the File Copy command, or press F8, to display the Copy dialog box. In the To text box, type the new path and

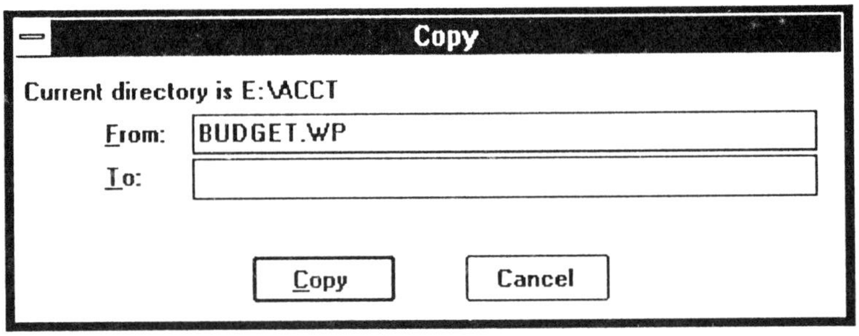

Figure 3-12 The Copy dialog box

name you want to use for the file. Finally, select the Copy button to complete the operation.

Moving Files and Directories

You can also move files and directories with File Manager by using your mouse or your keyboard. In fact, the sequence of steps required to move files and directories is very similar to copying files and directories. However, File Manager handles the files and directories involved differently. First, it copies the files and directories you specify to a new destination of your choosing. That being done, File Manager then deletes the files and directories in the old source location.

Moving with the Mouse

To move files and directories with the mouse, begin by making sure the destination directory is represented somewhere on the File Manager work surface. The destination directory can be any one of the following:

- An icon on the directory tree
- A directory icon in an open directory window
- The directory represented by an open directory window
- A minimized directory window
- A drive icon

Remember, if you decide to move to a drive icon, File Manager will move the files and directories in the current selection to the last directory that was used on that drive.

Once you've decided on your destination directory, select the files and/or directories that will be the source data for the move. Your source data can be one or more files and directories in an open directory window or a directory icon on the directory tree. When you are ready, hold down the **ALT** key and use your mouse to drag the source icon or selection to its new location. When you get to the destination, release the mouse button and then release the ALT key. File Manager displays the dialog box shown in Figure 3-13. Select Yes to complete the move. Windows copies the files and directories you've selected to the new location. (If you move a directory, the directory itself is copied along with any files and subdirectories it may contain.)

Once the copying aspect of the move is completed, File Manager attempts to delete the old source files and directories from their old locations. If only files are involved in the move, File Manager simply deletes them from the old location. However, if one or more directories are involved, File Manager displays the dialog box shown in Figure 3-14 before deleting each directory. If you want to keep the old empty directory, select No. To remove the directory from your hard disk, select Yes. To cancel the move operation at that point, select Cancel.

100   Windows 3 Power Tools

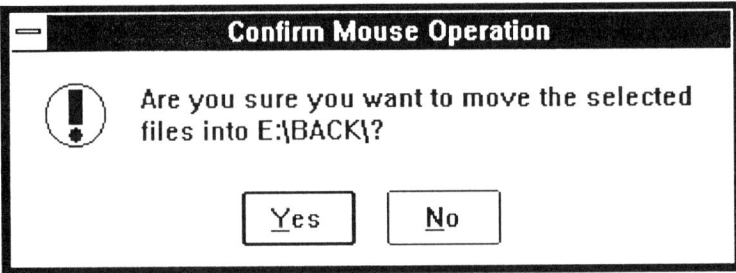

Figure 3-13 File Manager asks you to confirm a move operation performed with the mouse

Note: You do not have to use the ALT key if you are moving files and directories to a destination on the same disk drive. Instead, you can simply drag the current selection with your mouse.

Moving with the Keyboard

To move files and directories with the keyboard, begin by selecting the files and/or directories you want to move. You can make your selection either from an open directory window or from the directory tree. When you're ready, select the File Move command from File Manager's menu, or press F7. File Manager displays the dialog box shown in Figure 3-15. In the From text box, File Manager displays all the files and directories you have previously selected. To specify a new directory for these files and directories, type the path and name of the appropriate directory in the To text box. To complete the move, select the Move button. File Manager moves the files and directories referenced in the From text box to the directory you've specified in the To text box. Once again, if any directories are involved in the move, File Manager displays the dialog box shown in Figure 3-14 for each of the directories. Selecting No from this dialog box each time lets you keep the directories in the old location, but the directories are left empty.

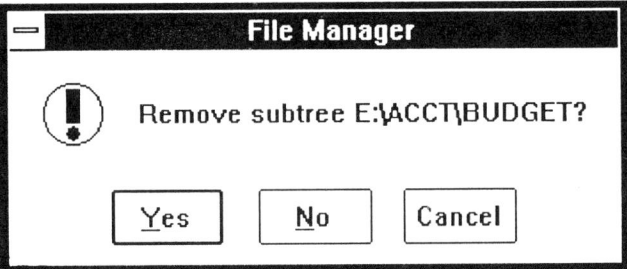

Figure 3-14 File Manager asks you to confirm the deletion of directories after a move operation

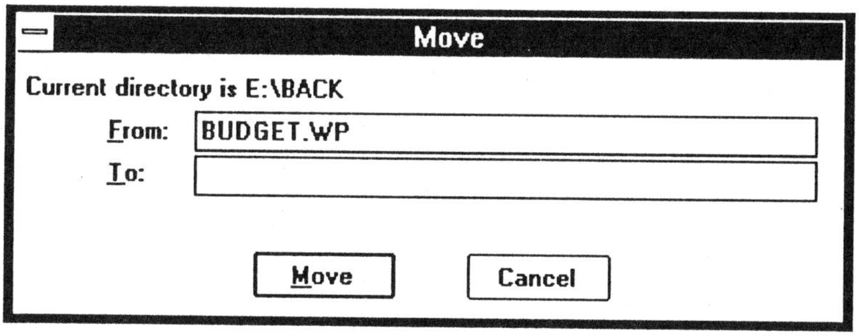

File Manager Techniques 101

Figure 3-15 The Move dialog box

Renaming Files and Directories

Renaming files and directories with File Manager couldn't be easier. To rename a file or directory, begin by selecting the icon for the file or directory you want to rename. You must select the name of a file from an open directory window. However, you can select the icon for a directory from either an open directory window or from the directory tree. Once you've made your selection, choose the Rename option from the File menu. File Manager displays the Rename dialog box shown in Figure 3-16. The current name for the file or directory is displayed in the From text box. Type the new name for the file or directory in the To text box. To rename the file or directory, select the Rename button.

Deleting Files and Directories

File Manager also lets you delete files or directories. To do this, select one or more files or directories from an open directory window. You can also select a directory to delete from the directory tree. After you've made your selection, select the Delete option from the File menu, or simply press DEL. File Manager displays the dialog box shown in Figure 3-17, asking you to confirm the deletion. The files and directories in the current selection are shown in the Delete text box. To delete these files or directories, select the Delete

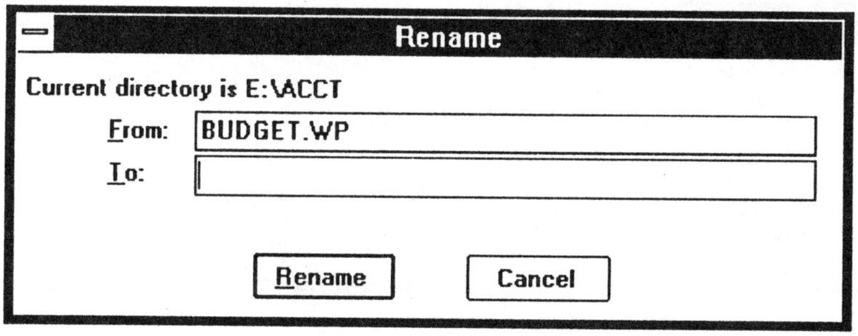

Figure 3-16 The Rename dialog box

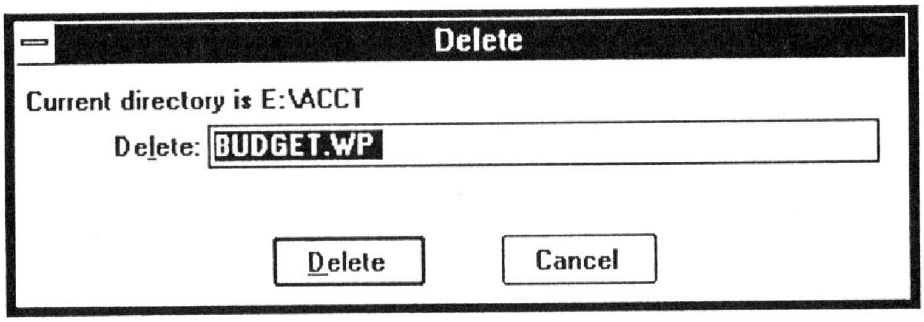

102   *Windows 3 Power Tools*

Figure 3-17 The Delete dialog box

button. File Manager displays the dialog box shown in Figure 3-18 asking you to confirm the deletion again. Select Yes to proceed with the deletion.

Note: As you know, you should always exercise special care when using any command that deletes files or directories. However, this is especially true with File Manager's File Delete command. Unlike DOS, which will not allow you to delete a directory that contains files, File Manager will not only delete the directory, but also delete all the files and subdirectories in that directory as well. You will, of course, be asked to confirm the deletion of each and every file and directory involved, starting from the last file in the last subdirectory and working backward toward the root. And you can cancel the operation at any time. Nevertheless, you should exercise the utmost care when using the File Delete command.

Searching for Files and Directories

Even the most organized PC user occasionally forgets where he or she has stored a file. Poking around from directory to directory looking for a file will eventually get the job

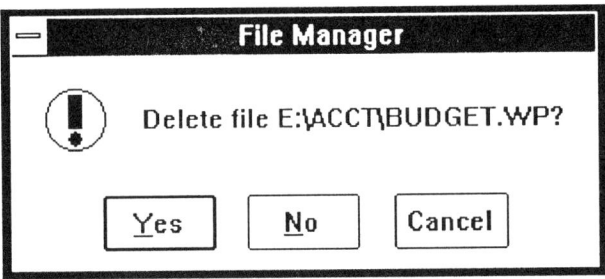

Figure 3-18 File Manager asks you to confirm the deletion of a file or directory

done, but precious time is lost in the search. To cut down on the time you spend searching for files, File Manager provides a way for you to quickly search a disk drive for files or directories that you specify. The results of the search are displayed in a search-results window. In addition, by using conventional DOS wild-card characters (* and ?), you can search for files and directories when you are not completely sure of how their names are spelled. This also allows you to search for multiple files and directories that have something in common. For example, imagine you give all your WordPerfect correspondence files a .WP extension. By using the search reference *.WP, you can search for and display the locations of all your WordPerfect correspondence files on the current drive.

As mentioned, when you search for files and directories, File Manager displays the results of the search in a search-results window. The path to each file appears on a separate line in the window. Once files and/or directories are displayed in this window, you can select them and apply File Manager commands to them, just as though they were located in a directory window.

To search for files or directories, first select the drive and directory that you want to search. When you are ready, select the File Search command from File Manager's menu. File Manager displays the Search dialog box shown in Figure 3-19. In the Search For text box, type the name of the file or directory you want to search for. You can also use DOS wild-card characters to describe a set of files with similar names or extensions. If you only want to search the current directory and any subdirectories it may have, clear the Search Entire Disk check box. Otherwise, File Manager will search the entire drive. To begin the search, select the Search button. File Manager hesitates for a moment and then displays the results of the search in the Search Results window shown in Figure 3-20. The path and name of each file or directory found is displayed on a separate line in this window.

The Search Results window has the same attributes as any other window in File Manager. Therefore, you can move it, resize it, minimize, close it, and so on. You can also select the name of a file or directory from the window and apply a File Manager command to it. For example, you can copy, move, or rename a file. However, you cannot copy or move files to the Search Results window.

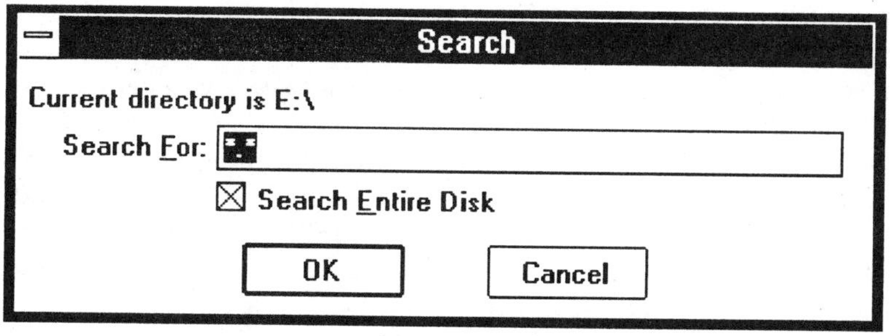

Figure 3-19 The Search dialog box

104   *Windows 3 Power Tools*

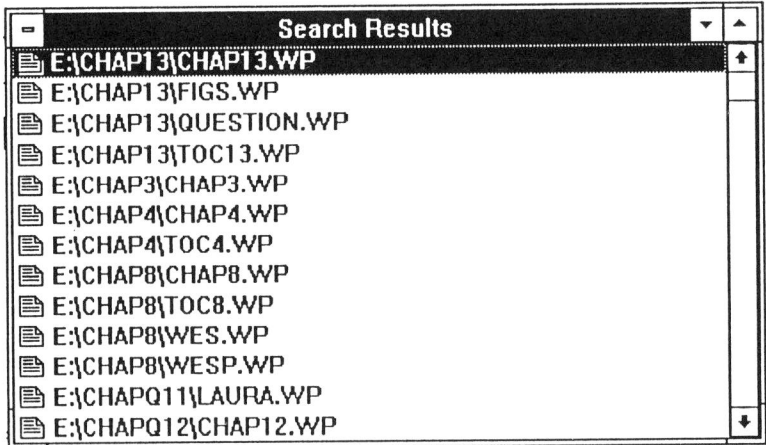

Figure 3-20 The Search Results window

CREATING ASSOCIATIONS

You can also use File Manager to create associations between files with a given extension and the application that supports those files. For example, you might create an association between files with a .WK1 extension and Lotus 1-2-3. Once this association exists, you can double-click on any .WK1 file in any directory window to have Windows automatically start Lotus 1-2-3 and load the file you've selected.

To create an association between a data file and an application, you use the File Association command. In preparation for this command, though, first select an appropriate data file from an open directory window. For example, if you always give your WordPerfect files a .WP extension, highlight any WordPerfect file that has that extension. When you are ready, select the File Associate command. File Manager displays the Associate dialog box shown in Figure 3-21. In the text box provided, type the path and name of the executable file for the application that you want to associate with the currently selected data file. To create the association, select OK. File Manager creates the association.

When you create an association between a data file and an application, Windows adds an entry to the [Extensions] section of your WIN.INI file. In fact, if you use Notepad or SysEdit to look at this file, you'll see that associations are already defined for some of the applications that come with Windows. For example, you'll see the line **wri=write.exe ^.wri**. This line defines an association between WRITE.EXE (Write) and files with a .WRI extension. Therefore, you can double-click on any .WRI file in an open directory window to have Windows start Write and load the file you've selected.

Because associations are recorded in the WIN.INI file, they can be used outside of File Manager. For example, as you learned in Chapter 2, you can use Program Manager's File Run command to start applications. This same command is available from File Manager's

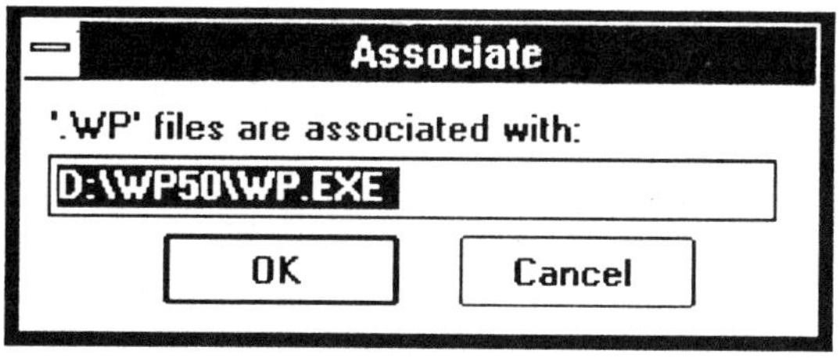

Figure 3-21 The Associate dialog box

menu. Nevertheless, if an association exists, you can simply select the File Run command, type the path and name of a data file, and press ENTER to have Windows start the appropriate application and load that data file.

Imagine you want to create an icon in a Program Manager group window that automatically starts a given application and loads a specific data file for the application. If an association has been created beforehand, you can use the File New command to set up the icon in the usual way. However, instead of supplying the path and name of the application's executable file for the icon, you can simply supply the path and name of a data file. That way, when you double-click on the icon in Program Manager, Windows will start the appropriate application and load that data file by association. For details on how you can set up icons for applications in Program Manager's group windows, see Chapter 2, "Program Manager Techniques."

RUNNING APPLICATIONS

As mentioned, you can double-click on the name of an executable file in one of File Manager's directory windows to run that application. However, you can also run applications by using other techniques. For example, you can simply highlight the name of an executable file and press ENTER to open the application. If an association exists between data files with a specific extension and an application, you can simply double-click on the name of a data file, or highlight it and press ENTER, to start the associated application and load the data file you've selected. See "Creating Associations" earlier for details on how you can create associations between applications and their data files.

Dragging with the Mouse

You can also start an application and load a specific data file for that application by dragging with your mouse. To do this, open a directory window that contains both the data file and the application file. (If these are located in separate directories, open a directory window for each of them.) When you are ready, drag the icon for the data file onto the icon for the application. For example, if you want to start Word for Windows (WINWORD.EXE) and load the file MYFILE.DOC, drag the icon for MYFILE.DOC onto the icon for WINWORD.EXE. File Manager displays a confirmation dialog box. Select OK to start the application and load the data file you've selected.

The procedure described in the previous paragraph usually works just fine for both DOS and Windows applications. However, under certain circumstances, problems may arise. For instance, problems often arise when the directory containing the executable file for the application is not in your path and the executable file and data file are in different directories.

For example, imagine you want to start a DOS version of WordPerfect, which is located in your C:\WP directory by dragging a file from your C:\LETTERS directory. The C:\WP directory is not in your path. Unaware of this, you open separate directory windows for C:\WP and C:\LETTERS. Once these windows are open, you drag the icon for a WordPerfect document from the C:\LETTERS window onto the icon for the executable file for WordPerfect in the C:\WP window. Windows displays a dialog box asking if you want to proceed with the operation. When you select OK to proceed, Windows displays an error message informing you that it cannot find the files it needs to complete the operation.

Further complications can arise where DOS applications are concerned. Once again, these problems tend to crop up when the data file and application file are in different directories. For example, some DOS applications expect certain driver and overlay files to be in a certain directory when you start the application. If that directory is not current at startup, the DOS application will crash.

For example, imagine you want to start Lotus 1-2-3 Release 2.2 located in your D:\LOTUS directory and load the file BUDGET.WK1 located in your E:\ACCOUNTI directory. To do this, you open a directory window for both of these directories and display them side by side. At that point, you drag the icon for the BUDGET.WK1 file in the E:\ACCOUNTI window on top of the icon for 123.EXE (1-2-3's executable file) in the D:\LOTUS window. Thus, the last active directory was E:\ACCOUNTI, not D:\LOTUS, which contains the needed driver and overlay files for 1-2-3. Windows displays a message box asking you if you want to proceed. When you select OK, Windows attempts to run 1-2-3. Things go along nicely until 1-2-3 looks for its driver files and cannot find them. An error message is then displayed informing you that a fatal error has occurred.

Using Commands

You can also run applications by using commands in File Manager's menu. For example, you can select an executable file from one of File Manager's directory windows and select the File Open command from File Manager menu to run the application. Alternatively, you can select the File Run command to have File Manager display the Run dialog box. Once this box is displayed, type the path and name of the executable file for an application and press ENTER to run the application. If you want to load a data file for that application as well, type the path and name of the application's executable file followed by a space and the path and name of the data file. If the application or its data file is in the current directory, or in a directory that is included in your path, you can simply use filenames without the preceding path information.

The Minimize on Use Option

Like Program Manager, you can have the File Manager window minimized to an icon whenever you run an application from within it. To do this, select the Options Minimize on Use command from File Manager's menu. From then on, the File Manager window is reduced to an icon whenever you start an application, and it remains iconized when you close the application. To save this setting for future File Manager sessions, select the Save Settings check box when you exit File Manager.

CHANGING FILE ATTRIBUTES

File Manager also allows you to set attributes for files. File attributes are actually determined by bits located in the file header. These bits are assigned a value of 1 (on) or 0 (off). They are used by DOS both to identify the type of file it is dealing with and to determine the type of operation that you can perform on that file.

For example, some files are of such importance that deleting them would cause your system to become permanently inoperable. These files are often hidden (the hidden bit is turned on). These files exist on your disk, but you can't find them with conventional DOS commands, and, therefore, they are very difficult to delete.

In other cases, although certain files are not critical to the operation of your system, you may still want to protect them. To do this, you can specify a read-only attribute for a file (flip the read-only bit). When a file is read only, you can see it in directories, read it into memory, and copy it, but you can't change its contents, and you can't delete it. This type of file attribute is often used in networking environments to make shared application files unchangeable by users.

You can use File Manager to see the attributes that are assigned to a file by opening a directory window containing that file. Once the directory window is displayed, select the View File Details command from File Manager's menu. This command causes File Manager to display all the available information for the files in the current directory, including their attributes. To see hidden files, however, you must also select the View Include command to display the Include dialog box and then select the Show/Hidden System File check box.

To change the attribute assigned to a file, first select it from an open directory window, then choose the Change Attributes option from the File menu. File Manager displays the Change Attributes dialog box shown in Figure 3-22. This dialog box contains four check boxes that define attributes you can assign to the currently selected file. The check boxes for those attributes that are currently assigned to the file appear preselected (contain an X). To assign other attributes, clear the currently selected check box, if necessary, and select the ones you want. The available choices are

- Read Only (R): Stops someone from changing the contents of the file. It can still be read into memory or copied from one location to another, but you can't change its contents. Further, if you attempt to delete the file, DOS will return the message "Access denied."

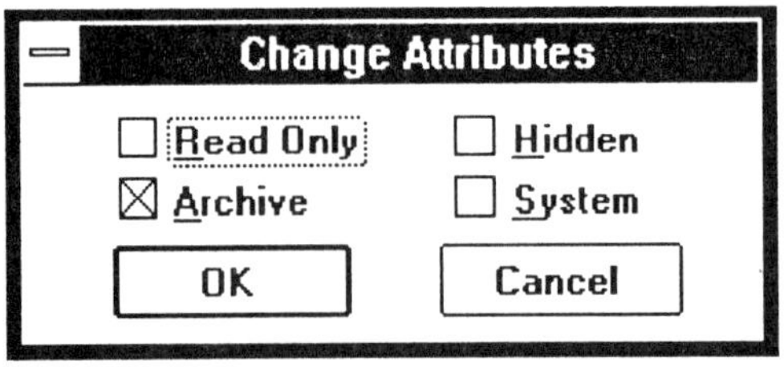

Figure 3-22 The Change Attributes dialog box

- Archive (A): DOS assigns an Archive attribute to any file you create or modify. However, when you use the DOS BACKUP or XCOPY commands with the /M switch, DOS turns off the Archive bit after it copies the file. That way, when you back up those same files the next time, DOS will skip over any files that you have not changed since your last backup.
- Hidden (H): Excludes a file from a directory search. Therefore, hidden files do not appear in DOS directory listings. If you attempt to list the file with the DIR command or delete it with DEL, DOS will return the message "File not found."
- System (S): Marks a file as a DOS system file. The System attribute is assigned to those DOS files that are critical to the operation of your system—such as DOS device drivers. This attribute prevents you from seeing these files or deleting them. Like hidden files, though, you can see these files in a directory window if you select the View Include command to display the Include dialog box and select the Show Hidden/System Files check box.

You can assign more than one attribute to a file. For example, you might select the Archive, Hidden, and Read Only check boxes from the Change Attributes dialog box. This selection leaves the archive bit for the file set to 1 (on) and assigns a value of 1 to the hidden and read-only bits as well. As a result, the file will not be listed in directory searches, and, although you can read the file into memory, you cannot delete it or change its contents.

Note: The DOS counterpart to the File Change Attributes command is the ATTRIB command. However, the ATTRIB command only lets you change the read-only and archive attributes for a file. To change the hidden or system attribute, you must turn to a utility program or be a programmer yourself. Therefore, File Manager's ability to not only let you view hidden files, but also to unhide them, gives it a distinct advantage over the conventional DOS command language.

PRINTING ASCII FILES

You can print ASCII files from within File Manager by using the File Print command. This command is only useful for printing files from applications like Notepad that save

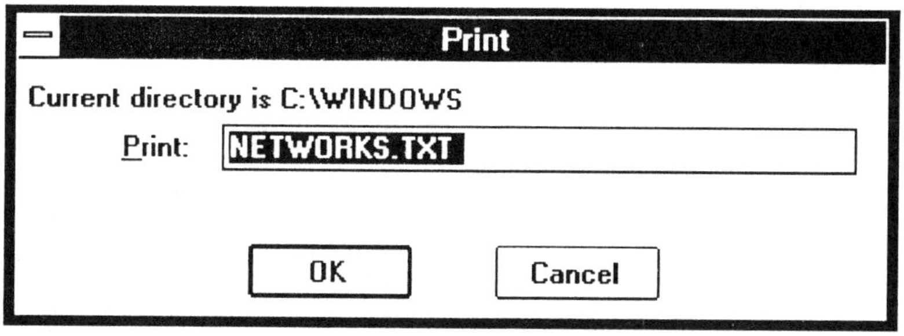

Figure 3-23 Print an ASCII file with File Manager

their files in a flat ASCII format. You should not use this command to print files from applications like Write that save their data files with both formatting and control codes. Instead, use the resident Print menu to print the files for these applications.

When you execute the File Print command, File Manager sends the file to the currently active printer. Therefore, before you use this command, you should use the Printers icon in the Control Panel to make sure the currently active printer is the one you want. See Chapter 4, "Of Fonts and Printing," for details on how to use the Control Panel to install and select printers.

To print an ASCII file, begin by selecting its name from any open directory window. For example, you might select the name of a .TXT file created in Notepad. When you are ready, select the File Print command from File Manager's menu. File Manager displays the dialog box in Figure 3-23. The name of the file you've selected appears in the Print text box. To print the file, select OK. File Manager sends the file to the currently active printer.

USING THE OPTIONS MENU

The Options menu in File Manager allows you to control various aspects of File Manager's operation. For example, you can turn off confirmation dialog boxes that are displayed when you delete or replace files. You can also have filenames in directory windows displayed in lower case, rather than the default upper case, and you can turn off the display of the status bar.

Turning Off Confirmation Messages

When you delete or replace files or directories with File Manager, a confirmation dialog box is displayed for each file and directory that is involved. Confirmation dialog boxes are also displayed when you copy or move files or directories with the mouse. These dialog boxes give you an opportunity to abort an operation gone wrong or to exclude selected files and directories from an operation. However, after you get used to how File Manager works, these confirmation dialog boxes can become unnecessary and even bothersome. To turn off the display of these dialog boxes, select the Options Confirmation

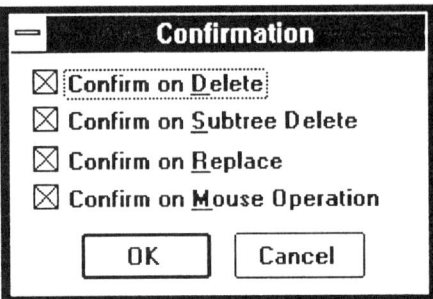

Figure 3-24 The Confirmation dialog box

command from File Manager's menu. File Manager displays the dialog box shown in Figure 3-24. This dialog box contains four check boxes that perform the following functions:

- Confirm On Delete: Suppresses the display of warning messages before deleting files.
- Confirm on Subtree Delete: Suppresses the display of warning messages before deleting directories.
- Confirm on Replace: Suppresses the display of a warning message before overwriting files.
- Confirm on Mouse Operation: Suppresses the display of warning messages before completing a copy or move operation initiated with the mouse.

Displaying File and Directory Names in Lower Case

By default, the names of files and directories in directory windows and the directory tree are displayed in upper case. If this is not to your liking you can have them displayed in lower case. To do this, select the Options Lower Case command from File Manager's menu. When you select this command, the names of all files and directories displayed on the File Manager screen are converted to a lower-case display.

Turning Off the Status Bar

You can also suppress the display of the status bar at the bottom of the File Manager window. To do this, select the Options Status Bar command. File Manager turns off the status bar. Turning off the status bar can give you slightly more room for the display of files and directories. However, this extra space is made available by sacrificing what is perhaps one of the most useful sources of information that File Manager has to offer.

WORKING WITH DISKS

File Manager allows you to work with floppy and hard disks. For example, you can format disks, create a system disk that you can use to boot your machine, copy information between disks, and change the volume label for a disk.

Formatting Disks

To format a disk, select the Format Diskette option from the Disk menu. This command is equivalent to using the FORMAT command at the DOS prompt. When you select this command, File Manager displays a dialog box that you can use to select from the drives that are available on your system. For example, if you want to format a floppy disk located in drive A, select A and then select OK. File Manager displays a second dialog box informing you of the gravity of the operation you are about to perform. To format the disk, select the Format button from this box. File Manager prompts you to insert a disk into the appropriate drive and asks you to specify whether the disk is a high-density disk (1.2 MB or 1.44 MB). (You can also elect at this time to make a system disk. See the next section for more details on creating a system disk.) To format the disk, select OK.

When formatting of the disk is complete, File Manager displays a Yes/No dialog box asking you if you want to format another disk in the same drive. Choose Yes to format another disk or No to return to the File Manager window.

Creating a Boot Disk

You can use the Make System Diskette option on the Disk menu to create a "system" disk that you can use to boot your computer. Selecting this option is equivalent to using the FORMAT command at the DOS prompt with the /S parameter. Having a system disk available for booting your computer can be handy in emergencies—for example, when your hard disk fails or when the network goes down.

To create a system disk, place a blank diskette in one of your floppy disk drives and select Disk Make System Diskette. File Manager presents a dialog box asking you to select the floppy drive in which the disk resides. Select the appropriate drive and select OK. File Manager presents another Yes/No dialog box asking you to confirm whether you want the system files copied onto the disk. Select Yes to have File Manager format the disk and copy the appropriate hidden system files along with COMMAND.COM to the disk. When the format is complete, you are returned to the File Manager window.

Copying Data between Disks

To copy information between diskettes, you can use the Disk Copy Diskette command. This command is equivalent to using the DISKCOPY command at the DOS prompt. This command copies all the information from the source diskette into memory and then places that information on the same tracks on the destination diskette. In the process, the contents of the destination diskette are erased. In addition, because copying takes place on a track-for-track basis, the source and destination disk must have the same capacity. For example, you cannot use the Copy Diskette option to copy information from a high-density diskette to a low-density diskette, or vice versa.

In preparation for the Disk Copy Diskette command, place the source diskette in the drive you want to copy from and place the destination diskette in the drive you want to copy to. If the source and destination drives are the same, simply place the source diskette in the drive. Next, select the icon representing the source drive from the top of File Manager's Directory Tree window. When you are ready, select the Copy Diskette option from the Disk menu. File Manager displays a dialog box that lets you choose the destination drive you want to copy to. Select the appropriate drive and then select OK. File Manager displays another dialog box asking you to confirm the operation. Select the Copy button from this box to proceed. File Manager copies the information from the source diskette and lays it down track-for-track on the destination diskette. If your source and destination drives are the same, File Manager will prompt you to remove the source diskette and insert the destination diskette at the appropriate time.

Changing the Volume Label

File Manager allows you to create a volume label for the disk. Or, if the disk already has a volume label, File Manager allows you to change it. To specify a volume label for a disk, you use the Label Disk option from the Disk menu.

Before labeling a disk, you must select the appropriate drive icon from the top of File Manager's window. For example, if you want to create or change a volume label for the disk in drive A, select the drive A icon. Next, select the Label Diskette option from the Disk menu. File Manager displays the Label Disk dialog box. Type a volume name of up to 11 characters in the Label text box. Choose OK to have File Manager label the disk. The volume name you define is then displayed at the top of File Manager's Directory window, just below the disk-drive icon section, when you select the icon for the drive.

SUMMARY

This chapter covers virtually every aspect of using File Manager. For example, you now know how to use the Directory Tree window to view the structure of your directories on different drives. You also know how to open a directory window that allows you to view the subdirectories and files in a directory. What's more, you can sort the files in a directory window in different ways, and you can limit the contents of a directory window to groups of files that you select. And, when the need arises, you know how to get information about the size of a file and the date it was last modified.

You also know how to use File Manager to manage files and directories. For example, you now know how to create a new directory as well as how to copy and move files between directories. In addition, you know how to delete or rename files when you need to.

This chapter also shows you various ways you can run applications from within File Manager. In addition, this chapter shows you how to create an association between an application and its data files. You now know how to start an application and load a specific data file by referring only to the name of the data file.

You also know how to use File Manager to work with disks. For example, you now know how to format a floppy disk in drive A, or back up a disk, without having to leave Windows.

4

Of Fonts and Printing

In Windows, you can install a single printer for use with all your Windows applications. You can also install more than one printer, each on a separate port, and choose from among your installed printers for the current print job. Moreover, you can install different fonts (different styles and sizes of type) for printing and screen display. In addition, with the aid of Print Manager (a print-spooler application), you can send multiple print jobs to a given printer from different applications and still keep working in Windows—printing takes place in the background.

This chapter brings you up to speed on all the printing features in Windows. For example, you'll learn how to install various types of printers, including laser, dot-matrix, and PostScript. You'll also learn how to install multiple printers and switch back and forth between them from within your applications. In addition, you'll learn about the role the Print Manager plays in printing and how you can use this application to monitor and control the output that is sent to your printer(s).

This chapter also shows you how to install fonts (typefaces in varying sizes) for both display and printing from Windows. As you'll see, Windows actually supports two types of fonts, screen fonts and printer fonts. As you might imagine, screen fonts are used to display data on the screen and printer fonts are used for printing.

Printer fonts can come from a number of sources including the printer itself, a cartridge that plugs into the printer, or soft fonts you've purchased from a third-party source. In fact, a growing raft of third-party soft-font packages are becoming available for Windows. Four of them are discussed in this chapter.

Screen fonts can also come from different sources. Of course, Windows supplies its own screen fonts for displaying text. However, because of the enormous number of printer fonts available, it would be impossible for Windows to provide a screen font that matches every available printer font. When a matching screen font is not available, Windows must substitute its closest available screen font. Therefore, what you see on your screen may not match what comes out on your printer. However, you can also purchase screen fonts from third-party sources and install them in Windows. In fact, all four of the third-party font packages discussed in this chapter include matching screen fonts for the printer fonts they supply.

Note: You can also print to a network printer from within Windows. In fact, Windows offers various features that allow you not only to send your output to a network printer, but to interact with the network print queue (depending on the type of network you have). However, this chapter covers printing from a standalone computer. Printing on a network printer is discussed in Chapter 13, "Networking."

INSTALLING PRINTERS

To print from Windows, you'll need to install a printer driver that supports your particular make and model of printer. Printer drivers are software programs that tell Windows how to interact with your specific make and model of printer. Windows comes with a large variety of printer drivers, most of which are capable of driving more than one type of printer.

To install a printer driver for Windows, you use the Control Panel shown in Figure 4-1. As you know, you can open the Control Panel by double-clicking on its icon, which is located in Program Manager's Main group window.

Normally, you install a printer driver for a particular printer when you install Windows. In fact, when you ran the Setup program to install Windows, you were given the option of installing a printer. If you elected to install a printer, Setup allowed you to select a particular make and model of printer. If you skipped this step, you can still install a printer

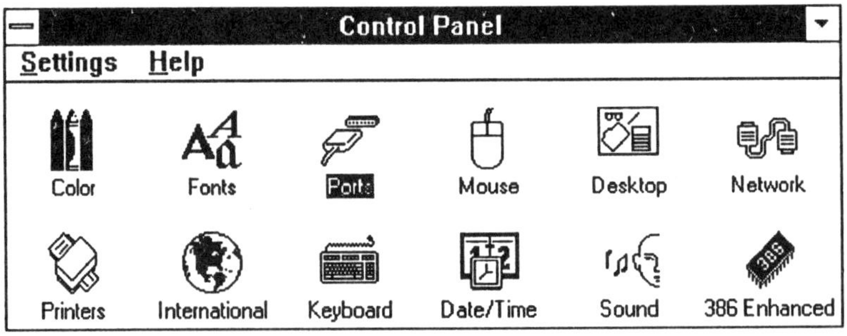

Figure 4-1 The Control Panel

without reinstalling Windows. Or, if you've already installed a printer, you can install a second one, if you so desire.

The sections that follow describe how to go about installing printer-drivers for Windows. Several popular printer types are discussed, including the HP LaserJet Series II, the Apple LaserWriter II NTX PostScript printer, and the Epson LQ2500 24-Pin dot-matrix printer. In addition to installing printers, you'll learn how to activate a specific printer when multiple printers are installed and how to choose a default printer for the entire system.

Configuring a Port

Before you install a printer for Windows, it's always a good idea to decide on the port that will be used to connect the printer to your computer. Once you've made your decision, you can configure that port, if necessary. That way, once you finally install the printer driver, you can begin using it immediately.

You only need to configure a port for a printer if it requires a communications (COM) port (also referred to as a serial port). Generally, the COM port settings for Windows are already properly set for most popular printer models. However, in case you do need to configure a COM port, the paragraphs that follow describe how to go about doing it. Naturally, Windows supports the same COM ports as its DOS host: COM1, COM2, COM3, and COM4.

Note: Some printers support both a communications port and a parallel port connection. For example, you can connect the HP LaserJet Series II to either a communications or a parallel port. Further, many of today's I/O cards have both a communications (COM1) and a parallel port (LPT1) available. Therefore, if you are fortunate enough to have two printers, you can configure the communications port for one printer, leaving the parallel port available for use by a second printer.

To configure a communications port, you double-click on the Ports icon in the Control Panel shown earlier in Figure 4-1. Windows displays the Ports dialog box shown in Figure 4-2. Select the particular communications port you want to configure and select Settings. Windows displays the Ports - Settings dialog box in Figure 4-3. This box allows you to specify the following settings for a communications port:

- Baud Rate: The speed at which data is transferred to the printer. The baud rate used by most printers is 9600, which just happens to be the default for Windows.

- Data Bits: The number of bits sent in a computer word. Common settings here are 7 or 8. Most popular printers require a setting of 8, which is the default.

- Parity: The verification bit. Printers do not need to verify to your computer that information has been sent to them. Therefore, a setting of None, the default, is common here.

118 *Windows 3 Power Tools*

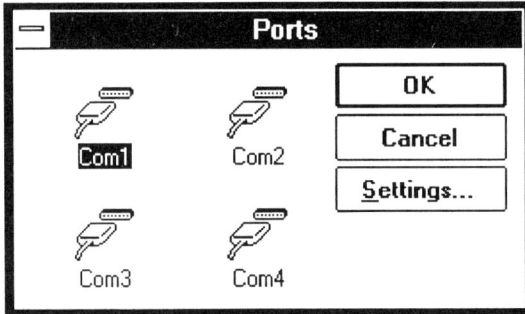

Figure 4-2 The Ports dialog box

- Stop Bits: The number of separator bits between words. The common setting here is 1, the default.
- Flow Control: The method of interaction between computer and printer.

The most common setting for Flow Control is Xon / Xoff. With this setting, the printer sends a message back to the computer that informs the computer when the printer is ready to accept more data. A common problem encountered, particularly with the HP LaserJet series, is that this setting is left at None (the default). Therefore, the printer's memory buffer becomes overloaded almost immediately, and, as a result, only part of a document is printed.

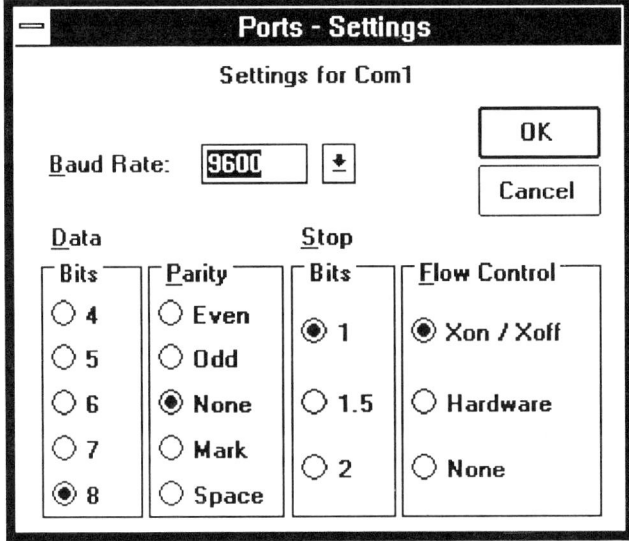

Figure 4-3 The Ports Settings dialog box

The Flow Control setting is also important if you intend to install a PostScript printer on a communications port. Most PostScript printers require either a software or hardware "handshake" in order to print properly. When you install a PostScript printer for Windows, you can specify either a software or hardware handshake, depending on the requirements of your printer. If you specify a hardware handshake, it is very likely that you'll also need to specify a setting of Hardware for the Flow Control setting. Conversely, if you specify a software handshake, you may also need to specify Xon / Xoff for your Flow Control setting.

Installing the LaserJet II Printer: An Example

The sections that follow take you through a sample printer-installation session. During this session, a printer driver for the HP LaserJet Series II printer will be installed. In general, most of the steps in this procedure are required to install just about any printer, including another laser printer, like the HP LaserJet III, a PostScript printer, or a dot-matrix printer. However, just as every printer is unique, so is every printer driver. Therefore, installation procedures will vary slightly from one printer driver to the next.

Selecting a Printer

The first step in installing a printer driver is to select the printer you want to install. To do this, you use the Printers icon in the Control panel. When you double-click on this icon, Windows displays the Printers dialog box in Figure 4-4. If you've already installed a printer, its name appears in the Installed Printers box. In fact, each of the printers you installed thus far are listed in the Installed Printers box.

As mentioned, in many cases, a single Windows printer driver is capable of supporting more than one printer. Therefore, generally, the name of the printer driver will appear in the Installed printers box, rather than the make and model of the printer itself. For example, this section will show you how to install the PCL/HP driver that comes with

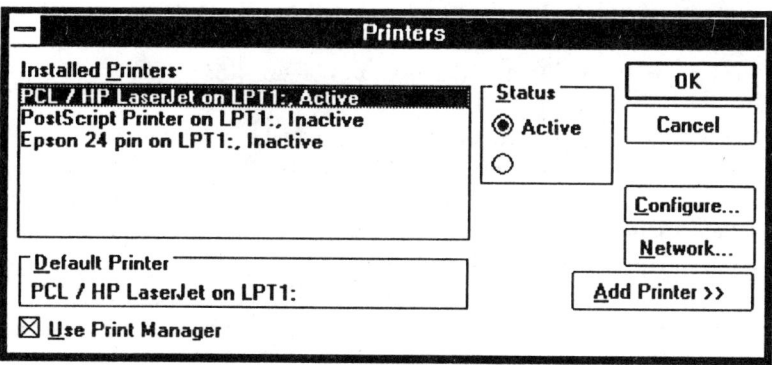

Figure 4-4 The Printers dialog box

120 *Windows 3 Power Tools*

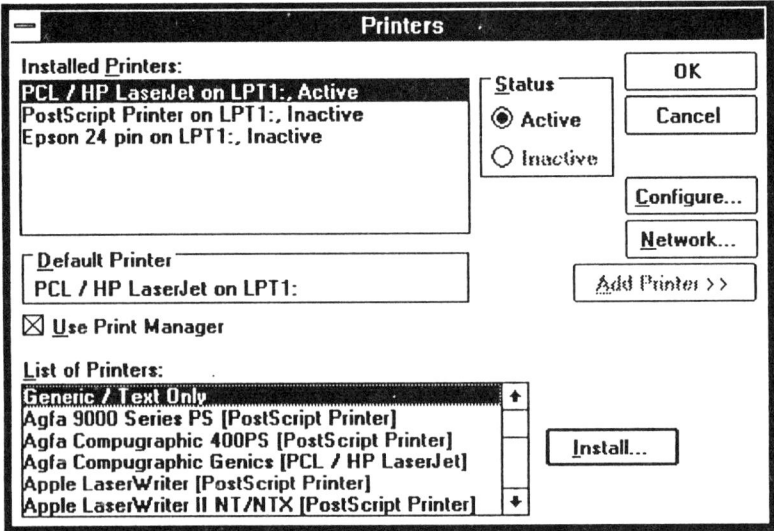

Figure 4-5 The expanded Printers dialog box

Windows. This driver supports a number of printers in the HP LaserJet family, as well as selected laser printers from other manufacturers.

To select a new or additional printer to install, click on the Add Printer>> button in the Printers dialog box. Windows expands the Printers dialog box so that it appears as shown in Figure 4-5. As you can see, the expanded dialog box includes the List of Printers box with an Install button right next to it. The List of Printers box includes the various makes and models of printers that Windows supports. You'll notice, in some cases, that a printer make and model is followed by the name of the printer driver that supports it enclosed in parentheses.

Work your way down through the List of Printers box until you find your particular make and model of printer. In this example, you'll select the listing for HP LasertJet Series II [PCL/HP LaserJet]. When you're ready, select the Install button. Windows displays the Control Panel - Printers dialog box in Figure 4-6.

Note: If you can't find your particular make and model of printer in the List of Printers Box, see "When Your Printer Model Isn't Listed" later in this chapter. Or, if you know that your printer is not in the list, but you've secured a Windows 3-compatible driver for it from a third-party source, select the Unlisted Printer option at the bottom of the List of Printers box.

The Control Panel Printers dialog box is prompting you to insert the disk that contains the printer driver file you want to install into drive A. You can, of course, modify the drive shown, or type the name of a directory on your hard disk in which the driver resides. Normally, however, the file you need is located on one of your Windows program disks.

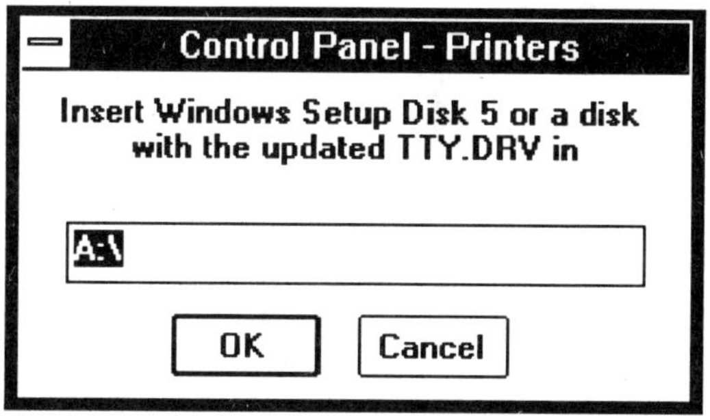

Figure 4-6 The Control Panel Printer dialog box

Windows will prompt you for the appropriate one. Insert the requested disk and select OK. Windows copies the needed driver file to your \WINDOWS\SYSTEM directory. The name of the printer driver then appears in the Installed printers box above.

For the first printer driver you install, Windows places the name of that driver in the Installed Printers box along with a port of *LPT1* and a status of *Active*. For example, if the LaserJet II is the first printer installed, you'll see a listing similar to **PCL/HP LaserJet on LPT1:,Active**. As you might imagine, this means the printer has been assigned to the LPT1 port and is the active printer for that port. This may or may not be what you want. However, you'll learn how to change this in a moment. Each subsequent printer you install will appear with *None* for a port assignment and *Inactive* as a status assignment.

You're not done yet. That is, the printer driver you selected has been installed, but it is not as yet ready for use with your particular printer. You must still configure the printer driver and set options for its use.

Configuring the Printer

To configure the printer driver, select the Configure button from the right side of the Printers dialog. When you make this selection, the Printers - Configure dialog box shown in Figure 4-7 appears on your screen. This dialog box lets you select a port for the printer and specify a timeout setting for the printer (if necessary). It also gives you access to a printer-driver-specific dialog box that lets you specify various settings for the printer. For example, you can select such things as a paper tray and size, printing orientation (portrait versus landscape), number of copies, print quality, and so on. Setting options for a printer driver is discussed in the next section.

To begin, use the Ports list box to select a port for the printer. The following options are available:

- LPT1-LPT3: These are the standard parallel ports, LPT1 through LPT3, supported by DOS.

- COM1-COM4: The standard communications (serial) ports supported by DOS. If you select a serial port, remember that you may need to configure that port, as discussed earlier in this chapter under "Configuring a Port."

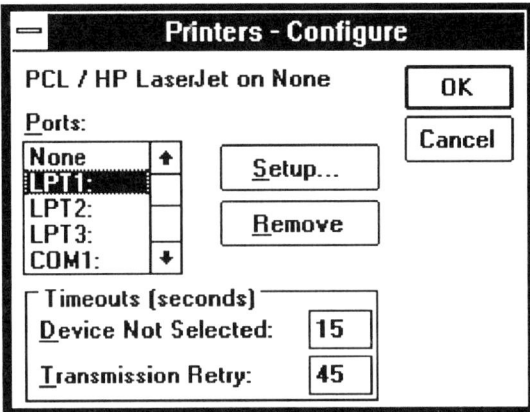

Figure 4-7 The Printers - Configure dialog box

- EPT: This port is reserved for such printers as the IBM Personal Pageprinter. You must have a special adapter card to use this port. In addition, you must have special software to configure that card. For example, the IBM Pageprinter Adapter Program Version 1.3.1 or later is required.

- FILE: Use this option when you want to print to a file. If you select this option, Windows will prompt you for a filename each time you print. The file created will have the same information that is normally sent to the currently selected printer. That way, you can print the file at a later time or in another location. For additional detail on this option, see "Printing to a File" later in this chapter.

- LPT1.OS2-LPT2.OS2: Use these if you want to run Windows from within the OS/2 operating system. OS/2 offers a DOS compatibility box that lets you run many popular DOS applications. Selecting either of these ports (instead of their DOS LPT counterparts) bypasses any special handling of your output by Windows.

The Timeouts (seconds) group box lets you set the number of seconds Windows will wait before displaying an error message regarding your printer. For example, before Windows will send data to a printer, it requests confirmation that the printer is available. The Device Not Selected setting determines the number of seconds that Windows will wait to receive the appropriate signal from your printer. If the signal is not received within the allotted time (15 seconds), Windows will inform you that the printer is not available.

In addition, printers normally process output from your computer in batches. After the first batch is processed, the printer signals your computer that it is ready for the second batch, and so on. If it does not signal for the next batch before the allotted time for Transmission Retry runs out, Windows will display an error message that a problem exists. You can, of course, change either the Device Not Selected or Transmission Retry setting by clicking on the appropriate box and typing the number of seconds you want Windows to use.

Generally, you won't need to modify the settings in the Timeouts group box except under special circumstances. For example, if you are printing a large graphics image through a serial port (often a slow process), you may need to increase the Transmission Retry setting. Further, PostScript printers may require that you increase the Transmission Retry setting. Or, if you are working on a network with a large number of logged-on users, you may need to increase the Device Not Selected and Transmission Retry settings to allow the network sufficient time to process your print request.

Tip: Setting up multiple printers for a single parallel port

Some users have access to multiple printers but only one parallel port. If you find yourself in this situation, you can make a minor modification to your WIN.INI file that will allow you to assign several printers to the same port.

DOS is not particular whether you call the first parallel port LPT1 or LPT1.*XXX* where *XXX* is an arbitrary word that you provide. Therefore, you can replace the LPT1:= statement in the [ports] section of WIN.INI with entries like the following:

```
LPT1.HP=LPT1:
LPT1.EPS=LPT1:
```

That way, when you access the Printers - Configure dialog box shown in Figure 4-7, the LPT1.HP and LPT1:EPS selections will be available in the Ports list box. You can select the first one for one printer and the second one for another printer. Further, this configuration allows you set the status of both of these printers as Active, which allows you to switch back and forth between them from within your applications. See "Activating a Printer" later for details on how to classify a printer as Active.

Setting Printer Driver Options

To set options for a particular printer driver, select the Setup button from the Printers - Configure dialog box shown in Figure 4-7. When you select this button, Windows displays a driver-specific options dialog box for the printer you happen to be installing. For example, if you are installing the HP LaserJet Series II driver, Windows displays the PCL/HP LaserJet dialog box shown in Figure 4-8.

The PCL/HP LaserJet dialog box allows you to set options that are specific to the printer you are installing. For example, you can select a paper tray and size. You can also specify the amount of memory you have installed in the printer. In addition, you can select a printing orientation setting (portrait versus landscape), the graphics resolution you want (dots per inch), and the number of copies you want printed of each page.

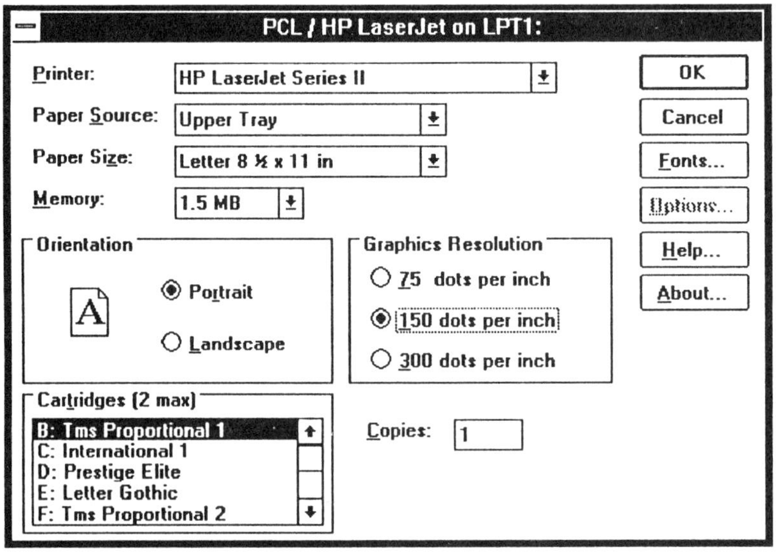

Figure 4-8 The PCL/HP LaserJet dialog box

The PCL/HP LaserJet dialog box in Figure 4-8 also allows you to select and install fonts for use with the printer driver. For example, the HP LaserJet Series II supports up to two plug-in font cartridges. You can select the font cartridges you have from the Cartridges list box at the lower-left corner of the dialog box. In addition, you can select the Fonts button on the right side of the dialog box to install soft fonts for use with the printer driver. Installing and using soft fonts, however, is discussed later in this chapter under "Installing Printer Fonts."

The Help button at the right of the Options dialog box in Figure 4-8 is more than just window dressing. This button gives you access to specific information about the printer driver you are installing. In fact, if a Help button is available, you should select this button for each printer driver you install.

You'll notice that the Options button at the right side of the PCL/HP LaserJet dialog box appears grayed. This button is not active for the HP LaserJet Series II. However, if you are installing the HP LaserJet IID, which supports duplex (double-sided) printing, this button gives you access to a dialog box that lets you set options for the duplex printing feature.

Once you've defined the options you want for the current printer driver, select OK twice. Selecting OK the first time saves the settings in the PCL/HP dialog box in Figure 4-8. Selecting OK again accepts the settings in the Printers - Configure dialog box shown in Figure 4-7, and returns you to the Printers dialog box. The printer driver is now properly installed and ready for you to use.

Activating a Printer

In Windows, the status of a printer is either active or inactive. You can only print to a printer whose status is active. If only a single printer is installed, it is, by default, the active printer.

However, if you have multiple printers installed, you may need to activate a printer in order to use it. Further, if you install more than one printer on the same port, you'll need to decide which printer will be the active printer. The current status for a printer appears at the end of its driver name in the Installed Printers box of the Printers dialog box.

To activate a printer, you use the Printers dialog box shown again in Figure 4-9. As you may recall, you can access this dialog box by selecting the Printers icon from the Control Panel. Once the dialog box is displayed, select the name of an inactive printer driver in the Installed Printers list box. Then, select the Active radio button from the Status section of the dialog box. Windows changes the status of the printer driver from Inactive to Active. If another printer driver assigned to the same port is also active, Windows changes its status to inactive.

Choosing a Default Printer

If only a single printer is installed, that printer will be used as the default printer for all your Windows applications. Further, its name will appear in the Default Printer box of the Printers dialog box shown in Figure 4-9. However, when you have more than one installed printer (and more than one active printer), you can choose which printer will be used as the default for your applications. To do this, double-click on the name of the driver for that printer in the Installed Printers box. (The printer must be active for this to work.) Alternatively, you can highlight the name and press ALT+D. Whichever method you select, Windows displays the name of the printer driver you selected in the Default Printer box. That printer driver will now be used by all Windows applications.

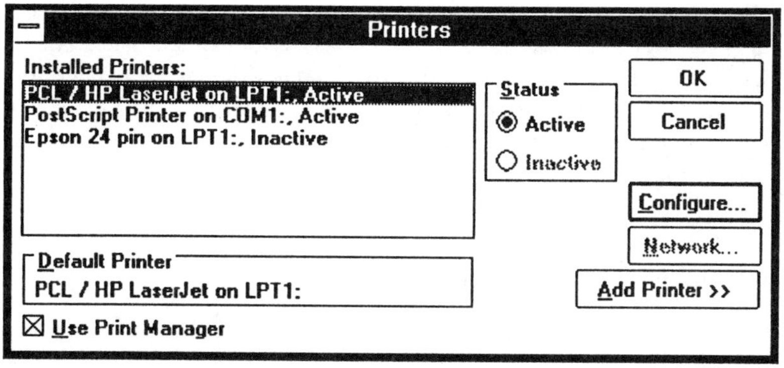

Figure 4-9 The Printers dialog box

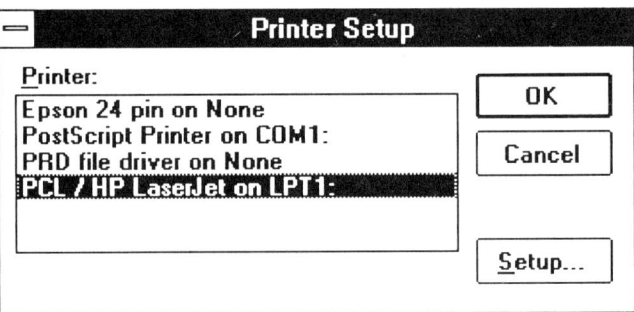

Figure 4-10 A sample Printer Setup dialog box

Changing the Default Printer from Within an Application

You can also select a default printer from within an application. For example, many Windows applications, including Notepad, Paintbrush, Microsoft Excel, and Word for Windows, have a File Printer Setup command. This command gives you access to a Printer Setup dialog box similar to the one in Figure 4-10. It displays the names of currently installed printers, whether they are active or not, and includes a Setup button. You can select the name of an active printer driver for use with both the current application as well as your other Windows applications. In addition, you can select the Setup button to access an options dialog box, similar to the one shown earlier in Figure 4-8, that lets you specify various options for the printer driver you've selected.

Note: The File Printer Setup command does not work the same way in all Windows applications. With some applications, you can use this command both to make a specific printer current and to change settings for that printer. In others, it only allows you to change settings for a printer, not select it for use with the current application. In these cases, you'll need to access the Printers dialog box from the Control Panel and declare the printer you want to use as the default printer for the system. You'll have to check the manual that came with your particular application to determine the functionality of its version of the File Printer Setup command.

Removing an Installed Printer Driver

You can also remove an installed printer driver. To do this, select the Printers icon from the Control Panel to display the Printers dialog box shown earlier in Figure 4-9. Highlight the name of the printer driver you want to remove in the Installed Printers dialog box and select the Configure button. Windows displays the Printers - Configure dialog box shown earlier in Figure 4-7. Once this dialog box is displayed, select the Remove button. Windows displays a message box asking you to confirm the removal. Select OK to have

Windows remove the installed printer driver and return you to the Printers dialog box. Select OK again to confirm your choice and return to the Control Panel.

When you remove a printer driver, the printer-driver files installed in your \WINDOWS\SYSTEM directory are not affected. Therefore, you can easily reinstall the printer driver at a later time. Or, if you need the disk space, you might want to use File Manager to erase the unneeded files from your hard disk. (File Manager is described in Chapter 3.) In general, printer driver files have a .DRV extension. However, so do other device driver files for Windows. Therefore, if you don't know the precise filename of the file you want to erase, you're better off sacrificing the disk space. Otherwise, you may delete a device-driver file that Windows needs to drive one of your other peripheral devices, such as your screen display.

Printing to a File

As mentioned, Windows also allows you to print to a file. The output sent to the file, however, is the same output that would normally be sent to the currently active printer. This means that, in addition to text and/or graphics, all the necessary control codes, formatting, and so on for the currently selected printer are included. Therefore, you can print the file at a later time or on another computer, provided that computer is connected to the same make and model of printer.

To print to a file, you'll need to activate the Control Panel and select the Printers icon. Windows displays the Printers dialog box shown earlier in Figure 4-9. Select the appropriate printer driver in the Installed Printers box and activate it, if necessary. Then, select the Configure button. Windows displays the Printers - Configure dialog box, shown earlier in Figure 4-7. Select FILE: from the Ports list box and select OK twice, once to confirm your selection in the Printers - Configure dialog box and again to confirm the Printers dialog box and return to the Control Panel. From then on, whenever you print using that particular printer driver, Windows will display a dialog box like the one in Figure 4-11, prompting you for the name of a file.

Once you have printed to a file, you can use the DOS COPY command to print that file. For example, to print the file REPT.PRN on the printer that is connected to the first parallel port, you would use following command at the DOS prompt:

```
COPY REPT.PRN/b LPT1
```

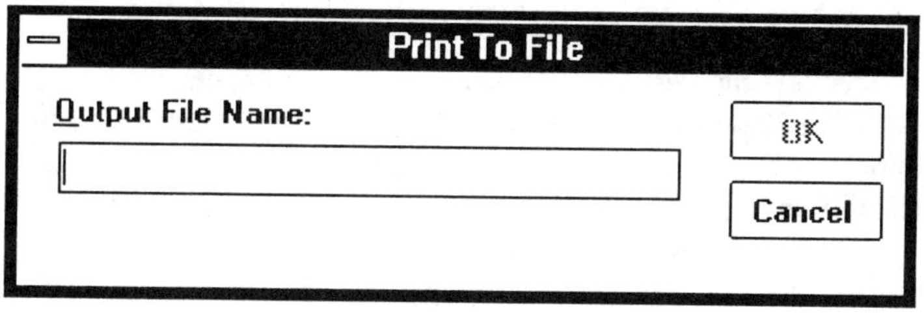

Figure 4-11 Printing to a file

Notice the use of the /b switch after the filename. This directs DOS to copy the file based on its physical size. Otherwise, COPY may quit copying when it encounters a CTRL-Z character, which normally marks the end of a file. However, this character may occur before the end of a document if the file contains graphics.

Printing to a file can be particularly useful when you want to print your work at a later time or on another printer that is not connected to your machine. For example, imagine that the Marketing department down the hall has an expensive PostScript printer that produces an excellent image. You can install the PostScript driver for Windows, activate that driver, and send your output to a file. By default, the file generated will be an Encapsulated Postscript (.EPS) file suitable for use with the PostScript printer. You can then take that file down the hall and use the DOS COPY command from one of the Marketing department's machines to get a top-notch printout.

Installing PostScript Printers

You install and configure PostScript printer drivers by using the same commands and techniques as you would for any other printer. However, because PostScript printers have capabilities over and above those of a laser or dot-matrix printer, they have their own special set of considerations. This section will familiarize you with those considerations by discussing the installation of the popular Apple LaserWriter II NTX PostScript printer.

Note: To have Windows print properly to your PostScript printer, it must be set for batch mode rather than interactive mode. However, this usually isn't a problem because most PostScript printers are set for batch mode as the default.

Selecting a Printer

To install a PostScript printer, open the Control Panel and double-click on the Printer icon to display the Printers dialog box. Select the Add Printer button to expand the Printers dialog box, which reveals the List of Printers box and the Install button. Highlight the name of the printer you want to install, in this case the Apple LaserWriter II NT/NTX [PostScript Printer], and select the Install button. Windows displays the Control Panel Printers dialog box, prompting you to insert the disk containing the driver file in drive A. Insert the appropriate disk and select OK. Windows copies the driver file to your \WINDOWS\SYSTEM directory and adds *PostScript Printer on None:,Inactive* to the Installed Printers box. Select the Configure button to display the Printers - Configure dialog box. Use the Ports list box to select a port for the printer and then select the Setup button. Windows displays the PostScript Printer dialog box in Figure 4-12.

Just like the PCL/HP LaserJet dialog box discussed earlier, the PostScript Printer box lets you set options for the printer you are installing. For example, you can select the appropriate paper tray and size, printing orientation, and number of copies. If your printer supports color (which the Apple LaserWriter II NTX doesn't), you can select the Use Color check box to take advantage of that feature. Otherwise, this selection appears grayed, meaning you can't select it.

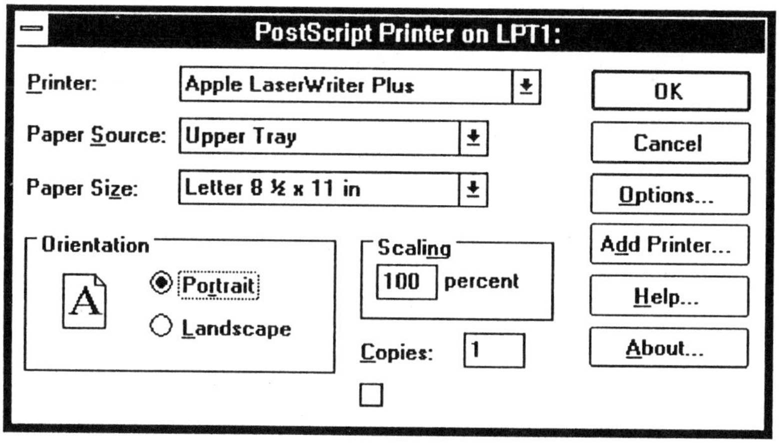

Figure 4-12 The PostScript Printer dialog box

You can also use the Scaling box to specify a scaling factor for the output sent to the printer. This allows you to increase or decrease the size of text and graphics sent to the printer. Normally, printed output is sent at 100% of its original size. However, if you specify a setting of 50%, it will be scaled down to half its normal size, and a setting of 200% will increase it to twice its normal size. The same page area is used, however. The only difference here is that, with reduced scaling, more information will fit on each page, and with increased scaling less information will fit on each page, thereby increasing the total number of pages.

Setting Options

To set additional options for the PostScript printer, select the Options button. Windows displays the Options dialog box shown in Figure 4-13. You can use the Print To section to determine the destination for the printed output. You can print either to your printer (the default) or to an Encapsulated PostScript (EPS) File. To print to an EPS file, select the Encapsulated PostScript File radio button and type the name of the target file. A number of popular applications, including PageMaker, that run under Windows are capable of reading this file format directly.

You can use the Job Timeout section to set the amount of time (in seconds) that your printer will wait to receive output from Windows. Normally, you should leave this option set to 0. That way, your printer will never time out. If you need to increase this setting, though, simply activate the Job Timeout section and type the number of seconds desired in the text box provided. You may want to compare this setting to the Transmission Retry setting in the Printers - Configure dialog box shown earlier in Figure 4-7. As you may recall, this option sets the amount of time Windows waits for a signal from your printer that it is ready to accept more data.

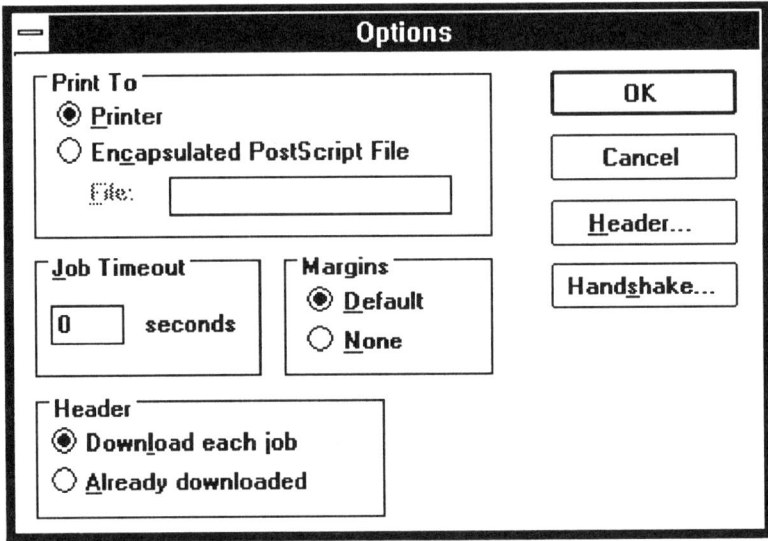

Figure 4-13 The Options dialog box

The Margins section lets you turn off the default margins defined by the printer itself. Generally, most printers will not allow you to print in the border area of the paper that is about 1/4 inch from each of its edges. This area is needed to feed the paper through the printer. However, an additional margin is often set beyond this. A selection of None in the Margins section sets the printer's margins to the largest possible paper area it is capable of printing. Microsoft recommends, though, that you use the Default setting, unless you are having difficulty setting the margins from an application.

Once you've set the additional options you desire, if any, you are ready to define the header file and handshake method that you need for your particular printer. The sections that follow describe how to do this.

Creating a Header File

PostScript printers are different from laser or dot-matrix printers in that they require a header file be sent to them in advance of a print job. Otherwise the printer may not print correctly. Windows automatically takes care of this for you by sending a header file to the printer whenever you print from a Windows application. To confirm this, check the Header section in the Options dialog box shown in Figure 4-13. You'll notice that the Download each job radio button is preselected. With this setting, the header file is sent to the printer in advance of each print job. This configuration works well for most printing situations, especially if your machine is connected to a network.

However, there may be situations where you do not want the header file to be sent to the printer each time you print. For example, if the PostScript printer is connected directly to your machine, you can download the header file once either manually or by including the appropriate commands in your AUTOEXEC.BAT file. Once the header is

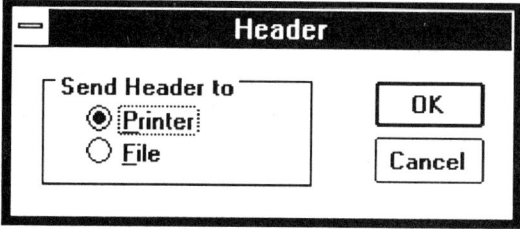

Figure 4-14 The Header dialog box

downloaded, it will remain in effect while the printer is turned on. In this instance, the header file is already downloaded to the printer and there is no need for Windows to download it again. In this case, you would select the Already downloaded radio button from the Options dialog box. Using this configuration can save you approximately 20 seconds per print job.

To set up this configuration, you'll need to create a header file and copy it to your printer at the beginning of a session. To create a header file, choose the Header button from the Options dialog box in Figure 4-13. Windows displays the Header dialog box shown in Figure 4-14. This dialog box contains two radio buttons, Printer and File. Select the File radio button and then select OK. Windows prompts you for the name of a file. Type the name you want to use and select OK to return to the Options dialog box. Windows creates a header file with the name you specified. Conversely, if you select the Printer radio button and then select OK, Windows presents a dialog box asking you if you want the header file downloaded to the printer now. This option is useful when you want to download the header file to the printer a single time.

If you've selected the Already downloaded radio button from the Options dialog box, you'll probably want to download the header file to the printer independently of Windows. The most common way of downloading a header file to your printer is to use the DOS COPY command either at the DOS prompt or in your AUTOEXEC.BAT file. For example, to copy the header file PSHEAD.HDR to the printer connected to the first parallel port, you would type **COPY PSHEAD.HDR LPT1** at the DOS prompt or include this entry in your AUTOEXEC.BAT file. However, whether you initiate this command from the DOS prompt or from your AUTOEXEC.BAT file, the printer must be turned on in advance of using the command. Otherwise, it will have no effect.

Setting the Handshake Method

Setting a handshake method is only appropriate when your PostScript printer is connected to a communications (COM/Serial) port with a conventional RS232 cable. Handshaking is a common term used to describe the interaction between your computer and your printer. Through handshaking, the printer informs the computer when it is ready to accept more data. Handshaking can be hardware- or software-based. You'll have to consult the manual that came with your printer to determine which method it uses.

In addition, you should also use the Ports icon in the Control panel to configure the port you assign to the PostScript printer for the appropriate handshake method (select

132   *Windows 3 Power Tools*

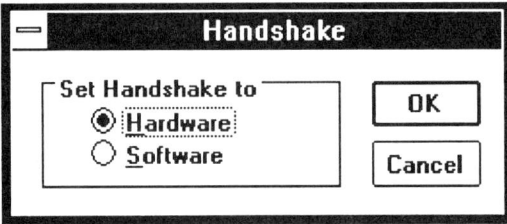

Figure 4-15 The Handshake dialog box

Hardware versus Xon/Xoff for the Flow Control setting). Using the Ports icon to configure printer ports is described at the beginning of this chapter under "Configuring a Port."

To set a handshake method, select the Handshake button from the right side of the Options dialog box shown in Figure 4-13. Windows displays the Handshake dialog box in Figure 4-15. Two radio buttons are available, Hardware and Software. Select the button that is appropriate for your printer and select OK to return to the Options dialog box. Select OK as necessary to return to the Control Panel. Your PostScript printer should now be properly installed for use with Windows.

Installing an Unlisted PostScript Printer

Windows comes with a single printer driver for PostScript printers. Although this driver supports a wide variety of printers, it doesn't support all of them. If your particular PostScript printer is not supported, you'll need to acquire a Windows PostScript Description (.WPD) file. You can usually get this file either from the manufacturer of your printer or from Microsoft. See "When Your Printer Isn't Listed" later in this chapter for more details on this.

To install the new .WPD file, first follow the steps above to install the PostScript Printer driver. Once the PostScript Printers dialog box in Figure 4-12 is displayed, select the Add Printer button. Windows displays the Add Printer dialog box in Figure 4-16. Insert the disk containing the .WPD file in drive A and select OK. A dialog box with a list box appears. Select the appropriate printer from the list box and choose the Add button. Windows copies the necessary files to your \WINDOWS\SYSTEM directory. Choose the Done button to return to the PostScript Printer dialog box. The printer is now listed in the Printer list box. Open this list box and select it. You can now complete the installation of the printer using the procedures described above.

Note: A number of third-party sources produce PostScript cartridges for HP LaserJet printers, especially the HP LaserJet III. To use these cartridges, you'll need to install the Windows PostScript Printer driver. Moreover, you'll need a .WPD file that supports the configuration of LaserJet III with a PostScript cartridge. See "When Your Printer Model Isn't Listed" later in this chapter for ideas on securing a .WPD file.

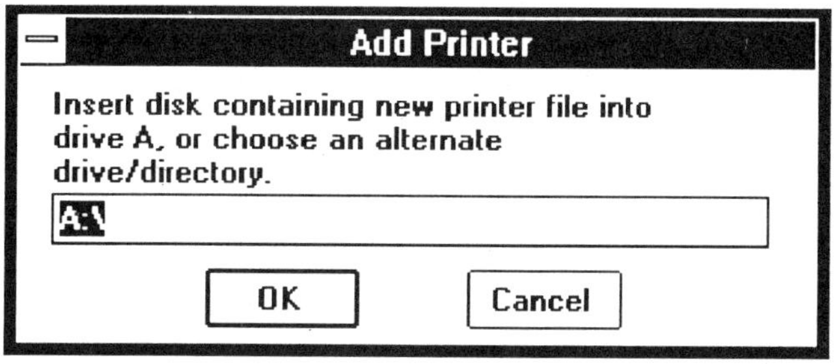

Figure 4-16 The Add Printer dialog box

Installing a Dot-Matrix Printer

Installing a dot-matrix printer for use with Windows is relatively easy in comparison with installing a laser or PostScript printer. To demonstrate just how easy, this section will take you through a sample install session for the popular Epson dot-matrix printer. Specifically, the Epson LQ2500 will be highlighted, because it is a near-letter-quality printer that supports graphics and has a color option.

To begin, double-click on the Printers icon in the Control Panel to access the Printers dialog box shown earlier in Figure 4-12. Select the Add Printer>> button to expand the Printers box to reveal the List of Printers box along with the Install button. Select the listing for the dot-matrix printer you want to install, in this case *Epson LQ 2500/2550 [Epson 24 Pin]*. When you're ready, select the Install button. Windows displays the Control Panel-Printers dialog box, prompting you to insert the disk containing the driver file in drive A. Insert the appropriate Windows program disk (Windows will tell you which one) and select OK. Windows copies the Epson 24-pin driver to your \WINDOWS\SYSTEM directory and adds the listing *Epson 24 Pin on None:,Inactive* to the Installed Printers box.

To Configure the printer, choose the Configure button to access the Printers - Configure dialog box. Choose a port for the printer from the Ports list box. When you're ready, select the Setup button. Windows displays the Epson 24-pin printer driver dialog box shown in Figure 4-17. This dialog box allows you to set options for the printer's operation. It is fairly representative in that it offers most of the options you can set for a dot-matrix printer.

To specify the Epson LQ2500, first use the Printer list box to select that printer. As soon as you make your selection the Color check box is activated. If you installed the color option kit for the LQ2500, you can select this option. Otherwise, ignore it.

You can also set various other options to properly configure the printer. For example, you can select a graphics resolution (dots per inch), printing orientation (portrait versus landscape), the type of paper feed that matches your equipment, a text mode setting (letter versus draft), and an appropriate paper height and width. Also, if your printer came with a font cartridge, you'll probably want to select one of the fonts listed in the Other LQ Fonts list box. That way, you can access those fonts from within your applications.

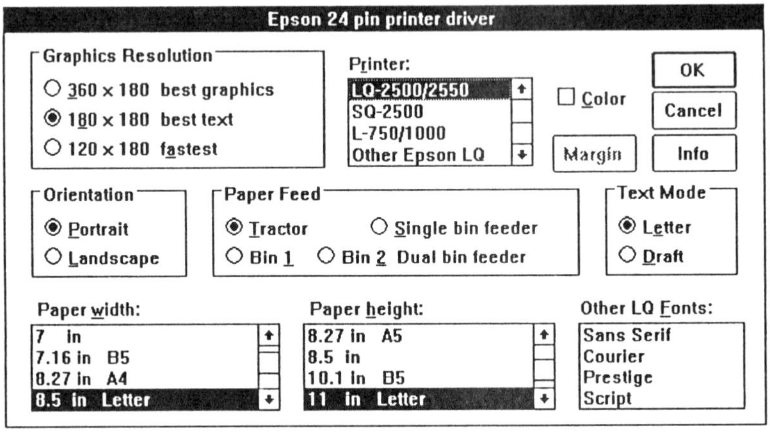

134 *Windows 3 Power Tools*

Figure 4-17 The Epson 24-pin printer driver dialog box

Although the Epson LQ2500 does not have minimum limits for top and bottom margin settings, other Epson 24-pin models do. To set the minimum top and bottom margins for these printers, select the Margin button. Windows displays the dialog box in Figure 4-18. Select the appropriate margin for the appropriate category. (The left and right margins are determined by the application you're printing from.) To save the new settings, select OK. Windows returns you to the Epson 24-pin printer driver dialog box.

Finally, before you select OK to leave the Epson 24-pin printer driver dialog box, take a moment to select the Info button. Windows displays an information dialog box as shown in Figure 4-19. This box shows you the dip-switch settings that are required on the printer to make it function correctly with this printer driver. Dip switches are either on or off. Consult the manual that came with your Epson to determine where the dip switches are located and how to go about setting them.

To complete the job, select the OK button. Windows returns you to Printers Configure dialog box. Select OK again to return to the Printer dialog box. Once there, select the

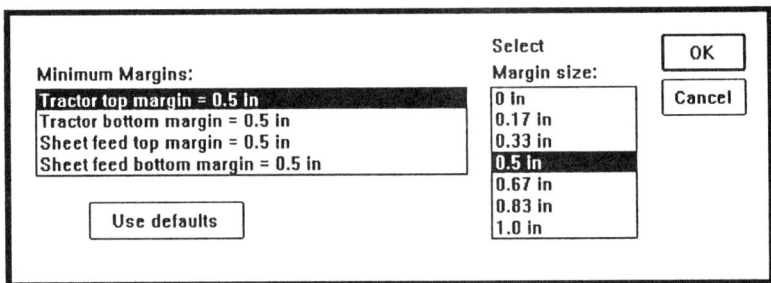

Figure 4-18 The Margins dialog box

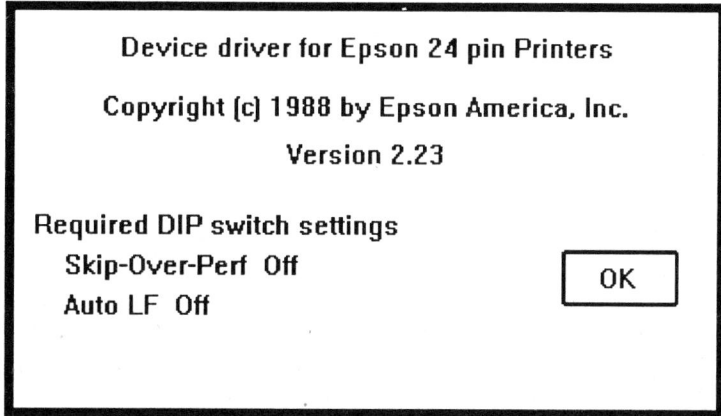

Figure 4-19 An information box showing dip-switch settings for an Epson Printer

Active radio button, if necessary, from the status section to activate the printer. Select the OK button to return to the Control Panel and begin using the printer.

When Your Printer Model Isn't Listed

If you don't see your printer make and model listed when you attempt to install it, it may mean that Windows doesn't have a driver that supports your particular printer. However, there are a number of things you can do about this. The first option is to check the Hardware Compatibility List that comes with your copy of Windows. If you know that your printer is 100% compatible with another printer for which Windows provides a driver, you may be able to use that driver. To see if your printer is compatible with another printer make and model, you'll probably end up having to check your manual.

Or perhaps your printer is capable of emulating another popular printer supported by Windows. For example, many laser printers are capable of emulating the HP LaserJet, and many dot-matrix printers can emulate a particular model of Epson printer. To determine this, though, you'll have to check the manual that came with your printer. If it can emulate a supported printer, you'll have to configure it accordingly. This may involve flipping some dip switches on the back of the printer or entering some commands using the buttons on the front of the printer.

If the compatibility route fails, there are still some steps you can take. For example, because of the popularity of Windows, new printer drivers are becoming available for it all the time. You may be able to contact the manufacturer of your printer and secure a Windows driver from that source. Often this can be inconvenient, though, especially if the manufacturer is located in a foreign country.

Another option is to call Microsoft. Microsoft maintains a Software Driver Library for Windows and adds drivers to that library as they become available. In addition, Microsoft has been known to upload Windows device-driver files to CompuServe. You may be able to find a driver this way. For example, Microsoft maintains a Windows-specific software library on CompuServe that you can access by typing GO MSL at the CompuServe ! prompt.

FONTS

Windows supports two types of fonts, Graphics Device Interface (GDI) fonts, often called "screen fonts," and device-based fonts, often called "printer fonts."

The GDI, or screen, fonts are provided by Windows and are stored in .FON files in your \WINDOWS\SYSTEM directory. Each of these .FON files contains a complete font (characters of a specific typeface, for example Roman or Courier, in various point sizes). Generally, GDI fonts are used for screen display (thus the term "screen fonts"). However, they can also be used for printing on certain types of printers including dot-matrix, ink-jet, and laser printers. To display these fonts on your screen, Windows accesses the currently installed video adapter in graphics mode and writes screen fonts to the screen through its internal GDI module.

Device-based, or printer, fonts, on the other hand, are provided by the printer, rather than by Windows. These fonts can come from three different sources. For example, they can come from the printer itself (the font is "burned" into the memory chip for the printer). Or, some printers support the use of cartridges that contain interface boards that plug into a slot on the front of the printer and provide additional fonts. Finally, fonts can be software-based, often called *soft fonts*. These fonts are stored on disk and are downloaded (sent) to the printer either at print time or beforehand (usually when you boot your computer). These types of fonts are provided either by the printer manufacturer or by a third-party source. Four such third-party soft font packages will be discussed later in this chapter.

As mentioned, in some cases, Windows uses screen fonts for printing to dot-matrix, ink-jet, and laser printers. However, this depends on the mode of the printer. If the printer is in text mode, Windows uses the printer's internal (resident) fonts. In this case, it need only send the appropriate ASCII values to the printer. If, on the other hand, the printer is in graphics mode, Windows uses screen fonts and sends bitmap pixel patterns to the printer.

About Windows Screen Fonts

Windows screen fonts come in two varieties, raster and vector. Both varieties are stored in .FON files in your \WINDOWS\SYSTEM directory. In raster fonts files, each individual character is stored as a bitmap pixel pattern. On the other hand, vector fonts are defined by strokes. Figure 4-20 show examples of both raster and vector fonts displayed in a larger size so that you can see how they are defined.

As mentioned, raster fonts are defined by bitmap pixel patterns. They are designed to be displayed at a specific aspect ratio (height to width) and in a specific size. Windows only provides a discrete number of sizes. When you increase the size of a raster font beyond that for which it was designed, Windows simply duplicates rows and columns of

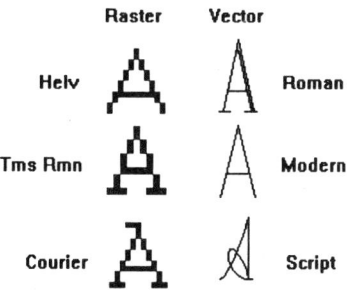

Figure 4-20 Examples of Windows screen fonts displayed in a large size

pixels to accommodate you. However, the end result is the much talked about stair-step effect (sometimes called the "jaggies") shown in Figure 4-20. And, because of their bitmap configuration, raster fonts tend to require more hard-disk space and more memory.

On the other hand, vector fonts are stroke-based fonts that are defined by line segments. This makes them more scalable than raster fonts. That is, the same font can be used to display a character in virtually any size by increasing or decreasing the length of the strokes that define that character. This means that less disk space is required to store the font and less memory is required to display it. In addition, the appearance of vector fonts tends to be more consistent than raster fonts as you scale them to larger sizes. On the downside, though, because vector fonts are defined by single line segments, their general appearance becomes weaker as you increase their size.

Figure 4-21 shows examples of the various default raster and vector screen fonts that are available in Windows. In addition, they are described in the following table:

Font	*Font Type*	*Description*
Helv	Raster	A Helvetica typeface. This is a proportional font in that its characters have varying widths. It is a sans serif typeface in that the characters do not end with serifs (small upward or sideways strokes).
Tms Rmn	Raster	A proportional Times Roman typeface with serifs.
Courier	Raster	A fixed-pitch Courier font with serifs. In contrast to proportional, fixed-pitch means that each character has the same width.
Symbol	Raster	A proportional font for mathematical symbols.
Roman	Vector	A proportional Roman font with serifs.
Modern	Vector	A proportional modern font without serifs.
Script	Vector	A proportional font composed of script characters that look like they were written by hand.

Helv
Tms Rmn
Courier
Roman
Modern
Script
Συμβολ

Figure 4-21 Examples of Windows' default screen fonts

Windows determines which screen font to display, based on your selection from an application menu. You'll find most, if not all, of Windows screen fonts available on the menus for your applications. However, as you'll soon see, you can also install printer fonts for use with Windows. When you install these fonts, they appear on your application menus as well.

However, due to the multitude of available printer fonts, Windows cannot hope to provide a matching screen font for all of them. Instead, when Windows does not have a screen font that matches the printer font you've selected, it substitutes the closest available screen font that it has. This may account for the disparity between what you see on your screen versus what actually comes out on your printer. Generally, though, the font substituted by Windows is of the same height and width as the printer font you've selected. As a result, you can usually trust that the character height, line length, and so on, that is displayed on your screen will be reflected in your printout.

This shortage of Windows screen fonts has generated an opportunity for third-party sources. Later, under "Third-Party Soft-Font Packages," four soft-font packages will be discussed. Each of these packages provide matching screen and printer fonts. Thus, your printed output matches what is displayed on your screen. In addition, some third-party vendors sell packages that include just screen fonts. These are useful in situations where numerous fonts are already resident to the printer, as is the case with PostScript printers and certain laser printers (like the HP LaserJet III). Once you acquire one of these packages, you may need to install the screen fonts provided. See "Installing Screen Fonts" later for more information on how you can install screen fonts for use by Windows.

In addition to its default screen fonts, Windows provides a system font. The system font is used to display messages, menus, and so forth throughout Windows. An example of the system font appears in the labels used to identify each of Windows screen fonts in Figure 4-20.

In Windows 3, the system font is proportional—the width and spacing of the characters varies—lending a more pleasing appearance to the display of the characters. This is an improvement in Windows 3. In older version of Windows, a fixed-pitch font (equal character widths and equal spacing) was used. However, to accommodate older Windows applications, Windows 3 still provides the fixed-pitch system font. In fact, if you run an older-vintage Windows application under Windows 3, you'll notice the characters displayed in menus and so on have a fixed pitch.

The files containing Windows screen and system fonts are identified by a .FON extension. Windows knows which files to use through listings in the WIN.INI and SYSTEM.INI files. The names of files containing Windows screen fonts are listed in the [Fonts] section of the WIN.INI file, and its system fonts are listed throughout the SYSTEM.INI file.

Installing Screen Fonts

You can install additional screen fonts from third-party sources. For example, if you are using a PostScript printer, which has 35 resident printer fonts, you can purchase a package of 35 matching screen fonts so that you get a true indication on your screen of how your printed output will appear. (See "Third-Party Font Packages" later in this chapter for more details on this.) Most third-party font packages will automatically install screen fonts for you. However, in case they don't, you can easily install them through Windows.

To install a screen font, you use the Fonts icon in the Control Panel. When you double-click on this icon, Windows displays the Fonts dialog box shown in Figure 4-22. This dialog box shows you the screen fonts that are currently installed for Windows. When you select the name of a font, Windows shows you a sample of what that font looks like in the list box below. To install additional screen fonts, select the Add button. Windows displays a dialog box that lets you specify the directory that contains the screen fonts. Normally, font files have a .FON extension. Specify the font file you want to add and select OK. Windows installs the font and returns you to the Fonts dialog box.

Each font that you install requires additional memory. Therefore, if you install a font and later decide you don't need it, consider removing it. To remove an installed screen font, select the name of the font you want to remove from the Fonts dialog box, then select the Remove button. Windows displays a Yes/No dialog box that asks you to confirm the removal of the font. Select Yes to remove the font and return to the fonts dialog box. Select OK to return to the Control Panel.

Font Terms

Up to now, the term *font* has been use to describe different styles and sizes of characters that appear on your screen. However, as you might imagine, there is a bit more to it than that. This section gives you a brief overview of some of the significant terms you'll encounter while working with fonts.

A font is a complete selection of characters in a specific typeface and size. The term "typeface" refers to a specific style of type, for example Courier or Helvetica. There are literally thousands of typeface designs. In addition to the typeface design, a typeface can

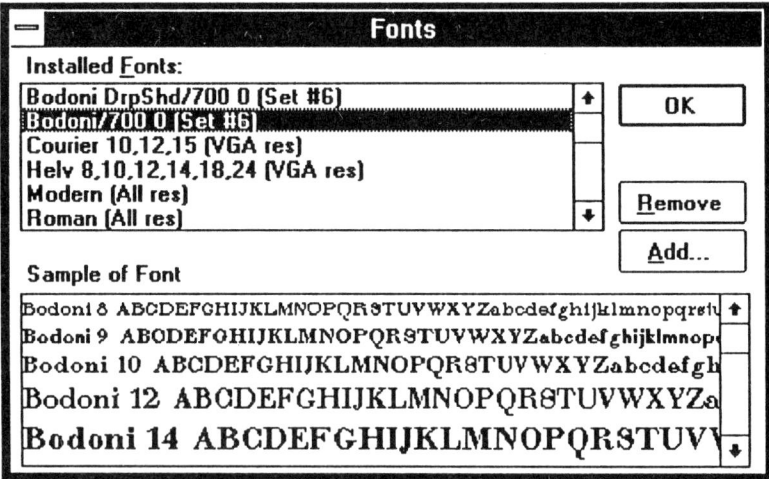

Figure 4-22 The Fonts dialog box

have an attribute, such as italic or boldface. For its screen fonts, Windows synthesizes these attributes by basically printing the same character right next to itself or by offsetting pixels. However, printer fonts are a different matter. For a printer, such as a laser printer, to print a typeface in bold or italic, it generally must have access to a separate font that has that attribute. Often the name of the attribute follows the name of the font, for example Times Roman Italic.

Because of the huge variety of typefaces available, they are often grouped into families. Each family contains a group of typefaces with strong design similarities. In fact, Windows itself groups fonts into families, including Roman, Swiss, Modern, Script, and Decorative.

Typefaces are also grouped in other ways. For example, you may have come across the term "serif." This refers to a final upward- or sideways-sloping tail on a character. It is believed that these are originally derived from brush strokes. However, they tend to make type appear more attractive. On the other hand, "sans serif" simply means without serifs. Other typeface groups include Script, which are cursive (handwritten-like) and Novelty, sometimes called Decorative, which includes odd typefaces or symbols that do not fit into any other category.

The size (or height) of a typeface is measured in points. A point is about 1/72 of an inch tall. Therefore, 12-point type is about 3/16 of an inch tall. Windows supports type sizes from 4 to 127 points. However, many of the applications that run under Windows have their own restrictions on the range of point sizes they support.

A font can have a fixed pitch, or it can be proportional. With a fixed-pitch font, all of the characters are of the same width and are equally spaced. On the other hand, with a proportional font, the width of the characters and the space is varied, lending a more pleasing appearance to the font. Varying the space between characters is called kerning.

Kerning involves reducing the space between specific pairs of letters and lends an even visual appearance to the type.

Font Technology

Windows raster and vector fonts are not the only types of fonts available. In fact, many of the third-party soft-font packages discussed later in this section use a newer font technology referred to as *scalable outline* fonts.

Outline fonts help to overcome the stair-step effect of raster type (bitmap) fonts. With outline fonts, an outline of a character is drawn first. Once that outline is drawn, it is filled in with dots. As a result, outline fonts are almost infinitely scalable. That is, once you choose the size, the outline is scaled to the size you've selected, and then the dots are filled in. Thus, outline fonts are generally more attractive and more flexible than bitmap fonts.

PostScript fonts are a form of outline font. As you know, PostScript fonts are supported and used largely by PostScript printers. (However, there are exceptions to this. See "Adobe Type Manager" later under "Third-Party Soft-Font Packages" for more details on this.) Most PostScript printers come with 35 resident PostScript fonts. To scale and define these fonts, an internal PostScript language interpreter is also supplied with the printer. This interpreter relies on the proprietary Adobe PostScript page-description language. This language provides the tools needed to define the shape of each character in precise mathematical curves. Once the shapes are defined, they are filled in with dots that are appropriate for the resolution of the printer. Although this technology results in spectacular output, it can take a long time to print even a simple document.

You can get PostScript cartridges for HP Series II, Series III, or 100% compatible printers. This new innovation allows you to transform your laser printer into a PostScript printer. Provided sufficient memory is available (usually 2+ MB) the cartridge loads the PostScript language interpreter into the printer's memory. It also makes the 35 resident fonts available. To run this printer from Windows, though, you must install the PostScript driver. Moreover, you'll need a special .WPD file for the PostScript driver that supports this configuration. See "Installing an Unlisted PostScript Printer" earlier in this chapter for more details on this.

Unlike PostScript printers, the industry norm is to use the bitmap file format to produce fonts for dot-matrix and laser printers. These bitmap fonts can be either resident to the printer (on its memory chip or supplied by a cartridge) or downloaded (sent) to the printer from an application. The file format for the bitmap varies from printer to printer. Therefore the bitmap must be sent to the printer in a form and resolution that the printer can support.

This norm is changing, however; laser printers are becoming available that have resident scalable outline fonts. The HP LaserJet III is a partial example of such a printer—along with supporting scalable outline fonts, it also allows you to download fonts in a bitmap format.

There are other advantages to using outline fonts beyond their improved appearance. Generally, outline font files are more compact than bitmap font files. As mentioned, each character in a bitmap font file is stored as a bitmap pixel image. Thus, by virtue of their design, bitmap font files tend to be much larger than outline font files, which contain a single character that can be scaled. This translates into increased use of disk space to store the files as well as a drain on your computer's memory to make these fonts available for display on your screen.

Some third-party font packages use the outline font technology to build the characters in your document at print time. These characters are then sent to the printer in graphics mode. In essence, each page is sent to the printer as one large bitmap.

Installing Printer Fonts

As mentioned, printer fonts can come from a variety of sources. For example, they can be resident to the printer (burned into its memory chip) or they can be supplied by a cartridge that plugs into a slot on the printer. Some printers have multiple slots to accommodate multiple cartridges. Finally, you can acquire soft fonts for Windows from third-party sources. Soft fonts are software-generated fonts that are downloaded to your printer either at print time or when you boot your computer.

When you install cartridge-based printer fonts or soft fonts, Window displays the names of those fonts in the appropriate menus in your applications. However, in Windows, printer fonts are always associated with individual printers. Therefore, to print from Windows in a specific font on a given printer, you must install that font for that printer. In addition, that printer must be both active (see "Activating a Printer," earlier) and selected (see "Choosing a Default Printer," earlier) for use by the current application.

Normally, when you install a printer driver for a given printer (see "Installing Printers," earlier), the resident fonts for that printer are installed automatically. However, if you want to install either cartridge-based fonts or soft fonts, you must take some extra steps.

Adding Fonts

Perhaps the best way to show you how to install cartridge-based and soft fonts for a printer driver is to take you through an actual example using the popular HP LaserJet Series II printer. Although each printer driver is different, this particular driver offers most of the font-related options you are bound to encounter, and it is thus fairly representative.

To begin, double-click on the Printers icon in the Control Panel. Windows displays the Printers dialog box. From the Installed Printers list box, select the name of LaserJet Series II driver, PCL/HP LaserJet. Then, select the Configure button from the right side of the Printers dialog box. Windows displays the Printers - Configure dialog box. From that dialog box, select the Setup button. Windows displays the PCL/HP LaserJet dialog box shown earlier in Figure 4-8.

At the lower left of the PCL/HP LaserJet dialog box is a list box entitled Cartridges. You can select up to two cartridges from this list box by simply clicking on them. At this point, you can select OK to confirm your selections, or you can install any soft fonts you may have.

> *Note:* Before going any further, an important point should be made. To install soft fonts for a printer, you must have secured a third-party soft-font package specifically designed for Windows. In addition, you must have already used the installation

program for that package to install it on your hard disk. Finally, for the HP LaserJet Series II printer, bitmap fonts are required. Generally, most third-party soft-font packages do not come with bitmap files pregenerated. Instead, you must run a specific program associated with the package that builds these fonts.

To install soft fonts, select the Fonts button on the right side of the PCL/HP LaserJet dialog box. When you select this button, Windows displays the Printer Font Installer dialog box in Figure 4-23. You'll notice this dialog box is composed of two blank boxes. Eventually, the box on the right will contain the fonts you want to install and the box on the left will contain the fonts that you have installed.

To select soft fonts to install, select the Add Fonts button from the Print Font Installer dialog box. Windows displays the Add Fonts dialog box in Figure 4-24. Insert the disk that contains the fonts into drive A, or, more commonly, type the name of the directory that contains your soft-font files. (Normally, these are downloadable bitmap font files you've created with a third-party font packaged and stored in a specific directory.) When you're ready, select OK. Windows reads the disk or directory you've specified and displays the names of the font files it finds in the right-hand box of the Printer Font Installer dialog box.

To install one or more of the fonts displayed in the right-hand box, click on each of their respective names. As soon as you make a selection, the Add button, between the left- and right-hand boxes, is activated. To install the fonts you've selected, click on the Add button. Windows displays a second version of the Add Fonts dialog box, this time reading "Copy to:" with a text box suggesting the name of a directory, usually C:\PCLFONTS. If this directory is to your liking, select OK. If the directory doesn't already exist, Windows prompts you whether it should create it. Select OK to create the directory. Windows copies the fonts you've selected to that directory and displays the names of the files you've selected in the left-hand box of the Printer Font Installer dialog box.

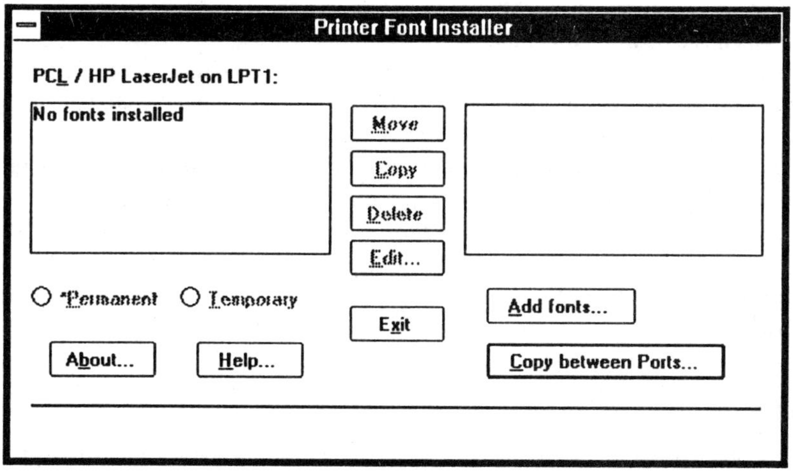

Figure 4-23 The PCL/HP Printer Font Installer dialog box

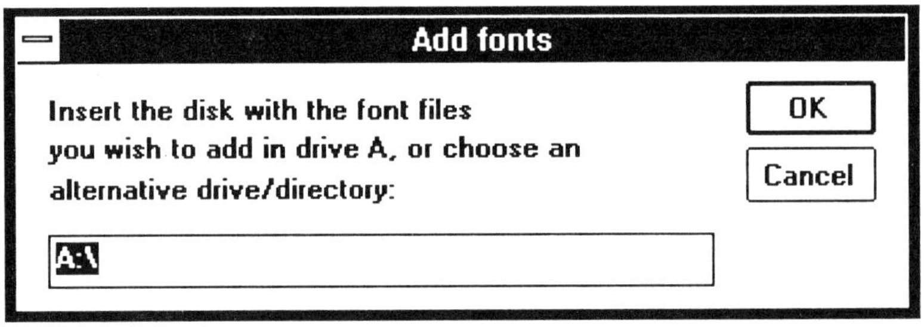

Figure 4-24 The Add Fonts dialog box

Choosing a Download Status

Your next job is to determine how you want each of the fonts used (downloaded). You can have each installed font downloaded (sent) to the printer either permanently or temporarily. Temporarily is the default; with this setting, Windows only downloads the font to the printer when you print with that font from a Windows application. On the other hand, if you select Permanent, Windows will make an entry in your AUTOEXEC.BAT that causes the font to be downloaded to your printer when you start your computer. Remember, each font that you download takes up printer memory. If you are printing a large graphics image, less available printer memory may mean that you will have difficulty printing that image.

If you've decided to have all fonts downloaded temporarily, do nothing. However, if you want to designate a permanent font, click on the name of that font in the left-hand box of the Printer Font Installer dialog box. When you make a selection, the Permanent and Temporary radio buttons below become active. Select the Permanent radio button, indicating that you want the font to be downloaded to the printer when you boot your computer. (You can, of course, change your mind on this at a later time by selecting the same font and selecting the Temporary radio button.)

When you specify a font as permanently downloadable and then select the Exit button to leave the Printer Font Installer dialog box, Windows displays the Download options dialog box shown in Figure 4-25. This dialog box contains two check boxes, Download now, and Download at Startup. If you choose Download now, the fonts you've installed will be downloaded to the default printer, in this case the HP LaserJet Series II. If you select the Download on startup check box, Windows will place a line in your AUTOEXEC.BAT file, similar to C:\PCLFONTS\SFLPT1.BAT. This calls a special .BAT file that Windows places in the directory in which the fonts are installed, usually C:\PCLFONTS.

Editing Fonts

You can also change the download status as well as other parameters for an installed printer font. To do this, select the name of an installed font in the left-hand box of the

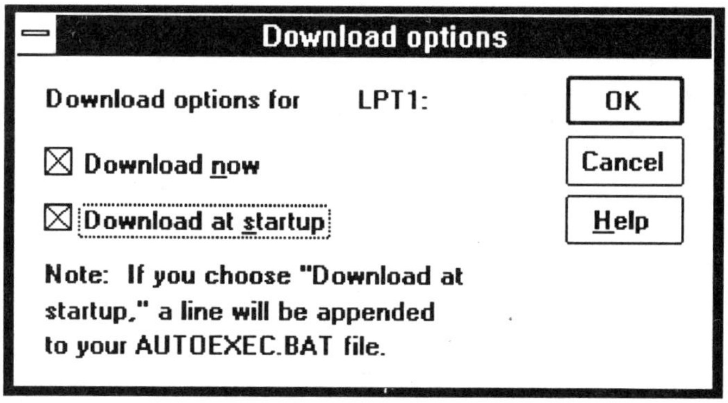

Of Fonts and Printing 145

Figure 4-25 The Download options dialog box

Print Font Installer dialog box. Then select the Edit button. When you select this button, Windows displays the dialog box shown in Figure 4-26. The top two lines of this box give the official name and filename for the font. You cannot change these. However, the next line is a text box, entitled Name, that shows the name of the font. You can change this name if you want to. The name you provide will appear in your application menus. For example, if you have two soft fonts with the same name from different manufacturers, you can change one of them so that it appears in your Windows application menus under a different name.

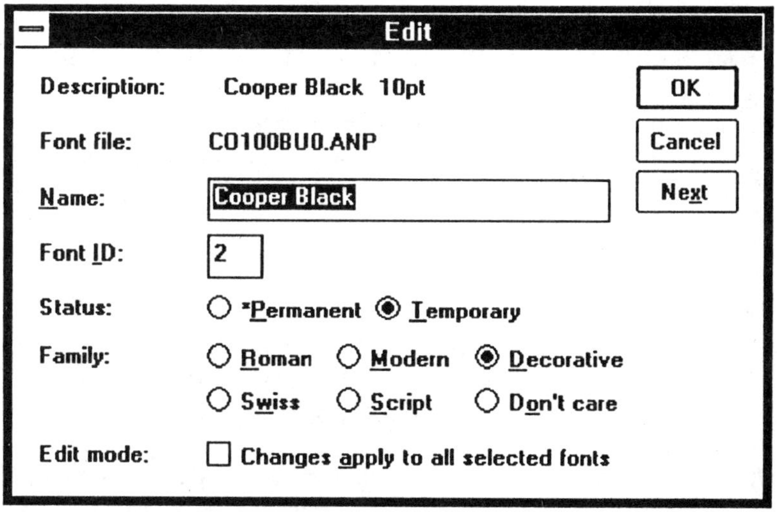

Figure 4-26 The fonts Edit dialog box

The next line in the Edit dialog shows the Font ID number that is assigned to the font in the WIN.INI file. You shouldn't have a need to change this setting. In fact, you should avoid doing so unless you are familiar with the font parameters in the WIN.INI file.

Below the Font ID# line is a line entitled Status. This line shows the current download status for the font. You can choose from Temporary or Permanent. As you might imagine, these settings have the same effect as the Temporary and Permanent settings described earlier.

Below the Status line is a section entitled Family. This section is composed of a series of radio buttons that show the Family to which the font is currently assigned. You can assign the font to a new family by clicking on the appropriate radio button. Or if you don't care about the family to which the font is assigned, you can select the Don't care radio button. Generally, though, you should choose a family whose attributes most closely match those of the current font. As mentioned, Windows groups fonts into five common families as follows:

- Roman: Serif fonts with proportional spacing such as the Times Roman type face. This is the most common font family.
- Swiss: Sans serif fonts with proportional spacing, such as Helvetica
- Modern: Serif or sans serif fonts. Many fonts with fixed spacing and character widths, such as Courier, fall into this class.
- Script: Cursive fonts like Script or Park Avenue.
- Decorative: Unusual fonts, like Old English or Zapf Dingbats

The last line in the Edit dialog box, entitled Edit mode, is only active if you've selected multiple installed fonts before entering the Edit dialog box. In addition, if you've selected multiple fonts, a Next button is added to the OK and Cancel buttons in the upper-left corner. Selecting the Next button allows you to move sequentially through each of the selected fonts. Nevertheless, returning to the Edit mode line, if you select the check box labeled "Changes apply to all selected fonts," the changes you've made, other than Name and Font ID, will apply to all the fonts you've previously selected.

Once you've recorded the changes you want for the currently selected font(s), select the OK button to confirm those changes and return to the Printer Font Installer dialog box.

Removing Soft Fonts

You can easily remove an installed soft font. To do this, select the name of the font you want to remove from the list of installed fonts in the left-hand box of the Printer Font Installer dialog box. When you make a selection, the Delete button between the left- and right-hand boxes becomes active. Select the Delete button. Window displays a Yes/No/Cancel dialog box asking if you want the file deleted from the disk as well. Select No to simply remove the font without deleting it from the disk. Windows returns you to the Print Font Installer dialog box. Select OK to return to the PCL/HP LaserJet dialog box.

Copying Fonts between Ports

The HP/PCL LaserJet driver also provides a facility for you to copy and move fonts between ports. To do this, you use the Copy between ports button in the Printer Font Installer dialog box. This option is handy when you are installing a second printer supported by the HP/PCL driver on another port, or when you want to change the port assignment for the current printer.

To copy or move fonts between ports, select the Copy between Ports button from the Printer Font Installer dialog. Windows displays the Copy between ports dialog box shown in Figure 4-27. Choose a port to which you want the fonts copied or moved and then select OK. Windows returns you to the Print Font Installer dialog box. A listing now appears at the top of the dialog box showing the port you're copying the fonts from on the left and the port you're copying the fonts to on the right. Also, the name of the Copy between ports button has changed to End between ports.

Next, select those fonts you want to copy or move from the left side of the Printer Font Installer dialog box. When you make a selection, the Copy and Move buttons between the left- and right-hand boxes become active. Select either Copy or Move. Windows copies or moves the fonts you selected from the left-hand box to the right-hand box. (To cancel the operation at any time, select End between ports. Choose Exit to leave the Printer Font Installer dialog box and return to the PCL/HP LaserJet dialog box.)

When you select Exit, Windows records the new assignments for the fonts you've copied or moved. You can now install another printer supported by the PCL/HP driver on that port, or change the port assignment for the current printer.

However, if you've copied or moved a permanent font, Windows displays the Download options dialog box, shown earlier in Figure 4-25, when you select Exit to leave the Printer Font Installer dialog box. As mentioned, if you select the Download at startup check box, Windows will update your AUTOEXEC.BAT file so that the fonts are automatically downloaded to your printer when you start your computer. In fact, if you've moved all the fonts for a port, to make it available for use by another device other than a printer, make sure you perform a little maintenance on your AUTOEXEC.BAT file. When you open this file using Notepad or another ASCII editor, you'll find two clearly identifiable statements inserted by Windows, one for the old port and a second one for the new port. Simply delete, or comment out, the statement for the old port.

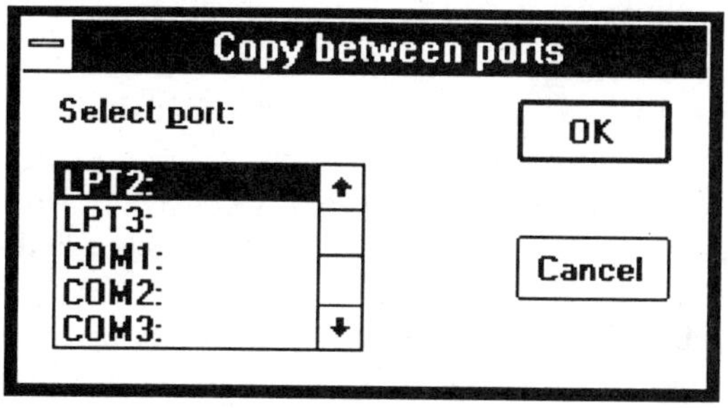

Figure 4-27 The Copy between ports dialog box

Formatting with Installed Fonts

Once you install printer fonts, soft or otherwise, they are usually displayed on the menus for your applications. Nevertheless, before you can select a font, the printer to which those fonts are assigned must be the currently active printer. Most applications include a File Printer Setup command that lets you choose from among the active printers you've installed. Otherwise, you can use the Printers icon in the Control Panel to select a default printer for the system.

Even when you select the appropriate printer, though, your installed printer fonts may not appear to be available from the menus for an application. Often you have to make them current by using a submenu to access a dialog box that lets you select them. For example, in Write, you use the Character menu option to format text in a given font. However, when you select this option, only three fonts appear to be available. To see the other printer fonts you've installed, you must select the Fonts option from the Character menu. A dialog box is then displayed that lets you choose from among the printer fonts you've installed.

Using Fonts with Dot-Matrix Printers

If you have a laser printer installed, most Windows applications allow you to select a font and then to select a point size for that font as well. For example, when you select a Times Roman typeface, you can then select various gradations of point size for that type face. However, dot-matrix printers can be a different matter.

Many dot-matrix printers measure fonts in characters per inch (CPI) rather than in point size. CPI is a horizontal as opposed to a vertical measurement. Thus, each font is generally the same height and only the width between the characters is varied. When this is the case, an application may list each different font as a font name, for example Roman 10cpi, Roman 12cpi, and so on. When you select the font, only a single point size is available, for example, 10.

Printing ANSI Characters

As you know, Windows supports the ANSI character set. This character set includes all the characters that appear on your keyboard and some that don't. A listing of these characters appears in the back of the *Windows Users Guide*. You can produce any of the Characters in the ANSI set by holding down the ALT key and typing zero followed by the appropriate ANSI character number on your numeric keypad. For example, the ANSI number for Japanese Yen symbol is 165. To produce this character, hold down the ALT key, type **0165** on the numeric keypad, and release the ALT key.

Although you can display ANSI characters on your screen, you may not be able to print them. When you print a file, Windows translates each of the characters in that file from an ANSI character to a character that is appropriate for your printer. If your printer has an appropriate character, it will be printed. Otherwise, another character may be printed. This only happens, though, when Windows is relying on the fonts that are resident to the printer. When a Windows screen font is used for printing, all ANSI characters will be faithfully replicated.

Third-Party Soft-Font Packages

As mentioned, a growing number of third-party soft-font packages are becoming available for Windows. In fact, four of them are discussed in this section, including FaceLift from Bitstream, Inc.; Type Manager from Adobe Systems; SoftType from ZSoft Corporation; and Intellifont for Windows from Hewlett Packard.

Note: If you decide to purchase a third-party soft-font package for use with Windows, make absolutely sure that it is compatible with Windows 3. Font files must meet certain requirements before you can use them with Windows. In addition, font files traditionally require a significant amount of hard-disk space to store them. The amount you'll need depends, of course, on the number of fonts you acquire. In addition, printer memory can be an issue. For example, if you have a LaserJet Series II with 512K of memory, printing can be very slow with some of these packages. In fact, consider checking the amount of recommended printer memory before you buy a font package. It may be that part of the cost of acquiring a font package is the cost of upgrading your printer's memory.

Most of the third-party font packages discussed below allow you to generate both printer and screen fonts for Windows. That way, what you see on your screen is replicated on your printer. However, as you'll soon see, each package has a different way of doing this.

FaceLift from Bitstream

FaceLift from Bitstream, Inc. is perhaps the most versatile of the soft-font packages discussed in this section. Much of the work on FaceLift was done by a German firm called GCA, which, among other things, specializes in developing Windows and Presentation Manager applications.

FaceLift is specifically designed for use with Windows. It offers "on-the-fly" font generation for Windows applications. That is, it generates screen fonts only for the characters that you type, as you are typing them. These characters are then saved to a memory cache, so that FaceLift can instantly recall them when you move from one part of a document to another. FaceLift also generates printer fonts on the fly for Windows-supported dot-matrix, LaserJet, and PostScript printers.

FaceLift dovetails nicely into the Windows environment. For example, when you install the product, it updates your SYSTEM.INI and WIN.INI files so that FaceLift comes up when you start Windows and its fonts are displayed on your application menus. You can also turn off FaceLift whenever you want to.

The base FaceLift package comes with 13 Speedo scalable outline fonts as well as 13 PostScript Type 1 fonts. You can, of course, acquire additional Speedo and PostScript fonts as well as upgrade from the earlier Bitstream Fontware products to the new Speedo technology. The Speedo fonts from Bitstream are proprietary. However, you can procure over 200 typefaces from Bitstream for use with FaceLift.

FaceLift relies on its internal Speedo engine to generate both screen and printer fonts. This is done with the aid of separate screen and printer "shells" (.DLL libraries) that sit

150 *Windows 3 Power Tools*

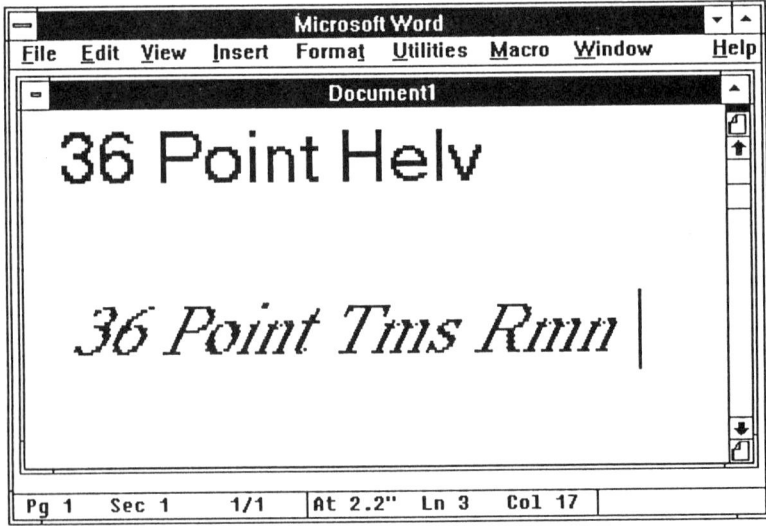

Figure 4-28 Default Windows screen fonts

between the Windows Graphics Device Interface (GDI) and the currently selected screen and printer driver. Thus, everything coming from the GDI to your screen or printer is intercepted, after a fashion, so that FaceLift can perform its font magic on that output.

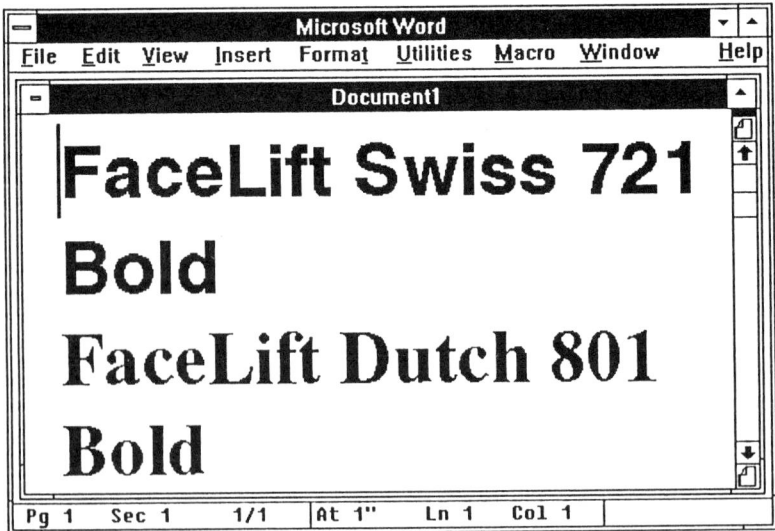

Figure 4-29 Screen fonts generated by FaceLift

The Speedo technology allows Facelift to use a single .SPD font file to generate fonts for both your screen and your printer. These font files contain scalable outline fonts. That is, when you choose a font for a character, FaceLift generates an outline for the character and then scales it to the appropriate size. Once the outline has been generated, it is filled in with pixels (in the case of your screen) or dots (in the case of your printer).

The result is an attractive screen display (minimal "jaggies") as well as quality output from your printer. For example, Figures 4-28 and 4-29 show before and after views of the effect using FaceLift can have with Word for Windows. Figure 4-28 shows two default Windows raster (bitmap) screen fonts. Notice the jagged stair-step-like edges for the characters. On the other hand, Figure 4-29 shows two of FaceLift's scalable outline fonts. Notice the smoother edges and the overall improvement in appearance.

Actually FaceLift generates its fonts twice, once for your screen and again for your printer. That is, when you select a font from an application menu for screen display, FaceLift generates the outline font for each character as you type it. The font is generated in a resolution that is suitable for your installed video adapter. However, when you print the document, FaceLift generates a whole new set of characters in a format and resolution that is appropriate for the printer you are currently using. For example, if you are using a laser or dot-matrix printer, FaceLift sends the characters to your printer in graphics mode. In effect, each page is sent to the printer as one large bitmap. On the other hand, if you are using a PostScript printer, FaceLift sends its fonts in a format that is appropriate for the PostScript interpreter.

In addition, FaceLift lets you create documents that contain a mix of font types. For example, you can print Speedo-generated fonts, pregenerated bitmap fonts that are downloaded to the printer, as well as resident printer fonts, all on the same page.

FaceLift comes with its own control panel containing six icons. This control panel appears in the upper-left corner of Figure 4-30. Each of FaceLift's icons lets you control a specific aspect of its operation, as follows:

- Typefaces: Lets you install and remove fonts.
- Printers: Lets you add to the list of printers for which FaceLift will generate fonts.
- PS-Outlines: Lets you download Bitstream Type 1 PostScript fonts to your PostScript printer to supplement the 35 that are already resident.
- Parameters: Gives you access to the window shown at the lower right of Figure 4-30, which lets you control the size of the character cache, save the character cache to a file on disk, or disable FaceLift.
- Name Table: Lets you match resident printer fonts to scalable screen typefaces and print documents on different printers without having to reformat them.
- HP-Softfonts: Lets you create (build) HP bitmap fonts for those printers (such as the HP LaserJet Series II) that can use them. Once those fonts are built, you can install them by using the procedure described earlier under "Installing Printer Fonts." Although this step is not necessary, it can be a time saver. That is, rather than waiting for FaceLift to generate fonts using the Speedo technology, you can download them to the printer in a bitmap format at or before print time. This can result in a substantial decrease in printing time.

Perhaps one of the most interesting features of FaceLift, though, is the way it allows you to control the character cache. As mentioned, when you select a font from an application menu, FaceLift generates that font as you are typing characters. These formatted characters are then stored in a memory cache. That way, if you are moving around in a large document, FaceLift can instantly display its fonts without having to load them from disk and potentially slow down your application. Obviously, though, this cache requires valuable memory that might otherwise be used for applications.

However, through the Parameters icon, you can control the size of the cache. When you select this icon, FaceLift displays the Parameters window at the lower right of Figure 4-30. This window lets you set the size of the cache in kilobytes, specify the maximum number of fonts it can contain, and save the cache to disk. When you save the cache, it is automatically reloaded the next time you start Windows.

If you have an HP LaserJet III, which has some resident scalable outline fonts already on board, Bitstream offers the Hewlett Packard LaserJet III Companion pack. This package offers screen fonts that are compatible with the fonts that are already resident to the printer. That way, what you see on your screen matches the output for your printer. Or, if you have a PostScript printer, Bitstream offers the PostScript Companion Pack. Once again, it includes only screen fonts; but it allows you to match what appears on your display with the output from your printer.

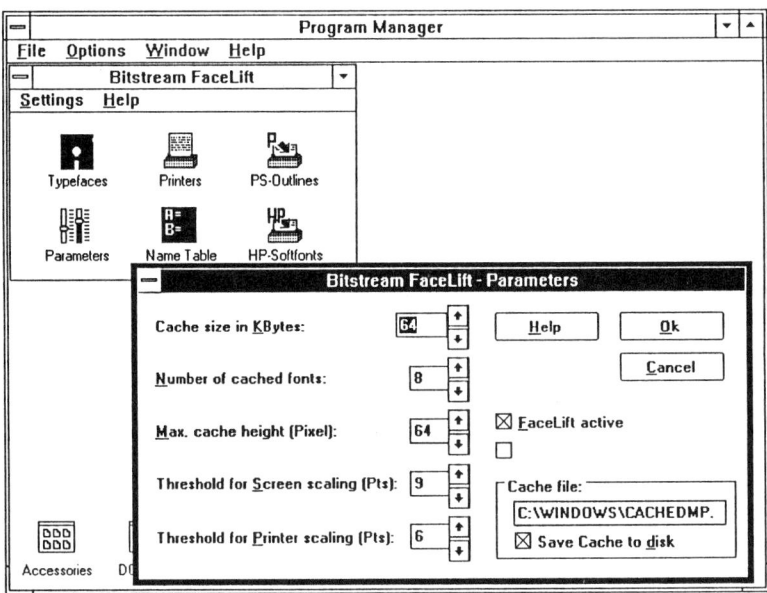

Figure 4-30 Bitstream FaceLift icons and Parameters dialog box

Of Fonts and Printing 153

Adobe Type Manager

Although not quite as flexible, Adobe Type Manager (ATM) offers many of the same features as Bitstream's FaceLift. For example, it offers on-the-fly font generation for screen fonts and a character cache to store them. It also supports a large variety of the laser, dot-matrix, and PostScript printers supported by Windows.

The base ATM package comes with 13 scalable outline fonts. However, you can also choose from over 700 PostScript typefaces available from the Adobe Type Library for use with ATM. Each face is licensed from its respective vendor. These include such notables as LinoType AG, Monotype, Agfa-CompuGraphic, and ITC. Therefore, you can be sure you are getting the original. When you purchase additional fonts, Adobe sends along a copy of the Adobe Font Foundry, which allows you to use those fonts with ATM. What all this means for the average user is that a huge variety of PostScript Type 1 fonts are made available for low-cost laser and dot-matrix printers.

For laser and dot-matrix printers, ATM generates the appropriate bitmap fonts at print time and sends them to the printer. However, you can also build independent bitmap font files for downloading to laser printers. These can be installed through the PCL/HP printer driver (see "Installing Printer Fonts" earlier). That way you can have the font either downloaded to the printer at print time or when you boot your system. In addition, ATM allows you to take advantage of any fonts that may be resident to the printer (burned into its memory or supplied by a cartridge).

ATM also comes with a control panel, which is shown in Figure 4-31. Among other things, this control panel lets you turn ATM on and off, adjust the size of the character cache from 64K to 8192K, as well as add and delete fonts from ATM's installed base.

When you install ATM, all the necessary files are copied to a directory on your hard disk. A special driver for ATM is copied to your \WINDOWS\SYSTEM directory. In addition, an entry is made to your SYSTEM.INI file referencing this driver so that ATM comes up automatically when you start Windows. Two files, ATMCNTRL.EXE and ATM.INI, are also installed in your WINDOWS directory. The ATMCNTRL.EXE file corresponds to the ATM control panel and provides an icon that you can install in a Program Manager group window. The ATM.INI file is a default configuration file for ATM. You can modify the entries in this file to do such things as substitute an ATM font in place of a Windows vector or raster font or change the directory in which ATM looks for its font files.

SoftType from ZSoft

SoftType from ZSoft comes with 62 scalable outline fonts from ZSoft's URW foundry. Like ATM and FaceLift, SoftType comes with a Windows application that lets you manage the package. Further, like other soft-font packages for Windows, SoftType lets you create and install both screen and printer fonts for use with your Windows applications. Once installed, the options for these fonts appear on the menus for your applications.

154   *Windows 3 Power Tools*

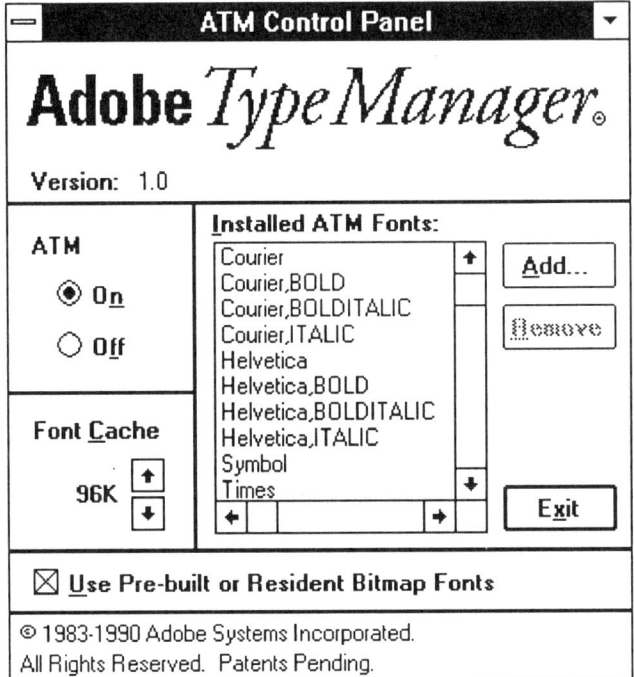

Figure 4-31 The Adobe Type Manager control panel

Like many of the packages discussed in this section, the fonts in SoftType are proprietary to ZSoft. However, you can purchase additional fonts from ZSoft. Further, you can purchase another Windows application from ZSoft called Publishers Type Foundry that lets you customize the fonts you have or design your own custom fonts from scratch. Once these fonts are created, you can use them with SoftType.

SoftType also includes a program that lets you customize the fonts that come with the package. For example, using the screen in Figure 4-32, you can change the appearance of the typeface. Letters can be black, white, or 100 shades of grey. You can extend, condense, slant (pseudo-italicize), rotate, outline, and add drop shadows to fonts. You can also modify drop shadows. For example, you can specify an angle for the shadows and set the point size for them. You can even specify a 3-D effect. However, when you edit fonts with SoftType, you see the effect of your edits on a rather bland sans serif typeface. Further, you must print with the custom font in order to see the true effect of your changes.

There are a few other minor shortcomings associated with SoftType. The printing of custom fonts, especially those with drop shadows, can take longer than noncustom fonts. In addition, the on-screen display of some of the fonts in this package does not appear as crisp, in some cases, as some of the other packages discussed here. However, because of

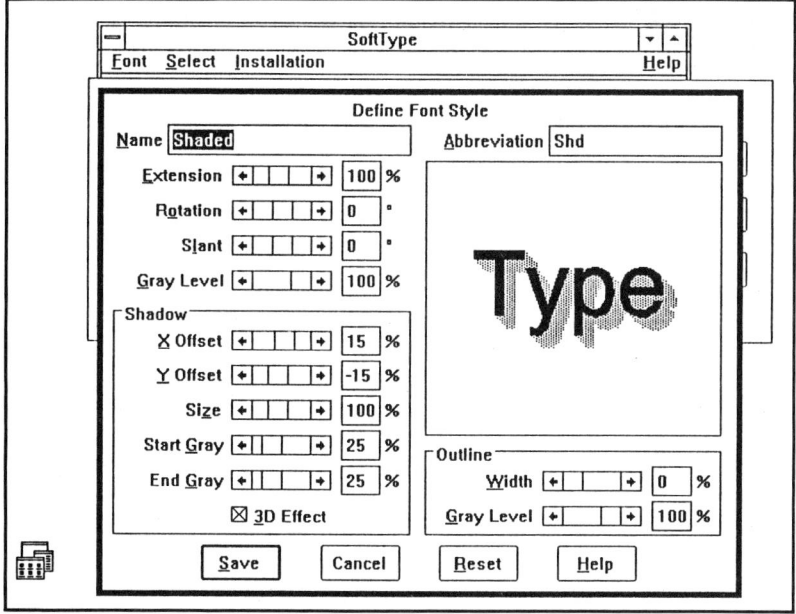

Figure 4-32 The SoftType Define Font Style dialog box

its font styling capabilities, SoftType is a serious contender in the Windows soft font market.

Intellifont for Windows 3 from Hewlett-Packard

Early releases of Intellifont for Windows 3 are intended for use with the HP LaserJet III and IIID printers. Both of these printers have scalable outline fonts that are resident to the printer. In support of these resident fonts, Intellifont comes with eight scalable screen typefaces. However, it also allows you to acquire and install additional type faces, in disk or cartridge form, from the HP Master Type Library.

Once Intellifont is installed, the names of its scalable fonts appear on the menus for your Windows applications. Like FaceLift and Adobe Type Manager, Intellifont offers font generation on the fly. That is, each character is generated and displayed on your screen as you type it. At print time, Intellifont does not have to generate a second set of printer fonts and download them to the printer. Instead, the fonts are already resident to the printer and print exactly as they appear on your screen.

Note: Hewlett-Packard is by no means a newcomer to the Windows soft-font business. In fact, a product called Type Director 2.0 has been commercially available for quite some time. This package lets you build matching screen and printer fonts for use with Windows applications. However, unlike the other soft-font packages discussed in this section, Type Director does not run under Windows. You must run it from the DOS prompt. Further, although Type Director supports most HP LaserJet printers, as well as Epson 9- and 24-pin dot-matrix printers, it does not support PostScript printers.

TrueType and TrueImage

No discussion of fonts in Windows would be complete without a brief mention of TrueType and TrueImage. TrueType is rumored to be coming in Windows 3.1. Supposedly, it will include an initial suite of approximately 13 fonts spread over four different typefaces. All of these fonts will be scalable with virtually no upper or lower limits. And, as you might imagine, there will be matching screen and printer fonts. Thus, there should be a very close relationship between what is displayed on your screen versus what comes out on your printer. TrueImage, on the other hand, is supposedly a form of device driver (not unlike the PostScript interpreter) that has built-in support for TrueType fonts.

Note: It bears mentioning again that the information just conveyed is rumor and nothing more. As of the writing of this book, it remains to be seen whether the TrueType technology is incorporated into Windows 3.1.

THE ROLE OF PRINT MANAGER

In Windows, you can print various documents from different applications and still keep working. Printing takes place in the background. To accomplish this, Windows stores each print job in a print queue (an area of your computer's memory). To control that queue, Windows employs a print-spooler application called Print Manager. This application releases print jobs from the queue to the printer in a sequential fashion. That is, the second print job is not released until the first one has been completed

Print Manager is always active as a transparent background application, unless you disable it. However, you can display Print Manager at any time. Further, you can use this application to manage the contents of the print queue. For example, you can view the contents of the print queue, reschedule print jobs, suspend a print job in midstream, or remove it from the queue altogether.

Viewing the Print Queue

To view the contents of the print queue, you'll need to open the Print Manager window. To do this, you can use the Print Manager icon located in Program Manager's Main group window. Alternatively, when you print from an application, the Print Manager icon is displayed at the bottom of the Windows desktop. You can double-click on this icon to open the Print Manager window. When you open the Print Manager window, it appears as shown in Figure 4-33.

As you can see, the Print Manager window displays lines of information regarding the print jobs that are currently underway. The first line (highlighted in Figure 4-33) is the

Of Fonts and Printing   157

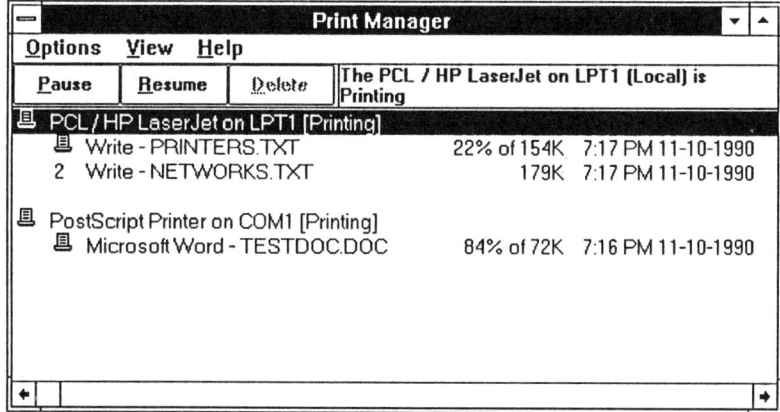

Figure 4-33 The Print Manager window

printer information line. This line contains information about the printer that is currently printing as well as the port to which it is connected. In addition, the status of that device is shown. In this case, the PCL/HP LaserJet on LPT1 is in the process of printing.

Beneath the printer information line appears a list of print jobs that are currently waiting in line for that printer. As you can see, only two print jobs are scheduled for the PCL/HP LaserJet printer. The first of these has a small printer icon next to it, which indicates that this job is currently printing. The next listing, however, begins with a number (2), which indicates that this job is the next one scheduled in that printer's queue.

Each print job listing shows information about that particular print job. Working from left to right, each listing begins with a number, identifying the position of the print job in the print queue. Next, the source (application) that sent the print job is shown along with the name of the file that is to be printed. To the right of this, Print Manager shows the size of the file in kilobytes and the percentage of that file that has been sent to the printer so far. This is followed by the time and date that the print job was sent to the queue.

If you are printing to more than one printer at a time, Windows starts a new section for each printer and its associated print jobs. For example, as you can see in Figure 4-33 about halfway down the Print Manager window, a second printer information line is shown for a PostScript Printer connected to COM1. Only a single job is scheduled for that printer, and that job is currently underway.

Rescheduling Print Jobs

You can easily change the order of print jobs in the print queue. To do this, simply click your mouse on the line that identifies a print job and drag that line to a new position in the Print Manager window. When you release your mouse button, Windows updates the numeric sequence of pending print jobs accordingly. However, you can only reschedule a print job like this if the file has not as yet begun to print.

You can also perform this operation with your keyboard. To do this, highlight the file information line that identifies the print job you want to move. Then, hold down the CTRL key and use the arrow keys to move the line to its new position. When you're ready, release the CTRL and arrow key. Windows updates the queue accordingly.

Pausing and Resuming a Print Job

You can also stop printing for a particular printer and then resume printing. To do this, click on the appropriate printer information line and then select the Pause button from the top of the Print Manager window. Windows temporarily suspends further printing. Alternatively, you can use the arrow keys to highlight the appropriate printer information line and type ALT+P to suspend printing. To resume printing again, click on the Resume button or type ALT+R.

Being able to temporarily suspend printing can be very handy when your printer needs maintenance. For example, if you run out of paper or you need to replace a ribbon or cartridge, you can stop printing while you do this and start it again when you're done.

If, for one reason or another, your printer stops working (you've run out of paper, for example), Windows will usually suspend printing for you. To signify this, it changes the suffix in the printer information line from [Printing] to [Stalled], indicating the printer is stalled for some reason. This gives you a chance to correct the problem. To resume printing again, select the Resume button or type ALT+R.

Removing a Print Job

If you change your mind about a print job, you can easily cancel it and remove it from the print queue. To do this, click on the listing for the print job to select it and then select the Delete button. Alternatively, you can highlight the appropriate print job and press ALT+D. Whichever method you choose, Windows displays an OK/Cancel message box asking you to confirm the selection. When you select OK, Windows deletes the print job from the print queue.

If you delete a print job that is in progress, Windows will stop printing that document at the point where you deleted it. However, your printer's memory buffer may still contain information. Therefore, when you start printing again, your printer may print a small portion of the old print job before starting the new one. To avoid this, you must reset the printer. You can do this by turning the printer off and on again, or by using the reset button or the menu system available on some printers.

You can also delete all the print jobs in the print queue. To do this, simply select the Exit command from Print Manager's Options menu. When you select this command, Windows displays an OK/Cancel message box informing you that all of the print jobs in the print queue will be canceled when you leave Print Manager. Select OK to cancel all print jobs and leave Print Manager.

When Your Applications Get Sluggish

Print Manager is a resource-intensive application. When you think about it, not only is Print Manager itself always in memory, but each print job you send to the print queue is stashed in memory while it waits in line for the printer. This process of storing print jobs and releasing them to the printer poses a tremendous drain on Windows' resources, perhaps causing your applications to run sluggishly. However, Print Manager allows you to mitigate this effect by controlling the speed in which information is sent from the print queue to the printer.

To adjust the print speed, you use the Options command from Print Manager's menu. This command gives you access to three suboptions—Low Priority, Medium Priority, and High Priority—that let you specify the amount of resources you want Windows to devote to printing. If you select Low Priority, Windows uses the majority of your computer's processor time for your applications and slows down the operation of Print Manager. If you select Medium Priority (the default), processor time is shared equally between your applications and Print Manager. Finally, if you select High Priority, Windows devotes more processor time to Print Manager, which speeds up printing but slows your applications down considerably. Use your own judgment in choosing the setting that's best for you.

Controlling Print Manager Messages

Print Manager also allows you to control the method it uses to display its messages. Messages are displayed when a printer error (such as an out-of-paper condition) occurs. However, you can choose how obstinate you want Print Manager to be in bringing this condition to your attention. To do this, you use Print Manager's Options menu. This menu gives you access to three suboptions—Alert Always, Flash if Inactive, and Ignore if Inactive—that let you choose the method of communication you desire. If you select Alert Always, Windows will immediately display a message box, right in the middle of your application, informing you that a printer condition requires your attention.

If you select Flash if Inactive (the default), Windows is more subtle. With this setting, Windows will beep once and the Print Manager icon at the bottom of your screen will begin to flash on and off. Or, if the Print Manager window is displayed as an inactive application, Windows will beep and the title bar of the Print Manager window will begin to flash. When you select Print Manager's window or icon, the message will then be displayed.

Finally, if you select Ignore if Inactive, Windows does not inform you of problems with your printer. Messages will be displayed only if Print Manager happens to be the active window.

Print Manager's messages are limited to nonfatal printer errors, such as out-of-paper conditions. On the other hand, if your printer goes off line, this is a system problem. In this case, Windows, not Print Manager, will display an error message informing you of the condition.

Simplifying the Display

You can simplify the display of Print Manager's window by choosing whether you want the date, time, and file size of each print job displayed. Normally, Print Manager will display the date and time a print job was sent to the queue and its file size in the listing for the print job. However, by using the View menu in Print Manager, you can suppress the display of these attributes. To suppress the display of the date and time information, select View Time/Date Sent. To suppress the display of the file size as well, select View Print File Size.

Disabling Print Manager

You can also disable Print Manager. However, when you do so, background printing is disabled as well. Thus, when you print from an application, Windows will suspend all further activity until the print job is completed. To disable Print Manager, use the Printer's icon in the Control Panel to access the Printers dialog box (last shown in Figure 4-9). At the lower-left corner of this dialog box is a check box labeled Use Print Manager. By default, this box is selected (contains an X). Select it to remove the X, then select OK to leave the Printers dialog box and return to the Control Panel. You'll hear some disk grinding as Windows disables the Print Manager.

Disabling the Print Manager is rarely appropriate, except in certain situations. For example, if you are working on a network, you can save time by simply bypassing Print Manager so that your output goes directly to the network print queue. Or you may want to disable Print Manager in low memory situations. For example, imagine you are printing a large graphics image from Paintbrush. Rather than store that image twice, once in Paintbrush and again in Print Manager, you can disable Print Manager so that the output is sent directly to your printer.

PRINTING FROM DOS APPLICATIONS

Basically, Windows is not involved when you print from DOS applications. DOS applications do not use Windows printer drivers, nor do they take advantage of Print Manager. Instead, they rely solely on their own printer drivers and demand exclusive access to the printer when printing. Therefore, there is the potential for conflict if a DOS application attempts to print while Print Manager is printing. This is not a problem in real or standard mode where Windows applications are suspended while you're working in a DOS application. However, in 386 enhanced mode, where you can multitask a mix of Windows and DOS applications, there is a potential for conflict. Windows allows you to mitigate this by using the 386 Enhanced icon in the Control Panel. This icon gives access to a dialog box that lets you arbitrate device contention for DOS applications. See Chapter 8, "Using the Control Panel," for more information on using this feature.

SUMMARY

This chapter tells most of what you'll need to know about printing from Windows. For example, you now know how to install various types of printers in windows. You also know how to install more than one printer, each on a different port, and select a given printer from within an application.

This chapter also shows you how to install fonts for Windows. You now know how to install both screen fonts for display and printer fonts for printing. In addition, you are aware of various third-party soft font packages that will allow you to extend your font library and further enhance the appearance of your documents.

Finally, you know about the role Print Manager plays in printing from Windows. You now know how to change the order of print jobs that are sent to your printer as well as how to cancel a print job when you need to.

5

Recorder Techniques

The Recorder is a Windows 3.0 accessory program that lets you record a series of mouse and keystroke actions in Windows and assign them to a shortcut key (for example, CTRL+W). You can then play back those actions whenever you want by pressing the shortcut key you've assigned. In this way, the Recorder lets you perform many common Windows tasks by simply pressing a key or two.

Any sequence of keystrokes and mouse actions you capture with Recorder constitutes a *macro*. However, Recorder macros are not the same as those you might create with the programming commands in Microsoft Excel or Word for Windows. Unlike these applications, Recorder does not offer a scripted command language. Therefore, you cannot perform such operations as getting user input, storing values or strings to variables, or using logical (IF-THEN-ELSE) statements. Further, you cannot write macros from scratch with Recorder, nor can you edit them. Instead, you are limited to simply recording keystrokes and mouse actions and playing them back.

Because of this lack of a scripted command language, you'll find that you frequently "hit the wall" with Recorder. In fact, on the surface, its apparent limitations will seem to handicap its effective use within Windows. However, this chapter shows you various techniques that you can use to get around many of Recorder's shortcomings.

Despite its limitations, the Recorder can be used to automate many of your routine Windows tasks (and some that are not so routine). For example, if you always load a particular file in conjunction with a given application, you can create a macro to do this.

Or suppose you routinely use Terminal to dial a particular bulletin board such as CompuServe. You can record a macro to do this job for you, instead of manually entering all the commands required to perform this task.

This chapter covers the Recorder from the ground up. It gives you the basics you'll need and shows you how to push the Recorder to its limits. If you're already familiar with how to use the Recorder, you may want to skip the basic material in the early part of the chapter and jump directly to "About Shortcut Keys."

The Recorder is intended for use both with Windows itself and with other Windows applications. The Recorder will not work from within DOS applications. However, you can certainly use the Recorder to start DOS applications and to configure the parameters for the windows in which they operate.

Note: You should be aware that you can run your Recorder macros from within two of the applications that come with this book, Oriel and Command Post. These applications provide the more structured environment the Recorder lacks.

RECORDER BASICS

Using the Recorder is easy. All you do is activate the Recorder and select the Macro Record command. A dialog box then appears that lets you assign a shortcut key, specify various parameters for the macro, and then begin the recording process. Once recording has begun, you can start using Windows as you normally would—the Recorder captures your keystrokes and mouse actions as you go (including the speed at which you make your selections). When you're done, simply press CTRL-BREAK to stop recording. Recorder will then prompt you to save your new macro. From then on, you can repeat those same actions by simply pressing the shortcut key you've assigned.

To get you up and running with the Recorder as quickly as possible, the sections that follow will take you through three sample macro recording sessions. The macros you create in these examples will demonstrate three potential applications for a Recorder macro. The first macro is a simple text-input macro that works with Windows Write; it will quickly create a closing salutation for a Write document. Next, you'll create a macro that manipulates the command menu in Write to automatically create a custom footer. The third macro will start Write from the Program Manager desktop. In preparation for creating these examples, you'll need to start Recorder. The next section tells you how to do just that.

Note: In the examples that follow, you'll be asked to use keystrokes, instead of mouse actions, to record macros. When recording mouse actions, Recorder merely notes the position on the screen at which a mouse click occurs. Because Windows may open and position windows differently each time, mouse clicks are not always a reliable means of recording a macro. Therefore, you're always better off using the keyboard. For more information on this topic, see "Problems with Recording Mouse Actions" later in this chapter.

STARTING THE RECORDER

To start the Recorder, simply open the Accessories window and double-click on the Recorder icon. Alternatively, you can use the arrow keys to move to the Recorder icon and press ENTER. Whichever method you choose, the Recorder window in Figure 5-1 appears on your screen. Now that you've got the Recorder up and running, put it aside temporarily by minimizing it to an icon.

Note: The Recorder must be active in order to either record a macro or to play back a macro.

RECORDING A SIMPLE TEXT-INPUT MACRO

In this example, you'll record a simple text-input macro that works within Windows Write. This macro will quickly generate a closing salutation for a Write document.

Setting Up the Macro

Before you're ready to record a macro, you must set up the environment in which the macro will run. That same environment must also be present when you later run the macro. As you'll soon see, the default for Recorder is to create macros that will only run in the application in which they were recorded. Thus, most of the macros you create will be application-specific. However, you can also create macros that will run in any application that is open on the desktop. See "Deciding Where a Macro Plays Back" later in this chapter for more details.

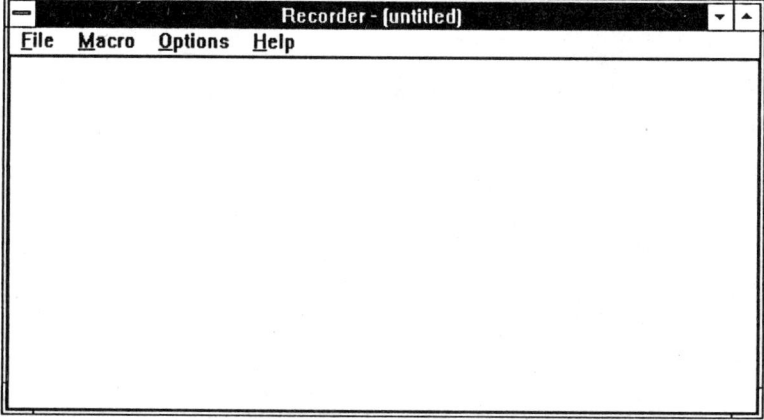

Figure 5-1 The Recorder window

To prepare the environment for this particular macro, begin by starting Write. When the Write window appears on your screen, minimize Program Manager to an icon. (This gets the Program Manager out of the way temporarily.) Now, three objects appear on your screen: the Write window, the Recorder icon, and the Program Manager icon. You're ready to record your first macro.

Recording the Macro

To begin Recording, start by double-clicking on the Recorder icon to restore the Recorder window. Next, select Macro Record from Recorder's main menu. The Record Macro dialog box in Figure 5-2 appears on your screen. This dialog box allows you to control most of the recording and playback options the Recorder has to offer. Each of these options will be discussed in detail throughout the balance of this chapter. However, for now, let's stick with the default settings and concentrate on naming the macro and assigning it a shortcut key.

You must assign either a name or a shortcut key to a macro in order to run it. It is not necessary to assign both. However, it is recommended that you do. In most cases, you'll use the shortcut key to run the macro, and the name will simply serve to help you identify the macro when it later appears in the Recorder window.

To assign a name to the macro, type a name of up to 40 characters in the Record Macro Name text box. For example, you might type the name **Write Salutation**. To assign a shortcut key, click on the Shortcut Key drop-down list box, or press TAB to move to it. Next, type a letter that you want to use to start the macro, for example S. Notice that the Ctrl check box appears checked already and that the Shift and Alt check boxes do not. Because of this configuration, you'll later run the macro by pressing CTRL+S.

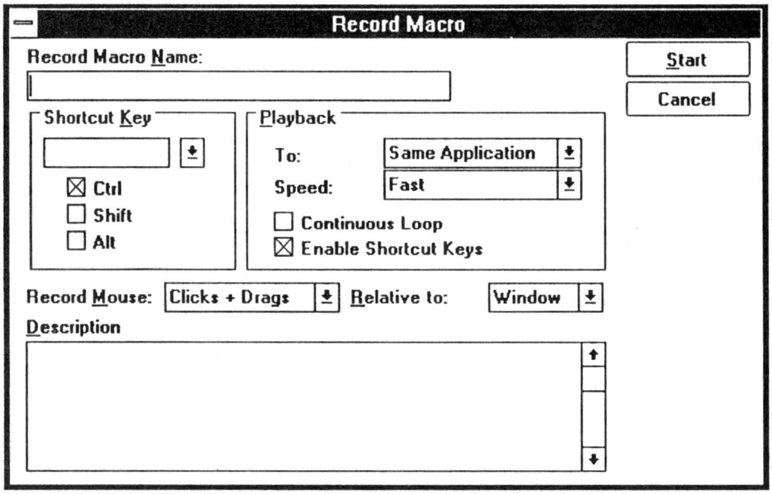

Figure 5-2 The Record Macro dialog box

To start recording the macro, select the Start command button. The Recorder window is minimized to a flashing icon at the lower left portion of your screen. The Write window is now the active window. (You can tell this by the blinking cursor on the first line of the document window.) You're now ready to record the actions that make up your macro. To do this, put your mouse aside for a moment and perform the following steps:

1. Type **Sincerely,**.
2. Press ENTER four times.
3. Type your name, for example **John C. Haenszel**, and press ENTER.
4. Type your title, for example **Vice President**.
5. Press CTRL-BREAK to stop recording. Alternatively, you can click on the flashing Recorder icon to stop recording.

Whichever method you choose to stop recording, the Recorder dialog box in Figure 5-3 appears on your screen. This dialog box contains three command buttons: Save Macro, Resume Recording, and Cancel Recording. These commands perform the following functions:

- Save Macro: Saves the current macro temporarily in RAM
- Resume Recording: Allows you to resume recording
- Cancel Recording: Cancels what you've recorded thus far

For now, select the Save Macro command, then select OK or press ENTER. You are returned to the currently active window (in this case the Write window), and your macro is saved for use while the Recorder remains open. To save the macro for use in future Windows sessions, you must return to the Recorder window and save the macro to a file. Before saving the macro permanently, however, it's always a good idea to test the macro to make sure it returns the results you want.

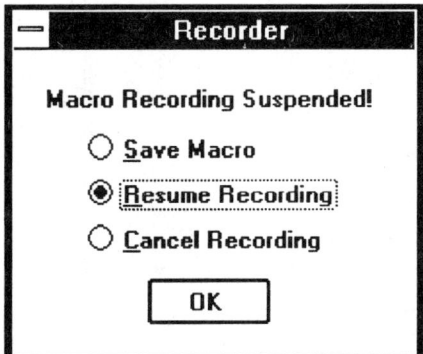

Figure 5-3 The Record dialog box

Running the Macro

Now that you've completed recording your first macro, you're ready to test it. To do this, type **CTRL+S**. The macro executes and repeats your keystrokes in the Write document window exactly as you typed them. You can use this macro in Write whenever you want to sign off on a finished document.

You can also test the macro by using the Macro Run command from Recorder's main menu. However, to use this command, you must return to the Recorder window.

When you restore the Recorder window, it appears as shown in Figure 5-4. The shortcut key (CTRL+S) for the macro appears on the first line of the Recorder window along with its name. To run this macro, make sure the CTRL+S macro name is highlighted, activate Recorder's menu, and select the Macro Run command. The Recorder window is minimized and the CTRL+S macro is executed in the Write window.

> **Tip: Double-click on a macro name**
>
> As an alternative to the Macro Run command, you can simply double-click on the name of a macro in the Recorder window. Recorder will then run the macro.

If you've been following along, you've probably got several closing salutations in the Write window. If you want to clear this text from the Write window, simply select the File New command from Write's main menu. When you are prompted whether you want

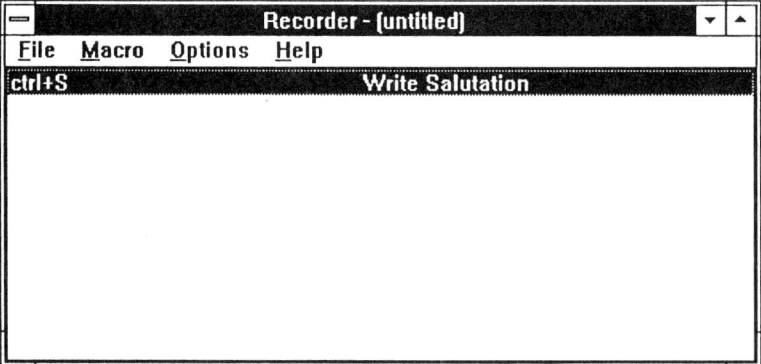

Figure 5-4 Macro names displayed in the Recorder window

to save your changes, simply select the No command button. A fresh document now appears in the Write window.

If You Make a Mistake

Suppose for a moment that you discover an error in the macro you've just recorded. Unfortunately, you cannot fix that specific error. Instead, you must return to the Recorder window, delete the macro, and record it all over again. To delete a macro, restore the Recorder window and make sure the macro (in this case, CTRL+S) is highlighted. Next, select Macro Delete from Recorder's main menu. Recorder asks you to confirm the deletion and then deletes the macro you've specified. You can now use the Macro Record command to re-record the macro.

Saving the Macro

To save a macro permanently, you must return to the Recorder window and save the macro to a file. As mentioned, when you return to the Recorder window, it appears as shown earlier in Figure 5-4. The shortcut key for your new macro (CTRL+S) is listed on the first line of the Recorder window followed by its name. As you record new macros, each will be added to the Recorder window in the order in which you record them.

To save the macros listed in the Recorder window, select the File Save As command from Recorder's menu. The dialog box in Figure 5-5 now appears on your screen. Type the file name of your choice in the Filename text box, for example **WINMACS**, and press ENTER. Windows saves the macros you've created thus far to a file with the name you've specified. That file is automatically given a .REC extension, for example WINMACS.REC. To use the macros in this file in a future Windows session, simply use Recorder's File Open command to open the WINMACS.REC file.

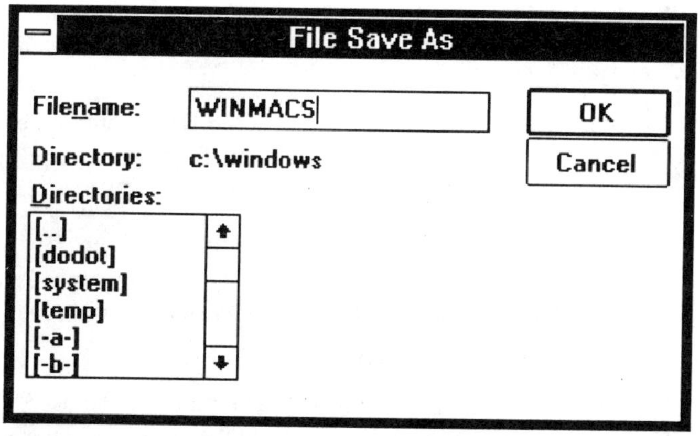

Figure 5-5 Recorder's File Save dialog box

MANIPULATING COMMAND MENUS: AN EXAMPLE

This next macro example will show you how to manipulate the command menu in a Windows application. This particular macro will manipulate the Write menu to create a custom footer. The techniques you'll learn here can be used to manipulate the command menu in virtually any Windows application.

Setting Up the Macro

In preparation for recording this macro, you'll need to set up the environment in which it will run. To do this, simply open Write (if you haven't already). In addition, make sure the recorder is up and running. Also, if you have applications other then Program Manager open, close those applications now. Finally, if the Program Manager is currently displayed, you'll probably want to minimize it to an icon, so that you can more easily see what you are doing. That way, the Recorder and Write windows are basically the only things on your screen.

Recording the Macro

Make the Recorder window the active window and perform the following steps:

1. Select Macro Record from Recorder's menu. The Macro Record dialog box shown earlier in Figure 5-2 is displayed.

2. In the Record Macro Name text box, type the macro name of your choice, for example **Write Footer**.

3. In the Shortcut key drop-down box, type the letter you want to use to start the macro, for example **F**.

4. To begin recording, select the Start button. The Recorder window is minimized to a flashing icon located at the lower left of your screen. The Write window then becomes the active window. As before, put your mouse aside for the balance of this recording session.

5. Press F10 to activate Write's main menu and select the Document Footer command. The Footer dialog box appears, as shown in Figure 5-6. The cursor, however, remains in the document window.

6. Type **Page** and press the space bar. This is the text portion of the footer.

7. Press F10 to activate Write's main menu and select the Paragraph Centered command. The "Page" text string is shifted to the center of the current line.

8. Press ALT+F6 to move to the Footer window.

9. Press TAB twice to move to the Insert Page # command button and press ENTER. This action inserts a (page) reference in the document that will reflect the current page number for each successive page that you print.

10. Press TAB twice to move to the Return to Document button and press ENTER. You are returned to the document window

11. Press CTRL-BREAK to stop recording (or click once on the flashing Recorder icon). The Recorder dialog box, shown earlier in Figure 5-3, appears on your screen asking you if you want to save the macro, resume recording, or cancel recording.

12. Select Save Macro and then select OK or press ENTER. You are returned to the Write Window.

Testing and Saving the Macro

To test the macro, simply press the CTRL+F shortcut key sequence. A second footer is inserted into the current Write document window. If the macro performs as you expect, you can now save the macro. On the other hand, if the macro contains errors, you must return to the Recorder window, use the Macro Delete command to delete it, and record the macro again.

To save the CTRL+F file to the same file (WINMACS.REC) as the CTRL+S macro you created earlier, you can use virtually the same procedure as described above. That is, double-click on the Recorder icon to restore the Recorder window. It should appear as shown in Figure 5-4. Notice that the shortcut key sequence you selected (CTRL+F) now appears on the second line of the Recorder window along with the name you assigned (Write footer).

Save the macro permanently by selecting the File Save command. The dialog box in Figure 5-5 is not displayed this time. Instead, Recorder simply overwrites the old version of WINMACS.REC with the new version and you are returned to the Recorder window.

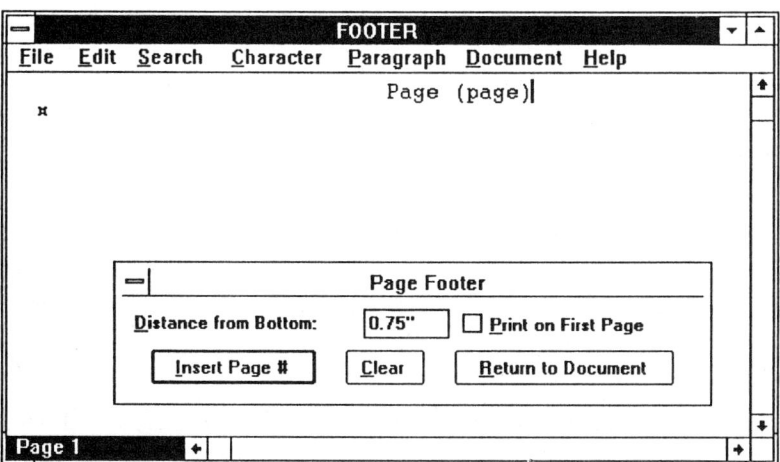

Figure 5-6 The Write window with the Footer dialog box displayed

LOADING AN APPLICATION: AN EXAMPLE

Another useful feature of the Recorder is its ability to create macros that allow you to quickly load applications at the touch of a key or two. In this next macro example, you'll create a macro that will automatically load Write. You can use the techniques described here to load virtually any Windows application or even a DOS application.

Setting Up the Macro

This macro will run within Windows Program Manager itself. Therefore, make sure the Program Manager is open. Also, if Write is open, close it now. Next, start the Recorder, if you haven't already. Further, leave the Recorder window displayed on your screen.

Recording the Macro

Now that you've set up the environment in which the macro will run, perform the following steps:

1. Select the Macro Record command from Recorder's menu. The Record macro dialog box shown earlier in Figure 5-2 is now displayed on your screen.

2. In the Record Macro Name text box, type the name of your choosing, for example **Write Start**.

3. In the Shortcut Key drop-down list box, type the name of the key that will be used to start the macro, for example **W**. Also, make sure the Ctrl check box is selected and that the Alt and Shift boxes are not. That way, you'll use CTRL+W to start this macro.

4. To begin recording, select the Start button. The Recorder window is minimized to an icon. As before, put your mouse aside for a moment.

5. Press F10 to activate Program Manager's main menu.

6. Select the File Run command. Program Manager presents the File Run dialog box shown in Figure 5-7.

7. Type **WRITE** and press ENTER. Windows runs Write, and its window is now displayed on your screen.

8. Press CTRL+BREAK to stop recording, or click on the flashing Recorder icon. The Recorder dialog box shown earlier in Figure 5-3 is now displayed.

9. Select Save Macro followed by OK.

10. Press CTRL+ESC to activate the Task List and select Recorder. The Recorder window appears on your screen.

11. Select the File Save command from Recorder's menu to save the CTRL+W macro to the WINMACS.REC file.

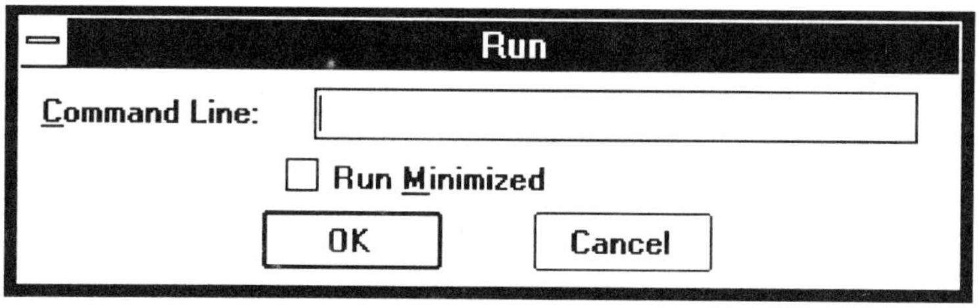

Figure 5-7 Program Manager's File Run dialog box

To test this macro, you'll need to close the Write window. (Otherwise, the macro will open a second copy of Write.) In addition, make sure the Program Manager is displayed. Then, press CTRL+W to run the macro. The Write window appears on your screen. To run this macro in future, the Program Manager must be displayed, so that your macro can access its File Run command.

Notice in the above example that the File Run command was used to start the Write accessory program by using its filename, WRITE.EXE. You can use this method to run virtually any Windows or DOS application. In fact, you will find this technique is more reliable than recording mouse selections to start your applications. That way, if you change Program Manager's layout (you move the Write icon to another location or window, for example), your macro will still function correctly. See "Any Application Macros " under "Deciding Where a Macro Plays Back" later in this chapter for a table of Windows executable files that you can run by using the File Run command.

ABOUT SHORTCUT KEYS

Just about any key on the keyboard can be used in conjunction with the CTRL, ALT, or SHIFT keys as a shortcut key. To assign a shortcut key, you use the Shortcut Key group box in the Record Macro dialog box shown earlier in Figure 5-2. For example, if you want to start your macro by using CTRL+C, type **C** in the Shortcut Key text (the case doesn't matter). Notice that the Ctrl check box below is already turned on by default. Therefore, the macro is assigned the CTRL+C shortcut key sequence. If you want to use ALT+C to start the macro, turn off the Ctrl check box and turn on the Alt check box. Finally, to use SHIFT+C to start the macro, make sure the Shift check box is selected and that the others are not.

It's best to make sure that only one of the Ctrl, Alt, or Shift check boxes is selected. Otherwise, you'll end up assigning a combination of the CTRL, ALT, and SHIFT keys to the shortcut key sequence. For example, you might end up assigning CTRL+ALT+C as a shortcut key. Although this is a legal macro shortcut key name that can be used to start a macro, it is unwieldy. However, you can use this option to avoid conflicts with other Windows applications. See "Conflicts with Other Windows Applications" later in this section for more details on this subject.

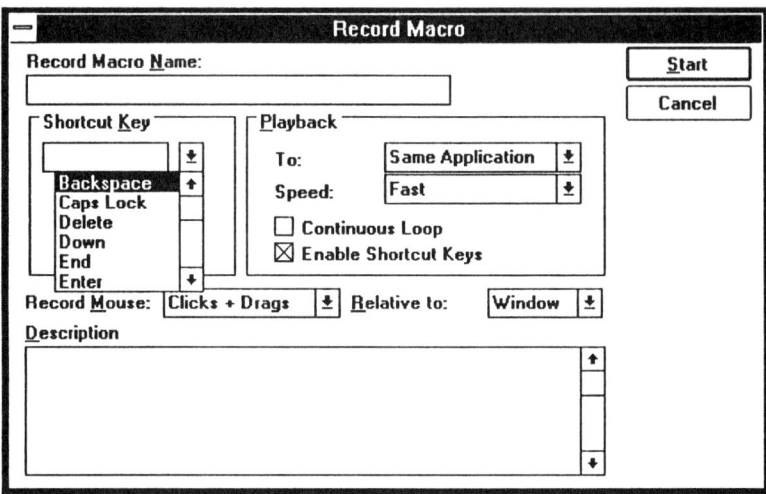

Figure 5-8 Use the Shortcut Key drop-down list box to select from a list of non-alphanumeric shortcut keys

Note: Technically, you do not have to assign either the CTRL, ALT, or SHIFT keys to an alphanumeric letter to create a shortcut key. For example, you could create a shortcut key of just "C". However, this disables the "C" key on your keyboard for any other purpose while the Recorder is active and the .REC file that contains the "C" macro is loaded.

Using Other Non-Alphanumeric Shortcut Keys

In addition to the alphanumeric keys, you can use many of the non-alphanumeric keys as shortcut keys. To see a list of these keys, open the Shortcut Key drop-down list box. Recorder displays a list of non-alphanumeric keys for your selection, as shown in Figure 5-8. (The keys in this list box are also summarized in Table 5-1.) As you page down though this list of keys, you'll notice that many of the cursor movement keys, for example HOME, END, ↓, and so on, are included in the list. In addition, you'll notice that the function keys, F1 through F12, are included. All of these keys can be used either individually or in conjunction with the CTRL, ALT, or SHIFT keys to start your macros.

If you decide to use the CTRL or ALT key in conjunction with a non-alphanumeric key, keep in mind that Windows itself makes extensive use of these keys. For example, ALT+ESC activates the next window, ALT+TAB lets you cycle through applications and choose one, CTRL+ESC brings up the Task List, ALT+F4 closes a window, and so on. If you assign one of these key sequences to a Recorder macro, the Recorder key sequence will take precedence over the same key sequence used in Windows. On the other hand, the function keys, F1 through F9, are used only infrequently by Windows and are therefore prime candidates for shortcut keys. (F10, like ALT, is reserved as a menu summoning key by Windows and should not be used as a shortcut key.)

BACKSPACE	ENTER	NUMLOCK	SPACE
CAPS LOCK	ESC	PAGEDOWN	TAB
DELETE	HOME	PAGEUP	↑
↓	INSERT	→	F1 - F10
END	←	SCROLL LOCK	

Table 5-1 Keys Names Listed in the Shortcut Key List Box

Conflicts with Other Windows Applications

When you assign shortcut keys, keep in mind the shortcut keys you've assigned to macros in other Windows applications such as Microsoft Excel or Word for Windows. Both of these applications have a Recorder-like feature, as well as a full-blown macro command language, that allows you to create macros. In addition, both applications allow you to use the CTRL key in conjunction with a letter to run those macros. What's more, if one of these applications is present in memory along with the Recorder, and both have a macro with the same name, for example CTRL+C, Recorder will win every time. That is, Windows will always run the Recorder's CTRL+C macro, rather than that of another Windows application.

Fortunately, however, there are various techniques you can use to avoid conflicts between the Recorder and other Windows applications. For example, instead of assigning a shortcut key to a Recorder macro, you can assign only a name and run the macro by using that name. (See the next section for more about macro names.) Or, you can assign a shortcut key to a recorder macro that is not likely to be used in another application, such as CTRL+ALT+C. Alternatively, both Word for Windows and Excel have a Macro Run command that allows you to run a macro by its name instead of its shortcut key. Finally, if none of these solutions is acceptable, you can disable the Recorder's ability to detect shortcut keys by using the Options Shortcut Keys command. See "Disabling Recorder Temporarily" later in this chapter for more details on this command.

Conflicts with DOS Applications

In general, when you use a Recorder shortcut key within a DOS application to do anything other than load the application, that shortcut key has no effect. (As mentioned, the Recorder is not intended for use with DOS applications.) However, there might be a conflict if you designate a shortcut key as part of a PIF (Program Information File) setting for a DOS application.

As you'll learn in Chapter 10, you can create custom PIF files that contain settings that tell Windows how to run a particular DOS application. That way, whenever you start that application, Windows automatically uses the .PIF file associated with it and sets up the application accordingly. As part of this .PIF file, you can specify a shortcut key that will be used to quickly switch to the application, once it has been loaded into memory. If the shortcut key you designate in the .PIF file matches a shortcut key in the Recorder, and both applications are in memory at the same time, the DOS application will always take precedence over the Recorder. In other words, rather than run the Recorder macro, Windows will activate the DOS application. However, you can still run the Recorder macro by simply double-clicking on its name in the Recorder window.

ASSIGNING NAMES AND DESCRIPTIONS

You must assign either a name or a shortcut key to a macro in order to run it. However, earlier, you were encouraged to assign both. That way, the name appears next to the shortcut key in the Recorder window to remind you of what the macro does. In a file that contains multiple macros, you'll no doubt find these names indispensable.

You can, however, assign only a name to a macro. To do this, simply type a descriptive name of up to 40 characters in the Record Macro Name text box of the Record Macro dialog box, shown once again in Figure 5-9. When you finish recording the macro, the name you assigned will appear on a line in the Recorder window. If the macro does not have a shortcut key, you can run it by simply highlighting its name, pressing F10 to access Recorder's main menu, and selecting the Macro Run command. Alternatively, you can simply double-click on the macro's name and Recorder will run the macro.

In addition to assigning a name to a macro, you can also provide a description for it. To do this, you use the Description box at the bottom of the Macro Record dialog box in Figure 5-9. You can enter a virtually unlimited amount of text in this box. For example,

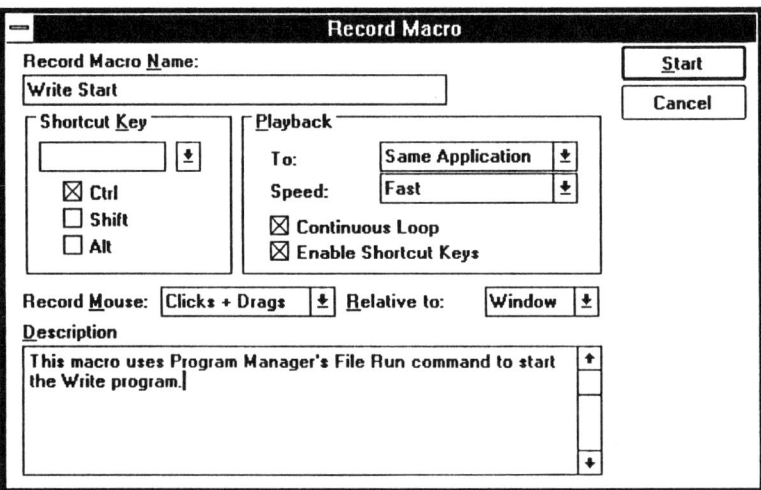

Figure 5-9 The Record Macro dialog box with a sample name and description displayed

you might enter a detailed description of what the macro does, the date it was created, and a list of applications that it uses. To see this description at a later time, and possibly to edit it, you can use the Macro Properties command. This command displays a dialog box that displays the operational properties for a particular macro and allows you to edit some of them. See "Modifying Macro Properties" later in this chapter for more information on how to modify a macro's properties.

DEALING WITH ERRORS

One problem that you must constantly face with Recorder is that it does not allow you to edit a macro. Because Recorder has no scripted command language, the individual events in a macro are all recorded as a single event. If an error is present in a macro, you cannot edit that specific section of the macro. Instead, you must delete the original macro (see the next section) and record it all over again. This can be particularly maddening if you've just recorded a long and complex sequence of commands.

Tip: Changing selected macro properties

Although you cannot edit the actions in a macro after it has been recorded, you can alter selected property settings for the macro. For example, you can change the name or shortcut key you've assigned, as well as certain other operating parameters. To do this, you use the Macro Properties command discussed later in this chapter under "Modifying Macro Properties."

Deleting Macros

To delete a macro, you use the Macro Delete command from Recorder's main menu. In preparation for this command, highlight the name of the macro in the Recorder window either by clicking on it or by using the arrow keys to move to it. When you are ready, select the Macro Delete command. Recorder displays an OK/Cancel message box asking you to confirm the deletion. Select OK to delete the macro or Cancel to abort the delete operation.

Changing the Playback Speed

Sometimes you cannot figure out exactly what is wrong with a macro. That is, it plays back so fast you can't quite see what happened. All you know is that you didn't quite get the results you expected. In these cases, you can slow down the playback speed of the macro so that it executes at the speed at which you recorded it. That way, you can better determine what went wrong.

To change the playback speed for a macro, begin by highlighting the name of the macro in the Recorder window. Then select the Macro Properties command from Recorder's main menu. Recorder displays the Macro Properties dialog box. This dialog box is very similar in appearance to the Record Macro dialog box shown in Figure 5-9. However, it allows you to change some of the properties for the macro you've selected, including its playback speed.

To change the playback speed, open the Speed drop-down list box in the Playback section. Recorder presents a two-option list with Fast (the default) and Recorded Speed. Select Recorded Speed followed by OK to return to the Recorder window. When you run the macro again, it will be played back at the speed at which you recorded it. (You can also select the Recorded Speed option when you record the macro the first time.) See "Modifying Macro Properties" later in this chapter for more information on other playback options that you can change.

MANAGING YOUR MACROS

You can store a virtually unlimited number of macros in the same macro file. As you record each new macro, it is added to the list in the Recorder window. To save that group of macros permanently, simply use the File Save or File Save As command from Recorder's main menu. Either of these commands lets you save the current group of macros to a file with a .REC extension. To use the macros in that file at a later time, simply start the Recorder and use its File Open command to load that particular file. The macros in that file are then available whenever you need them. If you later decide that you no longer need a particular macro, you can use the Macro Delete command, as described in the previous section, to delete that macro from the file.

Organizing Recorder Files

Although you can store a virtually unlimited number of macros in a macro file, you should avoid doing so. As a macro file grows in size, it can become difficult to keep track of what is in the file. Instead, you might consider organizing your macro files by the applications in which those macros execute. For example, if you have recorded a set of macros for Write, you can store these in a separate macro file. That way, you can start the Recorder and load that particular file before starting Write.

Merging Recorder Files

The Recorder also allows you to merge macro files. This feature can be very handy when you develop macros that you want to use in more than one file. To merge two macro files, you use the File Merge command from Recorder's menu. In preparation for this command, use the File Open command to open one of the files you want to merge in the Recorder window. Then, delete any macros in that file that you know are duplicated in the file you are about to merge. When you're ready, select the File Merge command. Recorder displays the dialog box in Figure 5-10. Select the name of the file you want to merge with the current file from the Files list box. Alternatively, you can type its name

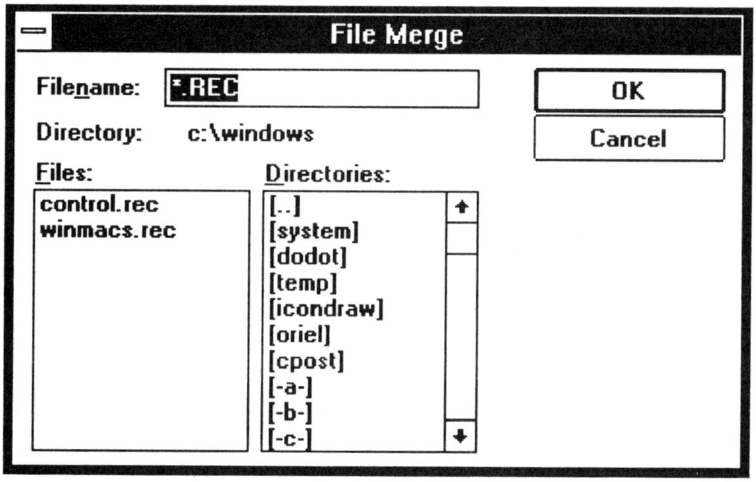

Figure 5-10 Recorder's File Merge dialog box

in the Filename text box. To complete the File Merge command, select OK. Recorder merges the file you selected with the current file.

When you merge two Recorder files, make sure there are no duplicate shortcut keys between the two files. If Recorder detects duplicate shortcut keys in the file you are merging with the current file, it will display an error message informing you that those shortcut keys have been cleared. When you select OK to clear the message box, Recorder will merge the incoming macros by using their names. The shortcut key column will be left blank. If the macro has no name, Recorder will insert a message in the name column of the Recorder window informing you that you must assign a new shortcut key to the macro. You can assign a new shortcut key to a macro by using the Macro Properties command. See "Modifying Macro Properties" later in this chapter for more details on how to use the Macro Properties command to change the shortcut key for a macro or assign a new one.

PROBLEMS WITH RECORDING MOUSE ACTIONS

Up to this point, you have been encouraged to record macros by using the keyboard instead of the mouse. However, the Recorder is also cable of recording mouse actions, including selections (clicks and double-clicks), pointer movement, and clicks and drags.

Be aware, though, that when you record a mouse action, Recorder simply notes the position (coordinates), either relative to the screen or relative to the active window, where the action occurred. Thus, when you click a button, only the position of the mouse pointer is recorded, not what was beneath it. Therefore, if the window in which you recorded the mouse action is a different size, or in a different location, you may not get the results you expect when you run the macro. For example, normally, when you select a main menu option, a pull-down menu of suboptions is presented that pops downward. However, if you move a window down to the very bottom of your screen, the menu of suboptions may pop upward instead of downward, causing your recorded mouse selection to become invalid.

Recording mouse actions can also present a problem if you intend to have your macro used across different computers. To guarantee that your macro will work properly on another computer, that computer should have a video adapter that is identical to the one on your computer. Otherwise, your macro may not perform as intended.

As mentioned, when you record a mouse selection, Recorder simply notes the position in the current window (so many columns across and so many rows down) where the action occurred. This "hit test" is then translated into numeric coordinates. If another computer's video adapter is of a different type (Super VGA versus VGA versus EGA, and so on), or of the same type but from a different manufacturer, it may display a different number of columns and rows. Therefore, it may display Windows objects at different locations on the screen. Thus, when your macro is executed, the coordinates it selects may refer to entirely different objects from those you intended.

Fortunately, however, Windows provides a keystroke alternative for virtually everything you can do with the mouse. Although running Windows with the keyboard may seem awkward at times, you need only do so for a brief period while recording your macros. Further, as a reward for your diligent efforts, you'll have a bullet-proof macro that will perform reliably every time you use it.

Deciding What Mouse Actions to Record

In some cases, though, you may need to record a mouse action. For example, you might want to record a drawing action in Paintbrush. In these cases, the Recorder allows you to choose what types of mouse actions are recorded. To control the types of mouse actions that are recorded in the current macro, you use the Record Mouse drop-down list box in the Record Macro dialog box. This list box appears open in Figure 5-11. It contains the following selections:

- **Clicks and Drags**: Records all keystrokes and all mouse actions while a button is pressed. Pointer movements when a button is not pressed are not recorded. (This is the default setting.)

- **Ignore Mouse**: Only keystrokes are recorded. Mouse actions are ignored. Use this option as a safeguard when you want to be absolutely sure that no mouse actions are recorded.

- **Everything**: All keystrokes and mouse actions are recorded. You may want to use this option in certain applications that respond to mouse movements even when a button has not been pressed. For example, in some applications, you can move the highlight to different menu options simply by moving the mouse. Once an option is highlighted, you can click your mouse button to select it.

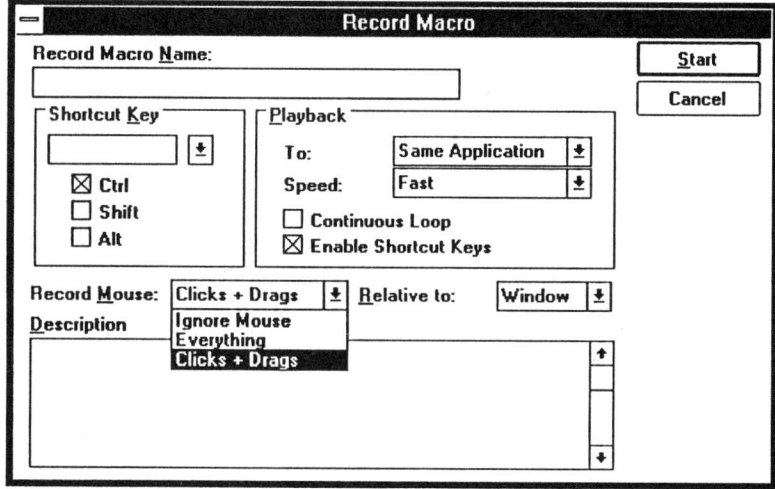

Figure 5-11 Using the Record Mouse drop-down list box to select the type of mouse actions that will be recorded

Note: If you decide to use the Everything option, make sure you press CTRL+BREAK to stop recording, rather than clicking on the Recorder icon. Otherwise, the last recorded action will be the movement of the mouse pointer to the area of the screen previously occupied by the Recorder icon and then clicking on whatever happens to be there at the time.

Deciding Where Mouse Actions Are Recorded

You can also control whether Recorder records mouse movements relative to the current window or relative to the entire screen. By default, Recorder assumes you want to record mouse actions relative to the current window. However, at times you may want to record mouse movements relative to the entire screen. For example, you might be recording a macro in a full-screen application. As a general rule, though, mouse actions recorded relative to the current window are more reliable, especially when the window is of a fixed size, such as a dialog box.

To select where mouse actions are recorded, you use the Relative to drop-down the list box shown open in Figure 5-12. You can choose from either Screen or Window. The Recorder will then use the setting you select both for recording the macro as well as playing it back. Unfortunately, you cannot change this setting once the macro has been recorded.

182   *Windows 3 Power Tools*

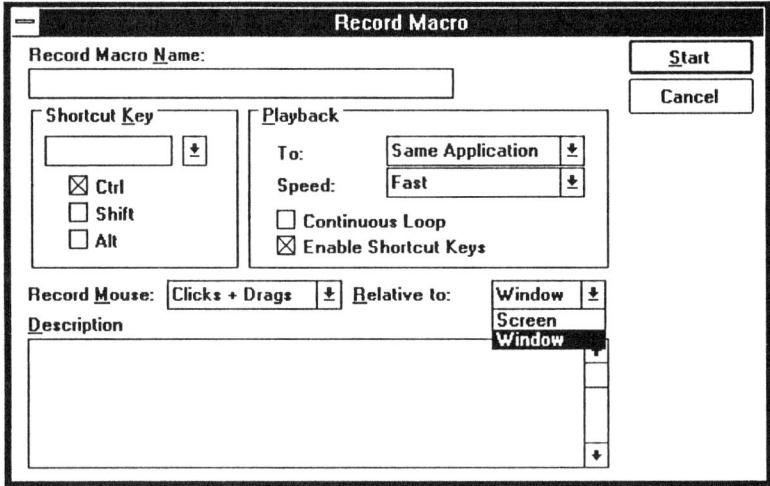

Figure 5-12   **The Record Macro dialog box with the Relative to box opened**

> *Tip: Selecting icons with the mouse*
>
> If you do record a macro that uses mouse actions to select icons for open applications, position those icons manually before you record or run the macro. That way, if you open the application associated with an icon and then minimize it, Windows will put that icon back in its original position. Otherwise, Windows may change the position of the icon when you minimize the window, making your macro unreliable.

STOPPING A MACRO

You can stop a macro from executing at any time by pressing CTRL+BREAK. The Recorder will complete the most recent macro instruction and then display a message box that says "Macro playback aborted". When you select OK or press ENTER to clear this message box, you will be returned to the window most recently activated by the interrupted macro.

You can also disable the CTRL+BREAK key. In fact, you may prefer this—particularly if you've set up a multiple-stage macro in which one stage must be completed before the next begins. To disable the CTRL+BREAK key, select the Options Control+Break Checking command from Recorder's menu. This removes the check mark next to the command name and disables the CTRL+BREAK key for the current Recorder session. The next time you start Recorder, however, it will once again honor the CTRL+BREAK key sequence.

Note: You can also use the Recorder to create a continuously running demo program (see "Creating Continuous-Loop Macros for Demonstrations" later in this chapter for more details). When you disable CTRL+BREAK checking before starting such a demo, the only way to stop it is to reboot the computer.

PAUSING AND RESUMING RECORDING

There may be times when you want to pause recording temporarily and then resume recording the same macro at a later time. For example, imagine you are in the middle of recording an extensive macro and the phone rings. To stop recording, simply press CTRL+BREAK. Recording is temporarily suspended and the Recorder dialog box shown earlier in Figure 5-3 is then displayed on your screen. Your hands are now free to perform other tasks. To resume recording, select the Resume Recording option button from the Recorder dialog box and then select OK or press ENTER. The Recorder will resume recording the same macro.

DECIDING WHERE A MACRO PLAYS BACK

When you record a macro, the Recorder assumes that you want to play that macro back only in the application in which you recorded it. If you try to run it anywhere else, Recorder issues an error message. However, you can also create a macro that will play back from within any application. The choice you make comes down to a matter of common sense. For example, a command macro you create in Write may not be at all appropriate in another application whose menu selections are different. On the other hand, Windows also offers applications such as Print Manager or File Manager that you can access from within any application.

To specify where a macro plays back, you use the To drop-down list box from the Playback area of the Record Macro dialog box shown in Figure 5-13. When you open this box, Recorder presents two options for your selection, Same Application and Any Application. The Same Application option is the default and confines playback to the application in which the macro is subsequently recorded. The Any Application option allows the macro to be played back from (you guessed it . . .) any application.

There are a number of issues to consider when you create an any-application macro versus an application-specific macro. The sections that follow explore these issues in detail.

Application-Specific Macros

As you know, when you record an application-specific macro, you must set up the environment for that macro both before you record it and when you play it back. For example, if you record a macro in Write, the Write window must be open, *and active*, when you play the macro back. Otherwise, Recorder issues the "Playback window does not exist" error message.

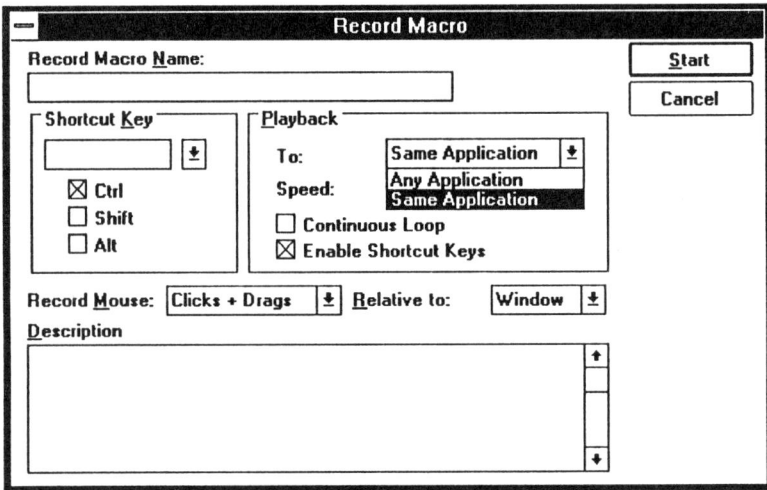

Figure 5-13 Use the Playback To box to select where a macro is played back

If you record an application-specific macro, and later on you change your mind, you can always modify this Playback setting. To do this, you use the Macro Properties command. See "Modifying Macro Properties" later in this chapter for more details on this command.

Any-Application Macros

You must also prepare the environment in advance for an any-application macro. Otherwise, you may not get the results you expect. For example, imagine you want to create a macro that will disable the Print Manager from within any application. (This often allows you to regain the memory needed to print a large file.) That macro would open the Control Panel, select the Printer icon, disable Print Manager, close the Control Panel, and return to your application. Sounds simple enough. Yet, there are a multitude of issues to consider when recording a macro of this kind.

When you select Any Application from the Playback To drop-down list box, the macro you subsequently record is licensed to run anywhere. Therefore, if for some reason the macro were to end up running in the wrong window, it would keep entering the keystrokes you've recorded, regardless of whether they are appropriate or not. The results might surprise you, or, worse, result in a loss of data. Therefore, it is to your advantage to make absolutely sure that the right conditions are present before you run the macro or that the right conditions are set up by the macro itself.

One of your main allies in creating any-application macros is Task List, which allows you to switch to applications that are already open on the desktop. To access Task List, simply press CTRL+ESC. The Task List window in Figure 5-14 then appears on your

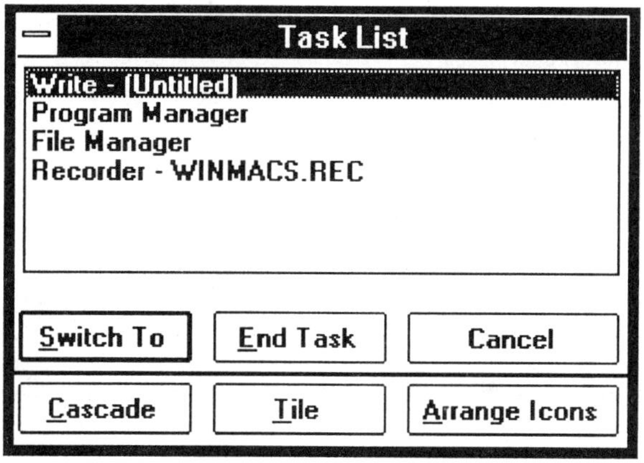

Figure 5-14 The Task List window

screen. The names of various applications that are open on the desktop appear in this window. The order of the names is determined by the order in which the applications were activated. The last application activated appears at the top of the list, the one before that is second in the list, and so on. We'll make use of this ordered listing later on. However, for now, be aware that this listing of window names is constantly subject to change.

To have Task List switch the focus to a particular application by using the keyboard, you have two choices. On the one hand, you can use the arrow keys to move to an application name and press ENTER. Or, you can select an application and press ALT+S to select the Switch command button. Windows will then activate and display the window you selected. From a macro recording standpoint, however, these methods will not always allow you to reliably select a particular window, unless you know the order in which the windows were activated (stacked on the desktop).

A second method for selecting a particular window in Task List is to type the first letter of its name and press ENTER. For example, with the list in Figure 5-14, typing **f** and pressing ENTER will activate File Manager. However, from a recording standpoint, if two open window names begin with same first letter, for example **Program Manager** and **Paintbrush**, this method is not always reliable either. But if the first letter of an application's name is unique among open Windows applications, as is the case with File Manager, this method can return reliable results.

A second ally for the any-application macro programmer is the File Manager. This is true for two reasons. On the one hand, its name is unique among the applications that come with Windows so that you can reliably switch to it by using Task List. On the other hand, it gives you direct access to the File Run command, which allows you to run specific applications by their filenames. Therefore, as long as the File Manager is open, you can reliably switch to it by using Task List and run virtually any application you want.

Before going any further, let's take a moment to record the macro referenced at the beginning of this section which disables the Print Manager. This will serve to illustrate the points made thus far in this section. To record this macro, perform the following steps:

1. Make sure the File Manager is active, either as a window or an icon.
2. Make sure the Recorder is open, either as a window or an icon.
3. Start another application of your choice, for example Write.
4. Press CTRL+ESC to access Task List, type **R** for Recorder and press ENTER. The Recorder window is now active.
5. Select the Macro Record command. The Record Macro dialog box is displayed on your screen.
6. Assign a name and shortcut key. For example, in the Record Macro Name text box type **Disable Print Manager** and in the Shortcut Key drop-down list box type **D**.
7. Open the To drop-down list box in the Payback section and select Any Application.
8. Select the Start button to begin recording. The Recorder is minimized to an icon and you are returned to the most recently activated window, in this case Write.
9. Press CTRL+ESC. Windows displays the Task List.
10. Type **f** to select File Manager and press ENTER. The File Manager window is now displayed.
11. Press F10 and select the File Run command. The File Run dialog box is displayed.
12. Type **CONTROL** and press ENTER. The Control Panel is displayed.
13. Press ↓ to move to the Printer icon and press ENTER. The Printers dialog box is displayed.
14. Press TAB twice followed by the space bar. This action disables the Print Manager.
15. Press ENTER to save the setting and return to the Control Panel window.
16. Press ALT+F4 to close the Control Panel window.
17. Press CTRL+ESC to open Task List. Notice that the list of window names begins with File Manager followed by Write (untitled). (The Program Manager was removed from the top of the list, because the Control Panel was closed in the previous step.)
18. Press ↓ once to move to Write (untitled) and press ENTER.
19. Press CTRL+BREAK to stop recording. The Recorder dialog box is displayed.
20. Select Save Macro and then select OK. The macro is now saved temporarily and you are returned to the Write window.

Test the Macro by pressing CTRL+D. The macro executes and the Print Manager is re-enabled. You are then returned to Write. If you want, you can close Write, open another Windows application, for example Paintbrush, and try it there. When you are finished testing, use the Task List, as described in step 4, to return to the Recorder, and save the macro to disk in the usual way.

OK, so what, if anything, did we learn? For one thing, you can execute this macro from any application. However, the File Manager must be open for this macro to work. In fact, don't attempt to run this macro unless the File Manager is open. Otherwise, you may not get the results you expect. In fact, the Recorder may well play back keystrokes you've recorded in the currently active application and attempt to remove that application from the desktop.

Step 10 of the above example illustrates another point made earlier in this section. In this step, the Task List is activated using CTRL+ESC, and the f key is pressed to activate File Manager by using the first letter of its name. Since the first letter of File Manager's name is unique among the open applications, this method should work every time. However, if you are running another DOS or Windows application whose name begins with *F*, like Framework, this method may break down. For instance, imagine File Manager is at the top of the Task List window, and Framework is at the bottom. When your macro types the f key, Windows will jump past File Manager and select Framework.

Steps 11 and 12 of the above example also illustrate the use of File Manager's File Run command to start a specific application, in this case CONTROL.EXE. This method allows you to select and run a specific application from among all the applications Windows has to offer. For your convenience, Table 5-2 shows a list of applications that come with Windows.

Note: As you know, the File Run command is also available from the Program Manager menu. However, because the first letter of Program Manager's name is not unique among other available Windows applications, its name cannot be reliably selected by using Task List during a macro.

The File Run method for launching Windows applications also has its share of drawbacks. For example, imagine the application you are attempting to run is already open. If this application is one of those included in Program Manager's Main group window (Control Panel, File Manager, Print Manager, and so on), Windows will either activate the current copy of the application, issue an error message, or do nothing at all. On the other hand, with some of the applications in the Accessories window, such as Notepad, Write, or Paintbrush, Windows will open a second copy of the application. This may, or may not, be what you want. Unfortunately, Recorder does not allow you to check if a specific application window is already open.

Finally, the macro in the above example takes advantage of the order of window names in the Task List window. As mentioned, the order of these names is determined by the order in which the applications were activated. The last application activated appears at the top of the list, the one before that is second in the list, and so on. In this case, you know the order of the names at the top of the list, because you put them there with your macro. Therefore, in steps 17 and 18 of the above example, you activated the Task List, pressed ↓ once, and then pressed ENTER to return to the original application from which the macro was started.

Filename	Application	Filename	Application
CALC.EXE	Calculator	RECORDER.EXE	Recorder
CALENDAR.EXE	Calendar	REVERSI.EXE	Reversi
CARDFILE.EXE	Cardfile	SETUP.EXE	Setup
CLIPBRD.EXE	Clipboard	SOL.EXE	Solitaire
CLOCK.EXE	Clock	SYSEDIT.EXE	System Editor
CONTROL.EXE	Control Panel	SWAPFILE.EXE	Swapfile
MSDOS.EXE	MS DOS Executive	TASKMAN.EXE	Task List
NOTEPAD.EXE	Notepad	TERMINAL.EXE	Terminal
PBRUSH.EXE	Paint Brush	WIN.COM	Windows 3.0
PIFEDIT.EXE	PIF Editor	WINFILE.EXE	File Manager
PRINTMAN.EXE	Print Manager	WINHELP.EXE	Windows Help
PROGMAN.EXE	Program Manager	WRITE.EXE	Write

Table 5-2 Windows Executable Files

COMBINING MACROS

You can also combine up to five macros into a single macro. When you combine macros, they are executed one right after the other in the order in which you combine them. For example, imagine you want to combine the CTRL+W, CTRL+F, and CTRL+S example macros discussed at the beginning of this chapter. That way, the Write accessory program will be loaded, a custom footer will be inserted into the new document, and a closing salutation will be typed automatically, all at the touch of a single shortcut key.

To combine two or more macros, those macros must be included in the same macro file. Further, that file must be open in the Recorder window. For example, the CTRL+W, CTRL+F, and CTRL+S example macros are all stored in the WINMACS.REC file. To combine these macros, open the Recorder window and use the File Open command to load the WINMACS.REC file. Then, select Macro Record to display the Record Macro dialog box. In the Record Macro Name text box, type a name—for example, **Write Setup**. In the Shortcut Key text box type the letter you want to use to start the macro—for example **A**. Also, make sure the Ctrl check box is selected and that the Alt and Shift check boxes are not. Then, select the Start button to begin recording. The Recorder window is minimized to an icon and the Program Manager window is in full view.

To record the macro, simply press CTRL+W followed by CTRL+F followed by CTRL+S. As you press these keys, Recorder performs the macros assigned to them. When you're done, press CTRL+BREAK to stop recording. The Recorder dialog box is displayed on your screen. Select Save Macro and then select OK. Activate the Recorder window and use the File Save command to save the CTRL+A macro along with the rest of the macros in the WINMACS.REC file. When you're done, minimize the Recorder to an icon.

To test the macro, begin by closing the Write window. Then, type **CTRL+A**. The macro you've just recorded is executed. Write is opened on the desktop, a custom footer is inserted into the new document, and a closing salutation is typed as you watch.

Combining macros can be useful when you are recording a particularly complex operation. That way, you can record individual sections of the macro, testing each of them as you go. Once you're sure the individual sections are working properly, you can combine them into a single macro.

Setting Up for Combining Macros

When you combine macros, make sure that the environment for each macro is set up before you run the macro. Otherwise, Recorder will display an error message. For instance, in the above example, the Write window is opened first with the CTRL+W macro prior to running the CTRL+F and CTRL+S macros to insert a footer and a closing salutation. If you were to run either the CTRL+F or CTRL+S macros before the CTRL+W macro, Recorder would display an error message box that says "Playback window does not exist."

Changing Combined Macros

You can change combined macros rather easily. When you record a combined macro, the Recorder captures only the shortcut keys you used to execute each individual macro (not the actions associated with each macro). Therefore, to change a combined macro, you need only change the individual macros that make up the combined macro.

Creating a Macro That Cannot Combine Other Macros

You can also disable combining when you create a macro. To do this, you must turn off the Enable Shortcut Keys check box located in the Playback section of the Record Macro dialog box. Once this is done, the CTRL, ALT, and SHIFT shortcut keys associated with the current Recorder file are ignored during macro recording. However, you can still use the CTRL, ALT, and SHIFT keys either in Windows itself or in Windows applications. The actions associated with these keys will be recorded in your macro.

MODIFYING MACRO PROPERTIES

The Recorder's Macro Properties command allows you to change selected settings for a macro after it has been recorded. In preparation for this command, first use the File Open command to load the file that contains the macro whose properties you want to change. Then, make sure that the macro is highlighted. Finally, select the Macro Properties command. Recorder displays the dialog box in Figure 5-15, which shows the current property settings for the macro you have selected. You can use this dialog box to alter any of the following settings:

- The name.
- The description.
- The shortcut key assignment.
- Where the macro plays back. (That is, whether it plays back in the application in which it was recorded or in any application.)
- The playback speed (fast versus recorded speed).
- Whether the macro plays back a single time or continuously.
- Whether the macro can contain other shortcut keys.

After you make your settings changes, select OK to return to the Recorder window; then save the file containing the macro so that your changes are saved permanently.

You cannot change mouse-related settings for a macro with the Macro Properties command. For example, notice in the middle of the dialog box in Figure 5-15 that the Record Mouse and Relative to boxes do not appear. Instead, these are replaced with textual information showing the settings used to record the macro. You cannot change this text. Thus, you cannot change what mouse actions are used by the macro or whether those actions are performed relative to the entire screen or to the current window. However, you are given information about the resolution of the video card present when the macro was recorded. Therefore, if you got this macro from someone else, you could compare this resolution data to that of your own video card to determine if the macro has a chance of working on your machine.

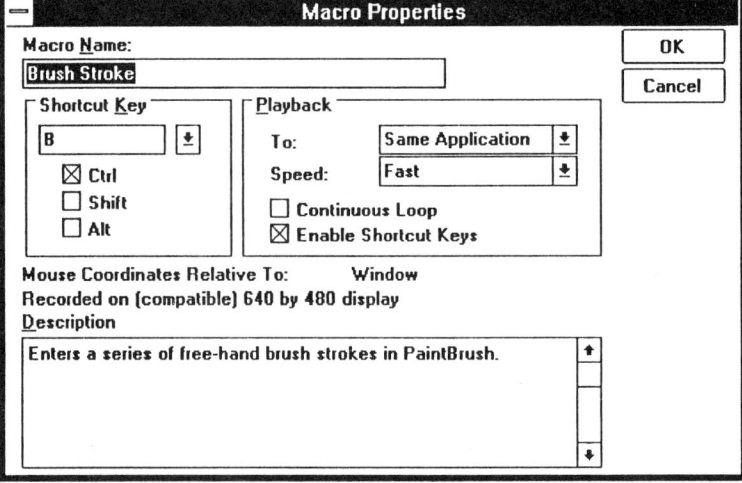

Figure 5-15 The Macro Properties dialog box

EVEN MORE OPTIONS

You can use Recorder's Options menu to control various aspects of Recorder's operation, as well as its default record and play back settings. For example, the Options Control+Break Checking command discussed earlier allows you to disable the CTRL+BREAK key during a macro. Therefore, a user cannot press CTRL+BREAK to stop one of your macros. However, you can also use the Options menu to disable Recorder temporarily, control whether it is minimized on use, and to change certain default settings for all Recorder sessions.

Disabling Recorder Temporarily

As mentioned, if the current Recorder file contains the same shortcut key as another open application, Windows will always run Recorder's macro. The other application's shortcut key will be ignored. However, you can avoid these conflicts by temporarily disabling Recorder, rather than closing it. To do this, you use Recorder's Options Shortcut Keys command. Selecting this command simply removes the checkmark next to the command name, thereby disabling Recorder's ability to detect shortcut keys. To turn shortcut key detection back on, select the Options Shortcut Keys command a second time.

The Minimize on Use Option

Normally, when you start recording a macro, the Recorder window is minimized to an icon located at the lower left portion of your screen. However, if you want the Recorder window to remain displayed during recording, select the Options Minimize on Use command to remove the checkmark next to the command name. The next time you record a macro, the Recorder window will remain open. Select this command again to return to the default setting of minimizing the recorder window during recording. The Options Minimize on Use command applies only to the current Windows session.

Setting Recorder Defaults

You can also control many of the default settings that Recorder uses to record your macros. To do this, select the Options Preferences command from Recorder's menu. When you select this command, Recorder displays the dialog box in Figure 5-16. This dialog box contains four drop-down list boxes that let you change the following default settings:

- The Playback To setting: Select Same Application to limit playback to the application in which the macro was recorded or select Any Application to play the macro back in any application.

- The Playback Speed setting: You can choose from Fast (the default) to play back the macro at full speed or you can choose Recorded Speed to have the macro play back at the speed at which you recorded it.

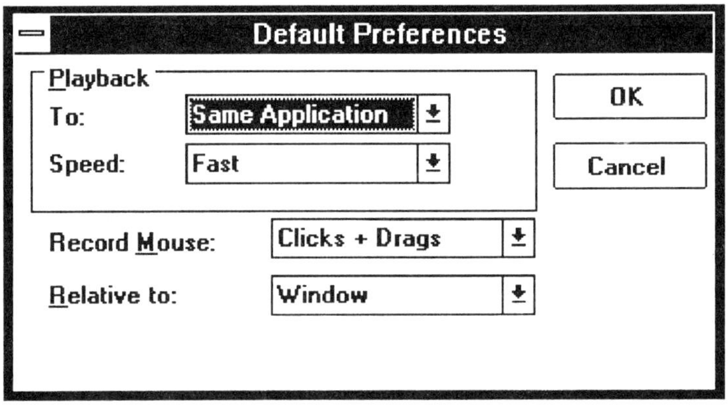

Figure 5-16 The Options Preferences dialog box

- Record Mouse settings: You can choose from Clicks+Drags, Everything, or Ignore Mouse. These options determine what mouse actions, if any, are recorded and are explained in detail earlier in this chapter under "Deciding What Mouse Actions to Record."

- Relative To settings: You can choose from Window (the default) or Screen. If you select Window, mouse actions are recorded relative to the current window. On the other hand, if you select Screen, mouse actions will be recorded relative to the entire screen. This applies to both recording and playback.

When you select OK to leave the Options Preferences dialog box, Windows saves the settings changes you've just made for both the current session as well as future Recorder sessions.

STARTING AN APPLICATION IN A SPECIFIC DIRECTORY

You can also create a macro that starts a given application and references a specific directory for that application's use. Normally, when you run an accessory program such as Write, Paintbrush, or Note, the default working directory for that application is your Windows program directory. Therefore, when you use the File Open or File Save command for the application, you get to look at your Windows program files. If you store the working files for that application in another directory, you have to make a concerted effort to reference that directory for the current Save or Open command. To avoid all this bother, you can create a macro that opens a specific application and references a specific directory for that application.

To control where an application starts up, you can use the File Run command from either File Manager or Program Manager. When you select this command, Windows

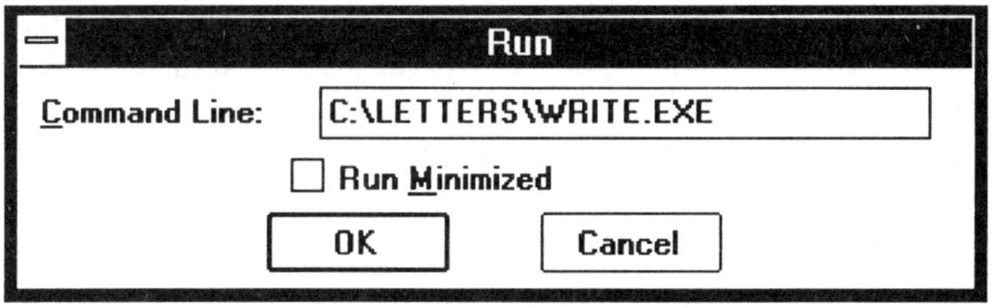

Figure 5-17 The File Run dialog box

displays the File Run dialog box shown once again in Figure 5-17. In the Command Line text box, enter a command line that takes the following form:

```
Drive:\Directory\...\Application-filename
```

For example, to start Write with your C:\LETTERS directory as the default working directory, you would enter:

```
C:\LETTERS\WRITE.EXE
```

For this command line to work, though, the application program must be either in the current directory or in a directory that is included in the PATH statement in your AUTOEXEC.BAT file. Otherwise, Windows won't be able to find the application and will issue an error message. To complete the command, press ENTER.

To record the actions just described in a macro, begin by making sure the Program Manager window is the only window displayed on your screen. Then open the Recorder window and select the Macro Record command to display the Record Macro dialog box. Enter a name and shortcut key for the macro and select Any Application from the Playback To drop-down list box. Finally, select the Start button to begin recording.

Now that Recorder is ready to capture your keystrokes, perform the actions previously described. That is, use Program Manager's File Run command to run the application file of your choice preceded by the appropriate directory name. When the application window is displayed, press CTRL+BREAK to stop recording. Then save the macro in the usual way.

CONTINUOUS-LOOP MACROS

You can also create continuous-loop macros for demonstrations. Continuous-loop macros are performed again and again until you press CTRL+BREAK to stop them. You can also disable CTRL+BREAK checking for continuous-loop macros; in this case, the only way to stop the demo is to reboot the computer. A continuous-loop macro might be useful when you want to demonstrate one of your own macro applications or when you want to teach someone else how to use Windows.

To create a continuous-loop macro, you turn on the Continuous-Loop check box in the Playback section of the Record Macro dialog box. The macro you subsequently record will be a continuous-loop macro.

A Continuous-Loop Example

The following example will create a continuous-loop macro that uses Paintbrush to display four of the bitmap images that come with your copy of Windows. Although this macro is not terribly useful, it is pretty and will show you how to create a continuous-loop macro.

To prepare the environment for this macro, begin by opening Paintbrush; then open the Recorder, if you haven't already. Next, minimize the Program Manager to an icon. Finally, activate the Recorder by clicking on its window or by using Task List to switch to it. When you're ready, perform the following steps:

1. Select Macro Record to display the Record Macro dialog box.

2. Assign the name and shortcut key of your choice. For example, in the Record Macro Name text box, you might enter **Paintbrush Display** and in the Shortcut Key text box, you might enter **P**. That way, you can start this macro by pressing CTRL+P.

3. Open the Speed drop-down list box in the Playback section and select Recorded Speed. The macro will then play back at the speed at which it was recorded, allowing the viewer to see the various bit maps you're about to display.

4. Select the Continuous Loop check box in the Playback section, so that the macro will be a continuous-loop macro.

5. Select Start to begin recording. The Paintbrush window is activated automatically.

6. Select the File Open command, type **PAPER**, and press ENTER. The PAPER.BMP bitmap is loaded into the Paintbrush window.

7. Repeat step 6 using the PARTY.BMP, RIBBONS.BMP, and CHESS.BMP files. Keep in mind that the macro will be played back at recorded speed. Therefore, don't dally about. Keep those bitmaps coming.

8. When the last bit map (CHESS.BMP) is loaded, press CTRL+BREAK to stop recording. The Record dialog box is then displayed.

9. Select Save Macro to save the macro.

10. Return to the Recorder window and use the File Save command to save the macro permanently.

Test the macro by pressing CTRL+P. The Paintbrush window is activated and the slide show begins. You can stop the macro whenever you want by pressing CTRL+BREAK.

Setting the playback speed to recorded speed can be important in continuous-loop macros. It gives Windows the time it needs to complete one operation before starting the next. In addition, it gives the viewer of the demonstration the time needed to actually see what is going on.

Running a Nonstop Demo

As mentioned, you can also run a nonstop demo by disabling CTRL+BREAK checking. That way, a continuous-loop macro cannot be stopped, except by rebooting the computer. Before you do this, however, make sure you've saved your work in any other applications that may be open on the desktop. Then activate the Recorder window and select the Options Control+Break Checking command. The CTRL+BREAK key sequence is now disabled from a Recorder standpoint. When you're ready, press the shortcut key that starts the continuous loop macro. The macro will now run continuously.

RUNNING A MACRO ON START-UP

You can also run a particular macro on Windows start-up. To do this, you must use some special command line parameters when you start windows from the DOS prompt. Further, the macro you elect to run must also have some special features.

Start-up Macro Considerations

When you run the Recorder on Windows start-up, the Program Manager is automatically minimized to an icon. Therefore, for a startup macro to be able to do anything, its first official act must be to restore the Program Manager. To do this, the macro must press CTRL+ESC to activate the Task List, type **P** to select Program Manager, and then press the ENTER key to restore Program Manager. The rest of the macro can then ensue.

Note: Normally, the Options Minimize on Use command from Program Manager's menu gives you control over whether Program Manager is minimized when another application runs. However, this command has no effect when you run an application on Windows start-up.

Entering the Command Line

As mentioned, to run a macro on Windows start-up, you must use special parameters in your DOS command line. This command line takes the following form:

```
WIN [Application Name] -h[Shortcut key] [Filename]
```

where WIN starts windows, [Application Name] is the executable filename of Recorder, -h[Shortcut Key] identifies the macro you want to run, and [Filename] is the name of the file that contains that macro. For example, to run the CTRL+A macro in the WINMACS.REC file on start up, you might use the following command line.

```
win recorder -h^a winmacs.rec
```

This command line breaks down as follows:

- win: Starts Windows.
- recorder: Refers to the RECORDER.EXE file.
- -h^a: The -h signifies a shortcut key and ^a is the equivalent of CTRL+A. Make sure you type a caret (^) symbol here followed by the letter "a". (Pressing CTRL+A produces what looks like ^a, but Windows won't interpret it properly.)
- winmacs.rec: Refers to the WINMACS.REC file.

> *Tip: Put your Windows start-up command line in a .BAT file*
>
> Since Windows start-up command lines can be rather long and drawn out, typing them at the DOS prompt can be somewhat inconvenient. Therefore, you may want to consider placing these command lines in .BAT files. That way, you can execute them with fewer keystrokes.

LOADING YOUR MACROS ON START-UP

Perhaps the best way, though, to have your macros available on Windows start-up is to use the load= statement in the WIN.INI file. In fact, this choice is recommended above all others. The load= statement allows you to load a given application, and open a specific file in its window. Therefore, you might use this statement to load Recorder and open a specific macro file. Although you cannot use this method to run a specific macro on Windows start-up, your macros will always be there whenever you need them.

When you start Windows, the application you specify through the load= statement is opened in the background. Further, any file you specify as part of the load= statement is loaded into that application's window. However, the Program Manager window remains the active window. The application you opened with the load= statement remains inactive in the background, awaiting your use. Thus, the load= statement lets you automatically set up the Recorder at the start of a Windows session. In addition, the first macro you run has the effect of minimizing the Recorder window to an icon, lending a further air of polish to this setup.

To modify the load= statement in your WIN.INI file, you can use the SYSEDIT.EXE program. This program is located in your Windows System directory, usually C:\WINDOWS\SYSTEM. In fact, you may have already assigned this program to an icon. If you have, double-click on that icon now. If not, select Program Manager's File Run command, type **C:\WINDOWS\SYSTEM\SYSEDIT**, and press ENTER. The SysEdit Window in Figure 5-18 appears on your screen. Click on the window entitled WIN.INI. The load= statement should appear near the top of this file. When you find it, click on it. A blinking cursor should now appear in the file. Edit the load= statement to equal the RECORDER.EXE filename followed by a space and the filename of your most commonly

Recorder Techniques 197

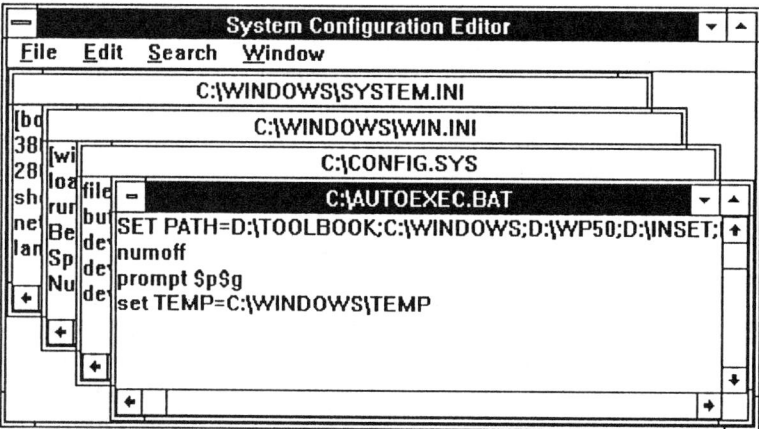

Figure 5-18 The SysEdit window

used macro file. For example, if you frequently use the WINMACS.REC macro file, you might set up the following load= statement:

```
load=RECORDER.EXE WINMACS.REC
```

When you complete editing, select the File Save command to save your changes. Then close the SysEdit window. The next time you start Windows, the Recorder will be loaded automatically and placed in the background, and the file you specified will be opened in its window.

Note: For a complete discussion of how you can use the WIN.INI file to customize your system, see Chapter 12, "Customizing Your .INI Files."

ASSIGNING AN ICON TO A MACRO

You can also assign an icon to a macro. This method of running a macro is more in keeping with the visual interface offered by Windows. In addition, since icons normally have capsule descriptions that describe what the icon does, you don't have to memorize as many shortcut keys. In fact, if you are preparing macros for use by others, you may want to consider using icons.

There is a minor problem associated with running a macro from an icon, though. When you run a macro in this way, you can only run a single macro. You must then close the Recorder before you can run another macro by using an icon. (See the next section entitled "Closing the Recorder with a Macro" for a solution to this problem.)

However, for now, imagine you want to attach the CTRL+A macro to an icon. As you may recall, this macro was created earlier in this chapter under "Combining Macros." It starts Write, inserts a custom footer into the new document, and types a closing salutation. This macro should be located in your WINMACS.REC file.

To attach the CTRL+A macro to an icon, begin selecting the group window where you want to locate the icon. Next, select the File New command from Program Manager's menu. Windows displays the New Program Object dialog box. Make sure the Program Item radio button is turned on and then select OK. Windows displays the Program Item Properties dialog box. In the Description text box, type a description, for example **Write Setup**. Press TAB to move to the Command Line text box and type the command line you'll use to run the CTRL+A macro, for example **WINMACS.REC -h^A**. (We'll talk more about this command line in a moment.) Next, select the Change Icon command button. Windows displays the Select Icon Dialog box. Click on the View Next command button until you find an icon you like. Then, select OK to return to the Program Item Properties dialog box. Finally, select OK again to create the icon. Windows creates the icon in the group window you selected. You can now run the CTRL+A macro by double-clicking on this icon.

Notice that the command line you just entered takes a slightly different form than that used earlier under "Running a Macro On Start-up." In that section, the command line format took the following form:

```
WIN RECORDER.EXE -h^a WINMACS.REC
```

where WIN started windows, RECORDER.EXE ran the recorder, -h^a selected the CTRL+A shortcut key, and WINMACS.REC is the file that contains the CTRL+A shortcut key. Here, however, the command line is abbreviated to read simply:

```
WINMACS.REC -h^a
```

When you run a macro from within Windows by using a command line, you need only provide the .REC filename that contains that macro and its shortcut key. Windows will automatically start the Recorder by association. That is, when Windows encounters the .REC file extension, it assumes you want to run the application associated with that extension and therefore starts Recorder. For information on how to create associations between files and applications, see Chapter 3, "File Manager Techniques." For additional information on this topic, see Chapter 12, "Customizing Your .INI Files." This chapter shows you how to create an association between an application and its data file extension by modifying the [Extension] section of the WIN.INI file.

CLOSING THE RECORDER WITH A MACRO

As mentioned, a minor drawback is associated with attaching macros to icons. That is, when you run a macro from within Windows by using an icon, you can only run one macro. After that macro executes, the Recorder will remain open. The second time you double-click on the icon to run the macro, Windows will activate the Recorder and will even load the appropriate macro file, but it will not run the macro. This is simply a glitch with the Recorder. You can overcome this glitch, though, by creating a macro that closes the Recorder itself.

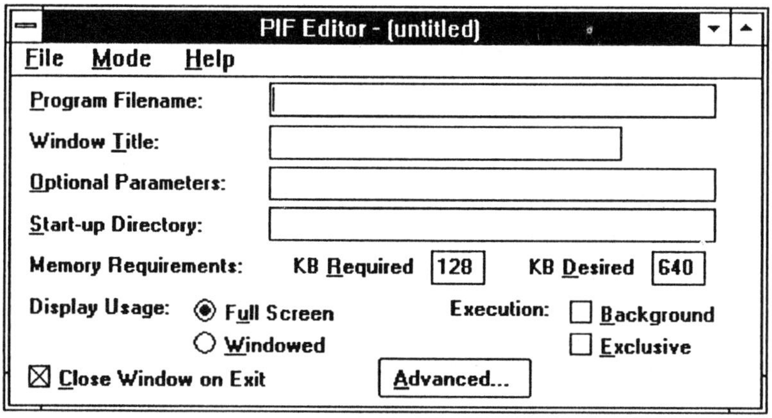

Figure 5-19 The PIF Editor window

Creating a macro that closes the Recorder will take a bit of extra work on your behalf, but it is well worth the effort. The best way to close the Recorder with a macro is by using the Task List to display the names of open windows. Once these names are displayed, you can highlight the Recorder window name by pressing **r** (the first letter of Recorder's name) and then pressing ALT+E to select the End Task command button. This action closes the window you've selected. The problem you run into, however, is that you cannot close the Recorder itself. If you do, you won't be able to save the macro you've just recorded. Therefore, you'll need to set up a "dummy" application whose window name begins with the letter *r*, and close that window instead. That way, you can save your macro. When you later run the macro without the dummy application present, it will perform its prescribed function of closing the Recorder.

To set up a dummy application, you'll need to use the PIF editor to create a .PIF file for a DOS application. To begin, double-click on the PIF Editor icon in the Accessories group window. The PIF Editor window in Figure 5-19 now appears on your screen. In the Program Filename text box, type **C:\COMMAND.COM**. Press TAB to move to the Window Title text box and type **RCOM**. Then, select the File Save As command from PIF Editor's menu. PIF Editor displays the File Save dialog box and suggests a name of COMMAND.PIF. Ignore this name and type **RCOM.PIF** instead, then select OK to save the file.

Now that you've set up the dummy application, you're ready to record the macro. To prepare the environment for recording, close everything except Program Manager. When you're ready, perform the following steps:

1. Select the File Run command from Program Manager's menu. Windows displays the File Run dialog box.

2. Type **C:\RCOM.PIF** and press ENTER. Windows launches a copy of COMMAND.COM and shows you the C> DOS prompt.

3. Press ALT+ESC. You are returned to Windows, and the RCOM (DOS) icon appears at the lower left of your screen.

4. Start the Recorder and use the File Open command to load the macro file of your choice. For example, you might load WINMACS.REC.

5. Select the Macro Record command to display the Record Macro dialog box.

6. In the Record Macro Name text box, type **Close Recorder**.

7. In the Shortcut Key text box, type **Z**.

8. Open the To drop-down list box in the Play back section and select Any Application.

9. Select the Start button to begin recording. You are returned to the Program Manager.

10. Press CTRL+ESC to display the Task List. The order of window names appears as follows: Program Manager, RCOM, and Recorder.

11. Type **R**. The Task List highlight jumps to RCOM.

12. Press ALT+E to select the End Task button. Windows displays the message "Application still active; choose OK to end it." Do *not* select OK.

13. Press CTRL+BREAK to stop recording. Windows displays the Record dialog box.

14. Select Save Macro followed by OK. The Recorder dialog box is cleared and the message box is re-displayed.

15. Select OK to clear the message box, and then close the RCOM program.

16. Activate the Recorder and use the File Save command to save your new macro.

When you've created this macro, you can combine it with your other macros. (See "Combining Macros" earlier in this chapter for information on how you can combine two or more macros into a single macro.) However, make sure you have the dummy program open when you are recording. Otherwise, you'll end up closing Recorder and you won't be able to save the macro.

Note: You'll also find the technique just described to be invaluable for use with the Oriel software that comes with this book. The Oriel command language includes a RUN command that lets you run macros as well as other applications from within your programs. However, once you run one macro, you cannot run another unless you close the Recorder or the macro itself closes the Recorder.

SUPPLEMENTING THE RECORDER WITH DOS .BAT FILES

Many people use DOS .BAT files to automate routine file management chores, start applications with specific parameters, and so forth. In fact, if you've spent any time creating DOS .BAT files, you know that the dozen or so commands in the DOS batch language can give you a surprising degree of control over your system. You should be aware that you can run batch files without having to leave Windows. In addition, if you want, you can link your DOS .BAT files to macros.

You can run a DOS .BAT from within Windows by using any one of several techniques. For example, you can use the File Run command from either Program Manager or from File Manager to run a .BAT file. When you run a .BAT file in this way, Windows will disappear from your screen temporarily while the .BAT file executes. When the .BAT file is finished running, you are automatically returned to the Windows environment.

You can easily use the Recorder to record the procedure just described and save it to a macro file. Simply open the Recorder and use the Macro Record command. Recorder displays the Record Macro dialog box. Assign a name and shortcut key in the usual way, and select the Start command button to begin recording. Then, use Program Manager's File Run command to run the .BAT file of your choice. However, when you press ENTER after the File Run command to execute the .BAT file, Recorder will suspend further recording until you are returned to Windows. At that point you can either use the File Run command to run another .BAT file or you can press CTRL+BREAK to stop recording. When you press CTRL+BREAK, Windows displays the Recorder dialog box. Select Save Macro and then select OK. Finally return to the Recorder and use the File Save command to save the macro to a file in the usual way.

Tip: **Entering DOS commands from within Windows**

You can execute DOS commands from within Windows by running the COMMAND.COM with the /C switch. For example, imagine you want to copy the file MYFILE.TXT from your Windows program directory to a floppy disk in drive A. To do this, select the File Run command from either Program manager or File Manager. Windows displays the File Run dialog box. Type COMMAND.COM/C COPY MYFILE.TXT A:. Your screen flutters for a moment while the command is executed and you are returned to Windows. If you perform this type of operation frequently, you want to use the Recorder to record this procedure as a macro.

A second way to run a .BAT file from within Windows is to run a Windows .PIF file that calls the .BAT file. When you use this method, you can pass parameters directly to the .BAT file. To do this, start the PIF Editor in the Accessories group window. Windows displays the PIF Editor window shown earlier in Figure 5-19. In the Program Filename text box, type the path and name of your .BAT file. In the Window Title text box, type the name that you want to appear in the title bar of the window in which the .BAT file will run. Then specify any additional parameters you may require for the .BAT file. (For a complete discussion of how to set up a .PIF files for DOS applications, see Chapter 10, "Using Non-Windows Applications.") When you're done, use the File Save command to save the new .PIF file to disk.

To run the actual .BAT file, use the File Run command from either Program Manager or File Manager to run the .PIF file you've just created. You can, of course, use the Recorder to record this procedure as a macro.

SUMMARY

Having read this chapter, you now know how to get the most out of the Recorder. The examples in this chapter have shown you both its strengths and its weaknesses. At this point, you can capture almost any routine Windows operation and store it as a macro. You can then repeat that operation quickly and efficiently whenever you want to by simply pressing a key or two. From here, you may want to refer to Chapter 14, which is about the Oriel software that comes with this book. In that chapter, you'll learn how to call Recorder macros from within your Oriel programs.

6

Sharing Data between Applications

In Windows, the primary means for transferring data between applications is the Clipboard. However, the Clipboard is not an application. In reality, it is an area of your computer's memory that Windows uses temporarily to store text or graphics images that have been cut (removed from) or copied from either a Windows or a DOS application. In general, once data has been cut or copied onto the Clipboard, you can then paste that data into another application. In this way, the Windows Clipboard provides a handy "middleman" that lets you easily share text and graphics between applications.

Windows also provides an application that lets you view the contents of the Clipboard—a "Clipboard Viewer," if you will. This application is appropriately called Clipboard, and its file name is CLIPBRD.EXE. You'll find the icon for this application in Program Manager's Main group window. Using this application to manage the contents of the Clipboard will be discussed at various points throughout this chapter.

The Clipboard is directly available to all Windows applications that choose to use it. However, there are a number of issues you should be aware of when cutting and pasting data between Windows applications. This chapter discusses those issues in detail.

On the other hand, the Clipboard is not directly accessible to DOS applications. Instead, Windows itself provides a means for you to cut and paste data between DOS applications. However, there are a number of limitations you'll run into when you try this. This chapter tells you what those limitations are and suggests ways you can best deal with them.

Another aspect of sharing data between applications in Windows involves a much-talked-about concept called Dynamic Data Exchange (DDE). DDE is not related to the

Clipboard in any way. Instead, DDE is a messaging system that allows Windows applications to communicate with one another to exchange data. Through DDE, you can link the data file for one application to the data file for another application. For example, you might display a graph in a Word for Windows document that relies on the numbers from a Microsoft Excel spreadsheet. When the numbers in the Excel spreadsheet change, the graph in the Word document is automatically updated to reflect the change. DDE is discussed toward the end of this chapter.

AN OVERVIEW OF USING THE CLIPBOARD

To conform to the Systems Applications Architecture (SAA) standard proposed by IBM, programmers must use certain conventions when developing applications that access the Clipboard. For example, the application should have an Edit Copy command. The purpose of this command is to copy selected data from the application's work area to the Clipboard. The application should also have an Edit Cut command, whose purpose is to remove (or cut out) selected data from the application's work area and copy it to the Clipboard. Finally, the application should have an Edit Paste command. The purpose of this command is to copy (paste) information that is on the Clipboard into the application's work area. You'll notice that Microsoft embraces the SAA standard for those Windows applications where use of the Clipboard is appropriate.

Note: As an alternative to the Edit Copy and Edit Cut commands, you can usually use CTRL+INS to copy selected data or SHIFT+DEL to cut selected data to the Clipboard. Further, most Windows applications support the use of the SHIFT+INS key sequence for pasting data into the current application's work area. Once again, these key sequences are recommended in the SAA literature as being the appropriate keys to use for these respective functions.

When you start Windows, the Clipboard is empty. However, when you use the Edit Copy or Edit Cut command from within any application, the text or graphics you've previously selected from that application's work area are copied to the Clipboard. Any information you copy to the Clipboard remains there until you use the Edit Cut or Edit Copy command again, or until you delete the contents of the Clipboard. (See "Deleting the Contents of the Clipboard" later for details on clearing the Clipboard.)

Therefore, using the Clipboard is an "all or nothing" proposition. That is, every time you use the Edit Cut or Edit Copy command from within an application, the old information on the Clipboard is completely replaced by the new information. However, you can also save the contents of the Clipboard to a file on disk before you replace it (or before you turn off your machine). See "Saving Clipboard Data to Disk" later for details on how to do this.

As mentioned, once you copy information to the Clipboard, it remains there (unless you replace or delete it). The downside of this arrangement is that memory is required to store the information—memory that could potentially be used by applications. (See

"Memory Considerations," later.) However, on the upside, that information is always there whenever you need it.

Once information is on the Clipboard, you can use the Edit Paste command from within any Windows application to paste that information wherever it is needed. In this way, you can easily transfer information between applications. Or, you can use the same information multiple times in the same application. For example, imagine you are developing a procedures manual for your company using Write. The same block of text will appear in several places throughout the document. Rather than retype the text each time you need it, you can type it once and copy it to the Clipboard. Whenever you need to, you can use the Edit Paste command to copy the block of text into the document.

Another common use of the Clipboard is to move information from one location to another. That new location can be within the same data file, another data file for the same application, or a data file associated with an entirely different application.

WORKING WITH WINDOWS APPLICATIONS

As mentioned, you can copy information to the Clipboard from a standard Windows application by using either the Edit Copy or Edit Cut command. The Edit Copy command simply copies information to the Clipboard, whereas Edit Cut removes the information from the application's work area and places it on the Clipboard. However, before you can use either the Edit Copy or the Edit Cut command, you must first select the information you want to copy or cut.

Selecting Data to Copy to the Clipboard

Usually, the easiest way to select information to copy or cut data to the Clipboard is by using your mouse. In most applications, all you need do is click your mouse on the upper-left corner of the data block you want to copy and hold your mouse button down. Then drag your mouse pointer to the lower-right corner of the information you want to copy. As you drag, the information within the data block is highlighted. When you release your mouse button, the data block is selected. You can then use the Edit Copy or Edit Cut command to copy or cut the data to the Clipboard. Although this method will work in most cases, an application may have a slightly different method for selecting text or graphics from its work. For example, in Paintbrush, you must select a cutout tool before highlighting a data block with the mouse.

You can also use your keyboard to select text or graphics to copy or cut to the Clipboard. In fact, Table 6-1 shows a list of common keyboard selection sequences supported by most Windows applications. Obviously, not all of these key sequences will work in every Windows application. You'll need to try them out in your specific application. Or (as a last resort) read the manual that came with the application. It will undoubtedly contain a list of acceptable keyboard sequences that let you select data from the application's work area.

Keyboard Action	Result
SHIFT+→	Extends the current selection to the right.
SHIFT+←	Extends the current selection to the left.
SHIFT+↓	Extends the current selection to the next line. Or, if the next line is already selected, cancels the selection.
SHIFT+↑	Extends the current selection to the previous line. Or, if the previous line is already selected, cancels the selection.
SHIFT+END	Extends the current selection to the end of a line.
SHIFT+HOME	Extends the current selection to the beginning of a line.
SHIFT+PGDN	Extends the current selection downward to include the next windowfull. Or, if the next windowfull is already selected, cancels the selection.
SHIFT+PGUP	Extends the current selection up to include the previous windowfull. Or, if the previous windowfull is already selected, cancels the selection.
CTRL+SHIFT+→	Extends a selection to include the next word. Or, if the next word is already selected, cancels the selection.
CTRL+SHIFT+←	Extends a selection to include the previous word. Or, if the previous word is already selected, cancels the selection.
CTRL+SHIFT+END	Extends the current selection to the end of a document.
CTRL+SHIFT+HOME	Extends the current selection to the beginning of a document.

Table 6-1 Common Keyboard Sequences for Selecting Data

Checking What Is on the Clipboard

You can easily check the contents of the Clipboard. To do this, simply start the Clipboard Viewer application. As mentioned, you'll find the icon for this application in Program Manager's Main group window. Alternatively, you can select the File Run command from either Program Manager or File Manager and specify a filename of CLIPBRD.EXE. Whichever method you use, Windows will display the Clipboard Viewer application window shown in Figure 6-1. Anything currently on the Clipboard is displayed in this window. For example, notice that the File Run dialog box appears in the Clipboard Viewer window in Figure 6-1. Later, under "Capturing Screens," you'll learn how you can capture a graphics image of a specific window or the entire screen and copy it to the Clipboard.

Note: Sometimes the line length of text that you copy or cut to the Clipboard may appear shorter when you look at the text in the Clipboard Viewer window. This is often necessary to fit the text within the window. However, when you paste the data into an application, your original line length should be restored.

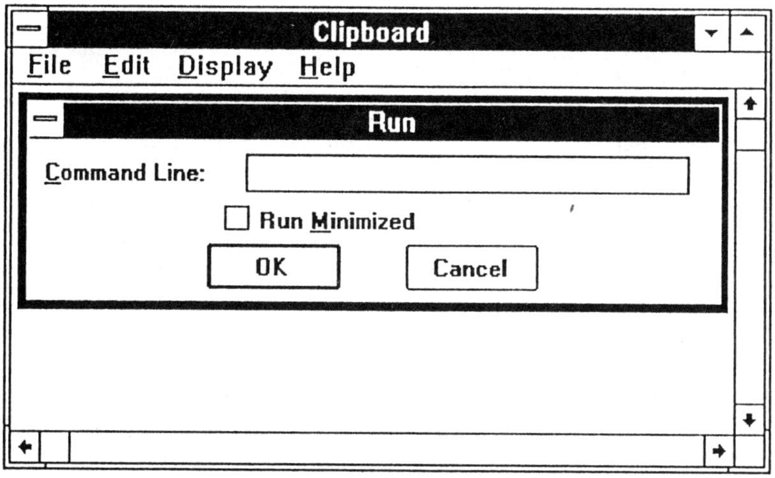

Figure 6-1 The Clipboard Viewer window

Pasting Data to Other Windows Applications

To paste the data that is on the Clipboard to another Windows application, you must first switch to that application. Once the destination application is current, select the spot where you want pasting to begin. Then, select the Edit Paste command from that application's menu. Windows pastes the information currently on the Clipboard into the application's work area.

With most applications, you can control the starting point at which pasting begins. For example, with word-processing packages, you can position the cursor prior to using the Edit Paste command. That way, the incoming text is pasted starting at the location of the cursor. Or, if you're pasting into a spreadsheet application, you can position the cell pointer where you want pasting to begin. As yet another example, if you're pasting a graphics image into Cardfile, you can choose the appropriate card prior to pasting the data.

Certain other Windows applications allow you to position pasted data once it is copied into the application. For example, when you paste a graphics image into Paintbrush, pasting begins at the upper-left corner of the application work area. However, the image is surrounded by a dotted line. You can click your mouse button within the image area and drag the image to its ultimate destination. When you release your mouse button, the dotted line disappears, and the image becomes part of the picture you're working on.

Note: At times, the Paste option in an application's Edit menu may appear grayed (meaning you cannot select it). This can occur for several reasons. The most obvious of these, of course, is that there is nothing on the Clipboard. However, the Paste option may also appear grayed when the data on the Clipboard is not in the right file format for the application. For example, you may be attempting to paste text from a word-processing package like Write into a graphics-based application like Paintbrush. See "Displaying Different File Formats" later in this chapter for a discussion of this topic.

When you paste text that has been formatted from one Windows application to another, the text takes on the formatting of the receiving application. For example, imagine you are pasting some text from a Word for Windows document into a Write document. When the text was copied from Word to the Clipboard, it was formatted as Modern with a bold attribute. However, when you paste the data into the Write document, it will take on the current font setting for Write. For example, if Write is set for Times Roman with an italic attribute, the incoming text will take on that font.

Note: In some cases the receiving application will not override the formatting of text copied from the Clipboard. Those applications that support the Rich Text Format (RTF) are capable of retaining the formatting of text copied from the Clipboard. You'll have to check the manual that came with your particular application to see if it supports RTF.

Saving Clipboard Data to Disk

As mentioned, when you cut or copy information to the Clipboard, it replaces any information already on the Clipboard. Therefore, the information already on the Clipboard is lost. However, rather than lose the information already on the Clipboard, you can save it to disk before replacing it. This is a rather subtle, yet powerful, enhancement to Windows. In versions of Windows prior to 3.0, it was not possible to save the contents of the Clipboard. In these releases, it was necessary to paste the information to an application data file to avoid losing it.

To save the contents of the Clipboard, start the Clipboard Viewer application and select the File Save As command from its menu. When you select this command, the dialog box in Figure 6-2 appears on your screen. You can use this dialog box to save the contents of the Clipboard to a file on disk with a .CLP extension. Only the Clipboard Viewer is capable of reading this particular file format. To restore the file at a later time to both the Clipboard Viewer window and to the Clipboard itself, simply use the File Open command from the Clipboard Viewer's menu.

When you attempt to save the contents of the Clipboard, Windows suggests a name of DEFAULT.CLP. You can, of course, accept this filename or change it. However, there is a plausible argument for accepting it. For example, imagine you only want to save the data on the Clipboard temporarily for a one-time transfer. Rather than create a separate file for each case, you can use DEFAULT.CLP as your one-time transfer file, overwriting it each time. This can help you save precious hard disk space. Further, if you do this consistently, the number of files listed for the Clipboard Viewer's File Save and File Open commands can be cut substantially.

There are a number of reasons why you might want to save the contents of the Clipboard. The most obvious of these is simply to have the data available for future reference. However, there are other issues to consider as well.

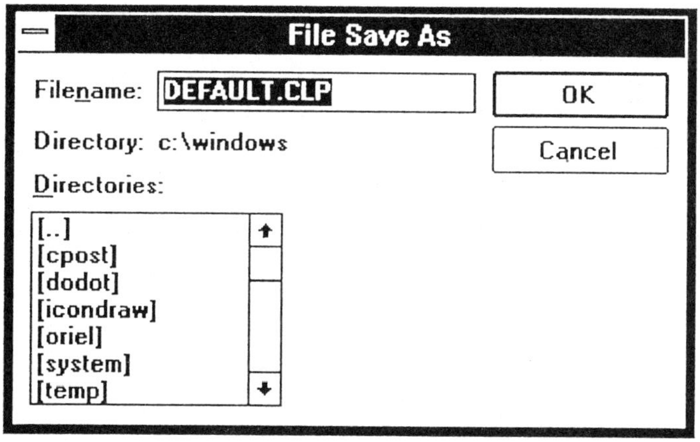

Figure 6-2 You can save Clipboard contents to a file on disk

Regaining Memory

Anything stored on the Clipboard requires memory that could potentially be used by applications. Frankly, if you have only a small text passage on the Clipboard, the memory required to store this data is probably negligible. However, if you have a large graphics image on the Clipboard, the memory required to store this image can be substantial (See "Memory Considerations," later). You can, of course, regain this memory for use by applications if you delete the contents of the Clipboard (see "Deleting the Contents of the Clipboard," later). However, by using the Clipboard Viewer's File Save As command, you can save the contents of the Clipboard to disk. You can then delete the contents of the Clipboard and regain the use of that memory for your applications.

Sharing Data between Applications Running in Different Modes

Saving the contents of the Clipboard also lets you easily share data between applications that run in different modes. For example, imagine you have an older Windows application that you must run in Real mode. Imagine further that you wish to use some data from that application with another newer Windows application that you can run in 386 Enhanced mode. To do this, start Windows with the /R switch so that it comes up in Real mode. Start the older application, load the subject data file, and copy the needed information onto the Clipboard. Invoke the Clipboard Viewer and save the data to disk. Then, leave Windows and start it again, so that it comes up in 386 Enhanced mode. Invoke the Clipboard Viewer and load the .CLP file you saved while in Real mode. You can now start the newer Windows applications and use its Edit Paste command to transfer the data on the Clipboard to the appropriate data file.

Deleting the Contents of the Clipboard

As mentioned, you can easily delete the contents of the Clipboard whenever you want to. In fact, deleting the contents of the Clipboard can help you to regain valuable memory needed by other applications. To delete the contents of the Clipboard, you must do so from within the Clipboard Viewer application. Once this application is current, open the Edit menu. This menu contains a single option, Delete. When you select this option, Windows displays an OK/Cancel message box asking you if you really want to delete the contents of the Clipboard. Select OK to delete both the contents of the Clipboard Viewer window and the contents of the Clipboard itself.

Note: You can also press DEL when the Clipboard Viewer application is current to delete the contents of the Clipboard.

CAPTURING SCREENS

You can also copy the contents of your screen to the Clipboard. You can capture either a single window or the entire screen. The sections that follow explain how.

Capturing the Whole Screen

You can copy the entire screen to the Clipboard by pressing the PRINTSCREEN key. If the Windows desktop is displayed when you press this key, the entire content of the desktop is copied to the Clipboard as a bitmap. If you press PRINTSCREEN while running a DOS application as a full-screen display, the entire contents of the current screen will be copied to the Clipboard.

The PRINTSCREEN key will work, regardless of the mode in which you are running Windows. In fact, as you'll soon see, if you are running Windows in real or standard mode, this is the only way to copy information from a DOS application to the Clipboard.

Note: If Windows is running in Real or Standard mode, and you are running a DOS application in graphics mode, the PRINTSCREEN key will not work. Windows simply ignores it. However, if Windows is running in 386 Enhanced mode, you can press PRINTSCREEN to copy an entire DOS graphics screen to the Clipboard.

As mentioned, when you copy the entire Windows screen to the Clipboard, it is copied as a bit map (a rectangular array of bits in which one or more bits correspond to the pixels in a graphics image). The file format for these bitmap images corresponds to the Windows 3 .BMP file format used in Paintbrush. Therefore, you can paste these bitmap images into Paintbrush or into another application that supports the Windows 3 .BMP file format. However, if the application is not capable of recognizing the Windows 3 .BMP file format, you cannot paste Clipboard bitmaps directly to that application.

A workaround for this, though, is to paste the bitmap into Paintbrush and save it as a .PCX file. Many popular paint and graphics packages are capable of reading .PCX files directly, or, in some cases, an application will come with a conversion utility that allows you to convert .PCX files to a format the application can use. To save a .PCX file from Paintbrush, first paste the image from the Clipboard into Paintbrush. Then, select the File Save As command from Paintbrush's menu. A dialog box is displayed that lets you name and save the file. However, before you select OK to save the file, select the push button entitled Options. This expands the dialog box to show you the different file formats in which Paintbrush can save its files. The .PCX file format is among the options displayed.

Capturing Just a Window

You can also copy just the currently active window to the Clipboard, rather than the entire screen, by pressing ALT+PRINTSCREEN. However, you must be running Windows in 386 Enhanced mode for this to work with a DOS application.

To select a particular application window to capture, begin by activating that window. If the application whose image you want to capture happens to be a DOS application that is running as a full-screen display, press ALT+ENTER to convert it to a windowed display. When you're ready, press ALT+PRINTSCREEN. Windows copies the window to the Clipboard as a bitmap image.

When you copy an individual window to the Clipboard, the entire window is copied. This includes the window frame, the title bar, scroll bars, and so on. For example, if you look at Figure 6-1 shown earlier in this chapter, you will see a shot of the Clipboard Viewer containing the File Run dialog box. The ALT+PRINTSCREEN key sequence was used to set up this figure.

Similar to copying an entire screen, when you copy an individual window to the Clipboard, it is copied as a bitmap file. The file format used conforms to the Windows 3 .BMP file format. Therefore, you can paste the image directly into those applications that support this format, but you cannot paste the image into those that don't. However, if you want to use the image with an application that does not support this format, you might be able to use the Paintbrush/.PCX file workaround discussed in the previous section.

> *Tip: If PRINTSCREEN or ALT+PRINTSCREEN won't work*
>
> If PRINTSCREEN or ALT+PRINTSCREEN will not copy screen images to the Clipboard, it may be that you are using an older style (un-enhanced) keyboard. If this is the case, try using SHIFT+PRINTSCREEN instead.

Memory Considerations

There are a few memory-related issues that you should know about when you copy graphics images to the Clipboard. First of all, graphics images (which are usually bitmaps, in the case of Windows 3) tend to require a fair amount of memory. For example, with a standard VGA display, copying a full-screen bitmap image to the Clipboard can take around 150K. Further, a full-screen bitmap from an IBM 8514/a display can take as much as 768K. Therefore, in situations where available memory is already tight, the contents of the Clipboard can play a significant role.

For this reason, it's always a good idea to leave graphics images on the Clipboard only as long as they are needed. If the need is only temporary—that is, you intend to paste the image into an application only once—get it over with. Paste the image into that application and then open the Clipboard Viewer and use the Edit Delete command to clear the contents of the Clipboard. If the need is longer term—you anticipate using the image multiple times—consider using the Clipboard Viewer application to save the contents of the Clipboard to a file on disk with a .CLP extension. Then clear the Clipboard. When a need for the image arises in the future, use the Clipboard Viewer's File Open command to load the image's .CLP file, thereby placing the image back on the Clipboard.

Note: If there is not enough memory to copy or cut an image to the Clipboard, Windows will not allow it. When this is the case, you may have to close some applications in order to free up sufficient memory to copy the image. See Chapter 7, "Memory Management," for other tips on how you can make more memory available to Windows.

WORKING WITH DOS APPLICATIONS

As mentioned, DOS applications do not have direct access to the Clipboard. However, Windows itself provides a means for you to copy or cut information from DOS applications onto the Clipboard. Once the data is on the Clipboard, you can paste that data either into another DOS application or into a Windows application.

Using the Windows Clipboard to copy text between DOS applications can be very convenient. Specifically, you don't have to worry about conflicting file formats, and you don't have to hassle with application-specific conversion utilities. However, there are a number of issues to consider when cutting and pasting data between DOS applications. The sections that follow discuss these issues in detail.

Capturing Data in Standard or Real Mode

As you know, if you're running Windows in Real or Standard mode, all your DOS applications will run as full-screen displays. However, you can still copy information from a DOS application to the Clipboard. To do this, simply press PRINTSCREEN. You'll notice a momentary flicker of your screen as its entire contents are copied to the Clipboard.

Note: The PRINTSCREEN method will not work if Windows is running in Real or Standard mode and the DOS application happens to be running in graphics mode at the time. Unfortunately, this means that you won't be able to copy graphics images from DOS applications to the Clipboard when Windows is running in Real or Standard mode. However, if you're fortunate enough to be running Windows in 386 Enhanced mode, this is not a problem. See "Capturing Data in 386 Enhanced Mode," later, for more details on this.

To see exactly what was copied to the Clipboard, press ALT+ESC to switch back to Windows and invoke the Clipboard Viewer. As you view its contents, you'll notice that all the text from the DOS application screen was copied. This includes text from the application work area as well as any displayed menu names, filenames, cursor position information, and possibly formulas, if the application happens to be a spreadsheet application. You can clean up some of this extraneous text by pasting the data into a Windows word-processing application like Write or Notepad and removing the unwanted text.

Note: When DOS text is pasted to the Clipboard, it is pasted as ASCII text. Therefore, no formatting is carried forward from the sending application. All fonts, control codes, and so on are ignored. Further, each line of text will end with a hard return (a carriage-return/line-feed character).

Pasting to DOS Applications in Standard or Real Mode

As mentioned, if you're running Windows in real or standard mode, your DOS applications must run as a full-screen display. To paste Clipboard data into a DOS application that is running full-screen, begin by positioning the cursor where you want pasting to begin. Then, press ALT+ESC to return to Windows. The DOS application now appears as an icon at the lower-left portion of the Windows desktop. To paste the data on the Clipboard into this iconized application, you must activate the icon, open its window Control menu, and select the Paste command. You can activate the icon by clicking on it, or by pressing ALT+ESC to move to it. If you activated the icon by clicking on it, the window Control menu is already displayed, and you can select Paste. If you activated by pressing ALT+ESC, press ALT+SPACEBAR to display the window Control menu and then select Paste.

Note: If the Clipboard contains no data, or it contains a graphics image, the Paste option in the window Control menu appears grayed, meaning nonselectable.

When you select Paste from the window Control menu, Windows restores the DOS application to a full-screen display. It then pastes the data currently on the Clipboard into that application's work area starting at the location of the cursor. All incoming data will be pasted as ASCII text, without any sort of formatting, and each line will end with a hard return.

> **Tip: Pasting to spreadsheet applications**
>
> Pasting more than a single line of text into a DOS spreadsheet application is not recommended. Most DOS spreadsheet applications like Lotus 1-2-3 or Borland's Quattro Pro require that you type an entry and press ENTER to place it in a cell. If you make a second entry to the same cell, the first entry is overwritten.
>
> As mentioned, when text is pasted from the Windows Clipboard to a DOS application, it comes in as ASCII text, each line ending with a hard return (the equivalent of pressing the ENTER key). Therefore, if you paste a multiple-line text entry from the Clipboard into a DOS spreadsheet application, the second line overwrites the first one, the third line overwrites the second, and so on. When the dust settles, only the last line of text is displayed in the cell.
>
> This is not true of Microsoft Excel, however. When you paste a multiple-line entry into Microsoft Excel, each line is pasted into a separate cell. The result is a column of consecutive cells, each containing a separate line of text. In addition, if you paste a single column of numbers from a Windows word-processing package (like Write) into Excel, each number is assigned a separate cell. The result is a column of consecutive cells, each containing a number. Moreover, those numbers are live values—that is, you can use them in calculations.

Capturing Data in 386 Enhanced Mode

If you're running Windows in 386 enhanced mode, your options for using the Clipboard with DOS applications expand dramatically. As you know, you can run your DOS applications in a window. As you'll soon see, this allows you to select a specific section of text to copy to the Clipboard, rather than copying an entire screenfull, as you must in real or standard mode. A final advantage gained from running in 386 enhanced mode is that you can copy graphics images from DOS applications to the Clipboard.

Note: Although you can copy a graphics image from a DOS application to the Clipboard in 386 enhanced mode, you can only paste that image into other Windows applications. Windows will not allow you to paste the image into other DOS applications.

To copy selected text or graphics to the Clipboard from a DOS application, you use the 386 Edit commands. These commands appear on the window Control menu for a windowed DOS application. Therefore, they are only available when Windows is running in 386 enhanced mode. To access the 386 Edit commands, open the Control menu for a windowed DOS application and select the Edit option. When you select this option, the window control menu appears as shown in Figure 6-3.

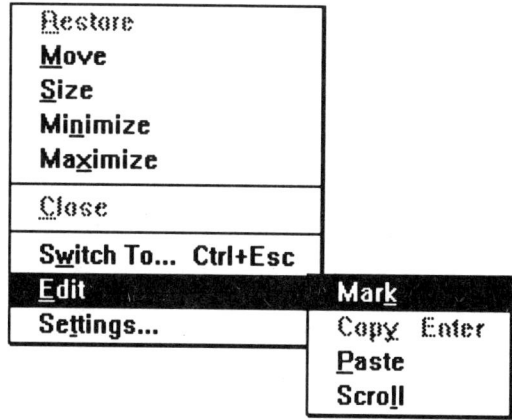

Figure 6-3 The 386 Edit menu for DOS applications

You can use the 386 Edit commands in conjunction with either your mouse or your keyboard to copy selected text or graphics images from a DOS application to the Clipboard. Both methods are discussed in the following paragraphs.

To copy selected text or graphics from a DOS application to the Clipboard with your mouse, the DOS application must be running in a window. Therefore, if the DOS application is currently running as a full-screen display, press ALT+ENTER to convert it to a windowed display. Once the application is running in a window, use your mouse to highlight a section of text or a graphics image. To do this, click on the upper-left corner of that area of the window you want to capture and hold the mouse button down. Then, drag to the lower-right corner of the area. As you drag, Windows creates a highlighted block. When you're ready, release the mouse button to select the block.

To copy the contents of the block to the Clipboard, open the window Control menu for the application and select the Edit option. When you select this option, the cascading submenu in Figure 6-3 appears. Select the Copy option from this menu. Windows copies the currently selected block to the Clipboard. You can now paste that block of data into other applications.

Copying a block of data from a DOS application to the Clipboard by using your keyboard is a bit more cumbersome. To begin, make sure the DOS application is running in a window and that the window Control menu is displayed. If the DOS application is currently running as a full-screen display, press ALT+SPACEBAR. This action has the dual effect of converting the application to a windowed display as well as opening the window Control menu. Select the Edit command from the window Control menu and then select the Mark suboption. The window Control menu disappears and a small rectangular cursor appears in the upper-left corner of the window. Use the arrow keys to move the cursor to the upper-left corner of the block you want to copy. To highlight the block, press the SHIFT key, and hold it down. Then, use the arrow keys to expand the highlight as needed. When you're done, press ALT+SPACEBAR to display the window Control menu again. From that menu, select the Edit Copy command. Windows copies the block you've selected to the Clipboard.

Note: Notice in Figure 6-3 that the accelerator key for the Edit Copy command is the ENTER key. This means that you can highlight a block of data from a DOS application window by using your mouse or the keyboard and simply press ENTER to copy it to the Clipboard.

The Scroll option on the 386 Edit menu is simply a keyboard alternative to using the mouse scroll bars to move around in a DOS application window. This command can be very convenient when you don't have access to a mouse. For example, when you press ALT+ENTER to display a full-screen DOS application in a window, that window serves simply as a viewer onto a larger work surface. Only the current full-screen view of the DOS application is contained in that window. When you select the Edit Scroll command from the window Control menu, you can then use the arrow keys to scroll around within the current full-screen view. However, when you reach the top, bottom, left, or right edges of the current full-screen view, scrolling stops. To see the next or previous full-screen view of the DOS application within the window, press PGDN or PGUP.

Tip: *Using graphics display drivers with DOS applications*

Many DOS applications come with graphics display drivers that let you run the application in graphics mode. Be aware, though, that if you are running a DOS application in graphics mode, and you copy information from that application to the Windows Clipboard, it will be copied as a graphics bitmap, not as text. To copy data from a DOS application to the Clipboard as text, the application must be running in text mode.

Some DOS applications, like Microsoft Word or Borland's Quattro Pro, allow you to switch back and forth between graphics and text mode by using commands. Others, like Lotus 1-2-3 Release 2.2, require you to leave the application and run the install program again, to select a graphics-mode driver. Still others, like Lotus 1-2-3 Release 3, run in graphics mode all the time and do not offer an option to run the application in text mode. Unfortunately, you will not be able to use the Windows Clipboard to transfer text from these applications to other applications. When you copy data from these applications to the Clipboard, it will be copied as a graphics bitmap.

Pasting Data in 386 Enhanced Mode

To paste data from the Clipboard into a windowed DOS application, you use the Edit Paste command from the 386 Edit menu. To do this, make sure the DOS application is displayed in a window. Next, move the application's cursor to the place where you want pasting to begin. When you're ready, open the window Control menu and select the Edit Paste command. Windows pastes the data on the Clipboard into the application's work area.

Note: As mentioned, you cannot paste graphics from the Clipboard into DOS applications. If you attempt to do so, Windows displays a message box that says "No appropriate data on clipboard."

When you paste text to a DOS application in 386 enhanced mode, the results are the same as in real and standard mode. For example, the text comes in as standard ASCII text. It has no formatting (fonts and so forth) and each line ends with a hard return. Further, if the original source of the text is another DOS application, the maximum amount of text you can transfer at a time is the equivalent of one full screen of that application.

Tip: **When pasting to a DOS Application is unsuccessful**

Not all DOS applications are capable of accepting data at the speed that Windows is capable of pasting it. Therefore, with some DOS applications, pasting may be unsuccessful. However, you may still be able to paste data into the application by disabling the Allow Fast Paste option in the application's PIF (Program Information File). This option is only available in an application's PIF when you are running Windows in 386 enhanced mode. For more on this topic, see Chapter 10, "Using Non-Windows Applications."

For example, imagine you are copying text between two DOS word processors, such as WordPerfect and Microsoft Word. Both of these applications appear side by side in Figure 6-4. While in WordPerfect, you can highlight a specific block of text, or you can highlight the entire windowfull, but no more. You can then use the Edit Copy command from the window Control menu to copy the selected block of text to the Clipboard. Once the data is on the Clipboard, you can switch to Microsoft Word, position the cursor, and use the Edit Paste command from the window Control menu. The text block from the Clipboard is then pasted into the current Word document. However, when it arrives in the Word document, each line ends with a hard return. Therefore, each line exists as a separate entity. To form the text into paragraphs, you must manually delete the hard returns at the end of each line and rely on Word's automatic justification to form the text into paragraphs.

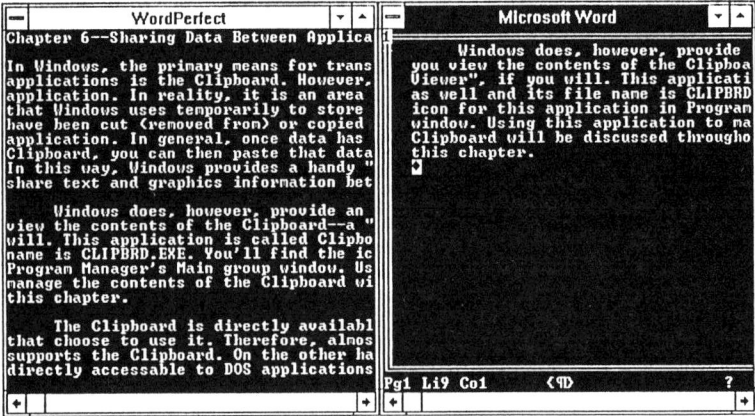

Figure 6-4 Two DOS Word Processors side by side

Tip: Sending Clipboard data to remote systems

You can also use the Terminal application to send Clipboard data to remote systems. The Terminal application offers an Edit menu that lets you copy information from Terminal to the Clipboard and a Paste option that lets you paste information to the terminal window. If you are properly connected to a remote system, the Edit Paste command has the same effect as the Transfer Send command—that is, the information you paste from the Clipboard to the Terminal window will be sent to the remote system.

CLIPBOARD FILE FORMATS

When you copy data from a Windows application to the Clipboard, that data may be sent to the Clipboard in more than one file format. When a Windows application is created, the developer can choose from a number of standard Clipboard file formats as well as define an entirely new file format that is specific to the application. Each of the file formats selected or created by the developer will be automatically copied to the Clipboard whenever you cut or copy data from the application. Supplying data to the Clipboard in several different formats at the same time can help to ensure that the data will be compatible with many different applications.

Some of the standard file formats that can be copied to the Clipboard, and displayed by the Clipboard Viewer, are as follows:

- Text: Null-terminated (ASCII) text.
- OEM Text: Null-terminated text in the OEM Character set.

- Bitmap: This can be a device-independent (.BMP) or device-dependent bitmap file. In general, a bitmap is a rectangular array of bits in which one or more bits correspond to the pixels in a graphics image.

- Metafile: A graphics metafile. In general, a graphics metafile is a collection of GDI drawing commands encoded in binary form. The commands in a metafile usually correspond to the drawing functions in the underlying application.

- Others: The Clipboard can also accommodate the SYLK, DIF, and TIFF file formats. However, the SYLK and DIF formats are rarely used in Windows 3 applications.

On the receiving end, the Windows application developer also controls the file format that is copied from the Clipboard to an application. Normally, when you select the Edit Paste command from within an application, the contents of the Clipboard are reviewed to see what file formats are there. If an acceptable file format is available, the pasting operation is allowed to occur.

As a user, you can check to see what file formats are on the Clipboard yourself. To do this, you use the Display menu option from the Clipboard Viewer application. When you select this menu option, a submenu is displayed that shows you the file formats that are currently available on the Clipboard. To see what a particular file format looks like, select the submenu option that corresponds to that file format. Windows will then show you what that file format looks like in the Clipboard Viewer window.

Essentially, the Display menu serves no purpose other than to show you what file formats are on the Clipboard and what they look like. Although you have no control over the format used to paste data to an application, you can at least see what is available. Further, if you know the exact file format supported by your application, you can determine if that format is available on the Clipboard. Some of the more common selections you'll see on the Display menu are as follows:

- AUTO—The default text format used for Windows applications.

- OEM—The default text format used for DOS applications.

- Bitmap—The standard device-independent (.BMP) bitmap file format supported by Windows 3.

- Owner display—This option is displayed only temporarily while the application that provided the information to the Clipboard is open. When you close the sending application, this option disappears.

Often, when you paste formatted text to the Clipboard, it retains its formatting when displayed in the Clipboard Viewer window. This is misleading. It implies that the formatting of the text will be retained when you paste it into another Windows application. This is not the case. Instead, the receiving application will determine the formatting of that text. For example, imagine you copy text from a Write document to the Clipboard that is formatted as Times Roman Italic. Imagine further that you then paste that text to a Word for Windows document, which is currently set for a Modern font. When the text arrives in the Word for Windows document, it will be formatted as Modern.

DYNAMIC DATA EXCHANGE

Dynamic Data Exchange, or DDE for short, is a messaging system that lets Windows applications communicate with one another to exchange data. In effect, DDE allows data fields to be passed automatically between two concurrently running applications.

DDE was first developed by Microsoft around the time that Excel was developed, and it was originally implemented in that application. Since that time, DDE has come a long way. Now in Windows 3, an open forum exists for applications to exchange data with one another.

By taking advantage of the DDE messaging system, a Windows programmer can create an application that is capable of sharing its data with other Windows applications that support DDE. However, not all Windows applications support DDE. Frankly, this is somewhat understandable in that properly implementing DDE within an application can take some doing.

From a user's viewpoint, however, DDE can be very powerful. It allows you to link a data file from one application to the data file for another application. When the information in one application changes, the other application's data file is automatically updated for the change.

For example, you might link a spreadsheet application to a communications package, which, in turn, has access to a service that supplies up-to-the-minute stock quotations. Therefore, when stock prices change, so does your spreadsheet. As yet another example, you can create a graph in a spreadsheet application and then link that graph to a document file in a word-processing application. The graph is then displayed in the word-processing document. As you change the underlying numbers for the graph in the spreadsheet application, the word processor's document is automatically updated for the change.

When you open an application that supports the DDE protocol, it immediately starts broadcasting messages about its name and data files to all open Windows applications that support DDE. At any time, another DDE application can request these messages be routed to one of its data files. Once such a request is made, a client/server relationship is established between the two applications. The application providing the information is the server, and the application requesting that information is the client. The interaction between the two applications (the exchange of data, that is) is often referred to as a conversation.

The client application always starts the conversation. It does this by making a request for messages from a specific server application and its associated data file. The server application, on the other hand, simply responds to that request. Of course, a client application can be involved in several conversations with different server applications at the same time.

Once you establish a "conversation" between two running applications, no further user interaction is required. When the data in the server application changes, the linked range in the client application is automatically updated for the change.

For example, imagine you want to start a conversation between Word for Windows and Microsoft Excel. The goal is to display a graph in the Word document that relies on the numbers in the Excel spreadsheet. In this case, Word is the client and Excel is the server. You, the user, would strike up a conversation between these two applications by supplying Word with the name of the application that will be the server (Excel) and the source of the information (an Excel chart file). When Word makes a request for a specific set of data, Excel responds by providing it.

Many Windows applications are capable of making two types of requests for data from other server applications: a one-time transfer or a permanent data link. With a one-time transfer, a client application requests and gets data from the server only once. This type of data transfer can be appropriate when the data doesn't change very often and a recent "snapshot" will do the job. On the other hand, with a permanent data link, a message is sent from the server application to the client whenever the data in the server application changes.

In addition, many DDE applications let you choose from two types of permanent data links, warm and hot. With a hot link, the information in the client's data file is immediately updated whenever the linked information in the Server's data file changes. With a warm link, updating only takes place when the client requests it.

Perhaps the best way to show you how DDE works is through an actual example. In truth, though, this example will illustrate just one scenario for DDE. Each DDE application will undoubtedly use a different set of commands and methods for taking advantage of DDE. You'll have to consult the documentation that came with your particular application for a list of the appropriate commands.

In this example, you'll take a graph from Microsoft Excel and link that graph to a data file in Word for Windows. The emphasis here will not be on teaching you how to use these two applications. However, along the way you'll learn about a few commands in these applications that are relevant to setting up a DDE link between the two.

To begin, start both Microsoft Excel and Word for Windows. Then, switch to Excel and create a graph. For example, you might create a graph similar to the one in Figure 6-5. Once you've finished creating the graph, make sure it is selected, and use Excel's Edit Copy command to copy the graph to the Clipboard.

Note: The Clipboard has nothing to do with DDE. However, many applications use it as an intermediary for transferring information about the server's application name and data filename to the client application for the first time.

When you are ready, switch to Word for Windows. Position the cursor where you want the graph to appear in the document. Then, open the Edit menu and select the Paste Link option. Word displays the dialog box in Figure 6-6. This dialog contains information about the link you will ultimately create. (This information is taken directly from the Clipboard.) At this point, if you select the Auto Update check box, Word will create a hot link. Otherwise, a warm link will be created. Select OK to create the data link. Word inserts a field code reference into the current document at the location of the cursor, as shown in Figure 6-7. This field code describes the nature of the link in terms that Word can understand. For example, it identifies the type of link as hot (DDEAUTO), the application source (EXCEL), and the data source for that application as follows:

```
D:\\EXCEL\\CHART4.XLC""\mergeformat
```

222 Windows 3 Power Tools

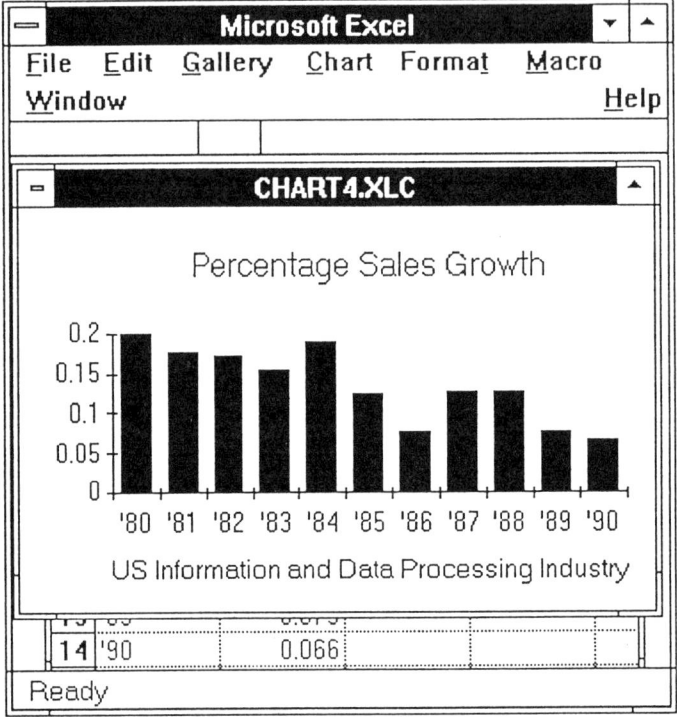

Figure 6-5 An example graph in Microsoft Excel

To display the actual graph in the Word document, select the View Field Codes command from Word's menu. This command removes the checkmark next to the command name and allows the graph to be displayed in the document, as shown in Figure 6-8.

To see DDE at work, switch to Excel and change the underlying numbers for the graph in that application; then switch back to Word for Windows. The changes you've made in

Figure 6-6 Word for Windows lets you choose whether you want a "hot" or a "warm" DDE link

Sharing Data between Applications 223

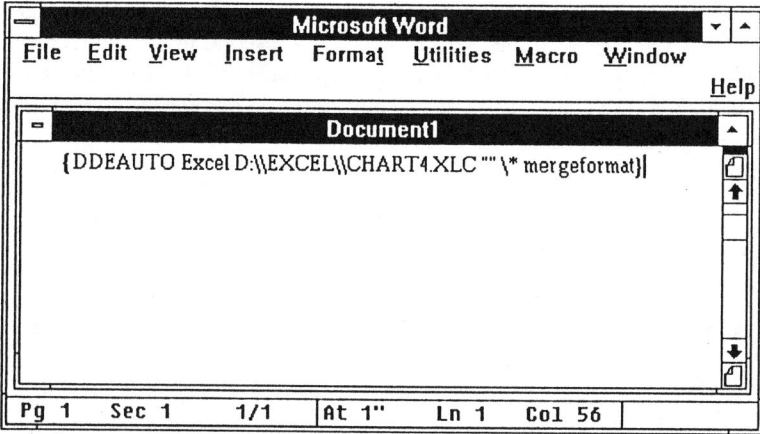

Figure 6-7 A field code reference in Word (the client application)

the Excel spreadsheet file are now reflected in the graph that is displayed in the Word for Windows document file.

Many Windows applications will inform you when a link exists in a data file. This usually happens when you open the linked data file in the client application. For example,

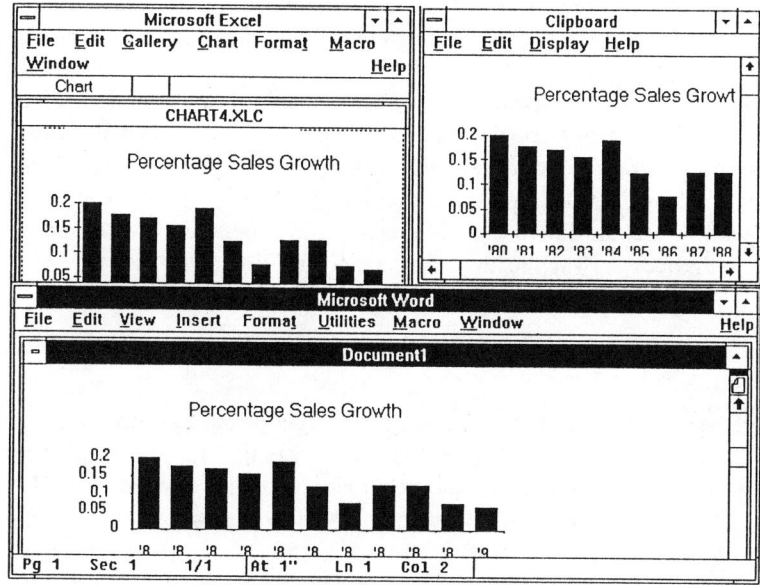

Figure 6-8 A graph in Word for Windows that is linked by DDE to a Microsoft Excel chart file

if the server application is not open when you open the client file, a message box is displayed that informs you of this. Often, when you respond to this message box, the client application will attempt to open the server application and load the appropriate data file. That way, both the client and server application will be running concurrently, and the appropriate data source will be available for the DDE conversation to continue.

OBJECT LINKING AND EMBEDDING

Shortly before this book went to press, Microsoft announced its intention to help developers implement object linking and embedding (OLE) for their Windows applications. Like DDE, the OLE technology will allow users to create links between applications for the purpose of sharing data between files. As with DDE, the application providing the data is referred to as the server and the application requesting the data is the client. Whenever the information in the server's data file changes, the client application's data file is automatically updated for the change.

Supposedly, though, the OLE technology will make it easier for users to implement links between applications. To set up a link, users must embed one or more objects—graphics, text, charts, spreadsheets, and so on—from other applications into the current application's data file. This embedding can be accomplished by simply pasting an object copied from another application into the data file for the current application. When the object is pasted, it brings with it all the necessary information about the application that created it. At that point, a link is formed between the two applications. At any time in the future, you can double-click on an object in a client application's data file to have Windows load the appropriate server application and open the data file that provided the object.

Microsoft is not the only proponent of the OLE technology. In fact, Microsoft enlisted the aid of several software heavyweights including Aldus, Lotus, and WordPerfect to codevelop the code libraries associated with OLE. Therefore, you might see evidence of the OLE technology in Windows applications developed by these companies in the not-too-distant future. In the case of Microsoft, you might see this technology implemented in the accessory applications that come with Windows 3.1.

SUMMARY

On the surface, the benefits of the Windows GUI (Graphical User Interface) are immediately apparent to the power user. Obviously, running multiple applications in overlapping windows can make for a very efficient working environment. However, beneath the surface, Windows also offers some of the most powerful data-sharing tools available.

For example, using the Clipboard, you can copy text or graphics from one application to another, without having to leave either application or create any additional files. In this way, the Windows Clipboard provides a seamless data-sharing mechanism that is available to all applications.

In addition to cutting and pasting data between applications via the Clipboard, you can also share data items between applications automatically. Through the DDE (Dynamic Data Exchange) messaging system, you can create a live link between the data files for two different applications. In this way, DDE lets you set up a running "conversation" between two open applications and pass live data from one to the other. When the data in one application changes, the other application is automatically updated for the change.

7

Windows Memory Management

Windows 3 memory management is one of the better juggling acts in the brief history of the IBM PC. Not only does it support Windows and non-Windows applications alike, but it also adjusts its behavior to take best advantage of your PC's unique hardware. The factors that most influence Windows memory management are your system's processor and the amount and type of memory available—but this is only part of the story.

Windows normally performs its memory management without assistance on your part. So, for most users, there is very little need to understand its inner workings. However, as a power user, if you want to optimize Windows as it performs its memory management feat, it's helpful to have at least a basic understanding of the mechanisms Windows uses. Given this knowledge, you can more easily intervene to improve Windows performance.

Intervening in Windows memory management means configuring your system's memory for maximum performance. The object is to strike a balance between Windows' own memory management needs and the needs of your applications. There are several levers at your disposal—for example, the amount of expanded and extended memory you configure your system for, setting up a permanent swap file for 386 enhanced mode, and controlling the size of the SMARTDrive disk-caching program. This chapter will help you understand what effect these levers will have on your system, and Chapter 11, "Improving Windows Performance," will help you fine tune them.

Intervening also involves configuring your DOS applications to make the best use of memory. You do this through the application's program information file (PIF) settings. PIF settings are covered in detail in Chapter 10, "Using Non-Windows Applications."

As you tweak a DOS application's PIF, however, it helps to have some grounding on the effect your changes will have. This chapter should help in that area.

This chapter begins by discussing the different types of memory available on the PC and some of the standards that have evolved for using that memory. It then describes the different memory configurations that Windows supports and the effect that these configurations have on Windows applications. How Windows handles DOS applications is then discussed, because this is one of the areas where you have the greatest control over Windows' performance. Finally, using software outside of Windows to affect Windows' memory management is discussed; more specifically, there are sections on QEMM-386 Version 5.1 from Quarterdeck and the improved memory management features of MS-DOS Version 5.0.

CONVENTIONAL AND RESERVED I/O MEMORY

There are two areas of memory in your PC's first megabyte—conventional and reserved I/O memory. *Conventional memory* is located in the memory addresses between 0K and 640K and is used to run DOS programs. This is the memory addressed by the 8086 processor, and in "real" mode of the 80286, 80386, and 80486 processors. As Figure 7-1 shows, the first 90K (or so) of conventional memory is used by the following:

- Interrupt vector table: A 1K table of interrupts that includes the address and name of the program providing the interrupt service.
- ROM BIOS tables: Used by the system ROMs for keeping track of the state of the system.
- MS-DOS: Includes the DOS kernel (usually IBMBIO.COM and IBMDOS.COM or their non-IBM-specific counterparts), DOS data (files, buffers, drive list, and the like), and device drivers.

The rest of conventional memory (approximately 550K) is available for programs.

Reserved I/O memory (also called *high memory*) is the memory between the top of conventional memory and 1 megabyte (1024K). Like conventional memory, reserved I/O memory can be addressed by DOS, but it has been traditionally reserved for use by the system (IBM did the reserving). The "system" includes the ROM BIOS and hardware adapters, such as the video display cards, network cards, and the like. As DOS programs have become larger and the need for multitasking greater, developers have endeavored to reclaim areas of reserved I/O memory for other uses. Figure 7-2 shows a detailed view of reserved I/O memory.

Note that your PC may not have actual physical memory for each memory address in reserved I/O memory. The physical memory that is present is a function of your ROM BIOS, video display cards, and other hardware adapters. Physical memory may also be provided by an expanded memory manager, a factor that makes it possible for programs such as Quarterdeck's QEMM-386 and Qualitas' 386Max to locate network drivers,

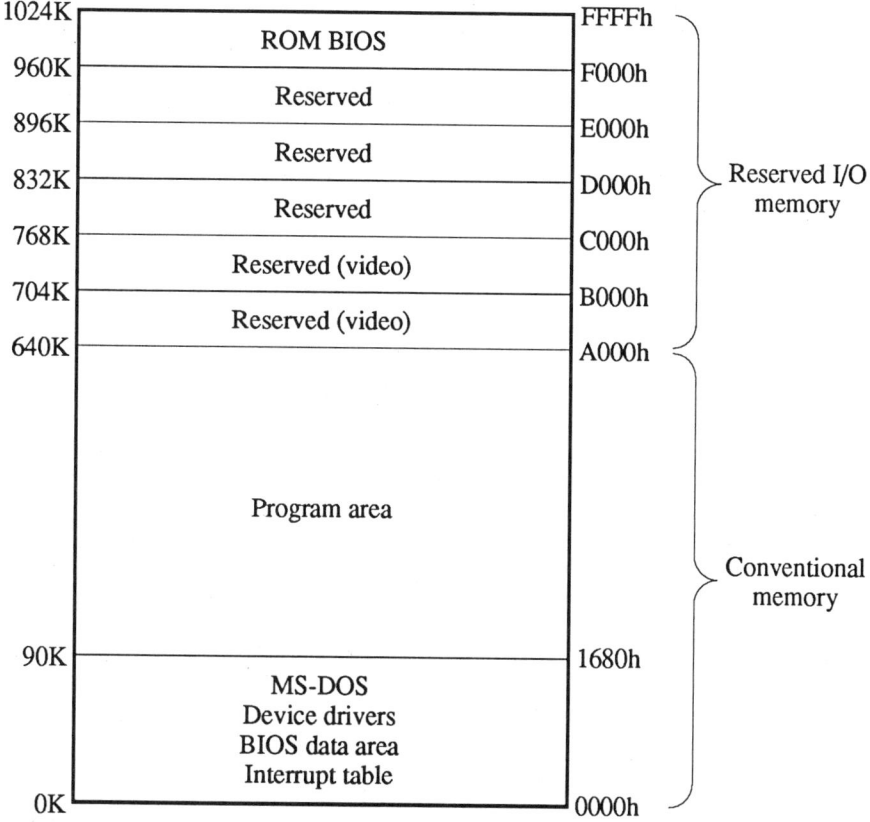

Figure 7-1 Conventional and reserved I/O memory

mouse drivers, and DOS resources (such as buffers) in reserved I/O memory (see the following for details).

Because of the 384K of reserved I/O memory, a machine that has 640K of memory has 1 megabyte of address space. Conventional memory occupies the first 640K of that space, and the reserved I/O memory occupies the area from 640 to 1 megabyte. This is not the same as a machine with 1 megabyte of physical memory. A machine with this amount of memory actually has 1408K of address space—640K of conventional memory, 384K of reserved I/O space, and 384K of extended memory (starting at 1024K).

EXPANDED MEMORY AND EMS

Expanded memory makes it possible to break the 640K barrier imposed by DOS. Expanded memory may seem hard to fathom at first because there are several expanded memory specifications, and the differences between them are rather subtle. This section should help you sort them out.

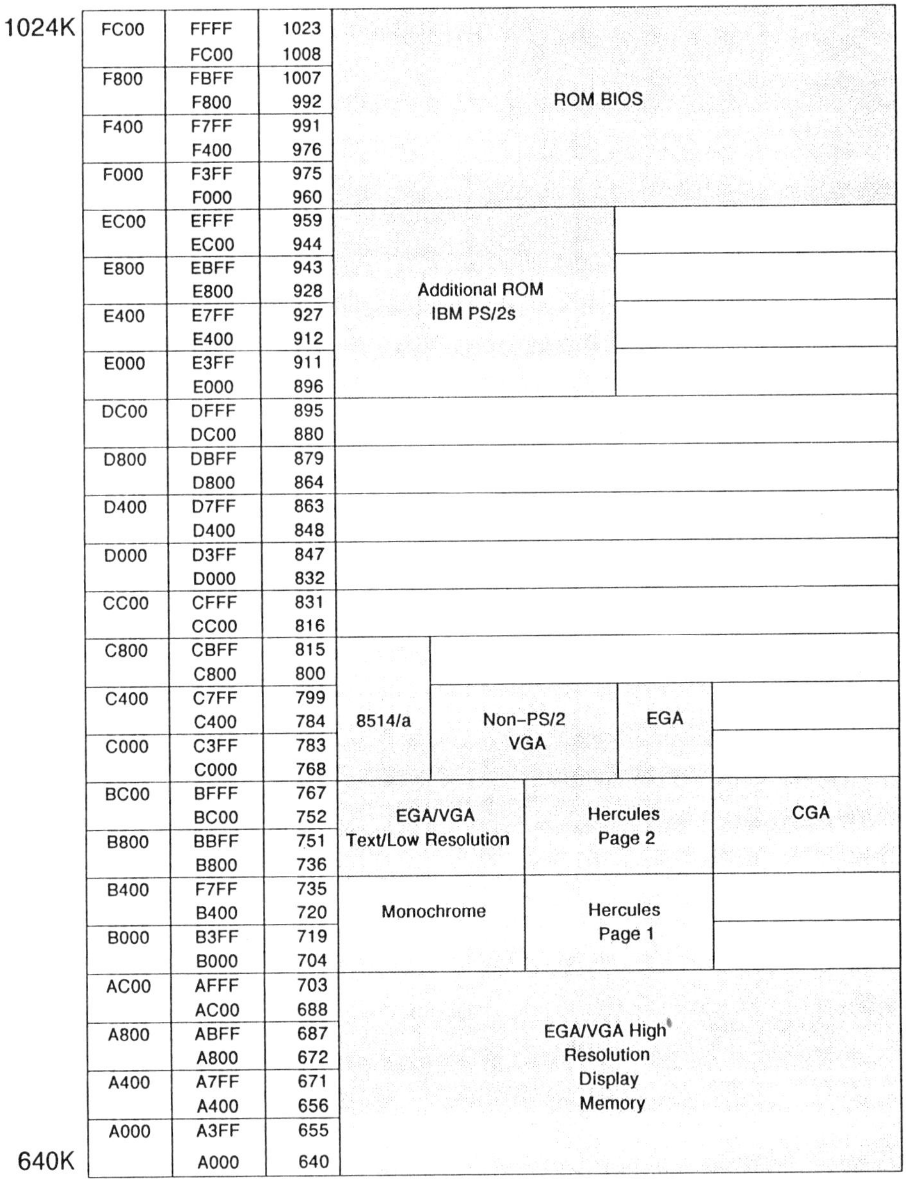

230 Windows 3 Power Tools

1024K				
	FC00	FFFF	1023	ROM BIOS
		FC00	1008	
	F800	FBFF	1007	
		F800	992	
	F400	F7FF	991	
		F400	976	
	F000	F3FF	975	
		F000	960	
	EC00	EFFF	959	Additional ROM IBM PS/2s
		EC00	944	
	E800	EBFF	943	
		E800	928	
	E400	E7FF	927	
		E400	912	
	E000	E3FF	911	
		E000	896	
	DC00	DFFF	895	
		DC00	880	
	D800	DBFF	879	
		D800	864	
	D400	D7FF	863	
		D400	848	
	D000	D3FF	847	
		D000	832	
	CC00	CFFF	831	
		CC00	816	
	C800	CBFF	815	
		C800	800	
	C400	C7FF	799	8514/a Non–PS/2 EGA
		C400	784	VGA
	C000	C3FF	783	
		C000	768	
	BC00	BFFF	767	EGA/VGA Hercules CGA
		BC00	752	Text/Low Resolution Page 2
	B800	BBFF	751	
		B800	736	
	B400	F7FF	735	Monochrome Hercules
		B400	720	Page 1
	B000	B3FF	719	
		B000	704	
	AC00	AFFF	703	EGA/VGA High* Resolution Display Memory
		AC00	688	
	A800	ABFF	687	
		A800	672	
	A400	A7FF	671	
		A400	656	
	A000	A3FF	655	
640K		A000	640	

Figure 7-2 A detailed view of reserved I/O memory

The need for expanded memory was spun out of the 8086 processor's limited addressing capability. The 8086 processor has a 1-megabyte (1024K) address space. DOS, however, can only use 640K of that space for running programs; the remaining 384K is reserved for system use. Although the 80286, 80386, and 80486 processors have far greater addressing capabilities, they must shift to *protected mode* to access that capability. To maintain compatibility with the 8086 processor, these processors offer *real mode* (see the tip). DOS runs your programs in real mode. Although the 80286, 80386, and 80486 processors all have greater addressing capabilities, in real mode they all share the 640K limitation that DOS imposes for running programs.

Tip: Protected versus real mode

When the processor is running in protected mode, applications must follow specific rules in the way they address memory. The purpose of these rules is to make sure that one application does not violate (overwrite) another application's memory area. If an application doesn't follow the rules and violates the integrity of another, the processor terminates it.

When the processor is running in real mode, no such rules apply. For example, any program can access free memory blocks wherever they may be, in conventional memory or in reserved I/O memory. These accesses are allowed in DOS because it is a single-tasking operating system. For example, a TSR program can be loaded into a free block of memory, do its work, and get out without another application even knowing it has been there.

Windows' real mode gets its name from the state in which it runs the processor. By contrast, Windows' standard and 386 enhanced modes operate the processor in protected mode. In theory, Windows' real mode applications could access another application's memory area. They usually don't, however, because this would prevent them from running in standard or 386 enhanced mode. In fact, when an application overwrites another application's memory area, the application is terminated, and you see a message like the one in Figure 7-3.

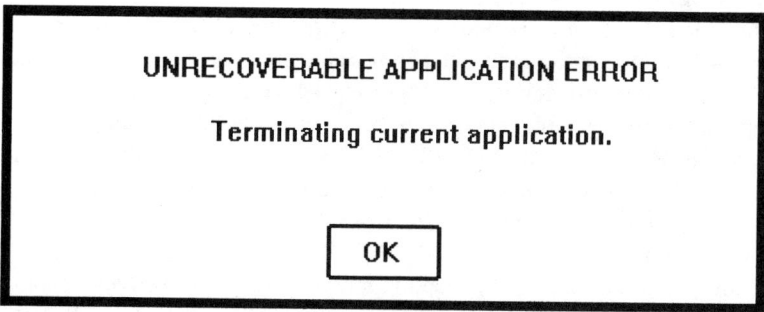

Figure 7-3 Unrecoverable error

In 1984, when Lotus Development Corporation was revising 1-2-3 Release 1A, they were aware that many 1A users had developed large spreadsheets that completely filled the 640K available in DOS. Yet the new version of 1-2-3, Release 2, would require about 60K more RAM than 1A. Unless something was done, users of Release 2 wouldn't be able to use the large spreadsheets they had developed for 1A.

Rather than disappoint their users, Lotus joined forces with Intel, and later Microsoft, and together they produced the Lotus-Intel-Microsoft (LIM) Expanded Memory Specification (EMS) 3.2. This specification outlines how a program can access add-on memory—so-called *expanded memory*—with the help of a control program, the *Expanded Memory Manager (EMM)*. (The EMM is in the form of a device driver.) By sending a series of requests to the EMM, a DOS program could access a large amount of data—well beyond the 640K limit of DOS—yet remain within the 1-megabyte address space of the 8086 processor.

The gist of the specification is that expanded memory would be provided by a special expanded memory card that would be divided into 16K-byte segments called *pages*. A DOS program could access up to 8 megabytes of expanded memory on the card through four contiguous pages (a total of 64K) located in the reserved I/O memory of the processor. It would be the responsibility of the EMM to map 16K pages from the expanded memory card into and out of the 64K area in reserved I/O memory. In this way, the 64K area in high memory would act as a "window" (called a *page frame*) onto the larger 8 megabyte address space of the expanded memory, in much the same way that with 1-2-3, for example, your screen is a window onto a large spreadsheet. Figure 7-4 shows a conceptual view of LIM EMS 3.2. The location of the page frame would be the responsibility of the EMM; it would scan the address space between C000 and F000 (768K and 960K) for an unused 64K-byte segment and automatically set up the page frame.

An important point to remember about EMS is that data is not physically copied from the EMS card to the RAM of the computer—that would be "swapping." EMS performs "bank switching." The EMM device driver simply changes the EMS card's page registers to make the pages in the page frame point to various pages in the EMS card. Once the page frame has been mapped to various locations on the EMS card, a DOS program can address the data on the EMS card—the data is now, for all practical purposes, located within the 1-megabyte address range of the processor.

The LIM EMS 3.2 standard was fine for storing data, such as spreadsheets, in expanded memory. However, DOS systems needed additional memory for purposes other than data storage. Programs were growing in size, and users were discovering multitasking in the form of terminate-and-stay-resident (TSR) utilities and task-switching environments that loaded more than one program at a time. LIM EMS 3.2 had the potential for running small programs, less than 64K in size, in expanded memory, but there was no provision for running larger programs. As a result, LIM EMS 3.2 provided little practical help for multitasking programs.

To provide for further use of expanded memory, AST, Quadram, and Ashton-Tate developed the Enhanced Expanded Memory Specification 3.2 (EEMS). This specification boosted the amount of expanded memory that a program could directly address by increasing the number of 16K pages from four to sixty-four. As a result, you could bank up to one full megabyte of memory at a time, the entire address range of an 8088

Windows Memory Management 233

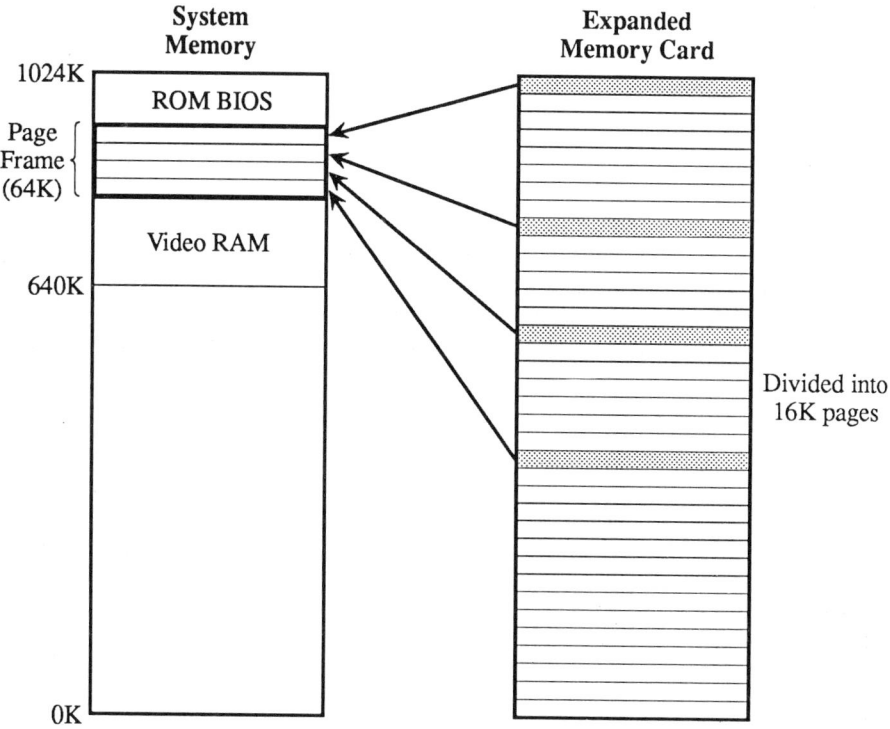

Figure 7-4 LIM EMS 3.2 requires a 64K page frame in reserved I/O memory consisting of four contiguous 16K pages

processor. In addition, the page frame itself no longer had to be four contiguous 16K pages. In fact, you needed no page frame at all.

To carry out this design, the EEMS specification provided for the ability to fill out or "backfill" conventional memory. Backfilling often required de-populating motherboard memory (pulling off chips or, on some older PCs, changing the motherboard switch settings), usually down to 256K, and letting the EMS card supply that memory instead. Figure 7-5 shows an example. As you can imagine, this would waste memory that you had paid for, but it had its advantages. By backfilling conventional memory, you could run multiple, large programs in EEMS memory. DESQview from Quarterdeck was the first program to take advantage of EEMS to multitask DOS programs.

In 1987, Lotus, Intel, and Microsoft expanded the EMS 3.2 specification to incorporate the EEMS provisions of direct access to up to one megabyte of memory and filling out or backfilling conventional memory. In addition, the new specification provided for up to 32 megabytes of expanded memory and added several other enhancements for improving multitasking. The resulting specification was christened the Lotus-Intel-Microsoft Expanded Memory Specification (EMS) 4.0.

To understand the benefit of backfilling expanded memory into the conventional 640K address space, and thus the real benefit of EMS 4.0 for multitasking, consider a system

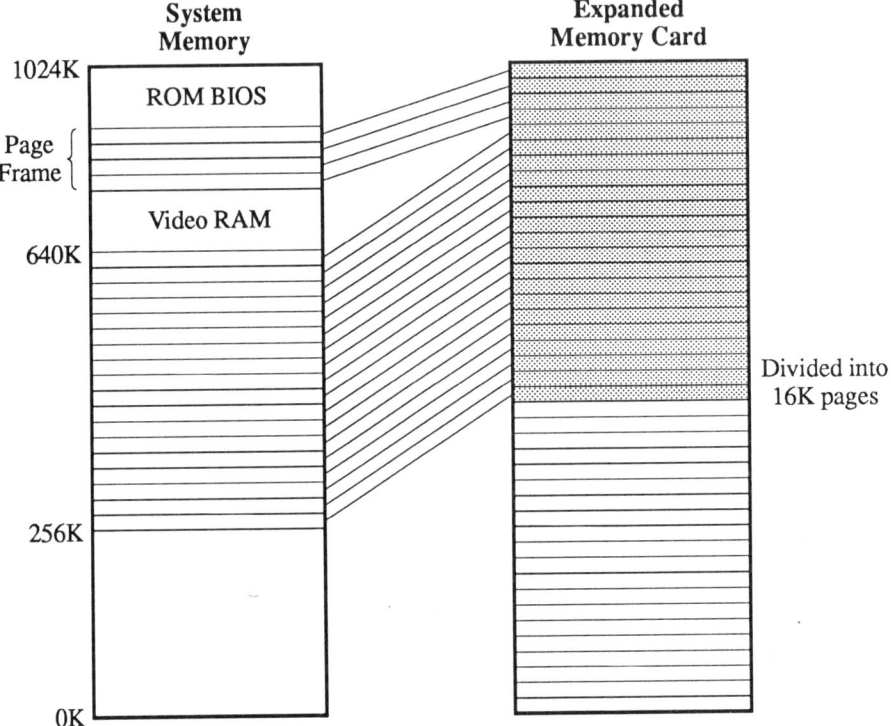

Figure 7-5 Backfilling conventional memory to 256K under EEMS 3.2 or EMS 4.0

like the one in Figure 7-5 with 256K of conventional memory on the motherboard and a fully populated 2-megabyte expanded memory board. The memory board is configured to backfill conventional memory to 640K. At the same time, the 384K used to backfill conventional memory remains in the expanded memory pool.

If an operating environment (such as Windows 3 in real mode) is running several applications at once that consume all conventional memory, and you try to start up another application, a program must be unloaded from memory to make room for the new one. However, because an application in the upper 384K of conventional memory already resides in expanded memory, all the operating environment has to do is allocate the appropriate number of 16K pages for the new application and map them into the 384K area in conventional memory. Pages formerly in that area are mapped out to expanded memory, and they retain their contents. Notice that this process avoids copying all the data through a 64K window. The process of switching between two previously loaded applications is similar. The pages holding the incoming application are mapped in, and the pages holding the suspended application are mapped out and retained.

Using a 64K page frame for mapping data into and out of expanded memory is known as *small-frame EMS*. Using bankable expanded memory pages in conventional memory is known as *large-frame EMS*. There are advantages and disadvantages to both as far as Windows is concerned. See "Real Mode with EMS 4.0 Memory" later for more on this.

> **Tip: The term "large-frame EMS" is a misnomer**
>
> The term "large-frame EMS" is a misnomer because the page frame is actually never any larger than four 16K pages and is always located in the 384K reserved I/O address space. Having additional bankable pages in conventional memory does not make the page frame any larger. Rather, it merely provides additional bankable pages.

EMS Emulators

From its first release in September 1985, the Expanded Memory Specification always has had two parts: a software specification for writing programs that interface with the Expanded Memory Manager and a hardware specification for designing expanded memory boards. What became clear to early readers of the specification, however, was that the hardware component of EMS didn't have to be supplied by an EMS board at all. Rather, it could be implemented in the form of software. When a program provides expanded memory services in place of expanded memory hardware, it is known as an *expanded memory emulator* or *simulator*.

The first EMS emulators were disk-based emulators. That is, they stored the data allocated to EMS pages to a swap file on disk. When an application requested that an EMS page be mapped into the page frame, the emulator read the page from the swap file on disk and mapped it to the page frame. Two examples of these early disk-based emulators are Above Disk and Turbo EMS, but these were only the ones that went to market. Just about anyone with a copy of the specification and an Assembler took a shot at it. There are two major problems with these programs: They usually place the EMS page frame and driver in conventional memory (eating up 80K and more), and they are pathetically slow compared to EMS hardware. Nevertheless, these programs continue to serve the needs of users who need EMS memory only occasionally and are not distressed by their slow speed.

Another form of EMS emulator that cropped up fairly early on was an extended-memory-based emulator. This type of emulator is similar to a disk-based emulator, except that the EMS pages are stored in extended memory rather than on disk. In other words, the EMS emulator allocates a block of extended memory and makes it look like expanded memory to programs that make EMS calls. EMS emulators of this type were first written for 286-based systems, but they never really caught on. There were two reasons why: The overhead required for copying data from conventional memory to expanded memory was prohibitive, and there were few 286-based systems with over 1 megabyte of extended memory—those that did usually got that memory from one of the newer EMS boards that could be configured as either expanded memory, extended memory, or both.

More recently, EMS emulators designed specifically for 386/486-based machines have come into being. These emulators use the protected mode and hardware paging capabilities of these chips and are, for the most part, extremely fast and reliable. Some examples of such emulators are 386Max from Qualitas, QEMM-386 from Quarterdeck, and CEMM from Compaq. In fact, these days, when you hear the term "EMS emulator," it usually means an 80386-based emulator.

Another advantage of EMS emulators like 386Max and QEMM-386 is that they can fill out unused memory addresses in your PC's reserved I/O memory with expanded memory. Therefore, you can load TSRs, network device drivers, mouse drivers, and DOS resources (for example, buffers) into that memory. This makes available somewhere between 30-130K more conventional memory in your system, depending on your video display and other hardware add-ons (see "Managing Memory with QEMM-386" for more details).

Windows 3 also offers its own EMS emulator, EMM386.SYS. If you have a 386/486-based system with plenty of extended memory, you can convert some of that extended memory to expanded using EMM386. (See Chapter 11, "Improving Windows Performance," for information on how to set up EMM386 on your system.) The only time you will want to use EMM386, however, is when you are running Windows in real mode, or when you need expanded memory when you are not running Windows. In real mode, Windows makes extensive use of expanded memory when it's available on your system (see "Real Mode with EMS 4.0 Memory"). On the other hand, if you are running Windows in 386 enhanced mode, you do not need EMM386; Windows can simulate expanded memory on its own without the help of an EMS emulator (see "DOS Applications in Windows").

Note: Unlike QEMM-386 or 386Max, the version of EMM386 that ships with Windows 3 doesn't let you relocate TSRs, device drivers, and DOS resources into your PC's reserved I/O memory area. However, when Windows is running in real mode, EMM386 does place EMS pages in the reserved I/O address space, boosting the size of Windows' global heap.

EXTENDED MEMORY

In 1984, the first PCs with 80286 processors were introduced. The 80286 processor could address up to 16 megabytes of memory. The 80386 processor made available in 1986 could address up to 4 gigabytes, over 4 billion bytes of memory. All the memory in these processors above the first megabyte is referred to as *extended memory*.

To access extended memory, the 286 and 386 processors must operate in *protected mode*. DOS cannot normally access this memory because it expects these processors to run in *real mode*—the mode in which the 286 and 386 processors can emulate the 8086. The 386 processor is also capable of running in a third mode, *virtual 8086 mode*, which has some features of real mode as well as protected mode; in particular, it has the ability to map memory (see "DOS Applications in 386 Enhanced Mode" later for more details).

Nevertheless, until recently, all the DOS programs you ran, or were likely to run, were limited to running in real mode and addressing memory in the first megabyte only. There were a few exceptions, however, in the form of RAM disks, print spoolers, and disk cache programs. One of the most well-known RAM disks is IBM's VDISK that is bundled with later versions of PC-DOS. VDISK uses a ROM BIOS call to temporarily switch the processor to protected mode, access some extended memory, and then switch the processor back to real mode. By placing a line like this in your CONFIG.SYS file, you could convert 384K of extended memory to a RAM disk:

```
DEVICE=C:\DOS\VDISK.SYS 384
```

Note: Windows comes with a RAM disk—RAMDrive—that lets you use expanded or extended memory. See Chapter 11, "Improving Windows Performance," for information on how to install RAMDrive on your system.

The eXtended Memory Specification (XMS)

The presence of extended memory, when combined with DOS's lack of support for it, proved too tempting for developers to pass up. The result was a hodge podge of approaches for accessing extended memory. In addition, applications often tried to use the same extended memory at the same time.

To overcome this disarray, Microsoft joined with Intel, Lotus, and AST Research to propose the eXtended Memory Specification (XMS). The purpose of XMS was to establish a uniform way for real-mode DOS applications to access extended memory as well as other areas of conventional memory that were not normally handled by DOS. The XMS standard deals with three types of memory blocks:

- Upper memory blocks (UMBs) in the 640K to 1024K range
- The *high memory area* (HMA) between 1024 and 1088 (described in the next section)
- Extended memory blocks (EMBs) above 1088K

To implement the XMS standard, Microsoft wrote the HIMEM.SYS eXtended Memory Manager (XMM). Windows/286 version 2.x used HIMEM.SYS to arbitrate the use of extended memory, and Windows 3 uses it as well. HIMEM.SYS is an installable device driver that allocates, resizes, and releases the memory blocks that XMS oversees. For example, whenever a program needs a chunk of extended memory (an *extended memory block* or *EMB*), it interacts with HIMEM.SYS to get it. Likewise, if a program wants to lay claim to a block of memory in the reserved I/O memory area (an *upper memory block* or *UMB*), it sends a request to HIMEM.SYS to allocate it. (See "The HIMEM.SYS Extended Memory Manager" later.)

The High Memory Area (HMA)

If you've followed the evolution of Windows over the last few years, you may recall that in 1987, when Microsoft introduced Windows/286, they announced that they had discovered a way to utilize 64K of extended memory as if it were conventional memory. Windows/286 used this memory to relocate Windows program code that was used for

238   *Windows 3 Power Tools*

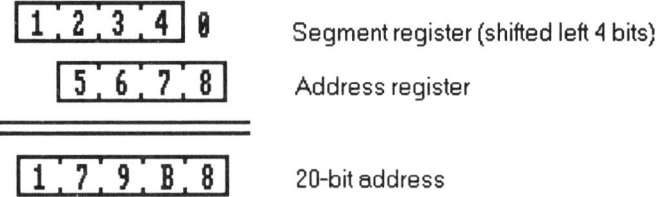

Figure 7-6 Memory addressing on an 8086-based PC

"user-related" functions, including code for handling windowing, menus, dialog boxes, and switching between applications. The upshot was that Windows/286 performed better in low memory situations and provided more conventional memory for running Windows applications (from 45K to 64K, depending on the system). How did Windows/286 access this extended memory while still remaining a real-mode program?

The answer lies in a programming trick that you might find interesting if you know a little hexadecimal arithmetic and are somewhat familiar with the way the PC addresses memory. You may recall that on an 8086 machine, memory addresses are 20-bits long and are calculated by shifting the contents of a 16-bit segment register 4 bits to the left and adding it to a 16-bit offset. For example, Figure 7-6 shows how the 8086 interprets the address 1234:5678H. (If you're interested in reproducing this example, try using the Calculator accessory in hexadecimal form—select View from Calculator's menu followed by Scientific, and then select the Hex radio button.)

If the result overflows the 20-bit address space, the upper 4 bits are discarded. For example, Figure 7-7 shows how the 8086 interprets the address FFFF:FFFFH.

On 80286-, 80386-, and 80486-based PCs, which have larger address spaces, 21-bit addresses are perfectly acceptable, provided the A20 line is enabled. The *A20 line* is a hardware address line in the processor that can be enabled or disabled through program control. If you repeat the operation in Figure 7-7 allowing 21-bit addressing, you get the result 10FFEFH. In fact, enabling the A20 line in these processors allows addresses in the range FFFF0H-10FFEFH. In other words, the first 65,520 bytes (64K less 16 bytes) of extended memory can be addressed without leaving real mode.

This 64K block that ranges from 1024K to 1088K is called the *high memory area (HMA)* and is an integral part of the XMS specification. (Note that the HMA should not

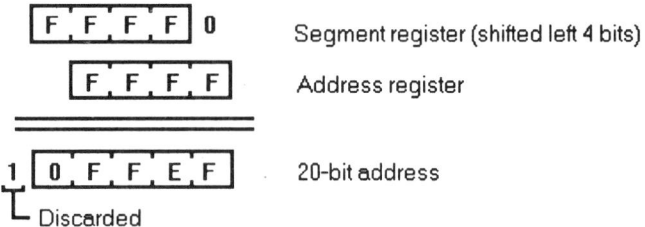

Figure 7-7 How the 8086 interprets the address FFFF:FFFFH

be confused with reserved I/O memory, called *high memory* by some, which is memory in the first megabyte above 640K.) The HIMEM.SYS driver arbitrates the use of the HMA between competing programs. In general, since the HMA is so small, it is mostly used by device drivers and TSRs. And because only one program at a time can use HMA, it is allocated as a unit on a first come, first served basis.

If a memory-resident program (such as a network device driver) uses the HMA before you load Windows, it is not available for Windows use. Therefore, if you know that a program uses the HMA before you load Windows and you want to run a DOS application from within Windows in 386 enhanced mode, you should turn off the Use High Memory Area check box in the DOS application's PIF (see Chapter 10, "Using Non-Windows Applications," for more details).

The HIMEM.SYS Extended Memory Manager

HIMEM.SYS is an extended memory manager that "administrates" the use of extended memory and reserved I/O memory (between 640K and 1024K) so that no two programs can use the same memory at the same time. HIMEM.SYS controls the use of extended memory according to the eXtended Memory Specification (XMS). If you do not use HIMEM, Windows 3 won't run in standard or 386 enhanced mode, nor will it use the high memory area (HMA) when running in real mode. Also, SMARTDrive and RAMDrive require HIMEM to be present when they are using extended memory (see Chapter 11, "Improving Windows Performance," for a complete discussion of these programs).

Note: You can, of course, substitute other XMS-compliant extended memory managers for HIMEM.SYS. For example, QEMM-386 is an excellent substitute (see "Managing Memory with QEMM-386").

When you install Windows, the Setup program detects whether you have a 80286-, 80386-, or 80486-based system, and automatically installs HIMEM.SYS. It does this by copying HIMEM.SYS to your root directory and placing a line like this in your CONFIG.SYS file:

```
DEVICE=C:\HIMEM.SYS
```

Setup always places this line before any other DEVICE= lines that install applications or device drivers that use extended memory (such as SMARTDrive). Otherwise, those utilities would not have the benefit of an extended memory manager and may not install properly. (See Chapter 11 for more on HIMEM.SYS.)

DOS Extenders

Although the first 80286-based system, the PC/AT, was introduced in 1984, the first DOS-compatible operating system to take advantage of the 80286 processor's protected mode, OS/2, didn't arrive until 1987. In the interim, DOS programs began to grow in size and complexity, and developers needed a way to access memory outside the 640K boundary of DOS. One creative solution was the DOS extender.

A *DOS extender* has many of the same features as an operating system—for example, the ability to shift the processor from real mode to protected mode and back, and to take advantage of extended memory. However, for many other tasks, such as file handling and device I/O, the DOS extender passes control back to MS-DOS and/or the BIOS. In addition, a DOS extender must be built into a DOS application. Therefore, the application must be specially written to take advantage of the DOS extender's unique capabilities. A DOS extender is really a hybrid program—it provides continued access to MS-DOS and BIOS services while allowing multimegabyte programs to run in protected mode.

One of the first programs to use DOS extender technology was 1-2-3 Release 3, which uses Rational Systems' DOS extender to access up to 16 megabytes of extended memory. Release 3 works its magic by placing a protected mode "shell" of about 30K into conventional RAM. The code in the shell then switches the processor to protected mode. Next it loads 1-2-3's program code and data at the top of extended memory, working its way downward toward conventional memory.

When you press a key in Release 3, or any other application for that matter, the processor is notified by an interrupt. The interrupt must be serviced by the keyboard-handling code that resides in the ROM BIOS, and this code must be run in real mode. The DOS extender handles this situation by intercepting the keypress interrupt from the BIOS in protected mode. It then saves the processor state and switches the processor back to real mode, where it reissues the interrupt so that it can be handled by the BIOS keyboard-handling routine. Next, the DOS extender switches the processor back to protected mode, restores the processor state, and picks up program execution where it left off—for example, recalculating the spreadsheet or updating the screen. A similar process happens with each timer tick, about 16 times a second.

With the delicate dance that DOS extenders must perform, it's a wonder that they work at all. The truth is that they work quite well and have become an integral part of many popular DOS applications that would otherwise be too large for DOS. Besides 1-2-3 Release 3, other programs that use DOS extenders are AutoCAD 386, Q&A 386, and Paradox 386.

By necessity, Windows 3 must work with programs that incorporate DOS extenders; but it doesn't work with all of them, and fewer still in 386 enhanced mode. In fact, for programs that incorporate DOS extenders to work in 386 enhanced mode, the DOS extender code must conform to a new set of rules that Microsoft established for that purpose. The next sections will give you some background on these new rules.

Virtual Control Program Interface (VCPI)

If a DOS extender's only job were to intercept DOS and BIOS interrupts and switch the processor from protected mode to real mode and back, that would be one thing. But the state of affairs gets more complicated when you are running an EMS emulator and a DOS extender at the same time and both are trying to switch the processor to protected mode and allocate extended memory.

It was for exactly this kind of contention that Quarterdeck (the developers of QEMM-386 and DESQview) and Phar Lap (the developers of 386|DOS Extender) joined together in 1987 to draft the Virtual Control Program Interface (VCPI). This is a program interface that allows EMS emulators and DOS extenders to live together peacefully on 80386- and 80486-based systems, avoiding the kind of chaos that befalls TSRs in DOS. The VCPI interface is designed so that when a DOS Extender makes VCPI calls (similar to LIM 4.0 calls), the EMS emulator provides support for them. Most EMS emulators (with the notable exception of Windows 3's EMM386) and DOS extenders are written to support VCPI, with the result that compatibility between the two is usually not a problem.

Compatibility between *multitaskers* and DOS extenders is another matter, however, even when both support VCPI. When a multitasker is character-based and includes the VCPI interface, there are usually no conflicts between it and a DOS extender that supports VCPI. For example, you can easily run 1-2-3 Release 3 and/or AutoCAD 386 under DESQview 386 because all these programs are VCPI compliant and DESQview is character-based.

There are two problems with VCPI as far as Windows 3 is concerned, however. First, VCPI was originally designed for 386/486-based systems and doesn't apply at all to 286-based systems, neglecting a significant portion of the Windows 3 user base. Second, even more restrictive, VCPI requires that DOS applications run in a full-screen display rather than in a window. (VCPI does not permit Windows to "virtualize" the screen—that is, for a DOS application that directly accesses the screen, Windows cannot remap its screen I/O to a buffer and then use the contents of that buffer in a window, as it typically does with this type of DOS application. Instead, extended DOS applications that directly access the screen must run full screen under VCPI.) For Windows 3, which is entirely graphics-based, these shortcomings were unacceptable, and Microsoft decided to support a different standard altogether in Windows 3—the DOS Protected Mode Interface (DPMI).

The DOS Protected Mode Interface (DPMI)

The DOS Protected Mode Interface (DPMI) was designed by Microsoft with the broad goal of letting extended DOS applications run within DOS-based multitasking environments and access up to 16 megabytes of extended memory directly. Implicit in this goal are support for Windows' graphics-based environment and control of any DOS software that uses protected mode, regardless of whether it's running on a 286, 386, or 486 processor.

DPMI Version 0.9 is built into Windows 3 and, as you can tell by its version number, is still in an early stage of development. Currently, the only program that supports DPMI is 1-2-3 Release 3.1, because of Lotus' and Rational System's early involvement with Microsoft in designing the DPMI specification. For other extended DOS programs to work in 386 enhanced mode, there must be voluntary cooperation of DOS extender developers; the needed cooperation seems more likely with the growing success of Windows. Beyond this, developers who use DOS extenders will need time to incorporate DPMI support into their products. Even with complete cooperation among all the parties involved, it is still likely to take quite a while before there are many extended DOS applications that work with Windows in 386 enhanced mode.

In the meantime, because of the XMS support provided to Windows by the HIMEM.SYS extended memory driver, extended DOS applications that do not support DPMI can run under Windows in real or standard mode.

WINDOWS MEMORY CONFIGURATIONS

In many ways, Windows 3 consists of four distinct and very different programs when it comes to memory management. These programs correspond to the three different configurations in which you can start Windows, plus one other.

- **Real mode**: The basic 640K memory configuration that provides compatibility with previous versions of Windows.
- **Real mode with EMS 4.0 memory**: The basic 640K configuration with Lotus-Intel-Microsoft (LIM) Expanded Memory Specification (EMS) 4.0 memory.
- **Standard mode**: The "normal" operating mode for Windows that accesses extended memory on 80286 and higher processors and lets you switch between DOS applications.
- **386 enhanced mode**: Provides access to the virtual memory capabilities of the 386 processor, which lets Windows access more memory than is physically available. This mode also lets you multitask DOS applications, each in its own 8086 virtual machine.

The sections that follow describe each of these memory configurations in detail. To keep the discussion intelligible, only the way in which Windows handles Windows applications is covered at first. Next, Windows' handling of DOS applications is covered.

REAL MODE

Windows' real mode assumes that your system has 640K of conventional memory, although it will actually run in as little as 384K of free conventional memory. (To force Windows to run in real mode, you use the /R switch on startup.) At the base of this memory are the following items:

- Interrupt vector table
- BIOS table
- MS-DOS
- Device drivers
- Any TSRs you loaded before starting Windows

Any conventional memory located above these items is available for loading Windows and applications and is called the *global heap*. Figure 7-8 shows a conceptual view of real mode.

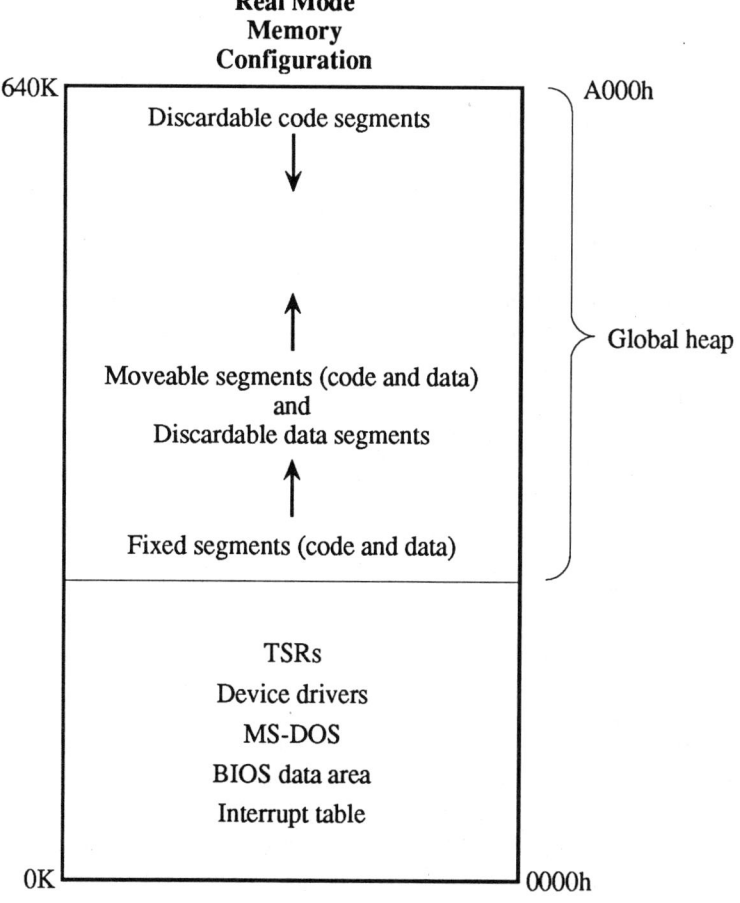

Figure 7-8 Real mode memory configuration

Note: If you've loaded HIMEM.SYS from your CONFIG.SYS file, Windows real mode memory configuration uses the high memory area (HMA) as part of the global heap. In this case, the top of the global heap is at approximately 704K, not 640K as shown in Figure 7-8. Of course, you must have a 286- or 386-based system with more than 640K in order to load HIMEM.SYS.

How Windows Manages Segments and Memory Blocks

Like DOS applications, Windows applications are divided into segments of 64K or less. Normally, one segment is used for code and another is used for data (although large applications often have more than one code segment). The code segment represents the program's instructions, and the data segment contains all the data for the program.

When you start an application in Windows, it loads the application's code and data segments using memory from the global heap. Because Windows can run more than one application at a time, memory becomes tighter as you load and run more applications.

To help minimize each application's impact on memory, Windows requires programmers to classify an application's segments as fixed, movable, or discardable. Most code and data segments are *movable*, meaning that Windows can rearrange them anywhere it wants in memory to make more room for other applications.

In addition, most code segments are *discardable*, meaning that Windows can move the segment in memory and/or destroy the segment's contents when either Windows itself or another application needs the memory it occupies. (To discard the segment, Windows simply reallocates it with a length of zero.) Fortunately, when a new code segment is needed, Windows can always load it from the application's executable file on disk. By contrast, data segments are rarely discardable, because destroying them would blow away your work.

Programmers may occasionally classify a code segment as *fixed*, meaning that it must remain at a fixed location in memory—Windows can neither move nor discard it. This is done to improve a program's speed, though fixing a segment in memory is frowned upon by Windows for reasons you'll see in a minute. Fixed code segments are primarily used for ISR (interrupt service routine) code to support devices like the mouse, keyboard, and the communication ports.

When an application needs a block of memory, it usually gets the block from the *local heap*, the free memory in the application's data segment. However, if an application needs a large chunk of memory (typically 1K or larger), it can use memory directly from the global heap. For example, when a program needs to read a bitmap from disk into memory, it usually allocates a chunk of memory from the global heap and reads the bitmap into it. Like segments, blocks of global memory that an application is using are classified as movable, discardable, or fixed, depending on how the program is using them at the time or the way a programmer has allocated them. In any case, when an application no longer needs a block of global memory, it frees the block so that other applications can use it.

The importance of classifying segments and blocks becomes more relevant as you look at how Windows manages them within memory. Figure 7-8 shows where Windows locates segments in the global heap (the same principles apply to blocks). When Windows loads applications into memory, it loads fixed segments (code and data) beginning at the bottom of the global heap and working its way upward. Movable segments (code and data) are then loaded above fixed segments. Discardable data segments are also loaded in the lower portion of the global heap above fixed segments. Discardable code segments, on the other hand, are loaded from the top of the global heap, working downward.

When you load a new application that has a fixed segment into memory, Windows relocates movable segments and discardable data segments in the global heap in order to place the fixed segment as low in memory as possible. Likewise, when you quit an application, Windows consolidates or "defragments" free memory by moving movable segments downward in memory.

In general, programmers are discouraged from using fixed segments because rearranging segments in memory takes away valuable processor time that could be used for applications. Therefore, using movable segments is far more common.

Suppose memory is tight and you load another application. Windows may need to discard segments to make room for new segments. It determines which segments to discard based on a least-recently-used (LRU) algorithm. If you haven't used an application for a while, its discardable segments are likely candidates for elimination. By discarding (and later reloading) segments, Windows can actually have more applications in memory than the amount of physical memory in the global heap would normally allow. These same mechanisms for compacting memory apply in all the different Windows memory configurations.

An important point to notice about real mode is that Windows does not perform any disk swapping in this mode (copying segments to disk and back). However, an application may swap its own data to and from disk without any special help from Windows.

How Windows Uses Extended Memory in Real Mode

When you run Windows in real mode, many segments are discarded, since Windows frequently needs the memory for some other purpose. For example, Windows typically discards all the discardable segments it can when you are running several Windows applications at once and they are larger than available memory.

However, if extended memory is available (through HIMEM.SYS), rather than eliminate a discardable segment, Windows copies it to extended memory. That way, instead of having to read a new copy of the discardable segment from disk, it can retrieve it from extended memory. The result is that Windows operates noticeably faster in real mode when you have extended memory available.

REAL MODE WITH EMS 4.0 MEMORY

If you are running Windows in real mode and your system has EMS 4.0 memory, either from an EMS board that you have used to backfill conventional memory or from an EMS emulator (such as EMM386.SYS), the size of the global heap grows substantially. As Figure 7-9 shows, the global heap now includes memory between A000H (640K) and F000H (960K); as is always the case, the memory between F000H and FFFFH is still reserved for the ROM BIOS. Some other areas between A000H and F000H are also reserved for video memory and other add-on hardware, such as a network card. So even though the amount of memory between A000H and F000H is 320K, the actual amount available is typically 288K or less.

Small- Versus Large-Frame EMS Mode

When Windows finds approximately 280K of free, mappable expanded memory pages in *conventional* memory, it will automatically switch into large-frame EMS mode. If it finds less than this amount available, it will automatically use small-frame EMS mode.

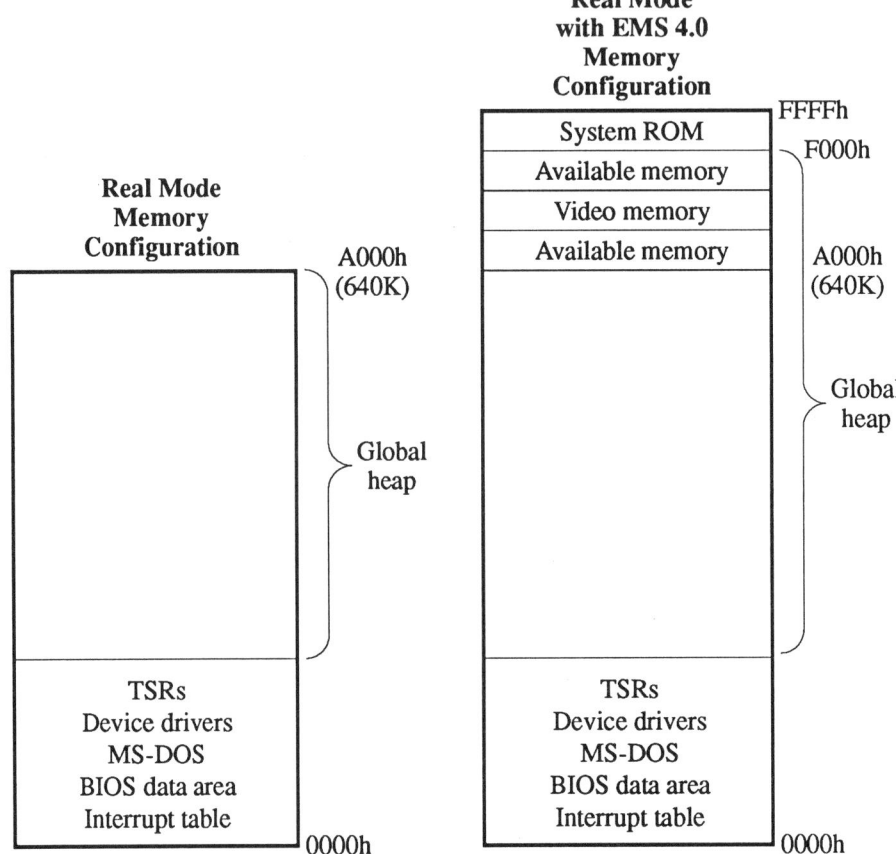

Figure 7-9 Real mode memory configuration with EMS 4.0 memory

You can use command-line switches to force Windows to operate in small- or large-frame EMS mode (see the following).

The value of having large-frame EMS 4.0 memory available in your system becomes most apparent when you are multitasking Windows applications in real mode. When you switch from one application to another, Windows maps the first application's code and data from the global heap into expanded memory. Next, it maps the second application's code and data from expanded memory into the global heap. Figure 7-10 shows how Windows handles the mapping or "banking" of applications when EMS 4.0 is available. As the figure indicates, the more expanded memory you have, the greater the number of applications you can run simultaneously.

Windows does not actually move data between expanded memory and the lower 1-megabyte address space. Rather, it modifies the EMS card's page registers to change the contents of that space. In addition, Windows only performs this feat when you switch between applications.

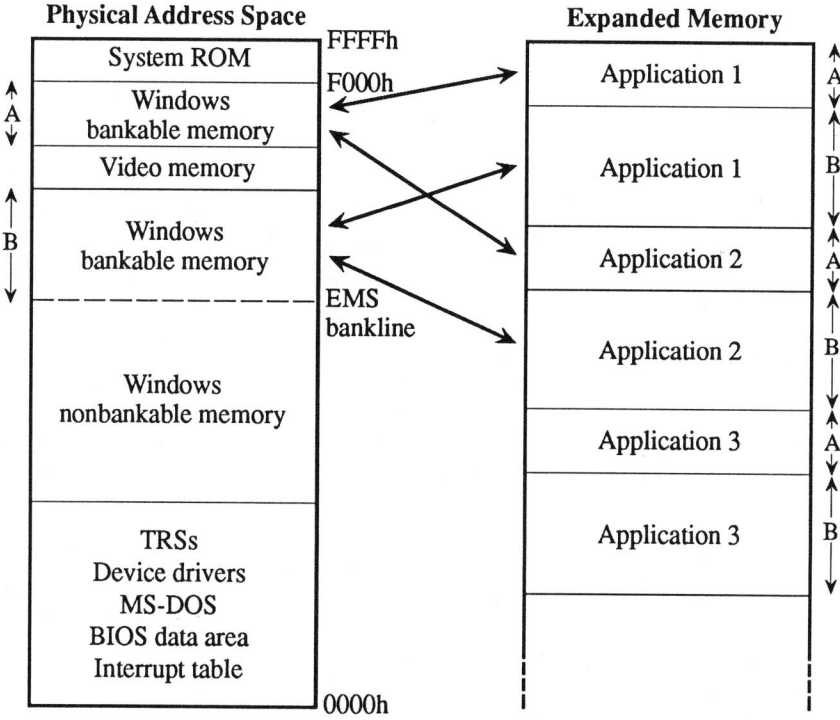

Figure 7-10 How Windows banks applications between expanded memory and the global heap

Adjusting the EMS Line: The /L Switch

Not all objects that reside in the global heap can be banked into expanded memory. For example, Windows creates application-specific data that it uses to manage applications, so-called *task databases*, which are never banked to expanded memory. The dividing line between those objects that can be banked and those that cannot is known as the *EMS bank line*.

Windows sets the EMS bank line automatically, based on the amount of memory available in the global heap; so there is no way to set the precise position of the EMS bank line. However, you can move the EMS bank line's relative position in 16K increments by using the /L switch when you start Windows. For example, the command line **WIN /R /L+16** moves the EMS bank line up 16K. Conversely, the line **WIN /R /L-16** moves the EMS bank line down 16K.

Note: Although it is possible to move the EMS bank line down, you should avoid doing so because it may impinge on the memory that Windows uses to store nonbankable data. When you impinge on this memory, Windows may have trouble printing or using fonts.

248   *Windows 3 Power Tools*

You can force Windows to start in small-frame EMS mode by using an arbitrarily high number with the /L switch. For example, the line **WIN /R /L+200** will usually do the trick.

Adjusting the Large-Frame EMS Point: The /E Switch

By using the /E switch when you start Windows, you can adjust the 280K default point at which Windows uses large-frame EMS mode. For example, the command line **WIN /R /E100** causes Windows to use large-frame EMS mode when at least 100K of free, mappable EMS pages is available in conventional memory. By contrast, the command line **WIN /R /E600** always forces Windows into small-frame EMS mode because there is never a case where a full 600K of free EMS pages is available.

Tip: Windows' choice of small- or large-frame EMS is usually the best choice

As a general rule, Windows normally chooses small- or large-frame EMS mode for a good reason. If you force Windows to use the opposite mode from what it chooses automatically, you may be preventing it from using memory efficiently. For example, when Windows runs in large-frame EMS mode, it is capable of placing more items above the EMS bank line and thereby banking those items out to expanded memory. However, if you force Windows to run in small-frame EMS mode, it is incapable of banking as many items, resulting in a less efficient use of memory.

Disabling Windows' Use of Expanded Memory: The /N Switch

By using the /N switch when you start Windows, you can disable Windows' use of expanded memory. Note that this does not disable expanded memory in your system. It merely prevents Windows from using it.

STANDARD MODE

Windows uses standard mode by default when your system has either of the following:

- An 80286 processor with 1 megabyte of memory or more.
- An 80386 processor with more than 1 but less than 2 megabytes of memory. (If your system has 2 megabytes of memory or more, Windows uses 386 enhanced mode.)

You can also force Windows to run in standard mode by using the /S switch on startup. The minimum requirement for running Windows in standard mode is an 80286 processor with 192K of free extended memory.

> **Tip: Actual standard mode memory requirements**
>
> As a general rule, Windows requires approximately 330K to 520K combined conventional and extended memory to run in standard mode. What's more, you typically need at least 128K of conventional memory available at the DOS prompt to start Windows in standard mode, assuming sufficient extended memory is available.
>
> For example, suppose you have 208K of extended memory available. You'll need at least 128K of free conventional memory to start Windows in standard mode. As another example, if you have 192K of free extended memory, you'll need approximately 322K of conventional memory to start Windows in standard mode.

In standard mode, the processor operates in protected mode and the global heap consists of three distinct areas of memory:

- **Conventional memory**: The amount of conventional memory available for the global heap is the same as when you are running Windows in real mode. It includes all conventional memory above MS-DOS—any TSRs you've loaded before starting Windows, device drivers, and the like.

- **Extended memory**: When you start Windows, it allocates *all* the extended memory in the system using the XMS driver (normally HIMEM.SYS). Windows then accesses the extended memory directly, without using the XMS driver. The theoretical maximum amount of memory you can have in the extended memory block is 15 megabytes (16 megabytes of address space less the lower 1 megabyte). On a more practical level, however, the size of the block available for the global heap depends on the amount of extended memory you have in your system and what you've loaded into that memory prior to starting Windows. For example, if you've loaded SMARTDrive from your CONFIG.SYS, you'll have a smaller block of extended memory available for the global heap.

- **High memory area (HMA)**: When you start Windows, it uses the XMS driver to determine if the high memory area (HMA) is available. If it is available, Windows adds it to the global heap. The only time it is not available is when another application has already used it before you start Windows, and since very few programs actually use the HMA, it is almost always available to Windows.

Figure 7-11 shows Windows standard mode memory configuration.

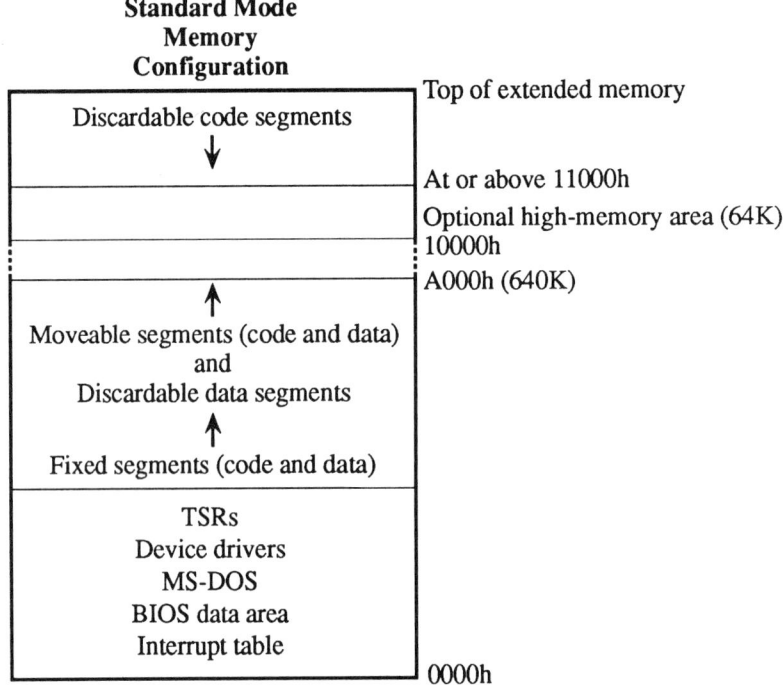

Figure 7-11 Standard mode memory configuration

When Windows runs in standard mode it makes no distinction between conventional and extended memory. Rather, it treats it all as one entity—the global heap.

Like the other memory configurations, Windows loads discardable code segments from the top of memory, working downward. Fixed code and data segments are loaded at the base of the global heap, and movable code and data segments are loaded above fixed segments.

386 ENHANCED MODE

If you have a 80386-based system with 2 megabytes of extended memory or more, Windows runs in 386 enhanced mode. You can also force windows to run in this mode by using the /3 switch on startup, provided you have at least 1 megabyte of extended memory.

In 386 enhanced mode, the 80386 processor operates in protected mode, which in theory allows Windows to address up to 4 gigabytes of memory. In addition, Windows takes advantage of the 80386 processor's native ability to work with *virtual memory* and perform disk swapping. In Windows's virtual memory scheme, the amount of memory available to applications equals the amount of free RAM in the system plus the amount of disk space allocated to a swap file. As a result, the amount of memory available to applications can be several times the amount of physical memory available in the system.

> **Tip: Actual 386 enhanced mode memory requirements**
>
> Windows requires approximately 580K to 624K of combined conventional and extended memory to run in 386 enhanced mode. In addition, you typically need a minimum of 182K of conventional memory available at the DOS prompt to start Windows in 386 enhanced mode. Be aware, however, that if you start Windows in a low memory situation, it may be extremely slow because it relies on virtual memory to make up the difference. When Windows relies heavily on virtual memory, it slows down because it spends a lot of time swapping to and from disk.

Although Windows can in theory address up to 4 gigabytes of memory in 386 enhanced mode, the actual limit is much smaller than that. In order to maintain compatibility with 286-based PCs, the standard Windows memory model is built around 16-bit segmented addressing, not the 32-bit flat addressing available to 386 and 486 processors. (The Windows SDK does provide 32-bit memory management functions, but few vendors take advantage of them today because it would mean that their applications could only run on 386- and 486-based PCs.) This means that Windows is actually limited to 16 megabytes of memory and 64 megabytes of virtual (disk based) memory in 386 enhanced mode.

Figure 7-12 shows a conceptual view of the 386 enhanced mode memory configuration. In many ways, this view resembles the real mode or standard mode memory configuration. Notice that Windows doesn't "bank" applications between the 1-megabyte address space and secondary memory as it does in real mode with EMS 4.0 memory. Rather, it treats the entire virtual address space (conventional memory, extended memory, and disk space available for swapping) as the global heap.

Like all the other memory configurations, Windows places fixed data segments at the base of the global heap and movable data segments directly above. Discardable code segments are placed at the top of memory, working downward. Windows defragments memory in 386 enhanced mode in the same way it defragments memory in the real-mode memory configuration.

How Virtual Memory Works in 386 Enhanced Mode

In real and standard mode, when memory gets tight and you launch a new application, Windows begins removing discardable segments to make room for the new application's segments. This usually means that the discardable segments are cast away, and when they are needed again, Windows must read them from the applications' executable files on

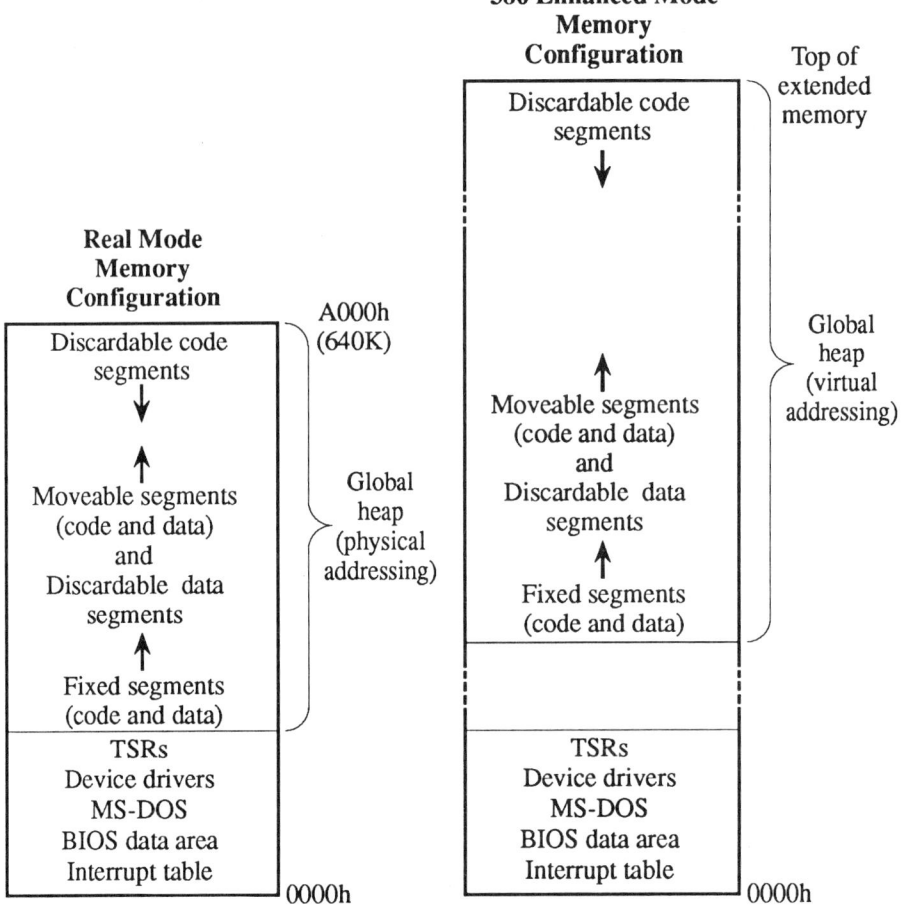

Figure 7-12 386 enhanced mode memory configuration

disk. (The one exception is in real mode when Windows copies the segments to extended memory.)

In 386 enhanced mode, Windows may remove discardable segments from disk when memory gets tight, but it does not cast them away. Rather it saves the segments to disk, so that they can be read back in later when they are needed.

Another important feature of 386 enhanced mode's virtual memory scheme is *paging*. The way paging works is that Windows keeps allocating physical memory until it runs out. When more is needed, Windows begins moving 4K pages of code and data from physical memory to disk to make more physical memory available. Windows "pages" 4K blocks because that is the fixed page size best suited to the architecture of the 80386 processor. The 4K block may be part of one code or data segment, or it may encompass part of one segment and part of another.

Later on, if an application should try to use a code or data segment and part of that segment has been paged out to disk, the 80386 processor issues a "page fault" to Windows. The *page fault* tells Windows to swap other 4K pages from physical memory to disk to make room for the application's pages, which it then swaps back in. The pages that Windows chooses for swapping out to disk are based on a least-recently-used (LRU) algorithm. If you haven't used an application for a while, blocks from its discardable segments are likely candidates for being paged to disk.

In 386 enhanced mode, Windows uses either a temporary or a permanent swap file when memory gets low. A permanent swap file is one you create with the SWAPFILE utility while running Windows in real mode. On the other hand, a temporary swap file is created automatically by Windows if it cannot find a permanent swap file. Windows creates the temporary swap file in your \WINDOWS directory and removes it when you exit Windows. The advantage of using a permanent swap file over a temporary swap file is that it is much faster because it consists of contiguous disk blocks, and because Windows can access it without calling MS-DOS. If Windows must create a temporary swap file, it grabs free disk blocks wherever it finds them—which, depending on the layout of your hard disk, may be scattered all over the place. As a result, accessing a temporary swap file can be relatively time consuming as the disk drive head may have to move all over the drive surface to read the file. See Chapter 11, "Improving Windows Performance," for a complete discussion of swap files.

Windows' management of code and data segments operates on top of its paging mechanism. In other words, Windows uses virtual memory as if it were physical memory for purposes of managing segments. Only when virtual memory is exhausted does Windows cast away discardable segments. When this happens, you can expect Windows to slow down considerably as it faces the dual responsibility of reading data from the swap file and restoring code segments from executable files on disk. The presence of SMARTDrive (the disk-caching program) can help speed up this process considerably. But when memory gets full, you face the dilemma of whether it is better to have more extended memory available for running applications or to allocate the memory to SMARTDrive for disk-caching. Chapter 11 will help you sort these issues out.

Windows paging mechanism is completely hidden from you as a user. (It's even hidden from programmers.) As a result, you cannot tell where a program resides in virtual memory at a given point in time. Nonetheless, you can guarantee that Windows is maximizing the use of virtual memory on your system by allocating a permanent swap file.

As a general rule, the maximum size of virtual memory is four times the size of the physical memory on your system. In other words, if you have four megabytes of physical memory on your system, the maximum size of virtual memory is 16 megabytes. This assumes, of course, that you have sufficient free disk space available to accommodate the swapped out pages. Figure 7-13 shows a view of this memory.

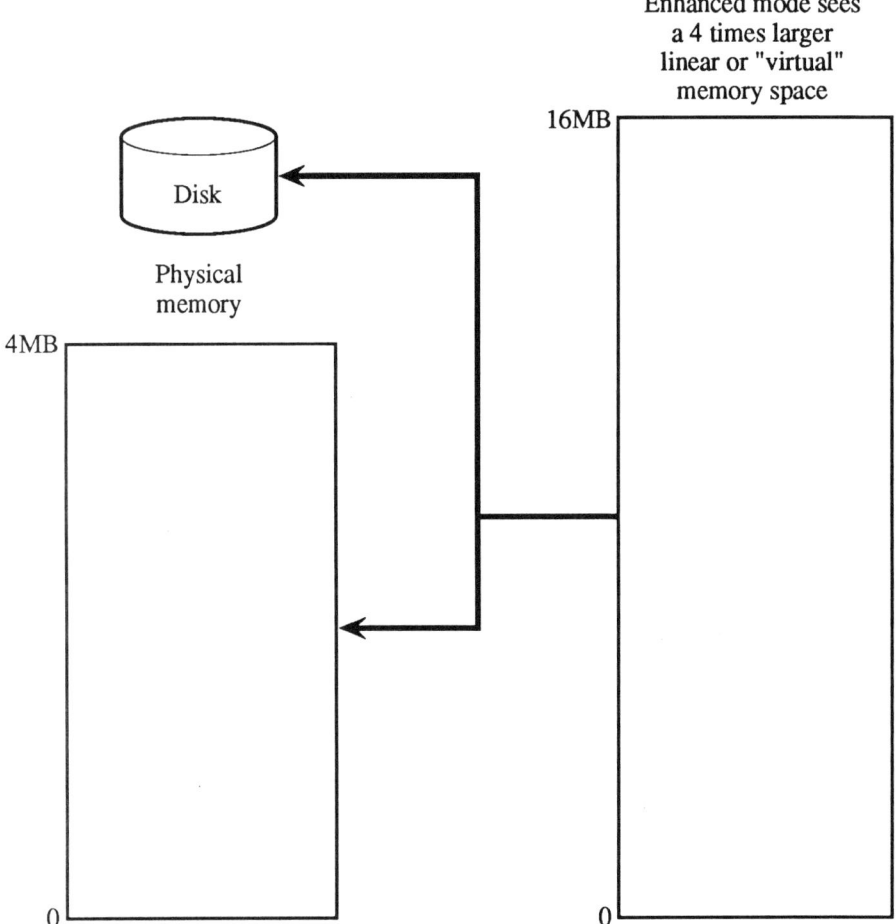

Figure 7-13 The relationship between physical and virtual memory in 386 enhanced mode

DOS APPLICATIONS IN WINDOWS

More than any previous version, Windows 3 provides a rich environment for running DOS applications and even for multitasking them in 386 enhanced mode. This section describes some of the more technical aspects of how Windows runs DOS applications. It begins by discussing how Windows/286 handled them and progresses into how Windows 3 handles them in all its different operating modes.

DOS Applications in Windows/286

To get a feel for how Windows 3 handles DOS applications, it's helpful to review how Windows/286 handled them. Windows/286 divided DOS applications into three groups: good applications, bad applications, and resource-intensive applications.

In Windows/286, a "good" (or "well-behaved") application was a character-mode application that made DOS and BIOS calls—the slowest form of video output, but the safest for compatibility's sake. Windows/286 would intercept many of these DOS and BIOS calls and translate them into Windows function calls. For example, when a DOS application made BIOS video calls to write text to the screen, Windows/286 would translate these calls into Windows function calls that would display the text in graphics form within a window. Examples of good applications were the basic DOS commands (for example, FORMAT and DISKCOPY) and early versions of WordPerfect and Microsoft Project. These programs could be run in a window in Windows/286.

The term "bad program" was first used to describe those programs that bypassed DOS and the BIOS and wrote directly to video memory. These programs were considered bad because IBM and Microsoft wouldn't promise upward compatibility for them in future versions of DOS, a posture that was later abandoned because so many programs broke the rules. In Windows parlance, the term "bad application" (or "bad app") had a slightly broader meaning and was used to describe any program that made use of graphics or directly accessed the machine's hardware (the screen or keyboard). Actually, many of the best DOS programs were considered bad apps for Windows/286. For example, Microsoft Word was considered a bad app when it was running in graphics mode. Some other bad apps were 1-2-3 and dBASE because they wrote directly to video memory. These applications could only run full-screen in Windows/286.

Resource-intensive applications were those that needed all the memory in the system, or on the graphics display card, such as early versions of AutoCAD and R:Base System V. When you wanted to run such an application in Windows/286, you would first have to close down all the other applications currently running, even Windows applications. Then, when you launched the resource-intensive application, Windows would remove itself from memory to give the application as much memory as possible in which to run. You as a user would have to identify a resource-intensive application to Windows/286 by turning on the Directly Modifies Memory option in the application's PIF (Program Information File). If you didn't, the application would very likely crash the system. Another point about resource-intensive applications is that you could not switch away from them without exiting from them first.

DOS Applications in Real and Standard Modes

One of the real problems with earlier versions of Windows was that it was hard for a user to know how to classify DOS applications as good, bad, or resource-intensive. As a result, you couldn't predict when a program would have problems with the screen or, worse yet, crash the system.

In Windows 3, Microsoft took a lot of the guesswork out of running DOS applications. In fact, it's pretty rare to have problems that afflict the screen or hang the system. Microsoft's strategy for making DOS applications and Windows more neighborly in real and standard modes is slightly different than for 386 enhanced mode.

In Windows 3 real and standard modes, Microsoft abandoned the idea of trying to keep Windows resident while DOS applications are running. Instead, all DOS applications are now treated like Windows/286 resource-intensive applications, and Windows moves itself out to disk, out of harm's way. However, unlike Windows/286, you don't have to leave all your other applications before launching a DOS application, and when a DOS application is running, you don't have to exit from it to switch away.

Another idea Microsoft abandoned from earlier versions was that of running DOS applications in a window. In real and standard modes, all DOS applications must run full screen—no great loss here, since you could run very few applications in a window in previous versions anyway.

To run your DOS applications, Windows in real mode uses a "shell" program, WINOLDAP.MOD, which acts as an interface between DOS applications and Windows (this is an updated version of the same program used in Windows/286). In the same way, Windows uses WINOA286.MOD for standard mode and WINOA386.MOD for 386 enhanced mode. In previous versions of Windows, WINOLDAP.MOD would provide cut and paste support for DOS applications that could be run in a window. In Windows 3, only WINOA386.MOD provides this support.

WINOLDAP.MOD (and friends) also provides support for the DOS application *screen grabber*, a special device driver that makes DOS applications that use graphics mode or write directly to screen memory visible on the screen. In previous versions of Windows, the screen grabber was found in WINOLDAP.GRB; the Windows Setup program created this file, which was specially tailored to your display type. In Windows 3, the WINOLDAP.GRB file has been replaced by two grabber files that are named in the [boot] section of your SYSTEM.INI file. One grabber file is used for real and standard mode and is named after the 286grabber= statement and another is used for 386 enhanced mode and is named after the 386grabber= statement. For example, if you have a standard VGA display, the grabber file for real and standard mode is VGACOLOR.GR2 and for 386 enhanced mode is VGA.GR3. Windows automatically changes the grabber file settings when you specify a new display type in the Windows Setup program.

Tip: Finding out which grabber is needed for a given display

If you want to see which grabber is needed for a given display, use Notepad to read the contents of the SETUP.INF file on your \WINDOWS directory (this file contains all the settings that Windows Setup uses when you install Windows on your system). By paging down to the [display] section of the file, you'll find the 286 grabber and 386 grabber settings for all the display types that Windows supports. (See Chapter 9, "Changing Your Setup," for information on the other settings in this section of the SETUP.INF file.)

When you launch a DOS application and Windows moves itself out of memory, it leaves behind a small footprint (of about 20K) so that it can reload itself. As a result, your DOS applications will have slightly less memory available to them when you are running them under Windows in real or standard mode than when you are running them under standalone DOS.

In the process of swapping itself out to disk, Windows creates a temporary hidden file for itself named ~WOA0000.TMP in the \WINDOWS\TEMP directory. This file holds the information that Windows needs to restore itself when you later switch back. In fact, if you have a DOS program that can view hidden files, such as the Norton Utilities, you can run it under Windows and see the ~WOA0000.TMP swap file that Windows creates. Windows eliminates this file when you switch away from the DOS application and back to Windows.

In the same way, Windows creates a temporary *application swap file* whenever you switch away from a DOS application. You can use File Manager to view these hidden files in the \WINDOWS\TEMP directory; make sure you select the View Include command and turn on the View Show Hidden/System Files option. Application swap files also begin with ~*WOA*—for example, ~WOA1DC0.TMP. WOA stands for Windows Old Applications. An application swap file remains until you exit the DOS application. However, if the system should crash before Windows has an opportunity to erase the application swap files, they will remain on your hard disk. Fortunately, Windows will overwrite them the next time you access a DOS application from real or standard mode. Figure 7-14 shows some examples of application swap files. Notice that each application swap file occupies about 530K on disk, although for small DOS applications, such as Procomm in this example, the amount is significantly less.

Along with the application swap files that begin with ~*WOA*, notice that there are other files that begin with ~*GRB*. These are temporary grabber files that house the information Windows needs to restore the display when you switch back to a DOS application.

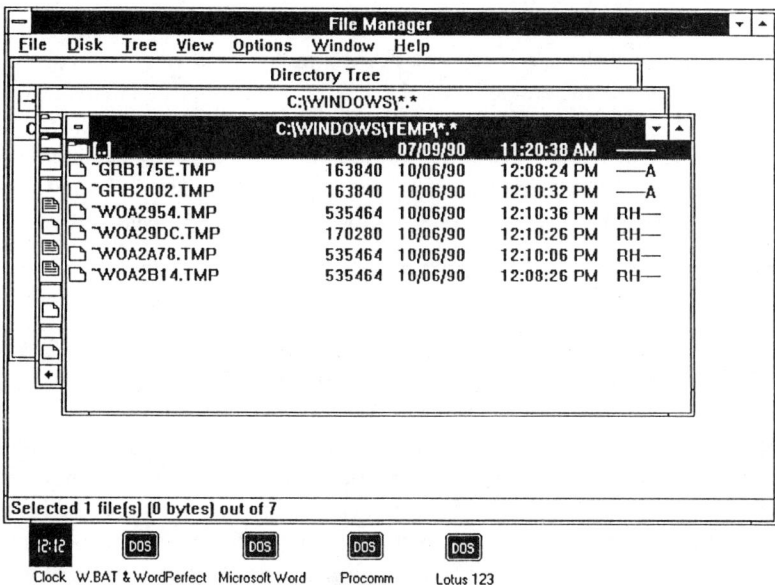

Figure 7-14 Windows application swap files and grabber files

Windows only creates a temporary grabber file when a DOS application uses low- or high-resolution graphics mode. If a DOS application runs in text mode, Windows can save all the information it needs in the application swap file.

Tip: *Controlling where Windows saves application swap files*

Power users who want to maximize their systems for speed in real or standard mode often set the TEMP environment variable in their AUTOEXEC.BAT files to use a fairly large RAM disk. This can create problems, however, when you try to run several DOS applications at once because Windows also saves application swap files in the directory named by the TEMP variable (if one exists). Because application swap files are quite large, you can quickly run out of RAM disk space and have trouble switching away. For example, if you have a 1-megabyte RAM disk and you are running one DOS application, you can usually switch back to Windows pretty quickly without any difficulty. But if you run two DOS applications and try to switch back to Windows, you typically have to exit the DOS application before Windows will let you switch back (the RAM disk won't hold all the application swap files that are required).

To have Windows store application swap files in another location, you can use a *swapdisk=* statement in your SYSTEM.INI file. Unfortunately, Windows automatically places a swapdisk= statement in your WIN.INI file that doesn't work at all. Use SYSEDIT or Notepad to enter one in the [NonWindowsApp] section of your SYSTEM.INI file—for example, swapdisk=C:. Storing application swap files on disk isn't as fast as a RAM disk, but what you lose in speed, you gain in space. For example, if you have 4 megabytes free on the disk named by swapdisk=, you can usually run 7–8 DOS programs simultaneously. Of course, the context switching will be slower. Note that if Windows cannot find a TEMP environment variable or a swapdisk= setting in your SYSTEM.INI, it uses the root directory of the disk on which Windows resides (usually drive C:).

When it comes to running DOS applications, Windows real and standard modes are remarkably similar. However, there are a few subtle differences. For example, although standard mode is well-suited for running Windows applications, it is not quite so ideal for DOS applications that require expanded memory. The reason is that Windows cannot take advantage of EMM386.SYS in standard mode, nor can it simulate expanded memory in this mode. If you want to use expanded memory with your DOS applications in standard mode, you must have an EMS board and configure it to provide the expanded memory. Another alternative is to use Quarterdeck's QEMM-386, which is capable of providing expanded memory to your DOS applications in standard mode. If neither of these options is open to you and you want to run DOS applications that require expanded memory, you are usually better off running them in real or 386 enhanced mode instead.

> **Tip:** *Windows 3 does not swap DOS applications to expanded memory, only Windows applications*

Windows/286 had the built-in ability to swap DOS applications directly to expanded memory. Because expanded memory is rarely used in Windows 3, Microsoft decided to remove this capability. If you still want to swap DOS applications to expanded memory, you can set up a RAM disk with RAMDrive (see the previous tip). Nevertheless, Windows 3 has retained the ability to swap Windows applications directly to expanded memory.

DOS Applications in 386 Enhanced Mode

Just as virtual memory lets the 80386 processor create the illusion of memory that really isn't there, virtual 8086 mode allows the 80386 to create the illusion of multiple 8086 processors. When Windows 3 is running in 386 enhanced mode, it uses this ability of the 80386 processor to give each application the equivalent of its own 8086 address space. Windows can multitask several applications at once this way, even when they are ill-behaved and directly access video memory. Even programs that use graphics mode can be run in a window.

Windows performs true *preemptive multitasking* of DOS applications in 386 enhanced mode. That is, Windows itself preempts—takes away—the CPU at anytime it desires and assigns the CPU to another application. Unlike Windows applications, DOS applications don't surrender the CPU; Windows preempts it. As a result, Windows lets you control the percentage of processing time each DOS application gets in relation to others (see Chapter 10).

When you run a typical program in standard DOS, it uses *physical addresses*. That is, the program assumes that it is running somewhere in conventional memory, with addresses that range from 0000H (0K) to A000H (640K). When the application requests a block of conventional memory from DOS, it expects the block to come from this same physical area. Likewise, if the program writes directly to screen memory, it knows that the screen memory is located at a particular address above A000H in the system (exactly where depends on the video hardware); and the program writes to that physical address.

When you run a DOS application in 386 enhanced mode, it is fooled into thinking that it is running on an 8086 and uses its standard physical addressing scheme. However, unbeknownst to the program, Windows maps the 1-megabyte 8086 address space that the application believes it is running under to the virtual memory space that Windows wants the application to use. To pull this off, Windows works together with the 80386 processor to translate the application's physical addresses to *virtual addresses*. The 80386's paging capability plays a part in this. When Windows runs out of extended memory, Windows begins paging applications out to disk in 4K chunks. As a result, some of the DOS application's 1-megabyte virtual address space may be located in RAM and some on disk. When you attempt to access a DOS application whose code is located on disk, the 80386 processor signals Windows in the form of a *page fault*, and Windows then pages that portion of a DOS application's code that resides on disk back into memory.

Here are some other unique features of the 80386 processor that Windows takes advantage of when running in 386 enhanced mode:

- The 80386's paging hardware isolates each virtual 8086 mode address space. This means that each DOS application runs in its own protected environment and cannot corrupt other DOS or Windows applications.

- The 80386 processor can perform I/O protection. This means that the processor intercepts all of an application's reads and writes to devices, allowing Windows to manage a program's memory access and to step in and arbitrate when more than one application wants to use the same device at the same time.

> **Tip: Each virtual machine inherits the DOS environment**
>
> Each virtual machine that Windows creates in 386 enhanced mode inherits the DOS environment that exists before you load Windows. In other words, if you have network device drivers, TSRs, and DOS resources occupying conventional memory before you load Windows, they also occupy the same memory in each virtual machine. That is why, for example, you can load a TSR before you load Windows and have it available for each DOS application you run. It is also why you can compound your memory savings by trimming down your use of conventional memory before loading Windows.

DOS Translation Buffers in 386 Enhanced Mode

As you know, when Windows runs in 386 enhanced mode, it switches the processor to protected mode so that it can gain access to extended memory. Nevertheless, whenever Windows needs DOS to perform a function (for example, to open a file or read a record from disk), it must switch the processor back to real mode so that DOS running in conventional memory can carry out the operation.

In order to communicate with DOS operating in real mode, Windows places translation buffers in the 384K of reserved I/O memory. Because reserved I/O memory is within the first megabyte, DOS can access it in real mode. In this way, the translation buffers act as a window through which Windows running in protected mode can pass information to DOS running in real mode. Besides DOS, Windows also uses these translation buffers to make real mode network calls.

On most machines with few adapter cards, Windows has no difficulty finding enough space in reserved I/O memory to place both the translation buffers and the EMS page frame. However, on some machines, Windows cannot find enough room. There are two options at this point: The expanded memory page frame can be eliminated, or the translation buffers can be allocated in conventional memory. When the translation buffers are allocated in conventional memory, they take up space in every virtual machine Windows creates, and you have less room available to your DOS applications. Another important point is that the translation buffers cannot be split, with part of them in reserved I/O memory and part of them in conventional memory. They must remain as a single unit in one location or the other.

By using the ReservePageFrame= setting in the [386Enh] section of your SYSTEM.INI file, you can directly control how Windows allocates the translation buffers and EMS page frame. If you use the setting ReservePageFrame=true, Windows allocates the page frame first and the translation buffers second (this is the default sequence). This makes it likely that Windows will use conventional memory for the translation buffers. However, you retain the ability to use expanded memory in your DOS applications.

If you use the setting ReservePageFrame=false, Windows allocates the translation buffers first and the page frame second. If little reserved I/O space is available, the EMS page frame does not get allocated, and you lose the ability to use expanded memory in your DOS applications. However, on the plus side, you do gain more room in each virtual machine. See Chapter 12, "Customizing Your .INI Files," for more on these settings.

Note: If you are using the EMM386.SYS expanded memory driver, it fills the reserved I/O memory area with expanded memory. When this happens, Windows always places the translation buffers in conventional memory.

Expanded Memory in 386 Enhanced Mode

Windows can simulate expanded memory in 386 enhanced mode without a DOS application's knowledge or cooperation. Because a DOS application runs inside a virtual machine, Windows can intercept its calls to the Expanded Memory Manager and use extended memory for storing the EMS pages. Windows does this by working with the 80386 processor to remap the "simulated" EMS pages into the DOS application's page frame when the DOS application issues the calls for them. Windows also lets you move the EMS page frame in 386 enhanced mode (see Chapter 12, "Customizing Your .INI Files," for more on this).

Note: If you are familiar with Windows/386, you may recall that it dynamically converted *all* the extended memory in your system that you were not currently using to expanded memory. The same is not true of Windows 3 in 386 enhanced mode. The amount it converts is a function of the DOS application's PIF settings (see Chapter 10).

FREE MEMORY AND FREE SYSTEM RESOURCES

When you run Windows in standard or 386 enhanced mode, Program Manager's and File Manager's Help About boxes have two settings that tell you the amount of available memory: Free Memory and Free System Resources. The Free Memory setting does just as it says—it reports the amount of free memory in the system, including virtual memory in the case of 386 enhanced mode. The Free System Resources percentage is the more cryptic of the two settings but is also the more important. To understand this percentage, it helps to know a bit about the structure of Windows.

The part of Windows that runs Windows applications is composed of the following three modules:

- USER.EXE—responsible for the keyboard, mouse, sound, communications hardware, timer hardware, and more.
- GDI.EXE—responsible for graphics and printing.
- KERNEL.EXE—responsible for memory management, loading and executing programs, and scheduling.

These modules are located in the \WINDOWS\SYSTEM directory, and Windows loads each of them on startup.

The USER and GDI modules together control the Free System Resources percentage. Each of these modules has a local heap (free memory in its data segment) that is limited to 64K in size. Every application you launch chips away at the local heap space. For example, each window that is created requires a block of data that is allocated out of USER's local heap. Likewise, each menu created eats up a chunk of the same heap. In the same way, every icon, pen (for drawing lines), and brush (for filling interiors) takes up space in GDI's local heap. The Free System Resources percentage is the remaining free percentage of USER's or GDI's local heap space, whichever is less.

In fact, if you've run several large Windows applications at once, you may have noticed that Free System Resources goes to zero long before you run out of free system memory. Once you have used up all the local heap space, you are effectively out of memory even though you still have gobs of free system memory available. If you try to run another application in this circumstance, Windows displays an out of memory error.

Once you've used up Free System Resources, the only way to run another application is to shut down another Windows application. In fact, the Windows documentation suggests that the time to start removing applications is when Free System Resources reaches about 15%. Another rule that power users often follow is to simply close any applications you don't currently need. This not only increases Free System Resources, but it also improves the performance of the applications that are currently running.

MANAGING MEMORY WITH QEMM-386

While Windows 3 is effective at multitasking DOS applications in 386 enhanced mode, problems can crop up when you have network drivers and TSRs that occupy a large portion of conventional memory. Because Windows replicates all these items in each virtual machine, you wind up with less memory available for running your DOS applications. QEMM-386 Version 5.1 from Quarterdeck helps you overcome this problem by relocating device drivers, TSRs, and DOS resources into reserved I/O memory (640K to 1024K) on 386- and 486-based systems.

Previous versions of QEMM were not compatible with Windows 3 in standard or 386 enhanced mode because both tried to access protected mode at the same time. (In fact, all expanded memory managers introduced before Windows 3 have this same drawback.) Therefore, you can only use these programs with Windows when it is running in real mode. This discussion pertains to the latest version of QEMM—QEMM-386 version 5.1—which works with all Windows 3 operating modes.

There are two aspects to QEMM-386's ability to access your system's reserved I/O memory. Like Windows' own EMM386, QEMM-386 is an *expanded* memory manager that supports EMS 4.0. What is unique about QEMM-386 is that it is also an *extended* memory manager, compatible with XMS. By using QEMM386.SYS in place of HIMEM.SYS, you get an XMS driver that supports all three forms of XMS memory—the high memory area (HMA), upper memory blocks (UMBs), and extended memory blocks (EMBs)—and is compatible with Windows 3 in all its different operating modes.

To access your system's reserved I/O memory, QEMM-386 ushers your system into protected mode in place of HIMEM.SYS. It then maps extended memory into the holes in the reserved I/O memory area and loads your TSRs, device drivers, and DOS system resources into these areas, making more conventional memory available in your system. These same savings are replicated within each virtual machine as you launch DOS applications in 386 enhanced mode.

Although QEMM-386 is a powerful program, it is also technical. There are many ways to fine-tune your system with QEMM-386 that this chapter doesn't deal with. The purpose of this section is to give you an appreciation of the benefits of QEMM-386 if you do not have the program, and to tell you some things to watch out for if you do.

Installing QEMM-386

When you run QEMM-386's installation program, it automatically reboots your system twice. It does this to determine the proper commands and parameters to add to your CONFIG.SYS and AUTOEXEC.BAT files that will optimize your system's use of the reserved I/O memory area. You can run the installation program either before installing Windows or after. This section assumes that Windows is already on your system, and that you run it after.

For example, here is a typical set of Windows-oriented CONFIG.SYS and AUTOEXEC.BAT files for a 386-clone with 8 megabytes of memory *before* running QEMM-386's installation program:

CONFIG.SYS

```
FILES = 30
BUFFERS = 10
DEVICE=C:\HIMEM.SYS
DEVICE=C:\WINDOWS\SMARTDRV.SYS 2048 1024
DEVICE=C:\MOUSE.SYS
```

AUTOEXEC.BAT

```
PATH C:\;C:\WINDOWS;C:\BIN;C:\WP50;C:\TOOLBOOK;D:\LOTUS...
SET TEMP=C:\WINDOWS\TEMP
PROMPT $P$G
```

Now, here are the same two files *after* you've installed QEMM-386 (located on the C:\QEMM directory):

CONFIG.SYS

```
DEVICE=C:\QEMM\QEMM386.SYS RAM
FILES = 30
BUFFERS = 1
DEVICE=C:\HIMEM.SYS
DEVICE=C:\QEMM\LOADHI.SYS /R:1 C:\WINDOWS\SMARTDRV.SYS
2048 1024
DEVICE=C:\QEMM\LOADHI.SYS /R:2 C:\MOUSE.SYS
```

AUTOEXEC.BAT

```
C:\QEMM\LOADHI /R:1 C:\QEMM\BUFFERS=10
PATH
C:\QEMM;C:\;C:\WINDOWS;C:\BIN;C:\WP50;C:\TOOLBOOK;D:\LOTUS...
SET TEMP=C:\WINDOWS\TEMP
PROMPT $P$G
```

Even with these very simple files, these changes result in a 39K savings in conventional memory. Actually, the savings are much greater when network drivers and associated TSRs are involved. In fact, when we used QEMM-386 to relocate network device drivers, the savings were from 110-146K. On one machine with over 200K of drivers and TSRs, over 600K of conventional memory was left when QEMM-386 had done its handiwork.

Here's an explanation of the changes to the two files:

- Notice that in the modified CONFIG.SYS file the installation program has placed the QEMM386.SYS driver before the HIMEM.SYS driver. Therefore, when you boot your system, HIMEM.SYS will see that another expanded memory manager is loaded and will not load. It also beeps and displays the message "ERROR: An Extended Memory Manager is already installed." This message isn't a problem because QEMM386.SYS provides all the features of HIMEM.SYS; and by failing to load, HIMEM.SYS does not use any memory. (After installing QEMM-386, you can usually remove the HIMEM.SYS line from your CONFIG.SYS file.)

- The RAM parameter in the QEMM386.SYS line tells QEMM-386 to "fill in" areas of memory above 640K and below 1024K that do not have RAM, ROM, or adapter RAM present. The LOADHI.SYS driver can then use these new RAM areas to load device drivers, in this case SMARTDrive and the Microsoft Mouse drivers. Without this step, these device drivers would occupy conventional memory.

```
C:\>QEMM TYPE

     Area         Size      Status
  0000 - 0FFF     64K    Excluded
  1000 - 9FFF    576K    Mappable
  A000 - BFFF    128K    Video
  C000 - CAFF     44K    ROM
  CB00 - CBFF      4K    Split ROM
  CC00 - DFFF     80K    High RAM
  E000 - EFFF     64K    Page Frame
  F000 - F7FF     32K    ROM
  F800 - F8FF      4K    Mapped ROM
  F900 - FFFF     28K    ROM

C:\>
```

Figure 7-15 A view of the first megabyte of memory as seen by QEMM-386

- The number of DOS sector buffers has been decreased to 1. If you look at the first line of the AUTOEXEC.BAT file, however, you'll notice that QEMM-386 provides the additional nine buffers, making a total of 10 buffers that Microsoft recommends you have when running Windows with SMARTDrive. These nine buffers are provided to DOS from the reserved I/O memory area using LOADHI.COM. (QEMM-386 does this by running its own BUFFERS.COM program, which allocates the additional buffers in the reserved I/O memory area; this "high memory" in the reserved I/O memory area is created by the RAM parameter following the QEMM-386's DEVICE= statement in your CONFIG.SYS.) When you have a BUFFERS= statement in your CONFIG.SYS, those buffers are allocated out of conventional memory. Therefore, by providing the sector buffers out of high RAM, you save 528 bytes of conventional memory per buffer.

Figure 7-15 shows an example of QEMM-386's view of the first megabyte of memory after you've installed the program. It lists different areas of memory, their size in kilobytes, and how they are being used. QEMM-386 is capable of detecting areas using a 4K granularity (this number comes up once again because it is the page size of the 80386). Here is an explanation of the different status conditions:

- Excluded: QEMM-386 automatically excludes the addresses from 0000 to 0FFFH because they contain the interrupt vector table, the BIOS data area, and other system data that QEMM-386 cannot remap.

- Mappable: An area of memory that is available for mapping QEMM-386's EMS memory into. QEMM-386 lets you map memory into this area in chunks as small as 4K. In this example, 1000 to 9FFFH represents all conventional memory below the HMA and above the excluded area (0000 to 0FFFH).

- Video: Areas of memory that are reserved for video display memory.
- ROM: Areas of memory in which the system's ROM resides and that QEMM-386 has not remapped. (You can usually remap some of these areas into RAM yourself using QEMM-386, particularly F000 to FFFF—but you have to experiment.)
- Split ROM: QEMM-386 can detect when an area of ROM occupies only part of a 4K segment. These areas are not available for remapping.
- High RAM: The addresses in high memory (the reserved I/O memory area) that QEMM-386 has already filled with EMS memory. Notice that QEMM-386 found an 80K chunk in this area where it will place TSRs, device drivers, and the like.
- Page Frame: The location of the 64K EMS page frame. QEMM-386 typically locates the EMS page frame as high as possible in reserved I/O memory, typically at E000H or higher.
- Mapped ROM: Areas of ROM that have been copied to RAM, then remapped back to the proper ROM locations by QEMM-386. By placing the ROM code in high-speed RAM, it runs much faster.

Fine-Tuning Your System with QEMM-386

When you install QEMM-386 on your system and use all of its defaults, you realize a lot of savings without much effort. As a power user, you may be inclined to fine-tune your system with QEMM-386 to pick up additional memory. QEMM-386's "Analysis" feature is the best way to fine-tune your system. It evaluates your memory and tells you what areas of reserved I/O memory are OK to use and what areas are not. As you exercise your system, being sure to run all your favorite programs and DOS commands, QEMM-386 records what areas of memory are being accessed. It then reports what areas may be available for remapping; these are areas that are not normally remapped by QEMM-386 when you first install the program.

For example, Figure 7-16 shows the results of the Analysis feature which reveals that certain areas of reserved I/O memory (marked Include) are available for mapping EMS memory into. By instructing QEMM-386 to include these areas when it maps EMS memory into the reserved area, you may be able to place additional drivers, TSRs, and DOS resources into the reserved area.

Special Considerations for Windows

QEMM-386 and Windows work amazingly well together, even in 386 enhanced mode. However, here are a few things to watch out for:

- QEMM-386 floats the 64K EMS page frame to the top of reserved I/O memory, and may place it above E000H on certain IBM clones (COMPAQ machines in

```
C:\>QEMM ANALYSIS
```

```
     Area        Size      Status
 0000 - C4FF     788K      OK
 C500 - C5FF       4K      Include
 C600 - C7FF       8K      OK
 C800 - CAFF      12K      Include
 CB00 - EFFF     148K      OK
 F000 - F1FF       8K      Include
 F200 - F2FF       4K      OK
 F300 - F7FF      20K      Include
 F800 - FAFF      12K      OK
 FB00 - FBFF       4K      Include
 FC00 - FCFF       4K      OK
 FD00 - FDFF       4K      Include
 FE00 - FFFF       8K      OK
```

```
C:\>
```

Figure 7-16 Areas in reserved I/O memory that are available for mapping

particular) if that memory is available. However, when the page frame is located higher than E000H, Windows will grind to a halt in 386 enhanced mode. If you notice that this is happening on your system, you should use QEMM-386's FRAME parameter to reset the page frame to E000H or lower.

- If you use QEMM-386 to fill in all the nooks and crannies of reserved I/O memory, be aware that you leave no room for Windows to place its DOS translation buffers when running in 386 enhanced mode. When this happens, Windows places the translation buffers in conventional memory, and they take up space (about 30K) in every virtual machine that is created. This is not to suggest that you should not have QEMM-386 make maximum use of reserved I/O memory; after all, any TSRs, DOS resources, and the like that you do not relocate in reserved I/O memory wind up using conventional memory anyway. You should be aware, however, that QEMM-386's recovery of conventional memory is not pure when it comes to Windows in 386 enhanced mode.

- When you run Windows in standard mode, it allocates for itself all the memory that QEMM-386 normally controls. Therefore, programs, like 1-2-3 Release 3.0, that use the Virtual Control Program Interface (VCPI) won't be able to access any extended memory. (This is the same reason that EMM386 does not run in standard mode.) To get around this problem, QEMM-386 offers an EMBMEM parameter that lets you set aside some memory for these programs.

MS-DOS 5.0

DOS version 5.0 offers a host of new features that any Windows 3 user will find attractive. However, there are two features in particular that relate to Windows memory management.

- Normally when you run DOS, it loads in conventional memory. With DOS 5.0, however, you can run DOS from extended memory, provided you've installed the HIMEM.SYS extended memory manager. To load DOS into extended memory, you use two command lines like these in your CONFIG.SYS file:

```
DEVICE=C:\HIMEM.SYS
DOS=HIGH
```

- The Windows 3 version of EMM386.SYS lets you simulate expanded memory using extended memory. However, in DOS 5.0, EMM386.SYS has been updated to also let you access unused portions of reserved I/O memory. Therefore, if you have an 80386- or 80486-based system, you can locate device drivers and TSRs into these nooks and crannies of reserved memory, just like you can with QEMM-386. After using EMM386 to map EMS memory into the available upper memory blocks (UMBs), you can then use the DEVICEHIGH= command from your CONFIG.SYS file or the LOADHIGH from the DOS prompt or AUTOEXEC.BAT file to specify which programs and device drivers should be loaded into the UMBs.

SUMMARY

Windows 3's memory management is an amazing accomplishment by Microsoft. In fact, Windows is really four distinct and very different programs when it comes to memory management. These programs correspond to Windows three operating modes, plus real mode combined with expanded memory.

Having read this chapter, you now know the ins and outs of Windows' four memory configurations and how you can take advantage of them to make the best use of Windows. You also have an appreciation of how to manage memory with QEMM-386 and the advantages of DOS version 5.0.

8

Using the Control Panel

Through the Control Panel, you can customize the appearance and operation of Windows. For example, you can use the Control Panel to do such things as change the default colors for the Windows desktop, set the spacing between icons in Program Manager, adjust the speed of your mouse, and set options for multitasking DOS applications in 386 enhanced mode.

This chapter discusses those aspects of the Control Panel that are not covered elsewhere in this book. The Control Panel can contain up to a dozen different icons, each of which lets you configure a different aspect of Windows. Two of these icons, labeled Fonts and Printers, respectively, let you install screen fonts and printers for use with Windows. Both of these icons are discussed at length in Chapter 4, "Of Fonts and Printing." Another icon that may be present in the Control Panel, labeled Network, allows you to control the connection between your PC and a network server. This icon is discussed in Chapter 13, "Networking Windows."

CONTROL PANEL BASICS

You can get to the Control Panel by double-clicking on its icon located in Program Manager's Main group window. Alternatively, you can use the File Run command from either File Manager or Program Manager menu to open the file CONTROL.EXE. When you open the Control Panel, it appears in its own window, as shown in Figure 8-1.

270 *Windows 3 Power Tools*

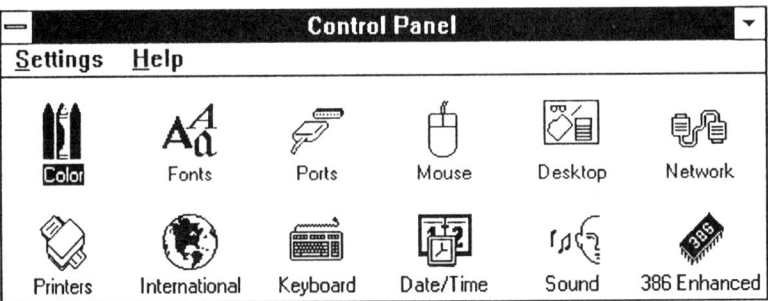

Figure 8-1 The Control Panel window

When you open the Control Panel, you'll notice its window looks a little different than a conventional window. Instead of the thick grey border you are used to, the border of the Control Panel window appears as a thin black line. This means that the Control Panel window is of a fixed size—that is, you cannot change its size and you cannot maximize it. However, in all other respects, the Control Panel window is just like any other window. For example, you can minimize it, restore it, move it, close it, and so on.

As you can see in Figure 8-1, the Control Panel window contains 12 different icons. Each of these icons gives you access to one or more dialog boxes that let you configure a different aspect of Windows. You can access any Control Panel option by double-clicking on the appropriate icon with your mouse or by highlighting the icon and pressing ENTER. Or, as an alternative keyboard method, you can use the Settings menu from the Control Panel. This menu gives you access to the same options as the icons visually displayed in the Control Panel window. If you need help at any time, the Help menu in the Control Panel opens up a wealth of useful information through the standard Windows Help facility.

The number of icons displayed in the Control Panel window may vary, depending on the options you've installed for Windows. Briefly, however, the function of each of the icons in the Control Panel window is as follows:

Color

Lets you change the colors for the Windows desktop. You can choose from pre-defined color schemes or make up your own custom colors.

Fonts

Lets you install screen fonts for use with Windows. The use of this icon is discussed in Chapter 4, "Of Fonts and Printing."

Ports

Lets you configure a communications port for a printer, mouse, or modem.

Using the Control Panel 271

Mouse

Lets you set options for the operation of your mouse. For example, you can set the tracking speed of your mouse—the rate at which the mouse pointer moves across the screen. You can also set the speed for double-clicking—the time between clicks—and you can swap the functions of your left and right mouse buttons.

Desktop

Lets you control various options for the desktop. For example, you can change the appearance of the desktop background (the grey area). Instead of the default grey, you can have a pattern displayed, or you can display wallpaper (a bitmap). You can also set the spacing between icons in Program Manager's group windows, and you can change the cursor blink rate.

Network

Lets you access specific features on a network. (This icon is only displayed if you've installed a network driver for Windows.) The use of this icon is discussed in Chapter 13, "Networking Windows."

Printers

Lets you install and configure printers for use with Windows. The use of this icon is discussed in Chapter 4, "Of Fonts and Printing."

International

Lets you set international options. For example, you can choose a different language and unit of measurement for Windows. You can also set options for the display of dates, times, and numbers.

Keyboard

Lets you set the keyboard repeat rate—the speed at which characters are produced when you hold down a key.

Date/Time

Lets you change the date and time both for Windows and for your system.

Sound

Lets you turn off the warning beep issued by Windows when you make a bad selection.

386 Enhanced

Lets you set options for the operation of Windows in 386 enhanced mode. (This icon only appears in the Control Panel when Windows is running in 386 enhanced mode.) For example, you can use this icon to handle device contention between applications and to adjust the amount of processor time Windows devotes to foreground versus background applications.

> *Tip: Changing the WIN.INI and SYSTEM.INI files through Control Panel*
>
> When you make a settings change through the Control Panel, Windows automatically updates the appropriate entries in either your WIN.INI or SYSTEM.INI file to reflect that change. That way, the settings you make are used both for the current Windows session and for future Windows sessions. See Chapter 12, "Customizing Your .INI Files," for more details on how you can customize the operation of Windows by manually editing your WIN.INI and SYSTEM.INI files.

CHANGING DESKTOP COLORS

To change the colors for the various elements that make up the Windows desktop, you use the Color icon in the Control Panel. When you double-click on this icon, Windows displays the Color dialog box shown in Figure 8-2. This dialog box lets you choose from a series of predefined color schemes for Windows as well as make up your own custom colors.

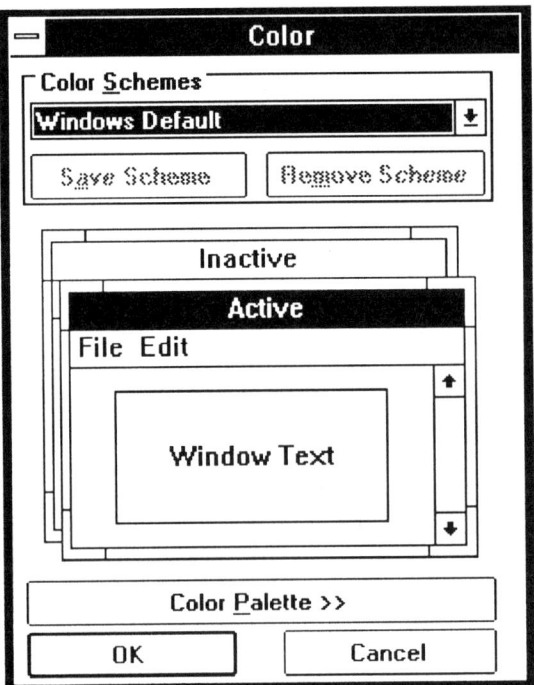

Figure 8-2 The Color dialog box

Choosing a Predefined Color Scheme

To choose from among the predefined color schemes that are available for Windows, you use the drop-down list box in the Color Schemes section of the Color dialog box. When you open this box, a list of names of available color schemes is displayed. When you make a selection from this list, Windows displays the colors for that scheme in the sample screen immediately below. You may want to snoop around in this list for a while until you find a selection that is to your liking. If you find one you like, select the OK button to return to Windows and have that scheme implemented. If you want to revert to the default Windows color scheme, select Windows Default from the Color Schemes drop-down list box.

Changing a Predefined Color Scheme

You can also take an existing predefined color scheme and change the color of one or more of its elements. To do this, begin by selecting a color scheme that is close to what you want from the drop-down list box in the Color Schemes section. Windows displays the colors for the scheme you've selected in the sample screen below. Next, select the Color Palette button at the bottom of the Color dialog box. Windows expands the Color dialog box to appear as shown in Figure 8-3.

To change the color of a specific element of the Windows screen, select that element from the Screen Element drop-down list box. When you open this box, Windows displays a list of screen elements that you can change. When you select a screen element from this list, Windows activates the Basic Colors palette below and shows you the color that is currently assigned to that element. To select another color, simply click on the appropriate block in the Basic Colors palette. Or, with the keyboard, press TAB to move the palette,

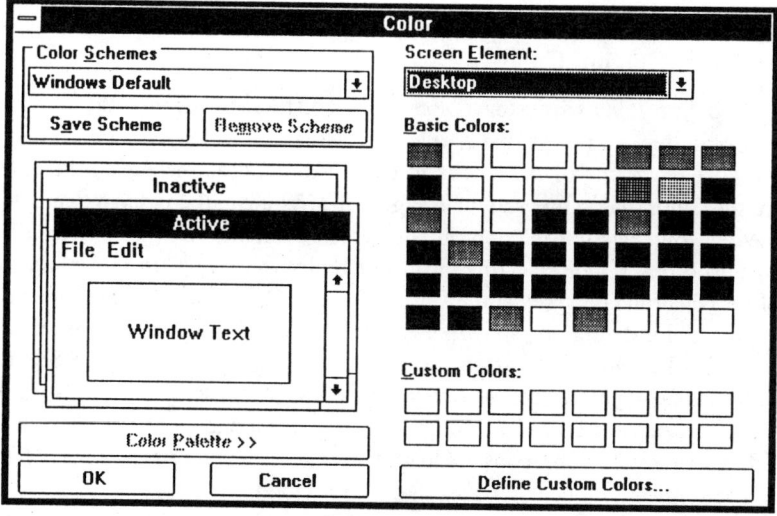

Figure 8-3 The expanded Color dialog box

use the arrow keys to move to a block, and press SPACEBAR to select it. When you select a block from the palette, Windows updates the sample screen to the left so that you can see the effect of your selection. To change the color of another screen element, first select it from the Screen Element drop-down list box and then choose a color for that element from the Basic Colors palette.

Note: You'll notice that the Basic colors palette contains both solid colors (uniform colors directly supported by your display) and nonsolid colors (nonuniform colors that are simulated by a pattern of red, blue, and green dots). If you attempt to assign a nonsolid color to the Window Frame, Window Background, Window Text, Menu Bar, Menu Text, or Title Bar Text selections in the Screen Element list box, Windows will substitute its closest solid color for the nonsolid color.

After you've worked out your new color scheme, you can save it under its own name and have Windows use it. To save your new color scheme, select the Save Scheme button from the Color Schemes section and type a name for your new color scheme. Then, select OK twice to return to Windows and implement that scheme. Once you've named a color scheme, its name appears in the Color Schemes drop-down list box. That way, if you want, you can define several different color schemes and select from among them.

If you don't want to assign a name to your new color scheme, you can still use it. To do this, simply select OK to return to Windows. Windows will use the colors you've selected for the current Windows session, as well as future sessions, until you change them.

If you decide to name your color scheme, but you decide later that you want to delete that name, simply select that name from the Color Schemes drop-down list box, then select the Remove Scheme button. Windows removes the name of the scheme from the list of predefined color schemes. At that point, you can select OK to return to Windows.

Creating Your Own Custom Colors

You can also define your own custom colors and assign them to different Windows screen elements. To do this, you must first define the custom color. Once that color has been defined, it appears in one of the blocks in the Custom Colors palette of the extended version of the Color dialog box shown in Figure 8-3. You can then assign that color to a screen element by selecting the appropriate screen element from the Screen Element drop-down list box and then selecting the custom color from the Custom Colors palette.

To define a custom color, select the Define Custom Colors button from the extended version of the Color dialog box shown in Figure 8-3. Windows overlays the left half of the Color dialog box with the Custom Color Selector dialog box shown in Figure 8-4. You can use this dialog box to define a custom color in one of two ways. On the one hand, you can select a custom color by manipulating the components of the Custom Color Selector dialog box with your mouse. Alternatively, you can enter values that define the custom color you want in the text boxes that are provided.

To select a custom color with your mouse, click anywhere on the large multicolored grid (the color-refiner box). Windows marks the position of your selection with an image of a crosshair (the color-refiner cursor). When you make a selection from the color-refiner

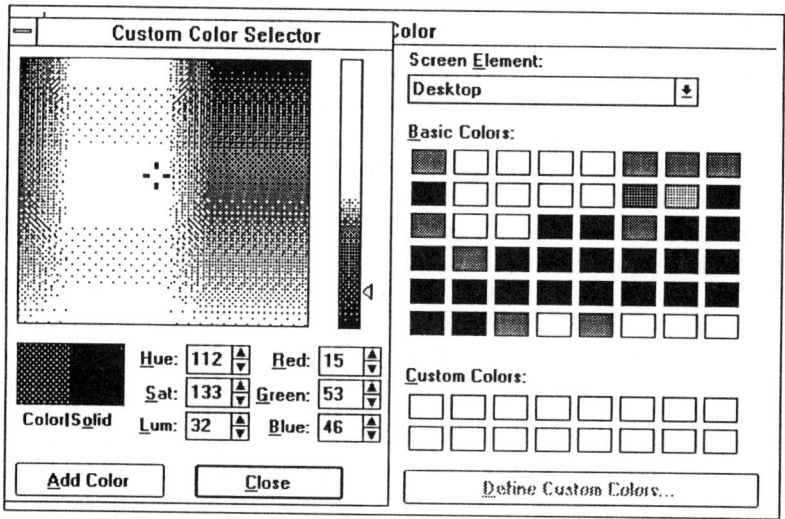

Figure 8-4 The Custom Color Selector dialog box overlaps the left half of the expanded Color dialog box.

box, Windows updates the Color/Solid box below, showing you the results of your selection. It also updates the values in the Red, Green, Blue, Hue, Sat, and Lum text boxes. To further refine the color you've selected, you can use the vertical luminosity bar to the right of the color-refiner box. To use this bar, grab the little arrow to the right of the bar and slide it up or down the bar. Sliding the arrow up makes the color appear lighter and sliding it down makes it appear darker. The changes you make are, of course, reflected in the text boxes below.

As an alternative to selecting and refining a color with your mouse, you can select a color by providing values in the Red, Blue, and Green text boxes. You can then refine that color by providing values in the Hue, Sat, and Lum text boxes. (The values you can enter in these boxes and their effect will be discussed in a moment.) Any changes you make to these text boxes are displayed in the Color/Solid box to the left.

When you've got the custom color you want, you can add it to the Custom Colors palette by using the Add Color push button. First, however, decide on which of the colors in the Color/Solid box you want to add. You'll notice that this box is split in half. The color on the left is the custom color you've defined. This is often a nonsolid color that is not directly supported by your monitor. Instead, the color is simulated by a pattern of red, blue, and green dots. Therefore, it may appear to have a pattern in it. The color on the right of the Color/Solid box, on the other hand, is the closest solid color supported by your monitor. To use this solid color when adding to the Custom Color palette, select it by double-clicking on it or by pressing ALT+O.

To add the custom color you've defined to the Custom Color palette in the Color dialog box, begin by clicking on a block in the palette. Otherwise, Windows will place the custom color in the upper-left block of the palette, if that block is available, or it will use the next empty block, working from upper-left to lower-right. (Choosing a block in advance also allows you to replace an existing color.) When you are ready, select the Add Color push button from the Custom Color Selector dialog box. Windows adds the color you defined to the Custom Colors palette in the Color dialog box. You can now choose the Close push button from the Custom Color Selector dialog box to remove it from your screen. You can then select a screen element from the Screen Element list box on the Color dialog box and apply your new custom color to that element by selecting the appropriate block from the Custom Color palette.

As mentioned, you can define a custom color in the Custom Color Selector dialog box by providing values in the Red, Blue, and Green text boxes. Knowing what values to provide in these boxes involves knowing a little about how Windows builds colors. Much like an artist, Windows builds custom colors through the use of the three primary colors—red, green, and blue. The shade of each of these primary colors is defined by a value ranging from 0 to 255. A setting of 255 defines the pure primary color. For example, a setting of Red = 255, Green = 0, and Blue = 0 (or 255, 0, 0) makes you see bright red. On the other hand, a setting of 50, 0, 0 shows dark red. On either side of the spectrum, a setting of 255, 255, 255 shows white, and a setting of 0, 0, 0 shows black. There are obviously many available colors in between. This is evidenced by the choice of colors in the color-refiner box in the Custom Color Selector dialog box. Each one of the dots in this grid represents a different combination of red, green, and blue.

The Hue, Sat, and Lum text boxes in the Custom Color Selector dialog box let you set the Hue, Saturation, and Luminosity of a color. You can make entries in these boxes ranging from 0 to 239. When you make an entry, Windows simply adjusts the values in the Red, Green, and Blue text boxes to reflect your selection.

Hue identifies the position of a color along the color spectrum. When you make an entry in the Hue text box, Windows moves the color refiner cursor horizontally on the color-refiner grid (0 = flush left and 239 = flush right). Saturation is the purity of the hue, ranging from grey to the pure color. When you make an entry in the Sat text box, Windows moves the color-refiner cursor vertically (0 = bottom and 239 = top). Finally, luminosity defines the brightness of a color, ranging from black to white. When you make an entry in the Lum text box, Windows slides the little arrow up and down the luminosity bar (0 = bottom and 239 = top). The Lum setting overrides the Sat setting and the Sat setting overrides the Hue setting. Therefore, in general, you'll have better luck defining a custom color if you define the hue first and then work on the saturation and luminosity.

CONFIGURING A COMMUNICATIONS PORT

To configure a communications port (often referred to as a COM or serial port), you use the Ports icon in the Control Panel. Communication ports are used to connect devices such as modems, serial mice, and some printers to your computer. Unlike devices that use parallel ports (LPT1, LPT2, and so on), devices that use COM ports require that you define communication parameters for the port. That way, when information is sent from your PC to the COM port, it is sent both at the proper speed and in the proper format for the device.

Using the Control Panel 277

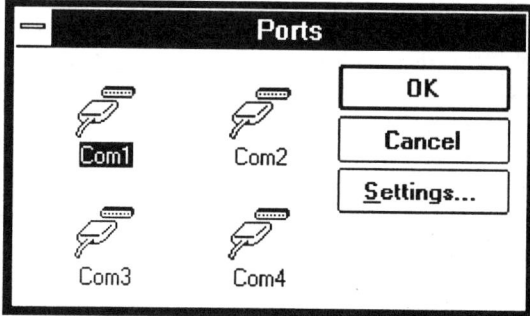

Figure 8-5 The Ports dialog box

When you select the Ports icon from the Control Panel, Windows opens up the Ports dialog box shown in Figure 8-5. An icon is displayed for each potential communications port supported by DOS (COM1 through COM4). Double-click on the port you want to configure. Alternatively, you can use the arrow keys to select a port and then press ALT+S to select the Settings push button. Either way, Windows displays the Ports - Settings dialog box in Figure 8-6.

The Baud Rate drop-down list box lets you select the speed at which data is sent to the COM port and thus on to the device. A standard setting for modems is either 1200 or 2400 baud; you'll have to check the manual that came with your modem to determine

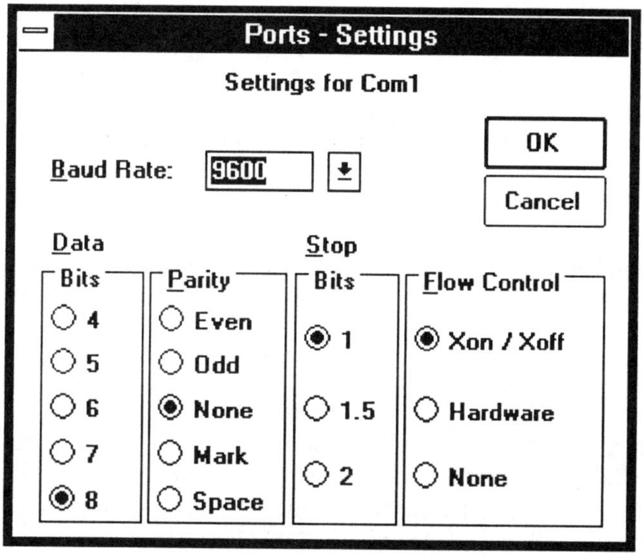

Figure 8-6 The Ports - Settings dialog box

the appropriate setting. On the other hand, a standard setting for printers is 9600 baud, the default setting.

The Data bits section lets you define the number of bits sent in a computer word. A common setting here is 8 (the default). However, some devices require a setting of 7. Once again, you'll have to check the manual that came with the device that is connected to the COM port.

The Parity section allows you to specify the verification bit that will be used for the port. The setting here can be Even, Odd, None, a Mark, or a Space. The most common setting here is None. However, some devices require a setting of Even.

The Stop Bits section lets you specify the number of separator bits between words in a communication. The most common setting here is 1, the default.

The Flow Control section lets you specify the method of interaction between your computer and the device connected to the COM port. For most modems and printers, the common setting here is Xon/Xoff. With this setting, the device tells your computer when it is ready to accept more data. The Hardware option, on the other hand, is suitable for those devices that require a hardware "handshake" to take place over one of the wires in the cable that connects the device to the port. The None option simply specifies no Flow Control setting.

Tip: Configuring for both a printer and a modem

Some users have only a single COM port to support both a printer and a modem. Most of the time the printer is connected to the COM port and the modem is connected only when it is needed. If you are configuring for both a modem and a printer, a Data Bits setting of 8, a Parity setting of None, and Baud setting of 9600 will be adequate for your printer, but not for your modem. However, most communications programs allow you to specify communications settings from within the program for the current communication. The settings you specify through the communications program will override the settings you make through the Control Panel. For example, the Terminal program that comes with Windows allows you to set parameters for the current session by using the Settings Communications command. Therefore, you may want use the Control Panel to specify settings that are appropriate for your printer and let those settings be overridden by your communications program when you are using the modem.

You can copy settings between ports by using the Ports dialog box. For example, imagine you have COM1 configured the way you want it and you want to copy those same settings to COM2. To do this, use the Ports icon in the Control Panel to open the ports dialog box. Drag the COM1 icon onto of the COM2 icon and release your mouse button. Windows copies the settings for COM1 to COM2. (Unfortunately, you cannot perform this operation with your keyboard.)

> *Tip: Windows will not recognize the DOS MODE command in your AUTOEXEC.BAT file for Windows applications*
>
> Some older laser printers require that you connect them to a COM port. If you have such a printer, your AUTOEXEC.BAT file might make use of the DOS MODE command to properly configure the printer when you boot your system. For example, your AUTOEXEC.BAT file might contain the following command lines:
>
> ```
> MODE COM1:9600,N,8,1
> MODE LPT1:=COM1:
> ```
>
> These command lines (1) set the communications parameters for COM1 to 9600 baud, no parity, 8 data bits, and 1 stop bit and (2) reassign the output for LPT1 to COM1. Therefore, you might assume that you can use the Printers icon in the Control Panel to assign the printer to LPT1, thinking that the output will be routed to COM1. However, when you attempt to print from a Windows application, nothing happens. A short time later, Windows displays an error message telling you it cannot print to LPT1. However, your DOS applications seem to print just fine. If this happens, use the Printers icon in the Control Panel to assign the printer to COM1. That way, you should be able to print from your Windows applications as well as your DOS applications. See Chapter 4, "Of Fonts and Printing," for information on how you can use the Printers icon in the Control Panel to change the port for a printer.

CONFIGURING YOUR MOUSE

The Mouse icon in the Control Panel lets you set options for the operation of your mouse. For example, you can change the speed of the mouse—that is, you can increase or decrease the distance traveled by the mouse pointer when you move the body of the mouse. You can also change the speed for double-clicking—the interval of time between clicks that causes Windows to register a double-click. Finally, you can swap the function of the left and right mouse buttons. For example, if you are left-handed, and you would like to use the index finger of your left hand to click the mouse, you can configure the right mouse button to register clicks rather than the left button.

When you double-click on the Mouse icon, Windows displays the Mouse dialog box shown in Figure 8-7. To change the speed of the mouse, you use the Mouse Tracking Speed scroll bar. You can either drag the scroll box to the left to go slower or to the right to go faster. Alternatively, you can press TAB to move to the Mouse Tracking Speed section and use the → and ← keys to set the mouse speed faster or slower. Increasing the speed of your mouse makes it more sensitive to movement. In fact, if you increase the speed of the mouse to the maximum setting, just a little movement on your behalf will send the mouse pointer shooting across the screen.

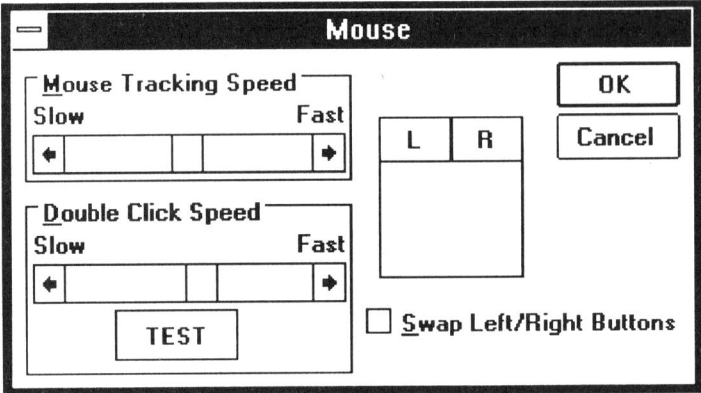

Figure 8-7 The Mouse dialog box

When you change the speed of your mouse through the Control Panel, Windows makes the appropriate entries in your WIN.INI file. That way, the settings you make are used both for the current Windows session as well as future sessions. For a detailed explanation of the changes made to the WIN.INI file, and a discussion of the technological issues behind changing the speed of your mouse, see Chapter 12, "Customizing Your .INI Files."

To change the double-click rate for your mouse, you use the scroll bar in Double Click Speed section of the Mouse dialog box. Simply drag the scroll box in the bar to the right to decrease the amount of time between clicks or drag to the left to increase the amount of time between clicks. Alternatively, you can press TAB to move to the Double Click Speed section and use the → or ← key to decrease or increase the time interval between clicks. If you move the scroll box all the way to the right (the fastest setting) you have to double-click awfully fast to have Windows register a double-click. To test whether Windows is registering your double-click as a double-click, use the Test box at the bottom of the Double Click Speed section. This box will invert (turn black on a color screen or reverse on a monochrome screen) if the test is successful.

To swap the left and right mouse buttons, select the Swap Left/Right Buttons check box. When you select this box, the right button on your mouse takes on all the same functionality formerly attributable to the left button. To test how the right and left mouse buttons are being read, click on the box marked L and R directly above. When you click the right button, the box marked R will invert, and when you click the left button, the box marked L will invert.

SETTING OPTIONS FOR THE DESKTOP

To set options for the Windows desktop, you use the Desktop icon in the Control Panel. When you select this icon, Windows displays the Desktop dialog box shown in Figure 8-8. With this dialog box, you can change the appearance of the desktop background (the

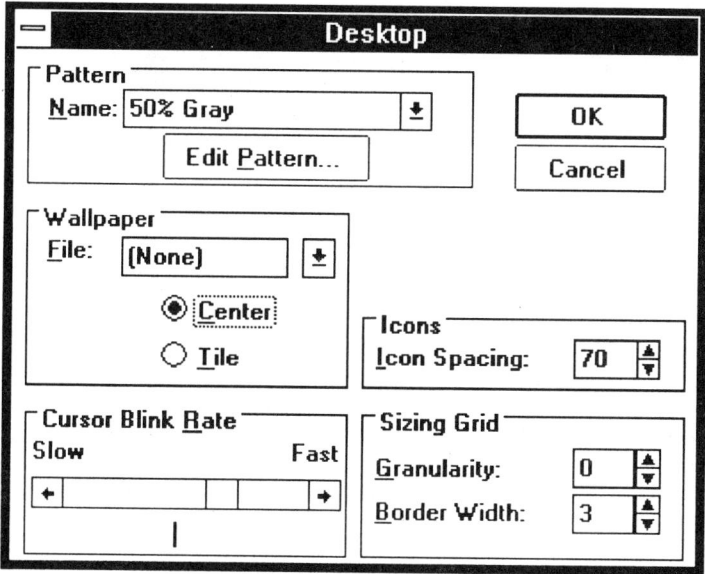

Figure 8-8 The Desktop dialog box

grey area) by displaying either a pattern or a bitmap image. You can also change the spacing between icons displayed in Program Manager and set the cursor blink rate.

Displaying a Pattern on the Desktop

You can display a pattern as a background for the Windows desktop. To do this, you use the Pattern section in the Desktop dialog box. You can either choose from predefined patterns or you can create a new pattern of your own. To choose from existing patterns, open the Name drop-down list box to display a list of names for predefined patterns. Make a selection and then select OK to return to Windows. The pattern you've selected is now displayed on the desktop background. You may want to experiment for a while to find a pattern that's right for you. Some of the available patterns are quite busy and can make your icons hard to spot on the desktop.

To preview a pattern or modify an existing pattern, select the Edit Pattern push button from the Pattern section of the Desktop dialog box. Windows displays the Desktop - Edit Pattern dialog box shown in Figure 8-9. To preview a pattern, open the Name list box and make a selection from the listed pattern names. When you make a selection, Windows displays an enlarged version of that pattern in the box immediately below. To the left of this box, a box labeled Sample shows you what that pattern will look like when it is displayed on the desktop. To modify the pattern, click on any spot in the box where the enlarged version of the pattern resides. (You cannot edit a pattern with the keyboard.) Each time you click, Windows places a contrasting square (an enlarged representation of a pixel) in the spot where you clicked. When you've got the pattern you want, choose the

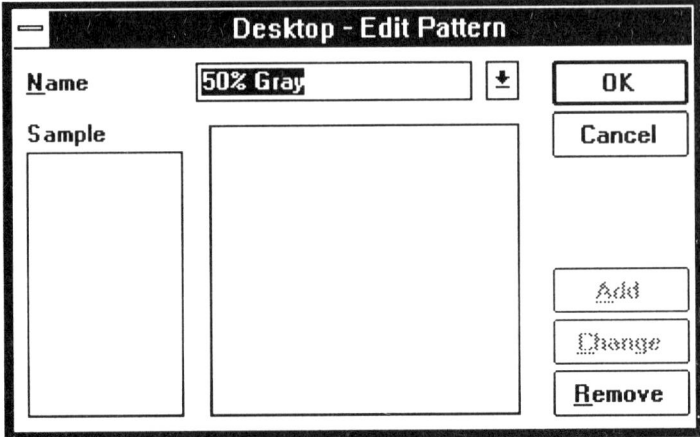

Figure 8-9 The Desktop - Edit Pattern dialog box

Change button and then choose OK. Select OK again to return to Windows and display the modified pattern.

To create a new pattern, use the Control Panel's Desktop icon to open the Desktop dialog box. Make sure that the (None) option is displayed in the Name box, then choose the Edit Pattern button. Windows displays the Desktop - Edit Pattern dialog box. Type the name you want to use for the new pattern in the Name box. Then, use the pattern box below to design your pattern. Click your mouse on each spot where you want an inverted (contrasting) pixel to appear. Each time you click your mouse, Windows updates the Sample window to give you an idea of what your pattern will look like when it is displayed on the desktop. When you've got the pattern the way you want it, select the Add button and then select OK to return to the Desktop dialog box. Once you've returned to the Desktop dialog box, open the Name drop-down list box and select the name for the new pattern you've just defined. Select OK to return to Windows and display your new pattern on the desktop background.

Hanging Wallpaper

You can have wallpaper (a bitmap) displayed for the desktop background rather than a pixel pattern. Wallpaper is displayed through the use of .BMP files, like the ones you create in Paintbrush. Windows comes with a variety of wallpaper (.BMP) files that you can choose from. Figures 8-10 and 8-11 show examples of the bitmap files that come with Windows. You can use one of these bitmap files as wallpaper or you can create your own wallpaper file with Paintbrush. In addition, there are a number of "interesting" wallpaper files that have been uploaded to bulletin-board services around the country that you may want to download and have a look at. For example, you might come across something like a full-screen shot of a sunset on a secluded beach that you can use as wallpaper for your desktop.

Using the Control Panel 283

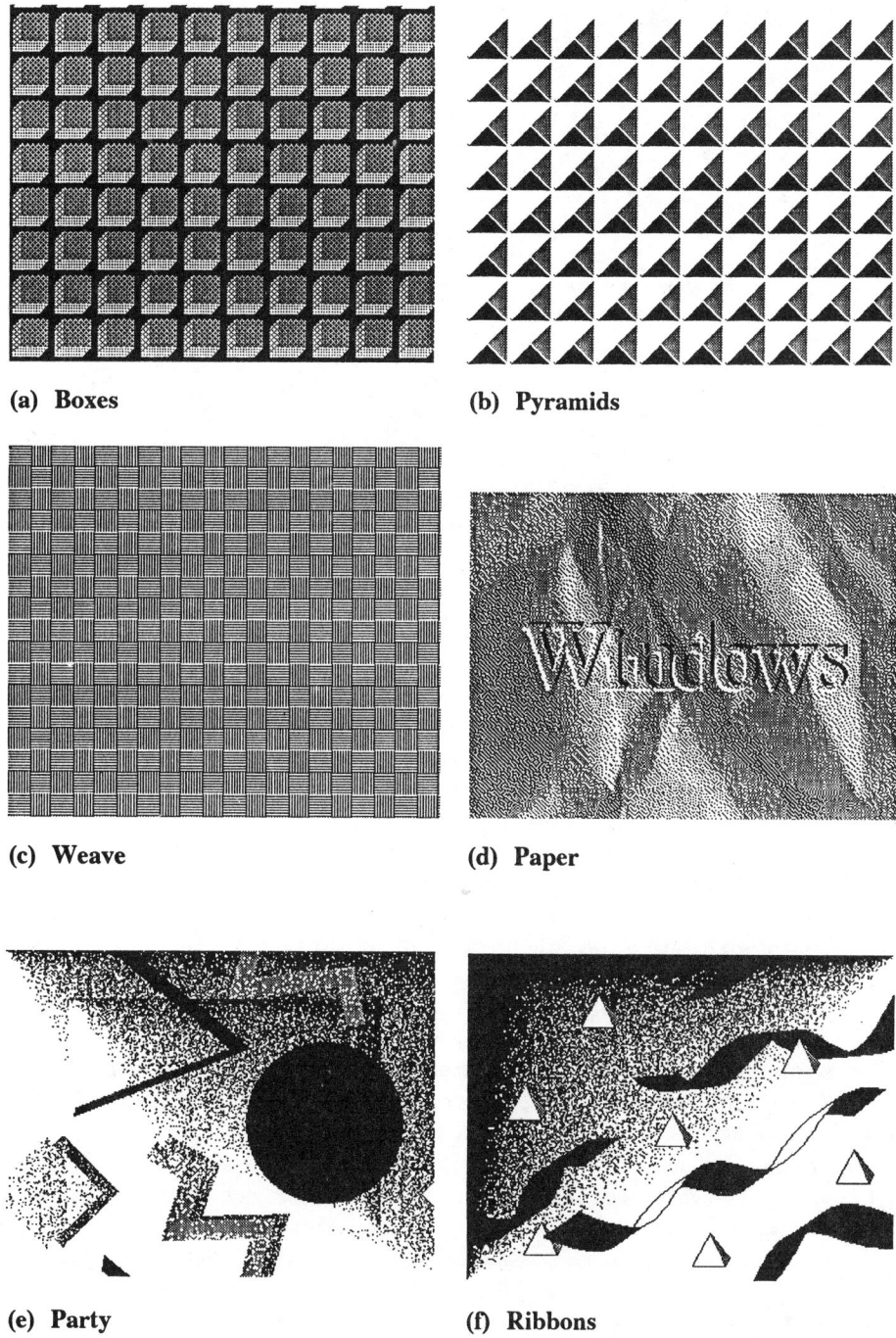

(a) Boxes

(b) Pyramids

(c) Weave

(d) Paper

(e) Party

(f) Ribbons

Figure 8-10 Samples of Windows wallpaper (.BMP) files

Figure 8-11 The CHESS.BMP file fills your entire screen

Note: If you decide to create your own .BMP file to use as wallpaper, or you procure one from somewhere else, make sure you copy that file to your Windows program directory. Otherwise Windows won't be able to find the file when you attempt to install it as wallpaper.

To select a bitmap file to be displayed as wallpaper, use the Desktop icon in the Control Panel to open the Desktop dialog box. Once this dialog box is displayed, open the File drop-down list box in the Wallpaper section to see a list of .BMP files in the Windows program directory. Select the one you want. Windows closes the list box and displays your selection in the File box. Next, use the Center or Tile radio buttons to specify how you want that bitmap displayed. If you anticipate that the bitmap will fill your entire screen, select Center. Otherwise, select Tile. With the Tile selection, Windows will display multiple copies of the bitmap in a tiled arrangement, so that your entire screen is filled. When you are ready, select OK to return to Windows. After a little disk grinding, Windows will display your bitmap as a backdrop for the desktop.

As you might expect, Windows requires an extensive amount of memory to display a full-screen (tiled) bitmap as wallpaper. Therefore, if available memory is already an issue, you might consider removing any wallpaper you may have installed. This will make more memory available for your applications. To do this, open the File drop-down list box in the Wallpaper section of the Desktop dialog box and select the (None) option, then select OK. Windows returns to its default setting of no wallpaper.

Setting the Distance between Icons

You can also use the Desktop dialog box to adjust the spacing between icons in Program Manager. The default spacing for icons is usually adequate, provided you keep the descriptions for your icons short. However, if you tend to use longer descriptions, you'll notice that the descriptions for adjacent icons are overlapping. You can solve this problem by increasing the spacing between icons so that your descriptions do not overlap.

On the other hand, perhaps the icons in Program Manager are spaced too far apart for your needs. For example, imagine you want to be able to see all of the icons in a particular group window without having to use the group window's scroll bar and without having to increase the size of window. In this instance, you might want to decrease the spacing between icons so that more icons can be displayed in less space.

To adjust the spacing between icons, select the Desktop icon from the Control Panel to display the Desktop dialog box. Once this dialog box is displayed, select the Icon Spacing text box from the Icon section. You'll notice that there is already a value of 75 in this box, meaning 75 pixels. To increase or decrease this value, click the up or down arrow beside the text box or type the new value you want to use. Since the distance between icons is measured in pixels, even a slight increase or decrease of 10 to 15 pixels will produce a noticeable difference. When you are ready, select OK to return to Windows.

To see the effect of your changes, activate Program Manager and click on any icon in an open group window or on a group window icon. Then select the Window Arrange Icons command from Program Manager's menu. Windows arranges the icons to reflect the new spacing setting you've defined. To arrange the icons for open applications located at the bottom of the Windows desktop to reflect the new setting, open the Task List window and select the Arrange Icons button.

Activating the Invisible Grid

You can also use the Desktop dialog box to activate an invisible grid that Windows will use to position application windows on your desktop. For example, normally, when you move a window, it stays exactly where you put it. However, if you activate the invisible grid, Windows will use that grid to position the window after you move it. When you let go of a window after moving it with the mouse, or after you press ENTER to confirm a move with the keyboard, windows adjusts the position of the window to place it on the nearest grid line.

To turn on the invisible grid and adjust the distance between grid lines, you use the Granularity text box in the Sizing Grid section of the Desktop dialog box. Normally, this box contains a value of 0, meaning the grid is turned off. However, you can use the up and down arrows next to the Granularity box to adjust the value in this box up or down. You can also manually enter a value in the Granularity box. The acceptable values range from 0 to 49. Each increment of 1 represents a distance of eight pixels between lines on the grid. Therefore, a setting of 3 will mean a distance of 24 pixels between grid lines. To determine the effect of your changes, select OK to return to Windows.

The effect of turning on and sizing the invisible grid will not be apparent until you actually move an application window. For example, when you grab a window's title bar and begin to drag with your mouse, you'll notice that the outline for the window moves a little farther and a little faster than you expected. When you release your mouse button to complete the move, the window "snaps" into position on the invisible grid.

Although the invisible grid is an interesting feature of Windows, it is not terribly useful. It tends to limit your flexibility in positioning windows on the desktop. It also has an impact on the size and aspect ratio of your windows when you open them. Nevertheless, you can try using the invisible grid feature for a while to see if you like it. If you don't, you can always turn it off by reducing the value in the Granularity text box to 0.

Setting the Width of Window Borders

The Desktop dialog box can also be used to adjust the width of window borders. The changes you make apply to all the windows displayed on the desktop whose size is adjustable. Those windows whose size is fixed, like the Control Panel window, are not affected.

To adjust the width of window borders, double-click on the Desktop icon in the Control Panel to display the Desktop dialog box. Once the dialog box is displayed, select the Border Width text box in the Sizing Grid section. You'll notice this text box already contains a value of 3. You can increase or decrease this value by using the up and down arrows next to the text box or by typing a value in the box. Acceptable entries range from 1 to 49, with 1 being the thinnest border setting and 49 being the thickest. To see the effect of your changes, select OK to return to Windows. The border widths of all displayed windows are adjusted to reflect the new setting.

Changing the Cursor Blink Rate

As you know, Windows displays a blinking cursor whenever it is awaiting a text entry. You can adjust the timing between blinks, if you so desire. To set the cursor blink rate, you use the scroll bar in the Cursor Blink Rate section of the Desktop dialog box. Simply drag the scroll box in the bar to the right to make the cursor blink faster or drag it to the left to make the cursor blink slower. Alternatively, you can press TAB to move to the Cursor Blink Rate section (or press ALT+R) and use the → and ← keys to speed up the cursor blink rate or slow it down. To save the new setting, select OK to return to Windows.

CHANGING INTERNATIONAL SETTINGS

You can use the International icon in the Control Panel to set various international options. For example, you can change such things as language, unit of measurement, date format, time format, currency format, number format, and so on. The changes you make affect all applications that use the items you change.

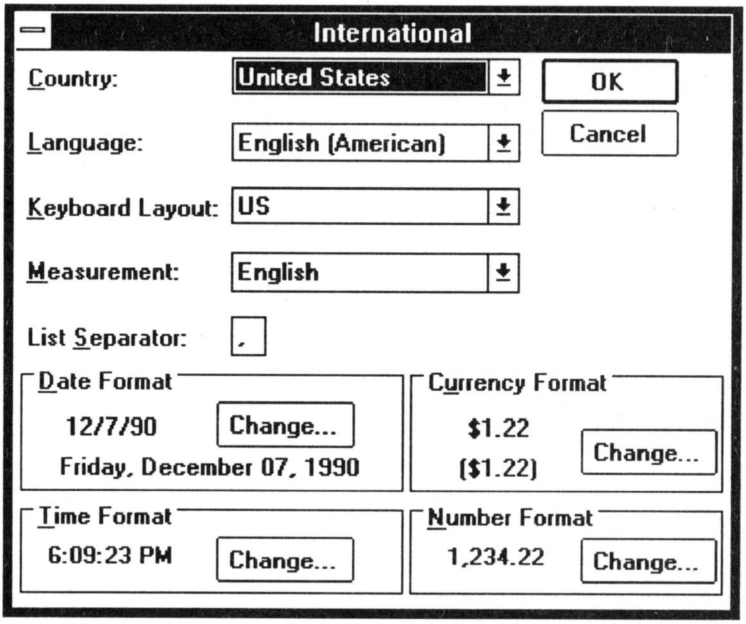

Using the Control Panel 287

Figure 8-12 The International dialog box with the default U.S. settings

When you double-click on the International icon in the Control Panel, Windows opens up the International dialog box shown in Figure 8-12. The first selection you'll want to make is from the Country drop-down list box. When you open this box, Windows displays the names of various countries throughout the world. Select the name of the country you are currently working in. Windows updates the other sections of the International dialog box to reflect the selection you've made. For example, Figure 8-13 shows the appearance of the International dialog box when you select Sweden from the Country drop-down list box. Notice that the settings for Measurement, Date Format, Time Format, Number Format, and Currency Format have all been changed to reflect the settings most prevalently used in Sweden. You can accept the current settings in the International dialog box by selecting OK to return to Windows.

You can change the various individual settings in the International dialog box to suit your particular needs. For example, you can use the Change button in either the Date Format, Time Format, Currency Format, or Number Format sections to change the format that is displayed. When you select the Change button from any one of these sections, Windows displays a dialog box that lets you alter the format for that particular section. You can also use the Language, Keyboard Layout, and Measurement drop-down list boxes to select a setting that is appropriate for each of these options. Finally, the List Separator text box allows you to specify a separator character that will be used to separate a series of words or numbers when they appear consecutively in a sentence.

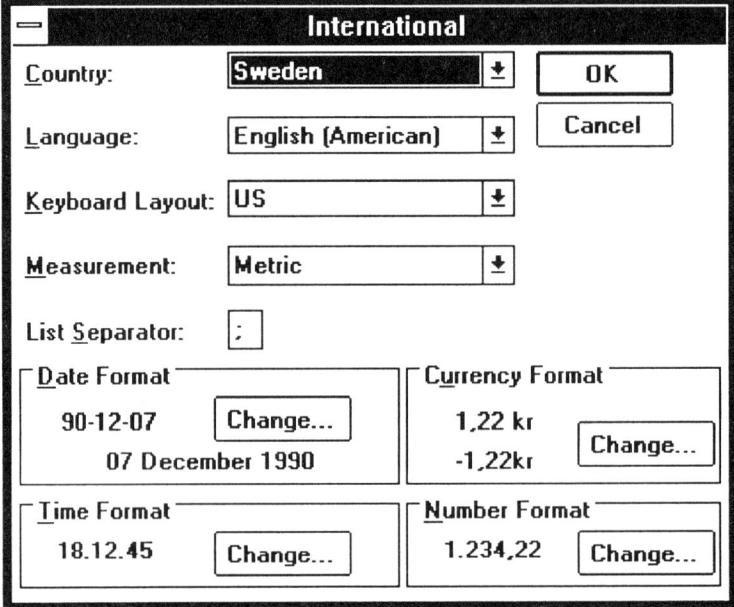

Figure 8-13 The International dialog box after selecting Sweden from the Country drop-down list box

SETTING THE KEYBOARD REPEAT RATE

You can also adjust the speed of your keyboard—how fast characters are produced when you hold down a key—by using the Keyboard icon in the Control Panel. When you double-click on this icon, Windows displays the Keyboard dialog box shown in Figure 8-14. To adjust the speed of your keyboard, use the Key Repeat Rate scroll bar. To increase or decrease the speed, drag the scroll box inside the bar to the right or left. Alternatively, you can press → or ← to increase or decrease the speed. To test the effect of the current setting, you can use the Test Typematic text box. Click on this box, or press ALT+T to move to it, and hold down any character key on your keyboard. Windows will repeat characters at the rate you've selected. To save the new setting and return to Windows, select OK.

CHANGING THE DATE AND TIME

You can change the current date and time for Windows by using the Date/Time icon in the Control Panel. However, be aware that any changes you make directly affect your system clock. Therefore, all Windows applications, like Clock and Calendar, as well as your DOS applications, that rely on your system clock will be affected by the change.

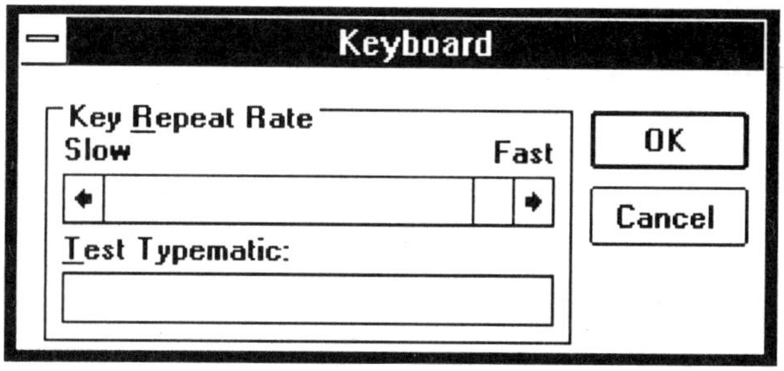

Figure 8-14 The Keyboard dialog box

When you double-click on the Date/Time icon, Windows displays the Date & Time dialog box shown in Figure 8-15. The current date is displayed in the Date section and the current time is displayed in the Time section. By default, the Date section is activated. To change a particular element of the current date, click on that element or press **TAB** to move to it. Once the appropriate element is selected, you can either type a new entry or use the up or down arrows to the right to adjust the entry. These same techniques can be used to adjust the time that is currently displayed in the Time section. To save your changes and return to Windows, select OK.

SUPPRESSING THE BEEP

Windows sounds a warning beep when you make a bad selection or attempt an operation that is not supported. For example, if you attempt to use an ALT+key sequence to make a selection from a dialog box when that selection does not exist, Windows will sound the warning beep. Frankly, the Windows warning beep is not that obtrusive. However, if you want to turn it off, you certainly can.

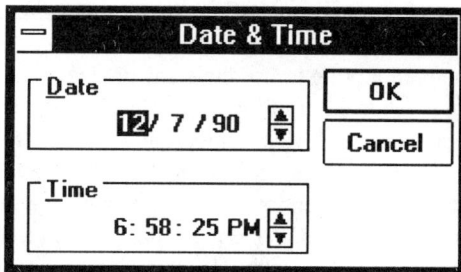

Figure 8-15 The Date & Time dialog box

290　*Windows 3 Power Tools*

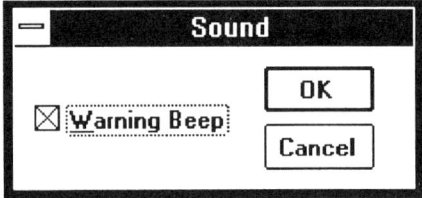

Figure 8-16　**The Sound dialog box**

To turn off the Windows warning beep, double-click on the Sound icon in the Control Panel. Windows displays the Sound dialog box shown in Figure 8-16. Clear the Warning Beep check box and select OK to return to Windows. The warning beep is now suppressed until you turn it back on again.

386 ENHANCED SETTINGS

If you are fortunate enough to be running Windows in 386 enhanced mode, an icon labeled 386 Enhanced appears in the Control Panel window. When you double-click on this icon, Windows displays the 386 Enhanced dialog box shown in Figure 8-17. You can use this dialog box to set options for the multitasking of DOS applications in the Windows environment.

Device Contention

When you print or send a modem transmission from a DOS application, that application automatically assumes that it has the exclusive use of an output device, be it a printer or a modem. In fact, when you start a DOS application, it automatically takes over the port for which it is configured. For example, if WordPerfect 5.0 is currently configured to send printed output to the printer connected to LPT1, it takes over that port for its exclusive use when you start the program. If another DOS application or a Windows application attempts to print to that same port, a situation known as *device contention* arises in which multiple applications are attempting to use the same device at the same time. The result may be as severe as an interrupted print job or a garbled transmission.

Where Windows applications are concerned, device contention is not a problem. Windows does not monopolize a device for its exclusive use. Instead, Windows maintains its own set of internal controls that let multiple applications share a given device without contention. For example, where printing is concerned, Windows relies on Print Manager to spool print jobs from different applications and release them to the printer sequentially. Thus, only when a DOS application is introduced into the multitasking picture is there a potential for device contention.

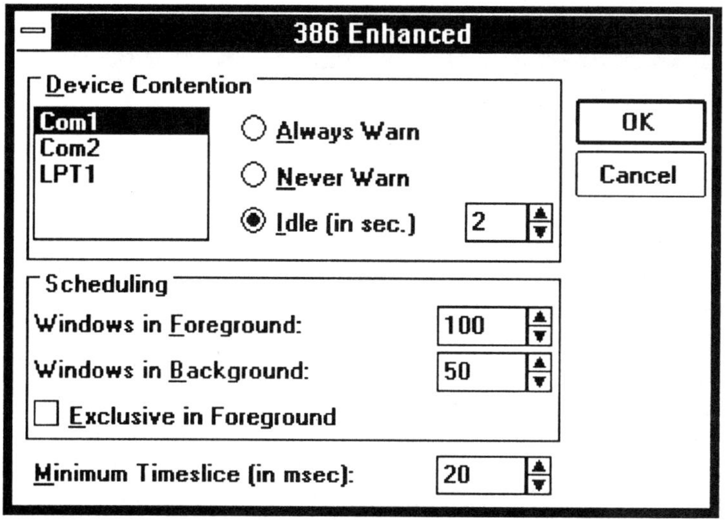

Figure 8-17 The 386 Enhanced dialog box

Although DOS applications access devices independently of Windows, Windows is capable of monitoring the devices for your system and of discerning when a device conflict exists. It is also capable of helping you to resolve the conflict by allowing you to assign the use of a device to one application versus another.

To arbitrate device contention between applications, you can use the Device Contention section of the 386 Enhanced dialog box. You can specify different settings for each port to which a device is connected. To begin, select the port to which a printer or modem is connected from the list box in the Device Contention section, then select from the Always Warn, Never Warn, or Idle (in sec.) radio buttons. These radio buttons have the following effect:

- Always Warn: Windows will warn you when a Windows application is infringing on a device that is currently in use by a DOS application. It will also warn you when a DOS application is attempting to use a device that is currently being used by Windows. It will even warn you when two DOS applications are contending for the same device. In each case, Windows will give you an opportunity to resolve the problem by letting you assign the device to the application of your choice.

- Never Warn: Windows will not warn you when a device conflict exists. You should only select this button if you are sure there is no potential for a device conflict.

- Idle (in sec.): This radio button in conjunction with the adjacent text box lets you set a time interval after which an application can access an idle port without Windows issuing a device-conflict error message. You can specify a time interval from 0 to 999 seconds. This option is explained in more detail toward the end of this section.

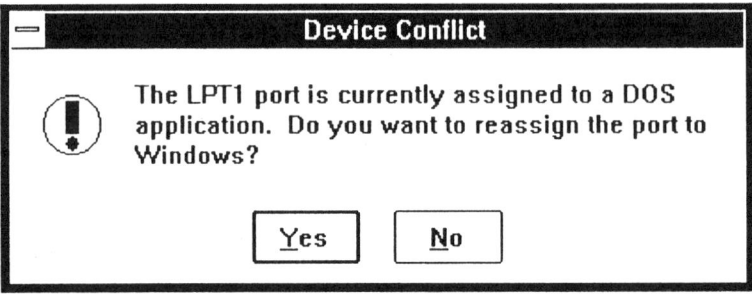

Figure 8-18 Windows detects a device conflict when printing to a port monopolized by a DOS application

The Always Warn option is your safest bet for detecting and dealing with device conflicts. For example, imagine that a DOS version of WordPerfect is currently sending data to a printer connected to LPT1. While that print job is taking place, you start a Windows application and begin printing to that same port. Windows detects that the LPT1 port is currently monopolized by WordPerfect and will display a message box similar to the one shown in Figure 8-18, asking you if you want the port assigned to Windows. If you select Yes, Windows will take over use of the LPT1 port for itself. Therefore the WordPerfect print job will be suspended, not because Windows stopped Wordperfect from printing, but because the port is no longer available. If you return to WordPerfect and check the status of the print job, a message similar to "Printer not accepting characters" will be displayed.

On the other hand, imagine that the LPT1 port is assigned to Windows and that Windows is currently sending a print job to that port. At that point, you switch to WordPerfect and start printing to LPT1. Windows will display a message box similar to the one shown in Figure 8-19, asking you to decide who gets the port, Windows or WordPerfect. If you select WordPerfect, Windows will release the port and suspend its print job so that WordPerfect can have the use of the port.

Windows can also help you to arbitrate device contention between two DOS applications when both are running under Windows. For example, imagine you are working on a document in WordPerfect and editing a long Oriel program file in WordStar at the same time. Imagine further that you initiate a print job from within WordPerfect. Shortly thereafter, you switch to WordStar and begin printing your program. Windows displays a dialog box similar to the one shown in Figure 8-20 asking you to resolve the device conflict that is currently taking place between the two DOS applications.

Windows can also detect when a port is idle (not being used by an application). If a port is idle, Windows will let an application have the use of that port without issuing an error message. However, for this to happen you must specify a waiting period, in seconds, after which an application can use that port. If the port is in fact idle, and another application accesses that port after the specified period of time has elapsed, Windows will simply let the application have the port and will not issue an error message. To specify

Using the Control Panel   293

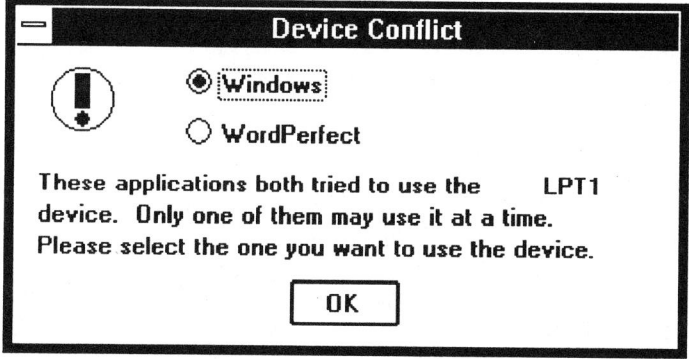

Figure 8-19 Windows detects a device conflict created by a DOS application attempting to print to a port it is currently using

a waiting period for a port, you use the Idle (in sec.) radio button in the 386 Enhanced dialog box. In the adjacent text box, specify the amount of time in seconds that you want Windows to wait before releasing an idle port to another application.

Delineating an idle-time setting can be useful when you anticipate that a DOS application and Windows will be accessing the same port, one right after the other. For example, imagine you use Cardfile to dial a phone number to connect your PC to an on-line service, such as CompuServe. Shortly thereafter, you switch to a DOS communications program to interact with that service. In this instance, you may want to set a relatively brief idle-time setting of 2 seconds. That way, Windows will not display a device contention error message when the DOS application attempts to use the port.

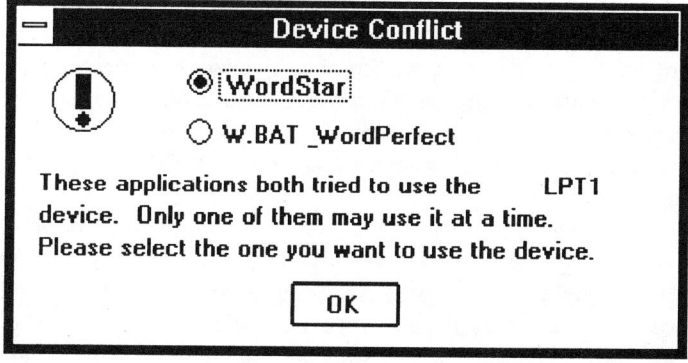

Figure 8-20 Windows detects a device conflict between two DOS applications

Setting Multitasking Options

When you run multiple DOS applications in 386 Enhanced mode, Windows keeps each of those applications separated from one another in memory. It does this by running each DOS application in its own virtual 8086 machine. At the same time, each of your active Windows applications run in a private protected-mode address space. In this way, your DOS applications remain separate both from each other and from Windows.

No matter how many applications you have in memory, all of them rely on the resources of a single processor. Since only a fixed amount of processor time is available, Windows uses a preemptive form of multitasking to allocate a fixed amount of processor time to each DOS application. Processor time is measured in units called time slices, which are measured in milliseconds. Windows gives the processor to each application for the duration of a time slice before taking it away and giving it to the next application. Since each DOS application resides in its own virtual machine, each is allocated a separate time slice. On the other hand, both Windows and Windows applications share a single time slice. Within this time slice, the scheduling for Windows applications occurs on a nonpreemptive, message basis.

The primary source of messages is you, the user. For example, when you activate an application, Windows creates a message to that effect and sends it to the appropriate application. It then gives that application the focus (the processor). Therefore, ultimately, the scheduling of Windows applications depends on what you, as the user, do.

You can set the duration of the time slice by using the Minimum Timeslice (in msec) text box located in the 386 Enhanced dialog box. The default value for the time-slice setting is 20 milliseconds. However, you can specify a value from 1 to 1000 milliseconds. If you decrease the time-slice setting, Windows will switch the processor between applications more frequently. If you have multiple applications in memory, they will appear to operate more smoothly. However, the overall performance of your system will decline. On the other hand, setting a larger time slice will increase the efficiency of your system, but the switching of the processor between one application and the next will become more apparent and your applications will appear to slow down.

In addition to setting the amount of processor time that is made available to each application, setting the priority for processor time can also be an important consideration. As you know, Windows applications can continue to process information, regardless of whether they are in the foreground (active) window or in a background (inactive) window. As you'll learn in Chapter 10, "Using Non-Windows Applications," this also is possible with DOS applications when Windows is running in 386 enhanced mode. You can activate background processing either through the application's PIF or while the DOS application is actually running.

Under normal circumstances, though, you'll probably want to give priority to the application in the foreground (the active window), because you are interacting with that application. Conversely, you'll want to give less priority to applications running in the background. However, if you have an important process running in a background window, such as a communications program, you may want to devote more priority to that operation to avoid having it interrupted.

To specify the percentage of processor time that will be devoted to applications running in the foreground versus those in the background, you use the Scheduling section in the 386 Enhanced dialog box. This section contains two text boxes, Windows in Foreground and Windows in Background, that allow you to specify the processing priority given to foreground versus background applications. However, these settings apply strictly to Windows applications. What's more, they are only used when one or more DOS applications are active. In addition, for purposes of these settings, Windows applications are treated as a group and DOS applications are treated as a separate group. The Windows in Foreground setting lets you specify the percentage of processing time devoted to a Windows application running in the foreground (the active window) relative to DOS applications running in the background. Conversely, the Windows in Background setting lets you specify the percentage of processor time devoted to Windows applications running in the background when a DOS application is running in the foreground.

The default value for the Windows in Foreground setting is 100 and the default value for the Windows in Background setting is 50. To determine the percentage of processor time devoted to applications running in the foreground versus those in the background, you must add these two figures together. For example, the total of these two figures is 150 (100 + 50 = 150). Therefore, the total amount of processor time devoted to foreground applications is 100 divided by 150 or 67%. Conversely, the total amount of time devoted to applications running in the background is 50 divided by 150 or 33%. You can change these percentages by changing the values in the Windows in Foreground and Windows in Background text boxes. You can adjust either of these values from 1 to 10,000.

You can also specify that Windows gets 100% of your computer's processing time whenever a Windows applications occupies the currently active window. To do this, select the Exclusive in Foreground check box in the Scheduling section of the 386 enhanced dialog box. When this box is checked, Windows applications will be allocated 100% of available processor time when a Windows application is activated, and background processing of DOS applications will be disabled.

SUMMARY

This chapter shows you how to use the Control Panel to customize the appearance and operation of Windows. For example, you can now change the colors for the various elements that make up the Windows desktop. You can choose from either the predefined color schemes that come with Windows or you can make up your own custom color scheme. You can also display different patterns or hang wallpaper on the Windows desktop, making it more attractive.

You also know how to use the Control Panel to configure various software-related aspects of Windows. For example, you can adjust the spacing between icons, activate the invisible grid, change the width of window borders, and adjust the cursor blink rate. In addition, you know how to handle device contention and set multitasking options for DOS applications running in 386 enhanced mode.

You also know how to use the Control Panel to configure many of the hardware-related aspects of Windows. For example, you know how to configure a communications port, adjust your mouse, set the keyboard repeat rate, change the date and time on your system clock, and turn off the Windows warning beep.

9

Changing Your Setup

In previous versions of Windows, if you wanted to change your setup, you had to reinstall Windows from scratch. With Windows 3, on the other hand, you can use the Setup program, and you don't have to suffer through the entire setup procedure again.

Using the Windows Setup program, you can

- Change your hardware options by changing device drivers.
- Automatically add applications to group windows.

When changing your hardware options, if you want to use any of the standard device drivers that come with Windows, you can run Setup from within Windows. However, if you want to install a new device driver that does not come with Windows, you must run Setup from DOS.

RUNNING SETUP FROM WITHIN WINDOWS

When you run Setup from within Windows, you can change your hardware drivers to any of the standard drivers that come with Windows, or you can set up new applications. To run the Setup program, simply click on its icon in the Main Group window. When the Setup window appears, it displays the status of your current hardware settings and swap file, as shown in Figure 9-1.

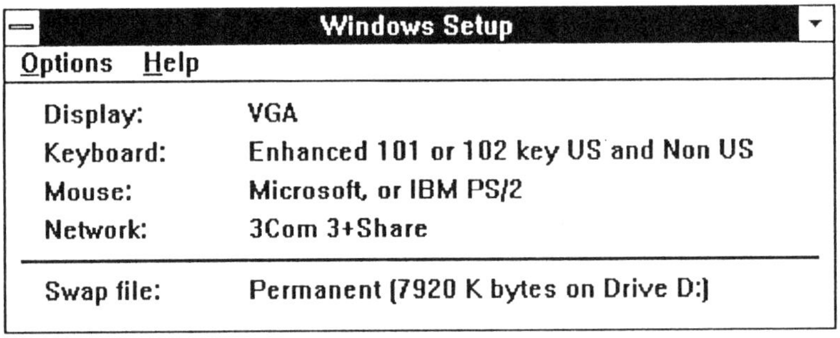

```
┌─────────────────────────────────────────────────────┬───┐
│                   Windows Setup                     │ ▼ │
├─────────────────────────────────────────────────────┴───┤
│ Options  Help                                           │
│                                                         │
│   Display:      VGA                                     │
│   Keyboard:     Enhanced 101 or 102 key US and Non US   │
│   Mouse:        Microsoft, or IBM PS/2                  │
│   Network:      3Com 3+Share                            │
│   ───────────────────────────────────────────────────   │
│   Swap file:    Permanent (7920 K bytes on Drive D:)    │
│                                                         │
└─────────────────────────────────────────────────────────┘
```

Figure 9-1 The Windows Setup window

Changing Hardware Drivers

To change any of your Windows 3 hardware drivers, select Change Systems Settings from the Options menu. Figure 9-2 shows the screen that appears. Here are the drivers you can change:

- The display driver
- The keyboard driver
- The mouse driver
- The network driver

The next few sections describe these drivers in more detail.

Note: If you want to change your printer driver, you must use the Printers icon in the Control Panel. See Chapter 4, "Of Fonts and Printing," for a complete discussion.

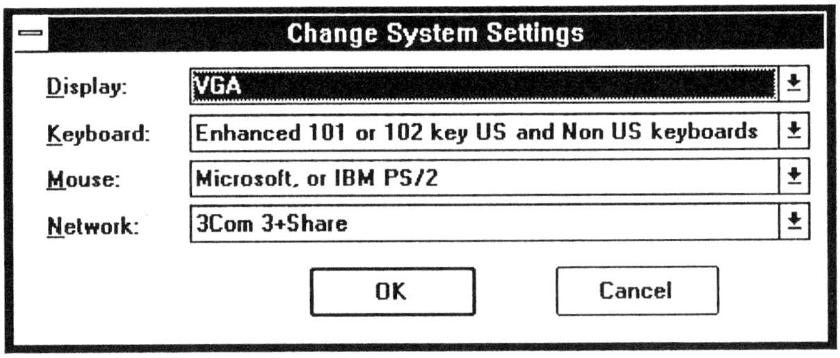

```
┌─────────────────────────────────────────────────────────┐
│                 Change System Settings                  │
├─────────────────────────────────────────────────────────┤
│                                                         │
│   Display:    │VGA                                 │ ±  │
│                                                         │
│   Keyboard:   │Enhanced 101 or 102 key US and Non US keyboards│ ± │
│                                                         │
│   Mouse:      │Microsoft, or IBM PS/2              │ ±  │
│                                                         │
│   Network:    │3Com 3+Share                        │ ±  │
│                                                         │
│              ┌──────────┐      ┌──────────┐             │
│              │    OK    │      │  Cancel  │             │
│              └──────────┘      └──────────┘             │
│                                                         │
└─────────────────────────────────────────────────────────┘
```

Figure 9-2 The Change Systems Settings dialog box

Changing the Display Driver

By far the most common driver you will want to change is your display driver. When choosing a display driver for Windows 3, it helps to know the resolution and color capabilities of your display card. Table 9-1 shows the most popular PC graphics standards and their resolutions.

By contrast, Table 9-2 shows the standard Windows 3.0 display drivers along with the resolution and colors they support. Notice that the Windows 3.0 drivers may not take advantage of the full resolution and color capabilities of your graphics card. For example, regardless of the VGA card you are using, all the standard VGA drivers support only 640 x 480 pixels.

Here are some notes on the various standard display drivers:

- 8514/a—The 8514/a display adapter offers a memory expansion kit that increases the total amount of memory on the board to 1 MB. Windows 3.0 senses whether the memory expansion kit is present and provides 256 colors if it is. Otherwise, Windows provides only 16-color support.

- CGA—The highest CGA resolution (640 x 200) is only available in black and white mode.

- Compaq Portable Plasma—This is the display on the Compaq Portable 3.

- EGA—If you have an XT-class machine (with an 8086/8088), you cannot run Windows in color when you have an EGA because the Windows EGA driver uses instructions in the 80286 instruction set; you can only use such systems in black and white. In addition, you may need to change the dip switch settings on the EGA board to operate in black and white mode. (This same restriction also applies to VGA boards on XT-class machines.)

- Olivetti/AT&T Monochrome or PVC Display—This display driver supports the 400 scan lines of Olivetti/AT&T monochrome and paper-white adapters (PVC), the Olivetti OEC in 400-line mode, and the AT&T VDC650. However, the fonts that Setup chooses are the standard EGA fonts, which appear smaller on a 400-line screen. If you want your fonts to appear larger on the screen, you can manually change to the VGA fonts instead. See "Changing Your Display Fonts Manually" for more.

- QuadVGA, ATI VIP VGA, 82C441 VGAs—These are older VGA cards that were among the first crop introduced; they offer 640 x 480 resolution only. (The "82C441" refers to the Chips and Technologies BIOS number on the VGA ROM chip. By pulling the card from your PC, you can usually see the BIOS number on the ROM chip.)

- VGA—This is the device driver that is used by Windows for almost all VGA cards, even if they support higher resolutions. If your VGA is capable of a higher resolution and your monitor will support it (see the tip later), you may want to use another display driver.

Standard	Resolution (in pixels)
8514/a	1024 x 768 in 256 colors
Extended (1K) VGA	1024 x 768 in 16 colors (512K RAM)
Super VGA	800 x 600 in 16 colors (256K RAM)
VGA	320 x 200 in 256 colors or 640 x 480 in 16 colors
EGA	640 x 350 in 16 colors
Hercules Monochrome	720 x 348 in 2 colors
CGA	320 x 200 in 4 colors or 640 x 200 in 2 colors

Table 9-1 PC Graphics Standards

- Video Seven VGA with 512K—Although this board is capable of supporting 1024 x 768 resolution in 16 colors, the standard Windows 3.0 display driver supports only 640 x 480 resolution in 256 colors. In other words, by choosing this display driver over the standard VGA display driver, you get no more resolution, but you do gain 256-color support.

Display Driver	Resolution (in pixels)
8514/a	1024 x 768 in 16 colors or 1024 x 768 in 256 colors
CGA	640 x 200 in 2 colors
Compaq Portable Plasma	640 x 400 in 2 colors
EGA	640 x 350 in 16 colors
Hercules Monochrome	720 x 348 in 2 colors
Olivetti/AT&T Monochrome or PVC Display	640 x 400 in 2 colors
QuadVGA, ATI VIP VGA, 82C441 VGAs	640 x 480 with 16 colors
VGA	640 x 480 with 16 colors
VGA with Monochrome display	640 x 480 with 2 colors
Video Seven VGA with 512K	640 x 480 with 256 colors

Table 9-2 Standard Display Drivers and Their Supported Resolutions

> **Tip: Even with the proper driver, you may not see 256 simultaneous colors**

Be aware that of the 256 colors available with certain display drivers, only 16 are used by the Windows system software. The other 240 colors are VGA palette colors that can only be accessed by Windows programs that are specially written to do so. For example, Microsoft PowerPoint takes advantage of the full 256-color palette, if it is available. But most Windows programs do not support this capability.

Changing the Keyboard Driver

In some rare instances, you may change the style of keyboard you are using and need to change the Windows 3 keyboard driver accordingly. For example, Windows has special drivers for the Enhanced 101-key keyboard, the AT-style keyboard (84-86 keys), the PC/XT style keyboard, and a variety of other more exotic choices.

Changing the Mouse Driver

If for some reason you change the mouse you are using, you will also need to change the Windows 3 mouse driver. Note that this driver only affects the mouse's behavior in Windows; if you want to use your mouse with DOS applications, you'll need to load a special mouse driver before loading Windows. See Chapter 10, "Using Non-Windows Applications," for more on using a mouse with DOS applications.

Changing the Network Driver

Setup also lets you change the device drivers for the network you are operating under. See Chapter 13, "Networking Windows," for a complete discussion.

An Example

Suppose you have just recently upgraded your system from an EGA to a VGA display, and you want to change your screen driver to take advantage of the new display. Follow these steps:

1. After starting the Setup program and selecting Change System Settings from the Options menu, pull down the Display drop-down list box.

2. Select VGA from the list and choose OK. Setup will request that you insert several Windows disks in drive A. After copying the appropriate drivers to your \WINDOWS\SYSTEM directory and modifying your SYSTEM.INI, Setup displays the message box in Figure 9-3.

3. Select a button to restart Windows or to return to DOS.

302 *Windows 3 Power Tools*

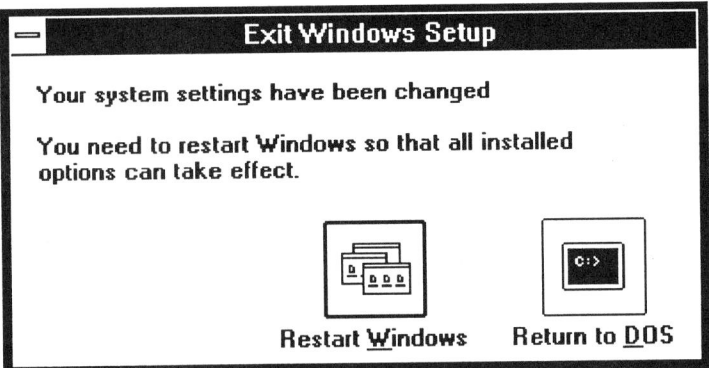

Figure 9-3 **After changing your screen display**

Note: If you cannot restart Windows because of the changes you've made with Setup, you'll need to run Setup from DOS.

Adding Applications

Whenever you add a new Windows application to your system, the easiest way to create an icon for it is to use Program Manager. However, if you have added several new Windows applications or a DOS application, you may be better off using Setup.

The reason that Setup is preferable for adding DOS applications is that it also supplies a PIF for each one, provided that it has PIF information for the DOS application. See Chapter 10, "Using Non-Windows Applications," for more information.

Note: One popular misconception about Setup is that as soon as you run it, it will somehow wreak havoc on your current arrangement of icons and group windows in Program Manager. On the contrary, Setup does not change this arrangement at all. It merely adds icons to group windows when and if you tell it to. In addition, there is no penalty whatsoever for running Setup then bailing out without adding any applications.

For example, suppose you've added a new copy of WordPerfect to your system. To add this application to Windows, perform the following steps:

1. Select the Set Up Applications option from the Options menu. Setup displays a pull-down list box that lets you choose whether you want to search all drives, a single drive, or the current path.

2. Select the search option you want and choose OK. When Setup completes the search, it lists all the names of the applications it found in the list box on the left,

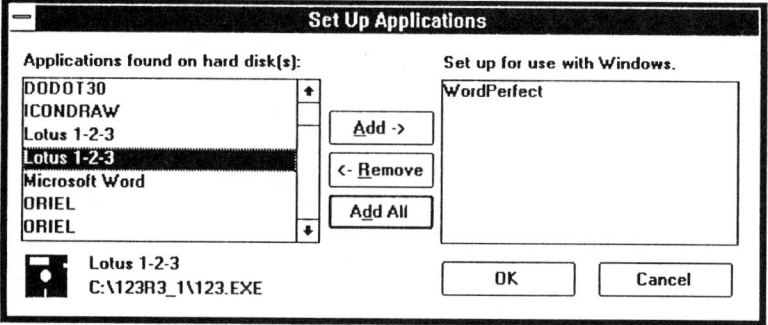

Figure 9-4 Setting up applications

as shown in Figure 9-4. When you highlight an application in the list, Setup displays its name and path. Setup also displays a disk icon for DOS applications and a window icon for Windows applications.

3. Select from the list box on the left the name(s) of the application(s) you want to add—in this example, WordPerfect.

4. Choose the Add -> button to move the name from the list box on the left to the list box on the right. If you decide you've made a mistake, you can return a name to the list box on the left by selecting it and choosing the <- Remove button.

5. Select OK to have Windows add icon(s) to group windows.

RUNNING SETUP FROM DOS

If you want to install a device driver that does not come with Windows, the only way to install that driver is to run Setup from DOS. The most common reason to run Setup in this way is to install a high-resolution display driver.

For example, when Windows 3.0 was first introduced, only the standard display drivers in Table 9-2 were available. Notice that the standard VGA drivers support only 640 x 480 resolution, the same resolution as the basic VGA originally introduced by IBM in 1987. Most VGA cards now available have higher-resolution Windows 3.0 drivers available. Therefore, if you have a Super VGA card or Extended (1K) VGA, you may want to use a Windows 3.0 VGA driver with a higher resolution.

If you are lucky enough to have recently purchased your VGA card, you are likely to find the high-resolution Windows 3.0 display drivers on a companion disk that comes with the card. If you already have a VGA card and you're wondering whether there's a new high-resolution driver available for it, you have two options: you can contact the manufacturer, or you can check the Windows 3.0 Supplemental Driver Library (SDL) (see the tip).

> **Tip:** *The Windows 3.0 Supplemental Driver Library (SDL)*

> The Windows 3.0 Supplemental Driver Library (SDL) is a library of device drivers that is maintained by Microsoft. The library includes the printer, display, network, mouse, and keyboard drivers. Each driver in the library either supports a new device or improves the performance of drivers already included in Windows 3.0. For example, Table 9-3 shows the display drivers available in the SDL as of the time of this writing.
>
> You can download sets of drivers from the SDL free of charge from CompuServe, GEnie, or Microsoft OnLine. (If you are using CompuServe, as we did, type "GO MSL".) You can also order the SDL directly from Microsoft for $20 by calling (800) 426-9400 in the U.S.A. and Canada. In other countries, contact your local Microsoft subsidiary.

> **Tip:** *To use a high resolution display driver, you need a compatible monitor*

> The Super VGA's 800 x 600 resolution requires a monitor that is capable of a 35-kHz horizontal scan rate, and this can be handled by many multifrequency monitors. One example is the NEC MultiSync/2A (the original NEC MultiSync is not capable of this rate). Monitors that are compatible with the basic VGA standard will not support this rate. If your card is capable of resolutions as high as 1024 by 768, your monitor must support a 49-kHz scan rate. In this case, you need a higher-end monitor like the NEC MultiSync XL or Taxan UltraVision 1000.

An Example

Suppose you have a Super VGA card by BOCA Research, an inexpensive though popular card, and you want to use one of the display drivers from the SDL. This card is capable of 800 x 600 resolution in 16 colors and uses a Chips and Technologies BIOS number 82C451. (In most cases, you don't need to know the BIOS number to get the right Windows 3.0 driver, but with inexpensive VGA cards it never hurts.) Here are the steps for installing the new display driver:

1. Exit Windows.
2. From the DOS prompt, type *setup* and press ENTER. Setup shows an initial screen like the one in Figure 9-5.
3. Use the arrow keys to highlight the "Display:" setting and press ENTER.

Displays supported

ATI Mode 54h (800x600 16 colors) v2.00
ATI Mode 55h (1024x768 16 colors) v2.00
CHIPS Super VGA 82C451 (800x600 16 colors)
CHIPS Super VGA 82C452 (800x600 16 colors)
CHIPS Super VGA 82C452 (1024x768 16 colors)
CHIPS Super VGA 82C452 (640x480 256 colors)
COMPAQ Integrated Video Graphics System
DGIS 3.x Medium Resolution w/VGA, Ver 1.01
DGIS 3.x High Resolution w/VGA, Ver 1.01
Paradise VGA (800x600 16 colors)
Paradise VGA (1024x768 16 colors)
Paradise VGA (640x480 256 colors)
Video Seven VGA (800x600 16 colors)
Video Seven VGA (1024x768 16 colors)
Video Seven VGA (640x480 256 colors)

Table 9-3 Display Drivers in the Windows 3.0 SDL

```
Windows Setup

     If your computer or network appears on the Hardware Compatibility List
     with an asterisk next to it, press F1 before continuing.

     System Information
        Computer:          MS-DOS or PC-DOS System
        Display:           VGA
        Mouse:             Microsoft, or IBM PS/2
        Keyboard:          Enhanced 101 or 102 key US and Non US keyboards
        Keyboard Layout:   US
        Language:          English (American)
        Network:           3Com 3+Share

        Complete Changes:  Accept the configuration shown above.

     To change a system setting, press the UP or DOWN ARROW key to
     move the highlight to the setting you want to change. Then press
     ENTER to see alternatives for that item. When you have finished
     changing your settings, select the "Complete Changes" option
     to exit Setup.

  ENTER=Continue   F1=Help   F3=Exit
```

Figure 9-5 The initial Windows Setup screen

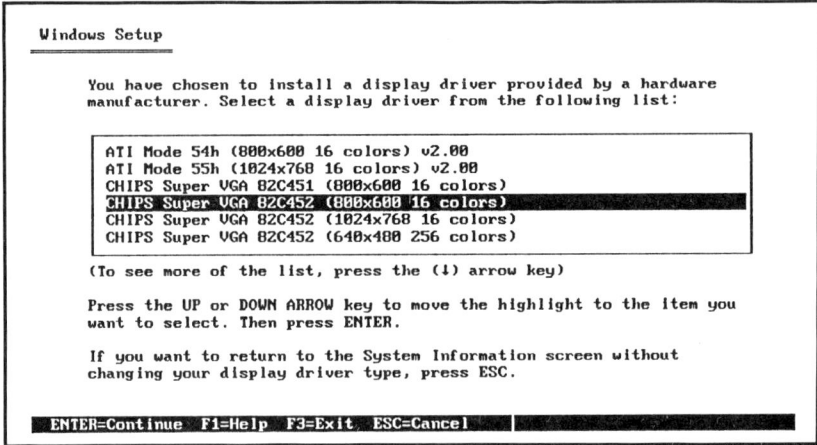

Figure 9-6 A sample list of display drivers

4. Select Other at the bottom of the list and press ENTER. Windows will prompt you to place the disk containing the device driver in drive A.

5. Insert the disk into drive A and press ENTER. Windows displays a list of the display drivers on the disk, as shown in Figure 9-6.

6. Select from the list the driver you want to add and press ENTER. After Setup copies the appropriate files to your \WINDOWS\SYSTEM directory, it displays an updated list of hardware.

7. Press ENTER to accept the settings and leave Setup.

You can now start Windows in the usual way, and it will use your newly installed display driver.

Tip: If your system hangs when you run Setup

If your system hangs when you run Setup from DOS, the most likely reason is that Setup senses a conflict between the driver you've chosen and your equipment. To prevent your system from hanging and install the driver anyway, run Setup with the /I switch. Typing **setup /i** prevents Setup from performing any hardware checking.

CHANGING YOUR DISPLAY FONTS MANUALLY

When Setup changes your display driver, it actually copies two types of files onto your system: driver files and font files. In addition, Setup makes several changes to your WIN.INI and SYSTEM.INI files, all related to the new files it has copied.

When you run Setup from DOS, it usually copies the driver files to your system without a hitch. If Setup has trouble, you can always resort to using the /I switch to force it through the process. When Setup copies font files, however, it is quite common to encounter problems. This is especially true if you are working with disks from the SDL (not one of Microsoft's better efforts). To work around these problems, it helps to know what Setup is actually doing when it changes your font files and their associated .INI file settings. That way, you can carry out the process manually if things go awry.

In addition, by knowing the changes that Setup makes, you can adjust your font files to make your screen more readable. The most common reason for doing this occurs when you have installed a high-resolution display driver—for example, an Extended (1K) VGA or 8514/a driver—but your fonts appear too small on the screen and you have to squint to see them. By changing your font files and .INI file settings, you can make your fonts more readable.

Changing Your DOS Application Font

When you run Setup to change your display driver, it usually copies four font (.FON) files to your system that are used for running DOS applications in 386 enhanced mode. These files control the fixed-pitch display font Windows uses when running a DOS application in a window. You can easily tell which files Windows is currently using by loading the SYSTEM.INI file into a text editor (we recommend SYSEDIT.EXE) and checking the following settings in the [386Enh] section:

- EGA80WOA.FON=<filename>—Names the file containing the fixed-pitch display font used for DOS applications with a display of 80 columns and more than 25 lines.

- EGA40WOA.FON=<filename>—Names the file containing the fixed-pitch display font used for DOS applications with a display of 40 columns and more than 25 lines.

- CGA80WOA.FON=<filename>—Names the file containing the fixed-pitch display font used for DOS applications with a display of 80 columns and 25 or fewer lines.

- CGA40WOA.FON=<filename>—Names the file containing the fixed-pitch display font used for DOS applications with a display of 40 columns and 25 or fewer lines.

For example, here are the SYSTEM.INI settings for a standard VGA display with a 640 x 480 resolution:

```
[386Enh]
EGA80WOA.FON=EGA80WOA.FON
EGA40WOA.FON=EGA40WOA.FON
CGA80WOA.FON=CGA80WOA.FON
CGA40WOA.FON=CGA40WOA.FON
```

Unfortunately, Windows uses these same settings if you've installed an 8514/a or Enhanced (1K) VGA adapter with a resolution of 1024 x 768. The result is that whenever you run a DOS application in a window, you get remarkably small text that may strain your eyes.

To increase the size of the fixed-pitch font that Windows uses, change the line that reads

```
EGA80WOA.FON=EGA80WOA.FON
```

to

```
EGA80WOA.FON=8514FIX.FON
```

If you've installed an 8514/a or Enhanced VGA, the 8514FIX.FON file should be located in your \WINDOWS\SYSTEM directory. If for some reason it is not, you can copy it from Windows Disk 1. To do so, you'll need a copy of the EXPAND.EXE utility on Windows Disk 2 (this utility expands the compressed files on the Windows disks). After copying this utility to your hard disk, place the Windows Disk 1 in drive A, and type the following command:

```
EXPAND A:8514FIX.FON \WINDOWS\SYSTEM\8514FIX.FON
```

From this point on, whenever you run a DOS application in a window, Windows will use the larger system font that is specially tailored for 1024 x 768 displays.

Changing Your System Fonts

Another common problem when you install a high-resolution VGA driver is having a System font that is too small, making your screen hard to read. As you know, the System font is used for menus, dialog boxes, and in several Windows applications, such as Notepad and Calendar.

To see what font files Windows is currently using for the System font, you can check the following settings in the [boot] section of your SYSTEM.INI file:

- fixedfon.fon=<filename>—Names the file containing the fixed system font used by Windows when it is running Windows version 2.x applications.
- oemfonts.fon=<filename>—Names the font file for the OEM character set.
- fonts.fon=<filename>—Names the file containing the proportionately spaced system font used by Windows 3.0.

For example, here are the SYSTEM.INI settings for a standard VGA display with a 640 x 480 resolution:

```
[boot]
fixedfon.fon=vgafix.fon
oemfonts.fon=vgaoem.fon
fonts.fon=vgasys.fon
```

When you use Setup to install an 8514/a or Extended (1K) VGA driver with 1024 x 768 resolution, here are the changes that Setup should make:

```
[boot]
fixedfon.fon=8514fix.fon
oemfonts.fon=8514oem.fon
fonts.fon=8514sys.fon
```

If for some reason Setup hasn't made these changes or copied the appropriate files to your \WINDOWS\SYSTEM directory, you can make the changes yourself, and then use the EXPAND utility to read the .FON files from Windows Disk 1. Use the following command from the DOS prompt:

```
EXPAND A:8514zzz.FON \WINDOWS\SYSTEM\8514zzz.FON
```

where *zzz* is the appropriate segment of the filename—fix, oem, or sys.

From this point on, whenever Windows uses the System font, it will appear larger on the screen.

Note: You may also find these 8514 font files helpful if you have installed a Super VGA display with 600 x 800 resolution and you are straining to see your display.

Changes to Your Raster Fonts

Besides the System font, you may also find that Windows raster fonts—Symbol, Tms Rmn, Courier, and Helv—are also too small for your screen when you install a high-resolution VGA driver. Windows names the font files it uses for these fonts in the [fonts] section of the WIN.INI file. For example, here are the settings for a standard VGA display with a 640 x 480 resolution:

```
[fonts]
Symbol 8,10,12,14,18,24 (VGA res)=SYMBOLE.FON
Tms Rmn 8,10,12,14,18,24 (VGA res)=TMSRE.FON
Courier 10,12,15 (VGA res)=COURE.FON
Helv 8,10,12,14,18,24 (VGA res)=HELVE.FON
```

Note: You do not need to change the font files for Windows vector fonts (Modern, Script, and Roman) because you can always scale these fonts to a larger size.

When you use Setup to install an 8514/a or Extended (1K) VGA driver with 1024 x 768 resolution, these are the changes that Setup should make to the WIN.INI:

```
[fonts]
Symbol 8,10,12,14,18,24 (8514/a res)=SYMBOLF.FON
Tms Rmn 8,10,12,14,18,24 (8514/a res)=TMSRF.FON
Courier 10,12,15 (8514/a res)=COURF.FON
Helv 8,10,12,14,18,24 (8514/a res)=HELVF.FON
```

If these settings were not made, you can make them yourself. In addition, use the EXPAND utility to read the following .FON files from Windows Disk 4 and place them in the \WINDOWS\SYSTEM directory:

```
SYMBOLF.FON
TMSRF.FON
COURF.FON
HELVF.FON
```

> **Tip: Reading SETUP.INF and OEMSETUP.INF to decipher Setup's actions**
>
> If you encounter trouble with Setup when installing a new display driver, you can usually determine the source of its trouble by delving into the SETUP.INF and OEMSETUP.INF files (both are ASCII files). Setup reads the SETUP.INF file for the appropriate settings whenever you install a display driver that comes with Windows. On the other hand, when you install a display driver that comes separate from Windows, Setup reads OEMSETUP.INF, which usually resides on the same floppy as the display driver. These files contain all the settings that Setup uses for establishing font and driver files as well as where to find them on the different Windows and driver disks.

SUMMARY

To change your setup in Windows 3, you use the Setup program. You can use this program to change your hardware drivers and to add applications to your system. When you use Setup to change your display driver, Setup normally performs its work automatically. But if for some reason the Setup program doesn't work properly when installing fonts, and it often doesn't, you now know how to manually change your font settings.

10

Using Non-Windows Applications

Windows 3 provides many advantages to programs that are written specifically for it. Not only do these programs share a consistent user interface, but they also use memory cooperatively, an important feature in a multitasking environment where memory can be tight. And because Windows provides all the screen and printer drivers, applications gain the benefit of device independence—programs will work unchanged on any hardware supported by Windows device drivers. Windows applications can also share text and graphs through the Clipboard or by using Dynamic Data Exchange (DDE).

DOS applications, on the other hand, are totally unaware of Windows' presence and were never designed to be multitasked. When you start a DOS program, DOS normally hands over all available memory to that program. And when a DOS program lays claim to memory, it holds onto that memory until you exit the program. In addition, all DOS programs must have their own video and printer drivers, creating a kind of criminal redundancy. Add to this the fact that there is no consistent way for DOS programs to share data with one another, and you have what amounts to a pretty antisocial group of programs.

Even with these inherent incompatibilities, Windows is capable of running DOS applications—even of multitasking them in 386 enhanced mode. To pull this off, Windows makes certain assumptions about how a DOS application behaves—for example, how much memory it needs and how it uses the video display. To make the most of DOS applications in Windows, it helps to know a bit about the basic mechanism that Windows uses to support them. Chapter 7, "Windows Memory Management," describes that mechanism in detail. Knowing the material in that chapter, you can more easily improve on how Windows works with DOS applications. That's what this chapter is all about.

This chapter begins by describing how to use memory-resident utilities with Windows. However, the bulk of the chapter is devoted to PIFs (program information files) and to customizing them for running DOS applications. The chapter also describes how to change the settings for an application running in 386 enhanced mode—for example, how to switch an application from the foreground to the background or how to change the amount of processor time an application receives. The final part of the chapter gives some advice on what to do when you try to use a DOS application and things go wrong.

USING MEMORY-RESIDENT UTILITIES

When you load a memory-resident utility in DOS, it's available from any program, even while that program is running. Memory-resident utilities fall into two categories: device drivers and pop-ups. A *device driver* acts as a bridge between DOS and hardware devices such as a mouse or network. You usually start device drivers from your CONFIG.SYS file so that they are loaded right as you boot your machine. A *pop-up*, on the other hand, usually lurks in the background until you access it, usually by a special key sequence. You typically load pop-ups from the DOS prompt, although it's common to place them in your AUTOEXEC.BAT if you use them all the time. When memory-resident utilities are loaded into RAM, they stay there until the system is reset, or until you remove them using a special parameter or a separate program designed for that purpose.

The critical issue for using memory-resident utilities with Windows is whether to load them before you load Windows or after. If a memory-resident utility is a device driver with a .SYS file extension, you haven't any choice—you must load it from your CONFIG.SYS file. With memory-resident utilities that are housed in executable files (.COM or .EXE), the choice isn't so clear. The sections that follow will help you make this decision.

Starting Memory-Resident Utilities Before You Start Windows

In general, if you want a memory-resident device driver to be available to any Windows or non-Windows application, or a memory-resident pop-up to be available to all non-Windows applications, you should load it *before* you load Windows. Here are three things you should be aware of, however:

- When you load a memory-resident utility before you load Windows, the memory that the utility occupies will not be available to Windows.

- When you run Windows in 386 enhanced mode, each DOS application runs in its own virtual machine, and each virtual machine inherits the DOS environment that was present before you started Windows. Therefore, when you load a memory-

resident utility before you start Windows, it occupies memory in each virtual machine, leaving less memory for each DOS application.
- If you load a pop-up like SideKick before you load Windows, Windows will not allow you to access the pop-up from the Windows desktop or from any Windows application. However, you can usually access the pop-up after you've switched to a full-screen DOS application or, in 386 enhanced mode, even to a DOS application running in a window. For example, after you've started WordPerfect, you can access SideKick from within WordPerfect.

Starting Memory-Resident Utilities Within Windows

Starting memory-resident utilities *after* you've started Windows is another option. You can load a memory-resident utility by itself, just as you would any other DOS application, or you can load it as part of a batch file.

Loading a Memory-Resident Utility by Itself

When you load a memory-resident utility by itself, Windows treats it like any other DOS application. For example, if you are running Windows in 386 enhanced mode, Windows gives the utility its own virtual machine and runs the utility within it. To use the utility, you must switch to it just as you would to any other DOS application—you cannot access the utility from within another application. When you quit the utility, Windows casts it away and frees the memory it once occupied.

To load a memory-resident utility by itself, you can use the File Run command from Program Manager (or File Manager) or launch it from an icon that you've added to a group window. Just as for any other DOS application, you run the utility directly from its executable file or from a PIF. Either way, after the utility loads, Windows displays the message shown in Figure 10-1. As this message indicates, when you're finished using a utility, you should press CTRL+C. When you do, Windows removes the utility from memory and (in 386 enhanced mode) closes its window.

Loading a Memory-Resident Utility with a Batch File

You can also load a memory-resident utility as part of a batch file. In fact, this is the preferred method when your intent is to access the utility from within a DOS application. The batch file should first load the memory-resident utility and then load the DOS application (see "Using DOS Batch Files" below for more details).

There are only a handful of memory-resident utilities that are accessible to Windows applications—for example, the IBM Personal Communications/3270 utility. If you want to load such a memory-resident utility so that you can access it from Windows applications, you can start the utility from WINSTART.BAT. This is a DOS batch file like any other, except that Windows always reads it after starting in 386 enhanced mode. In addition, when you start a utility from WINSTART.BAT, Windows makes it available to all Windows applications but not to non-Windows applications. The advantage is that

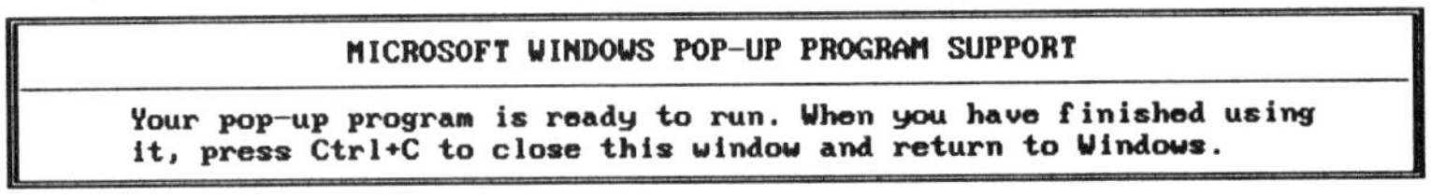

314 *Windows 3 Power Tools*

```
┌─────────────────────────────────────────────────────────────┐
│            MICROSOFT WINDOWS POP-UP PROGRAM SUPPORT         │
│   Your pop-up program is ready to run. When you have finished using │
│   it, press Ctrl+C to close this window and return to Windows.      │
└─────────────────────────────────────────────────────────────┘
```

Figure 10-1 The message Windows displays when you start a memory-resident utility

you can conserve memory for non-Windows applications, because the utility is not duplicated in each virtual machine.

WHAT IS A PIF?

A PIF—*program information file*—is a special file that provides Windows the settings it needs to run a DOS-based application. In general, the more Windows knows about an application, the better chance it has of running it properly. Whenever you start a DOS application, Windows looks for the PIF associated with that application. If Windows finds the PIF, it uses the information in the file instead of the *standard settings*, the default settings that Microsoft has determined work with the majority of DOS applications.

When you launch a DOS application, Windows looks for the PIF filename that exactly matches the application's name. For example, if you click on WP.EXE in the File Manager to launch WordPerfect, Windows looks for WP.PIF. This is true for both executable files (.EXE or .COM) and batch files (.BAT).

If Windows cannot find the PIF in the Windows directory or in the directory associated with the application, it uses the standard settings. (It does not search the directories provided in your PATH statement.)

Of course, you can also start an application directly from its PIF. For example, you can run WordPerfect (WP.EXE) simply by launching WP.PIF.

Note: The most important thing to remember about PIFs is that you usually don't need them. The easiest way to launch a DOS application is to run it from its executable file (.EXE or .COM), which usually works just fine. The time to use a PIF is when you're having trouble with the application—for example, the program won't load, the screen is flaking, or you can't switch back to Windows. PIFs are also helpful when you want to customize the way an application runs. For example, PIFs let you limit the amount of memory a program uses, adjust the rate at which an application accepts Clipboard text, and control whether a program runs in the background.

Using Predefined PIFs

As you may recall, when you use Windows Setup (SETUP.EXE) to install Windows on your system for the first time, you can elect to have it search your hard disk(s) for existing programs and add them to group windows. Setup adds icons for both Windows and DOS

Using Non-Windows Applications   315

applications. (Chapter 9, "Changing Your Setup," explains how to use Windows Setup to add predefined PIFs to your system and install applications.)

In the case of DOS applications, Setup adds only those applications for which it has PIF information. Setup stores the PIFs it creates in the Windows directory (usually C:\WINDOWS). If Setup does not create a PIF for an application, you have two options: you can run the application *without* a PIF, which usually works just fine, or you can create a PIF yourself.

Note: If you elected not to have Windows Setup install applications when you first installed Windows, you can use Setup later to install them. Chapter 9, "Changing Your Setup," explains how.

You may also find that your DOS application comes with its own PIF. For example, some recent versions of Quattro Pro and 1-2-3 Release 3.1 include their own PIFs. To install the PIF, you simply copy it to the Windows directory or the application's directory. In general, you are better off using the manufacturer-supplied PIF than the Microsoft-supplied PIF, since the manufacturer usually knows more about how the application uses extended memory, video memory, monitor ports, and the like.

When you run an application without a PIF, Windows uses the standard PIF settings.

Tip: *A list of Microsoft-supplied PIFs*

Unlike earlier releases of Windows, you will not find any PIFs on your Windows 3 distribution disks. If you are wondering what DOS programs Microsoft supplies PIFs for, you may be at a loss. Fortunately, you can see a complete list of those programs in the SETUP.INF file that Windows copies to your \WINDOWS\SYSTEM directory. The SETUP.INF file is an ASCII file that includes a plethora of settings that the Setup Program reads when it executes. To see the contents of this file, load it into Notepad. By searching for "[pif]", you can move to the section that lists the PIFs. Each line in the list includes the name of a DOS program, the name of the program's executable file (.EXE or .COM), and several other settings. At the top of the list is a guide to the settings. Here's an example of how to decipher the settings for WordPerfect:

Category	*Example Setting*	*Meaning*
description	"WordPerfect"	For WordPerfect.
exe	WP.EXE	The name of the program's executable file (.EXE or .COM).
pifname	WP.PIF	The name Microsoft assigns to the PIF it creates.
optional parameters	""	This program has no optional parameters (see "Optional Parameters").

(continued)

Category	Example Setting	Meaning
min mem	358	The minimum amount of memory that must be available in the system before Windows even tries to load the program (see "Memory Requirements: KB Required").
graphics	n	The program does not run in graphics mode (it runs in text mode). Therefore, in the standard mode PIF settings, the Video Mode option will be set to text (see "Video Mode"); and in the 386 enhanced mode options, the Video Memory option will also be set to Text (see "Display Options").
com	n	The application does not directly modify a COM port in standard or real mode (see "Directly Modifies").
fast_paste	p	Allows Windows to use a faster method when pasting information from the Clipboard to the application in 386 enhanced mode (see "Allow Fast Paste").
background bit set	n	The application does not normally run in the background. Therefore, do not turn on the Background check box in the application's 386 enhanced mode PIF settings (see "Execution").

Tip: Recovering predefined PIF settings

Suppose you have changed the settings for a predefined PIF that Windows Setup provided for you, but you later decide that you want to restore the PIF to its original settings. Rather than try to reconstruct the settings from memory, you can use the Setup program again to restore the PIF. Here's how:

1. Launch the Windows Setup program from the Main group menu.
2. Select Options from the main menu followed by the Set Up Applications... option.

Using Non-Windows Applications 317

3. Choose a drive or path from the drop-down box indicating where you want Windows to search for the application(s) to set up. You can have it search all drives, a single drive, or all the directories in your PATH statement. After Windows completes its search, it displays a dialog box showing all the applications it found.

4. Highlight the application name in the "Applications found on hard disk(s)" list on the left and click on the Add -> button. Windows moves the application name to the "Set up for use with Windows" column on the right.

5. Select OK to have Windows overwrite the existing PIF for that application.

Windows will also add an icon to your Non-Windows Applications group window.

THE PIF EDITOR

To work with PIFs, you use the PIF Editor, located by default in the Accessories group window. When you start the PIF Editor, it displays a new, untitled PIF in its window using the standard settings. You can create and modify PIFs just as you do other files in Windows. For example, to load an existing file into memory, you use File Open. To create a new unnamed PIF with all the standard settings, use File New. Most important, to save a PIF so that Windows will use it the next time you launch a DOS application, use File Save.

Tip: Changing the standard PIF settings

Suppose you are running Windows in 386 enhanced mode, and you decide that you want all the DOS programs for which you do not provide special PIFs to appear windowed rather than use a full-screen display. As mentioned, when Windows cannot find a PIF for a DOS application, it uses the standard settings. You can override these standard settings by changing the contents of the _DEFAULT.PIF file. When this file is present in the Windows directory, Windows uses its settings in place of the standard settings when it cannot find a PIF for a DOS application. In the current example, to have a DOS program appear in a window, you would open the _DEFAULT.PIF file, click on the Windowed radio button in the Display Usage options, and choose File Save to save the file.

If you no longer want to use the modified settings, you can delete the _DEFAULT.PIF file. Windows will then revert to using the standard settings. Of course, you can always recreate a _DEFAULT.PIF file by using the File New command to load a new, untitled PIF. Next, enter **_default.pif** in the Program Filename text box (don't forget the preceding underscore) and choose File Save to save the file.

CHANGING THE PIF MODE

Windows saves two sets of settings in a PIF file—those for standard (or real) mode and those for 386 enhanced mode. The options that appear within the PIF Editor window depend on the mode that Windows is currently in when you start the PIF Editor. For example, Figure 10-2 shows the settings that appear when you launch the PIF Editor in standard or real mode. The settings that appear for 386 enhanced mode are more extensive and include advanced options for controlling multitasking, EMS and XMS memory, display usage, and more.

Suppose you have started Windows in standard mode, but you want to create settings for 386 enhanced mode. To change the PIF mode, you use the Mode command from the PIF Editor's main menu. When you select this command, Windows shows a warning message like the one in Figure 10-3. This message simply indicates that you are about to switch to a different mode than Windows is currently in, and you should be aware that the settings you are about to make will not apply to the current mode.

Tip: **Windows duplicates many options between modes**

Many of the standard and real mode PIF options are automatically duplicated for 386 enhanced mode. For example, if you set the Program Filename option in standard/real mode and then use the Mode command to switch to the settings for 386 enhanced mode, Windows duplicates the same setting in 386 enhanced mode. This is especially helpful when you run Windows frequently in both real/standard or 386 enhanced mode and you need to set PIF options for both modes. The most notable exception, however, is the Optional Parameters setting, which you use to supply command-line parameters to a program when you start it—you must set this option independently for the two modes.

USING DOS BATCH FILES

If you want to run a DOS batch file from within Windows, you should normally create a PIF for it. In general, the settings for the PIF should match those of the largest and most video memory-intensive application you are launching from the batch file. For example, suppose you want to run Quattro Pro, and you want to use your Logitech bus mouse with the program. You can activate your mouse by using MOUSE.COM, the memory-resident mouse driver. Here's an example of the batch file you might use:

```
MOUSE.COM
Q.EXE
```

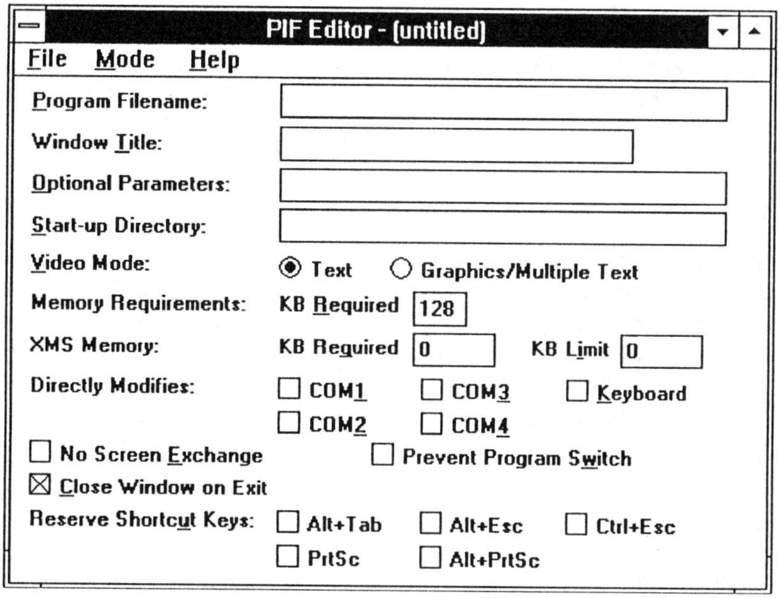

Figure 10-2 The PIF Editor in standard or real mode

The first line loads the memory-resident mouse driver (MOUSE.COM) and the second line loads Quattro Pro (Q.EXE). The settings for the PIF should match those you would normally use for Quattro Pro because it requires the most memory of the two programs and very likely uses graphics mode. (See "Special Considerations for the Logitech Mouse" for more on using that mouse with DOS applications.)

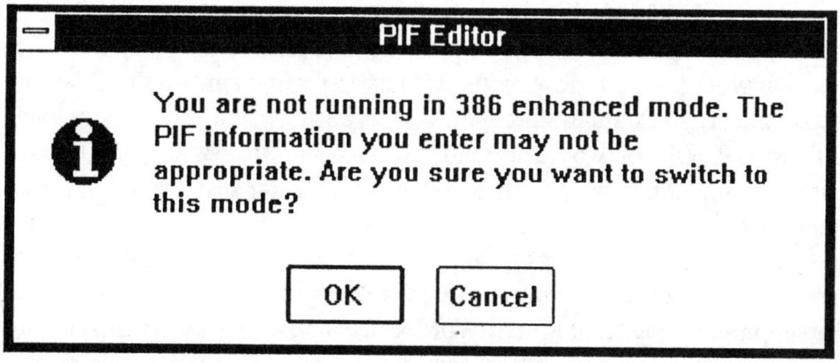

Figure 10-3 After switching the PIF Editor from standard to 386 enhanced mode

STANDARD AND REAL MODE PIF OPTIONS

The PIF Editor provides several options for running DOS applications in standard and real mode. Many of these same options appear when the PIF Editor is set for 386 enhanced mode.

Program Filename

The Program Filename text box should contain the path and name of the file that starts the application. For example, if you are creating a PIF for WordPerfect 5.1, you might type **c:\wp51\wp.exe** because WP.EXE is the file you use to start the program and c:\wp51 is the directory associated with WordPerfect's program files. If you have included the directory associated with the application in your DOS PATH statement, you do not need to enter the complete path in the text box—for example, **wp.exe** alone will suffice.

Window Title

The Window Title text box is where you place the name that you want to appear below the application's icon when you minimize the application. (In 386 enhanced mode, this text will also appear in the title bar at the top of the application's window.) For example, you might type **Quattro Pro V 2.0** to create a title for that application. If you leave the Window Title box blank, Windows uses the application's filename, without the extension, when you minimize the application.

Note: Do not confuse the Window Title text with the text that appears below an icon in Program Manager. To assign the latter, you use Program Manager's File New or File Properties command and enter a description for the icon.

Optional Parameters

If you want to supply any application-specific parameters to a program when you start it, place them in the Optional Parameters text box. The parameters you place here are the same ones you would enter following the application's filename on the DOS command line. For example, if you want to start WordPerfect and have it automatically load the file named STARTUP.WP, you would normally type **wp startup.wp** at the DOS prompt. To accomplish the same thing using a PIF file, you would enter **startup.wp** in the Optional Parameters text box.

By specifying a question mark (?), you can have Windows prompt you for optional parameters. This is an excellent way to provide information to the application on the fly. For example, suppose you want to start WordPerfect and have it load a different file each time. By placing a ? in the Optional Parameters text box, you can have Windows prompt you for the filename as shown in Figure 10-4.

Note: If you launch an application by choosing File Run from Program Manager or File Manager, any parameters you supply on the command line will automatically override those supplied in the application's PIF.

Using Non-Windows Applications   321

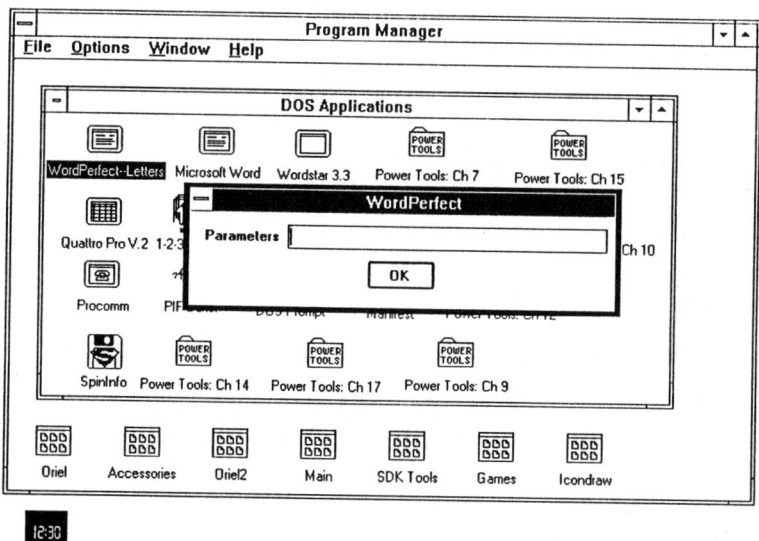

Figure 10-4 The effect of using a question mark (?) in the Optional Parameters text box

Start-up Directory

The Start-up Directory text box is where you enter the drive and directory you want Windows to make current when you start the application. The most common reason to use this setting is when an application needs access to other files—for example, configuration or overlay files. In this case, you should specify a start-up directory location that is the same as that of the needed files. If you want Windows to determine the start-up directory, leave this option blank.

> **Tip:** *How Windows determines the current directory when you do not specify a start-up directory*
>
> If no start-up directory is specified in a non-Windows application's PIF, the current directory depends on how the application is launched. If the program is started by calling its executable (.EXE, .COM, or .BAT) file, the current directory will become the directory containing the program; this will be true even if a PIF exists for that program in Windows' home directory. On the other hand, if the program is launched by calling its PIF, the current directory will become the directory containing the PIF. This applies for all three methods of launching a

322 Windows 3 Power Tools

> program: by clicking on an icon, by clicking on a filename in the File Manager or Program Manager window, or by using the File Run command available from the File Manager or Program Manager menu. However, if the current drive or directory is changed using File Manager, then that drive or directory will remain current when the program's executable file or PIF is called by using the Run command from the File Manager menu.

A Problem with Windows

As anyone who has worked at all extensively with applications programs knows, you can usually place a program's directory in your PATH statement and then execute that program from any directory you're located in. DOS checks for the program name in the current directory and, if it can't find it, looks for the program in the directories in your PATH.

On the other hand, when you launch a program from a PIF, Windows always changes the current directory to the directory containing the PIF. One way to have a program use another directory on start-up is to supply the directory name in the Start-up Directory text box. However, this forces you to have a separate PIF for each directory in which you want to use the program, a preposterous solution. Another is to change the current directory with File Manager and then run the program from the File Manager menu by calling either the executable file or the PIF.

There is, however, a third method that allows you to click on an icon to execute a program in the directory of your choice. Begin by creating a batch file that accepts two parameters on the command line: the directory and the drive. For example, here's the contents of a batch file named W.BAT that changes to the directory and drive supplied on the command line. The batch file then launches WordPerfect:

```
echo off
if %1!==! goto oops
If %2!==! goto skipdrv
%2
:skipdrv
cd %1
wp
goto end
:oops
echo You forgot to supply the directory and drive
:end
```

Suppose you ran this batch file from the DOS command line by typing **w \letters d:**. The program would change to the d:\letters directory and then start up WordPerfect. Notice that the batch file bails out if you do not supply any parameters on the command line. In addition, if you include only one parameter on the command line, the batch file assumes it is the directory parameter and skips around the line to change the drive.

After the batch file is created, the next step is to start the PIF Editor and load the application's PIF using the File Open command. Building on the current example, you might load the Microsoft-supplied PIF, WP.PIF. Place a question mark (?) in the Optional Parameters text box and the name of the batch file in the Program Filename text box, in this case W.BAT. To save the PIF, use the File Save As command and enter a name corresponding to the batch file (in the current example, W.PIF).

The last step in the process is to create an icon that launches the PIF. Select File New from the Program Manager menu, and choose OK to create a new program item. Next, enter the name of the program in the Description text box—for example, W.BAT & WordPerfect—and the name of the PIF in the Command Line text box—in this case, W.PIF.

When you click on the icon you've created, Windows prompts you for the command-line parameters. Remember that these are the parameters to the batch file, not the program.

Video Mode

The Video Mode option, which is available only in Windows standard and real modes, lets you tell Windows how much memory to set aside for saving an application's display so that you can switch back and forth between the application and Windows without any trouble. If you choose the Text button, Windows reserves the least amount of memory possible for saving the display (only about 4K). You should select this option when you know you'll be running the application in text mode only. The Graphics/Multiple Text button, on the other hand, causes Windows to set aside more memory for saving the display. Choose this button when you are running the application in graphics mode. If you have no idea what video mode your application is running in, choose Graphics/Multiple Text, because it's the safest choice.

> *Note:* Multiple text refers to an application that uses multiple text pages to display text. Almost no programs use multiple text pages—the only notable exception is BASIC programs that have been written specifically for the CGA adapter.

One thing to keep in mind as you choose a Video Mode setting is that the memory that Windows uses for saving the display comes out of the memory Windows allocates to the application. Therefore, if you select Graphics/Multiple Text, you will have slightly less memory available for the application and its data than if you select Text (about 8K less). This is usually not a big concern, but it may influence your choice of settings if, for example, you want to load a large spreadsheet into 1-2-3 and you have very little memory to spare.

In actual practice, it's extremely rare that the Video Mode settings will have any effect at all on Windows' behavior, so you'll rarely have to fool with them. In the vast majority of cases, selecting the Text button will not cause any problems if your application should happen to switch to graphics mode. Windows usually handles the mode change just fine, and you can still switch back and forth between the application and Windows without a hitch.

The time to try changing the Video Mode setting is when you are having trouble with the screen when switching between an application and Windows. For example, the screen may appear distorted or blank. If this is the case, try choosing the Graphics/Multiple Text button to have Windows set aside more room for saving the display.

Be aware, however, that these Video Mode settings are not a panacea for all video problems you may encounter when switching between applications and Windows. In fact, they are really only intended for EGA and VGA systems. If you are having trouble with another video adapter (for example, CGA or Hercules), these buttons usually won't help you much.

Memory Requirements

If you've created PIFs in previous versions of Windows, you may think that setting the memory requirements for a DOS application is part art, part science. Though this is still somewhat true in Windows 3, the guidelines are a bit clearer.

To begin with, whenever you start an application in standard or real mode, Windows gives it all available conventional memory. There's no way to limit the amount of conventional memory an application gets. (You can, however, limit the amount of conventional memory an application gets in 386 enhanced mode. See "386 Enhanced Mode Options" below.)

The Memory Requirements: KB Required text box lets you tell Windows how much *conventional* memory must be free in the system before it even attempts to load the application. If the memory is not available, you'll see an error message like the one in Figure 10-5 when you try to run the program from the PIF.

The standard setting for the KB Required text box is 128, which is a little low for most popular business applications. You may want to increase this setting to about 250, but each program is different. Try experimenting to find the best setting for a given application. You'll know that you've set KB Required too low when the application itself issues an error message indicating that there's not enough memory for it to load. (Of

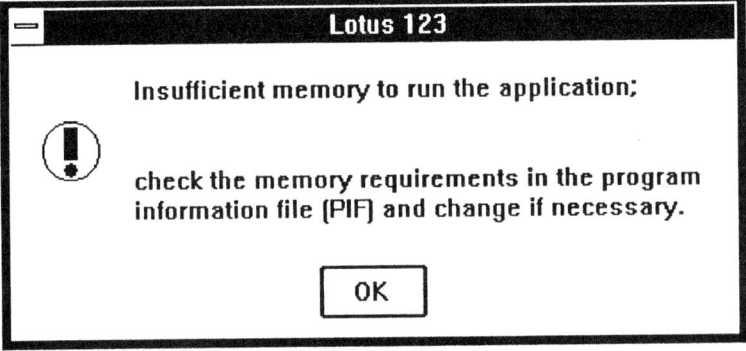

Figure 10-5 When there is too little conventional memory to load an application

course, the message only appears when there's enough conventional memory in the system to exceed the KB Required setting, but not enough to actually load the application.) You can easily simulate such a low memory situation in real mode by running several Windows accessories at once, then trying to load the DOS application.

Note that when the documentation for an application lists the memory required, the figure shown is not always a good indicator of the minimum amount of memory that Windows needs to have available to load the application. For example, the 1-2-3 Release 2.2 documentation states that the program needs a minimum of 320K of conventional memory to run; but this figure also includes the overhead required for running DOS and the utilities in your AUTOEXEC.BAT and CONFIG.SYS files. You can actually load 1-2-3 Release 2.2 in Windows with as little as 250K of conventional memory available (provided the undo feature is off). Of course, you'll have very little memory available for your spreadsheets.

XMS Memory

The XMS Memory settings let you tell Windows how much *extended* memory to allocate to an application that uses the Lotus/Intel/Microsoft/AST eXtended Memory Specification (XMS) standard. Only a handful of DOS programs take advantage of extended memory, and those that do incorporate a DOS extender of one variety or another. Programs written using conventional DOS extender technology, most notably 1-2-3 Releases 3 and 3.1, all access extended memory using the XMS standard. (See Chapter 7 for a more complete explanation of this standard.)

Windows supports these programs in real or standard mode. Recall that Windows itself does not have XMS support. Rather, it is provided to Windows through the HIMEM.SYS driver. Chapter 7 gives a detailed description of HIMEM.SYS.

Note: Unlike extended memory, Windows does not let you control the amount of *expanded memory* allocated to an application in real or standard mode. In fact, Windows exercises no control whatsoever over how an application uses expanded memory in real or standard mode; it's up to the application itself to handle this memory. Of course, if you want an application to be able to access expanded memory in either of these modes, you must have installed an expanded memory manager on your system, either from the disk that accompanies your expanded memory board or by using an expanded memory emulator. See "Expanded Memory" in Chapter 7 for a complete discussion of expanded memory. (In 386 enhanced mode, Windows can simulate expanded memory using extended memory. See "Advanced 386 Enhanced Mode Options" for more on this subject.)

KB Required

Use this setting to tell Windows how much extended memory must be available before it even attempts to the load the application. If the application uses extended memory, deriving this setting is usually quite easy—just check its documentation. For example, the documentation for 1-2-3 Release 3.1 states that the program requires a minimum of 384K to run. This is the setting you should use for XMS Memory: KB Required.

If an application does not use extended memory (and most do not), leave this setting at 0. Using a setting other than 0 significantly increases the time it takes to switch between the application and Windows. The time is required to write an image of the memory to an application swap file on disk, and to read it back in later when you switch back to the application. (See Chapter 7 for more details.)

KB Limit

Most of the current DOS applications that access extended memory are gluttons. They grab all of the extended memory they can get, even when they don't need it, and they hold onto it until you quit them. When one such program latches onto all the extended memory, another program can't get any if it needs some. What's more, if you have a lot of extended memory, and you switch away from the gluttonous program, Windows must write the contents of that memory to a temporary application swap file on disk, a time-consuming process at best. (When this happens, it's also not uncommon to run out of disk space, especially when you have a lot of memory on your system and you're a little short on disk space.)

Fortunately, Windows lets you limit the amount of extended memory that an application can get by using the KB Limit text box. A setting of 1024 works fine for most applications, provided you have that amount of extended memory (or more). If you want to prevent an application from accessing any extended memory at all, enter 0.

Tip: Changing the standard mode XMS settings for 1-2-3 Releases 1A and 2.x

If you look carefully at the Microsoft-supplied PIF for 1-2-3—123.PIF—you'll see that it is designed to work generically with all versions of 1-2-3 (Releases 1A, 2.x, and 3.x). You can significantly decrease the time it takes to switch between 1-2-3 Release 2.x (or 1A) and Windows in real or standard mode by optimizing 123.PIF for this release. For example, if you are using 123.PIF with 1-2-3 Release 2.x, you can change the XMS Memory: KB Required setting to 0, instead of the Microsoft-suggested setting of 320. These settings are possible because neither Release 1A or 2.x use extended memory. If you are using 1-2-3 Release 3.1, increase the XMS Memory: KB Required setting to 384 because the program needs this amount of extended memory to run.

Directly Modifies

Because DOS is a single-tasking operating system, most DOS applications assume that they can access all system resources at will. For example, if a communications program such as Procomm Plus needs to read and write to COM1, it simply does so, without any concern that another application might also be sharing the port.

The Directly Modifies check boxes let you tell Windows whether an application takes control of a system resource to the exclusion of other applications. For example, if you are creating a PIF for Procomm Plus, you might turn on the COM1 check box so that Windows will know that the program will be monopolizing that port.

In the same way that some applications monopolize a COM port, a few older programs monopolize the keyboard. They do this by reading keys directly from the PC's keyboard buffer. Fortunately, this type of antisocial behavior is the exception rather than the rule—it is very rare that you will ever encounter such an application today. To give such an application exclusive use of the keyboard, you can turn on the Keyboard check box. If you are not sure whether the application reads directly from the keyboard buffer, you should avoid turning on this check box.

Here's an example of when you might want to use a Directly Modifies option. Suppose you are using Procomm Plus to access an online service through your modem hooked to COM1. The settings you've chosen for the modem are 2400 baud, no parity, 8 databits, 1 stopbit. While you are in the middle of the online session, you decide that you want to switch to WordPerfect to dash off some notes. Suppose you normally have your laser printer hooked to COM1, not your modem, and WordPerfect is set to print to COM1 at 9600 baud. If you switch to WordPerfect, you may lose some data from WordPerfect's using the serial port previously used by Procomm Plus.

Rather than having the two programs compete for the same device, you can turn on the COM1 option button in Procomm Plus's PIF. The good news is that this lets you avoid any data loss that might occur if another application tries to interfere with Procomm Plus's setting for the device. The bad news is that Windows won't let you switch away from Procomm Plus without first quitting the program. In fact, whenever you have turned on any of the Directly Modifies check boxes (for example, COM1 or Keyboard), you will not be able to switch away from the application while it is running. Rather, you must first quit the program to return to Windows or use another application.

In standard or real mode, when you switch between two DOS applications that use the same communications port without either of their PIFs indicating this by having the Directly Modifies box checked, Windows does not warn you that the port is already in use. It simply makes the switch. However, if one of the applications is a Windows application, Windows displays the message shown in Figure 10-6 when you shift from the Windows application to the DOS application. You can then choose whether you want the DOS application's settings to override the Windows application's settings for the port.

If the communications port settings are the same between the two applications, you won't have any problem switching from one application to another. This means, for example, that you can use two different communications programs to access the same port. For example, you might use Terminal (TERMINAL.EXE) to dial up an on-line service, then switch to Procomm Plus to drive the communications session from that point forward.

Later on you'll see that the Directly Modifies options are not offered in the 386 enhanced mode PIF options because they are not needed. In 386 enhanced mode, Windows intercepts an application's I/O port reads and writes, a feat made possible by

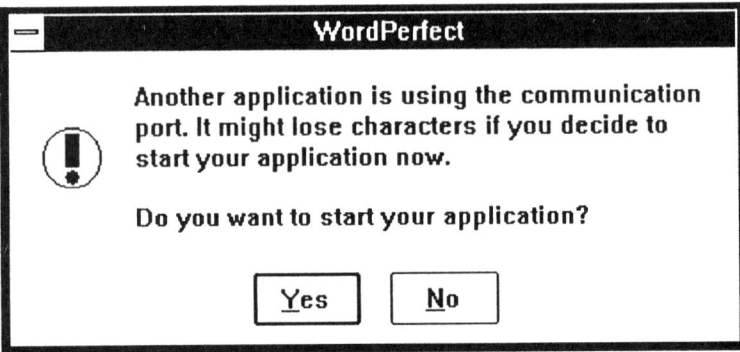

Figure 10-6 The warning that appears when a DOS application is about to override a Windows application's settings for a communications port (standard and real mode only)

the architecture of the 386 chip. If the two applications are Windows programs, Windows automatically handles the use of the device, and no contention arises. However, if one of the applications is a DOS program, problems can occur when they both try to read or write to a device. If Windows detects that two applications are in contention for a device, it can arbitrate between them. For example, Windows might warn you when an application tries to use a device that is already in use; you can then choose whether to proceed or cancel the interfering program's I/O. Alternatively, you can have Windows automatically interrupt the first application's I/O, allowing the second application to intercede. The way Windows behaves in this situation depends on the Device Contention settings. You can control these settings through the 386 Enhanced icon in the Control Panel. See Chapter 8, "Using the Control Panel," for a complete explanation of how Windows arbitrates device contention.

No Screen Exchange

If you want to copy text from a DOS application's window to the Clipboard, you can press PRINTSCREEN or ALT+PRINTSCREEN. When you press either key, Windows copies the text to a small buffer (about 4-5K) that it has previously set aside for holding the text. The memory that Windows uses for the buffer comes from its global heap, not from the application's memory.

By turning on the No Screen Exchange check box in the application's PIF, you can prevent Windows from allocating the buffer and thereby conserve a small amount of memory that Windows can use elsewhere. Of course, if you turn on this option, you will not be able to copy text from a DOS application's window to the Clipboard.

The important thing to remember about the effect of turning on the No Screen Exchange option is that it does not directly increase the application's available memory. Rather, it makes available a small amount of memory that Windows can use as a whole.

Note: Turning on the No Screen Exchange check box has the same effect as turning on the PrtSc and Alt+PrtSc check boxes in the Reserve Shortcut Keys options.

Tip: Using PRINTSCREEN for screen dumps

When you are running a program in DOS, you may be used to using PRINTSCREEN or SHIFT+PRINTSCREEN to print a quick screen dump—a copy of whatever is currently on your screen—to your printer on LPT1. (Both PRINTSCREEN and SHIFT+PRINTSCREEN usually work on newer 101-key keyboards, while SHIFT+PRINTSCREEN is required for older AT-style keyboards.) Unfortunately, in real or standard mode, Windows disables the screen dump feature; try as you might, you cannot get a screen dump in standard or real mode, even when you have turned on the PrtSc box in the Reserve Shortcut Keys section of the application's PIF. (The only exception is when the DOS program has its own PRINTSCREEN code, which very few programs actually do.)

Printing a quick screen dump is only a problem in real or standard mode. You can easily produce screen dumps in 386 enhanced mode with PRINTSCREEN or SHIFT+PRINTSCREEN. Whether you need the SHIFT key depends on the style of keyboard you have and your PIF settings. If you have an old AT-style keyboard, you must turn on the PrtSc box in the application's PIF. You can then get a screen dump by pressing SHIFT+PRINTSCREEN. If you have a newer 101-key keyboard, you can get a screen dump any time by pressing SHIFT+PRINTSCREEN (you don't have to change your PIF settings at all). If you turn on the PrtSc box in the application's PIF, you can also get a screen dump with PRINTSCREEN.

Prevent Program Switch

Whenever you start a DOS application in standard or real mode, Windows creates a temporary application swap file for the application. Then, when you switch away from a DOS application, Windows writes all (or part) of the application to the application swap file. To reconstruct the scene when you later switch back to the application, Windows must allocate a small chunk of memory (usually about 50K for the first application and 12K for each application thereafter) so that it can restore the context from the swap file.

Suppose you are running several DOS applications at once, and memory is tight. You can conserve memory by turning on the Prevent Program Switch check box in an application's PIF. Choosing this option prevents you from switching away from the application without first quitting the application. Windows never allocates the small chunk of memory required to restore the context from the swap file (it never gets the chance). Unless memory is especially tight, though, you will probably want to leave this box unchecked.

Close Window on Exit

As you're no doubt aware, whenever you're in standard or real mode and you quit a DOS application, Windows immediately closes the application's window. If for some reason you want to leave an application's window on the screen after you quit the application, you can uncheck the Close Window on Exit check box in the application's PIF. If you are running the application in text mode when you quit, Windows will display a message telling you that you need to press a key to exit. If you are running the application in graphics mode, you may or may not see a message, but you will need to press a key anyway to continue your work.

Reserve Shortcut Keys

Occasionally you may encounter a DOS application that uses one of the same key combinations that Windows uses as a shortcut key. For example, suppose your DOS program produces an Icelandic thorn (or some other special character) when you press ALT+TAB, but Windows uses this same sequence to switch to the next active application. Because Windows filters all the keystrokes as they come in, it intercepts the ALT+TAB and uses it for its own purposes; the sequence never makes it to the DOS application.

If you prefer to have the DOS application receive the keystroke sequence rather than Windows, you can use the Reserve Shortcut Keys options in the application's PIF. For example, to reserve ALT+TAB for the application, turn on that check box in the application's PIF. The next time you run the application, Windows will let the ALT+TAB sequence pass through to it. Of course, when you are running other DOS applications, Windows will still use ALT+TAB as a shortcut key.

386 ENHANCED MODE PIF OPTIONS

When Windows is running in 386 enhanced mode, it takes advantage of the 386 or 486 processor's native ability to run each DOS application you launch in its own "virtual machine." In other words, each DOS program has the illusion that it is running in the fixed, 1-megabyte address space of an 8086. And because the paging hardware built into the 80386 and 80486 processors allows the system to protect memory on a page-by-page basis, Windows can insulate DOS programs from one another and from itself.

To further guarantee its success in multitasking DOS applications, Windows makes certain assumptions about how a program writes to the screen, uses memory, and accesses other system resources. These assumptions are reflected in the standard PIF settings for 386 enhanced mode. For most programs, the standard settings are fine, and you won't need to change them. But occasionally you'll need to do some fine tuning of an application's PIF, especially when you are running several applications at once and memory is tight.

Here are some examples of the unique ways you can change an application's PIF for 386 enhanced mode:

- When you run an application in DOS, it may try to consume all the conventional memory available in the system. While this is fine in DOS, it can create special problems in Windows when you are running more than one application in 386 enhanced mode. Because Windows applications and DOS applications must share memory cooperatively, Windows offers PIF settings that let you limit the amount of memory a DOS application uses. By limiting a DOS application's use of memory, you can make more memory available to other programs (see "Memory Requirements," later).

- Windows normally runs DOS applications full screen; but if you like, you can have them run in a window, even when they write directly to screen memory or use graphics mode (see "Display Usage").

- The 386 enhanced mode PIF options include a handful of settings that control how an application runs when other applications are active. For example, you can have a DOS application continue to run in the background while you are using another DOS application in the foreground. You can also have Windows suspend all other applications while the current DOS application is running (see "Execution"). Windows also lets you control how much processor time an application gets in relation to others (see "Multitasking Options").

- In 386 enhanced mode, Windows simulates expanded (EMS) memory for those applications that need it. You can control the amount of EMS memory Windows makes available to the application through the application's PIF (see "EMS Memory").

- Windows can make extended (XMS) memory available for applications that use it, provided those applications conform to the DOS Protected-Mode Interface (DPMI) standard. Windows gives you direct control over the amount of extended memory allocated to an application (see "XMS Memory").

- If, before you load Windows, you load a memory-resident utility that uses the high memory area (HMA)—the first 64K of extended memory—you can tell Windows that your application should not use the HMA (see "Uses High Memory Area").

- Windows needs to reserve sufficient memory to save the application's display so that when you switch away from an application, it can restore the application's screen when you switch back. The amount of memory Windows initially reserves depends on the setting you provide in the application's PIF. You can easily increase the memory Windows initially uses to save the display if you are having trouble switching to and from the program (see "Display Options").

When Windows is running in 386 enhanced mode and you start the PIF Editor, you see the options shown in Figure 10-7. These are the *basic* options for 386 enhanced mode. The *advanced* PIF options appear when you click on the Advanced... button at the bottom of the window. The advanced options are covered in the next section.

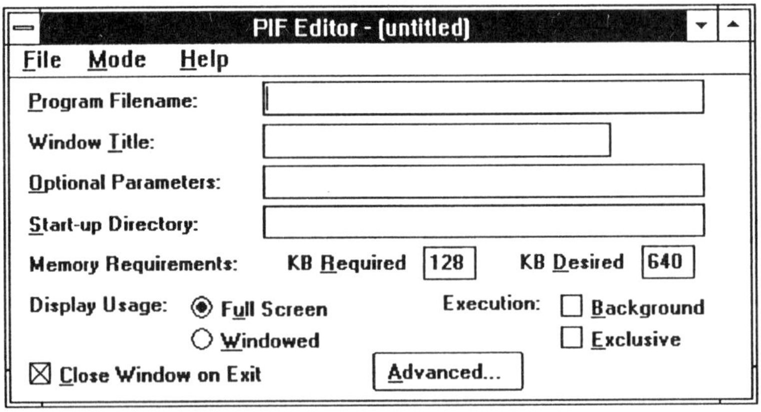

Figure 10-7 Basic PIF options for 386 enhanced mode

Duplicated Options

Many of the 386 enhanced mode PIF options are the same as for standard or real mode. For example, the Program Filename, Window Title, Optional Parameters, Start-up Directory, and Close Window on Exit options (all found on the basic options screen) and the Reserve Shortcut Keys option (found on the Advanced options screen) are all the same as the standard mode settings. In fact, if you make any of these settings for 386 enhanced mode and then use the Mode command to switch to the settings for standard mode, Windows mirrors the settings in standard mode. (The one exception is the Optional Parameters setting, which you must set independently for the two modes.) See the previous sections for descriptions of these options.

Memory Requirements

When you run an application in DOS, it may try to grab all the conventional memory in the system in the belief that, since no other programs are around to use leftover memory, it might as well have it all. When you are running Windows in standard or real mode, it's okay for an application to behave in this way because Windows moves itself out of memory to make room for the application. Besides, you can run only one DOS application at a time.

In 386 enhanced mode, both Windows applications and DOS applications must share memory cooperatively. If a DOS application uses too much memory, you may have difficulty running other programs with it. Therefore, Windows provides the Memory Requirements text boxes to let you control the amount of "conventional" memory a DOS application uses (see the tip). By limiting an application's use of memory, you can make more memory available to other applications.

> *Tip: How Windows and DOS applications view "conventional" memory*
>
> As you read these sections on 386 enhanced mode PIF settings, it's important to keep in mind the difference between how Windows and DOS applications view conventional memory. On the one hand, a DOS application has the myopic view that it is the only program running in the system and that it can use as much conventional memory—0K to 640K—as it wants.
>
> On the other hand, when Windows is running in 386 enhanced mode, it treats all memory—conventional, extended, and virtual (disk based) memory—as one large pool, the so-called "global heap." In addition, Windows places each DOS application in its own virtual machine within the global heap. When a DOS application makes a request for a block of conventional memory, Windows satisfies that request by giving it a block of memory from the global heap. Just where that block of memory resides in the physical address space of the processor is hidden from the DOS application.
>
> The Memory Requirements PIF settings let you limit the amount of memory that a DOS application uses. From the DOS application's standpoint, this is conventional memory. From Windows' standpoint, however, this is simply memory.

When your system is equipped with a lot of memory (for example, 4MB or more), putting a limit on a DOS application's use of memory is rarely that important. If each DOS application gets 640K of memory, it's normally not a problem. There's usually plenty of memory left over for other applications.

Placing limits on a DOS application's use of memory only becomes important when memory gets tight and Windows starts giving you messages like "This application has insufficient memory for its display"; or, even more significant, "Insufficient memory to run application." When you see messages like these, you should reduce the amount of memory each DOS application uses, making more memory available to the system as a whole.

KB Required

The Memory Requirements: KB Required text box lets you tell Windows how much memory must be free in the system before it should even try to load the application. If the memory is not available, you'll see an error message like the one in Figure 10-8. If other applications are running, you can try closing them to free up additional memory. Another option is to reduce the Memory Requirements settings in the PIF for each DOS application currently in memory. (See "When You Run Out of Memory" later for more suggestions.)

The standard setting for the KB Required text box is 128, which is a bit low for most popular business applications. You may want to increase this setting to around 250, but each application is different.

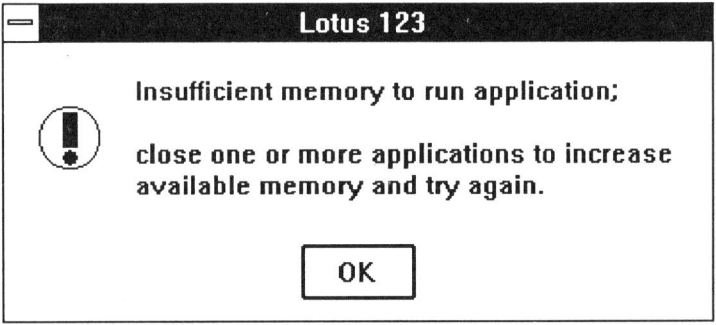

Figure 10-8 The error message you may see when there's not enough memory to launch an application

In general, you should use a KB Required setting that is just high enough to load the application without it issuing an insufficient memory error message, but low enough that you can still load the program when memory is relatively tight. As you can imagine, it's very difficult to simulate this kind of tight memory situation in 386 enhanced mode because you're shooting at a moving target. For one thing, Windows may or may not be using virtual (disk-based) memory, depending on the mix of applications you are running. Therefore, the easiest way to derive the proper KB Required setting is to run Windows in real or standard mode and set up a tight memory environment there. You can then experiment with the Memory Requirements: KB Required setting in the application's PIF. When you have the right setting, you can then use it for 386 enhanced mode.

Be aware that the KB Required setting does not limit the amount of memory that Windows gives an application (this is the purpose of the KB Desired setting). In fact, if enough memory is available to meet the KB Required setting, Windows immediately grants the application as much memory as it can up to the limit set by the KB Desired option. Therefore, you can think of KB Required as the option that controls the lower limit of the amount of memory that Windows will give an application, and KB Desired as the option that controls the upper limit.

By using a setting of -1 for KB Required, you can give an application all the available memory in the system, up to a limit of 640K. Although this setting looks handy, you should avoid using it. In most cases, using a setting of -1 sets aside a full 640K—too much for most applications. However, if you always use an application when memory is tight, a setting of -1 might be appropriate because it causes Windows to set aside as much memory as it can.

KB Desired

The Memory Requirements: KB Desired text box lets you limit the amount of "conventional" memory Windows will give a DOS application. When you launch the application, Windows immediately sets aside the amount of memory specified in this box for the program's exclusive use. If not enough memory is available in the system to meet the KB Desired setting, Windows sets aside as much memory as possible.

In general, you should be frugal with the KB Required setting. If a program doesn't need a full 640K to operate, don't set KB Desired that high. Of course many applications, such as WordPerfect, will use as much conventional memory as is available, and the more you have, the more their performance improves. With this kind of program, you'll have to balance the program's speed against your need to multitask several applications at once.

A setting of -1 tells Windows to give the application all the conventional memory in the system, up to the maximum of 640K. Because using a setting of -1 usually has the same effect as a setting of 640, you may wonder why you would ever use it. A setting of -1 is handy because Windows issues an error message and will not load the program when there is not enough memory to meet the KB Desired setting. If you use a setting of -1, Windows will load the program and grant it as much memory as it can up to 640K. Another point to consider is that if you set KB Required to -1, you must also set KB Desired to -1 or else Windows complains.

> *Tip: Setting KB Desired too high leaves less memory for other applications*
>
> If the amount of memory that you specify for KB Desired is available in the system at the time you load a DOS application, Windows immediately sets aside the memory for the application's exclusive use. What's more, the application retains exclusive use of that memory even though it may not use the memory.
>
> In general, you should set KB Required to the bare minimum required to load the program and use KB Desired to set the maximum amount of memory you think you'll need. If you follow this rule, you can guarantee yourself the maximum amount of memory available to all applications in the system.

Display Usage

As mentioned, one of the big advantages of 386 enhanced mode is that you can run DOS programs within windows, including those programs that are "ill-behaved" and write directly to screen memory or use graphics mode. When you run a DOS application in a window, you can copy and paste text between it and other applications using the Clipboard (see Chapter 6, "Sharing Data Between Applications," for details).

When you choose the Windowed radio button in the application's PIF, Windows will start the application in a window, complete with scroll bars and a window Control menu. When an application appears within a window, you can use the mouse to copy and paste text between it and other applications. However, if your program supports the mouse and you want to take advantage of it, you must run the application full screen. You must also run MOUSE.COM (from the DOS prompt or AUTOEXEC.BAT) or MOUSE.SYS (from your CONFIG.SYS). (See "Using the Mouse with DOS Applications" later for more details.)

Keep in mind that running a DOS application in a window requires just slightly more memory than running it full screen. If memory is very tight and you are having trouble running applications simultaneously, changing them to full screen may make the difference; but don't expect a huge memory savings (only about 3K per application).

A major disadvantage of running a DOS application in a window is the sluggishness that many DOS programs exhibit. Even with a fast processor, you are bound to find that you prefer to run your DOS applications full screen, and only run them in a window when you want to see them side by side or to copy and paste text between them.

Here are some tips for running DOS applications in a window:

- Once an application is running, the easiest way to switch it from a window to full-screen display, or vice versa, is by pressing ALT+ENTER.

- If you are running an application in a Window and are having trouble switching away from it, one of the first things to check is whether you have inadvertently made a selection by clicking the mouse in the window. Press ESC (sometimes more than once) to remove the selection, and you should then be able to switch away from the window. See "When You Cannot Switch Away" later for other ideas.

- If you have a VGA card, you may have trouble running DOS applications in a window. See "A Common VGA Error" for more details.

Execution

In 386 enhanced mode, Windows is a true multitasking environment for DOS applications. By default, however, Windows only runs one DOS application at a time. In other words, when you are working in one DOS application, all other DOS applications sit idle—Windows gives them no processor time.

If you want to run two DOS applications simultaneously with one continuing to operate while you are working in the other, you must tell Windows to run one in the foreground and one in the background. You must also tell Windows how much processor time to give one application in relation to the other.

Controlling how Windows multitasks DOS applications is the purpose of the Execution settings in the 386 enhanced mode PIF options. You can use these settings to control not only how much processor time a DOS application gets but also how the application runs in relation to others. For example, you can set up a program to run in the background, or you can have a program run exclusively, reserving all the system resources for itself.

Background

Suppose you want to set up your environment so that you can work on a spreadsheet while a communications program is running in the background, receiving data from an online service. By selecting the Background check box in the communications program's PIF, you can have it continue to run when you switch away from it. If you do not check the Background check box, Windows will suspend the program when you switch away from it (this is the standard setting).

Note: When you run an application in the background, the amount of processor time it gets depends on the priority settings. You control these settings through the Multitasking Options in the application's PIF (see "Advanced 386 Enhanced Mode PIF Options" later) or, once the program is running, through the Settings command in the application's window Control menu (see "Changing a Running Application").

As a general rule, you should almost always leave the Background check box unchecked. The two exceptions are communications programs that you know you'll want to leave running in the background, and other applications that always require background processing (for example, WordPerfect Office). By leaving the box unchecked, you can save a substantial amount of processing power and memory that Windows can use elsewhere. If you should ever need to run a DOS program in the background, you can always change its background setting after you've launched it. To do this, make sure the program is running in a window (press ALT+ENTER if it is currently running full screen), then open its window Control menu (press ALT+SPACEBAR), choose the Settings command, and turn on the Background check box. (See "Changing a Running Application," later, for more information.)

Exclusive

Occasionally, you may want to give a DOS application all the processor time in the system. By selecting the Exclusive check box in the application's PIF, you can have Windows suspend all other applications while the current one has the focus. Windows suspends both Windows applications and DOS applications, even those that have their Background check boxes on.

Like the Background check box, you are almost always better off leaving the Exclusive box unchecked in the application's PIF. If you should ever want to run a DOS program exclusively, you can always change its exclusive setting while it's running. To do so, select the Settings command from the application's window Control menu and turn on the Exclusive check box (see "Changing a Running Application" for more details).

When you run an application exclusively, you should always run it full screen. That way, you can guarantee that it's getting all the processing power in the system. If you should leave the program windowed, Windows will reserve some processing power for itself and Windows applications (so that it can respond to keyboard and mouse input, update the screen, and the like).

ADVANCED 386 ENHANCED MODE PIF OPTIONS

The advanced 386 enhanced mode PIF options let you control some of the more exotic and powerful aspects of how Windows runs a DOS application. Figure 10-9 shows the

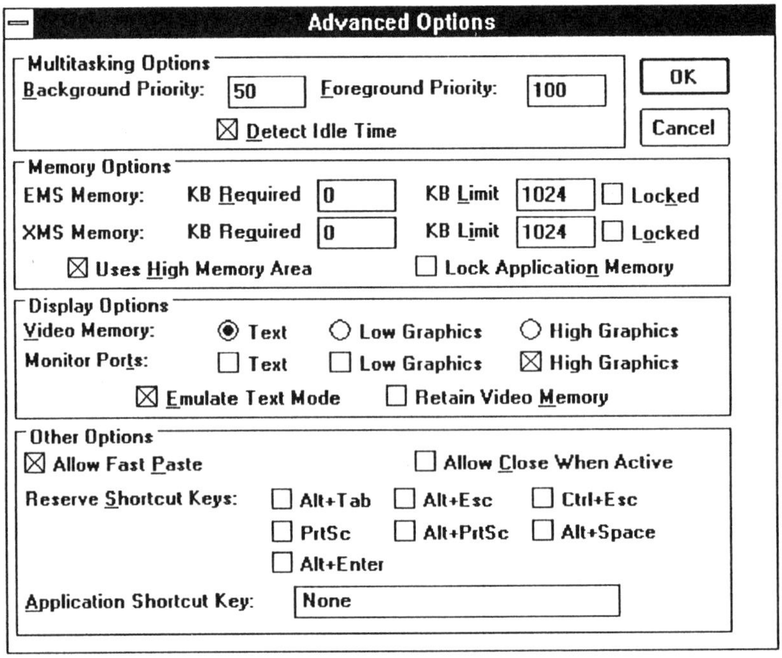

Figure 10-9 The Advanced 386 enhanced mode PIF options

Advanced options. For example, there's a setting for controlling the amount of processing power Windows gives a DOS application when you run it in the background and another for determining how much expanded memory a program can access. For most applications, you will never need to change the standard settings. But if you know how a program uses expanded or extended memory or how it uses the video display, you can usually benefit by rummaging around in its Advanced settings.

Multitasking Options

When you are running two (or more) DOS applications at once and one (or more) of them is running in the background, you need a way to control how much processor time each application gets in relation to the others. Windows lets you control this ratio through the Multitasking Options in the application's PIF.

Background Priority

When a program is running in the background, you can control the amount of processor time it gets by the number you enter in the Background text box. The standard setting is 50, but you can enter a value from 0 to 10000.

By itself, the number you enter in the Background text box doesn't mean anything. It only has meaning in relation to the Background and Foreground settings for the other

DOS applications. For example, suppose you have three applications in the system: one running in the foreground with a Foreground setting of 150 and two running in the background, each with a Background setting of 50. How much processor time does each application get? Adding all the priorities of the different applications together, you get a total of 250 (150 foreground priority + 2 * 50 background priority). The amount of processing time each background application gets is 50/250, or 20 percent of the processor time. The foreground application gets 150/250, or 60 percent of the processor time.

Note: If an application's Execution: Background check box is turned off, the application cannot run in the background. Therefore, any number you enter in the Background Priority text box will not have any effect.

You can always change an application's background or foreground setting after you've launched it by modifying the Priority options in its window Control menu (see "Changing a Running Application," later, for details).

Foreground Priority

The Foreground Priority text box lets you control the amount of processor time an application gets when it has the focus. The standard setting is 50, but you can enter a value from 0 to 10000. The value you enter has no meaning unless at least one other DOS application is running in the background. Also, the amount of processor time the application gets depends on the priority settings for the other applications in the system (see the previous section).

Tip: Giving maximum priority to a DOS application

If you want a DOS application to receive *all* the processor time in the system without interruption, set its Foreground Priority text box to 10000. This setting has the unique effect of giving background applications no processor time unless the foreground application is idle.

Detect Idle Time

If a DOS application is idle—that is, it is waiting for input—Windows can discern this and devote more processor time to other applications in the system. The applications that receive the increased processor time are DOS applications running in the background and Windows applications.

For the most part, Windows does a good job of detecting when a DOS application is waiting for input, and you will want to leave the Detect Idle Time box checked. However, in a few rare instances, Windows mistakenly interprets a DOS application's pauses for maintenance activity as idle time. When this happens, your DOS application usually runs abnormally slowly—Windows is giving away too much processor time. To prevent Windows from attempting to detect the program's idle time, and hopefully speed up the program, you can turn off the Detect Idle Time check box.

Memory Options

In 386 enhanced mode, Windows gives you a considerable amount of control over how much EMS and XMS memory are made available to a DOS application. The following sections describe how to control the amount of memory Windows allocates through the application's PIF.

EMS Memory

As you learned in Chapter 7, when you run Windows in 386 enhanced mode, it can simulate expanded (EMS) memory using extended memory. You do not have to have an EMS board or load any special drivers—Windows simply does the simulation on its own.

Tip: Don't use EMM386.SYS if you plan to use expanded memory in 386 enhanced mode

If you have used EMM386.SYS to emulate expanded memory, that memory is allocated before Windows is loaded, leaving less extended memory available to Windows. In addition, when you run Windows in 386 enhanced mode, your DOS applications cannot access the expanded memory that EMM386.SYS creates—Windows simply doesn't allow it. Therefore, if you want your DOS applications to be able to access expanded memory in 386 enhanced mode, you are better off not using EMM386.SYS. In fact, you should only use EMM386.SYS when you want to have expanded memory available in real mode, or if you need expanded memory when you are not running Windows. See Chapter 7, "Windows Memory Management," for more details.

The EMS Memory: KB Required setting lets you tell Windows how many kilobytes of expanded memory it must be able to provide before it should even attempt to load the DOS application. The standard setting is 0, but you can enter a number up to 16384 (for 16 megabytes).

Because some DOS programs, such as early versions of AutoCAD, gobble up all available expanded memory, Windows lets you limit the amount of EMS memory it provides to a given application. To do this, you use the EMS Memory: KB Limit setting. The standard setting is 1024, and the largest setting you can make is 16384.

When you run the application, Windows does not use the KB Limit setting to actually set aside that amount of memory for a program's exclusive use. Rather, it looks at the expanded memory available in the system and tells the program how much memory is available, up to the amount set by KB Limit. This memory is later made available to the application as the application requests it. However, if another program should happen to use the memory in the meantime, it will not be available to the application.

As an example of how these settings work, Table 10-1 shows the amount of expanded memory you get in 1-2-3 Release 2.2 using different KB Required and KB Limit settings. (You are bound to get slightly different results depending on your current setup; but you should see a similar trend.) Notice that while KB Required is 0, KB Limit is the factor controlling how much expanded memory 1-2-3 reports as being available. However, just as soon as KB Required is greater than 0, it becomes the controlling factor.

As Table 10-1 shows, you rarely get a one-for-one return on your EMS Memory settings. One reason is that EMS memory is always allocated in 16K pages. Another reason is that the KB Required and KB Desired settings usually have to reach a certain threshold before your program reports that expanded memory is available. For example, notice that when KB Required is 0, KB Limit must be set as high as 544 before 1-2-3 reports that any expanded memory is available.

One thing that Table 10-1 does not show is the effect that KB Required and KB Limit have on the memory available to other programs. For example, if you take this table too literally, you might think that the following sets of EMS Memory settings make no real difference, because they both have 507,656 bytes of expanded memory available to 1-2-3:

Set 1		*Set 2*	
KB Required:	0	KB Required:	1024
KB Limit:	1024	KB Limit:	1024

But, in fact, there is a difference: Set 1 does not set aside any memory for the application when you launch it, while Set 2 sets aside a full megabyte.

Here's a general rule of thumb: If you have an application that you know will require a lot of expanded memory (for example, a monster spreadsheet file), use KB Required to set aside this memory for the program's exclusive use. However, if you are building an application and may or may not need expanded memory as you go, set KB Required to 0 and use KB Limit to control the amount of expanded memory the application can ultimately access. That way, you can still have memory available for other applications.

Note: Just because Windows has allocated an application expanded memory, don't assume that the application can effectively use all of it. For example, 1-2-3 Release 2.2 can only support up to 4 megabytes of expanded memory. In addition, it can only place certain types of data in that memory (for example, labels, floating-point values, formulas, and functions); other types of data remain in conventional memory.

KB Required	KB Limit	1-2-3 R2.2 EMS Memory (in bytes)
0	0	0
0	544	16376
0	545	32752
0	560	32752
0	561	49128
0	1024	507656
0	2048	1555720
0	4096	3651848
1	1024	0
540	1024	0
541	1024	16376
556	1024	16376
557	1024	32752
1024	1024	507656
1024	2048	507656
2048	4096	1555720
4096	4096	3651848

Table 10-1 Effect of EMS Memory Settings on 1-2-3 Release 2.2

By turning on the Locked check box, you can make sure an application's expanded memory remains in physical memory and that Windows never pages it to disk. The advantage is that you improve the application's performance a little. The disadvantage (and it's a big one) is that you slow down the rest of your system because Windows cannot consolidate memory as it needs to (see Chapter 7 for more on how Windows consolidates memory). In general, you should leave the Locked check box turned off (the default setting).

XMS Memory

You might think that the XMS Memory settings let you tell Windows how much extended memory to allocate to an application that uses the Lotus/Intel/Microsoft/AST eXtended Memory Specification (XMS) standard. Unfortunately, it's not that simple. The reason is that the restrictions on how DOS applications can use extended memory are far tighter in 386 enhanced mode than in standard or real mode. To attain full compatibility with Windows 3 running in 386 enhanced mode, applications must support the DOS Protected

Using Non-Windows Applications 343

Mode Interface (DPMI), a relatively recent standard that was first developed by Microsoft for Windows 3.0 applications and that Microsoft is now hoping will become an industry-wide standard. For this to happen, manufacturers of DOS extender products must voluntarily support the new standard.

As mentioned, very few DOS programs take advantage of extended memory and fewer still conform to DPMI. Most current DOS extenders support the Virtual Control Program Interface (VCPI), which Windows does not support. However, Windows will run extended DOS applications when it is operating in real or standard mode (see Chapter 7 for more on VCPI and DPMI). If you should try to run such an application in 386 enhanced mode, you will see the message shown in Figure 10-10. This message was produced by attempting to run Lotus 1-2-3 Release 3.0 in 386 enhanced mode. At the time this book went to press, only one program supported DPMI—1-2-3 Release 3.1. However, it does not observe the XMS Memory settings. Rather, it limits its use of extended memory based on the SET123MEMSIZE= setting in your AUTOEXEC.BAT file.

If you happen to have a DOS application that supports DPMI better than 1-2-3 Release 3.1, you can use the XMS Memory: KB Required setting in the application's PIF to tell Windows how much extended memory must be available in the system before Windows should even attempt to load the application. You can enter a setting from 0 to 16384. For most applications, the standard setting of 0 is fine because they don't access any extended memory. If Windows doesn't have sufficient memory to meet the KB Required setting when you try to run the application, it issues an error message like the one shown earlier in Figure 10-8.

Because some applications that access extended memory grab as much as they can, Windows lets you limit the amount of extended memory an application gets by using the KB Limit option. Windows gives the application as much memory as it requests, up to the limit set by KB Limit, or until there is no more extended memory available. The standard setting for KB Limit is 1024, which causes Windows to provide as much memory to the application as it can, up to 1 MB. The maximum setting is 16384.

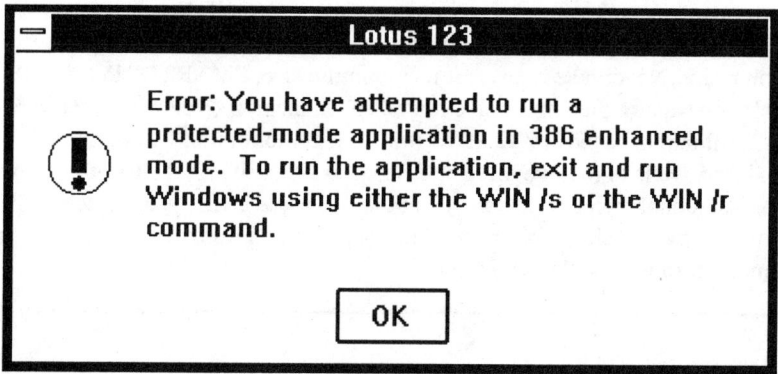

Figure 10-10 The error you see when you try to run a non-DPMI compliant DOS application in 386 enhanced mode

As you make your XMS settings, you should be aware that the extended memory you request in the KB Required text box is set aside for the application's exclusive use, regardless of whether the application actually uses it. By contrast, if you leave KB Required set to its standard setting of 0 and set KB Limit to the appropriate amount required for the application, Windows does not set aside the memory you request with the KB Limit setting for the program only. Rather, it looks at the extended memory available in the system and tells the program how much memory is available, up to the limit set by KB Limit. The memory is later made available to the application as the application requests it. However, if another program should happen to use the memory in the meantime, it will not be available to the application.

As with expanded memory, you can turn on the Locked check box to prevent Windows from paging the application's extended memory to disk. The advantage is that you can improve the application's speed somewhat, but the disadvantage is that you will slow down everything else in your system.

Tip: Getting more extended memory by reducing the size of SMARTDrive

If you want your DOS application to be able to access more memory, particularly expanded or extended memory, one way to increase the amount of memory available in the system is to reduce the size of SMARTDrive, or remove it from your system altogether. As you may recall, when you install Windows for the first time, the Windows Setup program usually places a line like this in your CONFIG.SYS file:

`DEVICE=C:\WINDOWS\SMARTDRV.SYS 2048 1024`

This statement causes DOS to load the SMARTDrive disk-caching program and set its normal size to 2048K and its minimum size to 1024K. When you run Windows in 386 enhanced mode, it always reduces the size of SMARTDrive to its minimum size. Nevertheless, even at its minimum size, SMARTDRIVE is rather large. If you want to pick up some extra extended memory, you may want to reduce the minimum cache size to 256K (the default minimum). Of course, another alternative is to remove this line from your CONFIG.SYS altogether and pick up additional memory that way. But the downside is that your system will have much slower disk performance. See Chapter 11, "Improving Windows Performance," for more on SMARTDrive.

Uses High Memory Area

As you learned in Chapter 7, the *high memory area* (HMA) is the first 64K of extended memory (from 1024K to 1088K) that, due to a special programming trick, is directly accessible by DOS programs even when they do not leave real mode. Because more than one program might want to use this area, Windows allocates each program its own private HMA, provided the HMA is available to Windows in the first place. The HMA is not available to Windows when you load a memory-resident utility that uses this area before you load Windows. For example, some network device drivers and TSRs use the HMA, making it unavailable to Windows. DOS Version 5.0 is also capable of using the HMA.

Because the HMA is usually available to Windows, and therefore available to your program, you should almost always leave the Uses High Memory Area check box turned on (the default). However, if you know that a utility uses the HMA before you load Windows, you should turn the check box off. An easy way to find out whether a utility grabs the HMA is to use Quarterdeck's Manifest program. This program gives a detailed report on your computer's memory, including the status of the HMA. Of course, the best time to run this program is after you load your network software and TSRs but before you start Windows.

> ### Tip: DOS 5.0 and the HMA
>
> If you are using DOS Version 5.0 and have it running in the HMA (the default for systems with extended memory), the HMA will not be available to DOS applications running in Windows 3. Therefore, you should always turn off the Uses High Memory Area check box in your DOS applications' PIFs. Note that in order for DOS 5.0 to use the HMA, you must have the command DOS = HIGH in your CONFIG.SYS file.

Lock Application Memory

By turning on the Lock Application Memory check box, you can lock an application in memory and prevent Windows from ever paging it out to disk. An application that is locked in memory can operate faster because Windows does not need to take the time to issue a page fault and read the program (or part of it) back from disk into memory. Of course, the only time that locking an application will result in increased speed is when you are multitasking several applications and memory is tight—this is the time that Windows swaps applications out to disk. In fact, if you have plenty of extended memory available, locking the application will not improve its speed at all because Windows never pages it to disk anyway. However, the problem with locking an application in memory is that Windows is unable to coalesce free blocks of memory, making it harder for it to manage memory for other applications that are running. The net effect is that you speed up one DOS application at the expense of all the other applications.

The Lock Application Memory check box controls only the application's conventional memory—the memory Windows stores inside the virtual machine. It does not affect the blocks of expanded or extended memory an application may use outside the virtual machine. If you want to lock any of these types of memory, use the Locked options in the EMS Memory and XMS Memory sections of the advanced PIF settings.

Display Options

The Display Options in the advanced options screen of a 386 enhanced mode PIF let you control the amount of memory Windows initially allocates to manage an application's display, as well as how Windows monitors an application's use of the display hardware. One of the most important things to remember about these options is that, regardless of how they are set, you will very rarely (if ever) need to change them.

Video Memory

The Video Memory radio buttons let you control the amount of memory Windows initially reserves for storing an application's video display when you first start the application. The only time you need to worry about this setting is when Windows is having trouble restoring the display when you switch away from an application and then switch back.

Windows offers the following three video modes:

- **Text**: Tells Windows that the initial display will be in text mode and to set aside 16K (or less) for storing the display.
- **Low Graphics**: Tells Windows that the initial display will be in low-resolution graphics mode and to set aside about 32K of memory for storing the display. This is the video mode that the CGA and Hercules cards use for displaying graphics; they cannot use high-resolution graphics.
- **High Graphics**: Tells Windows that the initial display will be in high-resolution graphics mode, the graphics mode that EGA and VGA video adapters use, and to set aside about 128K for storing the display.

The nice thing about these buttons is that if you don't choose the right one, it doesn't much matter because Windows adjusts the amount of memory for storing the video display dynamically. It does this by monitoring the video mode and providing additional memory when needed, or releasing unused memory. For example, suppose you choose the Text button, but your application runs in high graphics mode. Windows automatically provides the extra 112K (128K - 16K) of memory to store the display, provided, of course, that it is available in the system. On the other hand, if you choose High Graphics, but your application operates only in text mode, Windows releases the extra 112K for use elsewhere.

The only time you can get into trouble is when you choose a button that sets aside too little memory for storing the video display, and Windows is unable to provide the additional memory required when the application switches to a higher video mode. When this happens, Windows will have trouble restoring your display when you switch away and then switch back. You may get a partial or blank screen. The best way to prevent this from happening is to select the button that corresponds to the highest video mode the application will use, then turn on the Retain Video Memory check box (see the later section). With these settings, you can guarantee that Windows will have no trouble restoring the application's video display when you switch back to the application.

Monitor Ports

As you may know, most EGA cards (and VGA cards for that matter) are backwards compatible with earlier video modes. For example, an EGA card can typically emulate Hercules and CGA video modes, and the mode that the card operates in is often software selectable. In fact, your EGA card may come with a disk of utilities that you can run from the DOS prompt to change the video mode from EGA mode to some other mode of your choosing. This is especially nice if you want to run an older application that only supports an early video mode.

In addition, some EGA cards also have automatic mode switch circuitry that lets them switch to a video mode that differs from the video mode setting established in the ROM BIOS. When an application writes to a hardware port address that is unique to a display mode other than what the EGA card is currently operating in, the EGA hardware detects the write and changes the video mode automatically. For example, the card may be operating in EGA mode, and it detects a write to a Hercules port. When this happens the card automatically switches to Hercules mode.

The problem with this type of automatic video mode switching is that Windows takes its cue from the mode setting in the BIOS. If an application should happen to switch the video display to another mode, Windows cannot detect the switch and may have trouble restoring the display the next time you switch away from the application and then back again.

To get around this problem, Windows offers the Monitor Ports PIF options that tell it to monitor how an application writes to the video ports under different circumstances:

- **Text**: Tells Windows to monitor the video hardware ports when the application is running in text mode. This option is rarely needed.

- **Low Graphics**: Tells Windows to monitor the video hardware ports when the application is running in low-resolution graphics mode (CGA or Hercules mode). This option is also rarely needed.

- **High Graphics**: Tells Windows to monitor video hardware ports when the application is running in high-resolution graphics mode (EGA mode). This option is on in the standard PIF settings, and it is the one you will need to use most often.

The time to try turning one (or more) of these check boxes on is when you switch away from an application and then switch back and the display is lost or looks strange. Experimentation is about the only way to determine whether turning on a check box has any effect. When you turn one on, if Windows restores the display properly, you've found the solution.

You've probably noticed that this discussion centers around EGA cards rather than VGA cards, which are also backwards compatible with earlier video modes (including EGA). The reason is that the Monitor Ports settings do not affect the behavior of VGA cards. In fact, if you have any other card than an EGA, you should set all of these options off.

> **Tip: Turn off the Monitor Ports options to speed up DOS applications**
>
> The speed of DOS applications in 386 enhanced mode can be noticeably improved by turning off all the Monitor Ports options in the applications' PIFs. By default, the High Graphics option is on to guarantee the widest range of compatibility with DOS applications, but it is hardly ever needed.

Emulate Text Mode

By turning on the Emulate Text Mode check box, you can sometimes increase the speed at which a DOS application scrolls text. The time that this option is most beneficial is when the DOS program uses graphics mode for its text operations. Some examples that you may be familiar with are the Hercules 90x38 driver for 1-2-3 Release 2.2, all the graphics drivers for Quattro Pro, or almost all the drivers for 1-2-3 Release 3.1. If you've used any of these drivers you've probably noticed that when a DOS program runs in graphics mode, it must completely redraw the screen each time you scroll the contents of a window up or down a line. By contrast, when you use a text mode driver, the DOS program can scroll the screen more quickly. However, if you have a fast processor, you probably won't notice any difference at all in the behavior of the program.

Note: For most DOS applications you can leave the Emulate Text Mode check box turned on (the standard setting), regardless of whether the program is running in text or graphics mode. However, if you notice that the cursor appears in the wrong place or the text looks odd, you should turn this option off.

Retain Video Memory

As mentioned in the "Video Memory" section, turning on the Retain Video Memory option prevents Windows from releasing an application's extra video memory for use by another application. When Windows retains the video memory, you can be sure that it can always restore an application's video display when you switch away from the application and then switch back.

When the Retain Video Memory option is off and a DOS application switches video modes, Windows can automatically adjust the memory required to store the application's video display accordingly. For example, if an application switches from graphics to text mode, less memory is required to store the video display and Windows will automatically release the extra memory. If the application then shifts back to graphics mode, Windows automatically provides the additional memory required to store the display for this mode.

A problem occurs, however, when you run out of memory. When this happens and you switch back to a more memory-intensive video mode, Windows cannot provide the additional memory to save the video display. As a result, if you switch away from the application and then switch back, the application's display may be lost.

By choosing the right Video Memory option and turning on the Retain Video Memory option, you can always guarantee that Windows can restore an application's display, regardless of whether you run out of memory.

Other Options

The advanced 386 enhanced mode PIF options include a catch-all section called "Other Options." The settings in this section allow you to control the speed at which Windows pastes data from the Clipboard into a DOS application, to close a DOS application's window even when the application is still active, and to reserve certain Windows shortcut keys for use by a DOS application.

Allow Fast Paste

When you run a DOS application in a window, you can use the Edit Paste command from its window Control menu to paste text to and from the Clipboard (see Chapter 6 for details). The rate at which a DOS application can accept the text varies. Most can accept it at the fastest rate Windows can paste it without any difficulty. Therefore, the Allow Fast Paste check box is turned on by default. However, some require a slower rate, and Windows can usually sense this and automatically switch to a slower rate.

Nevertheless, you may find an application, such as PFS: First Publisher, that requires the slower pasting rate but Windows cannot tell. When this is the case, you may lose characters as Windows pastes text into the application. Alternatively, you may get no text at all. At this point, the best thing to do is to press ESC to stop pasting, turn off the Allow Fast Paste box in the application's PIF, save the PIF, and start the application again.

Allow Close When Active

If you've ever tried to quit Windows when a DOS application is still active, you've undoubtedly noticed that Windows won't let you. You get the same result when you try to close a DOS application's window when the application is still running—the Close option on the window Control menu is grayed. In either case, you must always quit the DOS application before Windows will close its window.

If you'd rather not go to the trouble of quitting a DOS application before closing its window, you can turn on the Allow Close When Active check box in the application's PIF. The problem with this setting, however, is that you can lose a lot of your work if you aren't careful. In fact, Windows makes a special point of this by showing the message in Figure 10-11 when you turn on the check box in the PIF Editor.

Using this option is actually quite safe as long as you realize that just because Windows can close an active DOS application, this does not mean that Windows also closes the application's open data files—quite the contrary. If you want to save your data files before Windows kills your program, you'll have to do it yourself. If you don't, you may lose them.

Even though you've turned on the Allow Close When Active check box, you must still respond to a dialog box like the one in Figure 10-12 when you try to close the application's

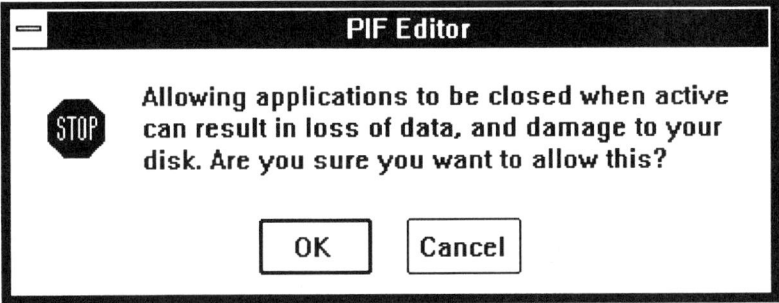

Figure 10-11 The warning you see when you turn on the Allow Close When Active check box

window or attempt to exit Windows. This message box is a nice safeguard if you haven't yet saved your data.

Another important point to consider before you select the Allow Close When Active check box is the method the DOS program uses for file access—that is, whether it uses file control blocks or file handles when it opens, closes, reads, and writes files. A *file control block* (FCB) is a data structure at the beginning of a file that maintains certain bookkeeping information about the open file, such as its drive identifier, filename, size, and the like. The FCB method of file access was the first method used in DOS and was a carryover from CP/M. On the other hand, all newer DOS programs work with file handles. A *file handle* is simply a number that DOS assigns to a file. DOS maintains tables that correlate the handles and the files (or devices) they refer to. The advantage of the file-handle method of file access is that it supports the hierarchical (treelike) file structure that was first introduced in MS-DOS version 2.0.

A good indication that a DOS program uses the FCB method and not the file handle method is if it cannot access files outside the current directory. An example of such a program is Wordstar 3.3 (and earlier), which still remains in use despite its advanced age.

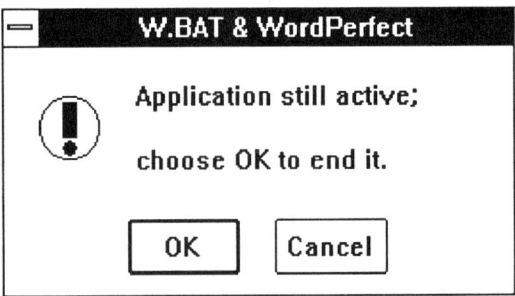

Figure 10-12 The message you see when the Allow Close When Active option is on and you close a DOS application's window

The problem with such a program is that when you turn on the Close When Active check box and close the program's window, Windows does not actually close the program's files. This can cause problems under MS-DOS version 3.0 and later, especially when files are being accessed across a network. The problems stem from the fact that DOS limits the number of FCBs that can be open at any one time in a shared environment to a default value of 4. As a result, if a program that uses the FCB method tries to open more than four files (or more than the number specified in the FCBS= statement in your CONFIG.SYS), DOS closes the least recently used files before opening any new files. When this happens, you start to see strange messages on your screen like "FCB unavailable—Abort, Fail?" You can avoid such messages by turning off the Allow Close When Active check box and quitting the DOS application in the usual way.

Reserve Shortcut Keys

The Reserve Shortcut Keys options in the advanced PIF settings have the same effect as they do in the standard PIF settings. The one difference is that there are two more shortcut keys available in 386 enhanced mode: Alt+Space (for activating an application's window Control menu) and Alt+Enter (for toggling a DOS application between windowed and full-screen display). See the "Reserve Shortcut Keys" section above for the effect of these settings.

Application Shortcut Key

When Windows is running in 386 enhanced mode, you can easily access a DOS application using an *application shortcut key*. When you press an application shortcut key, Windows instantly brings the program associated with that key to the foreground and gives it the focus.

To assign a shortcut key to an application, click on the Application Shortcut Key text box and press the key sequence you want. The sequence *must* include the ALT or CTRL key. However, it cannot include the ESC, ENTER, TAB, SPACEBAR, PRINTSCREEN, or BACKSPACE keys. For example, ALT+8, CTRL+R, and ALT+CTRL+F1 are all valid shortcut keys, but CTRL+PRINTSCREEN is not.

To delete an existing shortcut key setting, press BACKSPACE or SHIFT+BACKSPACE. Pressing BACKSPACE appears to clear the text box of any contents, but it actually returns the box to its previous setting; you'll see the previous setting the next time you access the advanced options screen. Pressing SHIFT+BACKSPACE replaces the existing setting with the default setting of "None," indicating that there is no shortcut key sequence for the application.

Be aware that when you assign an application shortcut key, it takes precedence over all other functions the key might have. For example, if you are familiar with Quattro Pro, you know that you can press CTRL+X to exit from that program. But suppose you have assigned CTRL+X as the shortcut for activating XyWrite. If both programs are active in Windows, and you are in Quattro Pro when you press CTRL+X, you'll switch to XyWrite, not exit Quattro Pro.

352 *Windows 3 Power Tools*

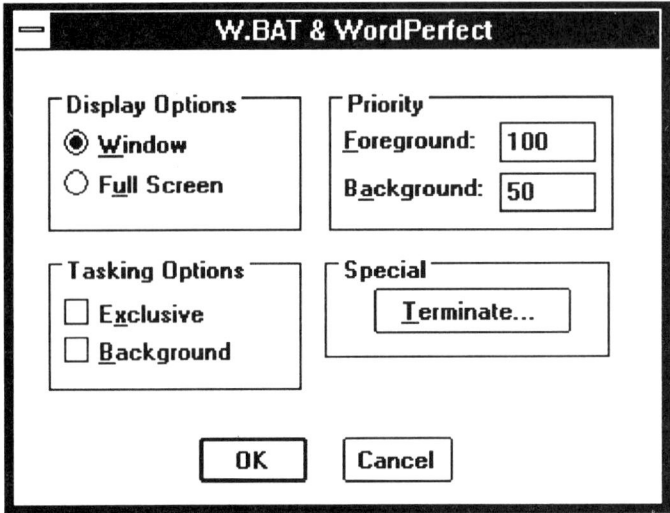

Figure 10-13 The dialog box that appears when you select the Settings command from a DOS application's window Control menu

CHANGING A RUNNING APPLICATION

Once you've started an application in 386 enhanced mode, you can use the Settings command from the application's window Control menu to change the way it runs in a handful of ways. Figure 10-13 shows the dialog box that appears when you select this command. For example, you can use this menu to toggle an application between a windowed and full-screen display, to switch an application from the foreground to the background, or to terminate an application that is not responding to your keypresses.

Most of the settings you can control through this menu can also be controlled through the application's PIF. When this is the case, you should read the appropriate section earlier in the chapter to get the whole story behind the setting.

Display Options

If an application is running full screen, you can switch it to a window by choosing the Window button in the Settings dialog box. Conversely, to switch an application from a window to a full-screen display, select the Full Screen button. Rather than use the menu at all, though, an easier way to switch from a windowed to a full-screen display, or vice versa, is to press ALT+ENTER. (If you want to control the display through the application's PIF, see "Display Usage" earlier.)

Note: If you want to use the mouse with a DOS application that supports it, you must run the application full screen. If the application appears in a window and you attempt to use the mouse, Windows assumes you want to copy and paste between applications, using the Clipboard. In fact, anytime you use the mouse in a windowed DOS application, Windows assumes you intend to copy and paste, and it registers all your mouse actions with that purpose in mind. (See "Using the Mouse with DOS Applications" for more details.)

Tasking Options

If you want to give a DOS application all the processing power in the system, turn on the Exclusive check box in the Settings dialog box and run the application full screen. Windows suspends all other applications in the system, both Windows applications and DOS applications, even those that are running in the background. (See "Execution" above for more details.)

If you want an application to run in the background while you are working on another application, select the Background option in the Settings dialog box. The amount of processor time the application receives depends on the Priority settings. (See "Execution" and "Multitasking Options" for more.)

Priority Options

When you're running more than one DOS application and you want to change the speed at which they crank away, you can control the amount of processor time each one gets using the Priority settings. If an application has the focus and you want to have it get more processor time in relation to the others, you should increase the Foreground setting. Likewise, if an application is running in the background (its Background check box is on) and you want to change the mix so that it runs faster, you should increase the Background setting. (See "Multitasking Options" above for all the details.)

Terminate Option

When a DOS application freezes in Windows, it's not a pretty sight. A typical sign is that the application stops accepting keyboard input. When this happens to you in DOS, you know it's time to press CTRL+ALT+DEL to reset the system. If the problem is bad enough to blow away the keyboard portion of the BIOS, you have to hit the power switch. Fortunately, Windows gives you an escape hatch. By selecting the Terminate... button in the Settings dialog box, you can sometimes exit a sinking DOS application while keeping the rest of Windows afloat around it.

The problem with the Terminate... button is that it usually makes Windows and DOS unstable. Therefore, the best thing you can do for the health of your data is to leave Windows as quickly as possible. Save your data and get out. When you're back at the DOS prompt, press CTRL+ALT+DEL to reset your system.

USING THE MOUSE WITH DOS APPLICATIONS

Windows incorporates its own mouse driver, called MOUSE.DRV located on the \WINDOWS\SYSTEM directory. This driver is actually a dynamic link library (DLL) that provides Windows with the information it needs to update the mouse pointer position on the screen and to react when the buttons are depressed and released. If none of your DOS applications supports a mouse, you don't have to worry about installing another mouse driver—Windows has you covered.

On the other hand, if a DOS application supports the mouse and you want to use the mouse with it, you must first run MOUSE.COM from the DOS prompt (or your AUTOEXEC.BAT) or include a DEVICE= statement in your CONFIG.SYS that loads the MOUSE.SYS device driver.

If you are using the Microsoft Mouse, make sure you use the latest version of MOUSE.COM and/or MOUSE.SYS that comes on the Windows distribution disks (see below). If you are using another brand of mouse, you should use the MOUSE.COM and/or MOUSE.SYS driver that accompanies it; do not use the Microsoft-supplied versions of these files.

Note: For a DOS application to receive your mouse input, you must run the program full screen.

MOUSE.COM

If you use the MOUSE.COM driver to install the mouse, you can run it either before you start Windows or after. Using it before usually meets with reasonably good success, although it impinges on memory that Windows could use for other purposes. To use MOUSE.COM after Windows is running, you must include the program in a batch file along with the name of the DOS application you want to run. You can then run the batch file each time you want to start the DOS application (see "Using DOS Batch Files" earlier for more details). The advantage of running MOUSE.COM from a batch file is that Windows casts away the mouse driver when the batch file is completed and, in the process, reclaims the memory that the driver occupied. You can usually save yourself about 13-15K of conventional memory this way and have few problems in the process. However, if you are using the Microsoft Mouse, you should avoid using MOUSE.COM *after* Windows is running. Conversely, if you are using the Logitech Mouse, you should avoid using its MOUSE.COM *before* Windows is running (see below).

MOUSE.SYS

Including a DEVICE= statement in your CONFIG.SYS file that loads the MOUSE.SYS device driver is usually the safest way of all to install your mouse. (The Logitech Mouse is an exception; see below.) The reason is because MOUSE.SYS conforms to the DOS standard for installable device drivers. That statement might look something like this

```
DEVICE=C:\MOUSE.SYS
```

if the driver is located on your root directory. By using such a statement, you give up about 13-15K of conventional memory that Windows could otherwise use. But you'll also have the fewest number of problems with different DOS applications. Of course, another advantage of using MOUSE.SYS in your CONFIG.SYS is that you make it available to DOS applications when you are not running Windows.

Special Considerations for the Logitech Mouse

If you are using a Logitech Mouse (bus or serial) and you want to use it with DOS applications, our experience indicates that you *should not* load its MOUSE.COM before you run Windows or load MOUSE.SYS from your CONFIG.SYS. If you do, you may have success using the mouse the first time you load a DOS application, but the next time you load the application, the mouse may not work. The Logitech mouse will work best if you load its MOUSE.COM as part of a batch file that also loads the DOS application.

Note: Make sure you are using the MOUSE.COM that accompanies the Logitech Mouse. Do not use the Microsoft-supplied MOUSE.COM or MOUSE.SYS with your Logitech Mouse—they won't work. In addition, Logitech recommends that you use Version 4.1 or later of MOUSE.COM for Windows 3.

Special Considerations for the Microsoft Mouse

If you are using the Microsoft Mouse (bus or serial) and you want to run it with DOS applications, you should read this section. Otherwise, if your DOS applications do not support a mouse or you're using a different brand of mouse, this section doesn't apply to you.

Use the Latest Version of MOUSE.COM or MOUSE.SYS

As mentioned, before you try to use the Microsoft Mouse with DOS applications, make sure that you are using the latest version of MOUSE.COM and/or MOUSE.SYS that are included on the Windows distribution disks. Older versions of these programs are notoriously troublesome with Windows 3.

Setup does not automatically install these programs when you install Windows. Therefore, you must install them manually.

To use the latest mouse drivers, you'll need to unpack them using the EXPAND utility located on Disk 2. The mouse drivers are called MOUSE.SY$ and MOUSE.COM and are located on Disk 4. MOUSE.COM doesn't look like it's packed, but it is. In fact, if you try to use MOUSE.COM from the Windows distribution disk before you unpack it, you'll crash your system.

Follow these steps to unpack the drivers and place them on your C:\WINDOWS directory:

1. Access DOS and place Windows Disk 2 in drive A.
2. Copy EXPAND.EXE to your \WINDOWS directory.
3. Replace the disk in drive A with Windows Disk 4.
4. Use these commands to unpack the mouse drivers:

   ```
   EXPAND A:\MOUSE.SY$ C:\WINDOWS\MOUSE.SYS
   EXPAND A:\MOUSE.COM C:\WINDOWS\MOUSE.COM
   ```

If you plan to use MOUSE.SYS, you can now update your CONFIG.SYS for the new driver. (Consider using SYSEDIT, a Windows accessory that is located on the C:\WINDOWS\SYSTEM directory. See Chapter 12, "Customizing Your .INI Files," for more on this program.) If you followed the steps outlined above, place this statement in your CONFIG.SYS:

```
DEVICE=C:\WINDOWS\MOUSE.SYS
```

When you reboot your system, the device driver will be loaded.

Serial Mouse Problems

If you are using the Microsoft Serial Mouse, here are two things to watch out for:

- MOUSE.COM may have problems if the number of buffers in your CONFIG.SYS is too high. Microsoft recommends a setting of BUFFERS=20, or less, for running Windows. If you have BUFFERS= set to anything over 20, you may have trouble with your mouse.
- In Windows, you cannot use COM3 or COM4 for mouse input, even though your computer's BIOS may support these ports.

Bus Mouse Problems

If you are using a Microsoft Bus Mouse, and you get the message "Driver not installed—interrupt jumper missing" whenever you try to run MOUSE.COM from a batch file in Windows, the jumpers on the bus interface board may be set improperly. The interrupt settings used by the mouse are controlled by jumper J4, and you may need to change the position of the plastic hood clip on this jumper.

Here are the rules for setting the interrupt jumper:

- If you have an XT-class machine, you should use interrupt 2 for the mouse. If there's a conflict with a network adapter, use interrupt 3, provided you're not using COM2. Otherwise, use interrupt 4, provided you're not using COM1. Do not use interrupt 5.
- If you have an AT-class machine, interrupt 5 is the first choice for the mouse. If this doesn't work, use interrupt 3 or 4 as outlined in the previous bullet. Do not use interrupt 2.

Problems with MOUSE.COM

If you are using MOUSE.COM in a batch file with the Microsoft Mouse, it usually works well the first time you run the batch file, but not the second. In fact, it freezes your mouse in Windows.

For example, suppose your batch file contains these statements:

```
C:\WINDOWS\MOUSE
Q
```

The first statement loads MOUSE.COM and the second statement loads Quattro Pro. The first time you run this batch file from within Windows, MOUSE.COM reports "Mouse driver installed," and the mouse works fine. However, if you quit Quattro Pro and run the batch file again, MOUSE.COM will report "Driver not installed—interrupt jumper missing." When you see this statement, your mouse will probably work fine in Quattro Pro, but when you switch back to Windows, the mouse pointer won't move.

One way around this problem is to run MOUSE.COM before running Windows. Using MOUSE.COM before you run Windows usually works pretty well, but occasionally you may find that it adversely affects the behavior of the keyboard, especially in applications that don't normally support the mouse, for example, WordPerfect.

The best alternative is to place MOUSE.SYS in your CONFIG.SYS file. Though you give up a little extra memory, you'll have the least amount of trouble with the Microsoft Mouse.

WHAT TO DO WHEN THINGS GO WRONG

One of the dilemmas with using DOS applications in Windows is that you can occasionally get some strange errors with little clue as to what went wrong. Some examples are insufficient memory error messages when there still appears to be plenty of memory left in the system, programs that slow to a crawl without any apparent reason, and strange error messages when you try to run a high-resolution program in a window. This section describes some of the most common problems with DOS applications and what to do about them.

When You Run Out of Memory

When you run out of memory in Windows, the first thing to think about is whether you have sufficient memory in your system. If you are running in 386 enhanced mode, and you have only 2 megabytes of RAM (the bare minimum), you're going to have memory problems. The simplest solution: Buy more memory.

If you think you have enough memory but you're still getting an out-of-memory error message when you try to run a DOS application, here are some quick fixes to try besides the patently obvious solution of closing other applications:

- If the problem occurs in 386 enhanced mode, try removing any TSRs that you've loaded prior to starting Windows. Windows places a copy of these TSRs in each virtual machine, and they may be impinging on the memory that your DOS application needs in order to load.

- Clear the Clipboard of its contents. If the Clipboard is holding a bitmap, you may be able to reclaim a substantial amount of memory this way, sometimes as much as 150K on a VGA system. Load the Clipboard accessory, press DEL, then close the accessory.

- If you are using wallpaper, remove it by setting the desktop wallpaper to None (see Chapter 8, "Using the Control Panel"). You might be surprised at the amount of memory you can save this way; for example, the chess bitmap (CHESS.BMP) supplied along with Windows will consume 150K.

- In 386 enhanced mode, you can save about 7K by running an application full screen rather than in a window.
- Try minimizing Windows applications to icons. Minimizing a Windows application to an icon can cause Windows to discard certain memory objects that the program has marked as discardable (see Chapter 7), making more memory available for loading your DOS application.

Changing Standard PIF Settings to Reclaim Memory

If none of the above suggestions do the trick and you are running Windows in standard or real mode, try modifying any of the following PIF settings:

- **Video Mode: Text**: By turning on the Text box in the Video Mode settings, you can have Windows set aside less memory for saving the application's video display. (Windows saves the display so that it can restore the display later when you switch away from the application then switch back). The advantage of selecting the Text option is that there is more memory available for the application itself. The disadvantage is that if the video mode changes while you are using the application (from text to graphics mode), Windows may have trouble restoring the application's display when you switch away from the application then switch back.

- **Memory Requirements: KB Required**: If you think you may be able to load the DOS application using less memory, try reducing the Memory Requirements: KB Required setting. If this works and you can load the application but it later issues its own error message saying it has run out of memory, you may need to increase the amount of memory available before you load Windows by removing device drivers or memory-resident utilities. After all, Windows is not the problem in this situation because it removes itself from memory, leaving only a small footprint behind.

- **XMS Memory**: If an application doesn't access any XMS memory (and most don't), set the XMS Memory: KB Required and XMS: KB Desired settings to 0. This has the added benefit of allowing you to switch away from the application faster.

- **No Screen Exchange**: By turning off the No Screen Exchange check box, you can save a small amount of memory that Windows allocates for saving the contents of the screen when you press PRINTSCREEN or ALT+PRINTSCREEN.

- **Prevent Program Switch**: By turning off the Prevent Program Switch check box, you can prevent Windows from allocating the small chunk of memory (usually about 50K) that it uses to restore the context from the application swap file when you switch away from an application and then back. The disadvantage, though, is that the only way to return to Windows is to quit the application.

Changing 386 Enhanced Mode PIF Settings to Reclaim Memory

When you're running multiple applications in 386 enhanced mode, memory can get tight very quickly. If you get an out-of-memory error message when you try to load a DOS application, you can usually pin the blame on two things: the size of the DOS application itself, and the size of all the other DOS applications that are currently running. Therefore, as you review the following suggestions on how to make more memory available by changing a DOS application's PIF, consider applying them to all the DOS applications that are currently running:

- **Memory Requirements**: If you get an out-of-memory error message from Windows when you try to load a DOS application, try decreasing the KB Desired setting. Along with this, try reducing the KB Desired settings for the other DOS applications in the system.

- **XMS Memory and EMS Memory**: If you are having trouble loading a DOS application, it may be because it's not getting enough expanded or extended memory. Try setting the XMS Memory and EMS Memory options higher.

- **Full Screen**: Windowed applications require slightly more memory than those that use a full-screen display. You can save about 3K per application by selecting the Full Screen radio button in the Display Usage options.

- **Exclusive**: If you don't mind suspending all other applications while the one you are about to start runs, turn on the Exclusive check box. This makes more memory available to the DOS application by suspending *all* other applications in the system.

- **Background**: If you have other DOS applications running in the background, consider turning off their Background check boxes. By doing so, you can make more memory (and processor time) available to the application you are about to run.

- **Video Memory: Text**: By selecting the Text box in the Advanced PIF's Video Memory options, you can decrease the amount of memory that Windows sets aside for storing the application's video display. (Windows uses this memory to restore the video display when you switch away from the application and then switch back.) In addition, turn off the Retain Video Memory check box so that Windows releases the extra memory used for storing the application's display when it's not needed.

   The disadvantage of selecting the Text box is that, if the program switches from text to graphics mode and there's not enough memory available for Windows to save the application's display, you may have trouble with the display when you switch away from the application and then switch back.

- **Lock options**: If you've locked any memory for a DOS application, turn off the lock. The options you should examine are Locked Application Memory (for locking conventional memory), EMS Memory: Locked, and XMS Memory: Locked. Any one of these options can create a logjam in memory, and you may be able to free enough memory to load the application you want to run.

If All Else Fails

Here are some other things you can try after you've tweaked the PIF settings, but you still can't get a DOS application to start:

- If you are using 386 enhanced mode, try reducing the size of SMARTDrive (see the previous tip "Getting more extended memory by reducing the size of SMART-Drive").

- If you have an EGA display and you always run Windows in 386 enhanced mode, try removing the EGA.SYS driver from your CONFIG.SYS file. Windows Setup always installs this driver if you have an EGA display. You can save about 2K by eliminating the driver without affecting Windows' performance at all in 386 enhanced mode. You may also be able to get by without using EGA.SYS in real or standard mode. However, you'll have to do some testing to make sure; removing it may prevent you from switching away from a DOS application. See Chapter 11, "Improving Windows' Performance," for more on EGA.SYS.

- If you are trying to start a DOS application in 386 enhanced mode that uses a lot of XMS memory, try running the application in standard mode. Because Windows occupies less space in standard mode, you have a little more physical memory available to the application.

- If you always run Windows in 386 enhanced mode, try removing EMM386.SYS from your CONFIG.SYS file. Because Windows can simulate EMS memory in 386 enhanced mode, you do not need EMM386.SYS (see the previous tip, "Don't use EMM386.SYS if you plan to use expanded memory in 386 enhanced mode").

- Some DOS applications that access XMS memory in 386 enhanced mode do not properly report that they have gobbled up that memory. As a result, Windows may report that plenty of memory is still available when you use the About Program Manager option from the Help menu. When this happens, the only thing you can do is to start removing other applications from the system.

- Some DOS applications that access extended memory are incompatible with the Windows 3 version of HIMEM.SYS. If your program tells you that there isn't enough extended memory available when you are running Windows in standard or 386 enhanced mode, first try all the suggestions in this section for making more memory available to the application. If these don't work, try removing the HIMEM.SYS statement from your CONFIG.SYS and start Windows in real mode.

- Try running QEMM or 386MAX to place some objects in high memory, making more memory available to Windows (see Chapter 7 for details).

See Chapter 11, "Improving Windows' Performance," for some other ideas.

When You Cannot Switch Away

If you're having trouble switching away from a DOS application, here are two things you might want to try, regardless of the mode you are running in:

- The DOS application may be using an unconventional video mode, and Windows doesn't know how much memory to set aside for saving and restoring the application's display. Try quitting the application and modifying its PIF to use a Video Memory setting (Video Mode in the standard mode PIF settings) that sets aside more memory.

- The settings in the application's PIF may cause it to reserve one or more of the Windows shortcut keys for its own use. Try quitting the application and modifying the Reserve Shortcut Keys options in the application's PIF. In particular, make sure the ALT+TAB, CTRL+ESC, and ALT+ESC boxes are turned off.

If you are running Windows in standard or real mode, here are some more things you may want to try:

- If you try to switch away from a large application—for example, one that uses XMS memory—you might see a message like the one in Figure 10-14. This message indicates that you do not have sufficient disk space for the application swap file. (Windows uses an application swap file to save the application out to disk so that it can load Windows back in.) One solution to this problem is to delete any unnecessary files from your hard disk to make more room for the application swap file. Another solution is to reduce the size of the permanent swap file you may have created for improving Windows' performance when running in 386 enhanced mode; start Windows in real mode and use the File Run command from Program Manager (or File Manager) to execute SWAP-FILE.EXE in the \WINDOWS\SYSTEM directory (see Chapter 11, "Improving Windows' Performance," for more details).

- Occasionally you may try to switch away from an application, and, after hitting the disk for a while, Windows beeps and returns you to the application without any explanation whatsoever. When this happens, it usually means that there is so little disk space available that Windows can't even start to create an application swap file. See the previous item for some suggestions on how to remedy the situation.

- Turn off the Prevent Program Switch check box in the application's PIF (real or standard mode only). When this option is on, it prevents you from switching away from an application; the only way to return to Windows is to quit the application.

- Change the Video Mode setting to Graphics/Multiple Text in the application's PIF (real or standard mode only). This setting will cause Windows to set aside more memory for storing the application's video display. That way, it won't have any trouble restoring the application to the screen when you switch away and then switch back.

```
            MICROSOFT WINDOWS DOS APPLICATION SUPPORT
Your program cannot be swapped out to disk. There is not enough space on
your  disk.  The suspended program will be restarted. You must free disk
space  to  switch  out  from this  application, or else you must end the
program before trying to go back to Windows.

                    press any key to restart the program....
```

Figure 10-14 The error message you see when Windows doesn't have enough room to store the application swap file

- If you have an EGA display, check your CONFIG.SYS file to make sure that the DEVICE= statement that installs EGA.SYS is correct. It should look like this:

  DEVICE=C:\WINDOWS\EGA.SYS

  Windows Setup automatically copies the EGA.SYS driver to your Windows directory and installs it in your CONFIG.SYS. See Chapter 11, "Improving Windows' Performance," for more on EGA.SYS.

- If you have turned on any of the Directly Modifies check boxes in the application's PIF (real or standard mode only)—for example, COM1 or Keyboard—you will not be able to switch away from the application while it is running. Turning off all these options will once again allow you to switch away.

- Some applications are impossible to switch away from because they intercept all the keyboard input before Windows ever gets a chance to read your keystrokes. If you've encountered one of these applications, your only choice is to quit the application when you want to return to Windows.

When You Cannot Switch to Full Screen Display

When you are running Windows in 386 enhanced mode, at some point you may find that you cannot switch a DOS application from a windowed to a full-screen display. Here are the two most common reasons why:

- If you've clicked the mouse anywhere in the window, Windows assumes that you want to transfer information from the window to the Clipboard. You can tell that this has happened when the application's title bar contains the word "Select." A similar situation occurs when you choose the Edit Mark command from the application's window Control menu. In this case, the title bar contains the word "Mark." When either word appears in the title bar and you attempt to shift the application from windowed to a full-screen display, you see an error message like the one in Figure 10-15.

  The easiest way to correct this situation is to return to the window and press ESC (or the right mouse button) to clear your selection. Windows removes the word "Select" or "Mark," and you can then switch the application to a full-screen display.

Using Non-Windows Applications 363

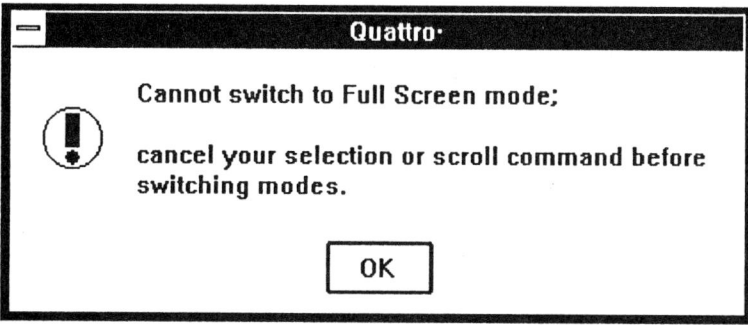

Figure 10-15 The message you see when you've selected something in a DOS application's window, and you try to switch to a full-screen display

- If you've selected the Edit Scroll command from the application's window Control menu, you'll also see the message in Figure 10-15 when you try to shift the application to a full-screen display. (In this case, the title bar contains the word "Scroll.") Return to the window and press ESC to tell Windows that you no longer want to scroll the information in the window.

When the Application's Display Is Lost

If an application's display is lost or looks odd when you are running Windows in 386 enhanced mode, it may be due to one of the following:

- If you have an EGA display, it may have automatically switched to a video mode that differs from the video mode setting in the ROM BIOS. Windows will not track this switch unless you tell it to. Try turning on one (or more) of the Monitor Ports check boxes in the application's PIF and then run the application again. (See the "Monitor Ports" section earlier for an explanation of the different options.)

- While you were running a DOS application, if it switched to a higher video mode (for example, from text to high-resolution graphics), there may not have been enough memory in the system for Windows to allocate additional memory for saving the application's video display. Try choosing a Video Memory option in the application's PIF that will set aside more memory. While you're at it, turn on the Retain Video Memory check box in the PIF so that Windows won't relinquish the extra memory.

A Common VGA Error

If you have a VGA display and you're running Windows in 386 enhanced mode, Figure 10-16 shows an error message you are likely to see at some point. This message rears its ugly head when you are trying to run a DOS application in a window and the application

364 *Windows 3 Power Tools*

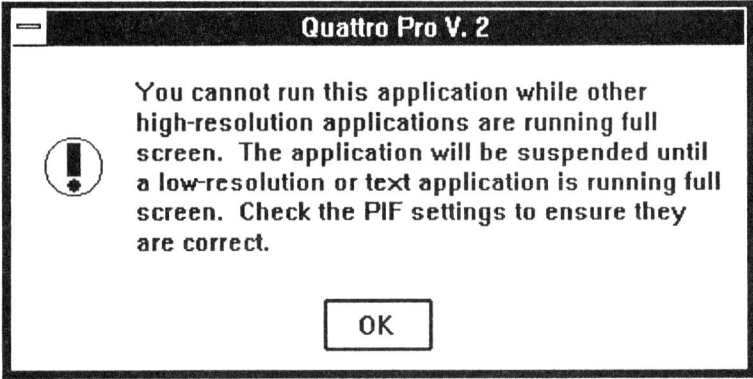

Figure 10-16 The message that appears when you run a DOS application in a window and it switches from text to high-resolution graphics mode (VGA only)

switches from text to high-resolution graphics mode. This occurs, for example, when you use print preview in WordPerfect or WordStar or view a graph in 1-2-3 or Quattro. Contrary to what the error message box says, there is no magic fix for your PIF (except setting the PIF to run the application full screen). There are some easy workarounds, however.

After you clear the error message box, you often see the information box shown in Figure 10-17, which provides the clue to the fix. This box indicates that the application will remain stalled until you switch the application to full-screen display. Press ALT+ENTER to switch to full screen. (You can also select the Settings option from the window Control menu and choose the Full Screen check box. See "Changing a Running Application" above.) After you switch to full screen, the application usually shows the high-resolution graphics screen (for example, the 1-2-3 graph) without any difficulty. You can then press ALT+ENTER a second time to return the application to a windowed

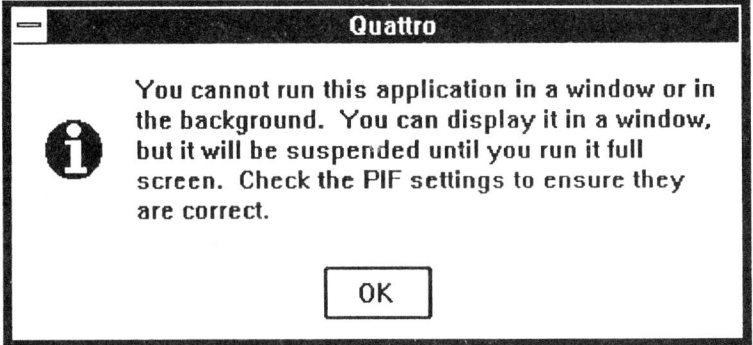

Figure 10-17 The information box tells you what to do when you get the error shown in Figure 10-16

display. When you do this, Windows will show the graphics screen in a window. However, the application will probably have trouble accepting keyboard input while the graphics screen is present. To get input, you will probably have to switch the application back to full-screen display.

Another way to get around this predicament, one that gets more to the heart of the problem, is to change the graphics display driver the DOS application uses to a low-resolution graphics driver. This will let you run the application in a window when it is running in graphics mode. Most applications will let you switch the graphics display driver either while the program is running or through its installation program. For example, to change 1-2-3 Release 2.2 to a low-resolution graphics driver when it is displaying graphs, you'll need to run 1-2-3's install program (INSTALL.EXE), select "Advanced Options," and choose CGA graphics for 1-2-3's graph display driver. Similarly, while you're running WordPerfect, select Setup (SHIFT+F1 for version 5.0) and select "IBM CGA 640x200 mono" for the graphics screen type.

Tip: Problem VGA cards

With some inexpensive VGA cards, the error message in Figure 10-16 appears every time you try to start up a DOS application in a window. The message surfaces immediately when the program tries to show its banner screen, and the application stops in its tracks. After clearing the error, press ALT+ENTER to switch the application to a full-screen display; the DOS program usually continues loading, though you may have trouble seeing it on your screen. To switch the application back to a windowed display, press ALT+ENTER again. From this point on, the program usually works just fine in a window.

When you have such a deviant VGA card, the only way to avoid getting this error message every time is to change the application's PIF so that the program always starts full screen (see "Display Mode" above). Another alternative is to see if the manufacturer has a Windows 3 driver for the card.

When Applications Are Running Too Slowly

When your Windows applications are running slowly, it usually means that memory is low. You'll see evidence of this when the light on your hard disk is flickering constantly, meaning that Windows is swapping applications to and from disk in an attempt to free up memory. When your DOS applications are running slowly, it's probably for the same reason. See "When You Run Out of Memory" for some ideas on how to increase available memory. After you've explored those ideas, here are some others you may want to try:

- If you shell to DOS from certain DOS applications, such as WordPerfect or 1-2-3, the application may slow down precipitously when you return to it. If this happens to you, the best way to handle the situation is to exit the application and start it back up again. You can avoid this problem by switching back to Windows and using the DOS icon rather than shelling to DOS from within an application.

- Some DOS applications, for example WordPerfect, operate faster the more conventional memory you give them. If you are running the application in 386 enhanced mode, try increasing the Memory Requirements: KB Required and KB Desired settings in the application's PIF. In standard or real mode, Windows cannot give the application any more conventional memory than Windows itself was given when it started (less about 20K). Therefore, the only way to increase the amount of memory that Windows can make available to a DOS application is to free up that memory before you run Windows. See "If All Else Fails" and Chapter 7, "Windows Memory Management," for some ideas on how to do this.

- If you are running multiple applications in 386 enhanced mode, occasionally a DOS application doesn't get enough processor time. When this is the case, you'll need to reapportion the processor time between DOS applications in either of two ways. The first way is to use the Settings command from the application's window Control menu and increase the number in the application's Background or Foreground text box. The second way is to increase the number in the Foreground Priority or the Background Priority text box of the application's PIF. Either way, a worthwhile companion step is to decrease the Priority options for other DOS applications that are currently running.

  If Windows applications are running concurrently with the DOS application, sometimes they get too much processor time, slowing the DOS application to a crawl. When this happens, you can make more processor time available to the DOS application by changing its Exclusive setting. To change this setting, select the Settings command from the application's window Control menu and turn the Exclusive check box on. Another alternative is to turn on the Exclusive check box in the application's PIF.

- Occasionally Windows will misdiagnose a DOS application's pauses for maintenance activity as idle time. When this happens, Windows will give away too much processor time to other applications in the system, slowing down the DOS application in the process. To prevent Windows from attempting to detect the program's idle time, turn off the Detect Idle Time check box in the application's PIF.

- If you are running Windows in 386 enhanced mode and all your applications are running slowly, try creating a permanent swap file or increasing the size of that file. Whenever you run Windows in 386 enhanced mode, if it cannot find a permanent swapfile, it creates a temporary swap file. The one disadvantage of a temporary swap file is that it may be broken into several noncontiguous locations on your hard disk. This can slow down the system substantially as Windows moves the drive head to read the noncontiguous blocks. To create a permanent Windows swap file that occupies one large contiguous block, start Windows in real mode and use the File Run command from Program Manager (or File Manager) to execute SWAPF-ILE.EXE in the \WINDOWS\SYSTEM directory (see Chapter 11, "Improving Windows' Performance," for more details).

- If you are running Windows in real or standard mode and switching away from a DOS application is very slow, try setting the XMS Memory: KB Required and KB Limit options to 0. Of course, you should only try this setting when the application doesn't need any XMS memory.

Communications Errors

When you are using a DOS communications program with Windows in 386 enhanced mode and your data appears scrambled, the first thing to check is the baud rate and the other communications settings. When you know your settings are right, but the data still appears scrambled, you may have two applications contending for the COM port. When this happens, you should access the Control Panel and check the Device Contention settings in the 386 enhanced icon (see Chapter 8, "Using the Control Panel," for a discussion of these settings).

When a Key Doesn't Produce the Desired Effect

If you press a key and Windows or your DOS application behaves differently than you expected, it may be due to one of the following:

- If you have a VGA display and you are trying to run a DOS application that uses high-resolution graphics mode, Windows may not be able to display it in a window in 386 enhanced mode. When you try to run it in a window, Windows issues the error message in Figure 10-16. After Windows issues the error message once, it doesn't issue it again. Instead, it merely beeps when you press a key. Press ALT+ENTER to switch the application to full screen. See "A Common VGA Error" above for another suggestion.

- If you are running a DOS application in real or standard mode and that application is large, Windows may not be able to create an application swap file when you press CTRL+ESC, ALT+ESC, or ALT+TAB in an effort to switch away from the application. This happens when you are low on disk space, and you usually see the error message shown in Figure 10-14. When you are very low on disk space, Windows doesn't show you the error message at all but merely beeps at you. See "When You Cannot Switch Away" for some remedies.

- If you are running a DOS application and you press a Windows shortcut key, such as ALT+TAB, but Windows doesn't respond to it, the likely answer is that the shortcut key has been reserved for the DOS application. To determine whether this is the case, check the Reserve Shortcut Keys settings in the application's PIF. If you are running Windows in 386 enhanced mode, you should also check the Application Shortcut Key option; this option lets you quickly access a DOS application by pressing a key sequence (for example, you can assign CTRL+W to access Word-Perfect).

- If you are running Windows in 386 enhanced mode and you press a key sequence that immediately switches you to another DOS application, that key sequence is probably assigned as an application shortcut key. One way to check this is to press the key sequence in different settings, and if it always takes you to the same application, it is very likely an application shortcut key. If you would rather not have the key sequence assigned in this way, you can change or eliminate it in the application's PIF.

When PRINTSCREEN or ALT+PRINTSCREEN Do Not Work

If you are running a DOS application and you press PRINTSCREEN or ALT+PRINTSCREEN to copy a snapshot of the screen to the Clipboard, these keys may have no effect in the following situations:

- If there is very little memory available in 386 enhanced mode, Windows may not be able to allocate sufficient memory for copying the screen to the Clipboard. If the application is running full screen, it's unusual to have this problem because Windows copies only text to the Clipboard, requiring less than 4K. However, if the application is running in a window, Windows tries to copy a bitmap to the Clipboard, which takes substantially more memory than text, sometimes as much as 150K for a VGA display. See "When You Run Out of Memory" for some ideas on how to free up memory.

- If you are running Windows in real or standard mode, you may have trouble copying a snapshot of the screen to the Clipboard if you've selected Text for the Video Mode setting in the application's PIF but the application actually runs in graphics mode. Try changing the setting to Graphics/Multiple Text.

- If PRINTSCREEN and ALT+PRINTSCREEN have been reserved for an application, they will not work as Windows shortcut keys. Check the Reserve Shortcut Keys settings in the application's PIF and turn off their check boxes.

- If you are running Windows in real or standard mode, PRINTSCREEN and ALT+PRINTSCREEN will never work if the No Screen Exchange check box is turned on in the application's PIF. In fact, the purpose of this option is to prevent you from copying to the Clipboard using these keys. Turn off the option to allow screen exchange.

When You Cannot Paste Information

If you try to paste information from the Clipboard to a DOS application but get poor results, here are the likely reasons why:

- The Clipboard may contain something other than text. When this is the case, you get the error message "No appropriate data in Clipboard." You cannot paste graphics, or anything other than text, into a DOS application.

- Some applications cannot accept data at the fast rate that Windows pastes it. When this is the case, the application may not respond at all when you try to paste text into it. With other applications, characters get dropped as Windows pastes text. Try turning off the Allow Fast Paste check box in the application's PIF.

When an Application Stays Around After You've Closed It

Typically, when you quit a DOS application, Windows instantly removes the application's window from the desktop. If the window still stays around, it usually means that you've turned off the Close Window on Exit check box in the application's PIF. To have Windows remove the application's window after you've quit the application, return this option to its standard setting of on.

When an Application Won't Let You Exit

When an application won't let you exit, here are some things to try:

- Press CTRL+C or CTRL+BREAK.
- Press CTRL+ESC to access the Task List, highlight the application in the list, and select End Task.
- As a last resort, if you are running Windows in 386 enhanced mode, switch the application to a window, if it isn't already (press ALT+ENTER or ALT+SPACEBAR); and select Settings in the application's window Control menu followed by Terminate.

When Your System Hangs

In 386 enhanced mode, because each DOS application runs in its own virtual machine, the rest of the system is protected from it. Therefore, if a DOS application hangs, you can usually press ALT+ESC, ALT+TAB, or CTRL+ESC to switch back to Windows and save your other work. You can then use the Terminate option from the application's window Control menu to kill the DOS application. As mentioned, whenever you use Terminate, you should exit Windows immediately after saving your other work, and then reboot your system.

SUMMARY

Windows gives you many ways to control DOS applications. PIFs are the primary tool for fine tuning a DOS application's performance. They let you tailor the application's environment to the particular machine on which Windows is running as well as establish the resources that the program will need. For example, you can set the application's memory requirements, adjust the amount of memory Windows uses to store the application's video display, and even allocate the amount of processor time an application will receive in relation to others. PIFs also let you make an application easier to operate. For example, they let you pass optional parameters to an application and access it through shortcut keys.

Windows also lets you change the way a running application operates on the fly. For example, you can move a DOS application to the background or toggle it between a full screen and a windowed display.

Now that you know how to customize a DOS application's performance in Windows, the next chapter will show you how to improve Windows' overall performance by optimizing its resources.

11

Improving Windows' Performance

The more you use Windows, the more you realize that it's not a single program. Rather, it is a collection of programs, device drivers, swap files, and settings that are all carefully crafted to work together harmoniously.

For the most part, Windows does a smooth job of adapting its various components to your system. Nevertheless, if one or two of them are operating at a substandard level, Windows won't function at its peak. Occasionally, the reason for Windows' substandard performance is its own doing. For example, it may have trouble recognizing your unique hardware. On the other hand, Windows may not have a fighting chance because your system is not configured properly in the first place. For example, you may have the settings in your CONFIG.SYS file improperly set so that Windows cannot use expanded or extended memory to its best advantage. However, by changing these settings, you can usually correct the situation. As another example, it's not unusual to find that your hard disk is operating well below par, and by fine-tuning it, you can speed Windows' disk I/O by as much as 300-500 percent.

This chapter will help you optimize Windows' performance on your system. Here are some of the topics it discusses:

- How to maximize Windows' use of swap files, including how to set up a permanent swap file for 386 enhanced mode.

- How to properly configure your system's memory, device drivers, and DOS resources for Windows, including how to streamline your CONFIG.SYS and AUTOEXEC.BAT files.

- Ways to make sure your hard disk is running at peak performance, including how to identify and delete unnecessary Windows files, how to defragment your hard disk, and how to optimize your hard disk's interleave.

- How to optimize SMARTDrive's disk-caching on your system.

- How to set up a RAM disk with RAMDrive, if it makes sense for your system.

- How to set the HIMEM.SYS extended memory manager to make sure Windows is using extended memory properly.

- Controlling how Windows uses expanded memory, including how to set up EMM386.

By reading this chapter, you'll gain the understanding you need to maximize Windows' performance on your system.

SWAP FILES

When you run Windows in 386 enhanced mode and memory gets tight, Windows starts paging information from memory to disk in 4K blocks. A *swap file* is a hidden file in which Windows stores the 4K blocks until it needs them again. Windows has two types of swap files: permanent and temporary.

A *permanent swap file* is one you create with the SWAPFILE utility while running Windows in real mode. A permanent swap file is somewhat faster than a temporary swap file primarily because it consists of contiguous disk clusters. One disadvantage of a permanent swap file is that it occupies a fixed amount of space on your hard disk, even when Windows is not running.

When you start Windows in 386 enhanced mode, if it cannot find a permanent swap, it dynamically creates a *temporary swap file*. Windows locates the temporary swap file in your Windows directory and removes it when you exit Windows.

You can tell what type of swap file Windows is using by selecting the Windows Setup icon from the Main group window. For example, Figure 11-1 shows that Windows is using a permanent swap file that is 7984K in size and located on drive C. If you are using a temporary swap file or no swap file, Windows does not show the swap file size or location.

When you run Windows in real or standard mode, it uses a third type of swap file, an *application swap file*. Application swap files are created only when you switch away from DOS applications (see "Application Swap Files" later).

The following sections describe how to set up permanent and temporary swap files. Application swap files are discussed afterward.

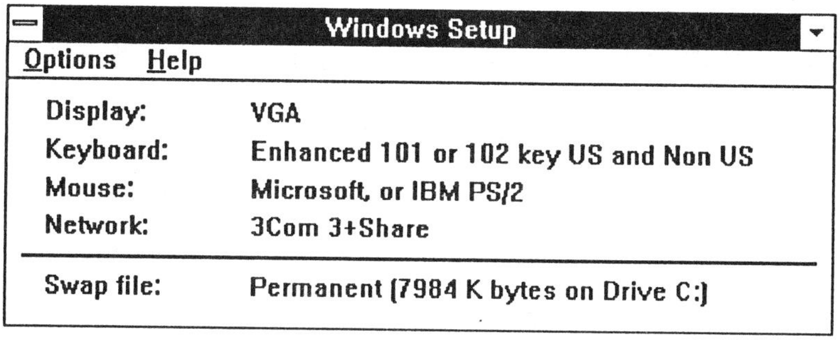

```
┌─────────────────────────────────────────────────────┐
│ ▬                    Windows Setup              ▼   │
│ Options   Help                                      │
├─────────────────────────────────────────────────────┤
│   Display:      VGA                                 │
│   Keyboard:     Enhanced 101 or 102 key US and Non US│
│   Mouse:        Microsoft, or IBM PS/2              │
│   Network:      3Com 3+Share                        │
│                                                     │
│   Swap file:    Permanent (7984 K bytes on Drive C:)│
└─────────────────────────────────────────────────────┘
```

Figure 11-1 The Windows Setup icon shows the type of swap file

Using a Permanent Swap File

As a power user, you should definitely set up a permanent swap file on your fastest hard disk if you use Windows in 386 enhanced mode most of the time. A permanent swap file is faster than a temporary swap file for two reasons: It consists of contiguous disk clusters, and Windows accesses it without calling DOS. A permanent swap file also has the advantage of allowing you to directly control how much disk space Windows uses for swapping.

When you create a permanent swap file, Windows actually places two files on your disk. The first one is SPART.PAR, a read-only file located in your \WINDOWS directory. The only purpose of SPART.PAR is to tell Windows where it can find the second file, 386SPART.PAR, and how large it is. 386SPART.PAR, the actual swap file, is a hidden file located in the root directory of the drive you specify in the SWAPFILE program. (If you look at this file in File Manager, you'll see that besides the hidden attribute, it also has the system attribute set.) You shouldn't try to move or rename these files. If you prefer to see what's consuming your disk space, though, you can change the hidden attribute of 386SPART.PAR without any ill effect. (To change 386SPART.PAR's attributes, run Windows in real mode, start File Manager, and select the Change Attributes command from the File menu. If you want to make 386SPART.PAR visible, you'll have to turn off both the hidden and system attributes.)

If you've been using your hard disk for a while and it is becoming full, it's also bound to be badly fragmented. If this is the case, you may have trouble creating a permanent swap file, since it requires contiguous disk clusters. When a disk is nearly full, the available clusters are usually scattered all over the drive. In this case, the best course of action is to compact or "defragment" your hard disk before trying to set up a permanent swap file (see "Compacting Your Hard Disk" later). Otherwise, you may see a message like the one in Figure 11-2, which indicates that SWAPFILE won't be able to create a permanent swap file until you defragment your drive. This message may appear even though you may have recently deleted several files and have vast amounts of space available on the disk. To create a permanent swap file, you must have at least 1024K of contiguous disk space available.

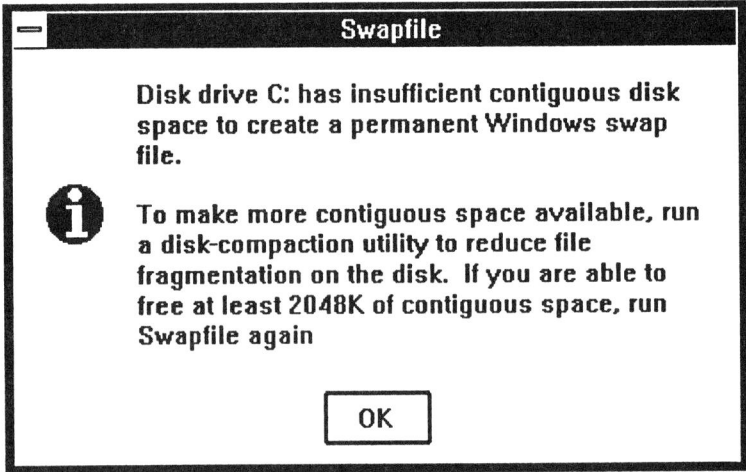

Figure 11-2 When you cannot create a permanent swap file

Figure 11-3 shows another message you might see if your drive is badly fragmented. As this message indicates, you may be able to create a permanent swap file, but it won't be as large as it ought to be. In this example, the message was produced when there were actually 13 megabytes available on the disk, but the largest contiguous block was only 1.7 megabytes.

Tip: SWAPFILE doesn't work with partitioning software

SWAPFILE only works with drives that have been partitioned using the DOS FDISK utility. Therefore, if you have partitioned your drive using third-party partitioning software—for example, Disk Manager from Ontrack Systems—you will not be able to create a permanent Windows swap file. In fact, if SWAPFILE sees that you have a partitioning driver in your CONFIG.SYS file (with the exception of COMPAQ's ENHDISK.SYS), it will display the error message in Figure 11-4.

Setting Up a Permanent Swap File

To set up a permanent swap file, you must start Windows in real mode and use the File Run command to launch the SWAPFILE.EXE utility on the \WINDOWS\SYSTEM directory. (Note that you don't have to enter the path information. Windows finds the file without it.) You must run Windows in real mode because SWAPFILE makes DOS calls that cannot be made from Windows when it is running in protected mode.

Improving Windows' Performance 375

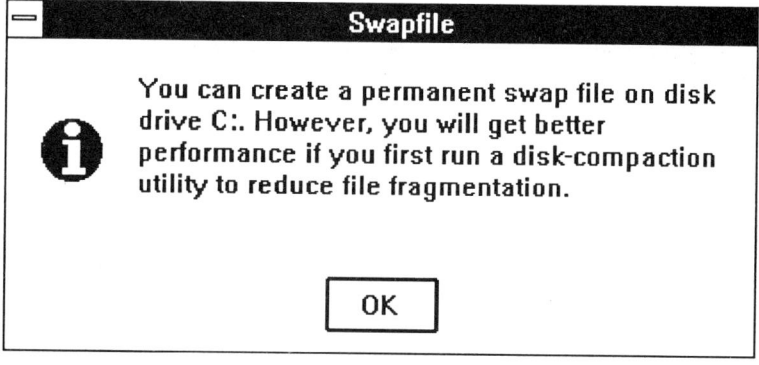

Figure 11-3 When you can create only a small permanent swap file

If you've already created a permanent swap file, SWAPFILE shows a dialog box that asks you whether you want to delete the current file and create a new one, or delete the current file only (see the next sections).

If a permanent swap file doesn't already exist, SWAPFILE examines your first drive (in this case, drive C:) and shows a dialog box like the one in Figure 11-5. The dialog box includes the following settings:

- *Largest possible swap file size*: This is the size of the largest block of contiguous unfragmented disk space.

- *Total free disk space*: This is the total amount of contiguous and noncontiguous disk space on the drive. It gives you a good indication of the degree to which your drive is fragmented.

- *Recommended swap file size*: SWAPFILE analyzes the two previous settings and recommends a swap file size that is no more than half the total free disk space. In

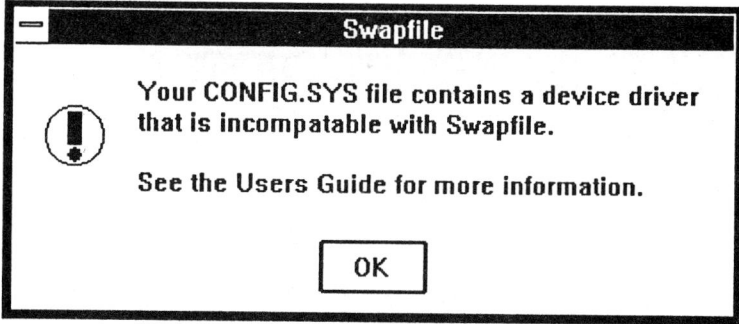

Figure 11-4 SWAPFILE dislikes partitioning software

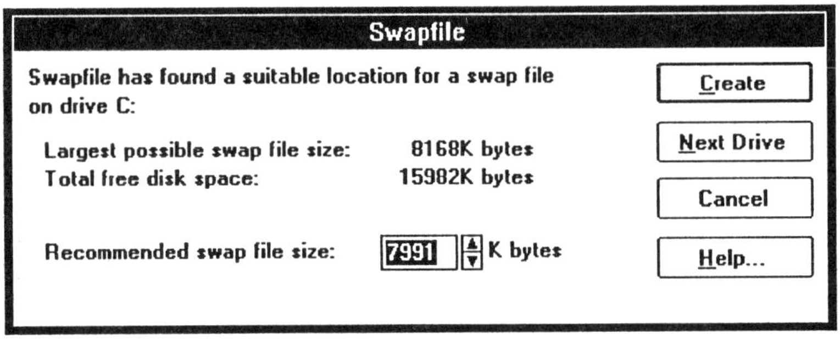

376   Windows 3 Power Tools

[Swapfile dialog box showing:
Swapfile has found a suitable location for a swap file on drive C:
Largest possible swap file size: 8168K bytes
Total free disk space: 15982K bytes
Recommended swap file size: 7991 K bytes
Buttons: Create, Next Drive, Cancel, Help...]

Figure 11-5 The dialog box for creating a new permanent swap file

the current example, the recommended swap file size is 7991K, exactly half of the total free disk space of 15,982K. If the largest possible swap file size had been less than half of the total free disk space (for example, 4098K), SWAPFILE would have used that setting as the recommended swap file size.

If you want to see if the next drive is a better candidate for a permanent swap file, select Next Drive. By selecting Next Drive repeatedly, you can cycle through the available drives.

In general, the larger the permanent swap file, the better. After all, if the file you set up is too large, you can always reduce its size later.

As you specify the swap file size you want, you can click the up or down scroll arrows to change the size in 10K increments. You can choose a size anywhere from 1024K up to the largest possible swap file size (the largest amount of contiguous disk space on the drive).

After you've chosen the drive and swap file size you want, select Create. SWAPFILE creates a hidden file of the size and on the drive you specify. It then shows a message like the one in Figure 11-6.

You can now exit Windows and start it in 386 enhanced mode. From this point forward, whenever memory gets tight, Windows will page information to the permanent swap file.

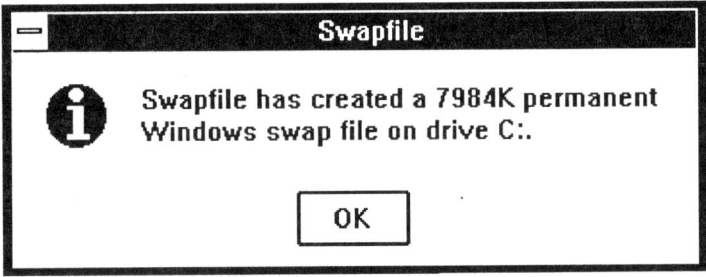

Figure 11-6 The message SWAPFILE shows when you select Create

Note: You cannot specify a network drive or a RAM disk for your permanent Windows swap file; SWAPFILE only lets you choose the physical drives on your system. You can, however, use either a network drive or a RAM disk for a temporary swap file (see the later sections).

Note: If you create a permanent swap file in real mode but get a message that your permanent swap file is corrupted when you start Windows in 386 enhanced mode, there is no cause for alarm. Just run the SWAPFILE utility again in real mode, delete the current swap file, and create a new one.

Changing Your Permanent Swap File

After you've set up a permanent swap file, you may decide that you want to change its size or location. Here are some likely reasons why:

- You've compacted your hard disk, and you now want to make a larger swap file available to Windows.
- You need more disk space for your data files, so you want to decrease the size of the permanent swap file or move it to another drive.

When you change the size of your swap file, the SWAPFILE utility actually deletes the existing swap file and creates a new one using the size and location you specify.

To change the size of your permanent swap file, start Windows in real mode and use the File Run command to launch SWAPFILE. You'll then see the dialog box in Figure 11-7. Next, turn on the "delete the current swap file and create a new one" radio button and select OK. SWAPFILE deletes the current swap file and shows a message confirming that it's deleted. After you respond to the message, Windows displays a dialog box like the one in Figure 11-5. You can now create a new swap file.

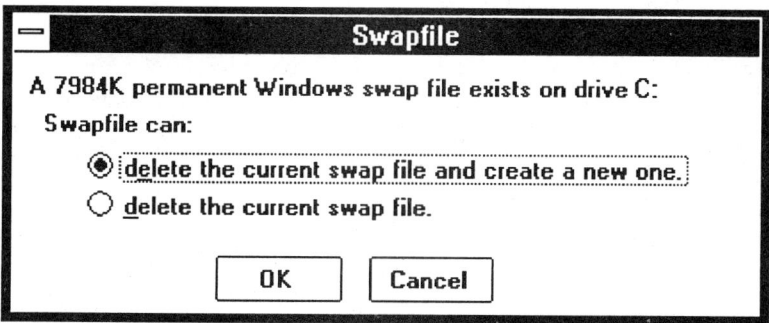

Figure 11-7 The dialog box when a permanent swap file already exists

Deleting Your Permanent Swap File

About the only time you will want to delete your permanent Windows swap file and use a temporary swap file instead is when disk space is so tight that you have no other alternative. To delete your permanent swap file, follow the same steps outlined in the previous section, except that when SWAPFILE displays the dialog box in Figure 11-7, select the "delete the current swap file" button.

Tip: Conserving disk space by preventing swapping

If you are running Windows in 386 enhanced mode and you want to conserve disk space, you can prevent Windows from swapping information to disk by placing the statement Paging=no in the [386Enh] section of the SYSTEM.INI file. Be aware, however, that although this statement limits Windows' use of disk space, it also severely limits its capacity. You should only use this statement if disk space is at a premium, and you need to use the space normally allocated for a temporary swap file.

Using a Temporary Swap File

When you run Windows in 386 enhanced mode, if you have not created a permanent swap file, Windows automatically creates a temporary swap file. Windows uses this file when memory gets tight and it needs to page information to disk. When you exit Windows, it automatically deletes the temporary swap file.

A temporary swap file is a normal DOS file that Windows can resize as it needs to. Because a temporary swap file does not require contiguous disk clusters, Windows can still create one when your disk is badly fragmented or disk space is relatively tight.

The name of the temporary swap file is WIN386.SWP, and it is located in your \WINDOWS directory. However, you can change the location for the temporary swap file by adding the PagingDrive statement to your SYSTEM.INI file (see "Changing the Location of the Temporary Swap File").

When Windows creates a temporary swap file, its size varies depending on the amount of memory in your system and the amount of free disk space. Windows usually starts with a file of about 1024K and increases (or reduces) its size as necessary. If disk space is tight and you want to limit the size of the temporary swap file, you can change the MinUserDiskSpace or MaxPagingFileSize settings in your SYSTEM.INI file (see "Restricting the Size of the Temporary Swap File").

Changing the Location of the Temporary Swap File

Normally, when Windows creates a temporary swap file, it places the file in the \WINDOWS directory. If you want to change the location that Windows uses to the root directory of the same or a different drive, you can enter the PagingDrive setting in the [386Enh] section of your SYSTEM.INI file. For example, by specifying Paging-Drive=D:, you can have Windows locate the file on the root directory of drive D. (There is no way to specify a subdirectory for the temporary swap file location.)

Tip: Choosing the "best" drive for your temporary swap file

If you have more than one drive on your system, there are two factors to consider when determining the PagingDrive setting: drive speed and free space. If you're concerned about Windows' speed, choose the drive with the fastest access time. If you're concerned about capacity, choose the drive with the most free disk space. (See "Improving Your Hard Disk's Performance" for some ideas on how to optimize your hard disk(s).)

Restricting the Size of the Temporary Swap File

If you are short on disk space, you may want to control the size of the temporary swap file that Windows uses. Windows provides two settings that you can place in the [386Enh] section of your SYSTEM.INI file to control the size of the swap file: MinUserDiskSpace and MaxPagingFileSize. Here's an explanation of the two settings:

- *MinUserDiskSpace* tells Windows to always leave a certain amount of disk space free instead of allocating it for a temporary swap file. For example, a setting of MinUserDiskSpace=1536 tells Windows to always leave 1.5 megabytes of disk space free.

- *MaxPagingFileSize* tells Windows the maximum size of the temporary swap file. For example, a setting of MaxPagingFileSize=2048 tells Windows never to enlarge the file beyond 2 megabytes.

You can use either setting or both in your SYSTEM.INI file.

Using a RAM Disk for Your Temporary Swap File

You should *not* use a RAM disk for your temporary swap file, because that would be a self-defeating exercise. Creating a RAM disk merely replaces physical memory with virtual memory that you have reassigned to physical memory. In other words, you're caught reusing as a RAM disk the same physical memory that would otherwise be available directly to Windows.

Using a Network Drive for Your Temporary Swap File

Although Microsoft does not recommend it, we've found that setting the temporary swap file to a network drive can be advantageous under the following limited circumstances:

- You have a fast file server.
- The root directory of the net drive does not have a DOS read-only attribute.
- You have Create and Write access to the net drive's root directory.
- The network drive has plenty of available free space.
- You are running several large DOS applications.
- You are *not* using Novell Netware (all versions).

To set the temporary swap file to a net drive, use the PagingDrive statement in the SYSTEM.INI file (see "Changing the Location of the Temporary Swap File" above).

Caution: If you are using a Novell network, *do not* set the temporary swap file to a net drive. Unlike other network vendors, Novell does not license Microsoft's MSNet Redirector module. Because Novell is not MSNet-Redirector compatible, the root directory of a Novell network drive is also the root directory of the server. What this means is that if more than one user tries to run Windows in 386 enhanced mode with their temporary swap files set to the same Novell drive, their systems will hang because the swap files will try to use the same name on the root directory of the server.

Improving Windows' Use of Application Swap Files

When you run Windows in real or standard mode and you launch a DOS application, Windows moves itself out of memory to make room for the DOS application. In the process of swapping itself out to disk, Windows creates a temporary hidden file for itself named ~WOA0000.TMP in the directory named by the TEMP environment variable, usually the \WINDOWS\TEMP directory. When you switch away from the DOS application and back to Windows, Windows restores itself from the information in this file and then deletes the file.

Windows also creates a temporary *application swap file* whenever you switch away from a DOS application back to Windows. Application swap files are hidden read-only files that also begin with ~*WOA* (for example, ~WOA2DC0.TMP) and are stored in the directory named by the TEMP environment variable. (When you install Windows, Setup usually sets the TEMP environment variable in your AUTOEXEC.BAT file to the \WINDOWS\TEMP directory.) If there is no TEMP setting, Windows places these files in the \WINDOWS directory. (See Chapter 7, "Windows Memory Management," for a more detailed explanation of application swap files.)

To have Windows store all of its application swap files in another location, you can place a SwapDisk statement in the [NonWindowsApp] section of your SYSTEM.INI file. For example, by using the statement **SwapDisk=D:**, you can have Windows store the application swap files on the root directory of drive D. Be sure to put the SwapDisk statement in the [NonWindowsApp] section; if you put it anywhere else, Windows will ignore it.

Note: Windows 3 also includes a SwapDisk setting in your WIN.INI file, but it does not do anything. Make sure to place SwapDisk in your SYSTEM.INI file, not your WIN.INI.

As a power user, you may want to maximize your system's speed in real or standard mode by having Windows swap DOS applications to extended memory. To do this, create a RAM disk in extended memory with the RAMDRIVE.SYS driver (see "Setting Up a RAM Disk with RAMDrive" later). Then set the SwapDisk setting in your SYSTEM.INI file to the drive created by RAMDRIVE.SYS. This technique works best if you have plenty of extended memory and you want to switch between relatively few DOS applications.

To determine the appropriate size for the RAM disk, you'll need to calculate the size of the Windows system swap file, ~WOA0000.TMP, plus the size of each DOS application's temporary swap file. As a general rule, ~WOA0000.TMP requires about 400-450K in real mode and only about 30K in standard mode. (Since the size of this file varies from one system to next, you should check it on your system. Double-click on the DOS icon and use the Norton Utilities, or another DOS program that can view hidden files to check this file's size.) You'll also need roughly 550K per DOS application—more if an application uses graphics mode and substantially less for small character-based applications. (An application that uses graphics mode usually has a temporary grabber file of about 165K with a name that begins with ~*GRB*. This file contains the information Windows needs to restore the display when you switch back to the DOS application.) To see the size of an application's temporary swap file, use File Manager and turn on the Show Hidden/System Files option in the View Include dialog box (see "DOS Applications in Real and Standard Modes" in Chapter 7 for more information).

For example, suppose you are running Windows in real mode, and you want to switch between two DOS applications. A RAM disk of about 1550K (450K + 2 * 550K) for character-based applications and 1830K (an extra 165K per application) for graphics mode applications will usually work, but you'll have to experiment. You'll know that the RAM disk is too small if Windows tells you that you have to exit a DOS application before you can switch back to Windows; this indicates that the RAM disk won't hold all the application swap files that are required.

Note: In standard mode, the size of temporary application swap files varies widely. Therefore, if you're setting up a RAM disk for swapping DOS applications in this mode, you'll need to check the size of the temporary application swap files carefully.

When you run Windows in real mode, it uses extended memory for caching discardable code segments for Windows applications. Be aware that using extended memory to create a RAM disk reduces the amount of memory that Windows can use for caching discardable segments. As a result, you will be sacrificing some of your ability to multitask Windows applications in order to load multiple DOS applications.

> **Tip: Swapping DOS applications to expanded memory**
>
> Windows version 2.x had the built-in ability to swap DOS applications directly to expanded memory. Because expanded memory is rarely used in Windows 3, Microsoft removed this capability. If you want to swap DOS applications to expanded memory, you must set up RAMDrive in expanded memory with the /A switch and then set the SwapDisk parameter in SYSTEM.INI to name the RAM disk created by RAMDrive.

CONFIGURING YOUR PC'S MEMORY

Making sure your PC's memory is properly configured is by far the most important step in optimizing Windows on your system. Configuring your memory properly means not only making sure that your system has the right amount of conventional, extended, and/or expanded memory but also using the right device drivers and DOS resources in your CONFIG.SYS file.

The following sections provide a list of memory and CONFIG.SYS settings that you can examine to make sure that Windows is running as efficiently as possible on your system. The sections are only slightly different depending on the processor you have, so you should skip to the appropriate one.

80386- and 80486-Based Systems

When you start Windows on an 80386- or 80486-based PC, it checks to see how much memory you have in your system and starts up in the most appropriate mode. If your system has 2 megabytes of memory or more, Windows starts in 386 enhanced mode. With between 1 and 2 megabytes of memory, Windows starts in standard mode. And with less than 1 megabyte of memory Windows starts in real mode.

To make the most of Windows, you should have the following amounts of memory:

- At least 640K of conventional memory.
- As much extended memory as possible. The more you have, the better Windows will run. (You'll need a minimum of 1024K to run Windows in 386 enhanced mode and 196K to run Windows in standard mode.)

If your system has a configurable expanded memory board, such as the Intel Above-Board or the AST Rampage board, you should configure it all as extended memory. The one exception is when you are running Windows in standard mode and a DOS application needs expanded memory. In this case, you should configure your board for as much expanded memory as the DOS application needs, and configure the rest as extended.

Check your CONFIG.SYS file for the following lines:

- **FILES=30**: This line sets to 30 the maximum number of file handles that can be open at once. Each file handle above eight consumes 48 additional bytes of conventional memory. Although you can increase this setting above 30 without much memory cost, you normally do not need to unless you are running large database applications. On the other hand, setting FILES below 30 may prevent Windows and applications from running.

- **BUFFERS=10**: If you are using SMARTDrive (and you should be), you should limit the number of buffers in your CONFIG.SYS file to 10. Using a greater number of buffers will actually decrease SMARTDrive's efficiency. In addition, because each buffer adds 528 bytes to the size of the resident portion of DOS, you'll save conventional memory by limiting your buffers. (If you are not using SMARTDrive, use BUFFERS=30.)

- **DEVICE=C:\HIMEM.SYS**: This line installs the HIMEM.SYS extended memory manager. Windows needs HIMEM.SYS (or a compatible driver, such as Quarterdeck's QEMM386.SYS) in order to use extended memory. This line should always come before other lines that install device drivers that use extended memory, such as SMARTDrive or RAMDrive. Setup automatically places this line in your CONFIG.SYS when you install Windows.

- **DEVICE=C:\EMM.SYS (or equivalent)**: You'll need a command line like this only if you are using an expanded memory board, such as the Intel Above Board.

- **DEVICE=C:\WINDOWS\SMARTDRV.SYS** $x\ y$: This line installs the SMARTDrive disk-caching utility, where x is the normal size and y is the minimum size (see "Using the SMARTDrive Disk-Caching Program"). Setup automatically places this line in your CONFIG.SYS when you install Windows.

- **DEVICE=C:\WINDOWS\RAMDRIVE.SYS** x **/E**: This line installs the RAMDrive RAM disk program, where x is the size of the RAM disk in bytes and /E places the RAM disk in extended memory. Don't use this line unless you run Windows in real mode most of the time and you want to speed up the rate at which Windows switches to and from DOS applications (see "Setting Up a RAM Disk with RAMDrive").

- **DEVICE=C:\WINDOWS\EMM386.SYS** x: This line installs the EMM386 expanded memory emulator, where x is the amount of expanded memory in kilobytes. Include this line only if a DOS application needs expanded memory in real mode, or if you are running such an application without Windows. Windows does not use EMM386-supplied expanded memory in standard or 386 enhanced mode.

- **DEVICE=C:\WINDOWS\EGA.SYS**: This line installs the EGA.SYS device driver. If you have an EGA card and you run Windows in real or standard mode, you may need a line like this in your CONFIG.SYS (see "The EGA.SYS Device

Driver" for details). If Setup detects that you have an EGA card, it automatically places this line in your CONFIG.SYS.

80286-Based Systems

When you start Windows on an 80286-based PC, WIN.COM determines whether your computer has at least 1 megabyte of memory, and starts up in standard mode if it does. With less than 1 megabyte of memory WIN.COM starts in real mode.

To optimize Windows' performance on your system, you should have the following amounts of memory:

- At least 640K of conventional memory.

- At least 192K of extended memory, but Windows' performance will improve the more extended memory you have.

If your system has a configurable expanded memory board, such as the Intel Above-Board or the AST Rampage board, you should configure it all as extended memory. The one exception is when you are running Windows in standard mode and a DOS application needs expanded memory. In this case, you should configure your board for as much expanded memory as the DOS application needs, and configure the rest as extended.

Check your CONFIG.SYS file for the following lines:

- **FILES=30**: This line sets to 30 the maximum number of file handles that can be open at once. Each file handle above eight consumes 48 additional bytes of conventional memory. Although you can increase this setting above 30 without much memory cost, you normally do not need to unless you are running large database applications. On the other hand, setting FILES below 30 may prevent Windows and applications from running.

- **BUFFERS=10**: If you are using SMARTDrive (and you should be), you should limit the number of DOS sector buffers in your CONFIG.SYS file to 10. Using a greater number of buffers will actually decrease SMARTDrive's efficiency. In addition, because each sector buffer adds 528 bytes to the size of the resident portion of DOS, you'll save conventional memory by limiting your buffers. (If you are not using SMARTDrive, use BUFFERS=30.)

- **DEVICE=C:\HIMEM.SYS**: This line installs the HIMEM.SYS extended memory manager. Windows needs HIMEM.SYS (or a compatible driver, such as Quarterdeck's QEMM386.SYS) in order to use extended memory. This line should always come before other lines that install device drivers that use extended memory, such as SMARTDrive or RAMDrive. Setup automatically places this line in your CONFIG.SYS when you install Windows.

- **DEVICE=C:\EMM.SYS (or equivalent)**: You'll need a command line like this only if you are using an expanded memory board, such as the Intel Above Board.

- **DEVICE=C:\WINDOWS\SMARTDRV.SYS** *x* *y*: This line installs the SMARTDrive disk-caching utility, where *x* is the normal size and *y* is the minimum size (see "Using the SMARTDrive Disk-Caching Program"). Setup automatically places this line in your CONFIG.SYS when you install Windows.

- **DEVICE=C:\WINDOWS\RAMDRIVE.SYS** *x* **/E**: This line installs the RAMDrive RAM disk program, where *x* is the size of the RAM disk in bytes and /E places the RAM disk in extended memory. Don't use this line unless you run Windows in real mode most of the time and you want to speed up the rate at which Windows switches to and away from DOS applications (see "Setting Up a RAM Disk with RAMDrive").

- **DEVICE=C:\WINDOWS\EGA.SYS**: This line installs the EGA.SYS device driver. If you have an EGA card and you run Windows in real or standard mode, you may need a line like this in your CONFIG.SYS (see "The EGA.SYS Device Driver" for details). If Setup detects that you have an EGA card, it automatically places this line in your CONFIG.SYS.

8086- or 8088-Based Systems

When you start Windows on an 8086- or 8088-based PC, WIN.COM runs in real mode only. To maximize Windows' performance on your system, you should have the following amounts of memory:

- At least 640K of conventional memory (Windows needs a bare minimum of 384K to run).

- As much expanded memory as you can provide. (Expanded memory will improve the performance of Windows applications, and if you set up RAMDrive in expanded memory, you can swap DOS applications to expanded memory.)

Check your CONFIG.SYS file for the following lines:

- **FILES=30**: This line sets to 30 the maximum number of file handles that can be open at once. Each file handle above eight consumes 48 additional bytes of conventional memory. Although you can increase this setting above 30 without much memory cost, you normally do not need to unless you are running large database applications. On the other hand, setting FILES below 30 may prevent Windows and applications from running.

- **BUFFERS=10**: If you are using SMARTDrive (and you should be), you should limit the number of DOS sector buffers in your CONFIG.SYS file to 10. Using a greater number of buffers will actually decrease SMARTDrive's efficiency. In addition, because each sector buffer adds 528 bytes to the size of the resident portion of DOS, you'll save conventional memory by limiting your buffers. (If you are not using SMARTDrive, use BUFFERS=30.)

- **DEVICE=C:\EMM.SYS (or equivalent)**: You'll need a command line like this only if you are using an expanded memory board, such as the Intel Above Board.

- **DEVICE=C:\WINDOWS\SMARTDRV.SYS *x y* /A**: This line installs the SMARTDrive disk-caching utility in expanded memory, where *x* is the normal size, *y* is the minimum size, and /A places the disk cache in expanded memory (see "Using the SMARTDrive Disk-Caching Program").

- **DEVICE=C:\WINDOWS\RAMDRIVE.SYS x /A**: This line installs the RAMDrive RAM disk program, where *x* is the size of the RAM disk in bytes and /A places the RAM disk in expanded memory. Use this line only if you want to speed up the rate at which Windows switches to and from DOS applications (see "Setting Up a RAM Disk with RAMDrive").

- **DEVICE=C:\WINDOWS\EGA.SYS**: This line installs the EGA.SYS device driver. If you have an EGA card, you may need a line like this in your CONFIG.SYS (see "The EGA.SYS Device Driver" for details). If Setup detects that you have an EGA card, it automatically places this line in your CONFIG.SYS.

Slimming Down Your CONFIG.SYS and AUTOEXEC.BAT Files

Before you run Windows, it's always a good idea to make as much conventional memory available as possible. In general, the more conventional memory Windows has, the better it will run. For example, when you run Windows in 386 enhanced mode, each virtual 8086 machine "inherits" the environment that was present before you started Windows. In other words, every device driver or TSR that was loaded before running Windows will consume memory in every virtual machine that Windows creates. Therefore, by freeing up conventional memory before starting Windows, you can make more memory available in each virtual machine.

The easiest way to free up conventional memory is to slim down your CONFIG.SYS and AUTOEXEC.BAT files to include only the bare essentials. The next two sections will show you how. As you read those sections, here are some recommendations to help make modifying your CONFIG.SYS and AUTOEXEC.BAT files a little easier:

- If you are modifying your CONFIG.SYS or AUTOEXEC.BAT from Windows, use SYSEDIT, the System Configuration Editor.

- Whenever you modify your AUTOEXEC.BAT and CONFIG.SYS files, it's always a good idea to keep handy a bootable DOS diskette that includes the original versions of these files. That way, you can always reboot from this diskette and restore the original files if your changes don't work out.

- By placing "REM" at the start of a command line in your CONFIG.SYS and AUTOEXEC.BAT files, you can disable that line. If you are using DOS version 3.3 or earlier, however, and you use "REM" at the start of a line in your CONFIG.SYS, DOS will issue the error message "Unrecognized command in CONFIG.SYS" when you boot your computer. Don't be concerned about this message;

you can always remove the offending line later, after you're sure that you no longer need it.

You can also preserve conventional memory by running memory-resident utilities after starting Windows and using batch files to pair them with the DOS applications that use them (see Chapter 10, "Using Non-Windows Applications," for more information).

CONFIG.SYS

As any power user knows, your CONFIG.SYS file, located in the root directory of your first hard disk (usually drive C), defines the device drivers and DOS resources that your system uses. Here are some pointers for optimizing your CONFIG.SYS for Windows:

- Disable any command lines that install device drivers that you do not need. For example, if your CONFIG.SYS has a line for a mouse driver (for example, DEVICE=C:\MOUSE.SYS) and you plan to use your mouse only with Windows applications, you can disable this line. Don't disable the lines for HIMEM.SYS or SMARTDRV.SYS, though, unless you're certain you have installed other compatible device drivers as alternatives.

- Set FILES=30 and BUFFERS=10 (see "Configuring Your PC's Memory").

- If you're using your PC on a network, your CONFIG.SYS may have a LASTDRIVE statement that places an upper limit on the number of network drives you can have, for example, LASTDRIVE=Z. Because each additional drive above E takes 81 bytes of RAM, you should set LASTDRIVE to the *actual number* of network drives you are using—for example, F or G—rather than some theoretical maximum like Z.

- If your CONFIG.SYS file has a SHELL command to increase the size of the DOS environment, consider specifying a smaller environment and removing the SHELL command. This will limit the number and length of the environment variables you can define using the SET command, but it will also save memory. The default size of the DOS environment is 160 bytes, but the SHELL command can increase its size to as much as 32,768 bytes, depending on the settings.

- If you have DOS version 3.3 or later, use STACKS=0,0 to stop DOS from allocating its interrupt stacks. Interrupt stacks are temporary data structures that DOS and applications use for processing hardware interrupts. These stacks are not needed because Windows automatically deals with the problem of choosing a stack for hardware interrupts. By using STACKS=0,0, you can save 3280 bytes of memory.

AUTOEXEC.BAT

Your AUTOEXEC.BAT file is a special DOS batch file that lists the commands that DOS executes after completing the commands in your CONFIG.SYS file. These lines typically start pop-up programs, such as SideKick, or initiate memory-resident programs, such as those associated with a network. Here are some ways to trim down your AUTOEXEC.BAT for Windows:

- If you are using your mouse only with Windows applications, you may want to disable your mouse driver, usually MOUSE.COM.
- If you have any command lines that launch pop-up programs or memory-resident utilities, you may want to disable them. In most cases, you are better off running them after you've started Windows and launching them from batch files that pair them with the DOS applications that use them (see Chapter 10). However, do not change any command lines that start your network.
- Make sure to disable the DOS APPEND, JOIN, and SUBST commands, because they can cause problems when you are using Windows 3.
- Consider setting your TEMP environment variable to a RAM disk if you are running applications that use the directory named by the TEMP variable for storing temporary files (see "Using the TEMP Environment Variable" later).

IMPROVING YOUR HARD DISK'S PERFORMANCE

Because Windows is a disk-intensive program, it's important that your hard disk be operating as well as it can. Here are some of the ways you can improve your hard disk's efficiency:

- Deleting unnecessary files.
- Running CHKDSK with the /F switch.
- Compacting your hard disk.
- Optimizing your hard disk's interleave.

Before you delve into these areas, though, it's helpful to know some hard disk fundamentals. This next section describes such basic terms as track, cylinder, and sector as well as the layout of a hard disk.

Hard Disk Fundamentals

While a floppy disk contains only a single magnetic disk, a hard disk is composed of several stacked disks, called *platters*, mounted on a central spindle. Each platter has two recording surfaces, called *sides*, on which information is stored. The sides are numbered sequentially starting with 0, as shown in Figure 11-8.

The *head* is the device that reads and writes data on a recording surface. Each side has its own read/write head. Therefore, if you see in your disk drive manual or CMOS setup program that your drive has six heads, you know that it also has six sides, or three platters.

Improving Windows' Performance 389

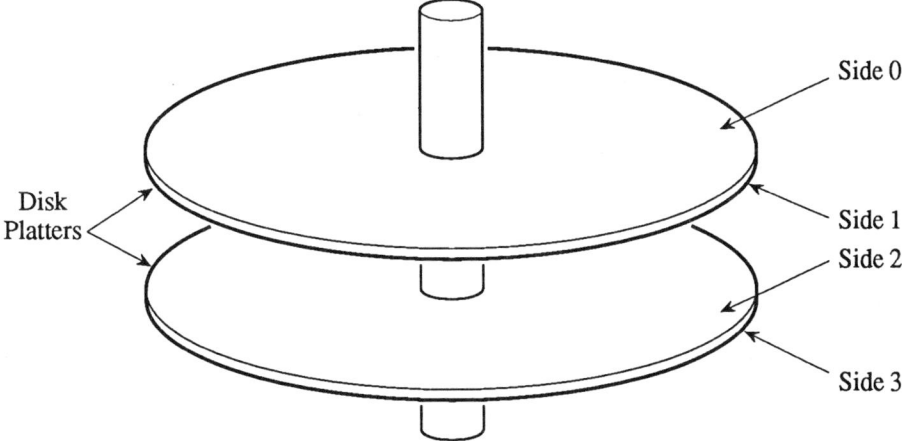

Figure 11-8 The platters of a hard disk

Like sides, the drive heads are numbered starting with 0, and the terms "side 2" and "head 2" are used interchangeably to refer to the third recording surface.

All the heads are mounted on a single arm that is similar to the arm on a phonograph. When the arm moves, all the heads move at once. But while a phonograph arm moves in one continuous sweep across a record album, a hard disk arm is driven by a stepper motor which moves the arm in discrete steps. Therefore, the surface of a hard disk platter is divided into concentric rings known as *tracks*. Standard 5.25" floppy disks contain 40 tracks, but hard disks may contain more than a thousand tracks. A *cylinder* is the term used for the set of tracks, one on each side, which are simultaneously accessible by the set of disk heads. Actually, the terms track and cylinder are used interchangeably and can be quite confusing. However, because all the heads are mechanically linked, you know that if one drive head is located over track 10, for example, all the other drive heads must also be located over that track.

Each track is broken down further into units called *sectors*, as shown in Figure 11-9. A sector is composed of 4096 data bits organized into 512 bytes. The original hard disks on the PC/XT, and most hard disks in existence today, use Modified Frequency Modulation encoding (MFM for short), which stores 17 sectors per track. Another popular encoding scheme that appeared after MFM was Run Length Limited (RLL) encoding, which stores 26 sectors within the same track space. By increasing the number of sectors, RLL drives achieve a 50-percent increase in the data transfer rate over MFM drives.

Locating Sectors

To achieve a high rate of data transfer, the hard disk is constantly spinning at 3600 RPM. When the read/write head is positioned over a track, an entire track's worth of data passes underneath the head 60 times a second. Any sector of data on the disk can be located by

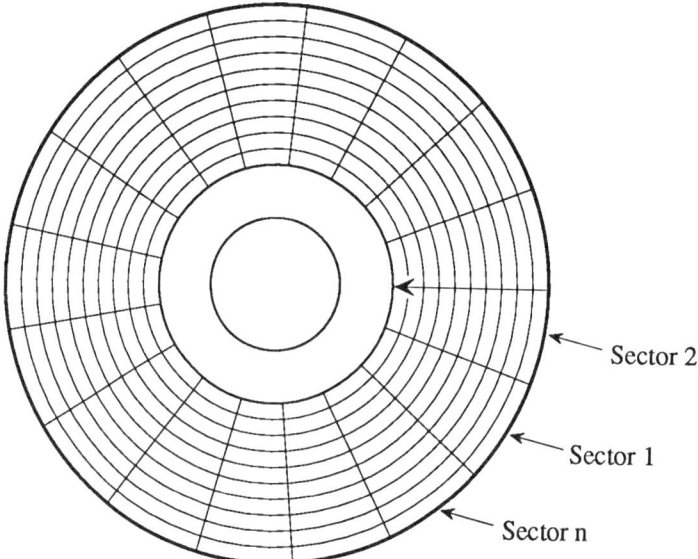

Figure 11-9 Sectors that make up tracks

moving the head to the proper track and waiting a maximum of one sixtieth of a second for the sector to revolve underneath the head.

At the start of each sector is a special nondata area known as the *sector ID header*. This ID header contains the sector's address, which consists of three coordinates: the cylinder, head, and sector number. By checking the sector ID header, the hard disk controller can verify that the proper sector has been chosen, in case the stepper motor has erred and "stepped" to the wrong track. When the controller wants to read or write a sector of data, the head is located over the proper cylinder, the proper head is electronically selected, and the appropriate track is read continuously until the proper sector ID header appears. If for some reason the sector ID header doesn't appear, you'll see the dreaded error message "Sector not found."

A disk drive's speed is measured by its *access time*. This is the average time it takes to switch between cylinders, one of the most time-consuming aspects of a disk's operation because the head must move mechanically across the platter. (When you hear a disk called "a 28-millisecond drive" this refers to the access time.) Another component of a drive's speed is the time spent waiting for the proper sector to rotate underneath the head. This can also be a significant cause of delay, depending on how the sectors are arranged or "interleaved" on the tracks (see "Optimizing Your Hard Disk's Interleave" for more on this).

How DOS Allocates Space

When a file grows in size, DOS must allocate space on the disk for the additional contents. The simplest way of allocating space would be a sector at a time. Although this sounds like a good idea, it's really not, because it would lead to disk fragmentation. Disk fragmentation occurs when several files are split into blocks that are scattered all over the hard disk, a phenomenon that occurs naturally the more you use your hard disk. (See "Compacting Your Hard Disk" for ways to combat disk fragmentation.)

To help cut down on fragmentation, DOS stores files in *clusters*. Clusters are typically four sectors long (2048 bytes) on most hard disks, though on the XT's original 10-megabyte hard disk they were eight sectors long. The one drawback of allocating disk space in clusters is that a file that requires only one sector has three sectors of wasted space. On the other hand, if space were allocated in smaller units, it's unlikely that they would be contiguous, and that would slow down the disk's access time.

Tip: Why Windows 3.0 and SMARTDrive have problems with partitioning software

When the IBM PC/AT was first introduced, hard disk drives were a new phenomenon in the world of PCs. All hard disks had 17 sectors per track, used MFM encoding, had 306 or 615 cylinders, and stored 10 or 20 megabytes. It was in this climate that IBM settled on a fixed number of drive types (17 to be exact) which were stored in an index table in the CMOS RAM. By choosing an integer from this table, you could pick your drive's configuration and store it indefinitely in the battery-driven CMOS. This same strategy was replicated by clone makers across the board. And although the number of entries in the CMOS index grew to around 46 on most systems, it could still never keep up with the steady proliferation of new drive sizes and types.

The industry attacked this problem from three different angles. The first and simplest solution was found by a few ROM BIOS makers who started adding the capability to enter "user-defined" drive types into the CMOS setup. For example, by selecting a drive type 47 on some BIOSes, you could enter a hard drive's cylinder, head, and sector counts into the system. Unfortunately, this solution was not immediately adopted by all BIOS makers, and many clones that exist today do not have it.

The second solution for non-CMOS-supported drive parameters was provided by hard disk controller manufacturers who built "smart" controllers that could read the drive parameters directly from the drive itself and automatically configure themselves. These controllers have been available for MFM, RLL, and ESDI (Enhanced Small Device Interface) drives for some time now.

The third solution to this dilemma was a software-only solution that is the cause of Windows and SMARTDrive's problem with certain hard drives. Many drives were shipped with third-party partitioning software that is installed as a device driver. When the system boots, the device driver immediately alters the system drive parameters to the correct settings for the drive. Because the system drive parameters are smaller than the actual drive and this inconsistency is tolerated temporarily by the system, the drive's C: partition could be booted. Then the third-party device driver would kick in to correct the inaccurate parameters, making the entire drive accessible.

Unfortunately, this last "solution" creates a discrepancy between the drive that DOS thinks it has booted and the drive parameters that the device driver has set up. Because the SMARTDrive disk-caching program takes its cue from DOS, when it writes to the drive, it scrambles the File Allocation Table (FAT), causing all the data on the drive to be lost.

This scrambling occurs under two scenarios. The first scenario is when the drive has less then 1024 cylinders but the BIOS settings don't match the actual driver parameters, and you are running DOS version 3.3 or later. The second scenario is when the drive has more than 1024 cylinders and you are using DOS version 3.3 or earlier. (Unfortunately, the BIOSes in PCs are only able to communicate with drives that have 1024 or fewer total cylinders.) In both cases, the scrambling only occurs when a partitioning device driver is present.

The third-party partitioning utility that creates the most havoc is Disk Manager (DMDRVR.BIN) from Ontrack Systems, because this is the utility usually shipped with Seagate drives (and many others). Other lesser-known though equally detrimental utilities are SpeedStor from Storage Dimensions, InnerSpace from Priam Systems, and Vfeatures Deluxe from Golden Bow Systems.

The short-term solution to this problem is to disable SMARTDrive by removing its DEVICE= line from your CONFIG.SYS file and placing the following line in the [386Enh] section of your SYSTEM.INI file:

`VirtualHDIrq=FALSE`

A better solution, if your drive has 1024 cylinders or less, is to re-initialize your drive using the fixed disk installation program that came with it (for example, Disk Manager), making sure not to allocate any partitions using this software. You can then partition the drive using DOS's FDISK, and reformat the partition(s) for DOS using FORMAT.

Two other reliable solutions are the first two solutions mentioned above: Get an upgraded BIOS or buy a "smart" controller.

Deleting Unnecessary Files

One of the easiest ways to improve your hard disk's performance is to delete any unnecessary files. Though this sounds patently obvious, several ways that Windows accumulates unnecessary files are less than obvious. This section explains those areas.

If you've been working with Windows for a while, including times when your system has hung, you can usually recover some disk space by deleting all the leftover temporary files in Windows' temporary directory (usually \WINDOWS\TEMP). To avoid deleting a temporary file that is currently in use, you should clean out the directory only when you are not running Windows.

Some of the temporary files in \WINDOWS\TEMP are likely to be old application swap files and grabber files. These files begin with ~WOA and ~GRB. But depending on the circumstances when your system crashed, there may also be leftover system and application files—for example, files that begin with ~DD or ~VD. Because many of these files are hidden, you will have to use a program like the Norton Utilities of PCTools that can view hidden files and either change their attributes or delete them. In general, you should clean out your \WINDOWS\TEMP directory on a regular basis.

If you do not have a \WINDOWS\TEMP directory (or a directory named by the TEMP environment variable in your AUTOEXEC.BAT), Windows places its temporary files in your \WINDOWS directory. In this case, you should remove the temporary files from this directory.

Note: Windows has three files in its system directory (usually \WINDOWS\SYSTEM) that may look like temporary application swap files but are not. These are WINOLDAP.MOD, WINOA286.MOD, and WINOA386.MOD. Under no circumstances should you delete these files. (See Chapter 7 for an explanation of these files.)

If your system crashes in 386 enhanced mode, Windows leaves behind the temporary swap file WIN386.SWP. You can safely delete this file if Windows is not running. You should never, however, delete the files associated with Windows' permanent swap file, 386SPART.PAR and SPART.PAR. If you want to delete these files, use the SWAPFILE utility.

Running CHKDSK with the /F Switch

When a new file is created, DOS allocates clusters of hard disk sectors as it writes the file to disk. DOS relies on a chart called the File Allocation Table (FAT) located at the start of the disk to remember where it stored the file clusters. It also uses a special nondisplaying part of the disk's directory to point itself to the first cluster of the file. So, while the directory contains the address of the first cluster, the FAT contains a "chain" of addresses of all the other clusters in the file.

In the interest of performance, DOS buffers its changes to the directory before writing them to the drive. Only when a file is properly closed by an application is the file's directory entry recorded. If the system crashes in the meantime, the directory is not properly updated. When the resulting chain of allocated clusters does not have a matching directory entry, it is known as a "lost chain."

You can have DOS "fix" any lost chains by using the CHKDSK command (short for CHeck DiSK) with the /F switch. When you run CHKDSK /F, DOS converts any lost chains to visible files that you can examine and delete. The files that DOS creates are placed in the disk's root directory and are named FILE0001.CHK, FILE0002.CHK, and so on. If you've been using your hard disk for a while, you may be surprised by the amount of disk space you can pick up by using CHKDSK /F.

Here are some recommendations for using CHKDSK /F:

- *Never ever run CHKDSK /F from within Windows.* If you do, you run the risk of damaging any open files.

- You should always run CHKDSK /F before compacting your hard disk or changing its interleave. By giving your disk a clean bill of health with CHKDSK, your compacting will be more efficient, and you won't run into any trouble should you decide to use a program that changes the interleave by low-level formatting your disk on the fly.

- If your system crashes unexpectedly, you might want to try running CHKDSK /F to see if you can recover any partially written files.

Compacting Your Hard Disk

Compacting (or defragmenting) your hard disk is probably one of those things you know you're supposed to do but have never done. Compacting a hard disk simply means consolidating its files into contiguous clusters.

Compacting a hard disk can significantly improve its performance no matter what software you are running. But it's particularly helpful for Windows. If your drive is badly fragmented, you'll have performance problems with Windows for the following two reasons:

- **The SWAPFILE utility has trouble creating a permanent swap file**: If you want to use the SWAPFILE utility to create a permanent swapfile for 386 enhanced mode but your hard disk is badly fragmented, you may not be able to create one. Figures 11-2 and 11-3 show the messages that SWAPFILE displays when your hard disk is badly fragmented (see "Using a Permanent Swap File" earlier).

- **SMARTDrive track-level buffering performs poorly**: The SMARTDrive disk caching program reads data from your hard disk a track at a time. If a hard disk is badly fragmented, SMARTDrive's track-level buffering breaks down because the clusters in which a file resides are not contiguous. By compacting your hard disk, you can ensure that a file's clusters are contiguous and that SMARTDrive will operate at its best.

One way to compact your hard disk is to back it up onto floppies, reformat your drive, and restore the data from the floppies. Although this technique works fine, it's time consuming and demands a lot of manual dexterity on your part.

A better alternative is to use a third-party program that can compact your drive on the fly. Some examples are Bridgeway Publishing's FastTrax, Symantec's Norton Utilities, Fifth Generation System's Mace Utilities, Golden Bow's VOpt, and Central Point Software's PCTools. All of these programs usually take quite a while the first time you run them on a badly fragmented drive. After the first time, though, regular subsequent runs take very little time.

Whichever technique you use, you'll be amazed at how much you can improve Windows' performance. To keep Windows operating at its peak, you should compact your drive regularly.

Optimizing Your Disk Drive's Interleave

Besides compacting your hard disk, another way to improve its performance is to optimize its interleave. To understand the importance of an optimal interleave, it's helpful to review how a hard disk controller reads the sectors on a drive.

A hard disk controller can read only one sector at a time. Because the drive is rotating at such a high rate of speed (3600 RPM), the controller may have trouble reading the next sector unless it is delayed until the current one is completely processed. Yet, if the next sector's ID header has already spun past the read/write head before the controller is ready to search for it, the disk must make another revolution before the sector comes around again. If the sectors are numbered sequentially around the disk (1, 2, 3, and so on), it takes 17 full revolutions before an entire 17-sector track (a mere 8K of data) can be read.

To get around this problem, sectors are often interleaved. A typical interleave is 3:1 where the sectors are arranged around the track in the order 1, 7, 13, 2, 8, 14, 3, and so on, as shown in Figure 11-10. If the computer can finish reading sector 1 by the time indicated as X, then it will be ready to read sector 2 when it comes around, and the entire track can be read in just three revolutions. A 3:1 interleave is the standard interleave used by most MFM encoded drives.

Nevertheless, not all computers with MFM encoded drives are capable of processing sectors until the time marked Y in the figure. When this happens, the disk must spin another revolution before the second sector comes by again. In this case, you return to the suboptimal condition of requiring 17 full revolutions to read a single track. However, if you change the interleave from 3:1 to 4:1, where every fourth sector is read as it goes by, the entire track can be read in just four revolutions. This results in a 425-percent increase (17 revolutions / 4 revolutions) in disk drive performance by optimizing the sector interleave.

Many newer generation RLL and ESDI drives and controllers are capable of using a 1:1 interleave, requiring only a single revolution to read an entire track (see Figure 11-10). But just because your hard disk controller documentation says that your controller supports a 1:1 interleave, don't automatically assume that your drive is also set for the same interleave. In fact, many system manufacturers mistakenly format drives for a 3:1 interleave even though the controller will support a 1:1 interleave. By changing the disk drive's interleave to 1:1, you can get a 300-percent boost in hard disk performance, and have the drive and controller perform the way they were intended.

Likewise, we've found that almost all the MFM drives in our shop can support a 2:1 interleave rather than the standard 3:1. Changing the interleave has resulted in a 150-percent increase in disk drive throughput, even on our oldest AT clones.

Note: Optimizing your disk drive's interleave is important for maximizing SMARTDrive's performance on your system, because SMARTDrive reads data a track at a time into its memory cache. If the interleave is not optimal,

396 *Windows 3 Power Tools*

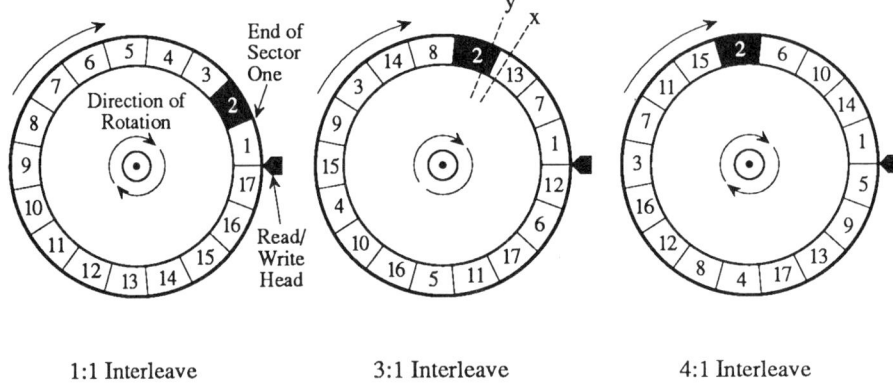

1:1 Interleave   3:1 Interleave   4:1 Interleave

Figure 11-10 Hard disk sector interleaving

SMARTDrive winds up waiting a lot longer than it should when reading data from your drive, reducing its benefit to your system (see "Using the SMART-Drive Disk-Caching Program").

Ways to Change the Interleave

There are two ways to change a hard disk's interleave. The first way is to use the fixed disk installation program that comes with your drive to low-level format the drive again with a new interleave. (For example, if you have a Seagate drive, you typically use Disk Manager from OnTrack.) The problem with this choice is that it requires all these steps:

- Backing up all your data onto tape or floppies.
- Low-level formatting your drive with a new interleave.
- Partitioning the drive with FDISK.
- High-level formatting each partition.
- Restoring all your data from tape or floppies.

And once you've done all these steps, you have no way of knowing whether you've chosen the optimal interleave.

A much better alternative is to use a program, like Spinrite II from Gibson Research, that will change your interleave for you. Spinrite II does a performance test on your drive and controller and determines the optimal interleave setting. It then changes the interleave by low-level formatting your drive on the fly, without destroying any of your data.

Besides changing your interleave, here are some of the other valuable services Spinrite II performs for your hard disk:

- Recovers many sectors that DOS previously diagnosed as unreadable and uncorrectable.
- Corrects low-level format aging by rescoring sector ID headers.

- Detects any new imperfections in the drive and relocates endangered data elsewhere.
- Corrects the drive alignment drift that naturally happens as a drive ages and its parts wear.

Spinrite has a few limitations. For example, it does not support drives that have more than 1024 tracks (neither does your BIOS), nor does it support some of the newer SCSI (Small Computer Systems Interface) and IDE (Integrated Drive Electronics) drives. It also takes quite a while to perform its most rigorous low-level formatting, several hours in most cases. But you can leave it on overnight.

None of these limitations amount to much. With all its benefits, no serious Windows user should be without SpinRite II.

When to Change Your Interleave

Microsoft recommends that the time to try changing your interleave is when you have compacted your hard disk and used SMARTDrive but your hard disk still responds slowly. The problem with this line of reasoning is that there is no way to tell that the disk is operating slowly if you don't know what its maximum speed is. The one thing to remember is that regardless of the age and speed of your hard disk, if you are using an improper interleave (and you probably are), the speed of your hard disk may be reduced by an average of 200 to 300 percent.

ADJUSTING THE HIMEM.SYS EXTENDED MEMORY MANAGER

The HIMEM.SYS extended memory manager must be present in your CONFIG.SYS file to start up Windows in standard or 386 enhanced mode. When you install Windows, Setup places a copy of HIMEM.SYS on the root directory of your first hard disk and adds a line like this to your CONFIG.SYS file:

```
DEVICE=C:\HIMEM.SYS
```

In most cases, you won't need to change this line. However, if HIMEM.SYS won't install, you may need to change the way it accesses extended memory.

The way that HIMEM.SYS accesses extended memory depends on your hardware. When you boot your computer, HIMEM.SYS displays a message like the following, which tells you the method that it is using to access extended memory:

```
Installed A20 handler number X.
```

where X is a number in the hardware list shown in Table 11-1.

If you cannot get HIMEM.SYS to work properly—that is, it issues the error message "Cannot install A20 line"—you can try another computer type by using the /M:X switch

Number	Name	Computer type
1	at	IBM AT or 100% compatible
2	ps2	IBM PS/2
3	ptlcascade	Phoenix Cascade BIOS
4	hpvectra	HP Vectra (A & A+)
5	att6300plus	AT&T 6300 Plus
6	acer1100	Acer 1100
7	toshib	Toshiba 1600 & 1200XE
8	wyse	Wyse 12.5 Mhz 286

Table 11-1 The Number Displayed by HIMEM.SYS

with HIMEM.SYS, where *X* is a number or name in Table 11-1. For example, if your computer is an Acer 1100, you can use either of the following lines in your CONFIG.SYS:

```
DEVICE=C:\HIMEM.SYS /M:6
DEVICE=C:\HIMEM.SYS /M:ACER1100
```

Either line tells HIMEM.SYS to use the method required by the Acer 1100 for accessing extended memory.

Caution: Use the /M switch with extreme care. If you use the wrong number or name with this switch (for example, you use the number for the PS/2 when your computer is an IBM AT or compatible), your File Allocation Table may be damaged, causing all the data on your drive to be lost. Before you try a switch, make sure you have a good backup of your hard drives.

HIMEM.SYS also accepts other optional switches on the DEVICE= line in your CONFIG.SYS, but they are rarely used. There is one, however, that may look inviting: /SHADOW:*ON/OFF*. This switch tells HIMEM.SYS to enable or disable shadow RAM. Some PCs copy ROM code into extended memory on startup to speed its operation—a process known as "shadowing" ROM in RAM. Although shadow RAM runs faster, it also eats up valuable memory that you might want to use for your applications. Of course, if you eliminate shadow RAM, your system will run slower because it must read the ROM code from the slower ROM chips.

Note: If your system has shadow RAM and the /SHADOW:OFF switch looks promising as a means of disabling it, don't get too excited. It rarely works, except on

COMPAQ 386 machines. If you try the /SHADOW:OFF switch with HIMEM.SYS and it doesn't work, it displays the message "Shadow RAM disable not available on this system."

If your PC has less than 384K of extended memory, HIMEM.SYS tries to disable shadow RAM automatically so that Windows can use the additional memory. You can prevent this behavior and keep the ROM code running from RAM with the following line:

```
DEVICE=C:\HIMEM.SYS /SHADOW:ON
```

Again, this line usually works only on COMPAQ 386 machines.

USING THE SMARTDRIVE DISK-CACHING PROGRAM

SMARTDrive is a disk-caching program that is specially tailored for Windows 3. And because it works closely with Windows, it can give you a significant increase in speed without taking memory away from Windows.

The purpose of SMARTDrive, and any other disk cache for that matter, is to accelerate data retrieval from your hard disk. SMARTDrive speeds system performance by anticipating what data Windows or a DOS application will need next.

SMARTDrive's disk cache operates under the principle that what Windows or a DOS application is likely to reach for next will be in the same neighborhood as what it reached for previously. By loading all the data within, let us say, a 256K vicinity from disk into a high-speed RAM cache, Windows and DOS applications run faster because they are performing disk I/O in and out of SMARTDrive's cache rather than directly with the much slower disk drive.

Note: Whenever Windows or a DOS application makes a request to copy new or modified information to your hard disk, SMARTDrive carries out that request immediately. Therefore, there is no danger of losing information if the power goes out.

If you're wondering why Windows needs a disk cache in the first place, you can easily satisfy your curiosity by temporarily disabling SMARTDrive's DEVICE= line in your CONFIG.SYS file and starting up Windows. When you hear your hard disk whir and thump like an old sewing machine and see Windows slow to a crawl, you'll know the reason—SMARTDrive makes Windows run a lot faster. What's more, SMARTDrive is especially helpful when you are running several DOS applications at once. As a general rule, if your system has at least 512K of extended memory or 256K of expanded memory, you will benefit by using SMARTDrive.

When you install Windows, Setup automatically installs SMARTDrive on your system. However, the settings that are provided are not always optimal for your system or for the applications you may run. This next section should help you adjust SMARTDrive's settings to your way of working with Windows.

How SMARTDrive Works

When you install Windows, Setup copies SMARTDRV.SYS to your \WINDOWS directory and places a line like this in your CONFIG.SYS file:

```
DEVICE=C:\WINDOWS\SMARTDRV.SYS 2048 1024
```

The first parameter following SMARTDRV.SYS is SMARTDrive's *normal size* (in kilobytes), which in this example is 2048K (2 megabytes). You can set the normal cache size anywhere from 128K to 8192K (8 megabytes). The second parameter is its *minimum size*, which is 1 megabyte here. You can also include a third parameter not shown here, /A; this parameter lets you tell SMARTDrive to use expanded memory for its cache. (Without the /A switch, Windows uses extended memory by default.)

When you boot your system, SMARTDrive makes a call to the extended memory manager (typically HIMEM.SYS), which allocates the amount of memory you've indicated by the normal size parameter. (If you use the /A parameter, a call is made to the expanded memory manager instead.) For example, if you have the DEVICE= line shown above, SMARTDrive's size is immediately set to 2048K, the normal size. If you do not include a normal size parameter, SMARTDrive's cache is set to 256K. The SMARTDrive cache always operates at the normal size when you are not running Windows.

What happens after you load Windows depends on the operating mode, as follows:

- If you start Windows in standard or 386 enhanced mode and the cache is using extended memory, Windows immediately reduces the size of the cache to the minimum size, making more room available to Windows. In the current example, the cache instantly shrinks to 1024K. If you do not provide a minimum size parameter, Windows reduces the cache to 0K, meaning that it uses no cache. (When Windows is running in standard and 386 enhanced mode, it cannot reduce the size of an expanded-memory cache.) Therefore, using a minimum-size parameter is always a good idea, since SMARTDrive is otherwise disabled in 386 enhanced mode.

- If the cache is using expanded memory and you start Windows in real mode, Windows reduces the cache to the minimum size, but not right away. Instead, it reduces the cache as it needs to use the expanded memory. (When Windows is running in real mode, it cannot reduce the size of an extended-memory cache.)

When you leave Windows, the cache always returns to the normal size.

SMARTDrive performs its magic by reading entire disk tracks into its cache. To do this, it must automatically determine your drive's track size and adjust its cache accordingly. For example, suppose you have a standard MFM-encoded drive (17 sectors per track) and the DEVICE= line shown previously that sets SMARTDrive's cache in extended memory, sets the normal cache size to 2048, and sets the minimum cache size to 1024K. When your system boots, you'll see a message like this on your screen:

```
Microsoft SMARTDrive Disk Cache version 3.03
     Cache size: 2048K in Extended Memory
     Room for 240 tracks of 17 sectors each
     Minimum cache size will be 1024K
```

This message tells you how SMARTDrive actually sizes its cache, given 2048K as the target for the normal cache setting. SMARTDrive begins by determining the track size, which in this case is 8704 bytes (17 sectors per track * 512 bytes per sector). It then divides the track size into the normal cache size and rounds down. In this case, SMARTDrive determines that it can read 240 tracks into its cache. Therefore, it sets its normal cache size to 2040K, not 2048K.

As another example, suppose you use the same DEVICE= line with an RLL-encoded drive (26 sectors per track). In this case, SMARTDrive's message will look something like this:

```
Microsoft SMARTDrive Disk Cache version 3.03
     Cache size: 2048K in Extended Memory
     Room for 157 tracks of 26 sectors each
     Minimum cache size will be 1024K
```

When there are 26 sectors per track, SMARTDrive determines that it can read 157 tracks into its cache, for a total of 2041K of memory.

Carrying this all just a bit further, suppose you have two drives on your system, one with a track size of 15K and the other with a track size of 10K. In this case, SMARTDrive uses the larger track size to determine the cache size. If you have set the normal cache parameter to 512K, Windows determines that it can fit 34 tracks into its cache. From that point on, Windows will cache only 34 tracks, even though it could actually fit as many as 51 of the smaller 10K tracks in its cache.

How to Set SMARTDrive

The proper way to set SMARTDrive depends on several factors, including your system configuration, the Windows operating mode, and the type of applications you are running. Because of all these variables, there is no single "best" way to set SMARTDrive. You'll have to experiment to determine what's best for your system.

Nevertheless, here are some general guidelines to start with:

- If you typically run Windows in standard or 386 enhanced mode, you should set SMARTDrive to run in extended memory (the default).

- If you run Windows mostly in real mode and your system has expanded memory, you should set SMARTDrive to run in expanded memory (use the /A switch).

- You should set SMARTDrive's normal cache size as high as possible, up to 2 megabytes. (Of course, the larger the cache, the more memory SMARTDrive uses.) Then, if you are having trouble running applications, you should gradually reduce the normal cache setting.

Memory Installed	Memory Available *	Normal cache Setting	Minimum cache Setting
1024K	1024K	320	0
2048K	1664K	768	0
4096K	3712K	2048	1024
6144K	5760K	2048	1024
8064K	8064K	2048	1024

Table 11-2 SMARTDrive Settings for Different Memory Configurations

- You should set the minimum cache size as high as possible, up to 1 megabyte. If you set the minimum cache size above 1 megabyte, you may make it harder for Windows to manage memory. On the other hand, setting the minimum cache size below 256K severely hampers SMARTDrive's performance—it cannot cache enough tracks to be useful.

- The most efficient value for SMARTDrive's normal cache size is 2 megabytes and for its minimum cache size is 1 megabyte. As you increase the settings over these target sizes, the improvements in SMARTDrive's performance are insignificant.

- SMARTDrive typically uses about 17K of conventional memory for a 256K cache. The larger you set the cache size, the more conventional memory SMARTDrive uses (about 500 additional bytes per megabyte of cache).

Table 11-2 shows some examples of the settings that are automatically assigned to SMARTDrive when you first install Windows. For example, if you have a 1-megabyte system, SMARTDrive is automatically assigned a normal cache size of 320K and a minimum cache size of 0K (no cache). At the other end of the scale, if your system has 8 megabytes of memory, the normal cache size is set to 2048K and the minimum cache size to 1024K.

Note: The difference between the "Memory Installed" and "Memory Available" columns in Table 11-2 is due to shadow RAM. If your system does not have shadow RAM, the memory available will be higher and the settings automatically provided for SMARTDrive may also be higher.

At the extreme ends of the memory scale, these standard settings are fine. However, if your system has 2 megabytes of memory and you use Windows to multitask DOS applications in 386 enhanced mode, a minimum cache size of 0 (essentially no cache) may be inappropriate. In this case, you may want to try setting the minimum cache size to 256. As another example, notice that the settings for a 4-megabyte system are the same as those for an 8-megabyte system. In this case, you may find that the cache occupies too much memory, especially when you are not running Windows. If your system has this amount of memory and you are having difficulty multitasking DOS applications, you should consider decreasing both cache settings.

Note: If you are using EMM386.SYS to emulate expanded memory, it is not a good idea to put SMARTDrive's cache into expanded memory. Although it is possible to run SMARTDrive's cache out of EMM386's memory, it is counterproductive because you lose a lot of speed. In general, you should use physical memory for SMARTDrive if you want maximum speed.

Tip: Disabling other caching programs improves performance

SMARTDrive is specially designed to work hand in hand with Windows, but it does not work well with other disk caching programs. For example, Quattro Pro will create its own cache with up to 512K of extended memory if you include a "/X" on the command line when you start the program. Unfortunately, if Quattro Pro uses its own cache when running under Windows and SMARTDrive is also installed, Quattro Pro runs unbearably slowly. You can correct this problem by eliminating Quattro Pro's cache. The net result is that to improve Windows' overall performance, you must give up the slight performance edge that a DOS application might otherwise gain by using its own specially tailored cache in standard DOS.

Tip: Windows reports the size of SMARTDrive in real mode

If you set up SMARTDrive to run in expanded memory and run Windows in real mode, Windows reports the amount of memory available in the cache when you select the About command from Program Manager's or File Manager's Help menu, as shown in Figure 11-11.

Improving SMARTDrive's Performance

Besides experimenting with different cache size settings, here are some ways to improve SMARTDrive's performance on your system:

- **Compact your hard disk**: If your disk is badly fragmented, the clusters in which a file resides may be scattered all over your hard disk. As a result, when SMART-Drive loads consecutive tracks, those tracks may not contain the needed data. Compacting your disk on a regular basis guarantees that your files will be located in contiguous clusters, and that SMARTDrive will operate at its best.

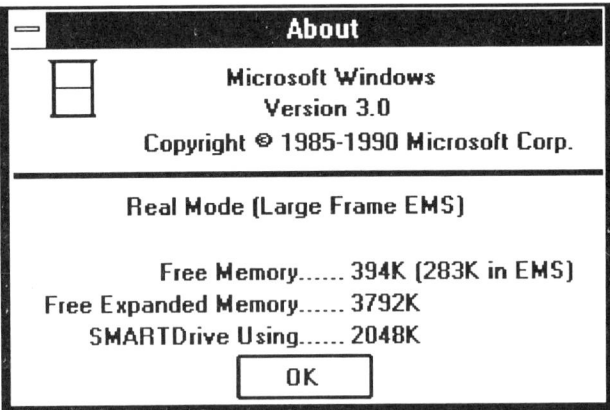

Figure 11-11 The size of the expanded memory cache in real mode

- **Optimize your disk drive's interleave**: Because SMARTDrive reads neighboring tracks into its memory cache, if the interleave is not optimal, SMARTDrive winds up waiting a lot longer than it should when reading data from your drive. This reduces its overall benefit to your system.

- **Set BUFFERS=10 in your CONFIG.SYS:** When you're using SMARTDrive, setting your buffers to more than 10 consumes memory without increasing your system's speed.

SETTING UP A RAM DISK WITH RAMDRIVE

As every power user knows, a RAM disk lets you imitate a disk drive in memory. RAM disks are much faster than even the fastest disk drives because there are no moving parts. In essence, you treat a RAM disk exactly as you would a disk drive. The only difference is that if your system crashes or the power goes out, the RAM disk loses its contents.

RAMDrive is a RAM disk that comes with Windows 3 and can operate in expanded or extended memory. When you install Windows, Setup copies RAMDRIVE.SYS to your \WINDOWS directory. You can set up RAMDrive to run on your system by placing a line like this in your CONFIG.SYS file:

```
DEVICE=C:\WINDOWS\RAMDRIVE.SYS 1024 /E
```

The first parameter sets the RAM disk's size to 1024K, and the second parameter (/E) causes RAMDrive to locate the RAM disk in extended memory.

When you boot your system, the RAM disk is assigned to the next available drive in your system. For example, if your system has physical drives C and D, the RAM disk is automatically assigned to drive E.

SMARTDrive provides many of the same benefits as RAMDrive, but operates much faster. Therefore, there are only a few cases where RAMDrive can be helpful.

- If you are running DOS applications in real mode, you may want to speed up the rate at which Windows switches back and forth between them. (See the earlier section, "Improving Windows' Use of Application Swap Files" for an explanation.)
- If you have a diskless workstation with plenty of memory but without a hard disk, you should create a RAM disk and assign it as much memory as possible.
- When an application reads and writes many small temporary files while it is running, RAMDrive may provide a greater speed advantage than SMARTDrive. For example, many applications create several temporary files and place them in Windows' temporary directory. When this is the case, you should set up a RAM disk of about 256K and set the TEMP environment variable to the RAM disk by using statements like this in your AUTOEXEC.BAT file:

```
MD E:\TEMP
SET TEMP = E:\TEMP
```

- If you start certain applications frequently, you might want to load them from a RAM disk rather than from the disk drive. By starting an application from a RAM disk, you can usually load it about three times faster. For example, to load Excel from a RAM disk, you would place a line like this in your AUTOEXEC.BAT file:

```
COPY C:\EXCEL\EXCEL.EXE E:\
```

This line copies Excel to your RAM disk (E:). You can then run Excel from drive E from within Windows.

The RAMDrive command line takes this form:

```
DEVICE=C:\WINDOWS\RAMDRIVE.SYS DiskSize SectorSize
    NumEntries /E /A
```

Here's an explanation of the parameters:

- *DiskSize*: This is the size of the RAM disk in kilobytes. If you don't include this parameter, RAMDrive creates a 64K RAM disk. The range is from 16 to 4096.
- *SectorSize*: This parameter lets you set the sector size for the RAM disk in bytes. You can use 128, 256, 512, or 1024. If you omit this value, RAMDrive uses a sector size of 512 bytes.
- *NumEntries*: Use this parameter to limit the number of directory entries (files and directories) you'll allow in the RAM disk's root directory. The range is from 2 to 1024. If you do not include this parameter, RAMDrive allows 64 entries.
- /E: Creates the RAM disk in extended memory.
- /A: Creates the RAM disk in expanded memory.

For example, the following command line creates a RAM disk in expanded memory, sets its size to 1024K, sets the sector size to 512 bytes, and limits the number of directory entries to 3:

```
DEVICE=C:\WINDOWS\RAMDRIVE.SYS 1024 512 3 /A
```

As you set up a RAM disk with RAMDrive, here are a few things to keep in mind:

- For RAMDRIVE.SYS to use extended memory, you must make sure to place RAMDrive's DEVICE= line after the line for the extended memory manager (typically, HIMEM.SYS); otherwise, RAMDrive will use conventional memory, if there's enough available. Likewise, if you are using RAMDrive in expanded memory, you must place it after the line for the expanded memory manager.

- If you omit both the /E and /A switch, RAMDrive will use conventional memory, which severely hampers Windows' performance.

- If you are using EMM386 to emulate expanded memory, don't use RAMDrive in EMM386's memory. If you do, you'll find that it runs quite slowly. In general, you should use physical memory for RAMDrive if you want reasonable speed.

Although you can use other RAM disks, none of them is specially tailored to work with Windows as well as RAMDrive. In fact, when you install Windows, Setup eliminates any RAM disks it knows about from your CONFIG.SYS file. If you are wondering what RAM disks Setup removes, check the SETUP.INF file in the \WINDOWS\SETUP directory.

USING THE TEMP ENVIRONMENT VARIABLE

When you install Windows on your system, Setup automatically places a line like this in your AUTOEXEC.BAT file:

```
SET TEMP=C:\WINDOWS\TEMP
```

This line uses the DOS SET command to set the TEMP environment variable to the C:\WINDOWS\TEMP directory.

Windows uses the directory named by the TEMP variable for locating temporary application swap files in real or standard mode. In addition, many applications themselves (particularly Microsoft applications) use the TEMP variable for locating temporary files.

If you want to maximize your system for speed, you might want to set the TEMP environment variable to a RAM disk, because it's much faster to read from memory than from a hard disk. Here are the steps for setting the TEMP variable to a 1-megabyte RAM disk in extended memory:

1. Modify your CONFIG.SYS file to include the following line, being careful to place this line after the line for HIMEM.SYS:

```
DEVICE=C:\WINDOWS\RAMDRIVE.SYS 1024 /E
```

When this line is executed, RAMDrive will create a RAM disk on the next available drive.

2. Assuming the RAM disk is assigned to drive F:, place the following lines in your AUTOEXEC.BAT file:

```
MD F:\TEMP
SET TEMP=F:\TEMP
```

These lines should replace the line that sets the TEMP environment variable to the C:\WINDOWS\TEMP directory.

USING THE EMM386 EXPANDED MEMORY EMULATOR

An *expanded memory emulator* is a utility that uses extended memory to simulate expanded memory. EMM386.SYS is an expanded memory emulator that comes with Windows 3. (When you install Windows, Setup copies EMM386.SYS to your \WINDOWS directory.) If you have a 80386- or 80486-based system with sufficient extended memory, you can convert some of that extended memory to expanded memory using EMM386.

The time to use EMM386 is when you are running Windows in real mode, or when you need expanded memory and you are not running Windows. In real mode, Windows makes extensive use of expanded memory when it's available on your system. It uses this memory for managing Windows applications and also makes it available to DOS applications.

On the other hand, if you are running Windows in standard or 386 enhanced mode, you do not need or want to install EMM386. In 386 enhanced mode, Windows can simulate expanded memory on its own without the help of an EMS emulator. In addition, when you run Windows in 386 enhanced mode or standard mode, if EMM386 is present, Windows turns it off. (Windows can turn off EMM386 even if expanded memory is being used at the time.) But even though Windows can turn off EMM386 in either mode, it cannot use the memory that EMM386 occupies. In this case, EMM386 takes up valuable memory without providing any benefit whatsoever.

Here are some things to remember if you use EMM386:

- Some 386 expanded memory managers, such as QEMM-386, provide the capability to load DOS device drivers into free areas of the 384K reserved I/O address space. However, EMM386.SYS does not provide this capability. (Fortunately, the new version of EMM386 that comes with DOS version 5.0, EMM386.EXE, does provide this capability.)

- You cannot use the Windows version of EMM386 to provide expanded memory to DOS applications when you are running Windows in standard mode. To provide expanded memory to DOS applications in this mode, you must supply it through an expanded memory board or by using a more sophisticated expanded memory manager like QEMM-386 that is capable of this feat.

Installing EMM386

To install EMM386, you place a line like this in your CONFIG.SYS file:

```
DEVICE=C:\WINDOWS\EMM386.SYS 4096
```

This line tells EMM386 to use 4096K (4 megabytes) of memory. When entering the number of kilobytes of memory you want EMM386 to use, you can specify a value from 16 to 32768. (EMM386 rounds down to the nearest multiple of 16.)

When you boot your system using this line, you see the following messages:

```
MICROSOFT Expanded Memory Manager 386 Version 4.10.0419
(C) Copyright Microsoft Corporation 1986, 1989, 1990

EMM386 successfully installed.

Available expanded memory . . . . . . . .  4096 KB
LIM/EMS version . . . . . . . . . . . . .  4.0
Total expanded memory pages . . . . . . .  280
Available expanded memory pages . . . . .  256
Total handles . . . . . . . . . . . . . .  64
Active handles. . . . . . . . . . . . . .  1
Page frame segment. . . . . . . . . . . .  D000 H
```

Here's an explanation of several of the messages:

- **Total expanded memory pages**: This is the number of 16K pages of memory that EMM386.SYS identifies as capable of being mapped. This area includes the 384K of reserved I/O address space. In this case, EMM386 recognizes a total of 4480K (280*16K) of expanded memory.

- **Available expanded memory pages**: This is the number of 16K pages that EMM386 determines are not currently being used. Because EMM386 counts the reserved memory area as being "used," this accounts for the discrepancy between the "Total expanded memory pages" and "Available expanded memory pages" settings. In this example, there is 4096K (256*16K) of expanded memory available.

- **Total handles**: This is the number of handles that EMM386 supports. This number affects EMM386's ability to honor requests for expanded memory.

- **Active handles:** This is the number of handles that have already been allocated.

- **Page frame segment**: This is the address in the reserved memory area that is assigned to the 64K expanded memory page frame.

Command-Line Options

EMM386 has several command-line options that you can use to control how it uses memory. Here are some of the more commonly used ones:

- **FRAME=***address*: This option lets you control the location of the 64K page frame. For example, to place the page frame at C000:0000H, you would use FRAME=C000 on the command line.

- **x=***addressrange*: Use this option to prevent EMM386 from using a particular range of addresses. For example, to prevent it from using the high memory area (HMA), FFFFH–10FFEFH, you would include x=FFFF-10FFEF on the command line.

- **l=***minXMS*: This option sets a minimum threshold in kilobytes for the amount of extended memory that must be available after EMM386 loads. For example, to make sure that 1 megabyte of extended memory is still available after EMM386 loads, you would include l=1024 on the command line.

THE EGA.SYS DEVICE DRIVER

EGA.SYS is a special device driver that Windows uses in real or standard mode to preserve the mode of EGA video cards when you are running DOS applications, such as Microsoft Word. It allows custom EGA palettes to be saved by maintaining an exact copy of the contents of your system's video control registers.

If Setup determines that you have an EGA monitor, it automatically installs a copy of EGA.SYS on your \WINDOWS directory. It also places a line like this in your CONFIG.SYS file:

```
DEVICE=C:\WINDOWS\EGA.SYS
```

Many power users remove this line because EGA.SYS is not necessary for their unique mix of DOS applications (their DOS applications do not create custom EGA palettes), or they always run Windows in 386 enhanced mode. You can save about 2K of conventional memory by eliminating EGA.SYS. However, you'll have to do some testing with your DOS applications to be sure that you can get by without it. If you find that you cannot switch away from a DOS application, it's likely that you need EGA.SYS.

386 ENHANCED MODE PERFORMANCE CHECK LIST

The following recommendations should help you maximize Windows' performance in 386 enhanced mode. Some of these suggestions also apply to real and standard mode.

1. **Create a permanent swap file.** Using a permanent swap file instead of a temporary swap file results in a tangible improvement in speed (see "Using a Permanent Swap File").

2. **Optimize SMARTDrive's settings.** The settings that are automatically provided for SMARTDrive may not be appropriate for your unique mix of applications, especially if you multitask DOS applications. Try experimenting with different minimum cache size settings (see "Improving SMARTDrive's Performance").

3. **Use BUFFERS=10 in your CONFIG.SYS file.** If you are using SMARTDrive, using more buffers than 10 actually decreases your system's efficiency.

4. **Keep your hard disk compacted.** See "Compacting Your Hard Disk."

5. **Use the proper disk drive interleave.** Use a program such as Gibson Research's Spinrite II to make sure you are using the optimal interleave. You may be able to improve your disk drive performance by as much as 300 percent (see "Optimizing Your Disk Drive's Interleave").

6. **Turn off the Monitor Ports options.** If you're running DOS applications, you can usually boost their speed by turning off all the Monitor Ports options in the applications' PIFs. By default, the High Graphics option is usually on, but it's rarely needed (see Chapter 10, "Using Non-Windows Applications," for more).

7. **Use a lower-resolution display driver.** If you have a high-resolution VGA card, such as the 8514/a or Video Seven, you can usually improve your system's speed by using a lower-resolution graphics driver, for example, the standard VGA driver. Although you lose the higher resolution and greater number of colors provided by the other drivers, you'll get quicker display performance.

8. **Turn off the ReservePageFrame= option.** If you don't use expanded memory for any of your DOS applications, you can gain some additional memory in each virtual machine by setting ReservePageFrame=no in the [386Enh] section of your SYSTEM.INI file. (See Chapter 7, "Windows Memory Management," for more on this subject.)

SUMMARY

In many ways Windows is like a finely tuned race car. For a race car to reach its maximum speed on any given track, all of its components have to be set just right; for example, its exhaust must be meticulously adjusted, its gear ratio properly set for both the turns and the straightaways, and its tires carefully chosen for the conditions.

In the same way, you must set up your system just right if you want Windows to reach its optimum performance. For example, you must configure your memory and DOS resources properly. You must also optimize your disk drive by compacting it on a regular basis and by optimizing its interleave. Other ways to improve Windows' performance include setting up a permanent swap file for 386 enhanced mode, adjusting the size of SMARTDrive's disk cache, and using EMM386 if you need expanded memory in real mode.

Having read this chapter, you now know all the tools at your disposal for improving Windows' performance. In the next chapter, you'll learn how to adjust Windows' performance even further by customizing your SYSTEM.INI and WIN.INI files.

12

Customizing Your .INI Files

There are five initialization (.INI) files in Windows 3: CONTROL.INI, PROGMAN.INI, WINFILE.INI, WIN.INI, and SYSTEM.INI. The first three contain the initialization settings for the Control Panel, Program Manager, and File Manager, respectively. Although you can change the contents of these three files by loading them into Notepad and editing them, it is actually far easier to control their settings through their respective programs.

The WIN.INI and SYSTEM.INI are a different matter, however. These files contain settings that control almost all aspects of the Windows environment, many of which you can only change by editing these files directly. Here's a summary of the type of settings each file controls:

- WIN.INI—In previous releases of Windows, there was no SYSTEM.INI file, and WIN.INI contained all the configuration settings. In Windows 3, however, WIN.INI contains almost all of the settings that let you personalize Windows. In addition, Windows applications often store their own settings in the WIN.INI file.

- SYSTEM.INI—This file contains mostly hardware-related settings. For example, there are settings for controlling the display, keyboard, mouse, and network drivers. There are also settings for controlling the system, OEM, and Windows 2.x application fonts.

WIN.INI and SYSTEM.INI are the focus of this chapter. Rather than cover all the settings that these two files offer, however, we've chosen only the most commonly used settings.

> **Tip: The WININI.TXT and SYSINI.TXT files**
>
> When you install Windows on your system, it copies several text files to your \WINDOWS directory that provide documentation on WIN.INI and SYSTEM.INI. The files that contain WIN.INI documentation are WININI.TXT and WININI2.TXT, and those that contain SYSTEM.INI documentation are SYSINI.TXT, SYSINI2.TXT, and SYSINI3.TXT. These files provide the most extensive list of WIN.INI and SYSTEM.INI settings found anywhere.

EDITING WIN.INI AND SYSTEM.INI

Both WIN.INI and SYSTEM.INI are ASCII files, so you can edit them with any text editor, such as Notepad. In fact, Windows 3 ships with a preestablished file association for .INI files so that when you open an .INI file, Windows automatically starts up Notepad.

Windows 3 also includes the System Configuration Editor (SYSEDIT.EXE), a little-known utility specially designed for editing your WIN.INI, SYSTEM.INI, AUTOEXEC.BAT, and CONFIG.SYS files. SYSEDIT resides in the \WINDOWS\SYSTEM directory, and most power users set up an icon for it in Program Manager. Figure 12-1 shows the SYSEDIT window.

> **Tip: SYSEDIT automatically saves backup copies**
>
> When you change a file with SYSEDIT, it automatically saves the previous copy of the file with an .SYD extension. That way, you can always recover the previous version if you need to.

THE STRUCTURE OF WIN.INI AND SYSTEM.INI

WIN.INI and SYSTEM.INI share the same overall structure. They are both divided into sections that use the following format:

```
[section name]
keyword=value
```

where *[section name]* is the name of the section (the brackets ([]) are required), and the *keyword=value* statement assigns a value to a given setting.

Customizing Your .INI Files 413

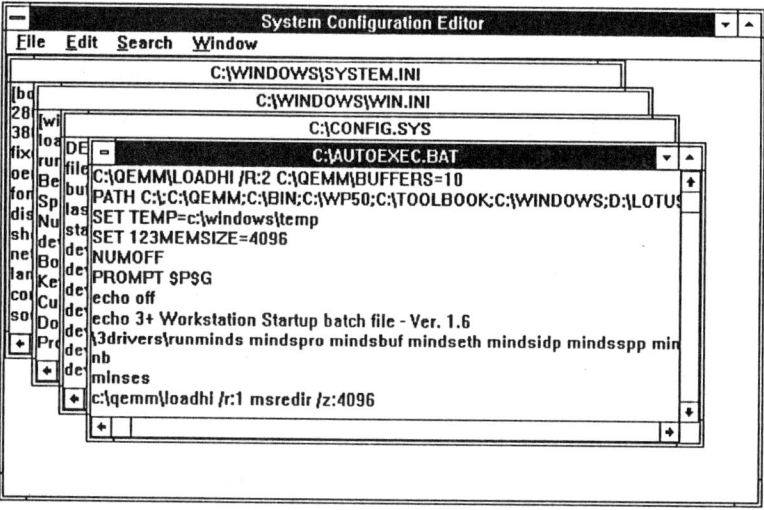

Figure 12-1 The System Configuration Editor (SYSEDIT.EXE)

> **Tip:** *Placing comments in your WIN.INI and SYSTEM.INI files*
>
> You can place comments in your initialization files by starting a line with a semi-colon. You may find this helpful if you make a change to an .INI file and want to keep a record of the rationale for the change.

WIN.INI

As mentioned, the WIN.INI file contains the settings that let you personalize Windows. WIN.INI is organized according to the following sections:

- [windows]—Affects a variety of elements in your Windows environment, for example, the border width of windows and the cursor blink rate.

- [desktop]—Stores settings that control the appearance of the screen background (desktop), like the current wallpaper setting and the spacing between icons. Stores all the settings you can modify through the Desktop icon in the Control Panel.

- [extensions]—Stores all the settings that link groups of documents with an application so that when you open a document, Windows automatically starts the application.

- [intl]—Stores country-specific settings.

- [ports]—Lists all available output ports, and, in the case of COM ports, their current port settings.

- [fonts]—Lists the screen font files that are loaded by Windows.
- [PrinterPorts]—Lists active and inactive printers that Windows can access.
- [devices]—This section lists the active printers and provides compatibility with Windows 2.x applications.
- [colors]—Lists all the color settings you can control through the Color icon in the Control Panel, and several more.

The ordering of these sections within WIN.INI is not important, nor is the ordering of the settings within a section. However, you must be careful to place settings in their preassigned sections. If you don't, Windows will not be able to find them, and you'll wonder why it isn't behaving properly.

Most Windows applications also store their own initialization settings in the WIN.INI file. These sections usually appear near the end of the file.

The [Windows] Section

The [windows] section of WIN.INI contains settings that affect your general Windows environment. Most of the settings can be controlled by other programs. However, some of them, like starting an application automatically as an icon, can only be controlled by editing your WIN.INI file.

Starting Applications as Icons

If you want to start up an application automatically as an icon when you start Windows, you can include its name in the load= line in the [windows] section. For example, this line automatically loads Clock, Clipboard, and COMMAND.COM when you start Windows:

```
load=clock clipbrd c:\command.com
```

You can also rely on a file association to load an application. For example, the following line automatically loads the document PROJECT.WRI into Windows Write on startup:

```
load=project.wri
```

Starting Applications as Windows

To have an application automatically execute as a window when you start Windows, include its name on the run= line in the [windows] section. For example, the following line runs Clock and Clipboard when you start Windows:

```
run=clock,clipboard
```

Note: Be aware that when you include an application's name in the run= line, Program Manager is automatically minimized when you start Windows.

Setting the Warning Beep

The Beep= line lets you control whether Windows sounds a beep when you press the wrong key or select the wrong option. When you first install Windows, Beep is active. You can deactivate it with the following line:

```
Beep=no
```

You can also control this setting through the Sound icon in the Control Panel.

Printing With or Without Print Manager

Normally, when you print output to the printer, it is sent through Print Manager. You can control whether Windows uses Print Manager with the Spooler= line in the [windows] section. For example, you can deactivate Print Manager with the following line:

```
Spooler=no
```

You can also control this setting through the Printers icon in the Control Panel.

Controlling the Name Used for a Null Port

When you select the Printers icon in the Control Panel, and then select the Configure button, Windows displays a dialog box listing all the available ports. At the top of this list is the null port, which is usually assigned the name "None." You can assign a different name to the null port by changing the NullPort= line in the [windows] section. For example, the following line changes the null port name to "No port":

```
NullPort=No port
```

Establishing the Default Printer

The device= line in the [windows] section controls what device Windows recognizes as the default printer. This line takes the form

```
device=<output-device-name>,<device-driver>,<port-connection>
```

where the elements of the line are defined as follows:

- <output-device-name>—One of the device names in the [devices] section of the WIN.INI.
- <device-driver>—The filename (without the extension) of the device-driver file.
- <port-connection>—The name of a port listed in the [ports] section of the WIN.INI.

For example, the following line establishes "PCL / HP Laserjet" as the default printer, uses HPPCL.DRV as the printer's device-driver file, and sets up LPT1: as the port Windows will print to:

```
device=PCL / HP LaserJet,HPPCL,LPT1:
```

Suppose you also have an Epson LQ-1500 installed on your system, and you want to make it the default printer instead of the HP. You might change the device= line as follows:

```
device=Epson 24 pin,EPSON24,LPT2:
```

This line establishes EPSON24.DRV as the printer's device driver and indicates that the printer is connected to LPT2:.

You can also control this setting through the Printers icon in the Control Panel. To make a printer the default printer, verify that its status is active and then double-click on its name in the Installed Printers list (you can also press ALT+D). When you select OK, Control Panel updates the device= line in WIN.INI for the new setting.

Changing the Width of the Window Border

By default, Windows uses a border width of 3 for all the windows on the desktop except those that have a fixed size. You can change the width of the borders with the BorderWidth= setting in the [windows] section. For example, the following setting assigns a width of 5:

```
BorderWidth=5
```

The range of values you can use is 1 (thinnest) to 49 (broadest).

You can also control this setting through the Desktop icon in the Control Panel.

Keyboard Speed

The KeyboardSpeed= setting in the [windows] section lets you control how quickly a key repeats when you hold it down. For example, the following setting sets the keyboard speed to the fastest setting, 31 (the default):

```
KeyboardSpeed=31
```

This setting affects both Windows and non-Windows applications when running Windows, but it does not work for all keyboards.

You can also control this setting from the Keyboard icon in the Control Panel.

Cursor Blink Rate

Using the CursorBlinkRate= setting in the [windows] section, you can control the number of milliseconds that elapse between blinks of the cursor. For example, the following line sets the rate to 530 milliseconds (the default):

```
CursorBlinkRate=530
```

You can also control this setting from the Desktop icon in the Control Panel.

Changing the Sensitivity Level of the Mouse

Normally, when you move the mouse quickly, the mouse pointer moves faster across the screen than when you move the mouse slowly. In other words, a quick jerk of the mouse may move the mouse pointer completely across the screen. By contrast, a slow, deliberate movement of the mouse may move the pointer only a couple of inches.

When you use the Mouse icon from the Control Panel and change the mouse tracking speed from the default, Windows places three settings in the [windows] section of your WIN.INI file: MouseSpeed=, MouseThreshold1=, and MouseThreshold2=. These settings are all interrelated and control how far the mouse pointer travels when you speed up your movement of the mouse. Here is an explanation of these settings:

- MouseSpeed= —This setting controls the relationship between mouse movement and mouse-pointer movement. If MouseSpeed=0, Windows does not accelerate mouse-pointer movement when you change the rate at which you move the mouse. If MouseSpeed=1, Windows moves the mouse pointer at twice the normal speed when mouse movement exceeds the value of MouseThreshold1. If MouseSpeed=2, Windows moves the mouse pointer at twice the normal speed when mouse movement exceeds the value of MouseThreshold1, and at four times the normal speed when mouse movement exceeds the value of MouseThreshold2.

- MouseThreshold1= —A mouse issues hardware interrupts at a specified rate. For example, the Microsoft Mouse issues interrupts at the rate of 30 Hz, or 30 interrupts per second. The MouseThreshold1 setting controls the maximum number of pixels that the mouse can move between mouse hardware interrupts before Windows speeds up mouse-pointer movement. If mouse movement exceeds this setting and MouseSpeed is greater than zero, Windows moves the mouse pointer at twice the normal speed.

- MouseThreshold2= —If mouse movement exceeds this setting and MouseSpeed=2, Windows moves the mouse pointer at four times the normal speed.

For example, suppose you have the following settings in your WIN.INI file:

```
MouseSpeed=2
MouseThreshold1=4
MouseThreshold2=12
```

Here's how you would interpret them: When you move the mouse pointer at a rate of less than or equal to 4 pixels per 1/30th of a second, mouse-pointer movement does not accelerate. On the other hand, if you move the mouse pointer at more than 4 pixels per 1/30th of a second, mouse-pointer movement accelerates to twice the normal rate. If you move the mouse pointer at more than 12 pixels per 1/30th of second, mouse-pointer movement accelerates at four times the normal rate.

Note: These settings appear in WIN.INI only when you change the mouse tracking speed from the default.

In general, you are better off using the Mouse icon from the Control Panel to change these settings rather than setting them manually in WIN.INI. That way, you can test the mouse at various speeds before accepting the one you like most.

Mouse Double-Click Speed

You can use the DoubleClickSpeed= setting in the [windows] section to control the speed at which Windows registers a double-click. The higher the value, the more time you have to click the mouse twice. For example, the following setting establishes the double-click rate at 300 milliseconds (452 is the default):

```
DoubleClickSpeed=300
```

You can also control this setting from the Mouse icon in the Control Panel.

Defining Program Files

By modifying the Programs= setting in the [windows] section, you can control which files Windows recognizes as program files. For example, the standard setting is as follows:

```
Programs=com exe bat pif
```

This setting causes Windows to recognize .COM, .EXE, .BAT, and .PIF files as program files. Therefore, these are the files that are displayed in File Manager (and in the MS-DOS Executive) when you select the View Include command and turn on the Programs check box.

If you want to include device drivers in the list of program files, you could change the setting to

```
Programs=com exe bat pif sys
```

From that point on, Windows would also include files with a .SYS extension in its list of program files.

Defining Document Files

By using the Documents= setting in the [windows] section, you can affect which files Windows recognizes as documents. By default, Windows treats as documents all the files whose extensions are listed in the [Extensions] section; these are the files that are displayed in File Manager (and in the MS-DOS Executive) when you select the View Include command and turn on the Documents check box. By default, the Documents= setting is left blank.

Suppose you want Windows to treat as documents all those files that have an .ASC extension. Here is how you would modify the Documents= setting:

```
Documents=asc
```

Device Timeout and Transmission Retry Timeout

When you use the Printers icon in the Control Panel to install a printer, Windows displays a dialog box that lets you establish the following two timeout settings:

- Device Not Selected—The amount of time Windows waits before notifying you that a printer is off-line. The default is 15 seconds.
- Transmission Retry—The amount of time Windows waits for a printer to accept output before notifying you that it cannot print to the device. The default is 45 seconds.

Windows gets the default settings for these options from the following two settings in the [windows] section of the WIN.INI:

```
DeviceNotSelectedTimeout=15
TransmissionRetryTimeout=45
```

By changing these settings, you can affect the default settings that appear in the Control Panel. Nevertheless, you are usually better off keeping these default settings as is in WIN.INI and modifying the settings for individual printers using the Printers icon from the Control Panel. Windows then saves the settings you make in Control Panel in the [PrinterPorts] section of your WIN.INI.

Using Expanded Memory for Windows 2.x Applications

In previous versions of Windows, you could place a swapdisk= setting in your WIN.INI file to change how Windows would swap applications to disk. You could even use this setting to have Windows swap applications to expanded memory.

In Windows 3, a swapdisk= setting appears in the [windows] section of WIN.INI for compatibility's sake, but it does not do anything. There is a swapdisk= setting in the [NonWindowsApp] section of the SYSTEM.INI file, however, that controls the location Windows uses for storing application swap files. See Chapter 11, "Improving Windows' Performance," for more on this.

Controlling the Network Warning

When you've installed Windows to run on certain networks, such as 3COM 3+ Share, it will warn you if the network is not running when you start up Windows. If you prefer that Windows not display a warning message, you can use the following line in the [windows] section:

```
NetWarn=0
```

You can also control this setting from the Network icon in the control panel window, except with Novell NetWare.

The [Desktop] Section

This section of the WIN.INI file stores settings that control the appearance of the screen background (desktop), the spacing between icons, and the positioning of windows. Most of these settings can be controlled by the Desktop icon in the Control Panel.

Controlling the Desktop Pattern

When you select the Desktop icon from the Control Panel, Windows lets you specify a desktop pattern. You can choose a predetermined pattern from the list (for example, paisley), or you can create your own pattern by selecting the Edit Pattern button and clicking on appropriate cells in the 8 x 8 matrix. Either way, when you select OK to accept a pattern, Windows stores this setting in the Pattern= statement of the [Desktop] section.

The setting is stored as a series of eight decimal numbers in the following form:

```
Pattern=b1 b2 b3 b4 b5 b6 b7 b8
```

where each decimal number represents a byte, and each byte represents a row of eight pixels. Here is the effect of setting a bit:

- 0—Assigns the background color (set in the [colors] section of WIN.INI).
- 1—Assigns the foreground color (set in the [colors] section).

For example, Figure 12-2 shows the relationship between the paisley pattern matrix, the bit pattern used to represent the matrix, and the decimal-number equivalents of each byte in the bit pattern. Windows stores this pattern in the [Desktop] section of your WIN.INI as follows:

```
Pattern=2 7 7 2 32 80 80 32
```

Changing the Wallpaper

As you know, you can use the Desktop icon in the Control Panel to display a bitmap as your wallpaper or desktop background. In addition, you select the Center or Tile radio button to control whether the bitmap is centered or tiled on the desktop.

When you make these choices, Windows stores them using the following settings in the [Desktop] section of your WIN.INI:

```
Wallpaper=<filename>
TileWallpaper=<0-or-1>
```

where <0-or-1> is 0 for centered (not tiled) and 1 for tiled.

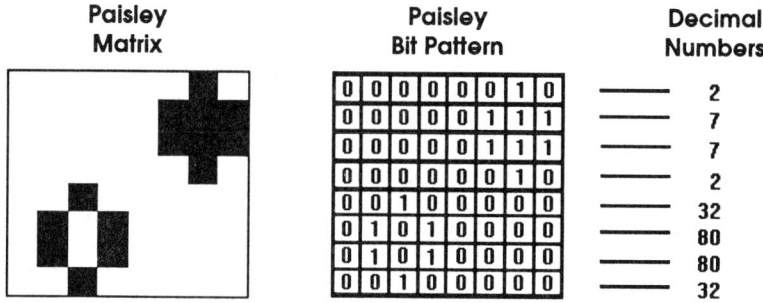

Figure 12-2 The paisley pattern in matrix, bit pattern, and decimal form

For example, here are the settings it stores when you specify the boxes bitmap (BOXES.BMP) and choose the Tile radio button:

```
Wallpaper=boxes.bmp
TileWallpaper=1
```

When you use the Desktop icon to specify the wallpaper, Windows displays a list of bitmap files in the \WINDOWS and \WINDOWS\SYSTEM directories for you to choose from. If you select a bitmap from another directory, Windows automatically copies that bitmap file to the \WINDOWS directory. If you modify WIN.INI directly, however, you can choose a bitmap from another directory and not have Windows copy it to the \WINDOWS directory. For example, suppose you have a \BITMAPS directory on drive D, and you move the chess bitmap to that location. You want to use this bitmap for your wallpaper, and you want it centered on the screen. Here are the [Desktop] settings you would use:

```
Wallpaper=d:\bitmaps\chess.bmp
TileWallpaper=0
```

Changing the Wallpaper Origin

By using the WallpaperOriginX= and WallpaperOriginY= settings in the [Desktop] section, you can control the precise position on the screen where Windows begins placing tiled wallpaper. The coordinates you use for these settings are expressed in pixels, where the upper-left corner of the screen is (0,0).

For example, suppose you want to use the boxes bitmap (BOXES.BMP) for tiled wallpaper. But rather than have Windows begin tiling the bitmap at the upper-left corner of the screen (0,0), you want to offset the starting location 10 pixels to the right and 10 pixels below the origin, at (10,10). Here are the settings you would use in the [Desktop] section:

```
Wallpaper=boxes.bmp
TileWallpaper=1
WallpaperOriginX=10
WallpaperOriginY=10
```

Note: By default, the WallpaperOriginX= and WallpaperOriginY= keynames do not appear in WIN.INI. If you want to use these keynames to control the positioning of your wallpaper, you'll need to add them yourself.

Controlling the Grid Granularity

Windows has an invisible grid system for controlling the alignment of windows on the desktop. Normally, the grid system is turned off. Therefore, when you drag a window to a new location on the desktop and release the mouse button, Windows places it exactly where you choose. By turning on the grid system, you can have Windows align windows in eight-pixel increments.

The typical way to turn on the grid system is to use the Desktop icon from the Control Panel and specify a Granularity setting that is greater than zero. For example, if you use a setting of 10, windows will be aligned using an 80-pixel wide (10 x 8 pixels) grid system.

Windows stores this setting in the GridGranularity= line of your WIN.INI file. The normal setting is GridGranularity=0 for no grid. On the other hand, Windows will use an 80-pixel wide grid if you change this setting to GridGranularity=10.

Changing Icon Spacing

By default, Windows leaves 75 pixels between icons. It stores this setting in the IconSpacing= line in the [Desktop] section of your WIN.INI. Suppose you want to change the icon spacing to 100 pixels between icons. You would use the following setting:

```
IconSpacing=100
```

Although you can change this setting directly in you WIN.INI, an easier way to change it is to use the Desktop icon in the Control Panel.

The [Extensions] Section

The [Extensions] section of your WIN.INI file stores all your file associations. Recall that a file association links a group of documents with an application so that when you open a document, Windows automatically starts the application. The typical way to set up a file association is to use File Manager, highlight a document, and select Associate from the File menu (see Chapter 3).

When you install Windows on your system, it automatically includes the following associations in WIN.INI:

```
cal=calendar.exe ^.cal
crd=cardfile.exe ^.crd
trm=terminal.exe ^.trm
txt=notepad.exe ^.txt
ini=notepad.exe ^.ini
pcx=pbrush.exe ^.pcx
```

```
bmp=pbrush.exe ^.bmp
wri=write.exe ^.wri
rec=recorder.exe ^.rec
```

Therefore, if you open a file with an .INI extension, for example, Windows automatically starts Notepad and loads the .INI file into it.

As another example, suppose you name all your Oriel script files with an .ORL extension. You want to add an association to your WIN.INI so that when you open an .ORL file, Windows automatically starts Oriel and passes it the name of the script file. Here is the line you would place in your WIN.INI:

```
orl=c:\oriel\oriel.exe ^.orl
```

Of course, this association will only work if you've placed Oriel in the C:\ORIEL directory.

The [Intl] Section

This section stores all the settings that control how Windows displays dates, times, currency, and other country-related settings. Because you can control all of these settings so easily through the International icon in the Control Panel, and there is no real advantage to modifying them directly in your WIN.INI, they are not covered here.

The [Ports] Section

This section lists all the available printer and communications ports that Windows can send output to. You can also use it to list files if you want to direct your output to a file.

The following is a list of the all default settings in the [ports] section:

```
LPT1:=
LPT2:=
LPT3:=
COM1:=9600,n,8,1
COM2:=9600,n,8,1
COM3:=9600,n,8,1
COM4:=9600,n,8,1
EPT:=
FILE:=
LPT1.OS2=
LPT2.OS2=
```

Here's an explanation of these settings:

- **LPT1:, LPT2:, and LPT3:**—These settings are the parallel ports that Windows can direct output to. They do not take any parameters after the equals sign.

- COM1:, COM2:, COM3:, COM4:—These are all the available COM ports. The easiest way to change a COM port setting is to use the Ports icon from the Control Panel. The general form of a COM port setting is

  `COMx:=<baud-rate>,<parity>,<word-length>,<stop-bits>[,p]`

  where <baud-rate> is the baud rate for the port; <parity> is the parity (for example, e for even parity); <word-length> is the length of a word in bits; <stop-bits> is the number of stop bits; and [,p] is an optional parameter describing the type of hardware handshaking. For example, the line COM1:=9600,n,8,1,x sets COM1 to 9600 baud, no parity, 8 bits, 1 stop bit, and Xon/Xoff hardware handshaking.

- EPT:—This is the port used for certain IBM printers, such as the IBM Personal Pageprinter (see Chapter 4, "Of Fonts and Printing," for more on this).

- FILE:—This setting is used for printing to a file. By configuring your printer to use this setting as the output port, you can have Windows prompt you for a filename at output time.

- LPT1.OS2 and LPT2.OS2—These ports are for when you are running Windows in the DOS compatibility box of OS/2.

By including a filename as a keyword in the [ports] list, you can have a printer print directly to a file in the current directory, as in the following example:

`PRINTOUT.HP=`

If you then use the Printers icon in the Control Panel and configure your printer for this port, the printer will direct its output to the file PRINTOUT.HP each time you print.

The [Fonts] Section

This section stores the display fonts that Windows uses. See "Changing Your Display Fonts Manually" in Chapter 9 for a complete discussion of these settings.

The [PrinterPorts] Section

This section lists the active and inactive printers that Windows can access. Windows automatically updates this list when you use the Printers icon from the Control Panel to configure a printer.

For example, here is a typical entry in [PrintersPorts]:

`PCL / HP LaserJet=HPPCL,LPT1:,15,45`

In this example, "PCL / HP Laserjet" is the name of the printer. It uses HPPCL.DRV as the printer's device-driver file and sets up LPT1: as the port to which Windows will print. In addition, this setting allows 15 seconds before Windows notifies you that the printer is off-line and 45 seconds for retries before Print Manager tells you that it cannot print to the device. (If you don't include either of the last two parameters, Windows uses the TransmissionRetryTimeout or DeviceNotSelectedTimeout setting in the [windows] section, respectively.)

The [Devices] Section

This section lists the same active printers as in the [PrintersPorts] section but without the timeout values. For example, here is the companion [devices] setting for the example shown in the previous section:

```
PCL / HP LaserJet=HPPCL,LPT1:
```

This section is provided for Windows 2.x applications only. Windows 3 applications do not use this section of WIN.INI.

The [Colors] Section

This section controls all the colors that are used for various parts of the Windows display. You can control most of the settings in this section through the Color icon in the Control Panel. However, there are six settings that you cannot change from the Color icon but must change manually add to WIN.INI. These are ButtonFace, ButtonShadow, ButtonText, GrayText, Hilight, and HiglightText. Table 12-1 shows a complete list of the available settings.

Each of the settings takes the following form:

```
Component=Red_value Green_value Blue_value
```

where Red_value, Green_value, and Blue_value control the intensity of the colors red, green, and blue. If all the values are set to zero, the component will be black. Conversely, if all the values are set to 255, the component will be white. To change the window frame to red, for example, you would use the following setting:

```
WindowFrame=255 0 0
```

Here are the default settings for the [colors] section if you've installed a color display:

```
ActiveBorder=128 128 128
ActiveTitle=0 64 128
AppWorkspace=255 255 232
Background=192 192 192
InactiveBorder=255 255 255
InactiveTitle=255 255 255
Menu=255 255 255
```

```
MenuText=0 0 0
Scrollbar=224 224 224
TitleText=255 255 255
Window=255 255 255
WindowFrame=0 0 0
WindowText=0 0 0
```

The settings will be slightly different if you've installed a monochrome display.

As mentioned, the Color icon in the Control Panel provides the easiest way to change most of these settings. However, suppose you want to change the color of button text to yellow. Because this is not a setting you can control through the Control Panel, the only way to change it would be to add the following line to WIN.INI:

```
ButtonText=255 255 0
```

Setting	Purpose
ActiveBorder	Border of the active window
ActiveTitle	Active title bar
AppWorkspace	Application workspace for Windows applications
Background	Screen background (desktop)
ButtonFace*	Button face
ButtonShadow*	Button shadow
ButtonText*	Button text
GrayText*	Grayed text (indicating that a command name is unavailable)
Hilight*	Background of highlighted text
HilightText*	Highlighted text
InactiveBorder	Border of the inactive window
InactiveTitle	Inactive title bar
Menu	Menu background
MenuText	Menu text
Scrollbar	Scroll bar
TitleText	Title-bar text
Window	Window workspace
WindowFrame	Window frame
WindowText	Window text

*Settings you cannot change from the Color icon in the Control Panel, but must add directly to WIN.INI

Table 12-1 Available [Colors] Settings

SYSTEM.INI

As mentioned, the SYSTEM.INI file contains mostly hardware-related settings. Windows reads the settings in SYSTEM.INI on startup. Therefore, if you make any changes to the file, be aware that they will not be recognized until you start Windows up the next time.

SYSTEM.INI is organized according to the following sections:

- [boot]—Lists device drivers, font files, and grabber files.
- [boot.description]—Stores the names of the devices you've installed. These are the names that appear in Windows Setup.
- [keyboard]—Stores information about the keyboard.
- [NonWindowsApp]—Lists information used by non-Windows applications.
- [standard]—Lists information used by Windows in standard mode.
- [386Enh]—Stores information used by Windows in 386 enhanced mode.

SYSTEM.INI has many exotic settings that most users will never need to know about. What's more, almost all of the settings in SYSTEM.INI are assigned automatically by Windows Setup. (For example, all the settings in the [boot] and [keyboard] sections are established by Setup, as are all the device= statements in the [386Enh] section.) Therefore, in most cases, you may be better off using Setup to change your settings.

There are, however, a handful of settings in SYSTEM.INI that are worthwhile changing yourself. These are the settings that we've concentrated our efforts on.

Caution: SYSTEM.INI is a power user's delight. It is also a potential minefield for the uninitiated—one incorrect setting can prevent Windows from starting. As you modify SYSTEM.INI, always keep a backup copy so that you can restore the file if you need to. If for some reason you don't have a backup and you're not sure which setting you've changed that is preventing Windows from restarting, try deleting SYSTEM.INI and WINVER.EXE and running Setup from DOS. Setup will create new versions of these files, and you should be able to restart Windows.

The [Boot] Section

This section is mostly a list of device drivers, grabber files, and font files. There is also a setting for controlling the default shell that appears when you start Windows.

Grabber Files

The [boot] section has two settings associated with grabber files: 286grabber and 386grabber. Grabber files are device drivers that make DOS applications visible when you run Windows in its various modes. The 286grabber= setting lists the grabber used for real and standard mode, and the 386grabber= setting lists the grabber used for 386 enhanced mode.

The grabber files vary with the type of display driver you are using. For example, here are typical settings for standard VGA, 8514/a, and Hercules displays:

VGA

```
286grabber=vgacolor.gr2
386grabber=vga.gr3
```

8514/a

```
286grabber=vgacolor.gr2
386grabber=8514.gr3
```

Hercules Monochrome

```
286grabber=hercules.gr2
386grabber=herc.gr3
```

Because Setup assigns these settings automatically based on your display type, there is usually no need to modify them yourself.

System Font Files

The [boot] section of SYSTEM.INI has three settings that control the System font used by Windows: fixedfon.fon, oemfonts.fon, and fonts.fon. All of these settings are assigned automatically by Setup based on the display type. See "Changing Your Display Fonts Manually" in Chapter 9 for a complete discussion of these settings.

Display Driver

When you install Windows for a particular display, Setup copies a display driver from your Windows Disk to the \WINDOWS\SYSTEM directory. It then stores the name of the display driver in the display.DRV= setting in the [boot] section of SYSTEM.INI. For example, here are the settings for VGA, 8514/a, and Hercules displays:

VGA

```
display.drv=vga.drv
```

8514/a

```
display.drv=8514.drv
```

Hercules Monochrome

```
display.drv=hercules.drv
```

Like most of the other [boot] section settings, Setup does a reliable job of maintaining the display.drv= setting, so there is usually no need to modify it yourself.

Changing the Default Shell

The shell= setting in the [boot] section controls the default shell that automatically appears when you start Windows. The standard setting

    shell=progman.exe

makes Program Manager the default shell.

Suppose you want to make File Manager the default shell. Here's the setting you would use:

    shell=winfile.exe

Tip: Making Command Post or Aporia the default shell

By using the shell= setting in the [boot] section of SYSTEM.INI, you can make Command Post or Aporia the default shell. For example, suppose Command Post is located in the \CMDPOST directory on drive C. Here is the setting to make it the default shell:

shell=c:\cmdpost\cmdpost.exe

Other Device-Driver Settings

The [boot] section also has settings for controlling the network, language library, communications, sound, mouse, keyboard, and system hardware drivers. For example, the following is a list of the typical settings for these drivers and how to change them:

Setting	How to change
network.drv=msnet.drv	Run Setup from Windows or DOS.
language.dll=	Use the International icon from Control Panel.
comm.drv=comm.drv	Use Notepad or Sysedit.
sound.drv=sound.drv	Use Notepad or Sysedit.
mouse.drv=mouse.drv	Run Setup from Windows or DOS.
keyboard.drv=keyboard.drv	Run Setup from Windows or DOS.
system.drv=system.drv	Run Setup from DOS.

The [Boot.description] Section

The [boot.description] section is merely a list of strings that are used by the Setup program to describe the various devices you've installed. These strings are copied by Setup from the SETUP.INF file (or from the OEMSETUP.INF file if you are using the Supplemental Driver Library) to SYSTEM.INI. There is no real benefit to changing these strings.

The [Keyboard] Section

The [keyboard] section holds the settings related to the keyboard. For example, there are settings for the dynamic-link library that defines the keyboard layout and the keyboard type. Because you can easily change these settings from Setup (or from the International icon in the Control Panel) and there is no reason to change them directly in SYSTEM.INI, they are not discussed here.

The [NonWindowsApp] Section

The [NonWindowsApps] section of SYSTEM.INI includes the settings that affect the behavior of DOS applications. Typically, this section is blank. However, there is one setting that you may want to use at some point. It controls the location that Windows uses for storing application swap files.

Changing the Location Used for Application Swap Files

When you run DOS applications in real or standard mode, Windows stores the temporary application swap files it creates in the directory named by the TEMP environment variable, usually \WINDOWS\TEMP. If there is no TEMP setting, Windows places these files in the \WINDOWS directory.

If you prefer that Windows use another directory for application swap files, you place a SwapDisk statement in the [NonWindowsApp] section of your SYSTEM.INI file. For example, by using the statement

```
SwapDisk=E:\SCRATCH
```

you can have Windows store the application swap files in the SCRATCH directory on drive E. See Chapter 11, "Improving Windows' Performance," for more on application swap files.

The [Standard] Section

The [standard] section controls settings that are specific to running Windows in standard mode. By default, Windows includes no settings in this section, and it's very uncommon to ever need any.

The [386Enh] Section

The [386Enh] section of SYSTEM.INI contains a wealth of settings related to running Windows in 386 enhanced mode. Most of the settings you will never need to know about. However, the following sections cover the handful of settings that you may want to consider using.

Controlling Your DOS Application Fonts

When Setup installs a display driver on your system, it copies several font (.FON) files to your \WINDOWS\SYSTEM directory. Four of these files contain the fixed-pitch display font that Windows uses for running DOS applications in a window in 386 enhanced mode. The names of these four files are stored in the [386Enh] section of SYSTEM.INI. For example, here are the settings for a standard VGA display with 640 x 480 resolution:

```
EGA80WOA.FON=EGA80WOA.FON
EGA40WOA.FON=EGA40WOA.FON
CGA80WOA.FON=CGA80WOA.FON
CGA40WOA.FON=CGA40WOA.FON
```

Oddly enough, these are the same settings that Windows uses for an 8514/a or Enhanced (1K) VGA adapter with a resolution of 1024 x 768. On these adapters, whenever you run a DOS application in a window, you may find the text so small that you have to squint to see it. Fortunately, you can easily increase the size of the font by changing the .FON file settings. See "Changing Your DOS Application Font" in Chapter 9 for a complete discussion.

Forcing DOS Applications to Run Full Screen

As you know, whenever you launch a DOS application in 386 enhanced mode, it runs in window or full-screen mode, based on the Display Usage setting in its PIF. By using the following setting in the [386Enh] section of SYSTEM.INI, however, you can override the setting in the PIF and force all DOS applications to run in full-screen mode:

```
AllVMsExclusive=yes
```

If you use this setting, be forewarned that your system may slow down substantially if you are running memory-resident and network software that is not supported by Windows.

Giving Preference to EMS Page Frame Space or Conventional Memory

Although Windows breaks the 640K barrier when running in 386 enhanced mode, it still must communicate with DOS running in conventional memory. To do this, Windows must allocate translation buffers in the 384K of reserved I/O address space. These buffers serve as a way station through which Windows running in protected mode passes information to DOS running in real mode.

On most machines, there is more than enough free space in reserved I/O memory to place both the translation buffers and the EMS page frame. On some machines, however, there simply isn't enough room. When this is the case, Windows uses conventional memory for the translation buffers instead of reserved memory. When the translation buffers are allocated in conventional memory, they take up space in every virtual machine Windows creates.

Through the ReservePageFrame= setting in the [386Enh] section of SYSTEM.INI, Windows gives you direct control over how it allocates the translation buffers and EMS page frame. If ReservePageFrame=true (the default), Windows allocates the page frame first and the translation buffers second. When reserved memory is tight, it is likely that Windows will use conventional memory for the translation buffers instead of reserved memory. The advantage, however, is that you retain the ability to use expanded memory in your DOS applications.

If ReservePageFrame=false, Windows allocates the translation buffers first and the page frame second, if there is still room in reserved memory. When there is little reserved I/O space available, the EMS page frame may not get allocated. The result is that you gain more room in each virtual machine, but you lose the ability to use expanded memory in your DOS applications. If your DOS applications do not need expanded memory, this is a good way to gain more conventional memory. See Chapter 7, "Windows Memory Management," for more on this topic.

Including and Excluding Adapter Memory

As you know, expanded memory requires a 64K contiguous page frame located in the 384K of reserved I/O memory. However, some adapter boards, such as network cards, ESDI disk controllers, and 3270 emulation cards, also vie for this space. One possible problem is that there simply isn't enough contiguous space available for the page frame. When this occurs, you usually have to reassign the address area of an adapter card (see Chapter 7 for more details).

Another possible problem is that there are mapping conflicts. Windows in 386 enhanced mode uses a search algorithm to locate a 64K block of unused memory between C000 and DFFF in the reserved I/O space. Yet some adapter boards do not reserve their chunk of this reserved memory until you access them. The result is that you get mapping conflicts between Windows memory manager and the adapter board, causing Windows to hang. Because Windows can recognize most adapter boards, this problem is fairly uncommon. When it occurs, however, you can use the EMMExclude= and EMMInclude= settings in the [386Enh] section of SYSTEM.INI to help control Windows placement of the EMS page frame. Besides controlling the position of the page frame, these settings also control the mapping of the DOS translation buffers (see the previous section).

For example, the following command causes the Windows memory manager to exclude the memory between E000—EFFF:

```
EMMExclude=E000-EFFF
```

You can also use the EMMInclude= setting to direct Windows to include certain areas of reserved memory in its search algorithm. This setting is rarely (if ever) needed, though, because Windows normally makes use of all available reserved memory.

Likewise, the EMMPageFrame= setting, which was available in Windows/386 for forcing a page frame at a specified address, is not used at all in Windows 3. Although this setting does move the page frame, it does not affect the position of the DOS translation buffers, making it useless in Windows 3. See Chapter 7, "Windows Memory Management," for more discussion of expanded memory.

Disabling Expanded Memory Support

By using the NoEMMDriver=yes setting in the [386Enh] section of SYSTEM.INI, you can disable Windows' use of expanded memory. (This setting prevents Windows from loading its expanded memory driver.) You may find this setting useful when you suspect that there are mapping conflicts between Windows' memory manager and an adapter board in your system, if you don't mind giving up expanded memory support for your DOS applications.

Controlling File Manager's Window Updates

In 386 enhanced mode, Windows is capable of monitoring a DOS application's disk access and notifying File Manager so that it can automatically update its window if directory information changes. By default, this capability is turned off and is stored in the following setting in the [386Enh] section of SYSTEM.INI:

```
FileSysChange=off
```

Because this option is off, you must manually refresh File Manager's window (using the Refresh option from the Window menu) after a DOS application has changed the directory information.

Note: Although you can turn this option on with FileSysChange=on, you should only do so if you are willing to put up with slower file access by your DOS applications.

Device Contention Settings

In 386 enhanced mode, Windows is capable of arbitrating between two applications when both are trying to access the same port and one of the applications is a DOS application. The way that Windows performs its arbitration is based on the COM*x*AutoAssign= and LPT*x*AutoAssign= settings in the [386Enh] section of SYSTEM.INI, where *x* is the number of the port. The easiest way to change these settings is to use the 386 Enhanced icon from the Control Panel. Of course, you can also edit them directly in SYSTEM.INI.

For example, here are some typical settings for a system with COM1, COM2, and LPT1:

```
Com1AutoAssign=-1
Com2AutoAssign=0
LPT1AutoAssign=2
```

In this example, because the COM1 setting is assigned a value of -1, Windows will display a warning message and ask you which application should be given use of COM1. (This is the setting that Windows assigns when you select the Always Warn radio button for the 386 Enhanced icon in Control Panel.) By contrast, because the COM2 setting is given a value of 0, an application can use a port at any time and no warning is given (the setting assigned when you select the Never Warn radio button in the 386 Enhanced icon). The positive value for the LPT1 setting represents the number of seconds after an application stops using this port before another application can use it (the setting assigned when you select the Idle radio button in the 386 Enhanced icon). See Chapter 8, "Using the Control Panel," for a complete discussion of device contention.

Minimum Disk Space Setting

The MinUserDiskSpace= setting in the [386Enh] section lets you control how much disk space (in kilobytes) Windows leaves free when it creates a temporary swap file. For example, the following setting tells Windows to leave 2 MB free:

```
MinUserDiskSpace=2048
```

The default value is 500. See Chapter 11, "Improving Windows' Performance," for more on swap files.

Preventing Windows from Paging to Disk

You can prevent Windows from swapping information to disk in 386 enhanced mode by placing the statement Paging=no in the [386Enh] section of SYSTEM.INI. Because this statement limits Windows' capacity, you should only use it if disk space is at a premium. Note that using this setting only makes sense when you need the disk space that would normally be allocated for a temporary swap file.

Changing the Paging Drive

By default, when Windows creates a temporary swap file in 386 enhanced mode, it places the file in the \WINDOWS directory. If you want to change the location that Windows uses to the root directory of a different drive, you can enter the PagingDrive setting in the [386Enh] section of your SYSTEM.INI file. For example, the following setting tells Windows to use drive E:

```
PagingDrive=E:
```

If drive E is full, Windows will disable paging.

Note: You cannot specify a subdirectory for the temporary swap file location.

Terminating Interrupts from the Hard Disk Controller

If you are using a third-party partitioning utility on your hard disk, for example Disk Manager (DMDRVR.BIN) from Ontrack Systems, you should place the following setting in the [386Enh] section of your SYSTEM.INI:

```
VirtualHDIrq=off
```

This setting terminates interrupts from the hard disk controller by bypassing the ROM routine that handles these interrupts. See Chapter 11, "Improving Windows' Performance," for more on third-party partitioning software and the importance of this setting.

SUMMARY

The WIN.INI and SYSTEM.INI files store settings that control nearly every aspect of the Windows environment. Although you can use Windows Setup and the Control Panel to change many of their settings, others you can only change by directly editing the files themselves.

Having read this chapter, you now have an appreciation for the division of labor between the two files. You also know the major sections within each one. Armed with this knowledge, you now know where to go when you need to modify a Windows setting.

13

Networking Windows

This chapter takes you on a tour of Windows networking features. As you'll soon see, you can access your network from File Manager, Control Panel, Print Manager, and Windows Setup. This chapter will explore each of these "hooks" into your network in detail.

You can network Windows 3 in one of two ways. On the one hand, you can have local copies of Windows on each workstation that can access files in shared directories on the network file server. On the other hand, multiple users with different workstation hardware configurations can share a single copy of Windows over the network. This is now possible because of improvements in the architecture of Windows 3 that allow device drivers to be stored locally on each workstation. Both methods of running Windows will be discussed in this chapter.

This chapter assumes you know a little about networking in general. For example, it assumes you know what a file server is, what a workstation is, and about the relationship between the two. Furthermore, it assumes you have at least a passing familiarity with the features that are available on your particular network. Therefore, all that remains is to familiarize you with how you can use Windows to interact with your network.

SUPPORTED NETWORKS

Not all networks are 100 percent supported by Windows. In fact, in order for Windows to work with your network, it must have access to a software driver that is compatible with your particular network. Windows comes with drivers for a variety of popular networks, including:

- 3Com 3+Open LAN Manager (XNS only)
- 3Com 3+Share
- Banyan Vines 4.0
- IBM PC LAN Program
- LAN Manager 1.x (or 100% compatible)
- LAN Manager 2.0 (or 100% compatible)
- LAN Manager 2.0 Enhanced (or 100% compatible)
- MicroSoft Network (or 100% compatible)
- Novell NetWare 2.01 or above or Novell NetWare 386

If Windows does not have a driver for your particular network, perhaps you can secure a driver from your network vendor. Or if your network is 100 percent compatible with a supported network, you can simply select the appropriate driver with the Windows Setup program.

Not all of the drivers provided by Windows support all of the features available on each network. In fact, this chapter will focus on two networks, one partially supported—3Com 3+Share—and one fully supported—Novell NetWare. See "Accessing Network Features from Windows" later in this chapter for examples of features that are, and are not, supported on these two networks.

Furthermore, to take advantage of the full functionality of Windows with your network, you must, in some cases, have the most recent version of the network software components. For example, with Novell NetWare, you must have version 3.01 or higher of the NetWare shell components (NET3.COM, NET4.COM, NETBIOS.EXE, and IPX.COM). Also, you should have Version 3.01 or higher of the NetWare utilities (such as BINDFIX.EXE and MAKEUSER.EXE) for use with the shell.

INSTALLING WINDOWS ON A WORKSTATION

Whether you run local copies of Windows, or a single shared copy on the server, the procedures for accessing the features of your network are the same. However, the procedure for setting up Windows is very different.

Note: The sections that follow assume you already have Windows installed either on your local workstation or on the network server. Therefore, the discussion that

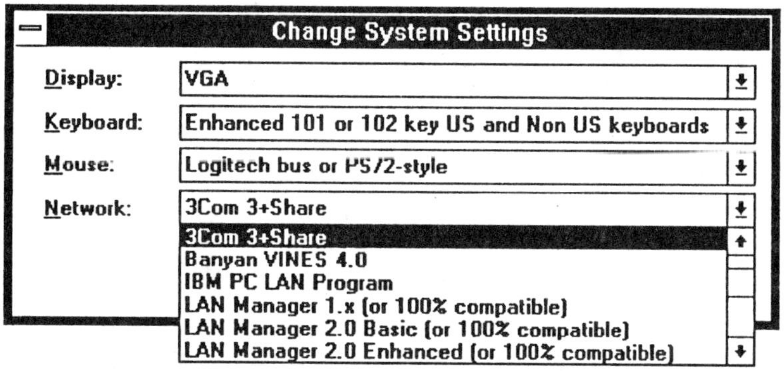

```
┌─────────────────────────────────────────────────────────────┐
│ ═                    Change System Settings                  │
├─────────────────────────────────────────────────────────────┤
│  Display:    │ VGA                                        │↕│
│                                                              │
│  Keyboard:   │ Enhanced 101 or 102 key US and Non US keyboards │↕│
│                                                              │
│  Mouse:      │ Logitech bus or PS/2-style                 │↕│
│                                                              │
│  Network:    │ 3Com 3+Share                               │↕│
│              ├────────────────────────────────────────────┤ │
│              │ 3Com 3+Share                               │↑│
│              │ Banyan VINES 4.0                           │ │
│              │ IBM PC LAN Program                         │ │
│              │ LAN Manager 1.x (or 100% compatible)       │ │
│              │ LAN Manager 2.0 Basic (or 100% compatible) │ │
│              │ LAN Manager 2.0 Enhanced (or 100% compatible) │↓│
└─────────────────────────────────────────────────────────────┘
```

Figure 13-1 The Change System Settings dialog box

follows takes place from the viewpoint of the user. If you want to install a shared copy of Windows on your server, see "Installing Windows on a Server," later in this chapter.

Setting Up a Local Copy of Windows

Setting up a local copy of Windows to recognize the network is fairly easy. To do this, start Windows and then start the Windows Setup program. (Before you do this, however, make sure you close any applications you may have open.) As you may recall, you can run the Windows Setup program by double-clicking on its icon located in Program Manager's Main group window. Once the Setup window is active, select the Options Change System Settings command from the menu bar. Windows displays the Change System Settings dialog box.

To configure your local copy of Windows to recognize the network, open the Network drop-down list box and select the type of network to which your computer is connected. For example, in Figure 13-1 the 3Com 3+Share network is selected. When you're ready, select the OK button from the dialog box. Windows displays the Windows Setup dialog box, prompting you to insert the appropriate Windows program disk that contains the driver for the network you've selected. Insert the appropriate disk into drive A and select OK. Windows copies the needed driver to your Windows program directory. It also makes the appropriate entries for that driver in your WIN.INI and SYS.INI files so that Windows will automatically activate the driver on startup. When it has finished performing these functions, Windows displays a dialog box that contains a Restart Windows button. Select this button to have Windows restart itself. Your local copy of Windows should now be properly configured to recognize the network.

Installing a Shared Copy of Windows on a Workstation

To install a shared copy of Windows on your workstation, you must get a copy of Windows from the network server. For you to do this, though, Windows must already be installed on the server. To determine if it has been installed, ask your network administrator. If you don't have a network administrator and you have to install Windows on the server yourself, see "Installing Windows on the Server," later in this chapter. When you have finished there, return to this section.

To get a copy of Windows from the network, start from the DOS prompt. Change to the directory on the server that contains the shared copy of Windows. Once there, type the following at the DOS prompt:

```
SETUP /N
```

When you press ENTER to confirm this entry, DOS runs the Windows Setup program. Follow the instructions on your screen. During the installation of Windows, you will be asked to specify a directory on your local hard disk that you want Windows to use. To this directory, Windows will copy only those files that are necessary to your system. The rest of the Windows program files will remain on the server for you to share with other users.

During installation, you will also be prompted to specify the type of equipment you have as well as the type of network to which you are connected. In addition, you will be asked to select and install a printer for printing on the network. When you select a printer, make sure you select the same make and model of printer that is used on the network. If you don't know which printer to install, contact your network administrator.

Note: When you install a printer with the Setup program, Windows actually opens the Printers dialog box for the first time. For detailed instructions on how to use the Printers dialog box to install a printer, see Chapter 4, "Of Fonts and Printing."

NETWORK BASICS

If you are logged onto the network when you start Windows, it recognizes your network connections automatically, regardless of whether you are using a shared copy of Windows or a local copy. For example, imagine that you have already logged onto the network, and, through your log-in script, you have established a series of connections to application directories on the network server. When you start either a local copy or a shared copy of Windows, it comes up recognizing both the network and the connections you've made to it. You can then access network resources—for example, shared applications and network printers—from within Windows.

Running a Shared Copy of Windows Versus a Local Copy

You won't notice any difference in functionality between a shared copy of Windows and a local copy. However, the way Windows interacts with your network will vary depending on (1) whether you are using a local copy of Windows versus a shared copy, and (2) the capabilities of the network driver you are using.

If you are running a local copy of Windows, most network drivers (including 3Com 3+Share) require that you log onto the network before you start Windows. That way, Windows comes up recognizing the network automatically. Further, with most network drivers, you should avoid logging off the network while Windows is running. For example, imagine Windows is running and that you are connected to the network. You then start a shared application—for example, Word for Windows. At that point, you double-click on the DOS icon in Program Manager to shell to DOS. Once the DOS prompt is displayed, you log off the network. When you type EXIT to return to Windows, all goes well until you start to use Word for Windows again. Within a short time, Word starts to display error messages informing you that it cannot find the overlay files and dynamic link libraries it needs to perform its operations. At that point you begin to run the risk that Word will crash and possibly take Windows with it.

On the other hand, some network drivers—for example, LAN Manager 2.0 and Novell NetWare—provide a special feature that lets you log on and off the network from within Windows. For example, if you are running a local copy of Windows, you can start Windows and then log onto the network. While you are logged on, Windows recognizes the network. When you are finished using the network, you can log off. At that point, Windows no longer recognizes the network. See "Accessing Network Features from Windows," later in this chapter, for more details on how you can log on and off the network from within Windows.

If you are running a shared copy of Windows, you must, of course, have already logged onto the network to start Windows in the first place. What's more, you cannot log off the network while Windows is running. If you do, you will break the connection between your workstation and the network directory that contains the Windows program files. After that, it is only a matter of time before Windows begins issuing error messages and eventually crashes.

Connecting to Network Resources

Normally, when you log onto the network, a log-in script runs that (1) connects your local workstation to the network and (2) sets up logical connections between your workstation and network resources. Network resources include such things as shared applications, printers, and modems. In addition to the connections established through your log-in script, you can set up additional connections to network resources by entering network-specific command lines at the DOS prompt.

If you have already connected to the network resources you require before starting Windows, Windows comes up recognizing those resources automatically. However, as you'll soon see, with most Windows network drivers, you can connect to the resources you require from within Windows itself. Therefore, you can start Windows and connect to the resources you need later. (See "Connecting to Network Drives" section.)

You connect to network resources from within Windows by using the same logic you would from either the DOS prompt or from a network menu. For example, normally, to access a network resource such as a shared application, you must set up a link between a logical drive (an unused address) on your PC and the network directory that contains that resource. Logical drives are identified by letters that often go as high as Z. Therefore, theoretically, you can establish up to 26 connections to the network. Logical drives normally start with the first letter after the last-used physical drive on your local PC. For example, if your last physical drive is drive D, theoretically your available logical drives are E through Z. Once you link a logical drive to a network directory, the network software will then accept input from your computer via the address specified by that logical drive. It will also route the output from the resource to that same address, allowing you to interact with the network resource.

Because the logic for accessing network resources varies from one network to the next, the sections below describe network linking logic for two popular networks, 3Com 3+Share and Novell NetWare. The same conventions described below can be applied when you are linking to network resources from within Windows for these networks. If you are already familiar with how to link to directories on these networks, you may want to skip the next two sections and go directly to the section "Connecting to Network Drives from Windows." That way, you can get started using Windows with your network right away.

3Com 3+Share

As a 3Com 3+Share user, you can only access those directories on the server that have been made shareable, usually by the network administrator. To make server directories shareable, the network administrator must have assigned sharenames to them. When setting up sharenames, the network administrator also assigns access privileges (read, write, create) to the directory referenced by the sharename and may even require a password, if he or she feels it is appropriate. Once the sharename has been defined, you can link one of your logical drives to that sharename. In this way, you can access the network resource in the directory that is defined by that sharename.

To make a directory on the server shareable, you, or your network administrator, must use the 3F.EXE program to assign a sharename to it. To use this program, you must enter a command line at the DOS prompt that takes the following form:

```
3F SHARE sharename=x:\dirpath [/rwc] [/pass=password]
```

The components of this command line break down as follows:

- 3F SHARE: Starts the 3F.EXE program and instructs it that a sharename is about to be defined.
- *sharename*: The name you want to assign the directory and its subdirectories, on the network that you are making shareable to users. Once the sharename is defined, the directory you specify will be known to the network by that sharename.
- *x*: The drive letter of the directory on the server that you are making shareable. Although this drive letter refers to one of the physical drives on the server, the actual letter you use may be one of your logical drives at the time.
- *dirpath*: The full path to the server directory that you are making shareable.
- /rwc: Optional keywords that you can assign to define access privileges to the directory. You can specify any combination of these keywords including r (read),

w (write), and c (create). With all three privileges, the user can read files, write to existing files, and create new files. If you do not designate a keyword here, the default is /rwc.

- /pass=*password*: An optional password that you can define in order for a user to access the directory.

For example, imagine you want to share a directory named \WINAPPS located on drive F. This directory has two subdirectories—\WINAPPS\WINWORD and \WINAPPS\EXCEL—that contain two Windows applications that you want to make shareable to users. To assign a sharename to this directory, you might use the following command line:

```
3f share wapps=f:\winapps /r /pass=win
```

This command line makes the server directory f:\winapps known to the network as wapps. The directory is read only (/r). Thus, you can read its files, but you cannot write to existing files in the directory or create new files. Finally, to access the directory, you must provide the password win.

Connecting to Server Directories

Connecting to a directory on the server allows you to associate one of your PC's logical drives with the contents of a directory on the network server. To connect to a server directory, you use the 3F.EXE program again. This time, however, the command line takes the form:

```
3F LINK x: \\servername\sharename [/pass=password]
```

This command line breaks down as follows:

- 3F LINK: Starts the 3F.EXE program and indicates a logical drive link is about to be set up

- *x:* : The letter that defines a logical drive on your PC that will be used to reference the shared directory on the server. Once the link is created, you can use this drive letter in command lines to access files on the network server. It's as though a whole new drive has been added to your hard disk.

- *servername*: The name of the server. Each server on a network is assigned a name that identifies it.

- *sharename*: The sharename that defines the directory you want to access.

- /pass=*password*: The password you need to access the server directory.

For example, imagine you want to link to the directory on the server that is defined by the sharename WAPPS and the password for this directory is WIN. Also, imagine that the name of that server is SERVER1. Further, imagine that your first logical drive (unused address) is E, which is linked to your home directory (your personal scratch directory) on the network. Thus, logical drives F through Z are available for linking to network resources. To link to this directory, you might use the following command line at the DOS prompt:

```
3f link f: \\server1\wapps /pass=win
```

When you enter this command line, the network establishes a logical drive F: for your PC and connects that drive to the directories defined by the WAPPS sharename on the server. At this point, you can use conventional DOS commands to access those directories, for example:

```
dir f:
```

Note: Setting up a network connection with the 3F command is only a temporary solution. When you log off the network or turn off your computer, the connection is lost. However, you can add the appropriate 3F command lines to your AUTOUSER.BAT file located in your home directory on the server. You can modify this file by using an ASCII text editor, like Notepad. The network reads this file, if it exists, each time you log onto the network. That way, the appropriate network connections are set up for you automatically. What's more, when you subsequently start Windows, it automatically comes up recognizing your connections to the network.

Connecting to Shared Printers

The network administrator can also make a printer shareable to users. To do this, he or she must execute the 3P.EXE program. The command line for this program takes the following form:

```
3P SHARE sharename=lptx: [/pass=password]
```

This command line breaks down as follows:

- 3P SHARE: Make the printer shareable.
- *sharename*: The name that identifies the printer to the network.
- lptx: The port to which the printer is connected. This corresponds to LPT1, LPT2, or LPT3.
- [/pass=password]: An optional password that you can define for access to the printer.

For example, to share the HP LaserJet Series II printer connected to the first parallel port on the server, you might use the following command line at the DOS prompt:

```
3p share laserjet=lpt1
```

As a user, you can connect to this printer by using its sharename. To do this, you must use the 3P.EXE program as well. However, this time, the command line will take the following form:

```
3p link lptx: \\servername\sharename [/pass=password]
```

This command line breaks down as follows:

- 3p link: Assigns a local printer device name to the network printer.
- lptx: : Defines the local printer device that you want remapped to the printer device on the server.
- *servername*: The name assigned to the server.
- *sharename*: The sharename assigned to the printer.
- [/pass=*password*]: The password required to access the printer, if any.

For example, imagine you want to print to the network printer, named LASERJET, on the server, named SERVER1, by using the first parallel port (LPT1) on your PC. To do this, you might use the following command line:

```
3p link lpt1: \\server1\laserjet
```

Novell NetWare

With the exception of the PUBLIC directory, server directories are not immediately shareable on Novell networks. However, the network administrator can change this by assigning trustee rights for them to users. To do this, he or she must use the System Console (SYSCON.EXE) utility. This utility allows the network administrator not only to assign trustee rights for server directories to users, but also to assign access privileges to those directories as well. See your Novell NetWare documentation for details on how to use the SYSCON utility.

Connecting to Server Directories

Once trustee rights and access privileges to server directories have been assigned, you can associate a logical drive on your PC with the contents of a network directory. To do this, you use the MAP utility. The command line for this utility takes the following form:

```
map x=servername/volume:directory/[pathname]
```

This command line breaks down as follows:

- map: Associates a logical drive letter on your PC with a directory and its subdirectories on the server.
- *x*: The logical drive letter you want to use. After you connect to the directory, you can use this drive letter in command lines to access files on the server.

- *servername*: The name of the server.
- *volume:directory*: The volume and home directory you want to connect to on the server. The default volume name is sys:.
- *pathname*: This argument is optional and can be used to specify subdirectories.

For example, to connect your G: logical drive to the directory SYS:WINAPPS/WINWORD on the server named MYSERVER, you might use the following command line:

```
map g:=myserver/sys:winapps/winword
```

Note: Using the MAP utility to map a logical drive on your PC to a network directory is only a temporary solution. Once you turn off your computer or log off the network, the connection is gone. However, you can set up the same connection each time you log onto the network by adding the appropriate line to your log-in script. To do this though, you must use the SYSCON utility. That way, each time you log on to the network, NetWare will read your log-in script and establish the appropriate connections for you automatically. When you subsequently start Windows, it will come up recognizing those connections. Consult your NetWare documentation for details on how to use the SYSCON utility.

Connecting to Network Printers

Novell automatically creates print queues and spoolers for each installed printer. In this way, each printer is automatically made shareable to you.

To connect to a network printer, you use the CAPTURE utility. This utility allows you to define a device (port) on your PC that represents a printer on the network. The command line for the CAPTURE utility takes the following form:

```
capture local=x queue=y
```

This command line breaks down as follows:

- capture: Routes the output from a local printer port to the network printer that is attached to the queue you specify.
- local=*x*: Specifies the local device from which to capture the output. The argument *x* can be 1, 2, or 3, meaning LPT1, LPT2, or LPT3.
- queue=*y*: Specifies the queue on the server that is used to stage print jobs for the printer. The *y* argument specifies the name of the queue that will hold the files to be printed to a particular port on the server.

For example, imagine you want to route your printed output from LPT1 on your PC to the PRINTQ_0 printer queue on the server. To do this, you might use the following command line:

```
capture local=1 queue=printq_0
```

This command line specifies that the queue named PRINTQ_0 will be the recipient of the output from your LPT1 port. After you enter this command, you can print to the PRINT_0 print queue by referring to the LPT1 port in your applications.

CONNECTING TO NETWORK DRIVES

To use shared network resources, such as applications, your PC must be connected to the network drive on which those resources reside. If these connections are already established before you start Windows, it comes up recognizing them automatically. However, if the appropriate network drive connections are not established, or you need to establish additional connections, Windows provides a facility that allows you to do this.

You can connect to network drives, and thus to shared network resources, through the use of File Manager. As you may recall, you can open File Manager by double-clicking on its icon, located in Program Manager's Main group window. If you are already linked to shared directories on the server, File Manager indicates this by showing little disk-drive push buttons for each logical drive across the top of its window. Network-related push buttons are labeled "NET" to identify them. For example, in Figure 13-2, four network-related push buttons—F, G, H, and I—are shown. You can click on any one of these buttons to display the directories on the server that are associated with these logical drives.

To connect to an additional shared directory on the server, select the Disk Connect Net Drive command from File Manager's menu. When you select this command, Windows displays the Connect Network Drive dialog box in Figure 13-3. The Drive text box at the top of this box shows the next unused logical drive that is available on your system. You

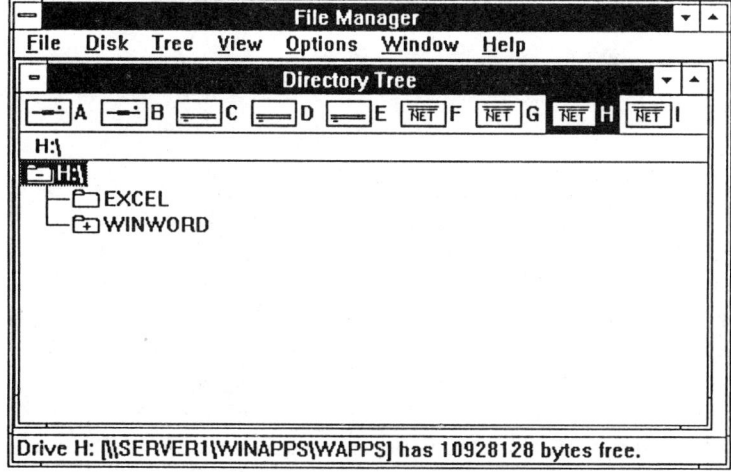

Figure 13-2 The File Manager window shows push buttons representing logical drives linked to the network

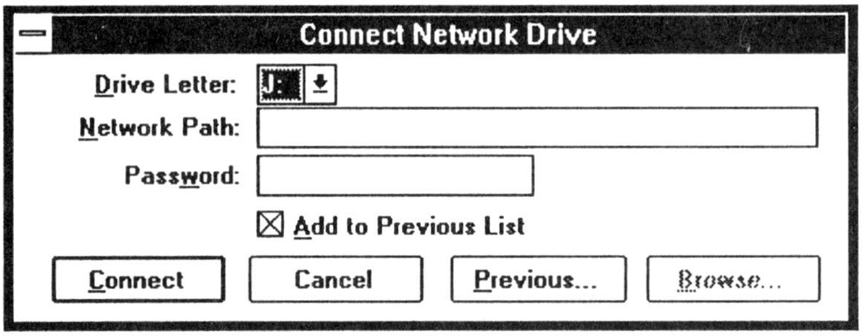

[Dialog box illustration: Connect Network Drive — Drive Letter, Network Path, Password fields; Add to Previous List checkbox; Connect, Cancel, Previous..., Browse... buttons]

Figure 13-3 The Connect Network Drive dialog box

can accept this drive or you can open the list box and select from among the drives that are available.

In the Network Path text box, specify the command line you would normally use at the DOS prompt to link to the shared directory. However, because Windows is network-aware, you do not have to supply the initial program or utility name for the command. For example, on a 3COM 3+Share network, you might use a command line similar to *3f link \\server1\wapps*. However, simply *\\server1\wapps* will do the job here. Or, on a Novell network, you might use a command like *map j:=myserver/sys:winapps/winword*. However, simply *myserver/sys:winapps/winword* will be sufficient here. Finally, if a password is required for you to gain access to the directory, type that password in the Password text box. When you are ready, select the Connect button. Windows links the logical drive you've selected to the shared network directory and returns you to File Manager. A push button for the new logical drive now appears at the top of File Manager's window. You can now use this push button to look at the contents of the network directory.

> *Note:* Some DOS applications allow you connect to network drives from within the application. However, if you decide to take advantage this option, make sure you also disconnect from the network drive before you leave the DOS application.

You can also have Windows remember your previous link commands so that you can easily recall them. Notice that the Connect Network Drive dialog box in Figure 13-3 contains a check box labeled Add to Previous List. When this check box is selected (contains an X), Windows stores each command line you enter in the Network Path text box. To see these command lines, select the Previous button from the Connect Network Drive dialog box. When you select this button, Windows displays the Previous Network Connections dialog box in Figure 13-4. Highlight the previous command line and choose from Select or Delete. If you choose Select, Windows returns you to the Connect Network Drive dialog box and displays the entry in the Network Path text box. You can then set up the connection in the usual way. On the other hand, if you choose Delete, Windows deletes the entry from the Previous Network Connections dialog box.

On some networks, you can also browse shared network directories and choose the one you want to connect to. To do this, select the Browse button from the Connect

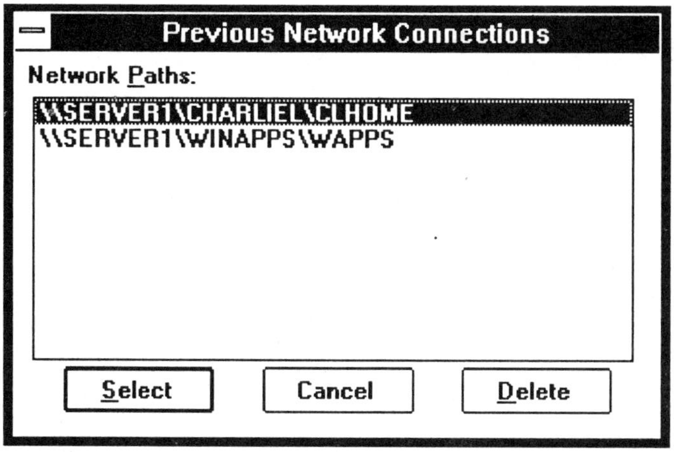

Networking Windows   449

```
┌─────────────────────────────────────────────┐
│ ─         Previous Network Connections      │
│ Network Paths:                              │
│ ┌─────────────────────────────────────────┐ │
│ │ \\SERVER1\CHARLIEL\CLHOME               │ │
│ │ \\SERVER1\WINAPPS\WAPPS                 │ │
│ │                                         │ │
│ │                                         │ │
│ │                                         │ │
│ └─────────────────────────────────────────┘ │
│   ┌────────┐    ┌────────┐    ┌────────┐    │
│   │ Select │    │ Cancel │    │ Delete │    │
│   └────────┘    └────────┘    └────────┘    │
└─────────────────────────────────────────────┘
```

Figure 13-4 The Previous Network Connections dialog box

Network Drive dialog box. (This button is not selectable for the 3Com 3+Share network, but it is selectable for Novell NetWare.) When you select this button, Windows displays a network-specific dialog box that allows you choose a network directory that you want to connect to. For example, Figure 13-5 shows the Browse Connections dialog box associated with the Novell NetWare driver. The Servers/Volumes box on the left shows the volumes available on the current server. When you click on the name of a volume, the directories in that volume are displayed on the Directories box on the right. You can then select the directory you want. To confirm your selection, select the OK button. Windows returns you to the Connect Network Drive dialog box and enters your selection in the Network Path text box. You can now select the Connect push button to connect to the directory.

Note: You should always use the same logical drive to link to a given network directory. This is especially important if you have set up an icon in Program Manager for that application. See "Running Applications" later in this chapter for additional details on running network applications.

Tip: When you have difficulty connecting to a network drive

If you are having difficulty connecting to a network drive, you may want to check for a lastdrive= statement in your CONFIG.SYS file. For example, you might find a statement similar to lastdrive=g, which tells DOS that the last available logical drive you intend to use is G. If you try to set up a logical drive H, Windows will not be able to accommodate you and will issue an error message when you attempt to make a connection.

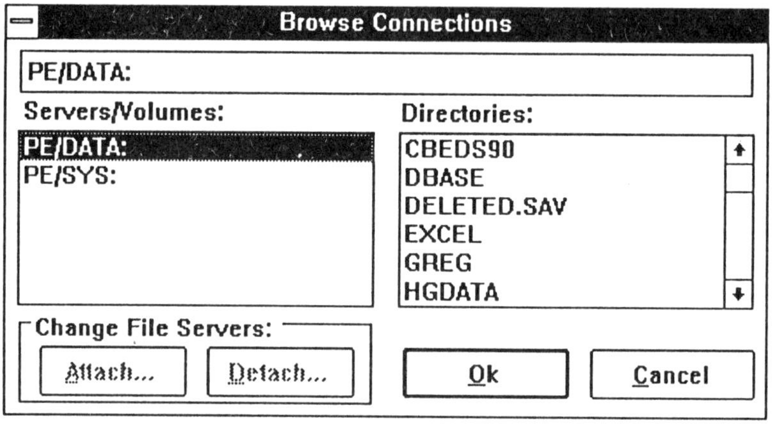

Figure 13-5 The Browse Connections dialog box

You can also disconnect from a network drive. To do this, select the Disk Disconnect Net Drive command from File Manager's menu. When you select this command, Windows displays the dialog box in Figure 13-6. Specify the letter of the logical drive that you want to disconnect and select the OK button. Windows breaks the connection to the shared directory on the file server defined by that drive and updates the File Manager window accordingly.

Caution: If you are using a shared copy of Windows, make sure that you do not disconnect from the drive that gives you access to the Windows program files. Otherwise, Windows will not run correctly.

Note: On some networks, you may not be able to disconnect from a network drive if you are running Windows in 386 enhanced mode. However, this only applies to network drives you were connected to prior to starting Windows.

PRINTING ON A NETWORK

As you might imagine, you can print to the network from your Windows applications. However, before you can print to the network printer from a Windows application, you must link your PC to the network printer. If a connection to a printer is already established before you start Windows, it comes up recognizing that connection automatically. On the other hand, if a connection has not been established, or you want to establish a new connection, Windows allows you to do this. The sections that follow explain how.

Note: If you are running a local copy of Windows as opposed to a shared copy, you can print from your Windows applications without having to exit them afterward. As you know, with many locally installed DOS applications, you must exit the

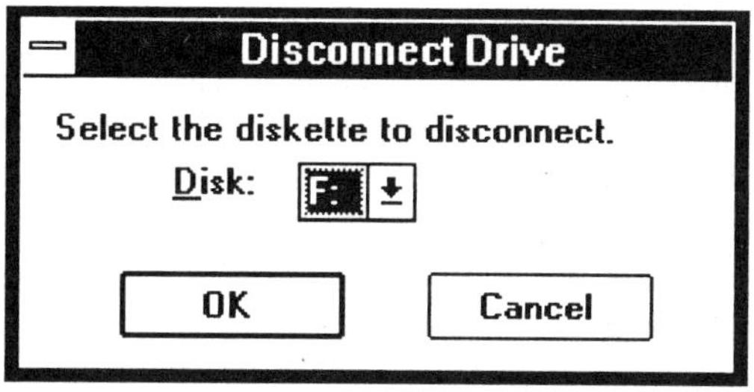

Figure 13-6 The Disconnect Net Drive dialog box

application in order to have the printed output released to the network printer. However, because Windows is network-aware, you do not have to exit a locally installed Windows application in order to release your printed output to the network printer.

Connecting to the Network Printer

To link to printers connected to the network, you use the Printers icon in the Control Panel. When you double-click on this icon, Windows displays the Printers dialog box. If you are connected to the network, the Network button on the right side of the Printers dialog box appears active. Select this button to display the Printers - Network Connections dialog box shown in Figure 13-7. In the Network Printer Connections box, Windows shows any connections that have been previously established with network printers. Further, if you were previously connected to a network printer before you started Windows, the name of that printer appears in this box.

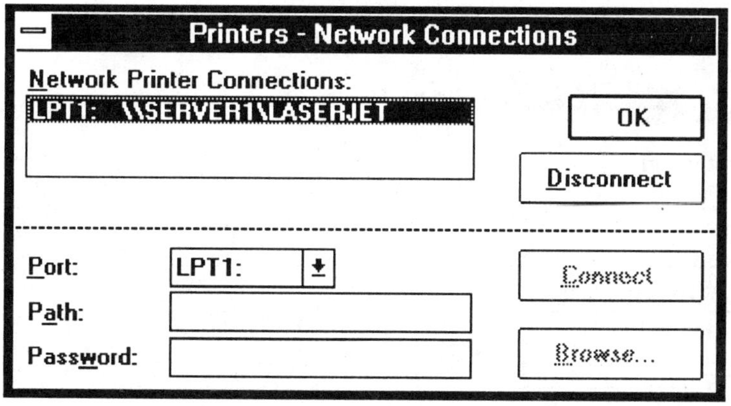

Figure 13-7 The Printers - Network Connections dialog box

To connect to a new or additional network printer, you use the bottom half of the Printers - Network Connections dialog box. From the Port list box, select the port on your local PC that you want to use to send printed output to the network. In the Path text box, specify the command line that you would normally use to connect to the printer. You do not have to supply the initial utility name for this command line. For example, if you are working on a 3Com 3+Share network, you might use a command similar to *3p link lpt1: \\server1\laserjet*. However, simply *\\server1\laserjet* will suffice here. Or, if you are working on a Novell NetWare network, type the name of the server followed by a slash (/) and the name of the print queue, for example *myserver/printq_1*. If a password is required to access the printer, type that password in the Password text box. When you're ready, select the Connect button. Windows links to the printer you've specified via the network driver.

Some network drivers, like the Novell NetWare driver, allow you to browse the printers available on the network and select the one you want. (This feature is not available for 3Com 3+Share.) To use this feature, select the Browse button from the Printers - Network Connections dialog box. When you select this button, Windows displays a network-specific dialog box that lets you select from among the printers currently available on the network. For example, Figure 13-8 shows the Browse Queues dialog box associated with the Novell NetWare driver. When you make a selection from this box, Windows returns you to the Printers - Network Connections dialog box and displays your selection in the Path text box. You can then select the Connect button to connect to the printer in the usual way.

You can also disconnect from a network printer by using the Disconnect push button in the Printers - Network Connections dialog box. First, highlight the description of the printer you want to disconnect in the Network Printer Connections box, and then select Disconnect. Windows breaks your connection with the printer you've selected.

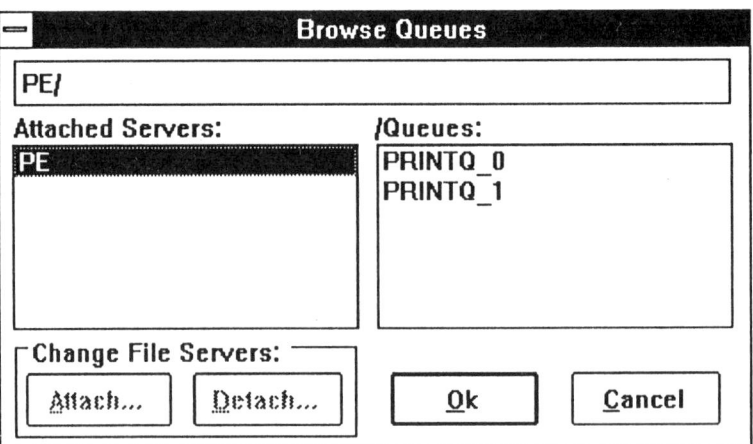

Figure 13-8 The Browse Queues dialog box

Printing from Windows

Once you are connected to a network printer, you can print from within your Windows applications as you normally would. However, to print successfully, you must make sure that the default printer for that application matches the make, model, and port of the network printer you are connected to.

For example, imagine you want to print a report from Write. To do this, first prepare the report in Write. When you are ready, use the File Printer Setup command to display the Printer Setup dialog box. Double check to make sure the current default printer matches the make and model of the network printer you are currently connected to. Also, make sure the port assigned to that printer matches the port assignment you've made in the Printers - Network Connections dialog box discussed in the previous section. For example, if you are connected to the HP LaserJet Series II printer on the network and specified LPT1 as the port for that printer, select PCL/HP LaserJet on LPT1 from the Printers Setup box. Then, select OK to return to Write. Finally, select the File Print command to print the report. Windows sends the report directly to the network print queue for that printer.

Some network drivers, like the LAN Manager 2.0 driver, will display a confirmation message box informing you that your print job has been processed. When you respond to this message box, Windows will display a second network-specific message box that gives you details about the execution of the print job. However, to display this message box, the WinPopup utility (NWPOPUP.EXE) must be installed for the current network driver. You'll learn more about this utility later under "Sending and Receiving Messages."

Viewing Network Print Queues

To manage multiple print jobs from various users, the network software must make use of print queues (memory or disk-based holding areas) for each printer that is connected to the network. These queues stage print jobs for the printer; as print jobs are received, they are logged into the queue and released sequentially to the printer in the order in which they were received. Therefore, if there is heavy traffic on the network, your print job may wait for quite some time before it is actually sent to the printer.

Most Windows network drivers allow you to view the contents of the network print queue to which you are currently connected. When you view a network print queue, Windows shows you all the files waiting in the queue, not just the ones you've sent. Thus, you can see where your files stand in relation to others in the queue. In addition, some network drivers allow you to browse the various network print queues and to view the contents of those queues to which you are not currently connected. This allows you to see which printer has the least activity. You might use this feature before sending a print job to the network. You can then send your print job to the printer with the least activity, thereby bettering your chances of getting your printed output just that much quicker.

454   *Windows 3 Power Tools*

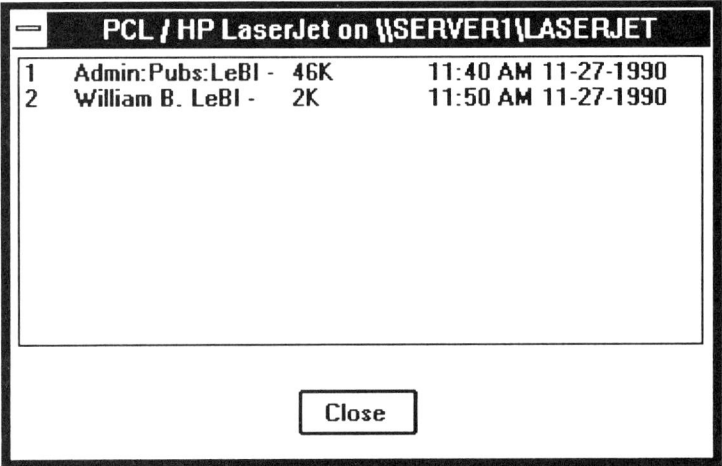

Figure 13-9 **Viewing the network queue from Windows**

Viewing the Network Queue

To view the contents of a network print queue from within Windows, you use **Print Manager**. As you may recall, you can open Print Manager by double-clicking on its icon, which is located in Program Manager's Main group window. Once the **Print Manager** window is displayed, select the View Selected Net Queue command from the menu bar. Windows displays a dialog box similar to the one in Figure 13-9. This dialog box shows the contents of the print queue to which you are currently connected. The extent of the information provided depends on the capabilities of the network driver you are currently using. However, generally each print job is identified by a title line that shows who sent it, when, and how big the file is. In addition, each title line for a print job begins with a number that identifies its position in the queue. To return to Print Manager, select the Close push button.

Viewing Other Net Queues

Some network drivers also allow you to view the contents of network print queues to which you are not currently connected. To do this, select the View Other Net Queue command from Print Manager's menu. (If your network does not support this feature, the Other Net Queue option appears greyed.) When you select this command, Windows displays a network-specific dialog box similar to the one in Figure 13-10. The Network Queue text box allows you to type the name of the network queue you want to view. After you make an entry in this box, select the View push button. Windows displays the contents of that queue in the box above. To see the contents of another queue, type its name in the Network Queue box and select View again. To return to Print Manager, select the Close button.

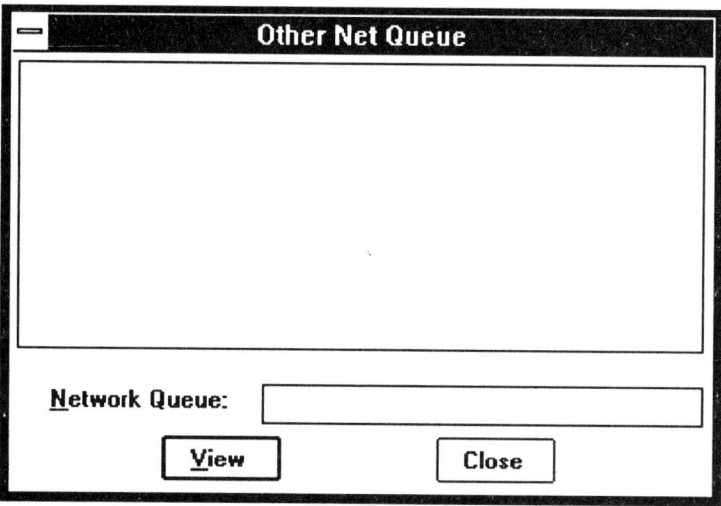

Figure 13-10 The Other Net Queue dialog box

Updating the Net Queue Manually

Windows periodically updates itself on the status of the network print queue while the Print Manager window is open. However, if you want to make absolutely sure you are viewing the most recent information in the network print queue, you can manually update Windows. To do this, select the View Update Net Queues command from Print Manager's menu. This command causes Windows to recheck the status of the print queue. That way, when you view the contents of the print queue, you can rest assured you are getting the most up-to-the-minute information.

Turning Off Print Queue Checking

As mentioned, Windows periodically checks the status of the network print queue while the Print Manager window is open. However, if you want to disable this checking during periods of heavy network traffic, you can select the Options Network command from Print Manager's menu. When you select this command, Windows displays the Network Options dialog box in Figure 13-11. Select the Update Network Display check box to clear its contents and select OK to return to Print Manager. Windows will now cease periodic print-queue status checking.

Enabling Print Manager

Normally, Windows bypasses Print Manager entirely when printing to the network. Since the network provides its own print queues, routing your printed output through Print Manager would result in an unnecessary delay in printing over the network. However, if

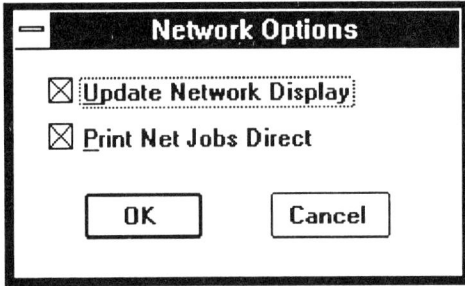

Figure 13-11 The Network Options dialog box

you want to use Print Manager as a staging area before your print jobs are sent on to the network, you can reenable it for network printing. To do this, select the Options Network command from Print Manager's menu. Windows displays the dialog box in Figure 13-11. Select the Print Net Jobs Direct check box to clear its contents and select OK to return to Print Manager. Windows will now route all outgoing print jobs through Print Manager.

The extent to which Print Manager is reenabled depends on the capabilities of the network driver you are using. With some drivers, like the 3Com 3+Share driver, your local print jobs are routed through Print Manager's print queue, but you lose the ability to control them—that is, the Pause, Resume, and Delete buttons in Print Manager's window remain greyed (unselectable). Therefore, you cannot pause, resume, or delete outgoing print jobs. However, with other network drivers, like the Novell NetWare driver, these buttons are activated, allowing you to manage your outgoing print jobs just as though they were being sent to a local printer.

ACCESSING NETWORK FEATURES FROM WINDOWS

You can access some of the features of your network through the Windows Control Panel. As you may recall, you can open the Control Panel by clicking on its icon located in Program Manager's Main group window. If you've previously installed a network driver for a local copy of Windows, or you've installed a shared copy of Windows on your PC, the Control Panel appears as shown in Figure 13-12. Notice that a Network icon now appears in the upper-right corner of the Control Panel. This icon serves as yet another gateway to the network.

The features available through the Network icon depend on the capabilities of your network driver. For example, with the 3Com 3+Share network driver, clicking on the Network icon results in the dialog box in Figure 13-13. Notice that this dialog box contains only a single check box, labeled "Disable warning when network not running." Normally, if you are on the network while running Windows and the network is disabled, Windows will warn you accordingly. To disable this warning, you can select the check box in Figure 13-13. This dialog box is typical of network drivers that provide only partial

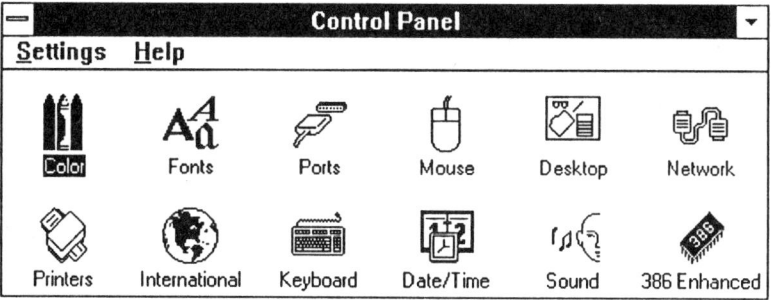

Figure 13-12 The Control Panel with the Network icon displayed

support for Windows' networking capabilities. However, other fully featured network drivers, such the Novell NetWare driver, provide a great deal of functionality through the Network icon.

For example, if you are running Novell NetWare, Windows displays the Network Utilities dialog box in Figure 13-14 when you select the Network icon. This dialog box offers options that are specific to Novell NetWare and are determined by your network administrator. The dialog box that appears for your network may be entirely different. Generally, though, you can use the dialog box that is displayed to do such things as log on and off the network, change your network password, send a message to another user on the network, or run a network-specific utility.

Logging On and Off the Server

As mentioned, many network drivers allow you to log on and off the network server from within Windows. However, each driver that supports this feature has a different way of going about it. The discussion that follows is conducted from the viewpoint of the Novell NetWare driver.

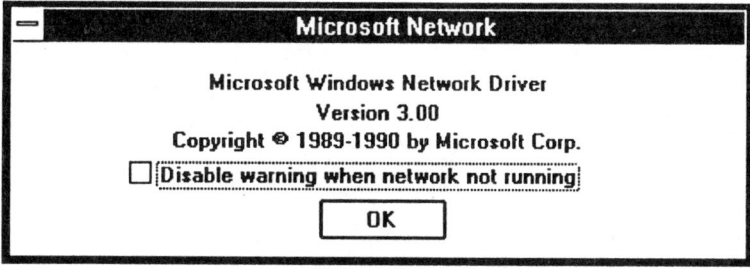

Figure 13-13 A network-specific dialog box for the 3Com 3+Share driver

458 *Windows 3 Power Tools*

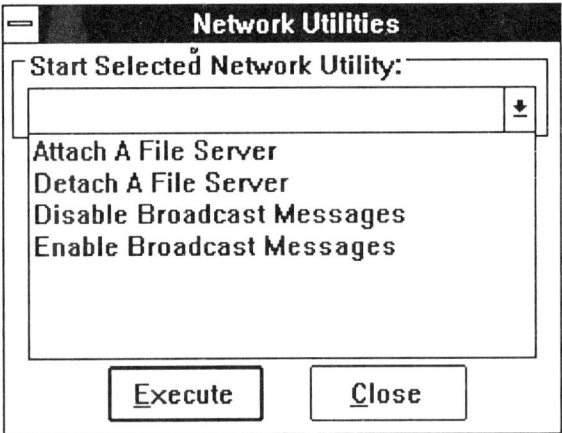

Figure 13-14 The Novell NetWare Network Utilities dialog box

If you are running a local copy of Windows, you can easily log on and off a network server. For example, if you are not currently connected to the network, select Attach A File Server followed by Execute from the Network Utilities dialog box in Figure 13-14. When you select this option, Windows displays the Attach File Server dialog box in Figure 13-15. In the File Server drop-down list box, specify the name of the server you want to attach to. In the Username text box, specify your log-on name. If a password is required, type that password in the Password text box. When you are ready, select the OK button. Windows logs you onto the File Server you specified.

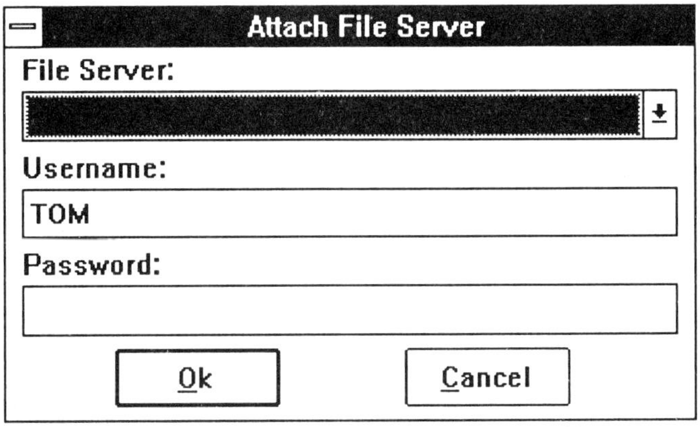

Figure 13-15 The Novell Attach File Server dialog box

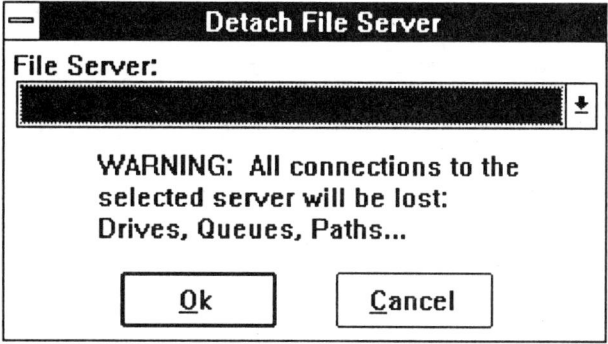

Figure 13-16 The Novell Detach File Server dialog box

Note: You can also access the Attach File Server dialog box in Figure 13-15 by selecting the Attach button from either the Browse Connections dialog box shown earlier in Figure 13-5 or from the Browse Queues dialog box shown earlier in Figure 13-8.

If you are running a shared copy of Windows, you must have already logged onto a network file server to run Windows in the first place. However, if you have access to another file server on your network, you can use the Attach File Server dialog box in Figure 13-15 to log onto that server.

You can also log off a network server from within Windows. To do this, select the Detach a File Server option followed by Execute from the Network Utilities dialog box in Figure 13-14. When you select this option, Windows displays the Detach File Server dialog box shown in Figure 13-16. Specify the name of the server you want to detach in the File Server drop-down list box and select OK. Windows logs you off the file server you specified.

Caution: If you are running a shared copy of Windows, do not log off the file server that provides you the shared copy. Otherwise, Windows will not run correctly. Also, if you are running either a shared or a local copy of Windows, avoid logging on and off the network from the DOS prompt. Instead, use the Network icon in the Control Panel to log on and off the network—provided, of course, that your network driver supports this feature.

Changing Your Password

Some network drivers allow you to change your password. Although the Novell NetWare and 3Com 3+Share drivers do not support this feature, the driver for LAN Manager 2.0 does. When this driver is installed, selecting the Network icon from the Control panel results in the display of a special Networks - LAN Manager window. This window offers an extensive menu system that allows you, among other things, to change your password.

Sending and Receiving Messages

Most networks offer some sort of simple messaging system that allows users to send short messages to one another. In support of this feature, some Windows network drivers (for example, LAN Manager 2.0) allow users to send and receive messages from within Windows. Others, like Novell NetWare, allow you only to receive messages. For example, if you are a Novell NetWare user, you know you can send a short message to another user by using the SEND utility. For example, if you want to send a message to the user named Tom, you might type the following at the DOS prompt:

```
send "Meeting at 2:30 in the small conference room" Tom
```

If Tom happens to be running Windows when you send this message, a message window with an OK button will pop up in the middle of whatever he happens to be doing at the time. The message window will list the log-in name of the person who sent the message followed by the message itself. To clear the message, the recipient need only select the OK button from the message window.

Exercise care, though, when sending messages to other users who are running Windows on a Novell network. Normally, when you use the SEND utility to send a message to someone who is running a graphics-mode application, their system will lock up. Windows itself, as well as most Windows applications, run in graphics mode all the time. Therefore, when the message window containing your message is displayed, the recipient's system will lock until they select OK to clear the message window. If they happen to be running a graphics-based communications package, like Terminal, at the time, you might interrupt an important transmission.

The Novell NetWare driver allows you to disable broadcast messages from other users. To do this, select the Network icon from the Control Panel to display the Network Utilities dialog box shown in Figure 13-14. Open the Start Selected Network Utility drop-down list box and select Disable Broadcast Messages. Then, select the Execute push button. The Novell NetWare driver executes the CASTOFF utility and disables the receipt of broadcast messages for your workstation. To reenable broadcast messages again, select Enable Broadcast Messages to have the Novell NetWare driver run the CASTON utility.

Note: To receive messages in Windows, the WinPopup program (NWPOPUP.EXE) must be referenced in your WIN.INI file. A copy of WIN.INI resides in your personal Windows directory. Normally, when you install the Novell NetWare driver, Windows modifies the load= statement in WIN.INI to read load=NWPOPUP.EXE. That way, the WinPopup utility is loaded automatically when you start Windows.

RUNNING NETWORK APPLICATIONS

You can run shared network applications from within Windows by using either File Manager or Program Manager. The sections that follow explain how.

Using File Manager

To run an application by using File Manager, begin by opening the File Manager window. As you may recall, you can open File Manager by double-clicking on its icon in Program Manager's Main group window. If necessary, use the Disk Connect Net Drive command from File Manager's menu to connect to the network drive that contains the application. (See "Connecting to Network Drives" earlier in this chapter for details on how to use this command.)

Once you are connected to the appropriate network drive, Windows displays a disk-drive button at the top of the File Manager window that represents that drive. (This disk-drive button will be labeled "NET" to identify it.) Double-click on this drive button to have File Manager display a directory tree for that network drive.

Once the directory tree is displayed, double-click on the name of the network directory that contains the application. Windows opens a directory window that shows the files in that network directory. Scroll through the directory window to locate the name of the executable file for the application. (To aid in this, you may want to use the View By Type command from File Manager's menu to sort the files by extension.) For example, if you are in the directory that contains Microsoft Excel, find the file named EXCEL.EXE. Or, if you are in the directory that contains Word for Windows, locate WINWORD.EXE. Once you find the filename, double-click on it. Windows opens the application you've selected on the desktop.

Using Program Manager

You can also set up icons for network applications in Program Manager's group windows. To do this, first connect to the appropriate network drive, if necessary, by using File Manager. (See "Connecting to Network Drives," earlier, for details on how to do this.) Once you are connected, use the File New command in the usual way to create a new program item for the application in a group window of your choice. You can then start the application by double-clicking on that icon.

However, if you decide to set up an icon for a network application, make sure you connect the same logical drive on your PC to the appropriate network directory for that application each time you use Windows. Otherwise, Windows will give you can "Invalid Path" error message the next time you attempt to use the icon. For example, imagine you are currently connected to the Microsoft Excel directory on the network through your logical drive F. At that point you set up an icon for this application. The next time you start Windows, you link your logical drive E to the Microsoft Excel directory on the network. When you attempt to use your Excel icon, Windows displays an "Invalid Path" error message.

Windows attempts to warn you of this problem when you set up an icon for a network application. In fact, when you select OK to create the icon, Windows displays the message box in Figure 13-17, asking if you want to continue. This is Windows' way of warning you that the potential exists for the path to the network application to change, making the icon invalid.

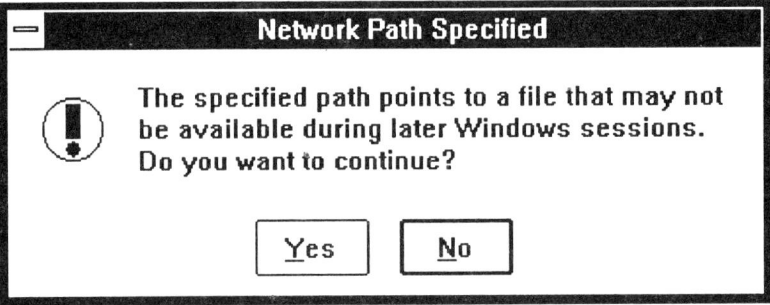

Figure 13-17 Windows displays a message box when you attempt to set up an icon for a network application

Note: If you are running a shared copy of Windows, it is possible that your network administrator used a special configuration file (SETUP.INF) that allows him or her to set up selected icons for shared applications in your Program Manager group windows. In addition, he or she may have modified your log-in script to preconnect your PC to the appropriate network drives for those applications. If this is the case, you do not have to use File Manager to establish connections to the network before you can use the network application icons in Program Manager.

NETWORK ADMINISTRATION

This section tells you how to install a shared copy of Windows on a network server. It also covers a few administrative topics you may find useful when setting up Windows on the network.

Installing Windows on the Server

As you might imagine, installing Windows on the server involves copying the files from the Windows program disks onto a shared directory on the server. However, most of the files on the Windows program disks are in compressed form. Therefore, to make those files usable, you must use the decompression program (EXPAND.EXE) that comes with Windows to expand the files. To make this process more efficient, you can create a special batch file that both copies the files from the program disks and expands them in the process.

Note: Before you begin the process of installing Windows on the server, make sure you have at least 5 to 6 megabytes of free disk space available for the program.

From a workstation, log onto the server under the appropriate administrative name. For example, if you are using a 3Com 3+Share network, log on as Admin. Or, if you are working on Novell NetWare, log on as the Supervisor.

Create a directory where you want the shared copy of Windows to reside. For purposes of this discussion, assume you create the directory \WINDOWS on an appropriate drive, for example F. (For the balance of this discussion, substitute the letter of the drive that you are actually using.) Once the directory is created, change to the directory to make it current.

At this point you are ready to create the batch file that will copy the Windows program file to the new directory on the server. The batch file you are about to create assumes that the drive you are copying the files from is drive A and the drive you are copying the files to is drive F. Substitute the drive letters you are actually using where appropriate. Perform the following steps:

1. In case you don't have an ASCII text editor handy, type the following at the DOS prompt:

    ```
    copy con expall.bat
    a:
    for %%i in (*.*) do f:\windows\expand %%i f:\windows\%%1
    f:
    ```

    When you press ENTER to complete the last line, type **CTRL-Z** and press ENTER. DOS creates the batch file EXPALL.BAT in the current directory.

2. Insert Windows Disk 2 into drive A and type:

    ```
    copy a:expand.exe f:\windows
    ```

    The expand decompression utility (EXPAND.EXE) is copied to the server directory.

3. Insert the Windows Disk 1 into drive A and type the following at the DOS prompt:

    ```
    expall a:*.* f:\windows
    ```

    When you press ENTER to confirm this command line, DOS runs the EXPALL.BAT file. This batch file copies all of the files on the disk in drive A to the \WINDOWS directory on drive F, expanding them in the process.

4. Repeat step 3 for the remaining Windows program disks.

As you're watching the Windows program files being copied onto the server, it begins to dawn on you that all the files from all the disks are being copied. Watching the last disk being copied can be especially frustrating as you see myriad .DRV driver files being copied for equipment you know you do not have. However, unless you know specifically which driver files are used for your equipment, you are better off resisting the temptation to delete these unneeded files. It is better to sacrifice a little disk space than to risk deleting a critical driver file.

Once all the Windows program files have been copied onto the server directory, you are ready to make that directory shareable to users on the network as read only. For example, if you are using a 3Com 3+Share network, you might create a sharename for the directory by using the following command line:

```
3f share windows=f:\windows /r
```

To safeguard this directory even further, you might want to make the files in this directory read only by using the DOS ATTRIB.EXE utility, for example:

```
attrib +r *.*
```

At this point, you might consider updating the AUTOUSER.BAT files for your various users so that they are automatically linked to the \WINDOWS directory.

If you are working on a Novell NetWare network, use the MAP SEARCH command to make the SYS:WINDOWS directory accessible through search drives, for example:

```
map search3: = sys:windows
```

Assign a drive letter to the directory, for example:

```
map f: = sys:windows
```

At this point, you can use the SYSCON.EXE utility to assign trustee rights for the directory. Remember to make the directory a Read-Open-Search directory. You may also want to use the SYSCON utility to modify the log-in scripts for users so that they are automatically mapped to this directory. See your Novell NetWare documentation for details on this.

Once the Windows program files have been installed and the directory has been properly shared, your users can get a copy of Windows from the network by using the SETUP /N command line. See "Installing a Shared Copy of Windows on a Workstation," earlier in this chapter, for more details on this.

Configuring Windows

When you use the SETUP /N command line to get a shared copy of Windows from the server, you are actually running the Windows SETUP.EXE program. This program takes you through a complete Windows installation session. To guide this session and configure Windows, SETUP.EXE relies on an ASCII text file called SETUP.INF. This file provides the necessary configuration information for setup and remains in the shared Windows directory on the server. It is through this SETUP.INF file that you can do a little configuring of your own.

Among other things, the SETUP.INF files determines the initial contents of Program Manager's group windows. If you installed Windows applications in shared directories on the server (for example, Word for Windows or Microsoft Excel), you can have the icons for these applications placed in one of Program Manager's group windows. To do this, use an ASCII text editor, like Notepad, to open the SETUP.INF file. Locate the section that begins with [progman.groups]. This section begins with a list of the default group windows in Program Manager. Beneath this, the applications to be located in each group window are defined. Each application has a listing that includes a description, path to the executable file, icon filename, and icon number. These elements are separated from one another by commas.

Locate the section that defines the group window to which you want to add an application. Enter a line that takes the following form:

`"Description",x:\dirpath\app-file,[icon-file],[icon-number]`

This command line breaks down as follows:

- "Description": The description you want to appear beneath the icon.
- *x:* The drive on the server that contains the application.
- *dirpath*: The directory path to the application.
- *app-file*: The executable filename for the application.
- *icon-file*: The file that contains the icon you want to use. This argument is optional; if you leave it out, Windows will default to using the icon for the current application or a PROGMAN.EXE icon, in the case of a DOS application. However, you can specify the name of any application you want as the source of an icon. You can also specify the name of a Windows icon (.ICO) file.
- *icon-number*: Some Windows applications contain more than one icon. If such is the case, you can use this optional argument to specify the number of the icon you want to use.

For example, imagine you want to have the icon for Microsoft Excel appear in the Main Group window of each of your users. Assume for a moment that this application is located on the shared directory G:\WINAPPS\EXCEL on the server. To use the default icon for Excel you might enter the following:

`"Excel",g:\winapps\excel\excel.exe`

Or if you wanted to borrow the third icon from PROGMAN.EXE, you might make the following entry:

`"Excel",g:\winapps\excel\excel.exe,progman.exe,3`

Configuring User Workstations

When users get a shared copy of Windows from the network, they are asked to specify a personal Windows directory on their local workstation or on the server. To that directory, Windows will copy only those files that are pertinent to that particular workstation. Examples of files that are copied include configuration files (WIN.INI and SYS-

TEM.INI), memory management files (EMM386.SYS or HIMEM.SYS), and the Windows executable file (WIN.COM).

Copying Selected Files to User Directories

However, as a system administrator, you can also have specific network-related files copied to users' personal directories when they install Windows on their workstation. To do this, you must once again use the SETUP.INF file.

For example, imagine you have created a series of custom Program Information Files (PIFs) for DOS applications. To have these files copied to a user's personal directory automatically, open the SETUP.INF file in Notepad and locate the section that begins with [net]. In this section, type a command line that includes a drive number, a colon, the name of the file, and an optional description for the file enclosed in quotes. The drive number you provide does not matter. You can use any number you want. For example, imagine you've created the file SPEC.PIF and stored it in the Windows program directory on the server. To have this file copied to all user workstations, you might include the following entry in the [net] section of the SETUP.INF file:

```
3:SPEC.PIF,"Network PIF File"
```

Setting Up Paths

Make sure that the user's personal Windows directory and the shared Windows program directory are in the user's path. The order in which they appear in the path is also important. Make sure the personal directory is listed first followed by the server directory. On many networks, you can control the path used by simply modifying the SET PATH statement in the user's AUTOEXEC.BAT file. However, with many networks, the user's path is changed after he or she logs onto the network. If such is the case with your network, make sure you update the user's log-in script to include the path to both the personal directory and the Windows directory on the server.

> **Tip:** Set up user's workstations in advance
>
> To make it easier for users to use Windows, you can create batch files (3Com) or log-in scripts (Novell) containing the appropriate linking (3Com) or mapping (Novell) information. You can include this batch file as part of the log-in process for each user. This will help to ensure that appropriate logical drives have been assigned to shared directories and the appropriate printer services are available. That way, when the user starts Windows, it will come up preconfigured to recognize the appropriate services on the network.

Getting Information about Your Network

As mentioned, every Windows network driver is designed to function with a particular type of network. When you install a network driver, the appropriate entries are made in the WIN.INI and SYSTEM.INI files in each user's personal Windows directory. These entries are required so that Windows will recognize the driver when you start the program and so that the driver will be properly configured to run on your system.

For most supported network drivers, there are various sources of information that can help you to understand how the entries in the WIN.INI and SYSTEM.INI files affect the configuration of your network driver. One of these sources of information is the NETWORKS.TXT file that comes with your copy of Windows. You can open this file and read its contents by using an ASCII text editor, such as Notepad. The file contains important notes about Windows networking in general and about configuring specific types of networks for use with Windows. You should read the contents of this file thoroughly before you install Windows on your network.

In addition to the NETWORKS.TXT file, some network drivers come with a Help facility. For example, the Novell NetWare driver comes with a help file called NETWARE.HLP. This file is automatically copied to the Windows program directory when you install the Novell NetWare driver. To open this file, select the Help Index command from Control Panel's menu. This causes Windows to open its standard Help window. Use the File Open command from this window to open the NETWARE.HLP file. Once the file is displayed, you can find information about different topics that are specifically related to the use and configuration of the Novell NetWare driver.

For example, you'll discover through NETWARE.HLP that a special file called NETWARE.INI is installed in each user's personal Windows directory. You can modify the contents of this file to have the names of different NetWare utilities (for example, SYSCON) appear in the Network Utilities dialog box when you select the Network icon from the Control Panel. You'll also learn about the WinPopup (NWPOPUP.EXE) program that comes with Windows and allows users to receive network broadcast messages while working in Windows.

SUMMARY

This chapter shows you how to get started using Windows on a network. For example, you now know how to set up a local of copy of Windows to recognize the network. You also know how to install a shared copy of Windows on your workstation by using the SETUP /N command.

You also know how to use Windows to connect your PC to shared resources on the server. For example, you can now link to directories that contain shared applications. And you know how to delete a network link when you need to.

This chapter also shows you how to print from Windows to the network. For example, you now know how to link to different printers on the network printer. You also know how to check the network print queues to see which printer is the least busy.

You also know how to access network-specific features from within Windows. For example, you now know how to use the Control Panel Network icon to open a network-specific dialog box that lets you log on and off the network, manage broadcast messages from other users, and change your password.

Finally, from this chapter, you know how to administer Windows on the network. For example, you know how to install Windows on the server and how to use the SETUP.INF file to configure individual user copies.

14

Oriel for Windows

Oriel for Windows is a graphics-based batch language for Windows 3 that gives you direct access to the Graphics Device Interface (GDI), the same tool Windows programmers use to create customized Windows programs. Oriel for Windows reads and acts on the commands contained in an ASCII file that can be created with any text editor, such as Notepad.

Oriel for Windows recognizes 33 different commands that let you perform such diverse functions as building custom menus, running executable programs, and drawing graphic objects on the screen using different shapes, colors, and patterns. Here are some examples of what you can do with these commands:

- Build Windows demo programs complete with custom screens, menus, and messages boxes.
- Create front-end shells for launching Windows and DOS applications.
- Write simple draw programs that accept keyboard and mouse input.
- Build hypertext-like programs similar to the ToolBook demo bundled with early copies of Windows 3.0, where you click on a region of the screen (a button, for example) and text pops up giving you more information.
- Experiment with the GDI interactively in a way that is simply not possible with the Windows 3.0 Software Development Kit (SDK).

HOW ORIEL FOR WINDOWS WORKS

If you've ever tried to create a simple Windows program using the Windows SDK and a C compiler, you know that it takes several pages of code just to put a simple message like "Hello world!" on the screen. With Oriel for Windows, creating such a program is easy. All you do is use a text editor (we recommend Notepad) and place the following two commands in an ASCII file:

```
DrawText(10,10,"Hello world!")
WaitInput()
```

If you then name the ASCII file HELLO.TXT and save it in the Oriel directory (for example, C:\ORIEL), you can run Oriel from File Manager and have it execute the contents of HELLO.TXT. To do so, you can start File Manager, navigate to the Oriel directory, and use the File Run command with the following command line:

```
ORIEL HELLO.TXT
```

Oriel creates the window in Figure 14-1.

Notice that what you've created is a true Windows application, complete with a resizable window, a window Control menu, and Maximize and Minimize buttons. As you can with any other Windows application, you can switch away from your Oriel program, perform work in another application, and then switch back. All the while, your Oriel program continues to execute, waiting for input.

From this point, you can add more Oriel commands to the ASCII file. The most convenient way is to use Notepad to make the additions you want and save the file. You can then execute the program again to see the effect of the new commands.

If you've made a mistake in the script, Oriel terminates it and shows a message, like the one in Figure 14-2, which identifies the errant line. By keeping Notepad open on the desktop, you can easily change your script and test it again.

Figure 14-1 Hello world! using Oriel for Windows

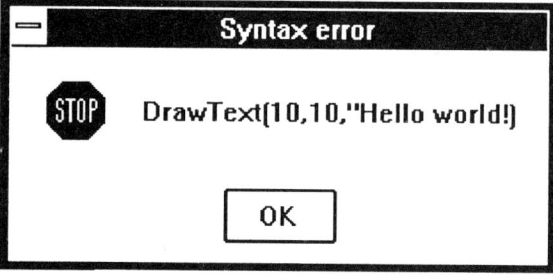

Figure 14-2 A sample syntax error message

Note: Oriel for Windows can accept ASCII files of up to 64K in size. However, Notepad can only work with ASCII files that are less than 50K. If you have a program that is larger than 50K, you'll have to use another editor besides Notepad to work with it.

MEMORY REQUIREMENTS

The Oriel for Windows executable file is quite small, only about 18K. However, the amount of memory that Oriel occupies in your system depends on the type of video display you have. Oriel for Windows uses a full-screen bitmap to store the contents of the screen so that it can restore the window when it needs to. Therefore, you can use the following equation to compute the amount of memory Oriel will require in your system:

```
Amount of memory = Size of ORIEL.EXE (18K) + Size of a
   Full-Screen Bitmap (.BMP) File
```

For example, on a standard VGA system, the size of a full-screen bitmap is approximately 150K. Therefore, the amount of memory that Oriel occupies is approximately 168K (18K + 150K). By contrast, on an EGA system the size of a full-screen bitmap is approximately 112K. Therefore, the amount of memory Oriel consumes on this type of system is about 130K (18K + 112K).

BASIC RULES AND SYNTAX

The basic rules and syntax for Oriel for Windows are quite simple. There are four classes of identifiers (names) in Oriel: commands, variables, tokens, and labels. These four kinds of identifiers are not case sensitive and can be any length. The sections that follow describe additional rules for the four classes of identifiers.

Commands

Commands are the basic building blocks of an Oriel script. Most Oriel commands follow the syntax shown in Figure 14-3, where a keyword is followed by parameters enclosed

Figure 14-3 The most common command syntax

in parentheses. The *keyword* names the action the command is to perform and can occur anywhere on a line. *Parameters* (also called arguments) provide the information necessary to execute the command and are separated by commas. Parameters can be integers, text enclosed in double quotes, variables, and tokens.

Other commands, such as If, follow the looser syntax shown in Figure 14-4. With these commands, the only rule is that the command elements must be separated by at least one space. You'll find the syntax for all Oriel commands in the command reference that follows and in the quick reference at the end of the chapter.

Variables

Oriel for Windows lets you create integer variables. To create an integer variable, all you have to do is use its name.

Variable names can be any length and can be upper or lower case. A variable name can use any of the characters A-Z, a-z, 0-9, or _ (underscore). However, it cannot start with a number. For example, the following are all valid variable names:

```
Mousex    _012       Foxtrot    y1         NEXT_LINE0
```

When you create a variable, Oriel automatically initializes it to zero. You can also initialize variables yourself using the Set command. For example, the following command initializes the variable named Counter to 6:

```
Set Counter=6
```

In many situations, you will not need to initialize a variable to a value. For example, some commands will set a variable for you, as in the following command, which lets you get mouse input:

```
SetMouse(1,1,10,10,Mouse_hit,x,y)
```

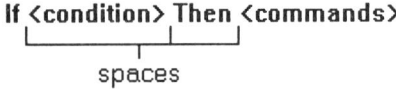

Figure 14-4 The syntax of the If command

In this command, the x and y variables are set automatically by Oriel; they indicate the point in the window where the mouse pointer was sitting when the user clicked the mouse button.

You can also perform simple mathematical calculations using integers and store the result in a variable. For example, the following command sets the variable Mouse_x2 to the value in Mouse_x1 multiplied by three:

```
Set Mouse_x2=Mouse_x1*3
```

See the Set command in the command reference for more details on variables.

Note: You can have a maximum of 500 variables in an Oriel program.

Tokens

Several Oriel for Windows commands require that you use tokens as parameters. A token is a special identifier that has been predefined by Oriel. For example, in the following command syntax, PIXEL and METRIC are tokens:

```
UseCoordinates(PIXEL/METRIC)
```

For this command, you *must* use either PIXEL or METRIC for the parameter, and you must spell the token correctly. No other parameter will be accepted.

When a command requires a token, the token appears in upper case in the command syntax. You'll find as you create your Oriel programs that it's a good idea to follow this same convention.

Labels

In Oriel for Windows, labels follow the same naming conventions as variables. For example, they can be any length and can be upper- or lower-case. Labels have the additional restrictions that they must be placed at the start of a line (in the first column of the line), and they must end with a : (colon). For example, here are some valid and invalid labels:

```
Next:                {A valid label}
  Wait_for_input:    {An invalid label because it isn't
                      located at the start of the line}
```

Note: You can have up to 500 labels in an Oriel program.

Comments

All characters between { and } are treated as comments by Oriel for Windows. You can place comments anywhere in an Oriel text file. You can also nest comments.

For example, the following program draws the pyramid bitmap (PYRAMID.BMP) located in the \WINDOWS directory in a continuous line across the screen. The program is generously commented to make it easier to read.

```
{------------------------PYRAMID.TXT---------------------------
This program draws the pyramid bitmap across the screen a set
number of pixels apart.
---------------------------------------------------------------}
{Initialize}
        UseCoordinates(PIXEL)       {Use pixels, not millimeters}
        Set x=30                    {Starting x-coordinate}
        Set y=20                    {Starting y-coordinate}
        Set Step=31                 {Step by 31 pixels at a time}

{Maximize the window}
        SetWindow(MAXIMIZE)

{Put up the pyramid bitmap for the first time}
        DrawBitmap(x,y,"C:\WINDOWS\PYRAMID.BMP")
        WaitInput(1000)             {Pause 1 second}

{Loop to draw the pyramid across the screen}
Next:   WaitInput(0)
        DrawBitmap(x,y,"C:\WINDOWS\PYRAMID.BMP")
        Set x=x+Step
        If x<600 Then Goto Next

{Leave the finished window up until the user kills it}
        WaitInput()
```

White Space

White space is a general term for the elements that Oriel ignores in a script. Oriel for Windows treats as white space all blanks, tab characters, carriage returns, line feed characters, split vertical bars (|), and comments. White space is ignored at any point in an Oriel script.

STARTING A PROGRAM

To start an Oriel program from the command line, you must provide the name of the Oriel executable file (ORIEL.EXE) followed by the name of the script file. For example, if Oriel for Windows is located in the C:\ORIEL directory and your script file is named SCRIPT.TXT and is located in C:\ORIEL\WORK, you would use the following command line:

```
C:\ORIEL\ORIEL C:\ORIEL\WORK\SCRIPT.TXT
```

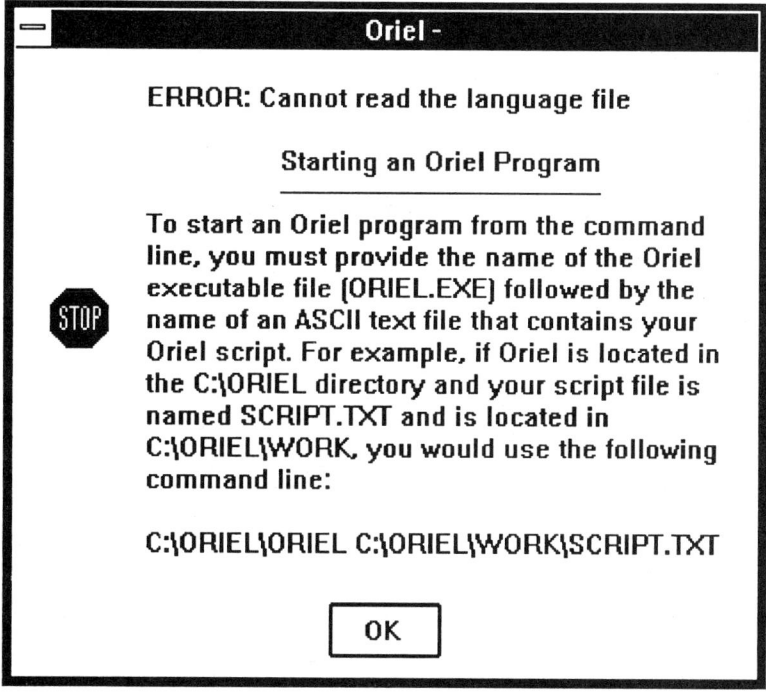

Figure 14-5 When Oriel for Windows cannot find your script file

If Oriel for Windows cannot find the script file, you'll see the message shown in Figure 14-5.

There are several ways you can simplify the Oriel command line. For example, if you have placed the Oriel directory in your DOS PATH statement (and you should), you can simplify the previous command line to read as follows:

```
ORIEL C:\ORIEL\WORK\SCRIPT.TXT
```

Another advantage of placing the Oriel directory in your DOS PATH statement is that you can invoke Oriel from another directory and have it look in that directory for the script file and any files that the script file might load, like bitmap (.BMP) files. Here's a variation of the example command line that uses this technique:

```
C:\ORIEL\WORK\ORIEL SCRIPT.TXT
```

Note: If you use this type of command line when creating an icon, Windows will issue a warning saying that the specified path is invalid. You can safely ignore this warning and accept the command line anyway. (See Chapter 2, "Program Manager Techniques," for more on this.)

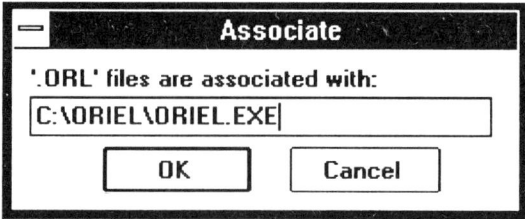

Figure 14-6 The File Associate dialog box

Yet another way to simplify the Oriel command line is to use File Manager to set up an association. For example, suppose you name all your Oriel script files using a unique extension like .ORL. You can create an association using the following steps:

1. Start File Manager.
2. Highlight a filename with an .ORL extension and select Associate from the File menu. Windows displays a dialog box like the one in Figure 14-6.
3. Type the path and name of the Oriel program file and select OK.

File Manager then updates your WIN.INI file with the association. From this point on, all you need to provide on the command line is the name of the Oriel script file, for example, SCRIPT.ORL. (If you use the Windows 3 Power Tools Setup program to install Oriel, a file association for ".ORL" is automatically set up.)

To create an icon for an Oriel program, you use the File New command from Program Manager. Chapter 2 gives a complete description of how to create icons.

Tip: When script files don't require path information

If a script file is located in the same directory as Oriel, you don't need to include path information for it.

STOPPING A PROGRAM

To stop an Oriel program at any point, press CTRL+BREAK. When you do so, Oriel for Windows displays the message box shown in Figure 14-7. To end the program, select Yes. To have the program resume where it left off, select No.

Oriel for Windows 477

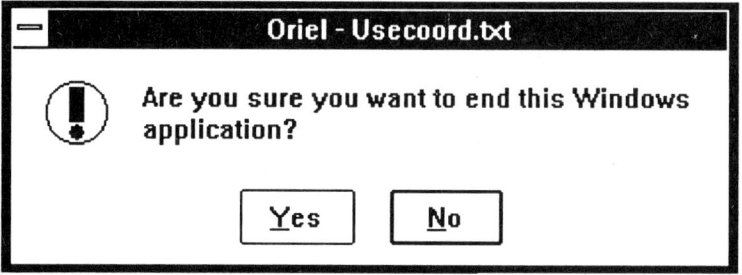

Figure 14-7 Stopping an Oriel for Windows program

THE ORIEL COORDINATE SYSTEM

In Oriel for Windows, the upper-left corner of a window is the origin, or point (0,0). Each millimeter to the right represents one unit along the positive *x*-axis. Each millimeter down represents one unit along the positive *y*-axis. Figure 14-8 shows the Oriel coordinate system.

You can modify the coordinate system to use pixels instead of millimeters (see the UseCoordinates command). Pixel coordinates are more accurate, but they are also device dependent. In other words, when you use pixel coordinates, an Oriel program you create for an EGA display will appear smaller when you run it on a system with a VGA display because there are more pixels per square inch on a VGA.

SELECTING DRAWING TOOLS

Oriel for Windows lets you use a variety of tools to draw within a window. It lets you set up pens to draw lines, brushes to fill interiors, and fonts to write text. To create tools for

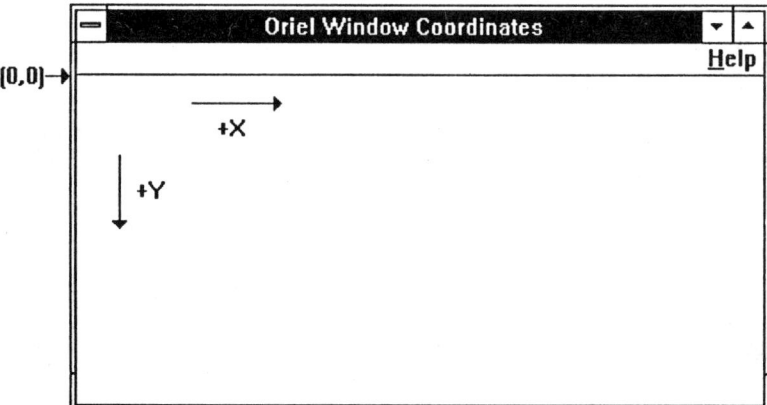

Figure 14-8 The Oriel coordinate system

drawing geometrical shapes, you use commands such as UsePen and UseBrush. To create fonts for writing text, you use the UseFont command.

Note: If you do not establish drawing tools before drawing in a window, Oriel uses these default drawing tools: a black pen, a white brush, and the System font.

Using Pens

The UsePen command lets you assign a pen for drawing lines and borders. Pens can be solid, dashed, dotted, and more. For example, the following example creates a solid black pen, two pixels wide:

```
Set Width=2
UsePen(SOLID,Width,0,0,0)
```

The Width argument controls the width of the pen in pixels. The three arguments following the Width argument specify the color of the pen. They control the intensity of the colors red, green, and blue, respectively. In this example, all the colors have 0 intensity, so the pen will be black. Conversely, the following line would create a white pen:

```
UsePen(SOLID,Width,255,255,255)
```

The pen you specify with UsePen will be used in all subsequent drawing operations, or until you use UsePen again to change the pen.

Note: The default pen is solid, black, and has a width of 1 pixel. If you use a command that draws a shape, but you haven't yet set up a pen with the UsePen command, Oriel for Windows uses the default pen.

Using Brushes

The UseBrush command lets you establish brushes for drawing and filling areas in rectangles, ellipses, pies, and the like. You can create brushes that are solid or hatched, have diagonal lines, horizontal lines, vertical lines, and more. For example, here's the command to create a solid blue brush:

```
UseBrush(SOLID,0,255,0)
```

As you might have guessed, the last three arguments control the color of the brush. The brush you specify with UseBrush will be used in all subsequent drawing operations, or until you use UseBrush again to change the brush.

Note: The default brush is solid white.

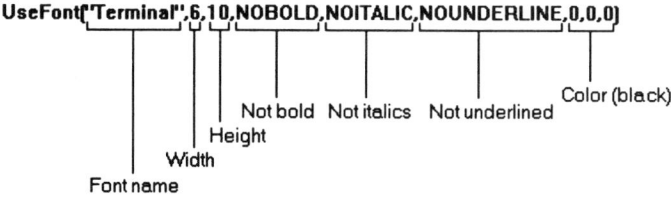

Figure 14-9 Command to select the Terminal font

Using Fonts

You establish a font in Oriel for Windows by using the UseFont command and giving it a series of font attributes, including the font name, width, height, style (bold, italics, or underline), and the color. Oriel for Windows uses the font you've established the next time you draw text or numbers on the screen. For example, Figure 14-9 shows a command that selects the Terminal font using different font attributes.

Note: Oriel for Windows lets you use fonts that are installed by third-party font packages, such as the Adobe Type Manager or Bitstream's Facelift. (See Chapter 4, "Of Fonts and Printing," for a description of these fonts.)

Note: By default, Oriel for Windows uses a black System font.

DRAWING AND WRITING

Oriel for Windows provides a variety of commands for drawing and writing output to the screen. The following sections give a brief overview of these commands. For more detailed descriptions of these commands, see the command reference.

Drawing Text

To draw text in a window, you use the DrawText command. For example, the following command displays the text "The ABC Company Shell" using the current font. The starting position of the text is at the point (20,10).

```
DrawText(20,10,"The ABC Company Shell")
```

If you want to display a number in a window, you can use the DrawNumber command. For example, the following command displays the number 200 starting at the point (50,60):

```
DrawNumber(50,60,200)
```

DrawNumber is also convenient for displaying the contents of variables in a window.

Command	Purpose
DrawArc	Draws an arc.
DrawChord	Draws a chord.
DrawEllipse	Draws an ellipse (or circle).
DrawFlood	Floods an area with color using the current brush.
DrawLine	Draws a line.
DrawPie	Draws a pie wedge.
DrawRectangle	Draws a rectangle.
DrawRoundRectangle	Draws a rectangle with rounded edges.

Table 14-1 Commands for Drawing Lines and Shapes

Drawing Lines and Shapes

Oriel provides several commands for drawing lines and shapes, as shown in Table 14-1. All of these commands use the current pen to draw borders and the current brush to fill interiors.

The following example shows how to use the DrawLine command to draw a line from the point (10,80) to the point (100,20):

```
DrawLine(10,80,100,20)
```

To draw a rectangle, you use the DrawRectangle command. The following command draws a rectangle that has its upper-left and lower-right corners at the points (15,25) and (75,110), respectively:

```
DrawRectangle(15,25,75,110)
```

This function uses the current pen to draw the border of the rectangle and the current brush to fill the interior.

The DrawEllipse command lets you draw a circle or an ellipse. The following example draws an ellipse that is bounded by the rectangle specified by the points (100,30) and (250,90):

```
DrawEllipse(100,30,250,90)
```

As with the DrawRectangle command, the DrawEllipse command uses the current pen to draw the border of the rectangle and the current brush to fill the interior.

Drawing Bitmaps

Oriel has two commands for placing the contents of bitmap (.BMP) files on the screen: DrawBitmap and DrawSizedBitmap. The DrawBitmap command is the simpler of the two. It lets you locate a bitmap starting at a specified point in a window. For example, the following program places the party bitmap (PARTY.BMP) starting at the point (10,10):

```
DrawBitmap(10,10,"C:\WINDOWS\PARTY.BMP")
WaitInput()
```

The DrawSizedBitmap command lets you stretch or compress a bitmap to fit within a specified rectangle. You indicate the upper-left corner of the rectangle using the first two parameters and the lower-right corner using the second two. For example, the following program places the party bitmap within the smaller rectangle specified by the points (10,10) and (50,60):

```
DrawSizedBitmap(10,10,50,60,"C:\WINDOWS\PARTY.BMP")
WaitInput()
```

You can also use the DrawSizedBitmap command to invert a bitmap as you place it on the screen (see the DrawSizedBitmap command for more details).

FLOW OF CONTROL COMMANDS

Oriel for Windows has three commands to control the flow of programs: If, Goto, and Gosub. The If command lets you make a decision when there are two alternative outcomes. It tests the value of a condition, and if that condition is true, the program continues executing commands on the same line following the Then. However, if the condition is false, the program begins executing commands on the next line following the If.

For example, the following If command tests the value of the variable Green to see if it is greater than 255. If it is, Oriel executes the Goto command on the same line. Otherwise, it executes the WaitInput() command on the next line.

```
If Green>255 Then Goto Exit
WaitInput()
Exit:
```

The Goto command transfers control unconditionally to a label. In the previous example, the Goto command causes the program to branch to the label Exit.

The Gosub command lets you execute a block of code as a subroutine. When the subroutine is completed, Oriel executes the next command following the Gosub.

MESSAGE BOXES

The MessageBox command lets you create your own customized message boxes. For example, the following command creates a message box with OK and Cancel buttons (the second parameter, 1, causes the OK button to be highlighted) and a question-mark icon. In addition, the message box displays the text "Do you want to exit?" and uses the caption "Exit box."

```
MessageBox(OKCANCEL,1,QUESTION,
           "Do you want to exit?","Exit box",Button)
```

The button you select is returned in the Button variable.

CONTROLLING THE WINDOW SIZE

The SetWindow command lets you maximize, minimize, or restore the Oriel window. For example, the following commands maximize the Oriel window, pause the program for 2 seconds, then restore the window to its original size:

```
SetWindow(MAXIMIZE)
WaitInput(2000)
SetWindow(RESTORE)
WaitInput()
```

PAUSING A PROGRAM

In Oriel, you can pause a program a specified number of seconds, or you can pause it indefinitely. Both require the WaitInput command.

Pausing a Specified Number of Seconds

By using the WaitInput command with an argument, you can pause an Oriel program a specified number of seconds. For example, the following program displays the message "Waiting...". Next, it pauses the program for three seconds then erases the window's contents.

```
DrawText(10,10,"Waiting...")
WaitInput(3000)    {Pause the program for 3 seconds}
DrawBackground    {Erase the window}
WaitInput()
```

As you may have guessed, the parameter for the WaitInput command is in milliseconds.

Pausing Indefinitely

By using the WaitInput command without an argument, you can pause a program indefinitely. In general, you should use WaitInput() whenever you are not performing any work in your Oriel window. This makes more system resources available to other Windows programs.

If you fail to use WaitInput() at some point in your program, one of two things will happen: either the window will disappear immediately after executing your script or, if you are stuck in a continuous loop, the hour-glass icon will always be present, and you may not be able to switch away.

The WaitInput() command is also important for building your own custom menus and for getting keyboard or mouse input. The next two sections will give you more information.

BUILDING MENUS

To build your own custom menus, you must use the SetMenu command to define a menu template. Then, when the program is pausing for input (a WaitInput() command is in effect) and the user selects a menu item, the program branches to the label associated with that menu item, as defined in the template.

For example the following program creates a simple menu with only two menu items: Write and Exit. If you select the Write option, the program branches to the Run_write label where Windows Write is launched. If you select the Exit option, the program ends.

```
{Define the menu template}
    SetMenu("Write",Run_write,
            ENDPOPUP,
            "Exit",Leave,
            ENDPOPUP)

Wait_for_input:
    WaitInput()

Run_write:
    Run("WRITE.EXE")
    Goto Wait_for_input

Leave:
    End
```

GETTING MOUSE INPUT

To get mouse input in an Oriel program, you use the SetMouse command and define rectangular regions on the screen as mouse hit-testing regions. Then, when the program is pausing for input and you click the left mouse button within a mouse hit-testing region, the program branches to the label associated with that region, as defined by the SetMouse command.

For example, suppose you want to modify the previous program to place some "buttons" on the screen and provide mouse support for when you click on a button. You could change the program as follows:

```
{Define the menu template}
    SetMenu("Write",Run_write,
            ENDPOPUP,
```

```
                "Exit",Leave,
                ENDPOPUP)

{Draw buttons with text}
    DrawRectangle(10,10,30,20)
    DrawText(14,12,"Write")
    DrawRectangle(10,25,30,35)
    DrawText(15,27,"Exit")

{Set up the mouse}
    SetMouse(10,10,30,20,Run_write,x,y,
            10,25,30,35,Leave,x,y)

Wait_for_input:
    WaitInput()

Run_write:
    Run("WRITE.EXE")
    Goto Wait_for_input

Leave:
    End
```

Figure 14-10 shows how the window appears.

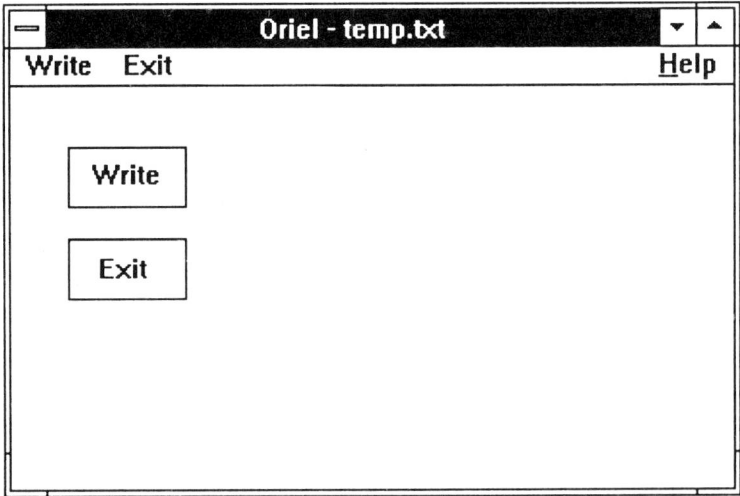

Figure 14-10 A sample program with a menu and "buttons"

In this example, two hit-testing regions are defined by the SetMouse command, both corresponding to the rectangles that were drawn with the DrawRectangle commands. The first hit-testing region is defined by the upper-left corner (10,10) and the lower-right corner (30,20)—the same area as the Write button. If you click the mouse within this region, the program branches to the Run_write label. In the same way, if you click the mouse button within the region defined by the points (10,25) and (30,35)—the same area as the Exit button—the program branches to Leave.

GETTING KEYBOARD INPUT

To read single keystrokes in an Oriel program, you use the SetKeyboard command to define the keys that you will accept. Then, when the program is pausing for input and you press a specified key, the program branches to the label associated with that key.

Building on the previous example, suppose you want to add keyboard support so that when you press *w* or *W* the program runs Write and when you press *e* or *E*, the program exits. Here's how you would modify the program:

```
{Define the menu template}
     SetMenu("Write",Run_write,
             ENDPOPUP,
             "Exit",Leave,
             ENDPOPUP)

{Draw buttons with text}
     DrawRectangle(10,10,30,20)
     DrawText(14,12,"Write")
     DrawRectangle(10,25,30,35)
     DrawText(15,27,"Exit")

{Set up the mouse}
     SetMouse(10,10,30,20,Run_write,x,y,
             10,25,30,35,Leave,x,y)

{Put up a message regarding keyboard support}
     DrawText(10,40,"Press W for Write or E to exit")

{Set up the keyboard}
     SetKeyboard("W",Run_write,
                 "w",Run_write,
                 "E",Leave,
                 "e",Leave)
```

```
Wait_for_input:
    WaitInput()

Run_write:
    Run("WRITE.EXE")
    Goto Wait_for_input

Leave:
    End
```

Note: By using virtual keys, you can read keys that are not on the typewriter portion of the keyboard (see SetKeyboard for more details).

RUNNING OTHER PROGRAMS

By using the Run command, you can execute Windows and non-Windows applications from within an Oriel program. For example, the following program starts Notepad and then launches a copy of COMMAND.COM:

```
Run("NOTEPAD.EXE")
Run("C:\COMMAND.COM")
WaitInput()
```

Each program you start takes on a life of its own independently of the Oriel script that invoked it. This means that, under normal circumstances, Oriel for Windows does not pause after executing a Run command, but continues with the next command in the script. For example, in the previous program, Oriel for Windows starts Notepad then immediately starts COMMAND.COM.

If you want Oriel to pause after starting Notepad, you would use the following script:

```
SetWaitMode(FOCUS)
Run("NOTEPAD.EXE")
WaitInput(1)
Run("C:\COMMAND.COM")
WaitInput()
```

By placing the SetWaitMode(FOCUS) command before and WaitInput(1) after Run("NOTEPAD.EXE"), you can have Oriel pause until it gets the focus back. That is, only when you close Notepad or switch back to your Oriel program does it execute the next Run command to launch a copy of COMMAND.COM. (See the WaitInput and SetWaitMode commands later for more information.)

COMMAND REFERENCE

The following is a list of commands that are supported by Oriel for Windows. The quick reference at the end of the chapter is handy if all you need to know is the syntax for an Oriel command.

Beep

This command sounds the bell.

Syntax: `Beep`

Example: This program puts up a message box with Yes, No, and Cancel buttons. It then beeps once if you select Yes, twice for No, and three times for Cancel.

```
{Put up a message box}
   MessageBox(YESNOCANCEL,1,QUESTION,
              "Did you vote?","Question",Button)
{Test for which button was selected}
   If Button=1 Then Goto Beep1
   If Button=2 Then Goto Beep2
   {Else} Beep
   WaitInput(500){Pause for 1/2 second}
Beep2:
   Beep
   WaitInput(500)
Beep1:
   Beep
```

DrawArc

This command draws an elliptical arc using the current pen. To draw the arc, you use the points $(x1,y1)$ and $(x2,y2)$ to define a rectangle that bounds the ellipse containing the arc, as shown in Figure 14-11. You then use the parameters $(x3,y3)$ to specify the point on the ellipse where the arc starts, and the parameters $(x4,y4)$ to specify where it ends. Note that when the GDI sweeps the arc, it begins at $(x3,y3)$ and moves in a counterclockwise direction towards $(x4,y4)$.

Syntax: `DrawArc(x1,y1,x2,y2,x3,y3,x4,y4)`

488   *Windows 3 Power Tools*

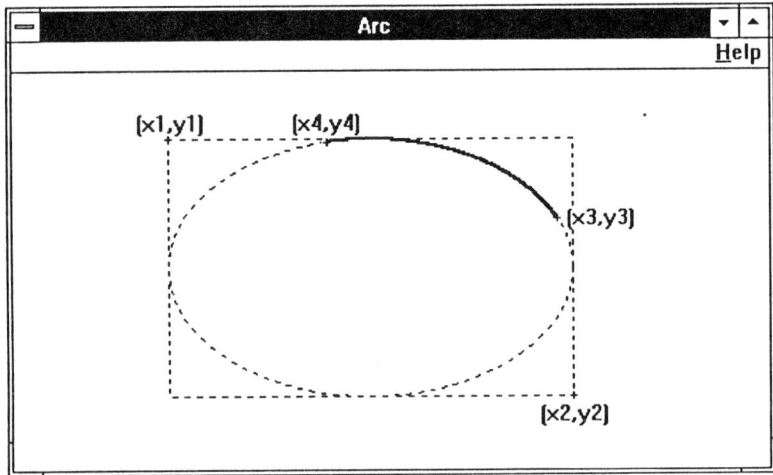

Figure 14-11 **The DrawArc coordinates**

Parameters:

x1,y1	The upper-left corner of the rectangle bounding the ellipse containing the arc.
x2,y2	The lower-right corner of the rectangle bounding the ellipse containing the arc.
x3,y3	The starting point of the arc on the ellipse.
x4,y4	The ending point of the arc on the ellipse.

Remark: The points (*x3,y3*) and (*x4,y4*) do not have to lie precisely on the ellipse. If they do not, however, the GDI uses points on the ellipse that are the shortest distance from (*x3,y3*) and (*x4,y4*).

Examples: This example sets the coordinate system to pixel, then draws an arc within the rectangle defined by the points (30,20) and (200,180). It sweeps the arc starting from the point (200,20) and moving in a counterclockwise direction to the point (30,20).

```
UseCoordinates(PIXEL)
DrawArc(30,20,200,180,200,20,30,20)
WaitInput()
```

The next program draws an arc by asking you to click on each of the four points needed to define an arc. The first point it asks for is the upper-left corner of the rectangle bounding the ellipse containing the arc, and the second is the lower-right corner of that same rectangle. The program then draws a temporary ellipse using the points you've defined so that you can select the third and fourth points needed for the arc—its starting and ending points. After you've clicked on these points on the ellipse, the program clears the screen and draws the arc using the DrawArc command. It then loops back up for you to specify another arc.

```
{Set up the environment}
   SetWindow(MAXIMIZE)
   UseCoordinates(PIXEL)
   UseFont("Terminal",10,10,NOBOLD,NOITALIC,NOUNDERLINE,0,0,0)

Arc1:
   UsePen(DOT,1,0,0,0)        {Use a dotted pen for the temporary ellipse}
   SetMouse(0,0,700,600,Arc2,x1,y1)
   DrawText(10,300,
     "Click on the upper-left corner of the rectangle bounding the arc ")
   Goto Get_Input
Arc2:
   SetMouse(0,0,700,600,Arc3,x2,y2)
   DrawText(10,300,
     "Click on the lower-right corner of the rectangle bounding the arc")
   Goto Get_Input
Arc3:
   DrawEllipse(x1,y1,x2,y2)        {Draw a temporary ellipse}
   SetMouse(0,0,700,600,Arc4,x3,y3)
   DrawText(10,300,
      "Click on the arc's starting point                              ")
   Goto Get_Input
Arc4:
   SetMouse(0,0,700,600,Arc_End,x4,y4)
   DrawText(10,300,
      "Click on the arc's ending point                                ")
   Goto Get_Input

Arc_End:
   DrawBackground                  {Clear the temporary ellipse}
   UsePen(SOLID,1,0,0,0)           {Use a solid black pen}
   DrawArc(x1,y1,x2,y2,x3,y3,x4,y4)
   Goto Arc1

Get_Input:
   WaitInput()
```

Related Commands: UsePen

DrawBackground

Draws a window's background using the current background color. If the window has any contents, they are overwritten in the process.

Syntax: `DrawBackground`

Remark: You control the current background color using the UseBackground command. (The current background mode, TRANSPARENT or OPAQUE, has no effect on the DrawBackground command's behavior.)

Example: This example sets the background color to green using the UseBackground command and then draws the background. Next, it draws some text in the window, waits for 2 seconds, and erases the text by issuing the DrawBackground command again.

```
UseBackground(TRANSPARENT,0,255,0)
DrawBackground
DrawText(10,10,"The effect of text")
WaitInput(2000)
DrawBackground
WaitInput()
```

Related Commands: `UseBackground`

DrawBitmap

This command places the contents of a bitmap (.BMP) file at a specified location on the screen.

Syntax: `DrawBitmap(x,y,"Filename")`

Parameters:

x	The x-coordinate of the upper-left corner of the bitmap.
y	The y-coordinate of the upper-left corner of the bitmap.
"Filename"	The name of the bitmap file, enclosed in quotation marks. Be sure to include the path if the bitmap file is not in the current directory.

Remark: You can use Paintbrush to get the size of a bitmap in pixels. To do so, begin by reading the bitmap into Paintbrush and choose Cursor Position from the View menu. When you move the cursor to the bottom right corner of the drawing area, Paintbrush will show the size of the bitmap as an x,y coordinate.

Example: This example reads the chess bitmap file (CHESS.BMP) on the \WINDOWS directory and draws its contents beginning in the upper-left corner of the window.

```
DrawBitmap(0,0,"C:\WINDOWS\CHESS.BMP")
WaitInput()
```

This next example places two bitmaps on the screen: the ribbons bitmap (RIBBONS.BMP) starting at (5,5), and the pyramid bitmap (PYRAMID.BMP) starting at (130,30):

```
DrawBitmap(5,5,"C:\WINDOWS\RIBBONS.BMP")
DrawBitmap(130,30,"C:\WINDOWS\PYRAMID.BMP")
WaitInput()
```

Related Commands: `DrawSizedBitmap`

DrawChord

This command draws a chord—a region bounded by the intersection of a line and an ellipse. To draw a chord, you use the points (*x1,y1*) and (*x2,y2*) to define a rectangle that bounds the ellipse that is part of the chord, as shown in Figure 14-12. You then specify the line that intersects the ellipse using the points (*x3,y3*) and (*x4,y4*). The command draws the chord's border using the current pen and fills its interior using the current brush.

Syntax: `DrawChord(x1,y1,x2,y2,x3,y3,x4,y4)`

Parameters:

`x1,y1`	The upper-left corner of the rectangle bounding the ellipse that is part of the chord.
`x2,y2`	The lower-right corner of the rectangle bounding the ellipse that is part of the chord.
`x3,y3`	A point on the line that intersects the ellipse.
`x4,y4`	A second point on the line that intersects the ellipse.

Remark: The points (*x3,y3*) and (*x4,y4*) do not have to lie precisely on the ellipse. If they do not, however, the GDI uses points on the ellipse that are the shortest distance from (*x3,y3*) and (*x4,y4*).

Examples: This example draws a chord by using the points (40,30) and (210,190) to define the rectangle that bounds the ellipse that is part of the chord. The points used for the line that intersects the ellipse are (210,30) and (40,30). The chord is drawn with the default black pen and a solid aqua brush.

```
UseCoordinates(PIXEL)
UseBrush(SOLID,0,255,255)
DrawChord(40,30,210,190,210,30,40,30)
WaitInput()
```

492   Windows 3 Power Tools

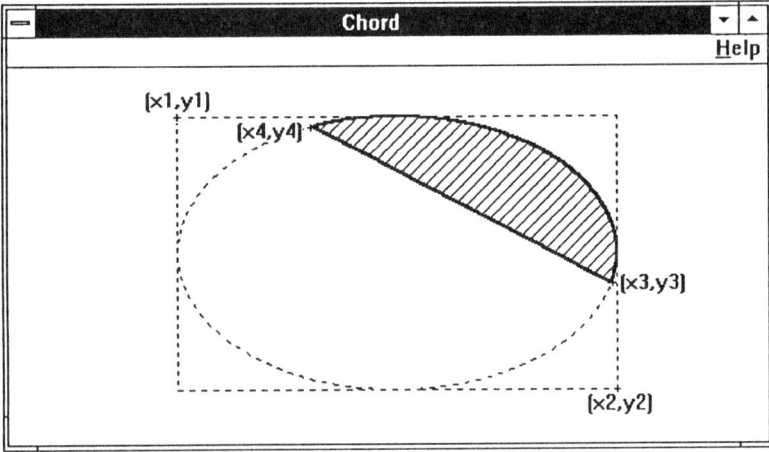

Figure 14-12 The DrawChord coordinates

This next example is a variation of one shown for the DrawArc command. It draws a chord by prompting you to click on the four points needed to define a chord. The first point is the upper-left corner of the rectangle bounding the ellipse that is part of the chord; the second is the lower-right corner of that same rectangle; the third is a point on the line bounding the chord; and the fourth is another point on that same line. After you've clicked on all four points, the program draws the chord using the DrawChord command, then loops back up for you to specify another chord.

```
{Set up the environment}
   SetWindow(MAXIMIZE)
   UseCoordinates(PIXEL)
   UseFont("Terminal",10,10,NOBOLD,NOITALIC,NOUNDERLINE,0,0,0)

Chord1:
   UsePen(DOT,1,0,0,0)        {Use dotted pen for temporary ellipse}
   UseBrush(NULL,0,0,0)       {Use hollow brush for temporary ellipse}
   SetMouse(0,0,700,600,Chord2,x1,y1)
   DrawText(10,300,
     "Click on upper-left corner of rectangle bounding chord ")
   Goto Get_Input
Chord2:
   SetMouse(0,0,700,600,Chord3,x2,y2)
   DrawText(10,300,
     "Click on lower-right corner of rectangle bounding chord")
   Goto Get_Input
Chord3:
   DrawEllipse(x1,y1,x2,y2)     {Draw temporary ellipse}
```

```
    SetMouse(0,0,700,600,Chord4,x3,y3)
    DrawText(10,300,
      "Click on one point of line defining chord              ")
    Goto Get_Input
Chord4:
    SetMouse(0,0,700,600,Chord_End,x4,y4)
    DrawText(10,300,
      "Click on second point of line defining chord           ")
    Goto Get_Input

Chord_End:
    DrawBackground              {Clear the temporary ellipse}
    UsePen(SOLID,1,0,0,0)       {Use a solid black pen}
    UseBrush(SOLID,255,0,0)     {Use a solid red brush}
    DrawChord(x1,y1,x2,y2,x3,y3,x4,y4)
    Goto Chord1

Get_Input:
    WaitInput()
```

Related Commands: UseBrush, UsePen

DrawEllipse

This command draws an ellipse (or circle). To specify the ellipse, you use the points $(x1,y1)$ and $(x2,y2)$ to define a rectangle that bounds the ellipse, as shown in Figure 14-13. The command uses the current pen to draw the border and the current brush to fill the interior.

Syntax: DrawEllipse(x1,y1,x2,y2)

Parameters:

    x1,y1   The upper-left corner of the rectangle bounding the ellipse.

    x2,y2   The lower-right corner of the rectangle bounding the ellipse.

Examples: The following example draws an ellipse that is bounded by the rectangle specified by the points (20,30) and (80,60). It draws the ellipse using a solid black pen (the default) and a solid yellow brush.

```
UseBrush(SOLID,255,255,0)
DrawEllipse(20,30,80,60)
WaitInput()
```

This second example prompts you to click on the points of the rectangle bounding an ellipse. It then draws the ellipse using the default pen and a solid green brush.

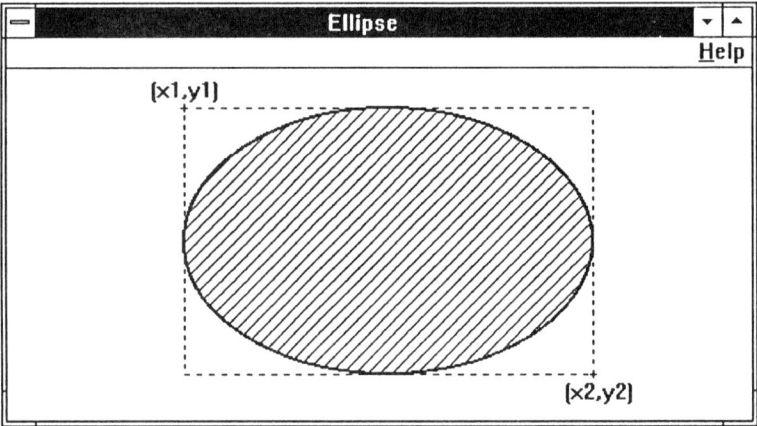

Figure 14-13 The DrawEllipse coordinates

```
{Set up the environment}
   SetWindow(MAXIMIZE)
   UseCoordinates(PIXEL)
   UseFont("Terminal",10,10,NOBOLD,NOITALIC,NOUNDERLINE,0,0,0)
   UseBrush(SOLID,0,255,0)    {Use a solid green brush}

Ellipse1:
   SetMouse(0,0,700,600,Ellipse2,x1,y1)
   DrawText(10,300,
     "Click on upper-left corner of rectangle bounding ellipse ")
   Goto Get_Input
Ellipse2:
   SetMouse(0,0,700,600,Ellipse3,x2,y2)
   DrawText(10,300,
     "Click on lower-right corner of rectangle bounding ellipse")
   Goto Get_Input
Ellipse3:
   DrawEllipse(x1,y1,x2,y2)
   Goto Ellipse1

Get_Input:
   WaitInput()
```

Related Commands: UsePen, UseBrush

DrawFlood

This command fills in any enclosed shape or area using the current brush. It begins at the point specified by the *x* and *y* parameters and fills in all directions until it reaches the color boundary specified by the *r, g, b* parameters.

Syntax: `DrawFlood(x,y,r,g,b)`

Parameters:

`x`	The x-coordinate of a point inside the area you want to fill.
`y`	The y-coordinate of a point inside the area you want to fill.
`r,g,b`	Specifies the color of the boundary up to which the command is to fill.

Example: This example draws a series of shapes on the screen using a blue pen and a hollow brush. It then sets the brush to solid red and asks you to click within an area to flood it with red. When you click on an area, the program branches to Flood_Mouse, where the DrawFlood command fills in the selected area using the current brush. (Notice that the *r, g, b* parameters are 0,0,255, causing the command to fill an area until it encounters a blue border.) The program stays in a loop, allowing you to flood as many areas as you like.

```
{Set up the mouse, pen, and brush}
    SetWindow(MAXIMIZE)
    SetMouse(0,0,700,600,Flood_Mouse,Flood_x,Flood_y)
    UsePen(SOLID,3,0,0,255)  {Use a 3-pixel wide blue pen}
    UseBrush(NULL,0,0,0)     {Use hollow brush for random shapes}

{Fill the window with random shapes}
    DrawRectangle(5,10,200,150)
    DrawRectangle(55,31,82,50)
    DrawRectangle(105,41,120,140)
    DrawRectangle(50,50,100,150)
    DrawRectangle(105,50,120,133)
    DrawRectangle(5,120,180,125)
    DrawEllipse(30,30,140,140)
    DrawEllipse(10,30,150,100)
    DrawEllipse(25,10,50,100)
    DrawEllipse(33,51,123,143)
```

```
            DrawText(5,3,"Click within an area to flood it with red")
            UseBrush(SOLID,255,0,0)     {Use a red brush for flooding}
            UseCoordinates(PIXEL)       {More accurate than metric}

    Flood_Wait:
        WaitInput()

    Flood_Mouse:
        DrawFlood(Flood_x,Flood_y,0,0,255)  {Flood till it meets blue}
        Goto Flood_Wait
```

Related Commands: UseBrush

DrawLine

This command draws a line using the current pen. The line begins at the point specified by $(x1,y1)$ and extends up to, but does not include, the point specified by $(x2,y2)$.

Syntax: `DrawLine(x1,y1,x2,y2)`

Parameters:

    x1,y1   The coordinates of the first point on the line.
    x2,y2   The coordinates of the ending point on the line.

Example: This program draws a series of five lines, each one using a different pen width. Figure 14-14 shows the results.

```
    UsePen(SOLID,1,0,0,0)
    DrawLine(10,10,40,10)

    UsePen(SOLID,2,0,0,0)
    DrawLine(10,15,40,15)

    UsePen(SOLID,3,0,0,0)
    DrawLine(10,20,40,20)

    UsePen(SOLID,4,0,0,0)
    DrawLine(10,25,40,25)
```

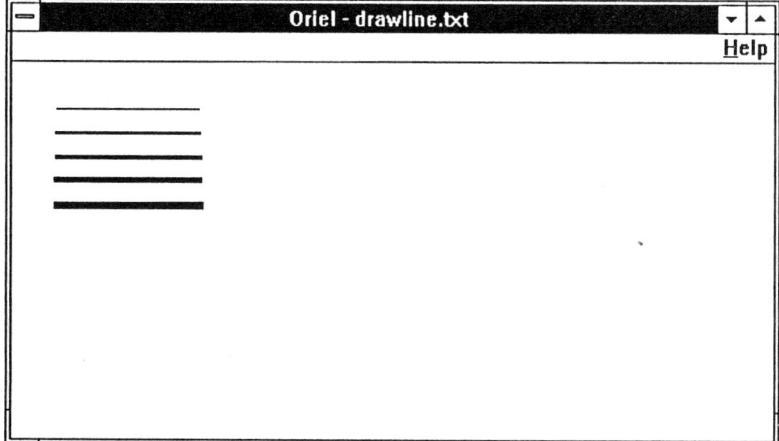

Figure 14-14 The effect of the DrawLine command with different pen widths

```
UsePen(SOLID,5,0,0,0)
DrawLine(10,30,40,30)

WaitInput()
```

See the UsePen command for another example of DrawLine.

Related Commands: `UsePen`

DrawNumber

This command displays an integer, *n*, using the current font. The starting position of the integer is given by the *x* and *y* parameters.

Syntax: `DrawNumber(x,y,n)`

Parameters:

x	Specifies the x-coordinate of the starting point of the integer.
y	Specifies the y-coordinate of the starting point of the integer.
n	The integer or the value of the integer variable you want to display.

Examples: This example changes Oriel's coordinate system from metric (the default) to pixel and then displays the integer 1000 starting 20 pixels to the right and 10 pixels below the upper-left corner of the window.

498 *Windows 3 Power Tools*

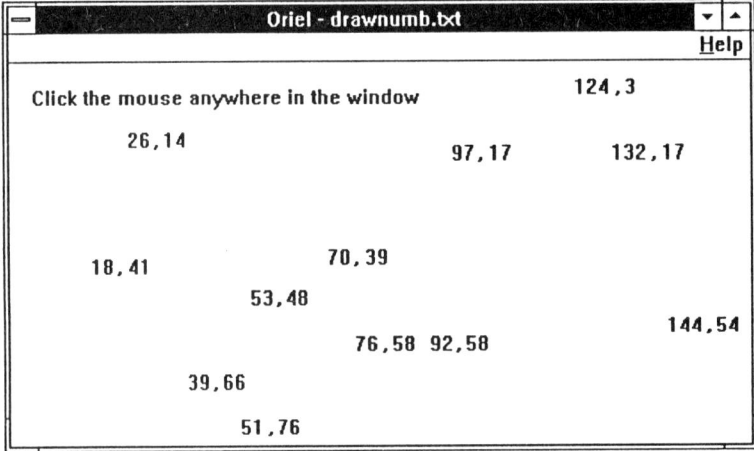

Figure 14-15 Using the DrawNumber command

```
UseCoordinates(PIXEL)
DrawNumber(20,10,1000)
WaitInput()
```

This next example reads a mouse click and uses the DrawNumber command to display the coordinates of where the mouse pointer was when the click took place. Figure 14-15 shows an example of how the window appears after you have clicked the mouse several times.

```
{Set up the mouse hit testing area and where to branch on a click}
    SetMouse(0,0,1000,1000,Draw_Coord,Mouse_x,Mouse_y)
    DrawText(5,5,"Click the mouse anywhere in the window")

Wait_Mouse:
    WaitInput()

{Draw the x-coordinate}
Draw_Coord:
    DrawNumber(Mouse_x,Mouse_y,Mouse_x)

{Increase the x-coordinate by 3 millimeters for each digit in Mouse_x}
    If Mouse_x>=100 Then Set x=Mouse_x+9 | Goto Draw_Comma {3 digits}
    If Mouse_x>=10  Then Set x=Mouse_x+6 | Goto Draw_Comma {2 digits}
    {Else}           Set x=Mouse_x+3                      {1 digit only}

{Draw the comma}
Draw_Comma:
    DrawText(x,Mouse_y,",")
```

```
{Increase x by 2 and draw the y-coordinate}
    Set x=x+2
    DrawNumber(x,Mouse_y,Mouse_y)
    Goto Wait_Mouse
```

Related Commands: UseFont

DrawPie

This command lets you draw a pie wedge using the current pen. A pie wedge consists of an arc whose center and end points are connected by lines. To draw the arc, you use the points (*x1,y1*) and (*x2,y2*) to define a rectangle that bounds the ellipse containing the arc, as shown in Figure 14-16. You then use the parameters (*x3,y3*) and (*x4,y4*) to specify the starting and ending points of the arc. Note that when the GDI sweeps the arc, it begins at (*x3,y3*) and moves in a counterclockwise direction toward (*x4,y4*). The current brush is used to fill the resulting pie-shaped area.

Syntax: `DrawPie(x1,y1,x2,y2,x3,y3,x4,y4)`

Parameters:

> `x1,y1`   The upper-left corner of the rectangle bounding the ellipse containing the arc.
>
> `x2,y2`   The lower-right corner of the rectangle bounding the ellipse containing the arc.

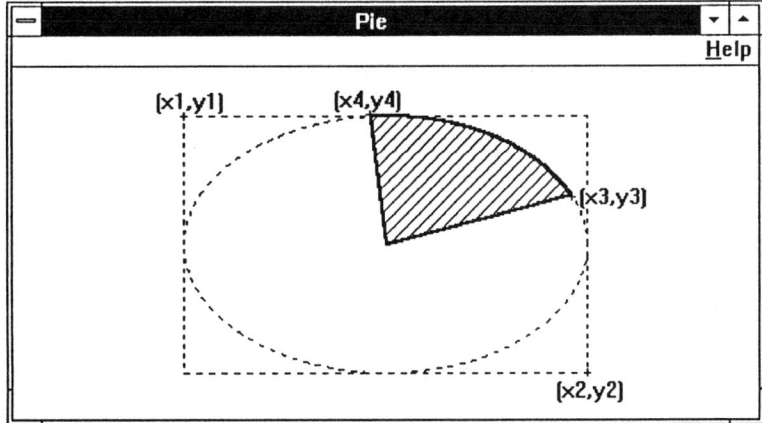

Figure 14-16 The DrawPie coordinates

x3,y3	The starting point of the arc. This point does not have to lie on the arc.
x4,y4	The ending point of the arc. This point does not have to lie on the arc.

Remark: The points (*x3,y3*) and (*x4,y4*) do not have to lie precisely on the ellipse. If they do not, however, the GDI uses points on the ellipse that are the shortest distance from (*x3,y3*) and (*x4,y4*).

Examples: This example draws a pie wedge using the default black pen to draw the border and an aqua brush to fill the interior. The pie wedge is bounded by the rectangle specified by the points (110,30) and (160,80). The pie's arc starts at the point (160,30) and ends at the point (160,80).

```
UseBrush(SOLID,0,255,255)
UseCoordinates(PIXEL)
DrawPie(110,30,160,80,160,30,160,80)
WaitInput()
```

This next program draws a pie wedge based on your mouse clicks. The first two clicks define the rectangle bounding the arc, and the second two define the lines connecting the points of the arc with its center.

```
{Set up the environment}
   SetWindow(MAXIMIZE)
   UseCoordinates(PIXEL)
   UseFont("Terminal",10,10,NOBOLD,NOITALIC,NOUNDERLINE,0,0,0)

Pie1:
   UsePen(DOT,1,0,0,0)       {Dotted pen for temporary ellipse}
   UseBrush(NULL,0,0,0)      {Hollow brush for temporary ellipse}
   SetMouse(0,0,700,600,Pie2,x1,y1)
   DrawText(10,300,
     "Click on upper-left corner of rectangle bounding pie ")
   Goto Get_Input
Pie2:
   SetMouse(0,0,700,600,Pie3,x2,y2)
   DrawText(10,300,
     "Click on lower-right corner of rectangle bounding pie")
   Goto Get_Input
Pie3:
   DrawEllipse(x1,y1,x2,y2)
   SetMouse(0,0,700,600,Pie4,x3,y3)
   DrawText(10,300,
```

```
      "Click on one end of arc defining pie                ")
    Goto Get_Input
Pie4:
    SetMouse(0,0,700,600,Pie_End,x4,y4)
    DrawText(10,300,
      "Click on other end of arc defining pie              ")
    Goto Get_Input

Pie_End:
    DrawBackground
    UsePen(SOLID,1,0,0,0)
    UseBrush(SOLID,255,0,0)
    DrawPie(x1,y1,x2,y2,x3,y3,x4,y4)
    Goto Pie1

Get_Input:
    WaitInput()
```

Related Commands: UsePen, UseBrush

DrawRectangle

This command draws a rectangle using the current pen and fills its interior using the current brush. You specify the upper-left corner of the rectangle using (*x1,y1*) and the lower-right corner using (*x2,y2*), as shown in Figure 14-17.

Syntax: DrawRectangle(*x1,y1,x2,y2*)

Parameters:

    x1,y1   The upper-left corner of the rectangle.
    x2,y2   The lower-right corner of the rectangle.

Examples: The following example draws a rectangle whose upper-left corner is located at (10,10) and lower-right corner is at (200,100). It uses a black pen that is three pixels wide and fills the interior using an orange brush.

```
UsePen(SOLID,3,0,0,0)
UseBrush(SOLID,255,128,0)
UseCoordinates(PIXEL)
DrawRectangle(10,10,200,100)
WaitInput()
```

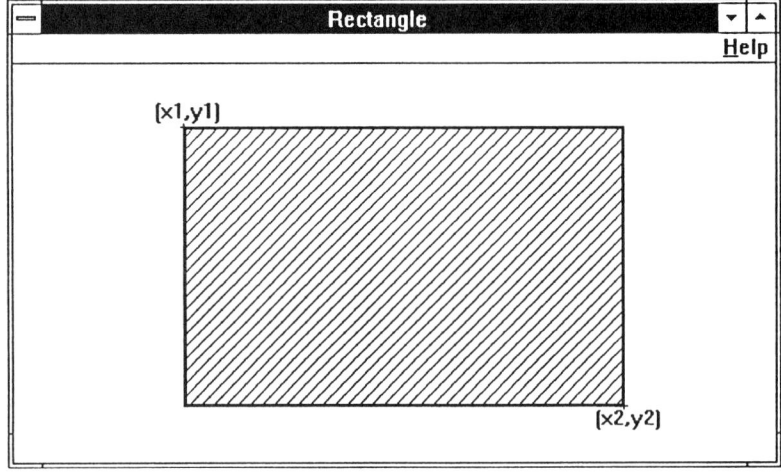

Figure 14-17 The DrawRectangle coordinates

This next example draws a rectangle based on two mouse clicks. The first mouse click defines the upper-left corner of the rectangle and the second one defines the lower-right. The rectangle is filled using a light cream-colored brush.

```
{Set up the environment}
   SetWindow(MAXIMIZE)
   UseCoordinates(PIXEL)
   UsePen(SOLID,3,0,0,0)
   UseBrush(SOLID,255,255,230)

Rect1:
   SetMouse(0,0,700,600,Rect2,x1,y1)
   DrawText(10,300,
      "Click on upper-left corner of the rectangle")
   Goto Get_Input
Rect2:
   SetMouse(0,0,700,600,Rect3,x2,y2)
   DrawText(10,300,
      "Click on lower-right corner of the rectangle")
   Goto Get_Input
Rect3:
   DrawRectangle(x1,y1,x2,y2)
   Goto Rect1

Get_Input:
   WaitInput()
```

Related Commands: `UsePen, UseBrush`

DrawRoundRectangle

This command draws a rectangle with rounded corners. It draws the border of the rectangle using the current pen and fills its interior using the current brush. You specify the upper-left corner of the rectangle using (*x1,y1*) and the lower-right corner using (*x2,y2*), as shown in Figure 14-18. You control the width and height of the ellipse used to draw the rounded corners using *x3* and *y3*.

Syntax: `DrawRoundRectangle(x1,y1,x2,y2,x3,y3)`

Parameters:

`x1,y1`	The upper-left corner of the rectangle.
`x2,y2`	The lower-right corner of the rectangle.
`x3`	The width of the ellipse used to draw the rounded corners.
`y3`	The height of the ellipse used to draw the rounded corners.

Examples: This example draws a rounded rectangle that resembles an OK button. The upper-left corner of the button is at (10,10) and the lower-right is at (20,17). The height and width of the ellipse used to draw the rounded corners are both 2.

```
UseBrush(SOLID,192,192,192)      {Use a light gray brush}
DrawRoundRectangle(10,10,20,17,2,2)
UseBackground(TRANSPARENT,0,0,0) {Make text background transparent}
DrawText(12,11,"OK")
WaitInput()
```

Related Commands: `UsePen, UseBrush`

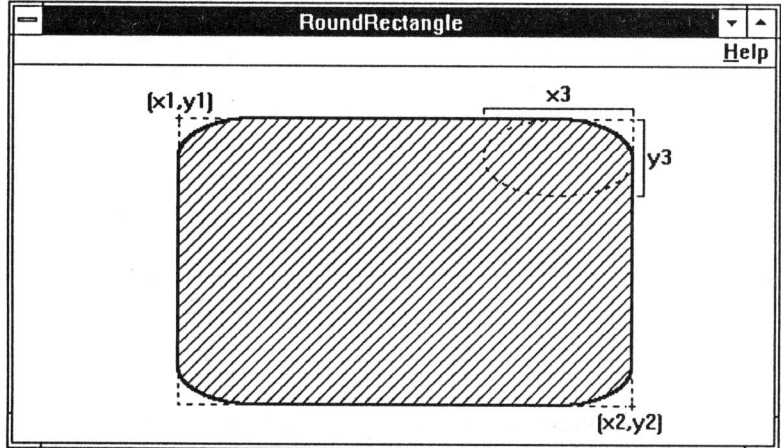

Figure 14-18 The DrawRoundRectangle coordinates

DrawSizedBitmap

This command reads the contents of a bitmap (.BMP) file and either stretches or compresses it to fit within a specified rectangle. You indicate the upper-left corner of the rectangle using (*x1,y1*), and the lower-right corner using (*x2,y2*). This command will create a mirror image of the bitmap if (*x1,y1*) is the lower-right instead of the upper-left corner.

Syntax: `DrawSizedBitmap(x1,y1,x2,y2,"Filename")`

Parameters:

`x1,y1`	The upper-left corner of the rectangle.
`x2,y2`	The lower-right corner of the rectangle.
`"Filename"`	The name of the bitmap file in quotes. Be sure to include the path if the bitmap file is not in the current directory.

Examples: The following program uses the DrawBitmap command to read the ribbons bitmap (RIBBONS.BMP) and place it on the screen. (This bitmap is located in the \WINDOWS directory.) Next, it uses the DrawSizedBitmap command to draw another copy of the bitmap next to the first one and reduce its size in the process.

```
UseCoordinates(PIXEL)
DrawBitmap(10,10,"C:\WINDOWS\RIBBONS.BMP")
DrawSizedBitmap(350,10,514,174,"C:\WINDOWS\RIBBONS.BMP")
WaitInput()
```

This next example is the same as the previous one, except that it flips the second copy of of the ribbons bitmap as it places it on the screen, as shown in Figure 14-19.

```
UseCoordinates(PIXEL)
DrawBitmap(10,10,"C:\WINDOWS\RIBBONS.BMP")
DrawSizedBitmap(514,174,350,10,"C:\WINDOWS\RIBBONS.BMP")
WaitInput()
```

Related Commands: `DrawBitmap`

DrawText

This command draws a character string in the window, using the current font. The starting position of the string is given by the *x* and *y* parameters.

Syntax: `DrawText(x,y,"Text")`

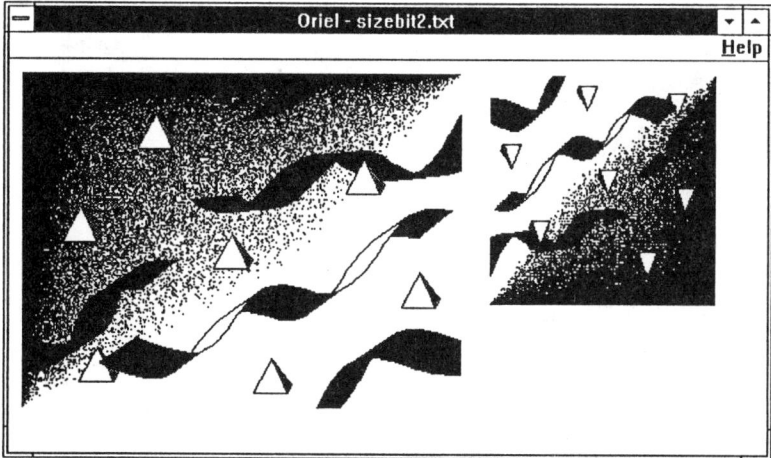

Figure 14-19 Flipping a bitmap with DrawSizedBitmap

Parameters:

x	The x-coordinate of the starting point of the string.
y	The y-coordinate of the starting point of the string.
"Text"	The character string to be drawn, in quotes.

Remark: By default, Oriel for Windows uses the System font in black when drawing text. You can change the font with the UseFont command.

Example: This example uses the Terminal font to draw the string "Windows 3 Power Tools" in a window in two different sizes. Figure 14-20 shows the results.

```
UseCoordinates(PIXEL)
UseFont("Terminal",10,20,NOBOLD,NOITALIC,NOUNDERLINE,0,0,0)
DrawText(10,10,"Windows 3 Power Tools")
UseFont("Terminal",25,40,NOBOLD,NOITALIC,NOUNDERLINE,0,0,0)
DrawText(10,30,"Windows 3 Power Tools")
WaitInput()
```

This next program shows the effect of the current background setting when you draw text. In this example, the first character string is drawn using the default background, opaque white. The second string is drawn after the background has been set to light grey. Before the third character string is drawn, the font is changed to white, creating a reverse effect. Figure 14-21 shows the results. (See UseFont and UseBackground for more on this.)

```
UseCoordinates(PIXEL)
UseFont("System",10,20,NOBOLD,NOITALIC,NOUNDERLINE,0,0,0)
DrawText(10,10,"Windows 3 Power Tools")
```

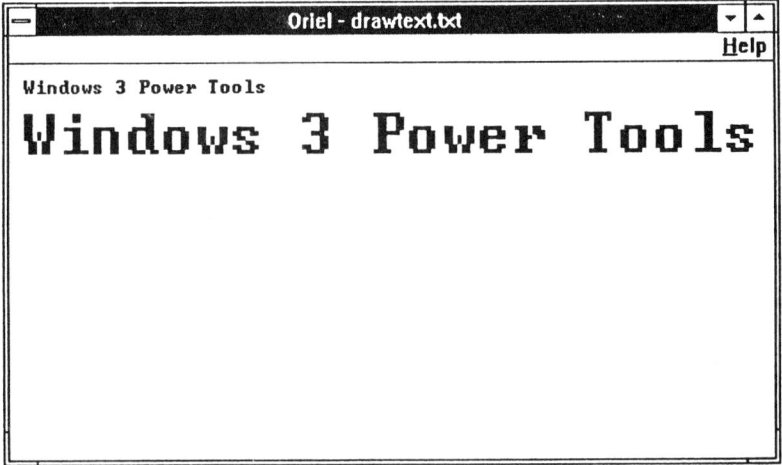

Figure 14-20 The effect of the DrawText command

```
UseBackground(OPAQUE,128,128,128){Light grey background}
DrawText(10,30,"Windows 3 Power Tools")
UseFont("System",10,20,NOBOLD,NOITALIC,NOUNDERLINE,255,255,255)
DrawText(10,50,"Windows 3 Power Tools")
WaitInput()
```

Related Commands: UseFont, UseBackground

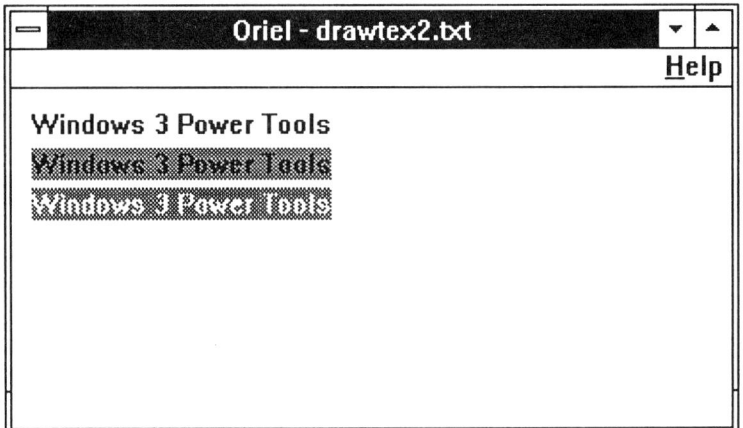

Figure 14-21 The current background affects your text

End

This command terminates an Oriel program. You can use End anywhere in a program, either in the main routine or in subroutine. If Oriel encounters an End in a subroutine, it will terminate execution not only for the subroutine but for the entire program as well.

Syntax: `End`

Remark: Oriel also ends a program when it encounters an end of file or CTRL-Z character (1AH).

Gosub

This command executes a block of code as a subroutine. When the subroutine is completed—that is, a Return command is encountered—control returns to the command following the Gosub.

Syntax: `Gosub label / Return`

Parameter:

>   *label*   The label in the current text file where the subroutine begins.

Remark: You can have up to 50 Gosub/Return nesting levels.

Example: This example uses a simple subroutine to draw text in different point sizes. The subroutine uses the Count variable to set the width of the font as well as the y-coordinate for each line that is drawn. Figure 14-22 shows the results. Notice that the text does not increase in size in smooth increments. Rather, it finds the closest match it can for the height and width you've chosen (see UseFont for more details).

```
{Initialize counter}
    Set Count=1

Next:
    If Count > 10 Then Goto Wait_for_Input
    Gosub Put_Line
    Set Count=Count+1
    Goto Next

Put_Line:
    UseFont("System",Count,1,NOBOLD,NOITALIC,NOUNDERLINE,0,0,0)
```

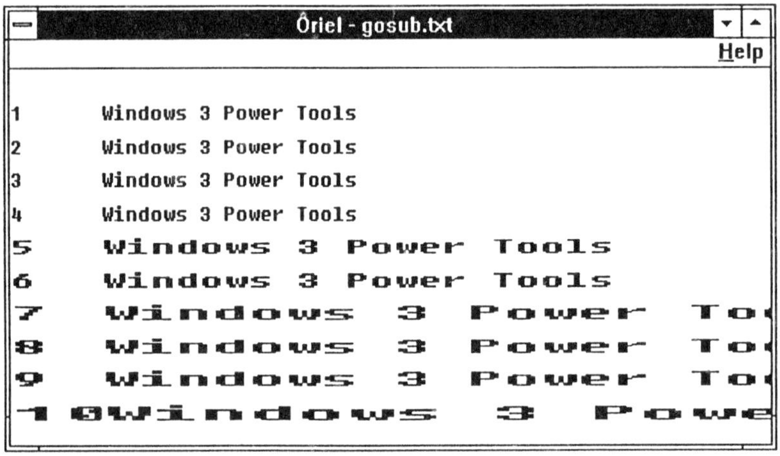

Figure 14-22 Using a subroutine to draw different font sizes

```
Set y=Count*7
DrawNumber(0,y,Count)
DrawText(20,y,"Windows 3 Power Tools")
Return

Wait_for_Input:
    WaitInput()
```

Related Commands: `Goto, Run`

Goto

This command transfers control unconditionally to a label.

Syntax: `Goto label`

Parameters:

    `label`   A label in the current text file.

Remark: You can use a : (colon) following *label* if you want. For example, Oriel treats the following two commands identically:

```
Goto Next
Goto Next:
```

Example: The following example launches Notepad and/or Calculator based on your responses to message boxes. The first message box asks whether you want to run Notepad and displays Yes and No buttons. If you select Yes (Button is set to 1), the program issues the Run command to launch Notepad. If you select No, the Button variable is set to 2 and the program uses a Goto to transfer control to the label Run_Calc; a similar message box then asks whether you want to run Calculator.

```
{Program to launch Notepad and/or Calculator}
     MessageBox(YESNO,1,QUESTION,"Run Notepad?",
                "Notepad?",Button)
     If Button=2 Then Goto Run_Calc
     Run("NOTEPAD.EXE")
Run_Calc:
     MessageBox(YESNO,1,QUESTION,"Run Calculator?",
                "Calculator?",Button)
     If Button=1 Then Run("CALC.EXE")
     End
```

Related Commands: `Gosub`

If

This command lets you execute commands conditionally. If the condition tested is true, execution continues on the same line, following the Then. If the condition tested is false, execution continues on the next line following the If; all commands on the same line as the If are ignored.

Syntax: `If <condition> Then <commands>`

Parameters:

`<condition>`   A conditional expression used to compare two integers taking the form

`Integer1 logical_operator Integer2`

where *Integer1* and *Integer2* are integers (or integer variables) and *logical_operator* is one of the logical operators in Table 14-2. For example, the following are all valid conditional expressions:

```
Red <= 255
Mouse_x1 <> Mouse_x2
10 > Counter
```

`<commands>`   One or more Oriel commands.

Remark: Because Oriel treats the split vertical bar (¦) as white space, it serves as a nice way to separate commands following the Then. Here's an example:

```
If x<10 Then Set x=x+1 | Set y=20 | Goto Next
```

Operator	Meaning
=	equal to
<	less than
>	greater than
<=	less than or equal to
>=	greater than or equal to
<>	not equal to

Table 14-2 Logical Operators

Without the split vertical bars, this line would be more difficult to read because the commands following the Then would be all jumbled together.

Example: This program draws an 8-by-8 matrix of colored boxes starting at (5,5). Figure 14-23 shows the positioning of the boxes in the window. The program uses several If commands to test the value of different variables and branch accordingly. For example, when you first start the program, it draws the first box in the window, increments the Color_Red variable by 64, and tests the value of that variable using the following If command:

```
If Color_Red<=255 Then Goto Color_Ready
```

In this case, if Color_Red is less than or equal to 255, the program branches to the Color_Ready: label. Otherwise, the program continues execution on the next line following the If.

```
{Initialize variables}
    Set Color_Red=63
    Set Color_Green=63
    Set Color_Blue=63
    Set Color_X1=5         {Start the matrix at (5,5)}
    Set Color_Y1=5

Draw_Color:
    UseBrush(SOLID,Color_Red,Color_Green,Color_Blue)
    Set Color_X2=Color_X1+8
    Set Color_Y2=Color_Y1+8
    DrawRectangle(Color_X1,Color_Y1,Color_X2,Color_Y2)

    Set Color_Red=Color_Red+64
    If Color_Red<=255 Then Goto Color_Ready
    Set Color_Red=63
    Set Color_Green=Color_Green+64
```

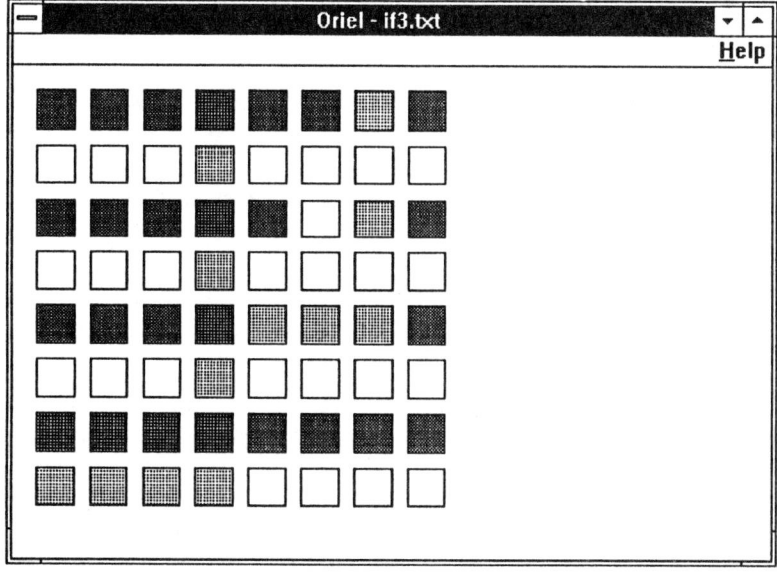

Figure 14-23 Using If to test variables and branch accordingly

```
        If Color_Green<=255 Then Goto Color_Ready
        Set Color_Green=63
        Set Color_Blue=Color_Blue+64
Color_Ready:

        Set Color_X1=Color_X1+11
        If Color_X1<=82 Then Goto Draw_Color
        Set Color_X1=5
        Set Color_Y1=Color_Y1+11
        If Color_Y1<=82 Then Goto Draw_Color

        WaitInput()
```

See MessageBox and Set for another example of the If command.

Related Commands: `Goto, Gosub`

MessageBox

This command lets you create a custom message box complete with your own prompt, caption, and push buttons.

Token	Meaning
OK	Causes the message box to display one push button: OK.
OKCANCEL	Causes the message box to display two push buttons: OK and Cancel.
YESNO	Causes the message box to display two push buttons: Yes and No.
YESNOCANCEL	Causes the message box to display three push buttons: Yes, No, and Cancel.

Table 14-3 Push Button Types

Syntax: `MessageBox(Type,Default_button,Icon,"Text","Caption", Button_pushed)`

Parameters:

Type Specifies the type of push buttons that appear within the message box. It must be one of the tokens in Table 14-3.

Default_button An integer indicating the button you want to appear as the default. The buttons are numbered left to right starting with 1.

Icon Controls the type of icon that appears in front of *"Text"* in the message box. You must use one of the tokens in Table 14-4.

"Text" The message to be displayed within the message box. *"Text"* can have multiple lines in the script (see the second example below). You can have as many lines as you like, but be aware that if you have too many, the message box may not fit on the screen.

"Caption" The text you want to place at the top of the message box.

Button_pushed A variable that returns a number corresponding to the button that the user pushed. The buttons are numbered left to right starting with 1.

Examples: The following program displays a message box that asks whether you want to change the background of the window to blue. The message box has Yes and No command buttons and a question-mark icon, as shown in Figure 14-24.

```
MessageBox(YESNO,1,QUESTION,"Change the background to blue?",
          "Background box",Button)
If Button=1 Then UseBackground(OPAQUE,0,0,255) | DrawBackground
WaitInput()
```

This next example displays three message boxes, each with more lines of text than the previous one.

Token	Meaning
INFORMATION	Causes the message box to display an icon consisting of a lowercase i in a circle.
EXCLAMATION	Causes the message box to display an exclamation-point icon.
QUESTION	Causes the message box to display a question-mark icon.
STOP	Causes the message box to display a stop sign icon.
NOICON	Causes the message box to display no icon.

Table 14-4 Icon Types

```
{Show a single-line message}
    MessageBox(OKCANCEL,1,QUESTION,
    "See a message box with a two-line message?",
    "One-line message",Button_mashed)
    If Button_mashed=2 Then Goto Wait_for_input

{Show a two-line message}
    MessageBox(YESNO,1,QUESTION,
"This box has two lines of text.
Do you want to see one with three?",
    "Two-line message",Button_mashed)
    If Button_mashed=2 Then Goto Wait_for_input

{Show a three-line message}
    MessageBox(OK,1,INFORMATION,
"This box has three lines of text.
You've now seen message boxes with,
one, two, and three lines of text.",
    "Three-line message",Button_mashed)

Wait_for_input:
    WaitInput()
```

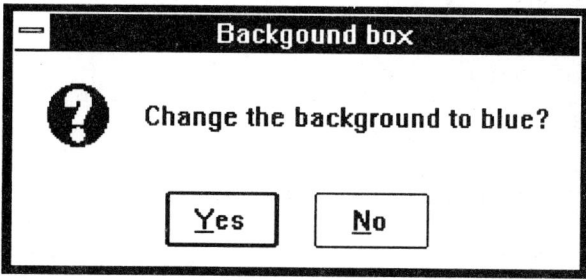

Figure 14-24 A sample message box

Run

This command lets you run a Windows or non-Windows application from within an Oriel program.

Syntax: `Run("Command_line")`

Parameter:

    `"Command_line"`   A string containing the command line (filename plus optional parameters) for the application to be executed.

Remarks: When Oriel for Windows encounters a Run command, it launches the program specified in *"Command_line"*, and then immediately executes the next command in the script without pausing. If you prefer that your Oriel program pause after executing a Run command, you must use a SetWaitMode(FOCUS) command before the Run command and a WaitInput(1) command immediately after (see the example below). This technique is particularly useful when you use the Run command to execute macros you've recorded with Recorder.

If *"Command_line"* does not contain a directory path, Windows searches for the executable file in the following order:

1. The current directory.
2. The Windows directory.
3. The Windows system directory (typically, C:\WINDOWS\SYSTEM).
4. The directories specified in the PATH variable.
5. The list of directories mapped in a network.

If you do not include an extension with the application filename, Oriel assumes an .EXE extension.

Examples: This example launches Notepad and has it automatically load the WIN.INI file on startup. Without pausing, the program then launches COMMAND.COM.

```
Run("NOTEPAD WIN.INI")
Run("C:\COMMAND.COM")
WaitInput()
```

This next example is a variation of the previous one. Rather than run the two programs in quick succession, however, it pauses after loading Notepad. Only after you leave Notepad (or switch back to Oriel for Windows) does the program pick up execution following WaitInput(1) and execute the second Run command to launch COMMAND.COM.

```
SetWaitMode(FOCUS)
Run("NOTEPAD WIN.INI")
WaitInput(1)   {Wait until the focus returns}
Run("C:\COMMAND.COM")
WaitInput()
```

Related Commands: `WaitInput`

Set

This command lets you assign an integer to a variable, or perform simple mathematical calculations using integers and store the result to a variable.

Syntax: `Set Variable = 0,1,2,3,...,65535`

or

`Set Variable = <math_expression>`

Parameters:

`Variable`	A valid variable name (see "Variables" earlier).
`<math_expression>`	A mathematical expression of the form

> `Integer1 math_operator Integer2`
>
> where *Integer1* and *Integer2* are integers (or integer variables) and *math_operator* is one of the mathematical operators in Table 14-5. For example, the following are all valid mathematical expressions:
>
> `Counter+3`
> `X2/18`
> `10*Box_size`

Remarks: In all cases, the results of a mathematical expressions are rounded down and stored as integers. For example, the command Set Green=2/3 results in the

Operator	Meaning
+	Addition
-	Subtraction
*	Multiplication
/	Division

Table 14-5 Mathematical Operators

variable Green being assigned a value of zero. Likewise, the command Set Green=3/2 results in Green being assigned a value of 1.

If you want to perform more than one mathematical operation at a time, the only way to do so is to break them up into separate operations. For example, the following command is invalid:

```
Set y=3*x+4
```

But you can accomplish the same thing using these two commands:

```
Set y=3*x
Set y=y+4
```

Example: The following program draws the 3-D ball in Figure 14-25 in red. By modifying the Set commands at the beginning of the program, you can change the size of the ball and its position on the screen.

```
{Initialize variables}
    UseCoordinates(PIXEL)
    UsePen(NULL,0,0,0,0)      {Use NULL pen for shading}
    Set Red=0
    Set Blue=0
    Set Green=0
    Set x1=150                {Starting x position}
    Set Final_x1=x1
    Set y1=160                {Starting y position}
    Set Final_y1=y1
    Set Ball_size=90          {Ball size}
    Set Count=1
Next_shade:
    If Count>10 Then Goto Flood
    Set x2=x1+Ball_size
    Set y2=y1-Ball_size
    UseBrush(SOLID,Red,Green,Blue)
    DrawEllipse(x1,y1,x2,y2)
    Set x1=x1+2
    Set y1=y1-2
    Set Red=Red+25
    Set Count=Count+1
    Goto Next_shade

Flood:
    UsePen(SOLID,2,0,0,0)
    UseBrush(NULL,0,0,0)
    Set x2=Final_x1+Ball_size
    Set y2=Final_y1-Ball_size
    DrawEllipse(Final_x1,Final_y1,x2,y2)
```

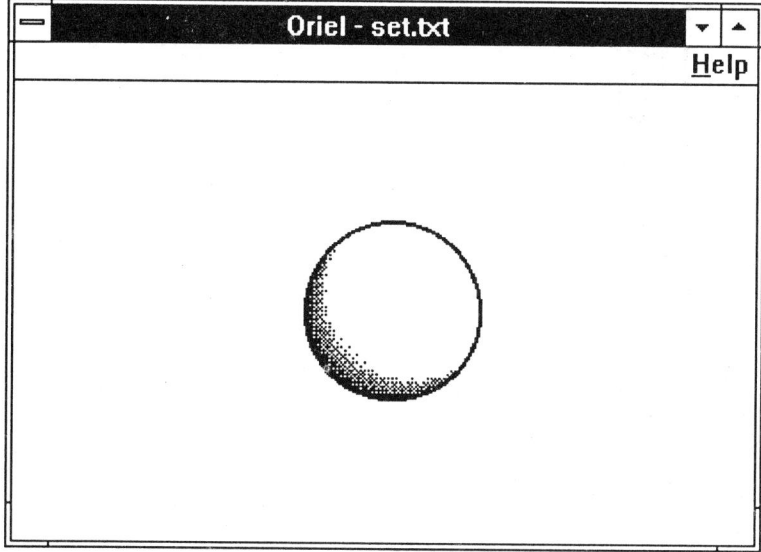

Figure 14-25 A 3-D ball

```
UseBrush(SOLID,255,255,255)    {White brush}
DrawFlood(1,1,0,0,0)           {Flood with white}
WaitInput()
```

Related Commands: DrawNumber

SetKeyboard

This command lets you get keyboard input from the user. When the program is pausing for input and the user presses a specified key, the program branches to the label associated with that key.

Syntax: SetKeyboard()
      or

      SetKeyboard("a",label,
                  "^a",label,
                  vkey,label)

Parameters:

"a"   Any white key on the keyboard (except function keys and certain keys on the numeric keypad) enclosed in quotation marks. For example, "a" represents lowercase *a* and "R" represents uppercase *R*.

518 *Windows 3 Power Tools*

    "^a"   Any white key on the keyboard (except function keys and certain keys on the numeric keypad) in combination with CTRL. For example, "^b" represents CTRL+b and "^V" represents CTRL+V.

    vkey   A virtual key number taken from Table 14-6. For example, the virtual key number for the F1 function key is 112. Using a virtual key number is the only way to test for certain keys, including function keys and several keys on the numeric keypad.

    label   A label you want Oriel to branch to when the user presses the preceding key. For example, the command SetKeyboard ("C",Run_calc) causes the program to branch to the label Run_calc when the user presses *C*.

Remarks: When Oriel encounters a SetKeyboard command in your program, it does not immediately branch anywhere. Rather, it waits until it encounters a WaitInput() command (which causes the program to pause indefinitely for user input) and the user presses a specified key. Only then does control transfer to the *label* associated with that key.

The syntax above shows only three keys in the SetKeyboard list. However, you can actually include as many keys as you want in the list.

A SetKeyboard command remains in effect until any of the following occurs:

- You use another SetKeyboard command.
- You use SetKeyboard without any parameters to reset the keyboard.
- The program ends.

Examples: The following example puts the message "Press E to end the program" on the screen, and then pauses the program indefinitely until you press *e* or *E*. When you press either key, the program ends.

```
DrawText(1,1,"Press E to end the program")
SetKeyboard("E",End_it,"e",End_it)
WaitInput()
End_it:
End
```

This next example places two buttons on the screen, as shown in Figure 14-26. When you click on a button with the mouse, or press the key associated with the button, the program runs the named Windows application. On the other hand, if you press F1, the program displays a message box with some simple help text.

```
{Draw Buttons}
    UseBrush(Solid,192,192,192)        {Grey brush}
    UseBackground(TRANSPARENT,0,0,0)   {Prevent white text background}
    DrawRoundRectangle(10,10,40,25,5,5)
```

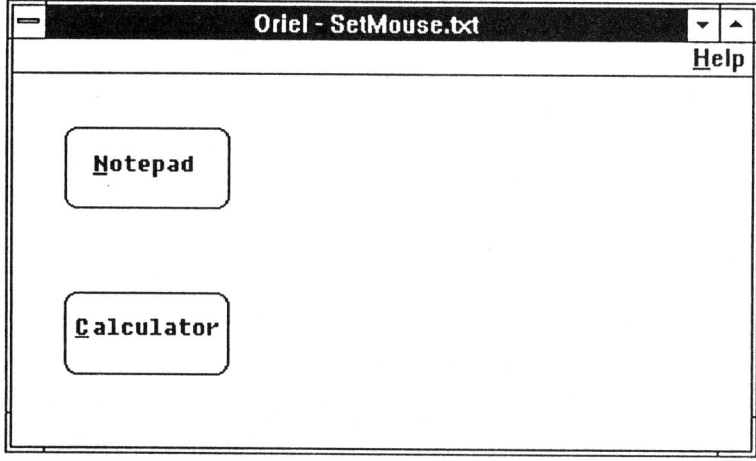

Figure 14-26 Getting keyboard input with SetKeyboard

```
        UseFont("System",1,3,NOBOLD,NOITALIC,UNDERLINE,0,0,0)
        DrawText(15,14,"N")

        UseFont("System",1,3,NOBOLD,NOITALIC,NOUNDERLINE,0,0,0)
        DrawText(18,14,"otepad")
        DrawRoundRectangle(10,40,40,55,5,5)

        UseFont("System",1,3,NOBOLD,NOITALIC,UNDERLINE,0,0,0)
        DrawText(12,44,"C")

        UseFont("System",1,3,NOBOLD,NOITALIC,NOUNDERLINE,0,0,0)
        DrawText(15,44,"alculator")

{Set up the mouse}
        SetMouse(10,10,40,30,Run_Notepad,Temp,Temp,
                 10,40,40,60,Run_Calc,Temp,Temp)

{Set up the keyboard}
        SetKeyboard("N",Run_Notepad,
                    "n",Run_Notepad,
                    "C",Run_Calc,
                    "c",Run_Calc,
                    112,Help_Box)     {112=virtual key for F1}

Wait_for_Input:
        WaitInput()
```

```
Run_Notepad:
    Run("NOTEPAD.EXE")
    Goto Wait_for_Input

Run_Calc:
    Run("CALC.EXE")
    Goto Wait_for_Input

Help_Box:
    MessageBox(OK,1,NOICON,
    "Pick a button to run the Windows application",
    "Help box",TEMP)
    Goto Wait_for_Input
```

Related Commands: `SetMenu, SetMouse, WaitInput`

Value	Description
8	BACKSPACE
9	TAB
12	5 on numeric keypad with NUMLOCK off
13	ENTER
16	SHIFT
17	CTRL
18	ALT
19	PAUSE (or CTRL+NUMLOCK)
20	CAPS LOCK
27	ESCAPE
32	SPACEBAR
33	PGUP
34	PGDN
35	END
36	HOME
37	LEFTARROW
38	UPARROW
39	RIGHTARROW
40	DOWNARROW
44	PRINTSCREEN
45	INSERT
46	DELETE
48	0
49	1

Table 14-6 Virtual Key Numbers

Value	Description
50	2
51	3
52	4
53	5
54	6
55	7
56	8
57	9
65	A
66	B
67	C
68	D
69	E
70	F
71	G
72	H
73	I
74	J
75	K
76	L
77	M
78	N
79	O
80	P
81	Q
82	R
83	S
84	T
85	U
86	V
87	W
88	X
89	Y
90	Z
96	Numeric key pad 0 (NUMLOCK must be on)
97	Numeric key pad 1 (NUMLOCK must be on)
98	Numeric key pad 2 (NUMLOCK must be on)
99	Numeric key pad 3 (NUMLOCK must be on)
100	Numeric key pad 4 (NUMLOCK must be on)

Table 14-6 Virtual Key Numbers (*continued*)

Value	Description
101	Numeric key pad 5 (NUMLOCK must be on)
102	Numeric key pad 6 (NUMLOCK must be on)
103	Numeric key pad 7 (NUMLOCK must be on)
104	Numeric key pad 8 (NUMLOCK must be on)
105	Numeric key pad 9 (NUMLOCK must be on)
106	Numeric key pad *
107	Numeric key pad +
109	Numeric key pad -
110	Numeric key pad . (NUMLOCK must be on)
111	Numeric key pad /
112	F1
113	F2
114	F3
115	F4
116	F5
117	F6
118	F7
119	F8
120	F9
121	F10
122	F11
123	F12
124	F13
125	F14
126	F15
127	F16
144	NUM LOCK
145	SCROLL LOCK

The following key codes apply to US keyboards only:

186	Colon/semi-colon
187	Plus/equal
188	Less than/comma
189	Underscore/hyphen
190	Greater than/period
191	Question/slash
192	Tilde/backwards single quote

Table 14-6 Virtual Key Numbers (*continued*)

Value	Description
219	Left curly brace/left square brace
220	Pipe symbol/backslash
221	Right curly brace/right square bracket
222	Double quote/single quote

Table 14-6 Virtual Key Numbers

SetMenu

This command lets you create your own custom menus. When the program is pausing for input and the user selects a menu item, the program branches to the label associated with that menu item.

Syntax: `SetMenu()`

or

```
SetMenu("Top1",IGNORE/label,
        "ItemA",IGNORE/label,
        "ItemB",IGNORE/label,
        SEPARATOR,
        "ItemC",IGNORE/label,
        ENDPOPUP,
        "Top2",IGNORE/label,
           .
           .
        ENDPOPUP)
```

Parameters:

"*Top1*","*Top2*"   The items that are to appear on the main or top-level menu bar, also called the *action bar*. You can have as many items as you like on the main menu bar. (If you have more than a single line's worth, Windows will extend the menu bar to a second line and beyond.)

"*ItemA*","*ItemB*", "*ItemC*"   The items that are to appear within a popup menu, also called a *pull-down menu*. You can have as many items as you like within a popup menu.

label	A label you want Oriel to branch to when the user selects a menu item.
IGNORE	Tells Oriel not to do anything when the menu item is selected. When IGNORE follows an item on the main menu bar, Oriel displays the item's popup menu, provided you've defined one.
SEPARATOR	Divides the items in a popup menu into groups.
ENDPOPUP	Ends a popup menu. In addition, this token is always the last argument in a SetMenu command.

Remarks: A top-level menu consists of one or more items— *"Top1"*, *"Top2"*, *"Top3"*, and so on. Below each top-level menu item is a popup menu. You can have one or more items within a popup menu— *"ItemA"*, *"ItemB"*, *"ItemC"*, and so on.

When you define a menu in Oriel for Windows, you define it sequentially. You begin by setting up the first top-level menu item and its popup menu. You then set up the second top-level menu item and its popup, and so on.

Following each top-level menu item (*"Top1"*) and popup menu item (*"ItemA"*) is a label you want the program to branch to when a menu item is selected. If you don't want the program to branch anywhere, use the IGNORE token instead; the IGNORE token is most often used following a top-level menu item when all you want Oriel to do is show the item's popup menu. (The IGNORE token is recognized even if you've created an IGNORE label.)

When Oriel for Windows encounters a SetMenu command in your program, it does not immediately branch anywhere. Rather, it waits until it encounters a WaitInput() command (which causes the program to pause indefinitely for user input) and the user selects a menu item. Only then does control transfer to the *label* associated with that item.

Here are some conventions you may want to follow when creating Oriel menus in order to give the user additional information about the items within the menu:

- An *underlined letter* in a menu item indicates that the letter can be used to select the menu item. You create underlined letters by placing an & in front of the letter you want underlined. For example, the parameter "&Notepad" underlines the letter *N* in the Notepad menu item. When a letter is underlined, it is known as a *mnemonic*. To select an item on the top-level menu using its mnemonic, you press ALT+mnemonic, for example ALT+N. Once a popup menu appears, you can select an item within it by pressing that item's mnemonic alone.

- By placing an *exclamation point* at the end of a top-level menu item, you can indicate that no pop-up menu will appear when the user selects the item.

- By using a *separator*, you can divide items within a popup menu into groups. You can have as many separators as you like within a popup menu.

Oriel for Windows 525

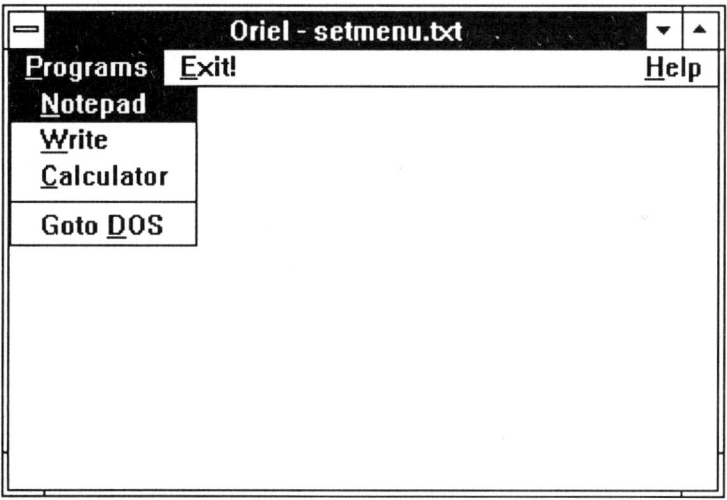

Figure 14-27 A menu created with SetMenu

Example: This example creates the simple menu show in Figure 14-27. As you can see, the menu has two top-level menu items, Programs and Exit!. (Because Exit! does not lead to a popup menu, it includes an exclamation point.) When you select an item from Programs' popup menu, the program branches to the associated label. For example, when you select Goto DOS, the program branches to the label DOS:, where it launches a copy of COMMAND.COM.

```
{Set up the menu}
    SetMenu("&Programs",IGNORE,
            "&Notepad",Run_Notepad,
            "&Write",Run_Write,
            "&Calculator",Run_Calculator,
            SEPARATOR,
            "Goto &DOS",DOS,
            ENDPOPUP,
            "&Exit!",Shut_Down,
            ENDPOPUP)

Wait_for_Input:
    WaitInput()

Run_Notepad:
    Run("NOTEPAD.EXE")
    Goto Wait_for_Input

Run_Write:
    Run("WRITE.EXE")
```

```
            Goto Wait_for_Input

    Run_Calculator:
        Run("CALC.EXE")
        Goto Wait_for_Input

    DOS:
        Run("C:\COMMAND.COM")
        Goto Wait_for_Input

    Shut_Down:
        End
```

Related Commands: `SetKeyboard, SetMenu, WaitInput`

SetMouse

This command lets you get mouse input. When the program is pausing for input and the user clicks the left mouse button within a specified rectangular region, the program branches to the label associated with that region.

Syntax: `SetMouse()`

or

SetMouse(region1_x1,region1_y1,region1_x2,region1_y2,label,x,y,
region2_x1,region2_y1,region2_x2,region2_y2,label,x,y,
        .
        .
regionn_x1,regionn_y1,regionn_x2,regionn_y2,label,x,y)

Parameters:

regionx_x1, regionx_y1	The upper-left corner of a rectangular mouse hit-testing region.
regionx_x2, regionx_y2	The lower-right corner of a rectangular mouse hit-testing region.
label	The label you want to branch to when the user clicks the mouse within the mouse hit-testing region (as defined by the previous four arguments).
x, y	The coordinates of the mouse pointer, as measured from the upper-left corner of the window.

Remarks: To get mouse input, you must set up rectangular areas in the window known as *mouse hit-testing regions*. When the user clicks the mouse within a hit-testing region, the program branches to the label associated with that region and saves the mouse pointer coordinates in the two variables that follow, x and y.

When Oriel encounters a SetMouse command in your program, it does not immediately branch anywhere. Rather, it waits until it encounters a WaitInput() command (which causes the program to pause indefinitely for user input) and the user clicks the mouse within a hit-testing region. Only then does control transfer to the *label* associated with that region.

You can have as many hit-testing regions as you like for a given SetMouse command. If two hit-testing regions overlap, Oriel will branch to the label for the first one in the list.

Example: The following program sets up two mouse hit-testing regions, a rectangle on the left-hand side of the screen and an Exit button on the right, as shown in Figure 14-28. When you click the mouse within the rectangle—the region (1,1) to (300,200)—the program saves the mouse pointer coordinates in Mouse_x and Mouse_y and branches to the Mouse_hit label, where it draws a small black rectangle at the location of the mouse pointer. If you click on the Exit button—the region (340,80) to (400,120)—the program branches to the Goodbye label where an End command ends the program.

```
{Set coordinate system to pixels}
    UseCoordinates(PIXEL)

{Draw the rectangle that will later become a hit-testing region}
    DrawRectangle(1,1,300,200)
    DrawText(30,210,"Click the mouse within the rectangle")

{Draw the Exit button using a grey brush}
    UseBrush(SOLID,192,192,192)
    DrawRoundRectangle(340,80,400,120,10,10)
    UseBackground(TRANSPARENT,0,0,0)
    DrawText(357,90,"Exit")

{Use a black brush}
    UseBrush(SOLID,0,0,0)

{Set up the mouse}
    SetMouse(1,1,300,200,Mouse_hit,Mouse_x,Mouse_y,    {Rectangle}
                340,80,400,120,Goodbye,Temp,Temp)       {Exit button}

Wait_for_Input:
    WaitInput()
```

528 *Windows 3 Power Tools*

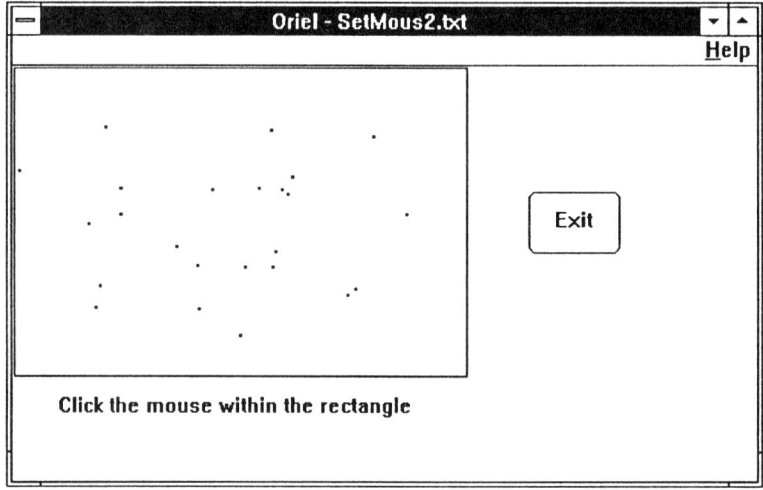

Figure 14-28 **Using SetMouse to get mouse input**

```
Mouse_hit:
    Set x2=Mouse_x+2
    Set y2=Mouse_y+2
    DrawRectangle(Mouse_x,Mouse_y,x2,y2)
    Goto Wait_for_Input

Goodbye:
    End
```

See the DrawNumber and SetKeyboard commands for other examples of SetMouse.

Related Commands: `WaitInput`

SetWaitMode

This command controls how Oriel for Windows behaves after a Run command starts another application and Oriel encounters a WaitInput command in your script.

Syntax: `SetWaitMode(NULL/FOCUS)`

Parameters:

NULL   Causes WaitInput to behave in the normal way. That is, WaitInput with an argument pauses Oriel a specified number of milliseconds, and WaitInput without an argument pauses Oriel indefinitely while it waits for user input. SetWaitMode(NULL) is the default.

FOCUS Causes Oriel for Windows to pause until the focus returns when it encounters a WaitInput(1) command.

Remarks: By default, when you use a Run command to start another application, Oriel for Windows does not pause after executing the Run, but immediately executes the next command in the script. By using SetWaitMode(FOCUS) before the Run command, and WaitInput(1) immediately after, you can have Oriel pause until it gets the focus back—that is, until you switch back to Oriel. It will then pick up execution after the WaitInput(1). (See the example below.)

If you want Oriel for Windows to pause until it gets the focus back, you *must* use a WaitInput(1) command following the SetWaitMode(FOCUS) command. Note that using *1* as the argument for WaitInput is critical. If you use WaitInput without an argument, Oriel will pause indefinitely and show no signs of continuing after it gets the focus back.

In most cases, you do not need to use the SetWait Mode command. The only time you will want to consider using it is when your program includes a Run command and the commands that follow it in the script create a confusing display—for example, an Oriel message box appears in front of another application's window.

Using SetWaitMode(FOCUS) and WaitInput(1) is particularly important when you use the Run command to start a macro that launches several applications. Without these commands bracketing the Run, your Oriel program will not pause and may create a confusing display as it horns in on the applications that are being launched by the macro.

Examples: The following program uses the Run command to start Notepad. Without pausing, the program then executes the MessageBox command, which causes it to display a message box in front of the Notepad window, as shown in Figure 14-29.

```
SetWaitMode(NULL)
Run("NOTEPAD.EXE")
MessageBox(OK,1,INFORMATION,"Comes up in front of Notepad",
          "Oriel message box",Temp)
```

This next example is a variation of the previous one. It uses SetWaitMode(FOCUS) to change the behavior of WaitInput so that when Oriel

530 *Windows 3 Power Tools*

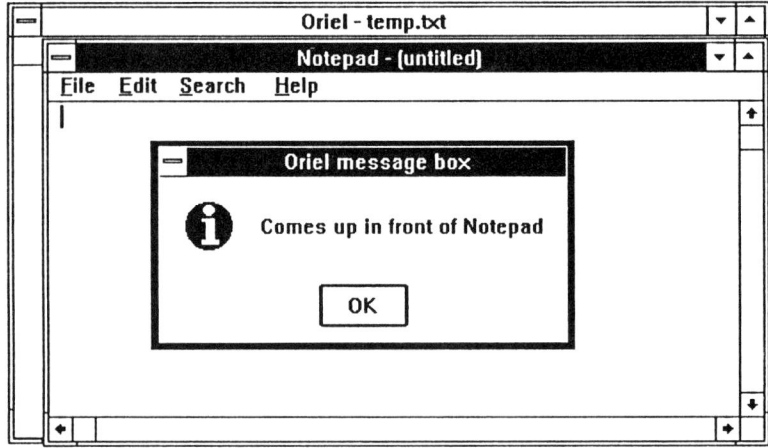

Figure 14-29 An Oriel message box appearing in front of another application's window

encounters WaitInput(1), it pauses until it gets the focus back. By doing so, the message box only appears after you return to Oriel for Windows.

```
SetWaitMode(FOCUS)
Run("NOTEPAD.EXE")
WaitInput(1)              {The 1 is necessary here}
MessageBox(OK,1,INFORMATION,"The focus is back","",Temp)
```

Related Command: WaitInput

SetWindow

This command maximizes, minimizes, or restores the Oriel window.

Syntax: SetWindow(MAXIMIZE/MINIMIZE/RESTORE)

Parameters:

MAXIMIZE	Maximizes the Oriel window.
MINIMIZE	Minimizes the Oriel window.
RESTORE	Restores the Oriel window.

Example: This program uses the SetWindow command to maximize, minimize, and restore the Oriel window in various ways, pausing for one second in between SetWindow commands.

```
SetWindow(MAXIMIZE)
WaitInput(1000)
SetWindow(RESTORE)
WaitInput(1000)
SetWindow(MINIMIZE)
WaitInput(1000)
SetWindow(RESTORE)
WaitInput()
```

UseBackground

This command has the dual role of controlling the background mode and the background color. The background mode establishes whether the GDI removes existing background colors before drawing any of the following:

- Text
- Shapes with a hatched brush
- Lines with a dotted pen

The GDI uses the background color to fill the small rectangles behind characters (called character cells), the gaps in dotted pens, and hatched lines in brushes.

Syntax: `UseBackground(OPAQUE/TRANSPARENT,r,g,b)`

Parameters:

OPAQUE	Causes the background to be filled with the current color specified by r, g, b.
TRANSPARENT	The background is left unchanged.
r,g,b	Specifies the color of the background using a combination of red, green, and blue. The default background color is white (255,255,255).

Remarks: When you draw a character on the screen, the GDI does more than draw the squiggles that make up the character. It actually draws a rectangular area enclosing the character, called the *character cell*, as shown in Figure 14-30. The current font color determines the color of the characters, but the current background color controls the color in the character cells.

When the background mode is set to OPAQUE, the GDI fills the character cells with the RGB value you've set with the r, g, b parameters. On the other hand, when the background mode is set to TRANSPARENT, the GDI does not change the color in the character cells.

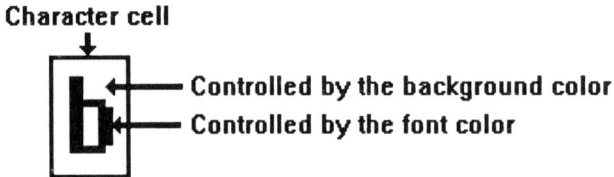

Figure 14-30 The character cell

These same principles apply to hatched brushes and dotted pens. That is, when the background mode is set to OPAQUE, the GDI fills the gaps in dotted pens and hatched brushes with the RGB value you've set with the r, g, b parameters. When the background mode is set to TRANSPARENT, the GDI does not change the color in the gaps.

You can change the color of the entire window's background using the DrawBackground command. This command also erases any window contents. (The background mode setting—OPAQUE or TRANSPARENT—has no effect on the DrawBackground command.)

Example: The following example shows the effect of the background mode and color settings when you draw text, draw lines with a dotted pen, and draw rectangles with a hatched brush (Figure 14-31). Notice that the white background only appears for character cells and the gaps in dotted pens and hatched brushes when the background mode is set to OPAQUE.

```
{Change window's background to light grey}
    UseBackground(TRANSPARENT,192,192,192)
    DrawBackground

{Change background mode to TRANSPARENT and color to white}
    UseBackground(TRANSPARENT,255,255,255)

{Draw text, dotted line, and hatched rectangle}
    DrawText(10,10,"Text with a TRANSPARENT background")
    UsePen(DOT,1,0,0,0)       {Dotted pen}
    DrawLine(10,21,40,21)
    UsePen(SOLID,1,0,0,0)     {Reset the pen to solid}
    UseBrush(CROSS,0,0,0)     {Cross hatched brush}
    DrawRectangle(10,30,40,40)

{Change back to default background mode and color (white)}
    UseBackground(OPAQUE,255,255,255)

{Draw more text and another dotted line and hatched rectangle}
    DrawText(10,60,"Text with an OPAQUE background")
```

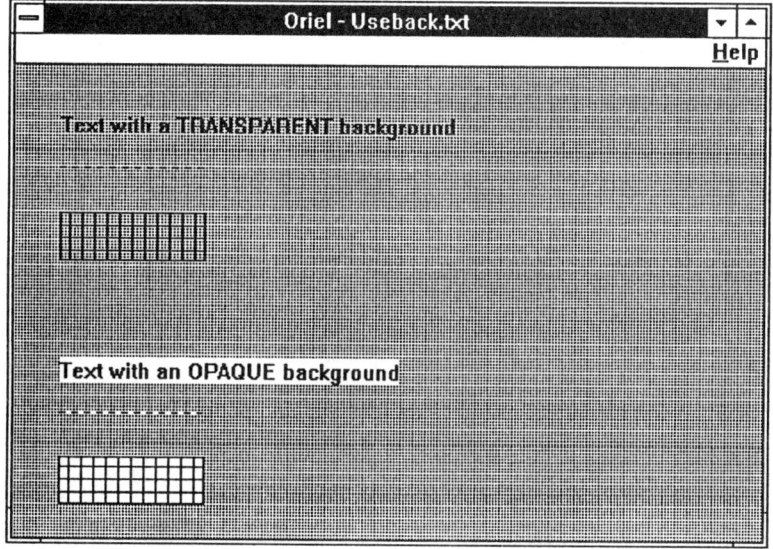

Figure 14-31 The effect of the background mode and color settings

```
UsePen(DOT,1,0,0,0)        {Dotted pen}
DrawLine(10,71,40,71)
UsePen(SOLID,1,0,0,0)      {Reset the pen to solid}
UseBrush(CROSS,0,0,0)      {Cross hatched brush}
DrawRectangle(10,80,40,90)

{Wait for input}
WaitInput()
```

See DrawRoundRectangle for another example of UseBackground.

Related Commands: DrawBackground, DrawText, UsePen, UseBrush

UseBrush

This command defines the style and color of the brush that will be used in subsequent drawing operations.

Syntax: UseBrush(SOLID/DIAGONALUP/DIAGONALDOWN/DIAGONALCROSS/
HORIZONTAL/VERTICAL/CROSS/NULL, r, g, b)

Parameters:

SOLID	A solid brush
DIAGONALUP	45-degree upward hatch (left to right)
DIAGONALDOWN	45-degree downward hatch (left to right)
DIAGONALCROSS	45-degree crosshatch
HORIZONTAL	Horizontal hatch
VERTICAL	Vertical hatch
CROSS	Horizontal and vertical crosshatch
NULL	A null or "hollow" brush (no color is drawn)
r,g,b	Specifies the color of the brush using a combination of red, green, and blue.

Examples: This program defines a crosshatched red brush and draws a round rectangle with it.

```
UseBrush(CROSS,255,0,0)
DrawRoundRectangle(10,10,40,40,10,10)
WaitInput()
```

This next program draws a series of circles using the eight available brush styles. Figure 14-32 shows the window that the program produces.

```
UseBrush(SOLID,0,0,255)
DrawEllipse(10,10,30,30)
DrawText(13,32,"SOLID")

UseBrush(DIAGONALUP,0,0,255)
DrawEllipse(49,10,69,30)
DrawText(45,32,"DIAGONALUP")

UseBrush(DIAGONALDOWN,0,0,255)
DrawEllipse(88,10,108,30)
DrawText(80,32,"DIAGONALDOWN")

UseBrush(DIAGONALCROSS,0,0,255)
DrawEllipse(127,10,147,30)
DrawText(119,32,"DIAGONALCROSS")

UseBrush(HORIZONTAL,0,0,255)
DrawEllipse(10,50,30,70)
DrawText(6,72,"HORIZONTAL")

UseBrush(VERTICAL,0,0,255)
DrawEllipse(49,50,69,70)
DrawText(49,72,"VERTICAL")
```

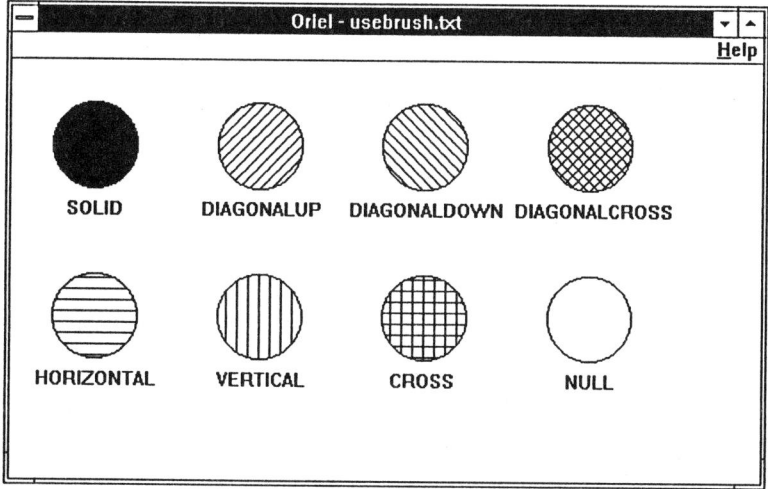

Figure 14-32 The eight different brush styles

```
UseBrush(CROSS,0,0,255)
DrawEllipse(88,50,108,70)
DrawText(90,72,"CROSS")

UseBrush(NULL,0,0,255)
DrawEllipse(127,50,147,70)
DrawText(131,72,"NULL")

WaitInput()
```

Related Comments: DrawArc, DrawChord, DrawEllipse, DrawFlood, DrawPie, DrawRectangle, DrawRoundRectangle

UseCaption

This command lets you place your own caption at the top of the Oriel window.

Syntax: UseCaption("*Text*")

Parameter:

"*Text*"   The text you want to use for the caption, enclosed in double quotes.

Example: This command places the caption "All that Jazz" at the top of the Oriel window.

```
UseCaption("All that Jazz")
WaitInput()
```

UseCoordinates

Specifies Oriel's coordinate system as either pixel or metric and controls the unit of measure that Oriel uses for all subsequent drawing operations.

Syntax: `UseCoordinates(PIXEL/METRIC)`

Parameters:

- PIXEL — Causes Oriel to use pixels as the unit of measure.
- METRIC — Causes Oriel to use millimeters as the unit of measure. METRIC is the default.

Remarks: By using metric coordinates, you can guarantee that your programs will be device independent. That is, your programs will appear the same regardless of the video display type.

On the other hand, programs written using pixel coordinates are device dependent, which may or may not be a problem for you. For example, suppose you have an EGA system and you write a program that draws shapes in a window. When you run that program on a VGA system, the shapes will appear much smaller. By the same token, pixel coordinates are much more accurate than metric. Therefore, if you need to address the screen with the highest precision, you'll want to use pixel coordinates rather than metric.

Example: The following program draws the same shapes using pixel and metric coordinates. The different results are shown in Figure 14-33.

```
UseCoordinates(PIXEL)
DrawEllipse(50,10,70,30)
DrawRectangle(50,30,70,50)
DrawText(50,55,"Pixel")
UseCoordinates(METRIC)
DrawEllipse(50,10,70,30)
DrawRectangle(50,30,70,50)
DrawText(50,55,"Metric")
WaitInput()
```

Related Commands: All Draw commands.

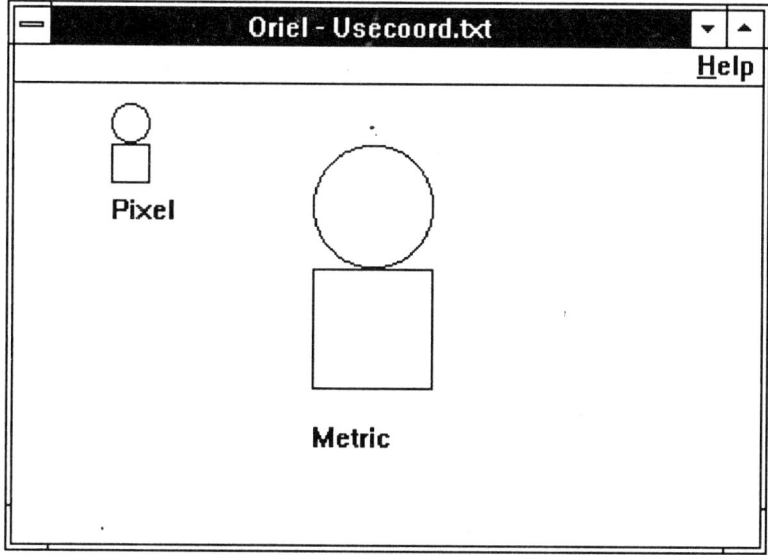

Figure 14-33 Pixel versus metric coordinates

UseFont

This command establishes the font that will be used for subsequent text-drawing operations. It lets you specify the width, height, style (bold, italics, and underlining), and color of the font.

Syntax: UseFont("Name",Width,Height,Set_bold,Set_italic,
 Set_underline,r,g,b)

Parameters:

"Name" The name of the font, enclosed in double quotes. The standard Windows screen fonts are Terminal, Roman, Script, Modern, Helv, Courier, Tms Rmn, Symbol, Digital, and System.

Width The width of the font using the current coordinate mode (either pixels or millimeters). If you specify a width of zero, then the default width is used for the given font.

Height The height of the font using the current coordinate mode (either pixels or millimeters). If you specify a height of zero, then the default height is used for the given font.

`Set_bold`	Specifies whether the font is bold and must be either of the following tokens:		
		BOLD	Font is bold
		NOBOLD	Font is not bold
`Set_italic`	Specifies whether the font is italic and must be either of the following tokens:		
		ITALIC	Font is italic
		NOITALIC	Font is not italic
`Set_underline`	Specifies whether the font is underlined and must be either of the following tokens:		
		UNDERLINE	Font is underlined
		NOUNDERLINE	Font is not underlined
`r,g,b`	Specifies the color of the font using a combination of red, green, and blue.		

Remarks: The GDI maintains all the fonts that are available in the system and their sizes in a font table. When you describe a font with the UseFrobe command, that font may or may not exist in the GDI's table. The GDI compares the font parameters you've supplied to the fonts it has in its table and returns the font with the closest match. This is a process known as font mapping.

The process by which the GDI chooses a font from the table that matches the font you've specified is based on a handicapping system. In short, it assigns certain penalties to the fonts in the table when they do not match the font you've specified. The font that has the fewest penalties is the font that the GDI selects, and is the one that is used the next time you draw text on the screen in Oriel.

In some cases, the GDI will synthesize a font to match the parameters you've supplied. For example, the GDI may determine that it can double the height and width of a font in its table to produce a font that is closest to the one you've asked for. In fact, the GDI is capable of quite complicated synthesis, including the ability to change the aspect ratio (the height to width ratio) of a font and to produce an italic or bold font from a standard font.

To see a list of names of the fonts available in your system, select the Fonts menu item in Paintbrush, as shown in Figure 14-34. You may also find the names of additional fonts by selecting the Fonts icon in Control Panel. To use one of the fonts you've identified, simply supply its name as the *"Name"* parameter in UseFont. Be sure to spell the name exactly as you see it on the screen.

Oriel for Windows also lets you access fonts you've added with third-party font packages. The names of these fonts may or may not be listed in Paintbrush or the Control Panel. See Chapter 4, "Of Fonts and Printing," for more on where to find font names.

The default font is the System font in black.

If you notice that the color behind each character is not what you intended, you may need to change the background mode or color. See the UseBackground command for more details.

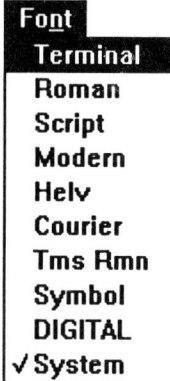

Figure 14-34 Font names in Paintbrush

Examples: The following program shows the effect of explicitly controlling the width and height of a font versus using the default width and height. Figure 14-35 shows the results.

```
{Set the coordinate mode to pixel}
    UseCoordinates(PIXEL)

{Set System font's width to 6 and height to 10 and draw text}
    UseFont("System",6,10,NOBOLD,NOITALIC,NOUNDERLINE,0,0,0)
    DrawText(10,10,"System font with specified height and width")

{Use the default width and height to draw text}
    UseFont("System",0,0,NOBOLD,NOITALIC,NOUNDERLINE,0,0,0)
    DrawText(10,30,"System font with default height and width")

    WaitInput()
```

This next program shows some samples of the standard fonts found on any system. Figure 14-36 shows the window the program produces.

```
UseFont("Terminal",0,0,NOBOLD,NOITALIC,NOUNDERLINE,0,0,0)
DrawText(10,10,"Terminal")
UseFont("Roman",0,0,NOBOLD,NOITALIC,NOUNDERLINE,0,0,0)
DrawText(10,18,"Roman")
UseFont("Script",0,0,NOBOLD,NOITALIC,NOUNDERLINE,0,0,0)
DrawText(10,26,"Script")
UseFont("Modern",0,0,NOBOLD,NOITALIC,NOUNDERLINE,0,0,0)
DrawText(10,34,"Modern")
UseFont("Helv",0,0,NOBOLD,NOITALIC,NOUNDERLINE,0,0,0)
DrawText(10,42,"Helv")
UseFont("Courier",0,0,NOBOLD,NOITALIC,NOUNDERLINE,0,0,0)
DrawText(10,50,"Courier")
```

540   *Windows 3 Power Tools*

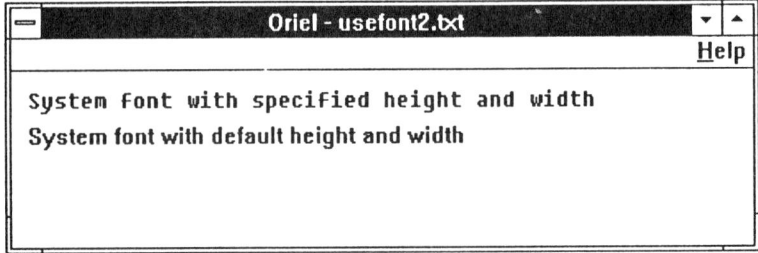

Figure 14-35 Controlling a font's width and height versus using the defaults

```
UseFont("Tms Rmn",0,0,NOBOLD,NOITALIC,NOUNDERLINE,0,0,0)
DrawText(10,58,"Tms Rmn")
UseFont("Symbol",0,0,NOBOLD,NOITALIC,NOUNDERLINE,0,0,0)
DrawText(10,66,"Symbol")
UseFont("DIGITAL",0,0,NOBOLD,NOITALIC,NOUNDERLINE,0,0,0)
DrawText(10,74,"DIGITAL")
UseFont("System",0,0,NOBOLD,NOITALIC,NOUNDERLINE,0,0,0)
DrawText(10,82,"System")
WaitInput()
```

Related Commands: `DrawText, UseBackground`

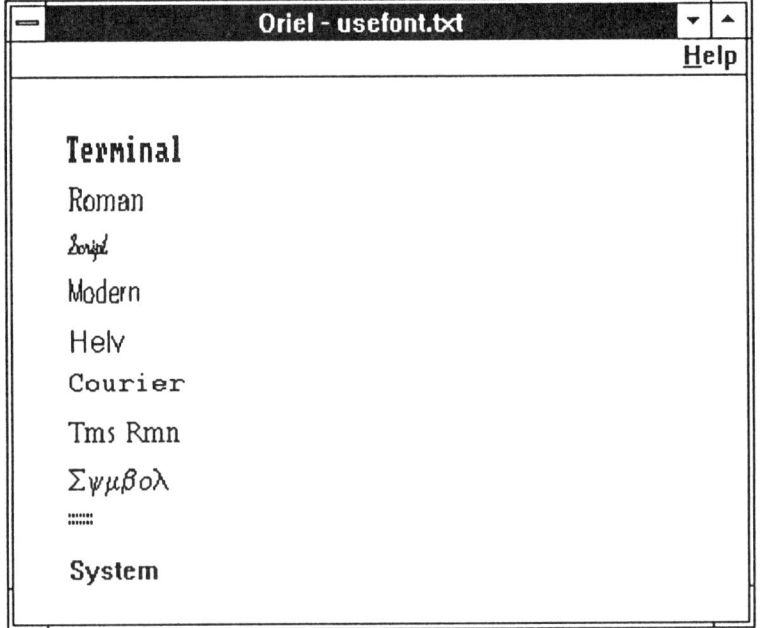

Figure 14-36 The standard fonts found on any system

Token	Description	Result
SOLID	Solid line	————
DASH	Dashed line	- - - - - -
DOT	Dotted line	. . . . . .
DASHDOT	Dash-dot line	_._._._._._
DASHDOTDOT	Dash-dot-dot line	_.._.._.._..
NULL	No line	

Table 14-7 Pen Styles

UsePen

This command establishes the pen that will be used for subsequent drawing operations. It lets you specify the style, width, and color for the pen.

Syntax: UsePen(Style,Width,r,g,b)

Parameters:

Style The style of the pen. It must be one of the tokens in Table 14-7. The default is SOLID.

Width The width of the line in pixels. It must be 1, unless the pen style is SOLID or NULL. The default width is 1.

r,g,b Specifies the color of the pen using a combination of red, green, and blue. The default is black (0,0,0).

Example: The following example draws five lines, each using a different pen style and color. Figure 14-37 shows the window that the program produces.

```
{Solid line in black}
UsePen(SOLID,1,0,0,0)
DrawLine(10,10,90,10)

{Dashed line in red}
UsePen(DASH,1,255,0,0)
DrawLine(10,20,90,20)

{Dotted line in green}
UsePen(DOT,1,0,255,0)
DrawLine(10,30,90,30)
```

Figure 14-37 The effect of different pens

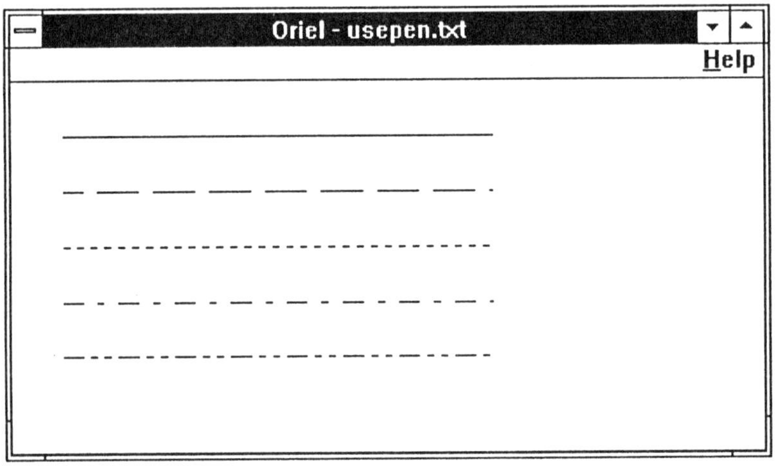

```
{Dash-dot line in blue}
UsePen(DASHDOT,1,0,0,255)
DrawLine(10,40,90,40)

{Dash-dot-dot line in pink}
UsePen(DASHDOTDOT,1,255,0,255)
DrawLine(10,50,90,50)
WaitInput()
```

WaitInput

This command lets you pause a program a specified number of milliseconds or pause it indefinitely to wait for user input.

Syntax: `WaitInput()`

or

`WaitInput(`*`milliseconds`*`)`

Parameter:

`milliseconds` The number of milliseconds you want to pause a program.

Remarks: WaitInput *without* an argument pauses a program indefinitely to wait for user input. When the user presses a key, clicks the mouse, or makes a menu selection and a SetKeyboard, SetMouse, or SetMenu command is in effect, Oriel for Windows immediately transfers control to the appropriate label specified in one of these commands. For example, if a SetMouse command is in effect and the user clicks the mouse within a specified hit-testing region, control transfers to the label associated with that hit-testing region.

WaitInput *with* an argument pauses a program a specified number of milliseconds. For example, WaitInput(1000) pauses Oriel for 1 second, WaitInput(3000) for three seconds, and WaitInput(250) for a quarter of a second.

Because the PC's clock ticks only 16 times a second, the granularity of the WaitInput command is not as fine as a *milliseconds* argument might have you believe. For example, WaitInput(1) has the same effect as WaitInput(62); they both pause your program for approximately 1/16 of a second.

If you use SetWaitMode(FOCUS) intending to pause an Oriel program until it gets the focus back, you must use a *milliseconds* argument with WaitInput, for example, WaitInput(1). If you do not use a *milliseconds* argument, your program will not pause (see the SetWaitMode command for more details).

WaitInput(0) is treated the same as WaitInput(1).

As a general rule, you should always use WaitInput() when you are not performing work in the Oriel window. This gives more of the system's resources to other Windows programs at a time when your Oriel program does not need them.

Example: The following program displays a message on the screen, pauses for 2 seconds, places another message on the top of the previous one, and then pauses indefinitely until you close the window.

```
DrawText(10,10,"Oriel will pause for 2 seconds")
WaitInput(2000)
DrawText(10,10,
   "Oriel will now pause indefinitely until you close the window")
WaitInput()
```

See the SetMenu, SetMouse, and SetKeyboard commands for other examples of WaitInput.

Related Commands: `SetWaitMode, SetMenu, SetKeyboard, SetMouse`

QUICK REFERENCE

```
Beep

DrawArc(x1,y1,x2,y2,x3,y3,x4,y4)

DrawBackground

DrawBitmap(x,y,"Filename")

DrawChord(x1,y1,x2,y2,x3,y3,x4,y4)
```

```
DrawEllipse(x1,y1,x2,y2)

DrawFlood(x,y,r,g,b)

DrawLine(x1,y1,x2,y2)

DrawNumber(x,y,n)

DrawPie(x1,y1,x2,y2,x3,y3,x4,y4)

DrawRectangle(x1,y1,x2,y2)

DrawRoundRectangle(x1,y1,x2,y2,x3,y3)

DrawSizedBitmap(x1,y1,x2,y2,"Filename")

DrawText(x,y,"Text")

End

Gosub label / Return

Goto label

If <condition> Then <commands>
   where <condition> uses <, >, <=, >=, <>, or =

MessageBox(OK/OKCANCEL/YESNO/YESNOCANCEL,Default_button,
           INFORMATION/EXCLAMATION/QUESTION/STOP/NOICON,
           "Text","Caption",Button_pushed)

Run("Command_line")

Set Variable = 0,1,2,3,...,65535
Set Variable = <math_expression>
   where <math_expression> uses +, -, *, or /

SetKeyboard()
SetKeyboard("a",label,
            "^a",label,
            vkey,label)

SetMenu()
SetMenu("Top1",IGNORE/label,
        "ItemA",IGNORE/label,
        "ItemB",IGNORE/label,
        SEPARATOR,
        "ItemC",IGNORE/label,
        ENDPOPUP,
        "Top2",IGNORE/label,
         .
         .
        ENDPOPUP)
```

```
SetMouse()
SetMouse(region1_x1,region1_y1,region1_x2,region1_y2,label,x,y,
         region2_x1,region2_y1,region2_x2,region2_y2,label,x,y,
                .
                .
         regionn_x1,regionn_y1,regionn_x2,regionn_y2,label,x,y)

SetWaitMode(NULL/FOCUS)

SetWindow(MAXIMIZE/MINIMIZE/RESTORE)

UseBackground(OPAQUE/TRANSPARENT,r,g,b)

UseBrush(SOLID/DIAGONALUP/DIAGONALDOWN/DIAGONALCROSS/
         HORIZONTAL/VERTICAL/CROSS/NULL,r,g,b)

UseCaption("Text")

UseCoordinates(PIXEL/METRIC)

UseFont("Name",Width,Height,BOLD/NOBOLD,ITALIC/NOITALIC,
        UNDERLINE/NOUNDERLINE,r,g,b)

UsePen(SOLID/NULL/DASH/DOT/DASHDOT/DASHDOTDOT,Width,r,g,b)

WaitInput()
WaitInput(milliseconds)
```

15

Command Post

When you use Program Manager or File Manager to launch programs or perform file management functions, you are using a *shell* program. These programs insulate you from having to type a command line with parameters to get MS-DOS to perform its functions.

As you discovered in Chapter 14, you don't *have* to use the standard Windows shells to launch your programs. The user can substitute alternate third-party shells, one of the most popular of which is Command Post by Wilson WindowWare. Command Post was created in 1987 by Morrie Wilson, an electronics engineer in Seattle. Like most of us, Morrie was frustrated by the lack of features in the MS-DOS Executive shell program that came with Windows 2.1.

Command Post allowed users to define their own custom menus in an ordinary text file and have them appear on the Executive window's menu bar along with the standard items. When the user selected one of these custom menu items, Command Post would jump in and launch a program, optionally changing directories or asking the user for a filename beforehand. Along with a menuing system, Morrie added many of the features of a batch language for Windows to Command Post that transforms its latest version, Command Post 7.0, into a very powerful shell that holds its own even in this new era of object-oriented Program Manager and File Manager.

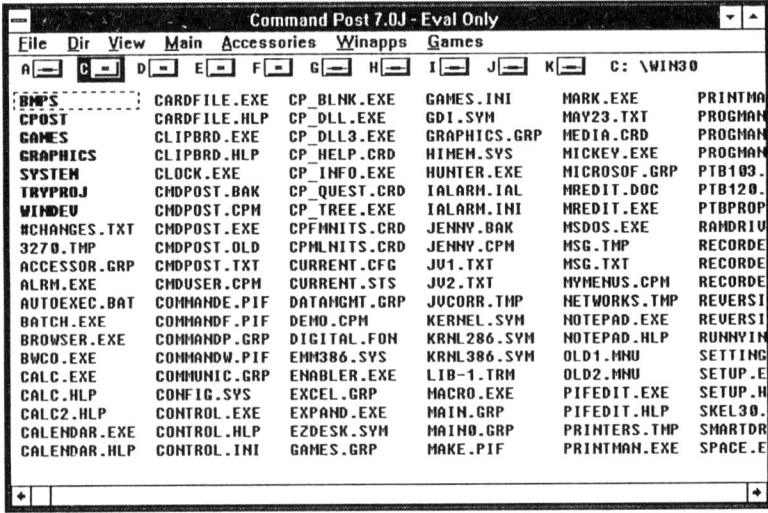

Figure 15-1 The Command Post window

IT'S A FILE MANAGER

As you can see from Figure 15-1, Command Post's heritage as an add-on to the MS-DOS Executive shows. They look deceptively similar. There's a menu bar across the top, little disk drive icons below it, the current directory path to their right, and below all this is a multicolumn listing of the current directory's files and subdirectories. You can copy, move, and delete files, and you can double-click on a filename to execute it.

But Command Post doesn't just attach menus to the MS-DOS Executive program like the earlier versions did; Command Post now has its own window. Several useful features have also been added that you won't find in the MS-DOS Executive, or even in Program Manager or File Manager. For instance, you can select all files having the same extension by simply double-clicking on one of the filenames with the right-hand mouse button.

IT'S A CUSTOM WORKSTATION BUILDER

But the real power of Command Post comes from your ability to define your own custom menu items. The new Command Post Menu Language (CPML) contains almost one hundred statements and functions. These statements can

- Launch programs.
- Copy, move, rename, or delete files.
- Create, delete, or change directories.
- Display messages, wait for you to type something in, and analyze what you entered.

- Perform arithmetic.
- Read and write to the WIN.INI file.
- Copy and paste strings to and from the Clipboard.
- Read DOS environment variables.
- Change the appearance of other programs' windows.

People have used Command Post menus for many different tasks. The most common uses of Command Post are to simplify daily procedures for clerical staff, or to make it easy to launch all your favorite programs from a central menu. You can also use Command Post to force programs to always come up full-screen, or even to create user-friendly Windows front ends for DOS utilities.

You can also simplify tasks that have nothing to do with launching programs. For instance, you can create a menu that simulates a "trash can" function to protect you from losing files when you delete them. Or you can have Windows automatically show a different wallpaper file each time it starts up.

Once you become familiar with CPML, you'll find yourself building bigger and more powerful menus to automate more complex tasks. Most of the time you'll find this menuing language meets the challenge. In fact, you could consider CPML a true batch language for Windows if it weren't for the fact that everything you create must be invoked from Command Post's menu instead of from its own icon.

Command Post is the type of program people either love or hate. There are no pretty icons to look at. You can't drag files around with the mouse. But many people have decided that when it comes down to accomplishing actual *work* with their computers, they prefer the organizational style implicit in the Command Post method of doing things.

USING COMMAND POST AS A FILE MANAGER

The basic look and feel of Command Post is similar to that of the MS-DOS Executive, which is still supplied with Windows 3.0. But Command Post is an even more powerful shell than either MS-DOS Executive or File Manager.

Selecting Files

Simple file selection is accomplished the same way in Command Post as it is in MS-DOS Executive and File Manager. You select an individual file or directory by clicking on its name with the left mouse button. You can also use the arrow keys to move the selection box through the list of files, or press a letter to select the next file in the list that starts with that letter.

In all three shells you run an application by double-clicking on it with the left button or pressing ENTER when the file is selected.

There are subtle differences among the three file managers when it comes to selecting more than one file at a time. With Command Post, as with the MS-DOS Executive, you can select multiple files by holding down the SHIFT key while you click on each additional filename with the left mouse button. File Manager has the same capability except that you press the CTRL key instead.

Command Post is one of the few Windows programs that make use of the right-hand mouse button. You can select additional filenames with the right button without having to remember which special key to press. You can also drag the right mouse button over a series of files at once. And if you double-click on a filename with the right-hand button, Command Post adds all filenames with the same extension to the list of selected files.

Selecting multiple files with the keyboard alone is similar to MS-DOS Executive. While using the arrow keys to move the selection box around, either hold down the SHIFT key to select each additional file or hold down the CTRL key to skip the file. You can toggle an individual file's selection with the SPACEBAR.

The Menus

All menu items on Command Post's main menu bar are defined in a text file using the CPML script language. Command Post comes with a set of menus already defined for you in the default menu files CMDPOST.CPM and CMDUSER.CPM. These are the menu files that are loaded by default when you run Command Post without specifying a menu file.

CMDPOST.CPM contains the definitions for the first four main menus: File, Dir, View, and Main. The other three default menus, Accessories, Winapps, and Games, are defined in CMDUSER.CPM. The default menus are split up in this way to encourage users to place their custom menus in the CMDUSER.CPM file instead of the larger and more confusing CMDPOST.CPM.

The sections that follow will examine each of the basic menu options defined in CMDPOST.CPM in turn. You may be tempted to skip this section if you will only be using Command Post with your own custom menus, but you should at least browse through these descriptions to get an idea of what you can accomplish with the menu language.

The File Menu

- **Run:** Launches a program in a window after showing you a small dialog box shown in Figure 15-2. Here you enter the pathname of the program to run, which defaults to whichever file has the highlight box around it. Although you can start a program more quickly by just double-clicking on it, this menu is useful for starting a program in another directory while still viewing the current one.

- **Load:** Similar to Run except the program is loaded as an icon.

- **Browse:** Calls up the Command Post Browser utility after displaying a dialog box like the Run and Load commands do. This program lets you view the contents of a file in ASCII or hexadecimal format. You can also view lines containing certain text while the rest is hidden. This feature that is very handy when working with large text files. Browser will be discussed in detail later.

Command Post 551

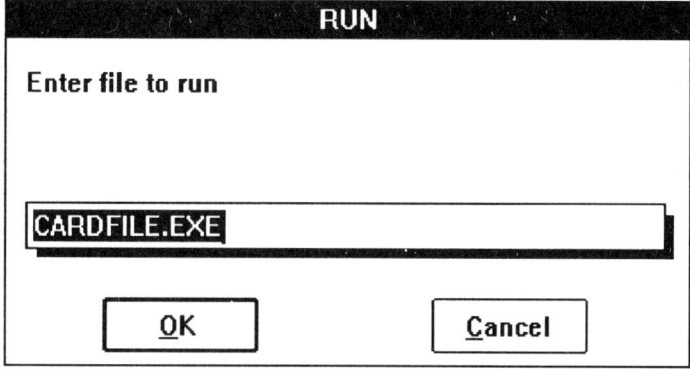

Figure 15-2 Run dialog box

- **Notepad Edit:** Runs the Windows Notepad editor after you confirm that the filename you selected is the one you want Notepad to open on startup.

Tip: Bypass the confirmation box

Run, Load, Browse, and Notepad Edit will all skip the confirmation dialog box if you press the SHIFT key or the right mouse button while making the menu selection with the left-hand mouse button.

- **Copy:** Copies all the files you've selected into the directory whose path name you enter in the dialog box shown in Figure 15-3. You can copy to a different filename by entering the new name as part of the directory path. If you've selected more than one file to copy at once, the destination filename must contain a wildcard. If the Copy command is about to overwrite a file, a warning box appears that offers you four choices: Overwrite, Overwrite all, Skip, and Cancel. Figure 15-4 shows what this warning box looks like.
- **Move/Rename:** Displays a dialog box similar to the Copy command in Figure 15-3, but here you enter either a destination directory path, in which case the selected files will be moved to that directory. You can also enter a new filename, which will cause the selected files to be renamed. You should use wildcards if you're renaming multiple files. You can also both move *and* rename files at the same time by specifying a destination filename within a different directory path.
- **Delete File:** Deletes the files you've selected. A confirming dialog box (Figure 15-5) appears here similar to the other File commands, except that you only get to

552 *Windows 3 Power Tools*

```
┌─────────────── Copy ───────────────┐
│                                    │
│  MAY23.TXT                         │
│                                    │
│  to                                │
│                                    │
│  ┌──────────────────────────────┐  │
│  │ C:\WIN30\                    │  │
│  └──────────────────────────────┘  │
│                                    │
│    ┌─────────┐      ┌─────────┐    │
│    │   OK    │      │ Cancel  │    │
│    └─────────┘      └─────────┘    │
└────────────────────────────────────┘
```

Figure 15-3 Copy dialog box

select Yes, No, or Cancel to confirm or deny the deletion. ("No" and "Cancel" mean the same thing here.)

- **Print:** Copies the selected file(s) to a printer port. This is useful for printing plain text files or files that contain control codes recognized by your particular printer.

Command Post does no formatting of the file whatsoever. It won't even advance the paper after printing a file. If you send two files to the printer at once, for instance, the second file won't start on a new page unless the first file ends with a page-eject code. It won't even start on a new *line* unless the first file ends with a carriage return.

The first time you select the Print command after installing Command Post, it asks you to confirm that your printer is a "standard" (i.e. non-Postscript) printer. If you choose "Yes" it displays a list box of printer ports for you to select. This information is saved in the WIN.INI file for subsequent Print commands, and if necessary it can be reset with the Reset Options selection in the Main menu.

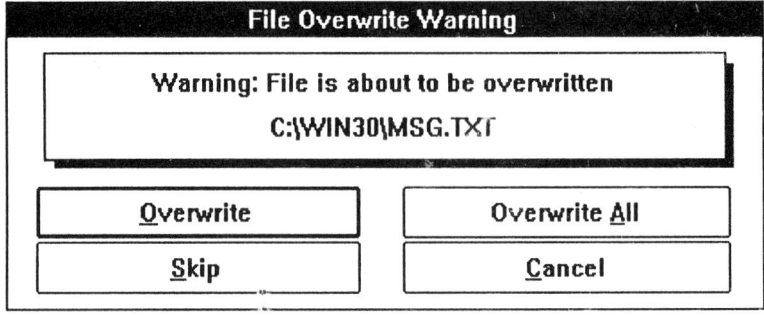

Figure 15-4 Overwrite warning dialog box

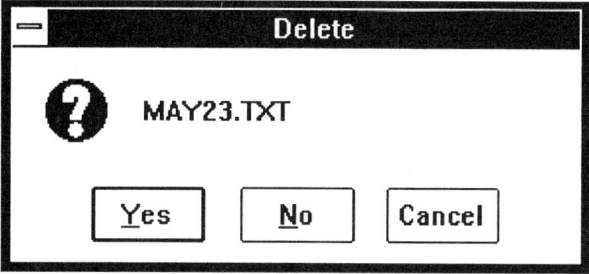

Figure 15-5 Confirming a delete request

- **Hilite Files:** Highlights the files you specify in the dialog box shown in Figure 15-6. The default is to highlight all files with the same extension as the file with the selection box around it. You can specify more than one set of filenames to highlight at a time.
- **Unhilite Files:** Removes the highlight from all the files you specify in a dialog box similar to Hilite Files. The default is to remove the highlight from all files with the same extension as the one with the selection box around it. You can specify more than one set of filenames at a time.
- **Size of Selected Files:** Sums the sizes of all the files that are currently highlighted and displays their total size, in bytes.
- **Freespace on Drives:** Displays the amount of space free on each of your hard drives. The first time you choose Freespace on Drives after installing Command Post, it asks you for the highest drive letter on your system so it knows which drives to examine for their free space. This information is saved in the WIN.INI file for

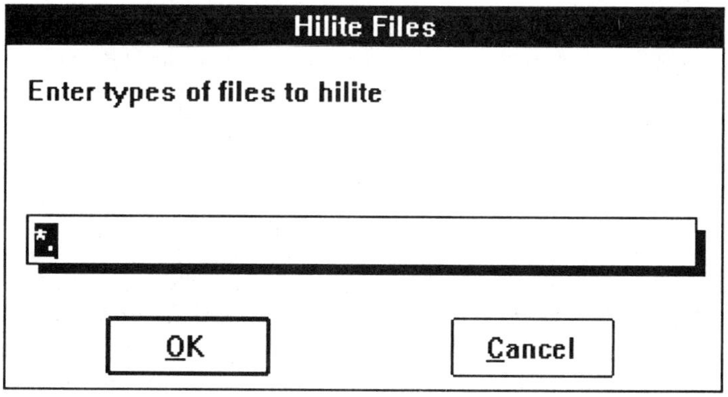

Figure 15-6 Highlighting files from the menu

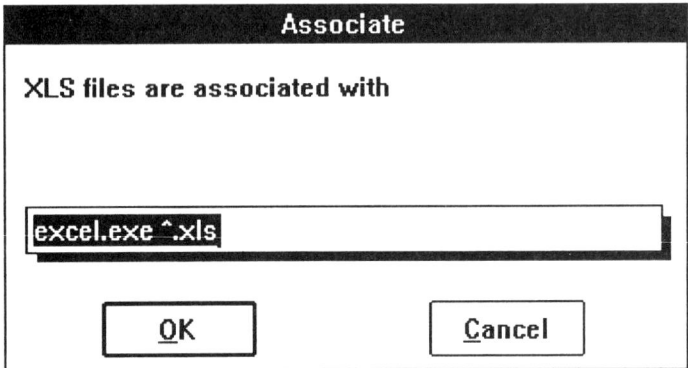

Figure 15-7 Associating extensions with programs

subsequent Freespace commands and can be reset, if necessary, with the Reset Options selection in the Main menu.

- **Space on A and size of files:** Shows you how much space the selected files take up, and also how much space is free on floppy drive A. Great if you want to copy or move files onto a diskette but aren't sure if they'll all fit on it.

- **Space on B and size of files:** Same as "Space on A" option, except this one compares the size of the files with the diskette in drive B.

- **Extensions:** This is Command Post's equivalent of File Manager's "Associate" command. It lets you create an association between the selected filename's extension and a program to execute with the file. Figure 15-7 shows the dialog box that prompts you for the program Windows should execute whenever you double-click on a file with this extension. You must change "???.EXE" to the desired program's filename. This association is stored in the WIN.INI file's [extensions] section.

  If there is already a program associated with that extension, its filename will show up in the edit box in place of ???.EXE.

- **Exit Windows:** Closes all application programs and exits Windows *without* making you confirm that you really want to do it.

Note: The accelerator key for Exit Windows is "X". In most Windows applications, pressing ALT+F X means "exit this program." Here it means "Exit *Windows* immediately," a somewhat different connotation. If you're hopelessly conditioned to hitting ALT+F X to end a program, you may want to change the accelerator key for Exit Windows by modifying the CMDPOST.CPM file.

The Dir Menu

- **Create Directory:** Creates a new subdirectory after displaying a dialog box for you to enter the new directory name.
- **Delete Directory:** Deletes whichever subdirectories are highlighted, after getting a confirmation from you. Unlike File Manager, which will delete both nested subdirectories and files without complaint, Command Post requires that directories be empty and do not themselves contain subdirectories. Because this is unlike File Manager, it could change in the future.
- **Change Directory:** Displays a dialog box for you to type in the name of the directory to make current.

Tip: Changing directories

There are easier ways to change directories. You can change to a subdirectory "beneath" the current directory by double-clicking on its name. You can move back toward the root directory by *single*-clicking on a portion of the pathname next to the disk drive icons. You can also back up one level to the parent directory by pressing the BACKSPACE key.

- **Format Diskette:** Formats a diskette in your A or B drive by calling the MS-DOS Format command.

    The first time you choose Format Diskette after installing Command Post, it asks you for the types of floppy drives on your system so that it knows what parameters to supply to the Format command. This information is saved in the WIN.INI file; it can be reset if necessary with the Reset Options selection in the Main menu. If your floppy drives are set up as something other than A: or B:, then you'll have to modify CMDPOST.CPM to format them.

- **Directory Tree:** Displays a map of the current drive's directory structure. Figure 15-8 shows what the tree looks like. You can click on a directory name to change to that directory or to select a new drive letter from the Disks menu. Clicking on a directory name with the *right*-hand mouse button brings up a new Command Post window with that directory showing.

Command Post's directory tree has a particularly good design feature: it always shows you *all* the subdirectories on the drive. When File Manager starts up, it only shows you the top level of the directory tree. You end up constantly clicking on folder icons in your quest for hidden lower-level subdirectories. There is a tradeoff, however: the Command Post directory tree takes longer to start up, since it has to search through all your directories right at the beginning.

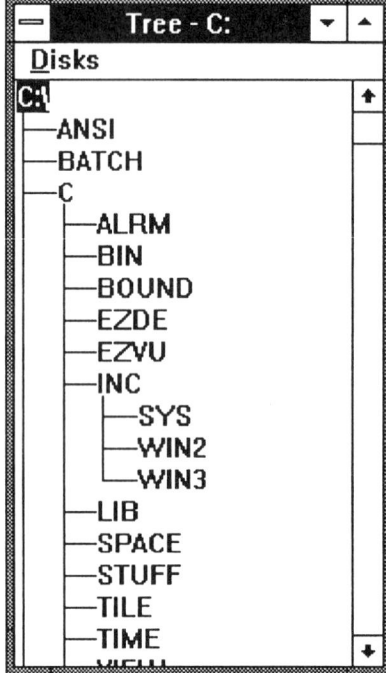

Figure 15-8 The directory tree

Tip: Load the tree from WIN.INI

The directory tree is actually a separate program. You may want to load it automatically each time you start Windows by adding the filename CP_TREE.EXE to WIN.INI's LOAD= or RUN= lines. You don't even have to load Command Post every time Windows starts. But if you select a directory name in the tree and Command Post is not currently running, it starts up automatically.

The View Menu

The View menu contains options that affect how the files appear in the directory listing and how the application windows should appear on the screen.

The first two items determine how much information gets displayed about each file:

- **Short:** Displays only the filenames in the directory list. This is the default.
- **Long:** Displays the filenames, their sizes, and the date and time they were last updated.

The next three items determine which files are displayed:

- **All:** Displays all the files and subdirectories.
- **Partial:** Displays a dialog box where you enter a series of file specifications to display. The default is whatever you entered the previous time you chose Partial.
- **Programs:** Displays only files with extensions of .EXE, .COM, .BAT, or .PIF.

There are five ways in which filenames can be sorted in the directory listing. (Subdirectories are always displayed first.)

- **By Name:** The files are sorted by filename.
- **By Date:** The files are listed from the most recently changed to least recently changed.
- **By Size:** The files are listed from the largest to the smallest.
- **By Kind:** The files are listed by extension.
- **Unsorted:** The files are listed in the same order they would be displayed by the MS-DOS DIR command.

The eight items in the right-hand column of the View menu will straighten up the display by rearranging (and resizing) all the application windows currently on the screen. These are handy when you have many programs open at once:

- **1 Stack:** Moves the windows so they are cascaded from the top right corner of the screen toward the bottom left corner. Figure 15-9 shows what the screen looks like after stacking.
- **2 Arrange:** Moves the windows into a tiled arrangement, as in Figure 15-10. Tiling the windows makes each one visible on the screen at the same time.
- **3 Arrange in Rows:** Tiles the windows one above the other, as in Figure 15-11.
- **4 Arrange in Columns:** Tiles the windows side-by-side, as in Figure 15-12.
- **5 (w/o CP) Stack:** Same as Stack, except the Command Post window is minimized.
- **6 (w/o CP) Arrange:** Same as Arrange, except the Command Post window is minimized.
- **7 (w/o CP) Arrange in Rows:** Same as Arrange in Rows, except the Command Post window is minimized.
- **8 (w/o CP) Arrange in Columns:** Same as Arrange in Columns, except the Command Post window is minimized.

558 *Windows 3 Power Tools*

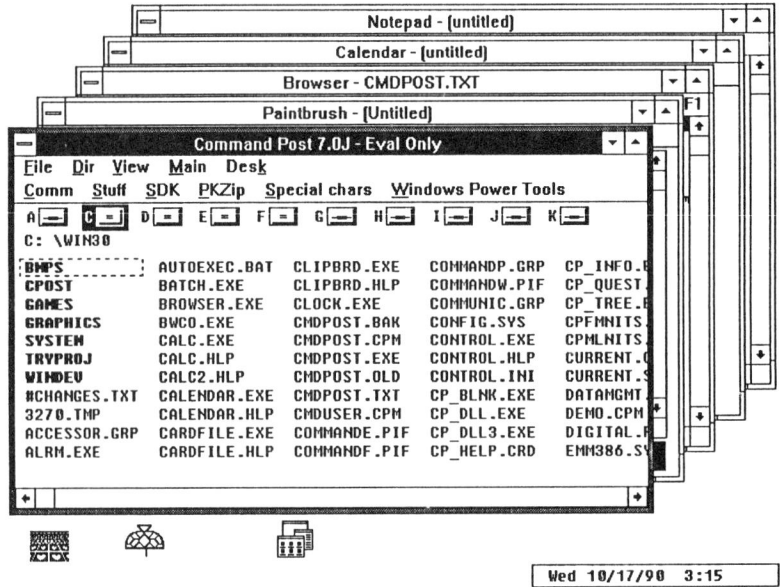

Figure 15-9 Cascaded ("stacked") windows

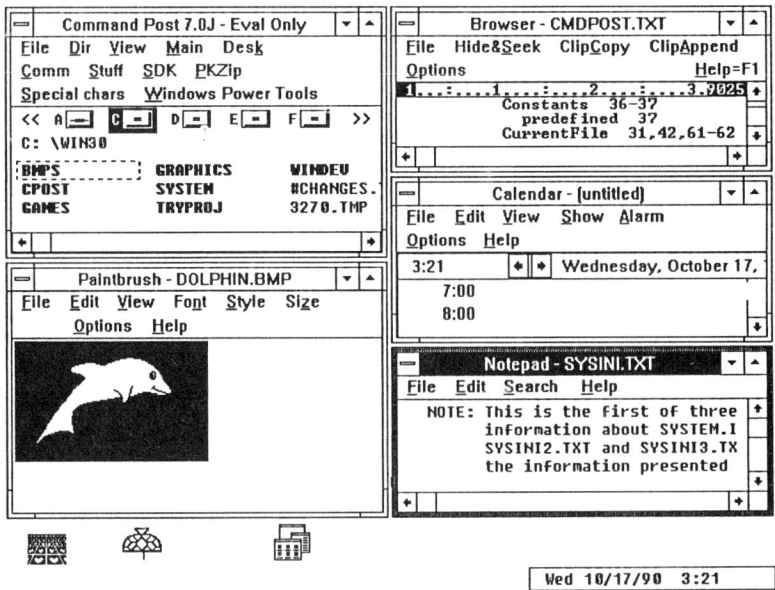

Figure 15-10 Tiled ("arranged") windows

Command Post 559

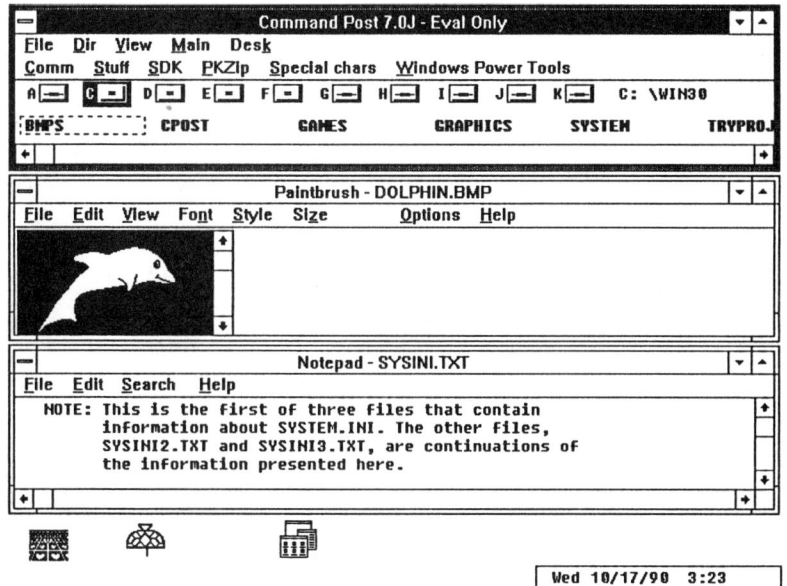

Figure 15-11 Windows tiled in rows

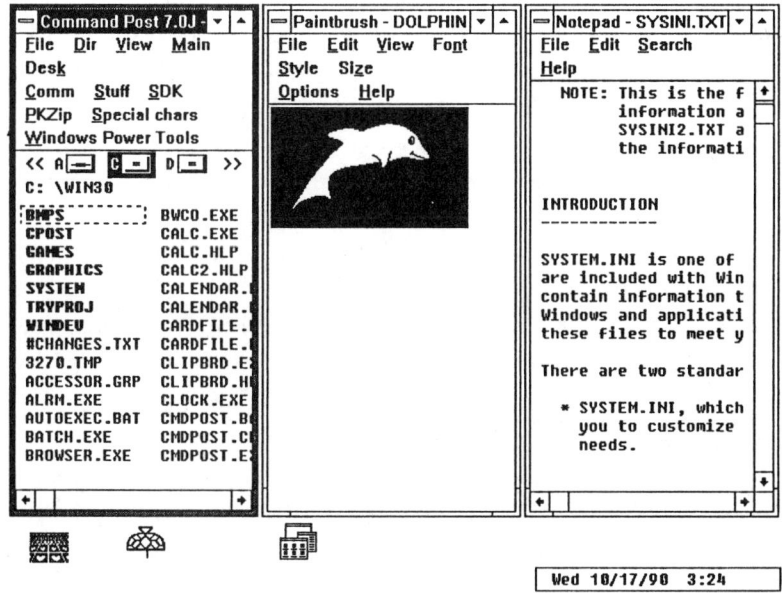

Figure 15-12 Windows tiled in columns

The Main Menu

The Main menu could just as easily have been called "Miscellany" or "Housekeeping." However the items on this menu are no less useful than the others.

- **Command Post:** Launches a second Command Post window. From here you can change to another directory to view two directories at a time. When a second copy of Command Post is running, the Copy and Move/Rename menu selections default to using the other Command Post directory as the destination.
- **Control Panel:** Launches the Windows Control Panel.
- **Clipboard:** Runs the Windows Clipboard viewer.
- **DOS Prompt:** Spawns a full-screen DOS session by executing COMMAND.COM.
- **Get Help Cardfile:** Brings up Cardfile and loads the file CP_HELP.CRD, which contains a short summary of each CPML function and statement.
- **Get Question 'n' Answer Cardfile:** Brings up Cardfile and loads the file CP_QUEST.CRD, which contains answers by Wilson WindowWare's technical support staff to some of the more common questions about Command Post.
- **Reset Options:** Resets information about your computer that some of the other menu items ask for. In particular, Print needs to know the name of the device your printer is attached to, Freespace on Drives requests the highest drive letter on your system, and Format Diskette needs to know the types of floppy drives installed.

    Reset Options also lets you set the number of minutes the Command Post screen blanker will wait after no keystrokes are detected before it blanks the screen.
- **System Information:** Displays a message box like that in Figure 15-13. It tells you what version of Windows is running, whether it's in real, standard, or 386 enhanced mode, the size of the screen, how much memory is free, etc.
- **Program Manager:** Launches the Program Manager. If it's already running (sitting at the bottom of the screen as an icon, for instance), it just activates that one copy rather than creating two copies of Program Manager.
- **File Manager:** Launches File Manager. If File Manager is already running, it just activates that copy of the program.
- **Print Manager:** Starts Windows' Print Manager. If it's already running, it just activates the current copy.
- **Windows Setup:** Runs the Windows Setup program. Chapter 9 deals with Windows Setup in depth.
- **Edit CmdPost menus:** This provides an easy way to get at all your .CPM files to change a menu's behavior. You're shown a list box of all the .CPM files in the Windows directory; if you choose one, Notepad is called up and loads the menu file you chose.

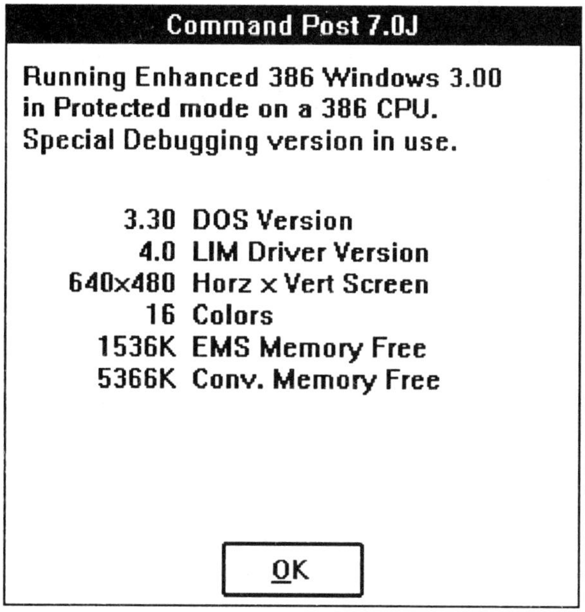

```
┌─────────────────────────────────────┐
│        Command Post 7.0J            │
├─────────────────────────────────────┤
│  Running Enhanced 386 Windows 3.00  │
│  in Protected mode on a 386 CPU.    │
│  Special Debugging version in use.  │
│                                     │
│       3.30  DOS Version             │
│        4.0  LIM Driver Version      │
│    640x480  Horz x Vert Screen      │
│         16  Colors                  │
│      1536K  EMS Memory Free         │
│      5366K  Conv. Memory Free       │
│                                     │
│                                     │
│              ┌──────┐               │
│              │  OK  │               │
│              └──────┘               │
└─────────────────────────────────────┘
```

Figure 15-13 System Information message box

- **Edit INI files:** In previous versions of Windows you only had to examine the WIN.INI file to find system parameters you could change. Now Windows 3.0 adds five more .INI files, and *any* application can create its own "private" .INI file in the Windows directory. Edit .INI files shows you a list box of all those files so you can quickly choose the one you want for editing.

- **Edit System Configuration:** This brings up the little-known Windows System Configuration Editor, or SysEdit. SysEdit is similar to Notepad, except it automatically opens four important files at once: SYSTEM.INI, WIN.INI, CONFIG.SYS, and AUTOEXEC.BAT. Chapter 12 goes into greater detail about SysEdit.

- **PIF Edit:** This opens the PIF Editor, which allows you to create or modify Program Information Files for DOS applications. The PIF Editor is explained in detail in Chapter 10.

The System Menu

The System menu contains the standard items found in almost all Windows 3.0 applications—Restore, Move, Size, Minimize, Maximize, Close, Switch To, and About. But this menu also contains some menu items specific to Command Post. This is the only menu in Command Post you *can't* change.

- **Enter License Info:** This is where you enter your license number when you register Command Post. Remember, Command Post is *shareware*. Think of it as a fully functional demo program that you still must purchase if you intend to use it. When you send in the registration fee, you get the latest version (WindowWare produces "silent upgrades" often, as new bugs get fixed) and an excellent 160-page typeset manual. Registration also entitles you to some very competent technical support by phone. And of course, once you enter your license number the "nag" screens, as well as the Enter License Info option itself, will mysteriously disappear.

Tip: Keep your registration card

When you register Command Post, you are sent a card titled, "KEEP THIS CARD." Keep it! The license number you enter from this card is encrypted and stored in the [CMDPOST] section of the WIN.INI file. If you accidentally erase this number or delete the WIN.INI file, Command Post will just assume it's an unlicensed copy until you find the card and enter the number again.

- **Reload Menu:** Whenever you make a change to an active .CPM file, you have to notify Command Post that it's been changed. This option allows you to do just that.
- **Exit Windows:** This is the same as Exit Windows in the File menu, except the accelerator key is "E" instead of "X".
- **The right-hand column** displays a list of all the Windows applications currently loaded, as illustrated in Figure 15-14. You can activate one of these applications by choosing its name from this list. This is much like selecting a program from Windows' Task Manager, except this list also gives each application a number so that you can easily select it from the keyboard.

COMMAND POST ACCESSORY PROGRAMS

In addition to the menuing system itself, Command Post comes with two useful accessories—a file browser and a combination clock and screen blanker.

Browser

Browser is a handy utility included with Command Post that lets you display the contents of files. It's normally used for viewing text files, but its extra features make it helpful for viewing other kinds of files that wouldn't normally be displayed.

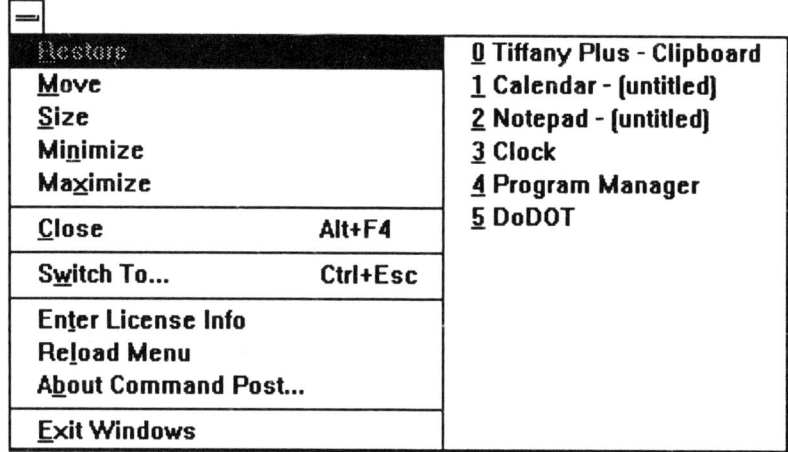

Figure 15-14 The right-hand column of the System menu

Browsing Text Files: An Example

Let's browse through a plain text file to get a feel for Browser:

1. Change to the Windows directory if you're not already there.
2. Select the WIN.INI file.
3. Choose Browser from the File menu.
4. Press ENTER at the dialog box to confirm you want to browse through WIN.INI.

At this point the Browser window comes up, looking like Figure 15-15. It looks much like what you would see in Notepad. The major difference is that there's no danger of accidentally changing the file's contents.

Changing the Display Format

Now let's change how you can view this file. Go to the menu bar and choose Options. Notice that the first menu item, ANSI Text, is checked. This means Browser is displaying the text in the standard Windows font. Let's choose the next item, ASCII Text.

Looks different, doesn't it? Browser is now showing the file in the "Windows OEM font". This font takes up somewhat less space than the standard ANSI font. In fact, on a standard VGA display you can see 37 lines of text if you maximize Browser to full-screen, as opposed to 29 lines using the standard font.

The other difference is that it interprets the special characters according to the ASCII standard instead of ANSI. This will become apparent when you look at an .EXE file.

564 *Windows 3 Power Tools*

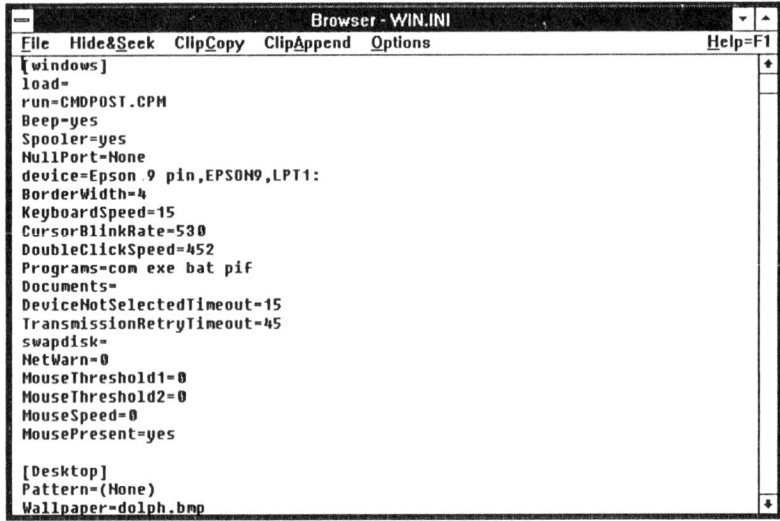

Figure 15-15 Command Post Browser

Basically ANSI displays many special characters as black boxes or foreign language characters, while the ASCII font interprets more of them as graphics characters such as smiley faces or as blanks.

Browser can display a simple ruler at the top of the window to help you find specific text columns. You select this from the Options menu, if it isn't already checked.

Hiding and Seeking

Browser has a unique feature for showing selected portions of a file. You can have it hide all text lines that contain a word or phrase you specify. Or you can hide *all* lines and then show only those lines containing the specified text. This is a great feature when you are trying to find information in a long text file. For instance, your WIN.INI file can easily end up with two dozen or more sections as applications dump their program options into it. Let's sort through that clutter and find a specific section:

1. Choose Hide all from the Hide&Seek menu.

2. Notice that the text has disappeared, except for a line in color stating that a certain number of lines have been hidden up to the end of the file (EOF).

3. Choose Show if from the Hide&Seek menu.

4. A dialog box appears as in Figure 15-16. Here you can tell Browser to show all lines that either do or don't contain whatever text you enter into the edit box. In our case, leave the radio buttons alone (the "do contain" button is selected by default) and type [into the edit box.

5. Select Show or press ENTER.

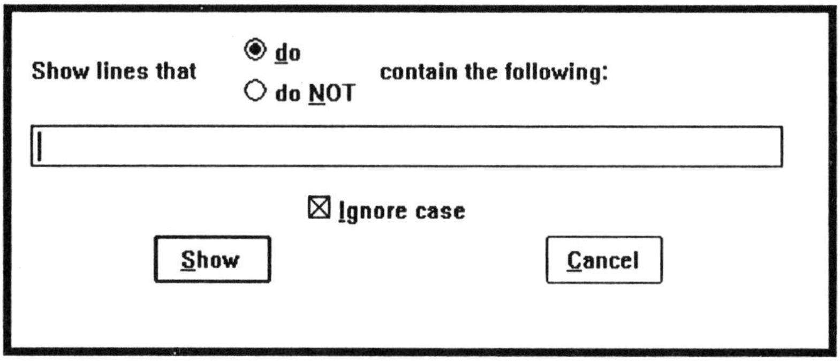

Figure 15-16 Hide&Seek dialog box

Now you see only the section headers—the lines starting with a section name in [] brackets. You probably also see some lines that aren't section headers but just happen to contain some text with square brackets. In between are more colored lines, again telling us how many lines are being hidden. Figure 15-17 shows what most WIN.INI files look like at this point.

Now let's look at the text hidden within one of these sections. Find the [Extensions] section in the Browser display. (It's the third section in a standard WIN.INI file.) Select the colored hidden-lines indicator by clicking on it. The line will change to reverse video. Browser refers to this as "marking" the text. Choose Show Marked from the Hide&Seek menu. The hidden lines within the [Extensions] section now appear in reverse video.

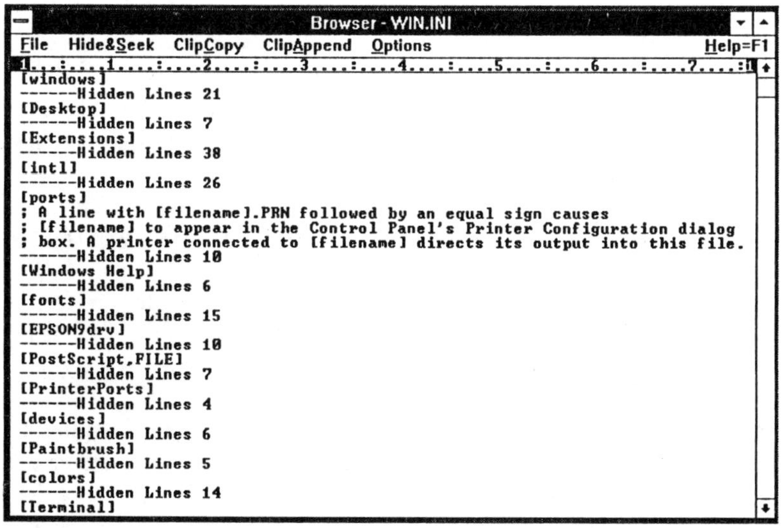

Figure 15-17 WIN.INI section headers

The ClipCopy and ClipAppend Menus

Once you've selected a subset of the file to view, you can copy or append it to the Windows Clipboard using the ClipCopy or ClipAppend menus. Other than copying versus appending the text to the Clipboard, these menus are very similar to each other. You can copy or append all the text in the file, only the nonhidden text, all the text within the marked lines, or only the nonhidden text within the marked lines.

Browsing Non-Text Files

Most of the time you won't have any reason to directly view nontext files, but it's always nice to have that capability. Browser has some features that greatly assist in viewing files full of nonprinting characters. As an example, we'll take a look at an .EXE file.

Tip: View files with Browser instead of Notepad

Try to get in the habit of using Browser to display a file instead of Notepad. Browser lets you look at *any* file—even if it's filled with control codes and unprintable characters or if it's a very large file. Notepad is often frustratingly picky about what it will or will not load. Notepad won't load files that contain anything other than plain vanilla text; it also cannot handle any files larger than approximately 50,000 bytes.

Select the Open menu item in Browser's File menu. The Open dialog box appears with a list box full of filenames to choose from. Choose the CALC.EXE file (the Windows Calculator program) and press ENTER to load the file. The Browser window will now look something like Figure 15-18. The file begins with the characters "MZ", denoting an MS-DOS executable file. Following that are lots of garbage characters. Some of these characters are being interpreted by Browser as the page-skip control code, and so you see some colored lines full of dashes with the note "New Page" in the center.

Here's where the Options menu comes in handy. First, choose Word Wrap. In a nontext file, the carriage return code has no significance, and so they may be few and far between. Without word-wrap, many characters will be scrolled off far to the right of the screen. With word-wrap on, you will see all the characters without having to scroll to the right all the time. In fact, now that you've turned word-wrap on, you may notice the message "This program requires Microsoft Windows," which is displayed if you try to execute the Windows Calculator from the DOS prompt.

If you're using ANSI text, you probably see most of the characters as black boxes. Choose ASCII Text if you'd rather interpret these special characters as graphics symbols.

You can use the Hide&Seek commands just like in a text file. For instance, let's look for all the copyright notices contained in the Windows Calculator. Select Hide if from the Hide&Seek menu. You want to hide all lines that do not contain the word "copyright,"

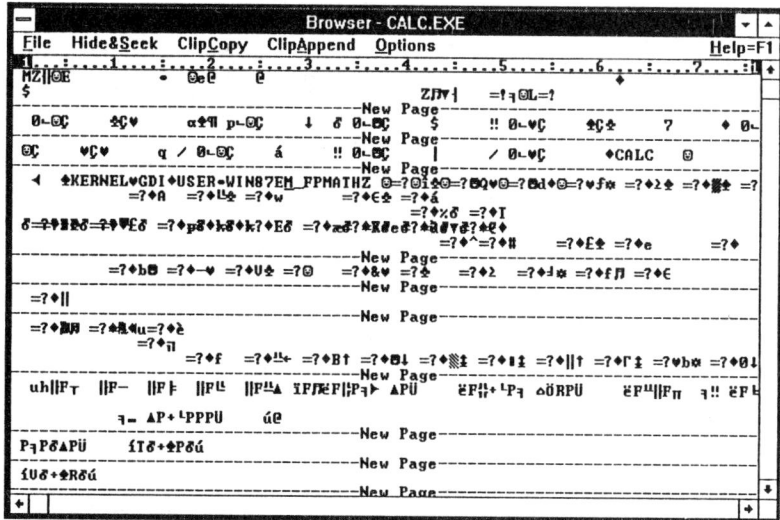

Figure 15-18 Browsing a program file

so click on the **do NOT** button and enter **copyright** in the edit box. Choose the **Hide** button, and then wait a few seconds while Browser searches for all occurrences of the word "copyright." Finally, you see one copyright notice in the .EXE file. Sure enough, Microsoft owns CALC.EXE.

Probably the most useful feature of the Options menu when you are browsing through a nontext file is the Hex Dump mode. This displays each character as its hexadecimal equivalent, as well as showing it as text on the right-hand side of the screen. Figure 15-19 shows what this looks like.

The Command Post Clock

As you've probably noticed by now, Command Post comes with its own clock that nestles down at the lower right-hand corner of the screen and displays the date and time. By clicking on the clock with the right-hand mouse button you can toggle between showing hours/minutes/seconds, just hours and minutes, or showing no date or time at all. Figure 15-20 shows the different ways the clock can look.

You can drag the clock to anywhere on the screen you want, and it will stay there the next time you run Command Post. You can also force the current Command Post window to the front by double-clicking the clock with the left button.

Note: When the Command Post Clock is displaying hours/minutes/seconds, it forces itself to the "front" of the display, on top of any other windows. This is a nice feature, because it means you can have an on-screen clock that's always visible. However this can also be annoying, as the clock is just tall enough to fit right

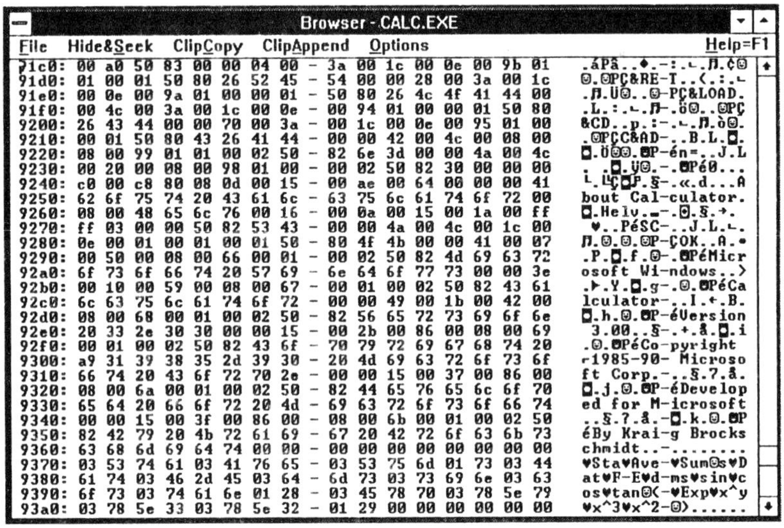

Figure 15-19 Viewing a nontext file in hexadecimal mode

over the horizontal scroll bar of a full-screen application. You can stop it from forcing its way on top of the application by toggling the display back to hours-and-minutes only.

USING COMMAND POST AS YOUR SHELL

As mentioned, Program Manager, File Manager, MS-DOS Executive, and Command Post are all considered "shell" programs. However, in Windows 3.0 "shell" has a specific meaning. Windows automatically starts one shell program before all the others. This program (which is usually Program Manager) is specified in the [boot] section of the SYSTEM.INI file:

```
[boot]
(other lines)
shell=progman.exe
(more [boot] lines)
```

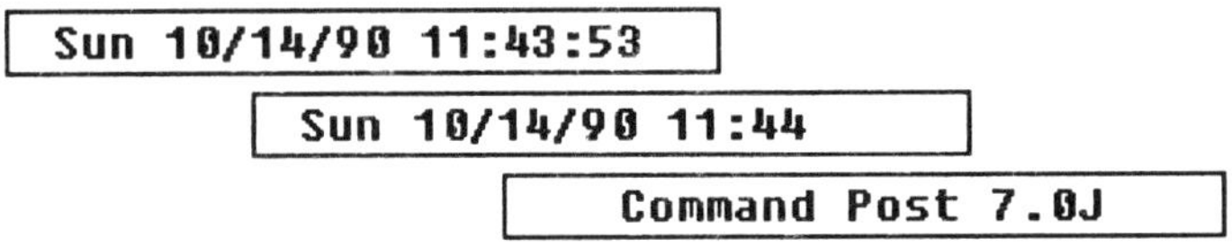

Figure 15-20 Command Post Clock

You can change this line yourself to make Command Post come up in place of Program Manager. From Command Post's Main menu, choose Edit .INI Files. Then choose SYSTEM.INI from the list box of .INI files. Command Post starts up Notepad, which loads SYSTEM.INI. Simply change the **shell=** line to

```
shell=cmdpost.exe
```

Choose Save from Notepad's File menu. The next time you run Windows, Command Post will start up automatically instead of Program Manager.

YOUR OWN MENUS

Here's where you get to make Command Post really lighten your load. Everyone's computer setup is different, and each of us has different needs and preferences when it comes to working with our machines. Now you can start customizing your own Windows workstation.

Setting Up a Menu File

Command Post's menus are defined in a script language called Command Post Menu Language, or CPML. You write a menu definition in a plain ASCII text file with an extension of .CPM. A .CPM file has two parts—an optional initialization section that is executed once when the menu is loaded, and the menu definitions themselves. These get called when their individual menus are selected from the menu bar.

We'll cover the initialization section later, but first let's make some menus.

Launching Programs

The simplest kind of menu to create is one that just launches a program when you select the menu item. Let's make a menu that does nothing more than start Notepad.

1. Start the Notepad application. (Don't open a file, as we're creating a new file from scratch.)
2. In the first column of the first line, type **&Editing**.
3. On the next line, starting in the *second* column, type **&Notepad**.
4. On the next line press TAB, and then enter **Run("NOTEPAD.EXE", "")**. Our menu description looks like this:

```
&Editing
 &Notepad
    Run("NOTEPAD.EXE","")
```

5. Now choose Save from Notepad's File menu. A Save As dialog box will appear since this is a brand-new file. Enter the filename **MYMENUS.CPM** into the edit box and choose **OK**.

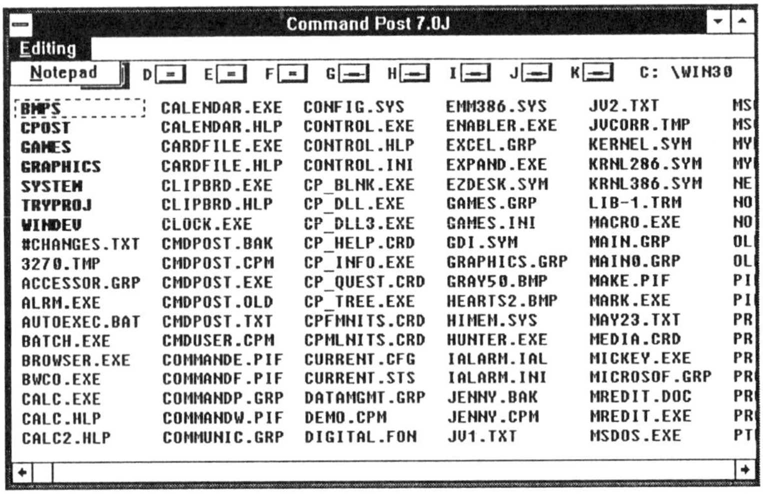

570 *Windows 3 Power Tools*

Figure 15-21 Our Notepad menu

6. Minimize Notepad to get it out of the way.
7. Find MYMENUS.CPM in the Windows directory listing and double-click on it.

A second copy of Command Post will appear, with a single menu name on the menu bar called **Editing**. If you select this menu, a drop-down menu will appear with one item in it: **Notepad**. Figure 15-21 shows what this looks like. Select this item, and Command Post will launch Notepad.

As you've probably realized by now, each main menu item is named starting in the first column of a line, and each item in its drop-down menu starts in the second column. The CPML statements that describe what to do when the menu item is selected start in at least the fifth column. You can also start the body of the menu with the TAB key, which will skip over to column eight. Each statement must go on one line; you can't split it up if it looks too long. However each line can be up to 256 characters long.

Each menu item can have an ALT-key combination attached to it, called an "accelerator." This is why Windows underlines one of the letters in the menu name. You specify which letter will become the menu's accelerator by placing an ampersand (&) in front of it. For example you can choose Notepad from our new menu by pressing ALT+E, then N.

Launching Programs with Parameters

Our menu used one CPML statement, "Run". This takes two parameters within the parentheses—the program's filename, and any command-line parameters you want to send to the program. In the case of Notepad, this parameter would be the name of an existing text file you want to edit.

Double-click on the Notepad icon so that you can add another menu to the MYMENUS.CPM file. Add a menu item after the Notepad menu and call it **Edit WIN.INI**, so the menu file now looks like this:

```
&Editing
  &Notepad
      Run("NOTEPAD.EXE","")
  Edit &WIN.INI
      DirChange("C:\WINDOWS")
      Run("NOTEPAD.EXE","WIN.INI")
```

Save the menu file and minimize Notepad. This time you already have a copy of Command Post running our MYMENUS menu file, so instead of double-clicking on MYMENUS.CPM to start up a third Command Post, just go to Command Post's System menu and choose Reload Menu.

This time our new menu makes sure we're in the Windows directory and then runs Notepad with the WIN.INI file loaded. (Changing the directory like this won't change the directory that Command Post displays.)

CPML contains four commands that launch programs. They all take the same two parameters in parentheses:

- **Run**(*program-name*, *parameters*): Launches a program in a "normal" window. Windows decides where to place the window and what size to make it.
- **RunZoom**(*program-name*, *parameters*): Launches a program full-screen. If you find yourself always clicking on the Maximize button whenever you start up a program in order to get some more space into your window, you'll probably end up using this statement often.
- **RunIcon**(*program-name*, *parameters*): Loads the program and displays it as an icon.
- **RunHide**(*program-name*, *parameters*): Launches a program, but doesn't show it on the screen. In fact you can't even find the program in the Task Manager's program list. You can still manipulate the window with Command Post's window statements, which we'll look at later.

Getting the Selected File

Instead of having Notepad load a specific file, you can have it load whatever file is currently selected in the directory listing. Bring up Notepad with our menu file again, and type in a new menu at the end of the file. This menu will be called **Edit Selected File**. It will be similar to the previous menu, except for two things: You don't have to change directories before running Notepad; and instead of using a filename in the second Run parameter, you want Notepad to load the currently selected file. It looks like this:

```
Edit &Selected File
    Run("NOTEPAD.EXE", CurrentFile())
```

CurrentFile is an example of a Command Post *function*. Functions are used in place of strings or numbers inside your menu scripts. CurrentFile returns a string with the name of whichever file has the dotted selection box around it. Now, whenever you select Edit Selected File, Notepad will appear and then load whichever file has the selection box around it.

Note: "Selected" files are different than "highlighted" files. Highlighted files are the ones you've clicked on; they are shown in reverse video. You can highlight more than one file at a time. On the other hand, there is always one (and only one) file with the dotted "selection box" around it.

Command Post provides seven functions you can use to get your commands to operate on files or subdirectories from the Command Post directory display:

- **CurrentFile( )**: Returns the file or subdirectory name with the selection box around it when the menu was selected.
- **FileItemize("")**: Builds a string containing all the filenames currently highlighted, separated by spaces. This function ignores any subdirectories that may be highlighted.
- **FileLocate(*filename*)**: Given a *filename*, this function searches the current DOS path for the file. It returns the full pathname if it finds one.
- **DirGet( )**: Returns the current directory path.
- **DirHome( )**: Returns the directory path that Command Post started from.
- **DirItemize("")**: Builds a string containing all the currently highlighted subdirectories, separated by spaces. It ignores any filenames that may also be highlighted.
- **OtherDir( )**: If there are other Command Post windows running, this function returns the current directory of the copy that was most recently invoked.

Variables and Expressions

Before you start creating more complex menus, let's stop and look at some of the basics of CPML syntax.

CPML contains many of the elements of a true programming language. We've already used strings and functions in our menus. CPML also provides you with integers, arithmetic expressions, logical expressions, and string expressions, as well as variables to put all of this information into. You can even compare values to each other, and branch to another part of the menu depending on the result.

Unless you use a number or a string directly in a function, you must store its value somewhere in order to use it later. This storage place is called a *variable*. The name you attach to a variable must start with a letter, but the rest of it can have letters or digits, up to 30 characters in all.

Variable names can be as simple as A, B, or N, or can suggest the information they hold, as in TextFiles, MyFile, OldName, and so on. You can capitalize variable names any way you like; Command Post doesn't care.

Arithmetic expressions are built from integers, variables containing integer values, and functions that return numbers. These building blocks can be combined with each other by using these standard arithmetic operators:

+: Addition. Adds two numbers together.

-: Subtraction. Subtracts the second number from the first.

*: Multiplication. Multiplies two numbers together.

/: Integer division. Divides the first number by the second, rounding down to the nearest integer.

mod: Modulo. Returns the remainder after an integer division.

-: Negation. When placed before an expression, this operator returns its negative.

Here are some examples of arithmetic expressions:

```
Counter = 1
NumFiles = NumFiles+1
OK = FileExist("MYDATA.TXT")
```

Some specific integer values can mean special things to CPML. The language contains a number of named integer constants that are used as switches by many functions. These all start with the @ sign. The most often used constants are @TRUE and @FALSE. You can also call them @YES and @NO, as well as @ON and @OFF. These are all defined as 1 and 0, respectively. The other predefined constants are just used by a few specific functions. These are described with the functions that use them.

Since constants are used as switches by the functions and commands, you normally don't have to be aware of what actual number each constant name represents.

String expressions don't have any operators of their own, although you can use the comparison operators such as < or == to compare strings as well as integers. CPML makes up for this by providing you with 13 powerful string functions. (The string functions' names begin with "str".) For example:

```
AllCaps = StrUpper(EnteredFile)
Name = StrTrim(Name)
```

Logical expressions (expressions that return either @TRUE or @FALSE) are built from comparing integer or string values to each other. CPML uses the same logical operators as the C language:

<: Less than.

<=: Less than or equal to.

==: Equal to.

>=: Greater than or equal to.

>: Greater than.

!=: Not equal to.

<>: Not equal to.

&&: Logical And. Returns @TRUE only if the first and second items both equal @TRUE.

||: Logical Or. Returns @TRUE if at least one of the items equal @TRUE.

!: Logical Not. Returns @TRUE only if the item following it *doesn't* equal @TRUE. Otherwise it returns @FALSE.

Logical expressions are usually found in IF-THEN statements, which we'll be covering later, for example:

```
If Answer==@NO then Exit
If FileExist(MyFile) && FileExtension(MyFile)=="TXT" then
Run("NOTEPAD.EXE",MyFile)
```

In complex expressions, you can put subexpressions in parentheses to force them to get evaluated before the other parts.

There are also several operators that work on numbers at a binary level. These take advantage of the fact that internally, Command Post stores numbers as 32-bit signed binary integers. You'll probably never use these operators, but it's nice to know they're available.

<<: Left shift. Shifts each bit of the first number to the left as many times as specified by the second number. In decimal, this results in multiplying the number by 2 for each time it's shifted. (Since Command Post stores numbers in signed format, the "leftmost" bit is reserved for denoting the numeric sign. If you left shift enough times, you can end up creating a negative number when a binary 1 gets shifted into the sign bit.)

>>: Right shift. Shifts each bit of the first number to the right, as many times as specified by the second number. In decimal, this results in dividing the number by 2 for each time it's shifted. (If you right shift a negative number, the "1" in the leftmost sign bit gets shifted out of its place, causing the value to be interpreted as some very large positive number.)

|: Bitwise Or. Returns a number whose bits equal 1 if either of the corresponding bits of the first and second numbers are 1.

&: Bitwise And. Returns a number whose bits equal 1 only if the corresponding bits of the first and second numbers are both 1.

~: Bitwise Not. Returns a number whose bits are the opposite of those of the number that comes after it.

Asking for Information

You aren't limited to running programs with specific filenames, or even passing programs the names of the currently selected files. You can actually prompt the user to enter a filename or other information into a dialog box before executing a program, just the way some of Command Post's default menus do. This adds a whole new level of flexibility to your menus.

CPML has two commands you can use to let the user select a file to process:

- **AskLine**(*title, prompt, default*): Displays a dialog box with the *title* and *prompt* string. Underneath the *prompt* is an edit box where the user can enter a line of information. The edit box initially contains the *default* string. The function returns whatever is in the edit box when the user presses the OK button, or it exits the menu selection entirely if the user presses Cancel. The Copy and Move/Rename menu options are good examples of AskLine in action.

- **ItemSelect**(*title, list, delimiter*): Displays a dialog box with a *title* and containing a list box. This list box is filled with strings taken from the *list* that are separated by the *delimiter* character. The function returns the item selected, or else exits the menu if the user presses Cancel.

In the next example we'll create a menu that acts pretty much like the last one did, but it also gives you the opportunity to enter a different filename for Notepad to operate on:

```
&Ask for File to Edit
   MyFile = AskLine("Entering a File", "Filename to edit:", CurrentFile())
   Run("NOTEPAD.EXE", MyFile)
```

Here we are using the AskLine command to display the dialog box in Figure 15-22. Notice that the edit box initially contains a filename (or possibly a subdirectory). This was supplied by CurrentFile, which provides the default value for the edit box. You could have used an empty string ("") here instead, in which case the edit box would always start out blank.

After the user chooses OK, AskLine returns the contents of the edit box. In this case we've assigned this string (which hopefully contains a valid filename) to a variable, which we've named "MyFile." Now when your menu runs Notepad, you pass it whatever is in MyFile instead of giving it a fixed filename like we did in Edit WIN.INI earlier.

Choosing from a List

Sometimes you would rather give users a list of filenames to choose from, instead of making (or letting) them type in a filename. The ItemSelect function lets you display a dialog box that has a list box filled with choices. This is mostly used for choosing from among filenames with the same extension, although you can actually put anything you want into a list box.

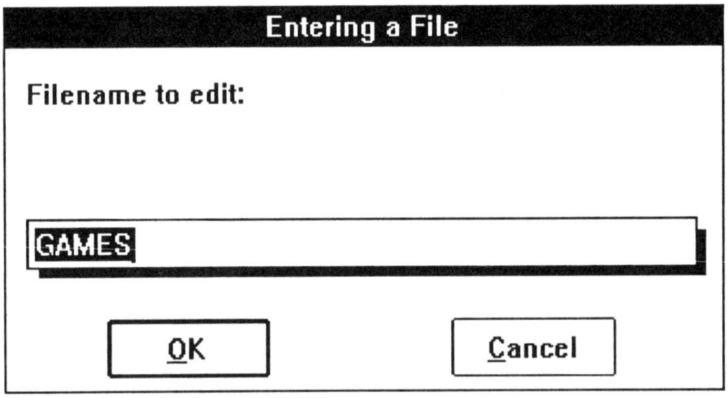

Figure 15-22 The AskLine dialog box

Enter this new menu item onto the end of your Notepad menu:

```
Edit .&INI Files
    DirChange("C:\WINDOWS")  ;your Windows path may be different!
    INIFiles = FileItemize("*.INI")
    MyFile = ItemSelect("Edit an INI file", INIFiles, " ")
    Terminate(MyFile=="", "", "")
    Run("NOTEPAD.EXE", MyFile)
```

After making sure we're in the Windows directory (where all the .INI files are located), this menu fills the variable INIFiles with a list of filenames that match the "*.INI" file specification.

The ItemSelect function creates the dialog box shown in Figure 15-23. It fills the list box with the filenames in INIFiles. ItemSelect puts each of these items on a separate line in the list box. It knows where to end one line and start the next because of the spaces between filenames in the INIFiles variable. In this case, the third parameter to the function (the *delimiter*) defines these spaces as the separators between items in the listbox. The entries are sorted alphabetically. After you select a filename from the list box, ItemSelect puts it into MyFile.

If the user doesn't select anything from the list box but instead presses OK or hits the ENTER key, then MyFile will equal ""; we assume this means the user made a mistake, so we just end the menu. Otherwise we have one filename sitting in MyFile, just like with our Ask for File to Edit menu, so we can use the same Run statement as before.

Also notice the *comment* at the end of the DirChange line. A comment is anything in the menu file that CPML ignores. Basically this means anything that comes after a semicolon, unless the semicolon is inside quotes or on the same line as a menu name. Also, you can insert blank lines anywhere in the menu file, since they're ignored too.

You aren't limited to filling a list box with just one set of wildcarded filenames. Here's a CPML menu that's very similar to Edit .INI Files, except that it displays a list box with several types of text files from the current directory:

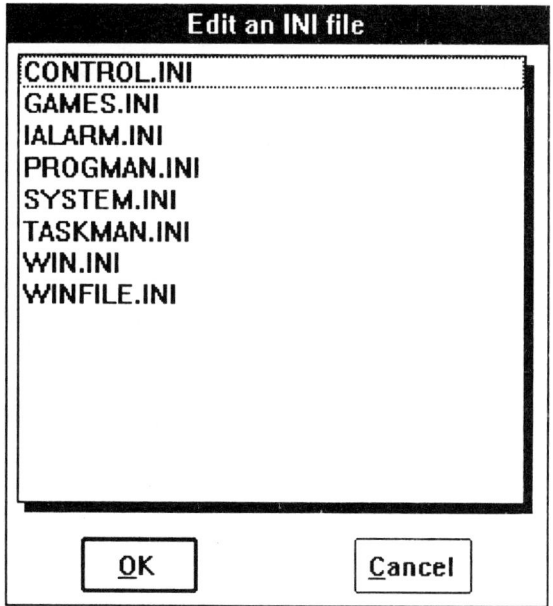

Figure 15-23 Selecting .INI files from a list box

```
Edit &Text Files
    TextFiles = FileItemize("*.BAT CONFIG.SYS *.DOC *.INI *.TXT")
    MyFile = ItemSelect("Edit a Text File", TextFiles, " ")
    Terminate(MyFile=="", "", "")
    Run("NOTEPAD.EXE", MyFile)
```

Note: If you're not careful, you can cause FileItemize to load a filename into its list box more than once. For example, you might want to add "READ*.*" to the list of text files in order to catch README.1ST, README.TXT, READ.ME, and all the other names that program developers have come up with for their read-me files. But if the current directory contains a README.TXT file, then it will be entered into the list box twice—once for READ*.* and once for *.TXT. There's nothing wrong with this, necessarily; just don't be surprised when it happens.

Stopping a Menu

As we've seen, the AskLine and ItemSelect functions will stop the menu option altogether if the user chooses the Cancel button. CPML provides you with two more ways to conditionally end an option:

- **AskYesNo**(*title, prompt*): This function displays a message box that looks just like the AskLine dialog box, but without the edit field. Also, instead of OK and Cancel buttons, the user gets to choose between Yes and No as well as Cancel. The function returns an integer—@YES or @NO, depending on the button pressed, or it just exits the menu if the user presses Cancel.

- **Pause**(*title*, *prompt*): This function looks and acts just like AskYesNo, except it gives you OK and Cancel buttons instead of Yes, No, and Cancel.

- **Terminate**(*expression*, *title*, *message*): Ends the menu's operation if *expression* equals @TRUE. If both *title* and *message* are empty strings, it just ends the menu option. But if either *title* or *message* contains something in them, a message box will appear to notify the user of what happened.

To demonstrate these functions, we're going to add a new "Maintenance" menu to the menu bar. We will add a menu item that deletes the backup files in the current directory. Go back to our menu file in Notepad, add a blank line at the end just for readability, and then type in the following menu definition:

```
&Maintenance
 &Delete Backup Files
    BAKfiles = FileItemize("*.BAK")
    Terminate(BAKfiles == "", "", "No backup files here!")
    Prompt = StrCat("Are you SURE you want to delete ", BAKfiles, "???")
    YesNo = AskYesNo("Delete Backup Files?", Prompt)
    Terminate(YesNo == @NO, "", "")
    FileDelete(BAKfiles)
    SetDisplay("", "", "") ;refresh directory listing after deletes
```

The first thing this menu does is to find all the .BAK files in the current directory and store them in the variable BAKfiles, separated by spaces. If there are no such files, BAKfiles will equal "". In this case Terminate will stop the menu right here with the message box shown in Figure 15-24.

If there are backup files to delete, we want to make the user confirm that he or she really *does* want to delete them. We want to display a YES/NO dialog box like the one in Figure 15-25. To build the prompt string, we use the *strcat* function, which is one of the simpler string functions in CPML. It takes two or more strings as parameters,

Figure 15-24 Terminate message box

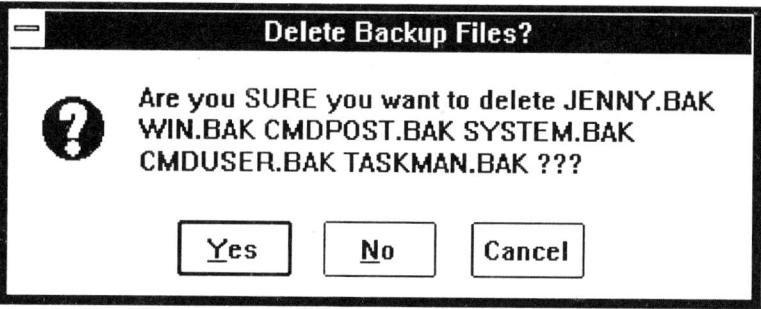

Figure 15-25 The AskYesNo dialog box

concatenates them, and returns the resulting string. Here we put the result into the variable Prompt and use it in the AskYesNo function on the next line.

At this point the user can choose Yes, No, or Cancel. If the user presses Cancel (or hits the ESC key) the menu stops automatically, but he or she might press No instead. In this case we want both actions to mean the same thing: Don't delete the files. So we have to test the result of AskYesNo, which we've put into a variable, YesNo. If YesNo equals @NO, we use the Terminate function again, this time stopping the menu with no message box at all.

If the user pressed Yes, then the menu goes on to delete all the .BAK files with the FileDelete command. Finally the SetDisplay command is called to update the directory listing to reflect the deletions.

Displaying Messages

In addition to having the user enter a line of text, your menu can simply display a message.

- **Beep**: This is the simplest command of all. It simply tells Command Post to beep at the user.

- **Display**(*seconds, title, text*): Displays a message box with the specified *title* in the title bar and *text* inside. This message box is displayed either for the specified number of *seconds* or until the user clicks on it.

- **Message**(*title, text*): Displays the *text* in a message box until the user presses the OK button.

Conditional Branching

Like a full-fledged batch language, Command Post gives you the ability to execute a different part of your menu code depending on a condition or relationship. This is accomplished with the IF and GOTO statements. With these commands you can infuse your menus with great power and flexibility.

The IF statement takes the form

`IF` *logical expression* `THEN` *statement*

where *logical expression* is any condition or expression that resolves to @TRUE or @FALSE (1 or 0). (Actually, if the expression evaluates to anything other than 0, it's interpreted as being true.)

You can conditionally execute one statement in this manner. If you need to execute more than one statement when the expression is true, you must use the GOTO statement to branch to another part of the menu, where you place the series of statements.

You specify the other part of the menu to go to by a label. A label is simply a name for a spot in the menu code. It uses the same rules as naming variables: It can be up to 30 letters and digits long, and must start with a letter.

At the point where the label announces the section of code, it is preceded by a colon. This is similar to denoting labels in MS-DOS batch files.

The following example shows IF-THEN and GOTO in action. This is a variation on our previous menu, Edit &Selected File, which calls Notepad to allow us to edit the currently selected file. The problem with using Notepad to edit text files is that Notepad will not accept files longer than approximately 50,000 characters. But if you have Microsoft Word for Windows, for example, you can edit a text file of any length. Our revised menu therefore checks the size of the selected file, and decides whether to run Notepad to edit it (if it's short enough) or else to invoke Word:

```
Edit &Selected File
    if (FileSize(CurrentFile()) >= 50000) then goto UseWinWord
    Run("NOTEPAD.EXE", CurrentFile())
    Exit
    :UseWinWord
    Run("WINWORD.EXE", CurrentFile())
```

First we use the **FileSize** function to find out how long the text file is. If it's greater than or equal to 50000 bytes, we branch to the section of code labeled "UseWinWord". Here we call Word for Windows and load the file.

If the file's size is less than 50000 bytes, execution "falls through" to the next statement after the IF, where we run Notepad with the selected file. At this point we don't want to fall through any further, or else we'd end up starting Word for Windows as well as Notepad, so we simply **Exit** the menu.

Unfortunately, Command Post does not allow you to branch to a label outside of the currently executing menu. All your GOTO's must be within the menu. Still, it makes for quite a powerful addition to the language.

Looping

Now that we can conditionally branch to another part of the menu, we can branch backward to a part of the menu we've already executed and do it again. Code that is performed more than once in this manner is called a **loop**. This is useful when performing some action on individual items within a group of data.

For instance, consider the Freespace on Drives selection in Command Post's default File menu. This menu option shows you the space available on each of your hard drives, in addition to showing you the total space you have available. For each drive letter, from C to the last one specified in WIN.INI, Command Post determines that drive's free space. It adds this number to a running total, and also concatenates that drive's letter and free space onto the message. After it has done this for the last drive, it branches out of the loop and continues on to display the message.

As another example of using loops to process information, consider this next menu that takes your DOS Path string and displays it in an easy-to-read fashion by breaking it up into separate lines for each component pathname:

```
DOS &Path
    Path = Environment("Path")
    CRLF = strcat(Num2Char(13), Num2Char(10))
    PrettyPath = ""
    Start = 1
    :Loop
    End = strindex(Path, ";", Start, @FWDSCAN)
    if (End==0) then End = strlen(Path)+1
    NextPathname = strsub(Path, Start, End-Start)
    PrettyPath = strcat(PrettyPath, NextPathname, CRLF)
    if (End>strlen(Path)) then Terminate(@TRUE, "DOS Path", PrettyPath)
    Start = strindex(Path, ";", End, @FWDSCAN)+1
    goto Loop
```

The first thing the menu does is to find the current DOS Path, using the **Environment** function. A user's DOS Path consists of a long string of directory paths separated by semicolons. In order to display the different directories on separate lines, we must build a new string consisting of each individual pathname separated by a carriage return/linefeed combination instead of a semicolon. We build this carriage return/linefeed string beforehand and place it into the variable CRLF.

Each time the Loop section of the program is executed, we want to take the next pathname (which ends just before the next semicolon we find) and copy it onto the end of our new PrettyPath variable. Then, instead of a semicolon, we concatenate CRLF to force the next pathname to the next line.

If we haven't come to the end of the Path string yet, we skip over the semicolon and loop back up to find the next pathname. When the end of this pathname is also the end of the Path string itself, then it's time to display our nicely formatted DOS Path. At this point we use the Terminate command, since we just want to display PrettyPath and exit. Figure 15-26 shows the resulting formatted DOS Path.

Note: When creating a loop in your menu, make sure it will eventually end. If your menu gets stuck in an "infinite loop," there is no way to get Command Post to gracefully break off from its processing. You will have to select Exit Windows from the System menu or you must end Command Post's task with Task Manager.

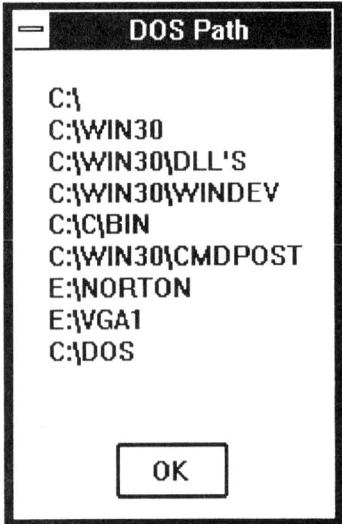

Figure 15-26 Displaying a pretty DOS Path

You can't even just close Command Post. If you try, Command Post will simply reply, "Previous menu selection still running."

File and Directory Handling

You can do more with files and directories than just getting their names and sizes. CPML has functions to copy, move, rename, and delete files, as well as to create and delete directories:

- **FileCopy**(*from-list*, *to-file*, *warning*): Copies files. *From-list* contains one or more filenames, which may contain wildcards.
- **FileDelete**(*file-list*): Deletes files.
- **FileMove**(*from-list*, *to-file*, *warning*): Moves files to another set of directories.
- **FileRename**(*from-list*, *to-file*): Renames files.

These are very useful functions to have. For instance, you can use FileCopy to automatically create a backup of a text file before you modify it with Notepad. You could take the Edit Text Files menu, for example, and add the following lines like this:

```
Edit &Text Files (w/Backup)
    TextFiles = FileItemize("*.BAT CONFIG.SYS *.DOC *.INI *.TXT")
    MyFile = ItemSelect("Edit a Text File", TextFiles, " ")
    Terminate(MyFile=="", "", "")
```

```
BAKFile = StrCat(FileRoot(MyFile), ".BAK")      ;New line
FileCopy(MyFile, BAKFile, @FALSE)               ;New line
Run("NOTEPAD.EXE", MyFile)
```

The first new line takes the filename you selected to edit (MyFile), extracts just the root portion of the filename using the FileRoot function, and sticks the extension ".BAK" onto the filename, thus creating the variable BAKFile. The FileCopy statement then copies the file to be edited over to the backup file. Now Command Post is ready to run Notepad.

Another safety-related feature you can add to your workstation is a "trashcan." A trashcan is just a holding area for files you want to delete. Instead of actually deleting the files, you can move them into a TRASHCAN subdirectory. The files are out of the way until you absolutely need to recover the disk space. If you need to restore one of these files, you select a Restore from Trashcan menu item. Finally, once you run out of disk space, you can select another menu item to "take out the trash." These would go well in our Maintenance menu, after Delete Backup Files:

```
_Move Files to &Trashcan
    TrashFiles = FileItemize("")
    Terminate(TrashFiles=="", "Trashcan", "No files to move!")
    ;If no trashcan directory on current drive, then create one...
    SaveDir = DirGet()
    If DirChange("\TRASHCAN") then goto OK
    DirMake("\TRASHCAN")
    :OK
    DirChange(SaveDir)
    FileMove(TrashFiles, "\TRASHCAN", @FALSE)
    SetDisplay("","","")
&Restore from Trash
    TrashFiles = FileItemize("\TRASHCAN\*.*")
    Terminate(TrashFiles=="", "Restore from Trash", "No files to restore!")
    TheFile = ItemSelect("Select file to restore", TrashFiles, " ")
    FileMove(strcat("\TRASHCAN\",TheFile), TheFile, @TRUE)
&Empty the Trash
    TrashFiles = FileItemize("\TRASHCAN\*.*")
    Terminate(TrashFiles=="", "Empty the Trash", "No files to delete!")
    Prompt = StrCat("Do you REALLY want to delete ", TrashFiles, "???")
    Confirmed = AskYesNo("Empty the Trash", Prompt)
    Terminate(Confirmed==@FALSE, "", "")
    FileDelete("\TRASHCAN\*.*")
    SetDisplay("","","")
```

Move Files to Trashcan finds all the filenames that are currently highlighted and stores their names in the variable TrashFiles. (If there aren't any highlighted files, the menu ends with a message.) Then it checks to make sure a \TRASHCAN directory exists on

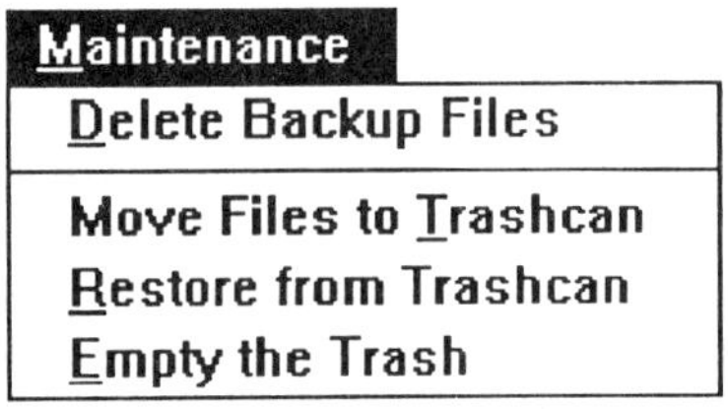

```
Maintenance
Delete Backup Files
Move Files to Trashcan
Restore from Trashcan
Empty the Trash
```

Figure 15-27 Separating menu items

the current drive, and creates it if there isn't one already. It then moves the files to the \TRASHCAN directory. Finally, it refreshes the directory listing with SetDisplay.

Restore from Trash gathers all the filenames in the \TRASHCAN directory (if any) into a list box for the user to choose from. The chosen file is then moved from \TRASHCAN into the current directory using the same filename. Then SetDisplay is called so the newly restored file will appear in the directory display.

Empty the Trash puts all the filenames in the \TRASHCAN directory into an AskYesNo dialog box to let you confirm that you really want to delete them. Then, if you haven't selected No or Cancel, it deletes the files. Empty the Trash also refreshes the directory display, just in case we're currently looking at C:\TRASHCAN.

You'll notice we put an underscore (_) at the start of the Move Files to Trashcan menu name. This causes the menu item to be separated from the previous item by a horizontal line, making the Maintenance menu look like Figure 15-27. You can also divide a popup menu into columns by starting a menu item with the vertical bar (|) character.

Note: You may have seen other Windows applications that have vertical lines separating some items on the main menu bar, or whose menu bar takes up multiple lines. While CPML doesn't let you separate main menu items with vertical lines, you can force a Command Post main menu item down to the next line by prefixing the menu name with a vertical bar.

Controlling Other Windows

Even after a program has started, you can still influence some aspects of its behavior. You do this with any of 15 "Win" functions. In using most of these functions, you identify the window or windows to act on by specifying a partial window title. The function will operate on all windows currently open on the screen (not icons) whose titles start with the title you pass to the function.

The basic window functions are similar to the Run functions. You can hide, restore, iconize, and zoom existing windows. In addition, you can place a window of a particular size at a particular position on the screen.

- **WinHide** (*partial-title*): Hides the application window matching *partial-title*.
- **WinShow**(*partial-title*): Restores hidden or iconized application windows to their "normal" state, as if you had chosen Restore from their System menus.

- **WinIconize**(*partial-title*): Minimizes (or "iconizes" the named application windows.
- **WinZoom**(*partial-title*): Maximizes application windows to full-screen.
- **WinPlace**(*left, top, right, bottom, partial-title*): Changes the size and position of an application window on the screen. The *left, top, right,* and *bottom* parameters are based on a coordinate system that is 1000 units wide by 1000 units high.
- **WinPosition**(*partial-title*): Returns a string consisting of the specified window's left, top, right, and bottom screen positions, all separated by commas. The positions are in the same units as are used in the WinPlace command.

When you place a window, you can specify the constant @ABOVEICONS for the *bottom* parameter. This sets the bottom of the window just above the row of icons along the bottom of the display. You can also use @NORESIZE for the right and bottom parameters. This would cause the window to be moved, while keeping the width and height constant.

Command Post comes with a utility program called WinInfo, which is a great help when you want a window to show up in a certain position. When you run WinInfo, it displays a window like the one shown in Figure 15-28. Then, as you move the mouse cursor over the various windows, WinInfo displays those windows' positions expressed in Command Post's coordinate system.

When the cursor is over the window you want to fix in its place, press the SPACEBAR. WinInfo will then build the appropriate WinPlace statement needed to move the window

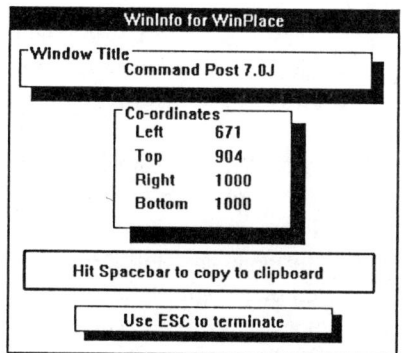

Figure 15-28 WinInfo

to that size and position, and will copy it to the clipboard. You can then paste it into your menu. Finally, unlike a standard Windows application, WinInfo will end only when you press the ESC key.

You can also force windows to become active:

- **WinActivate**(*partial-title*): Activates the application window whose title begins with *partial-title*.
- **WinGetActive**( ): Returns the title of the active window. When the menu starts, the active window will always be Command Post; but this would change once you execute a Run statement or a WinActivate function.

You can force other programs to shut down. Or you can simply wait until the user closes them manually:

- **WinClose**(*partial-title*): Closes an application whose window title begins with *partial-title*.
- **WinCloseNot**(*partial-title* [, *partial-title*]...): Closes all application windows *except* those specified.
- **WinWaitClose**(*partial-title*): Waits until the specified application windows are closed before executing the rest of the menu.

The Initialization Section

You can have your menu file do things when Command Post starts up, before any menus are even selected. Just add CPML statements to the beginning of the file, before the first menu is defined. This area of the file is called the *initialization section*.

As an example, we'll have Command Post start out by displaying only the menu instead of filling the screen with a directory listing. To do this, we'll make Command Post perform a WinPlace command on its own window. After it moves and resizes the window, the menu operates like any other.

The first thing you must do to create a floating menu is to find out its desired size and placement on the screen. Find the WININFO.EXE program in your Command Post directory and execute it. Next, grab the Command Post window by the "grow-bars" on the edge to adjust the window's size so that only the menu is visible. Drag the window over to the position where you want it to always start out. Click on the WinInfo window to make it the active window. Move the mouse cursor over to your Command Post menu and press the SPACEBAR to get the appropriate WinPlace statement into the Clipboard.

Now you can bring up Notepad with the MYMENUS.CPM file. Place the cursor at the very beginning of the file, before the first menu definition. Press SHIFT+INSERT to copy the WinPlace command from the Clipboard into the menu file. Assuming you dragged the menu down to the lower right-hand corner, you'll see something resembling this in the first line of the file:

```
WinPlace(479,860,1000,1000,'Command Post 7.0M - Eval Only')
```

Another popular use for the initialization section is to change the current Command Post window's title with the WinTitle command. However, Command Post will not let you change its own window title until you register it.

Tip: When a menu places its own window

If your menu is going to move or resize its own Command Post window, you should use an empty string ("") for WinPlace's *partial-title* parameter. This causes WinPlace to automatically refer to the current Command Post window regardless of the actual title. This way you don't have to worry about forgetting to change the title in the WinPlace statement if you later decide to change Command Post's title.

As a final example of the uses of the initialization section, later on in this chapter, under Faking Arrays, we'll look at how you can use the initialization section of your menu file to change your wallpaper bitmap each time you run Windows.

Note: When you make a change to a menu file's initialization section, you cannot just choose Reload Menu from Command Post's System menu to activate it, as you would if you had changed a menu. The initialization section never re-executes when a menu is reloaded. You'll have to quit Command Post and run it again to see the effect of your changes.

Linking Menu Files Together

So far we've been bringing up an extra copy of Command Post to run our MYMENUS.CPM menu file. But we don't have to run our custom menu in a separate window from the standard Command Post menu. CPML lets you build up a menu from two .CPM files. In fact, the standard Command Post menu is actually defined in two files—CMDPOST.CPM and CMDUSER.CPM.

You link two menu files by inserting the language directive statement

```
#NextFile second .CPM filename
```

somewhere in the first .CPM file. This is usually placed at the beginning of the file. After the first menu file is loaded but before its menu is executed, Command Post finds the #NextFile statement and loads the second menu file. Next, it executes the first and then the second file's initialization sections. The second file's menus are placed right after the first.

If you want the standard Command Post menu to link to MYMENUS.CPM, just load CMDPOST.CPM into Notepad, find the line that currently reads

```
#NextFile CMDUSER.CPM
```

and change it to designate MYMENUS.CPM instead. Then save CMDPOST.CPM. As we mentioned before, you cannot just choose Reload Menu from Command Post's System menu to reflect this change—you'll have to restart Command Post altogether.

WIN.INI Support

One of the more tedious aspects of using Windows is having to modify the WIN.INI file. Command Post can help you hide some of that tedium within a menu. With CPML, you can read and write a line to the WIN.INI file. (There is no support yet for reading or writing to the other .INI files.) You do this with the following functions:

- **IniRead**(*section*, *keyname*, *default*): Reads a string from WIN.INI. A *section* name is enclosed in square brackets inside the file, and *keyname*s are the words that begin each line within a section. If the specified *keyname* isn't found within the *section*, then the function returns the *default* string.

- **IniWrite**(*section*, *keyname*, *string*): This command writes a *string* that begins with *keyname* to the WIN.INI file within the *section* specified. The section and/or keyname will be created if they don't already exist in the file. If there already is such an entry, it will be replaced by the new value.

To demonstrate the WIN.INI commands, we'll create a menu item that lets you modify the RUN= line in WIN.INI. This is the line that specifies which programs to execute when Windows starts up. We want to use its current value as the default for an AskLine dialog box. If the user doesn't change the line, we simply terminate the menu; otherwise we'll write the new line back out to WIN.INI:

```
Edit WIN.INI &RUN= Line
    OrigLine = INIRead("Windows", "Run", "")
    NewLine = OrigLine
    NewLine = AskLine("RUN= Line", "Enter new RUN= line:", OrigLine)
     Terminate(NewLine==OrigLine, "", "")
    INIWrite("Windows", "Run", NewLine)
```

Password-Protecting Your Windows Environment

You're not limited to changing the standard sections of WIN.INI. You can, of course, create your own custom WIN.INI sections, just the way so many other Windows apps do. You could, for example, use Notepad to create a [This PC] section containing a line like "Owner=Joe Smith", or "password=bufkfd". Then when your menu file starts up, you could force the user to enter a password into an AskLine dialog box. If they enter it incorrectly, the menu terminates the current Windows session; otherwise, it continues normally. If you've included Command Post in the WIN.INI's RUN= line or have replaced Program Manager with Command Post as the Windows shell so that it will start up automatically whenever Windows does, you could use this to add a little security to your Windows workstation.

This one involves some complex programming, but even this isn't impossible to follow. At the very end of the second file's initialization section, type:

```
;Force user to enter a password to use the system...
     CurrPW = INIRead("This PC", "password", "")
     Terminate(CurrPW=="", "", "") ;no password found -- open system
     Owner    = INIRead("This PC", "owner", "somebody")
     Owner    = StrCat(Owner, "'s PC")
     EnteredPW = AskLine(Owner, "Enter Password:", "")
     Terminate(EnteredPW==CurrPW, "", "") ;correct pw entered
     EnteredPW = AskLine(Owner, "Enter Password (2nd try):", "")
     Terminate(EnteredPW==CurrPW, "", "") ;correct pw entered
     EnteredPW = AskLine(Owner, "Enter Password (3rd try):", "")
     Terminate(EnteredPW==CurrPW, "", "") ;correct pw entered
;else at this point they've tried to enter the password 3 times & failed,
;so...
     EndSession()
```

The first thing this code does is to read the system's current password from the WIN.INI file into CurrPW. If there was no password found, the menu assumes it's an open system and anybody can use it. If this is the case, Command Post simply terminates the initialization section and continues loading the rest of the menus. (This is why this code must be placed at the end of the second menu file's initialization section. Otherwise we would inadvertently skip over any other initialization we wanted to accomplish!)

Next we read the owner's name from WIN.INI for the title of the dialog box to follow. This isn't really necessary, but it looks impressive when the AskLine box is displayed. Then we have the user enter the password into the AskLine box, which looks like Figure 15-29. The entry is stored in EnteredPW, and if it's the same as CurrPW, we terminate the initialization section and let the user continue with the Windows session.

The user has three chances to enter the password. But if he or she goes through all three AskLines without entering the password correctly, we (meaning the programmer) put the EndSession command here to end the whole Windows session.

This method of password-protecting your Windows workstation has two limitations. The first one occurs if you haven't declared Command Post as your shell in the SYSTEM.INI file. In this case, the Program Manager icon is already displayed on the screen by the time the password dialog box appears. The user could open up Program Manager and just ignore Command Post altogether. This isn't a problem once you set the SYSTEM.INI's shell= line to use Command Post as your default shell instead of Program Manager.

The second limitation, on the other hand, is one we haven't been able to overcome: A person logging on can just press Cancel when the AskLine box comes up, and the initialization section will be terminated automatically, just as if the password had been entered correctly! This is why we said you can add "a little" security when we introduced this example.

If you actually want to use password protection with Command Post, you can set up a menu item that lets you change your password once you've logged in. First, display an

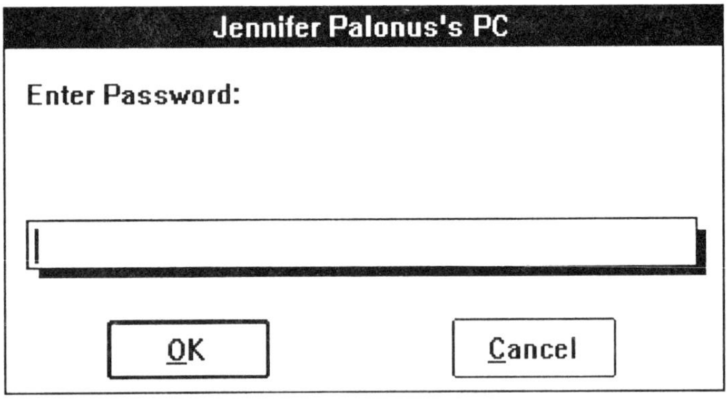

[Figure 15-29: Dialog box titled "Jennifer Palonus's PC" with "Enter Password:" label, text input field, and OK/Cancel buttons]

Figure 15-29 Asking for a password

AskLine box to confirm that the user knows the current password. If they enter it incorrectly, terminate the menu. Otherwise, prompt them for the new password and write it back to WIN.INI. The logic would look like this:

```
&Change PW
    CurrPW = INIRead("This PC", "password", "")
    UserPW = AskLine("Change PW", "Enter the current password:", "")
    Terminate(UserPW!=CurrPW, "", "")
    NewPW  = AskLine("Change PW", "Enter new password:", CurrPW)
    INIWrite("This PC", "password", NewPW)
```

Debugging Statements

Any self-respecting programming language should have a facility for helping you to debug your programs. CPML, even though as a language it's not nearly in the same league, nevertheless does provide a simple debugger.

You invoke the CPML debugger by going into the menu file and inserting a Debug command:

```
Debug(@ON)
```

While debug mode is on, the debugger dialog box, shown in Figure 15-30, is displayed. This lets you step through the menu one line at a time while viewing the menu line that has just been executed, the value of the line if an assignment was made, and the next line to be executed. The dialog box also lets you view the contents of a specific variable by entering its name into the edit box and pressing Show Var.

Debug mode is turned off automatically at the end of the menu item. You can also turn off debugging manually by inserting the command

```
Debug(@OFF)
```

into the menu file.

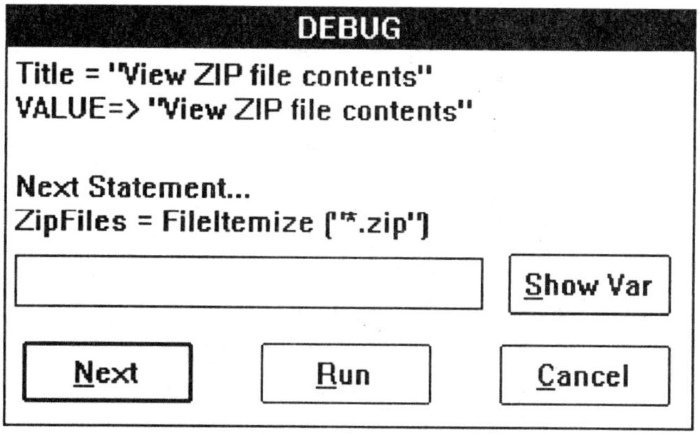

```
                    ┌──────── DEBUG ────────┐
                    Title = "View ZIP file contents"
                    VALUE=> "View ZIP file contents"

                    Next Statement...
                    ZipFiles = FileItemize ["*.zip"]

                    ┌──────────────────┐  ┌─────────┐
                    │                  │  │ Show Var│
                    └──────────────────┘  └─────────┘

                    ┌────────┐ ┌────────┐ ┌────────┐
                    │  Next  │ │  Run   │ │ Cancel │
                    └────────┘ └────────┘ └────────┘
```

Figure 15-30 The Debugger dialog box

PUSHING CPML'S LIMITS

Command Post Menu Language is so flexible you will soon be thinking of more complex operations to put into a menu. Unfortunately, CPML isn't *quite* a full-fledged programming language. To carry out your bigger and better ideas, you're going to have to resort to some sneaky methods to work around CPML's limitations.

In fact, as you eventually push CPML to the limit, you may end up putting as much effort into elaborate coding schemes to work around its limitations as if you were writing in a full-fledged programming language. Depending on how much you enjoy programming, you may become very discouraged by this feeling. Or perhaps you will merely hunger for more.

These next few sections demonstrate some extra CPML features and programming tricks you can use in your quest to build ever more powerful menus.

Building Statements with Substitution

The percent sign (%) has a special meaning in CPML. If you enclose a variable name within percent signs in a menu statement, Command Post will take whatever is in that variable and substitute it into the statement at that point. This happens before Command Post actually executes the statement.

The simplest way to demonstrate this feature is to look back at our Delete Backup Files menu item within the Maintenance menu:

```
&Maintenance
  &Delete Backup Files
     BAKfiles = FileItemize("*.BAK")
     Terminate(BAKfiles == "", "", "No backup files here!")
     Prompt = StrCat("Are you SURE you want to delete ", BAKfiles, "???")
```

```
YesNo = AskYesNo("Delete Backup Files?",Prompt)
Terminate(YesNo == @NO,"","")
FileDelete(BAKfiles)
SetDisplay("","","")
```

Instead of using the StrCat function to build the prompt string for AskYesNo, you can use this instead:

```
Prompt = "Are you SURE you want to delete %BAKfiles%???"
```

When this line gets executed, Command Post will substitute the one or more .BAK filenames from the variable BAKfiles directly into the string before assigning it to Prompt. The effect is the same as using StrCat, but as you can see it's a little easier to read. Using substitution helps readability even more when you need to build a string from two or more variables.

One thing to remember when using substitution is that whenever Command Post sees two percent signs together (%%) in a menu statement, it assumes you just want to use a percent sign *as a percent sign*, and not to trigger a substitution. For example, if you need to paste the variables AString and BString together, this line won't work:

```
CString = "%AString%%BString%"
```

You'll either have to put a space between %AString% and %BString%, or else resort to the StrCat function.

In some cases, using percent sign substitution is more than just a convenience. It's actually an integral part of being able to simulate arrays, as we'll see below.

Faking Arrays

Practically all programming languages give you the ability to create arrays of data. An array is a set of similar variables, all with the same name. You identify the specific element in the array by numbering them within parentheses or square brackets, depending on the language. For instance, in C you could build an array of bitmap filenames called "Bmp", and you would refer to each particular filename as Bmp[0], Bmp[1], Bmp[2], and so on.

Command Post doesn't directly support arrays. Fortunately, however, we can simulate an array by using the percent sign.

In the next example we will create some initialization code that will pick a bitmap file out of a preset list of filenames at random and cause Windows to use that bitmap file for the wallpaper background the next time Windows boots up. So fire up Notepad with the MYMENUS.CPM file in it. We'll be adding lines to the beginning initialization code. (You can put this before or after the other lines in the initialization section; it doesn't matter as long as it's not after the password logic.)

First, we create a set of variables containing the names of the wallpaper bitmap files that come with Windows. Then we create a variable with a random number from 0 to 5, which we will use to point to one of the six filenames:

```
;Change the Wallpaper for Next Time:
    Bmp0 = "BOXES.BMP"
    Bmp1 = "PAPER.BMP"
    Bmp2 = "PARTY.BMP"
    Bmp3 = "PYRAMID.BMP"
    Bmp4 = "RIBBONS.BMP"
    Bmp5 = "WEAVE.BMP"
    WhichOne= Random(5)     ;make random number from 0 to 5
```

The Random function returns an integer anywhere from 0 to whatever number we pass the function. We store the result in the variable WhichOne. Now we can use this random number to create a variable name "on the fly" and write this variable to the WIN.INI file:

```
IniWrite("Desktop", "Wallpaper", Bmp%WhichOne%)
```

Let's assume WhichOne is given the value of 3. When Command Post hits the "IniWrite" line, it takes "3" and pastes it onto "Bmp". Then Command Post in effect executes this line:

```
IniWrite("Desktop", "Wallpaper", Bmp3)
```

The next time we start Windows, we will see a wallpaper made from PYRAMID.BMP, the file whose name we had assigned to Bmp3.

It's also a good idea at this point to make sure Windows will tile the bitmap and not center it:

```
IniWrite("Desktop", "TileWallpaper", "1")
```

And finally, since we've created seven variables that we won't be needing anymore, we should drop them from memory:

```
drop(Bmp0, Bmp1, Bmp2, Bmp3, Bmp4, Bmp5, WhichOne)
```

The Execute Statement

Normally you write CPML statements into the menu definition and Command Post executes them. But CPML has a command called "Execute" that actually lets you store a CPML statement in a string variable and then execute that variable as if you had typed its contents into the menu definition itself.

This command can be used along with AskLine to let you enter CPML statements right from the Command Post window and run them, one at a time. First, we initialize a string variable, CPMLCmd, in the initialization section:

```
;initialize the interactive command...
    CPMLCmd = ""
```

Then we create a menu item (in our Maintenance menu, perhaps) that asks for a command line, and then executes it:

```
CPML &Interactive
    :Loop
    CPMLCmd = AskLine("CPML Interactive", "CPML line:", CPMLCmd)
    Execute %CPMLCmd%
    goto Loop
```

The first time you choose this menu item, CPMLCmd defaults to an empty string. Type in a command, and it will run immediately. You can even assign values to variables and use them again. The next time you select the menu, CPMLCmd will still contain the last statement you typed in as the default.

Each time after you execute a statement, the menu loops back and asks you for another one. When you're finished, simply press Cancel to exit the menu.

Running a Macro from a Menu

In Chapter 5 we discussed how to use Windows' Macro Recorder utility to send a batch of keystrokes to a program. You can combine this feature with Command Post to add more power to your menus. The technique relies on Recorder's ability to execute a macro immediately on being started.

In the following example we'll create a menu that starts Windows Write and then calls a macro that types in the salutation for a letter the user will finish manually.

First we need a Recorder macro. For this example we're using the first macro that was described in Chapter 5 under "Recording a Simple Text-Input Macro." This macro was titled "Write Salutation," has a shortcut key of CTRL+S, and was saved in the macro file WINMACS.REC. If you haven't already created that macro you should do it now.

Once you have the macro defined, debugged, and saved in a macro file, it's just a matter of creating a Command Post menu to launch the application program the macro acts on, starting Recorder, telling it to execute the CTRL+S macro immediately, and then closing Recorder when it's finished executing the macro:

```
&Letter w/Salutation
    Run     ("WRITE.EXE", "")
    RunIcon ("RECORDER.EXE", "WINMACS.REC -h ^s")
    Yield
    WinClose("Recorder")
```

After we run Recorder and have it execute the macro, we wait a bit to make sure the macro has finished; and then we close down Recorder. This is much simpler than creating a separate nested macro just to close Recorder, as you would have to do without Command Post.

Note: In the discussion of running a macro from an icon in Chapter 5, we said you can just specify the macro filename and shortcut key, and Windows will associate the .REC file with Macro Recorder. If you use the RunIcon command in this way, however, Recorder will load the WINMACS.REC file but won't execute the macro. You have to explicitly name RECORDER.EXE as the program to launch and put both the macro filename and the shortcut key in the command parameter.

TABLE OF CPML STATEMENTS

Abs(*number*)

Returns the absolute value of a *number*.

AskLine(*title, prompt, default*)

Displays a dialog box with the *title* and *prompt* string and lets the user enter a line of information into an edit box. The edit box starts off containing the value specified by *default*. The function returns whatever is in the edit box when the user presses the OK button, or else it exits the menu entirely if the user presses Cancel.

AskYesNo(*title, prompt*)

Lets user choose between **Yes**, *No*, and **Cancel** buttons after displaying a dialog box with the *title* and *prompt* strings. Returns an integer—@YES or @NO, depending on the button pressed—or else just exits the menu if the user presses Cancel.

Average(*number [, number]...*)

Returns the average of a series of *numbers*.

Beep

Beeps once at the user.

Char2Num(*string*)

Returns the ANSI code of the first character of a *string*.

ClipAppend(*string*)

Appends the *string* to the end of the Clipboard, if the Clipboard already contains a string or is empty.

ClipGet( )

Returns the Clipboard's contents, if it's a string.

ClipPut(*string*)

Replaces the Clipboard's contents with the specified *string*.

CurrentFile( )

Returns the file or subdirectory name that is currently selected.

DateTime( )

Returns the current date and time in a string.

Debug(*mode***)**

Turns Debug mode on or off. Arguments for (*mode*) can be @ON or @OFF.

Delay(*seconds***)**

Pauses menu execution for up to 15 *seconds*.

DirChange(*new-directory***)**

Changes the current directory to *new-directory* and, if necessary, logs to a different drive.

DirGet( )

Returns the current directory path.

DirHome( )

Returns the full pathname of the directory that Command Post originally started from.

DirItemize(*dir-list***)**

Builds a list of directories, similar to FileItemize.

DirMake(*new-directory***)**

Creates a *new-directory*. Returns @TRUE or @FALSE, depending on whether or not the directory was created.

DirRemove(*dir-list***)**

Removes an existing directory. Returns @TRUE or @FALSE, depending on whether or not the directory was removed. You can remove more than one directory at a time.

DiskFree(*drive-list***)**

Returns the amount of free space on a set of drives. *Drive-list* should contain drive letters, separated by spaces if more than one.

`DiskHide(drive-letters)`

Removes the disk drive icons corresponding to *drive-letters* from the directory display. This is especially useful if your PC is on a network with many remote drives you never use.

`DiskReset()`

Causes Command Post to re-examine all attached drives.

`Display(seconds, title, text)`

Displays a message box with the *title* and *text*. The message box is displayed for the specified number of *seconds*. The user can click on it to make it disappear before the time is up.

`DOSVersion(which-level)`

Gets the version of MS-DOS that is currently running. Acceptable *which-level* arguments are either @MAJOR or @MINOR, meaning either the integer part or the decimal part of the MS-DOS version number is returned.

`Drop(variable [, variable]...)`

Deletes *variable* to recover its memory.

`EndSession( )`

Ends the current Windows session.

`Environment(environment-variable)`

Returns the value of a DOS *environment-variable* in a string.

`ErrorMode(mode)`

Sets what happens in the event of an error. *Mode* can be either @CANCEL, @NOTIFY, or @OFF. @CANCEl cancels execution. @NOTIFY notifies the user, allowing them to continue. @OFF suppresses minor runtime errors.

`Execute statement`

Directly executes a Command Post statement.

`Exit`

Unconditionally ends the current menu item's operation.

`FileCopy(from-list, to-file, warning)`

Copies files. If *warning* is @TRUE, makes the user confirm if a file is going to be overwritten. *From-list* is a string with one or more filenames, which can contain wildcards. *To-file* may only contain one filename, but it can have wildcards. The function returns @TRUE if all files are copied successfully, or else it returns @FALSE.

`FileDelete(file-list)`

Deletes files contained in the *file-list* string. Returns @TRUE if successful; if not it returns @FALSE.

`FileExist(filename)`

Returns @TRUE if the *filename* exists; otherwise it returns @FALSE.

`FileExtension(filename)`

Returns the extension portion of *filename*.

`FileHilite(file-list,switch)`

Either highlights or unhighlights the filenames that match *file-list* depending on whether *switch* is @TRUE or @FALSE. *File-list* can contain wildcards.

`FileItemize(file-list)`

Builds a string containing a list of filenames separated by spaces. *File-list* may contain wildcards.

`FileLocate(filename)`

Finds a file within the current DOS path and returns its full pathname.

`FileMove(from-list,to-file,warning)`

Moves files to another set of directories. The syntax is the same as in FileCopy.

`FilePath(filename)`

Returns the full pathname of the file represented by *filename*.

`FileRename(from-list,to-file)`

Renames files to another set of names.

`FileRoot(filename)`

Returns the root portion of *filename*.

`FileSize(`*`file-list`*`)`

Adds up the total size of a list of files. This command doesn't recognize wildcards, but *file-list* can be the result of a FileItemize.

`IF(`*`logical expression`*`) THEN(`*`statement`*`)`

If (*logical expression*) evaluates to @TRUE, Command Post executes the (*statement*) following THEN. Otherwise, the next line following the IF statement is executed.

`GOTO(`*`label`*`)`

Causes Command Post to jump to (*label*) in the current program. This command is often used to create loops in Command Post program files.

`IniRead(`*`section, keyname, default`*`)`

Reads a string from the WIN.INI file. A *section* is a line surrounded by square brackets in the WIN.INI file, and *keynames* are the words that begin the lines within a section. If the specified *keyname* isn't found within the *section*, then the default is *returned*.

`IniWrite(`*`section,keyname,string`*`)`

Writes a *string* to the WIN.INI file under the *section* and *keyname* specified. The section and/or keyname will be created if they aren't already there.

`IsDefined(`*`variable`*`)`

Returns @TRUE or @FALSE, depending on whether or not the variable is currently defined.

`IsKeyDown(`*`special-key`*`)`

Returns @TRUE if *special-key* is pressed; otherwise it returns @FALSE. Special-key can be @SHIFT, @CONTROL, or both combined with the bitwise And (&) or Or (|) operator.

`IsLicensed( )`

Returns @TRUE if Command Post is licensed on this machine. Otherwise it returns @FALSE.

`IsMenuChecked(`*`menuitem-name`*`)`

Determines if a menu item is checked. Returns @TRUE or @FALSE.

`IsMenuEnabled(`*`menuitem-name`*`)`

Determines if a menu item is enabled. Returns @TRUE or @FALSE.

`IsNumber(`*`string`*`)`

Determines if a *string* represents a valid number.

`IsRunning( )`

Returns @TRUE if another copy of Command Post is running; otherwise it returns @FALSE.

ItemSelect(*title, list, delimiter*)

Displays a dialog box with a *title*, that contains a list box. The list box is filled with strings taken from the *list* that are separated by the *delimiter* character. Returns the item selected, an empty string if the user clicked OK without selecting anything, or else exits the menu if the user pressed Cancel.

LastError( )

Returns the number of the last error Command Post encountered.

LogDisk(*drive*)

Changes the logged disk drive to *drive*.

Max(*number [,number]...*)

Determines the highest of a series of *numbers*.

MenuChange(*menuitem-name,flags*)

Modifies the displayed characteristics of a *menu item. Flags* can be either @CHECK or @UNCHECK, @ENABLE or @DISABLE, or one from each set of flags combined with the Or (|) operator.

Message(*title,text*)

Displays *text* in a message box until the user presses the OK button.

Min(*number [,number]...*)

Determines the lowest of a series of *numbers*.

#NextFile(*menu-file*)

Declares a second Command Post *menu-file*, which will be loaded in after this one. You can only link one extra file in this way; if the second file contains another #NextFile declaration, it will be ignored.

Num2Char(*number*)

Converts a *number* to the ANSI character it represents.

OtherDir( )

Returns the current directory of the "other" running copy of Command Post, if there are any. This is the one copy that was most recently invoked.

`OtherUpdate( )`

Updates the display of another running copy of Command Post. This is useful after your menu copies or moves a file to the other Command Post directory.

`Pause(title,text)`

Same as the Message statement, except the user can press OK or Cancel. Pressing Cancel terminates the menu.

`Random(max)`

Generates a positive random number between 0 and *max*.

`Run(program-name,parameters)`

Runs program-name as a "normal" window, passing it the specified parameters, if any.

`RunHide(program-name,parameters)`

Runs *program-name* in a hidden window.

`RunIcon(program-name,parameters)`

Runs *program-name* as an icon.

`RunZoom(program-name,parameters)`

Runs *program-name* in a maximized window.

`SetDisplay(detail-level,sort-by,masks)`

Changes how the Command Post File Manager lists files. *Detail-level* is either "SHORT" or "LONG"; and *sort-by* can be "NAME", "KIND" (meaning by filename extension), "SIZE", "DATE", or "UNSORTED" (in the order that the MS-DOS DIR command would produce). *Mask* is a string containing one or more filenames to display (which can contain wildcards). If *detail-level*, *sort-by*, and *masks* are all empty strings, SetDisplay just refreshes the current directory listing.

`StrCat(string[,string]...)`

Concatenates one or more *strings* together.

`StrCmp(string1,string2)`

Compares two strings. The result is -1 if *string1* is less than *string2*, 0 if they're equal, or 1 if *string1* is greater than *string2*. You can also compare string expressions directly with the <, <=, ==, =>, >, and != operators.

`StrFill(string,string-length)`

Creates a string that is *string-length* characters long, which has been built up from repeating the (hopefully shorter) *string* parameter.

`StrFix(base-string,padding-string,length)`

Returns a string that is *string-length* characters long, which has been built up from either by padding the *base-string* with spaces or else by truncating it, so that it ends up a fixed *length*.

`StrICmp(string1,string2)`

Same as StrCmp, except that it ignores the strings' capitalization.

`StrIndex(main-string,sub-string,start-position,direction)`

Returns the position of *sub-string* within *main-string*. CPML searches for the *sub-string* starting at *start-position*, and looks either forward or backward within *main-string* depending on whether *direction* equals @FWDSCAN or @BACKSCAN. Returns 0 if *sub-string* was not found within *main-string*.

`StrLen(string)`

Returns the number of characters in a *string*.

`StrLower(string)`

Converts a *string* to all lower-case characters.

`StrReplace(string,old-substring,new-substring)`

Replaces all occurrences of *old-substring* within *string* to *new-substring*.

`StrScan(main-string,delimiters,start-position,direction)`

Looks for an occurrence of one or more characters in *main-string*. The characters to look for are grouped in the *delimiters* parameter. The *start-position* and *direction* of the search are determined the same way as for StrIndex.

`StrSub(main-string,start-position,length)`

Returns the substring within *main-string*, which starts at *start-position* and has *length* characters.

`StrTrim(string)`

Returns *string* after removing all the leading and trailing spaces from it.

StrUpper(*string*)

Converts a *string* to all upper-case characters.

Terminate(*expression,title,message*)

Ends the menu's operation if *expression* equals @TRUE. Also displays a notice unless both *title* and *message* are empty strings.

TextBox(*title,filename*)

Same as ItemSelect, except it fills the list box with text from the specified *filename*. Each string is assumed to be separated by a carriage return and linefeed.

Version( )

Returns the version of Command Post currently running.

WinActivate(*partial-title*)

Activates the application window whose title begins with *partial-title*.

WinArrange(*style*)

Arranges all running application windows on the screen. *Style* can be @STACK, @TILE, @ROWS, or @COLUMNS.

WinClose(*partial-title*)

Closes an application whose window title begins with *partial-title*.

WinCloseNot(*partial-title[,partial-title]...*)

Closes all application windows *except* those specified.

WinConfig( )

Returns the Windows configuration information as a number, which is built up from these individual flag bits:

1	Protect Mode	64	8086 CPU
2	80286 CPU	128	80186 CPU
4	80386 CPU	256	Large PageFrame
8	80486 CPU	512	Small PageFrame
16	Standard Mode	1024	80x87 Installed
32	Enhanced Mode		

WinExist(*partial-title*)

Returns @TRUE or @FALSE, depending on whether or not any application windows are running whose titles begin with *partial-title*.

WinGetActive( )

Returns the title of the active window.

WinHide(*partial-title*)

Hides the application windows matching *partial-title*.

WinIconize(*partial-title*)

Turns the named application window into an icon.

WinItemize( )

Builds a string containing the titles of all the applications currently running. Unlike FileItemize and DirItemize, these titles are separated by TAB characters since window titles often have embedded spaces.

WinPlace(*left,top,right,bottom,partial-title*)

Changes the size and position of an application window on the screen. The *left*, *top*, *right*, and *bottom* parameters are based on a coordinate system that is 1000 units wide by 1000 units high.

WinPosition(*partial-title*)

Returns a string consisting of the specified window's left, top, right, and bottom screen positions all separated by commas. The positions are in the same units as are used in the WinPlace command.

WinShow(*partial-title*)

Shows currently hidden application windows.

WinTitle(*partial-title,new-windowname*)

Changes the application windows' titles. Changes the current Command Post window's title if *partial-title* is a null string.

WinVersion(*which-level*)

Gets the version of Windows that is currently running. *Which-level* equals either @MAJOR or @MINOR, meaning either the integer part or the decimal part of the Windows version number is returned.

WinWaitClose(*partial-title*)

Waits until the specified application windows are closed.

WinZoom(*partial-title*)

Maximizes application windows to full-screen.

Yield

Pauses menu processing so other applications can gain control of the system for a while.

SUMMARY

As a shell for Windows, Command Post 7.0 isn't as pretty as Microsoft's Program Manager or File Manager, but it is actually much more useful. Unlike any of Microsoft's shells, Command Post lets you define your own menus with the robust Command Post Menu Language (CPML).

Windows' underlying philosophy of treating the user's environment as a collection of happily integrated objects on a seamless conceptual desktop is an admirable one. But let's face it, anyone who uses Windows regularly must still deal constantly with the myriad details of programs, windows, configuration files, subdirectories, data files, and the underlying MS-DOS operating system. By combining a good (if plain-looking) file manager with the flexibility of powerful custom menus, Command Post goes a long way in helping you deal with this reality. It also helps you create quite an efficient Windows workstation.

16

Aporia

Aporia is a shareware program from New Tools, Inc. that offers an alternative interface for Microsoft Windows. It combines many of the same functions as Program Manager and File Manager—launching programs and managing files—into a single package. Therefore, you might want to use it as a replacement for these two shells. However, unlike most Windows applications, which offer both a mouse and keyboard interface, Aporia caters primarily to the mouse.

Aporia provides an object-oriented approach to managing Windows. Like Program Manager, it presents program objects as icons. However, Aporia's icons are not confined to group windows. Instead, you can position them freely about the Windows desktop. Further, in Aporia, icons are called *tools*. The term "tool" is used to refer both to the icon itself and to the *object* that you attach to that icon. Objects can include such things as Windows or DOS applications, data files, directories, batch files and so on.

Aporia's tools are dynamic—that is, you can have them interact with one another. For example, you can use your mouse to drag a tool representing a data file onto another tool that represents an application. Aporia will then start that application and load the data file you specified.

Aporia also allows you to organize your tools into groups. One of the more commonly used tools in Aporia is called a *desk*. Desk tools are used to store groups of related tools. You can create multiple desks, each with a different name. In each desk, you can place one or more tools as well as other desks. For example, you could have a top-level desk called "Documents." Within this desk, you might have other desks like "WordPerfect" and "WordPerfect Files" or "Word for Windows" and "Word Files." To set up this same arrangement in Program Manager, you would either have to create one large group window or several smaller ones.

If you feel constrained by Program Manager and File Manager, Aporia may offer you a more free-form style of interface for organizing your desktop.

Note: Aporia is *not* public domain software—it is being distributed through this book as "shareware." See Appendix A for information on how to install Aporia and a summary of the registration procedure for the program.

APORIA BASICS

To install Aporia, you must run the Windows 3 Power Tools Setup program. (The use of this program is described in Appendix A.) This program copies Aporia's program files to a special directory on your hard disk, usually \AP-SETUP. Once this phase is completed, the Power Tools Setup program then runs Aporia's own version of Setup. This program, in turn, lets you choose the names of various directories in which Aporia's program files will ultimately be installed. (See Appendix A for a complete rundown on what these directories are.) Nevertheless, as a final step, the Aporia Setup program creates a Program Manager group window (entitled Aporia) and places an icon for the product in that window. Therefore, to run Aporia, you need only open this group window and double-click on the Aporia icon.

The first time you run Aporia, it will give you an opportunity to create a separate desk tool for each of your current Program Manager group windows. If you elect to take advantage of this option, it will present a dialog box showing the names of each of your Program Manager group windows. You can then select the ones you want. Aporia will then create a separate Desk Tool for each group window that you select. Within those desks, Aporia will place User Tools for each application in the group. This allows you to get a quick start with Aporia by creating tools for each of your applications.

The Default Tools

When you start Aporia, it displays a default set of tools on the Windows desktop, as shown in Figure 16-1. (You'll notice that the Program Manager window has been minimized to an icon, so that Aporia's tools are easier to see.) Each of the default tools is represented by an icon. Briefly, these tools perform the following functions:

- Tree: One of the most commonly-used tools in Aporia. You can use this tool to manage the files and directories on your hard disk. The use of the tool is covered in various spots throughout this chapter.

- Desk: The initial default desk tool for Aporia. This desk contains the default tools that are initially displayed by Aporia. You can, of course, add new tools or desks to this desk or create additional desks. See "Creating Desk Tools" later for a description of how you can use desk tools to organize your desktop.

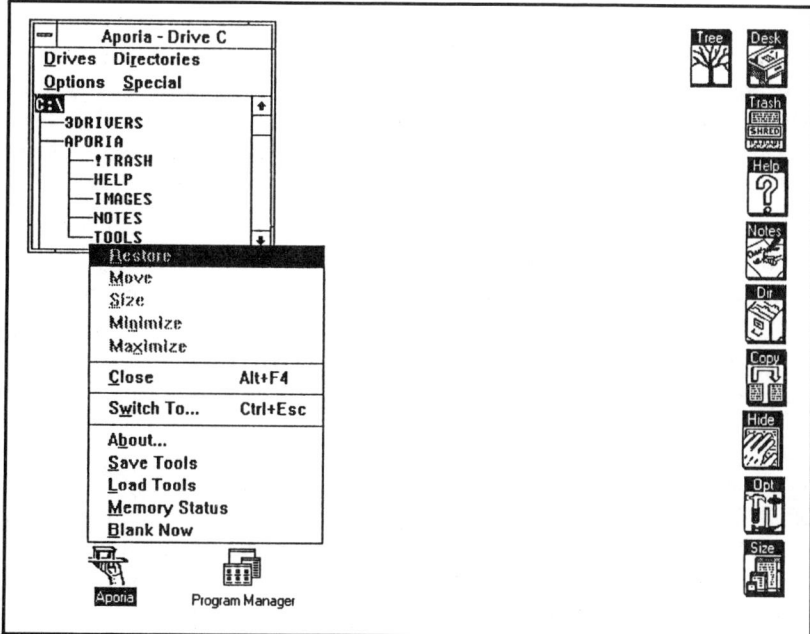

Figure 16-1 Aporia displays Tools on the Windows desktop that allow you to start applications and manage files and directories

- Trash: Lets you discard old and unneeded tools and erase their associated files on disk. All files that you delete with the aid of this tool are actually copied to a special \!TRASH directory on your hard disk. That way, if you change your mind, you can easily recover a file. However, if you leave Aporia without restoring the file, it will be gone forever. See "Removing Tools" later in this chapter for details on how to use this tool.

- Help: Provides access to on-line help for Aporia. See "Getting Help" later in this section for a description of how this tool is used.

- Notes: Lets you attach descriptive notes to Tools. See "Keeping Notes" later in this chapter for information on how to use this tool.

- Dir: Opens a Directory window that shows the files in the current directory. You can create and display up to 16 Directory Tools on the Windows desktop at any one time, each representing a different directory on your hard disk. Directory windows contain a special menu that lets you manage files (copy, move, rename, and delete them), sort the files in a directory, and create new User Tools.

- Copy: Lets you make copies of tools. See "Copying Tools" later for details on using this tool.

- Hide: You can use this tool to hide other tools that are displayed on the desktop. You can use this tool to help you avoid a cluttered display. See "Hiding Tools" later for information on how to use this tool to hide others.

- Opt: Lets you set various options for a tool. For example, you can change the name of the tool as well as its icon. Aporia comes with an assortment of icons from which you can choose. You can also use this tool to change the default settings for Aporia. See "Customizing Tools" later for a description of the various options you can set for a tool.

- Size: Lets you set the relative size and position of an application window. That way, each time you start an application, its window will always be displayed in a specific size and position on the desktop. See "Using the Size Tool" later for a description of how to use this tool.

The Aporia Menu

Unlike most Windows applications, Aporia does not run in a window. Instead, when you start Aporia, its tools are displayed on the Windows desktop. The only other evidence of Aporia is its icon, which appears at the bottom of your screen. When you click on this icon, a window Control menu is displayed, as shown in Figure 16-1. Because Aporia does not run in a window, all of the standard window manipulation commands (Restore, Minimize, and so on) appear greyed, meaning you cannot select them. However, the following menu options are available:

- Close: Closes Aporia, removing all its tools from the desktop. You can also use the ALT+F4 key sequence as an alternative to this option.

- Switch To: Displays the Windows Task List window, allowing you to quickly switch to a different application.

- About: Opens a dialog box that tells you all about Aporia and how you can become a registered user.

- Save Tools: Saves the tools that are currently displayed on the desktop. Normally, this is done when you close Aporia or when you leave Windows. However, this option allows you to guard against any data loss as the result of a system crash.

- Load Tools: Allows you to set up tools for each of the applications in your Program Manager group windows. A dialog box is displayed showing the names of your current group windows. You can select one or all of the names in the list. Aporia will then create a separate desk for each group window containing tools representing each application in the group.

- Memory Status: Displays a dialog box showing the free memory available to Aporia.

- Blank Now: Immediately turns on the Aporia screen blanker. The Windows desktop disappears momentarily and a small graphics image is displayed in its place. (Otherwise, by default, Aporia blanks the screen after five minutes of inactivity.)

Moving Tools

Aporia's tools can be moved to any location on the desktop by simply clicking on the tool and dragging it to its new location. To do this, begin by moving the mouse pointer

Figure 16-2 The "hot spot" for an Aporia tool is located in the upper-left corner of its icon

onto any tool. You'll notice that the shape of the mouse pointer changes to a hammer. When you click your mouse, the shape of the pointer changes to a pair of pliers. At that point, you can move the tool by simply dragging it to a new location and then releasing your mouse button.

Running Tools

You can run any tool by simply double-clicking on it. For example, if you have set up a tool representing an application, you can start that application by simply double-clicking on its tool. Alternatively, you can drag one tool on top of another. For example, as you'll soon see, you can create a user tool that represents a data file on your hard disk. Once that tool exists, you can drag it on top of an application tool and release your mouse button to have Aporia start the application and load that data file.

When you drag one tool on top of another, Aporia is rather particular about where you place the tool that is being dragged. The upper-left corner of each tool is referred to as the "hot spot," as indicated in Figure 16-2. You must position the hot spot of the tool you are dragging squarely on the tool you are dragging it to. Otherwise, if you just cover one tool with another, Aporia will respond by simply moving the tool you are dragging, and nothing will happen.

Getting Help

Aporia also offers an on-line help facility. However, Aporia does not use the standard Windows help program. Instead, through its Help tool, Aporia offers a series of windows that provide helpful information about each of its respective tools. For example, imagine you want to get help with the Tree tool. To do this, grab the Tree tool with your mouse and drag its upper-left corner on top of the Help tool. Aporia opens up a window that provides general information about how to use the Tree tool.

You can also set up custom help files for Aporia's Tools. For example, later, under "Creating User Tools," you'll learn how to create tools that represent applications and data files on your hard disk. To create a help file for one of these tools, simply drag it on top of the Help Tool. Aporia opens Notepad and passes it a parameter that includes the name of the tool followed by a .HLP extension. For example, if the name of the tool is WP.EXE, Aporia passes Notepad the parameter WP.HLP. If this Help file already exists, Notepad opens the file and displays it. On the other hand, if the file has not as yet been created, Notepad will inform you of this and give you an opportunity to create it. Once the file is displayed, you can type as much or as little text as you need. When you are done, save the file and close Notepad to return to Aporia. The next time you drag that same User Tool onto the Help Tool, Aporia will open Notepad and load the Help file you've just created.

Aporia also comes with two files, APORIA.INT and APORIA.MAN, that you can load into Write. APORIA.INT provides a topical tutorial-like approach to showing you how to use Aporia. APORIA.MAN, on the other hand, is a reprint of the Aporia manual without the illustrations.

USING TOOLS

As mentioned, Aporia is based on the concept of tools. Each tool is represented by an icon that is displayed on the Windows desktop. Aporia's tools can be used to represent programs, data files, and directories on your hard disk. Although Aporia comes with its own set of default tools, you can also create your own tools and link them to your applications, data files, and directories. In addition, you can organize tools into groups called desks. When you open a desk, its tools are displayed on the Windows desktop for your use. Conversely, when you have finished using the tools in a desk, you can close the desk, thereby removing its tools from the Windows desktop.

Aporia tools are separated into three groups: User Tools, Directory Tools, and Desk Tools. User tools provide access to your applications and their data files. Directory tools are used to provide access to specific directories on your hard disk. Desk tools are used to organize User Tools and Directory Tools into meaningful groups. The sections that follow show you how to create each of these kinds of tools.

Creating User Tools

To create user tools that represent applications and data files on your hard disk, you can use the Tree tool. When you double-click on this tool to run it, Aporia opens the Directory Tree window shown in the upper-left corner of Figure 16-1. This window contains a diagram of the directories on the current drive. Double-click on the name of directory that contains the executable file for one of your applications. For example, if you use WordPerfect as your word processor, you might double-click on the directory that contains WP.EXE. (You may have to use the Drives menu to change the drive for the Directory Tree window so that the appropriate directory is displayed on the directory tree.)

When you double-click on the name of a directory in the Directory Tree window, Aporia opens a Directory window displaying the names of files in that directory, as shown in Figure 16-3. This window is usually displayed immediately to the right of the Directory Tree window. Use the scroll bar to scroll the contents of the Directory window until the name of the executable file for your application appears, then click on the name of that file to select it. When you are ready, select the Special Make User Tool command from the Directory window's menu. Aporia hesitates for a moment and then creates a new user tool representing that application on the Windows desktop. The name of the executable file—for example, WP.EXE—appears as a description for the tool. You can now run the application by simply double-clicking on its tool.

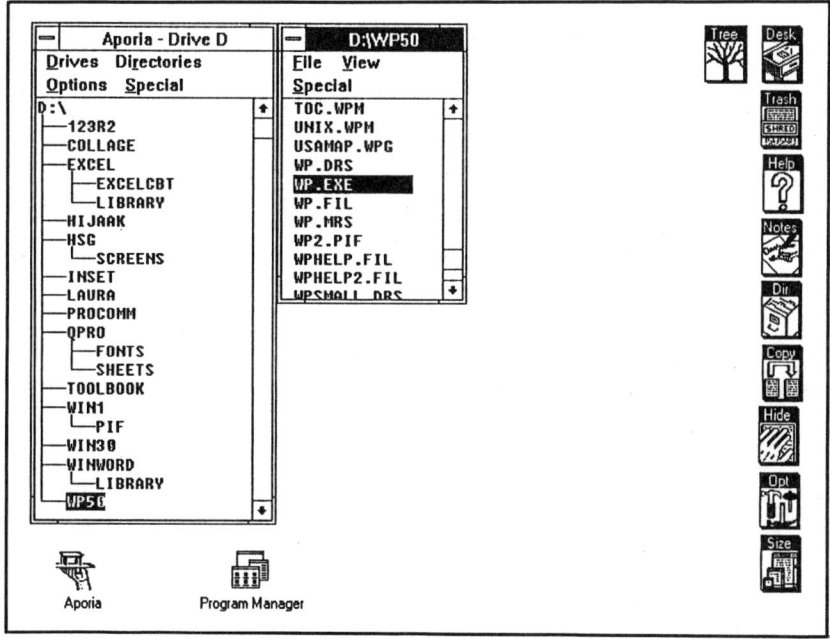

Figure 16-3 You can use Directory window to display the names of files in a directory and to create User Tools

Note: As an alternative to using the Special Make User Tool command to create a user tool, you can simply double-click your *right-hand* mouse button on the name of a file in a Directory window.

You can also create tools that represent data files for your applications. For example, imagine you want to create a user tool that represents a data file for the application user tool you've just created. To do this, double-click on the name of a directory in the Directory Tree window (left side of Figure 16-3) that contains the file you want to use. Aporia opens a second Directory window showing the files in the directory you've selected. Highlight the name of the data file you want to use and select the Special Make User Tool command. Aporia creates a tool that represents that data file.

If you've been following along, you now have two brand new User Tools displayed on the Windows desktop, one representing an application and the other representing a data file for that application. To give you an example of the interactive power of Aporia, drag the user tool for the data file onto the user tool for the application. Remember to locate the hot spot (the upper-left corner) of the data file's icon squarely on top of the icon for the application. When you release your mouse button, Aporia runs the application and automatically loads the data file into that application.

Note: See "Managing File and Directories" later in this chapter for additional ways you can use the Directory Tree window to manage the directories on your hard disk.

> **Tip: Running data files**
>
> You can also "run" a data file. That is, you can double-click on a User Tool that represents a data file. When you do this, Aporia loads the application that created the data file and then loads the data file into that application.

Creating Directory Tools

Directory Tools give you immediate access to the files in a specific directory without your having to use the Directory Tree window. When you run a Directory Tool by double-clicking on it, Aporia opens up a Directory window showing the files in a specific directory. This has two advantages. One the one hand, it has the effect of making that directory the current directory for Aporia's operations. On the other hand, it gives you instant access to the files in a specific directory without your having to navigate through the directory trees.

To create a Directory Tool, you must use the Tree Tool. Double-click on this tool to open the Directory Tree window (provided that it isn't open already) and select the name of a directory from the directory tree. When you are ready, select the Special Make Directory Tool command from the menu in the Directory Tree window. Aporia creates a Directory Tool for the directory that is currently selected in the directory tree and displays it on the Windows desktop. You can now double-click on that tool to open a Directory window for the directory whenever you want.

Note: As an alternative to the Special Make Directory Tool command, you can simply double-click your *right-hand* mouse button on the name of a directory in the Directory Tree window. Aporia will then create a Directory Tool for that directory.

Directory tools have a number of uses beyond that of simply opening a Directory window for a specific directory. For example, you can use a Directory Tool to make a specific directory current when you start an application. Earlier in this chapter you were encouraged to create a User Tool for one of your applications. If you want, you can drag the tool for that application on top of the Directory Tool you've just created. Aporia will make the directory represented by the Directory Tool the current directory for that application. You can then run the application by double-clicking on it, as usual.

You can also drag a User Tool that represents a data file onto a Directory Tool. This has the effect of copying the data file to the directory that is represented by the Directory Tool. See "Copying Files" later in this chapter for additional ways you can copy files with Aporia.

Note: A special Directory Tool is included in Aporia's default tool set. The name of this tool is simply Dir (Directory). Although it is a Directory Tool, it is not attached to any specific directory. When you run this tool by double-clicking on

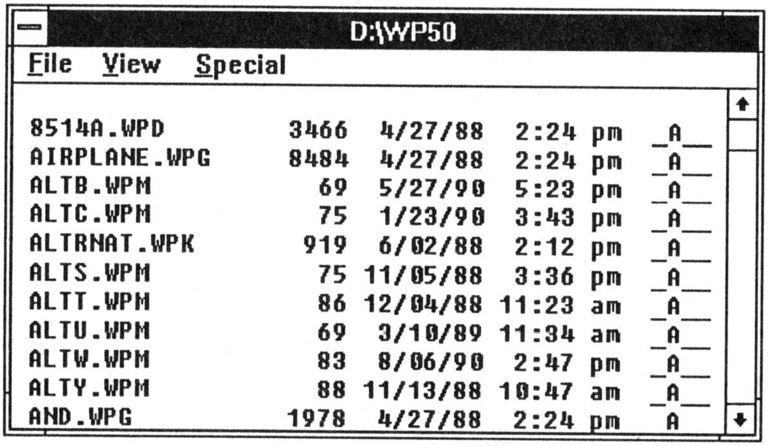

```
┌─────────────────────────────────────────────┐
│  —              D:\WP50                     │
│ File  View  Special                         │
├─────────────────────────────────────────────┤
│ 8514A.WPD      3466   4/27/88   2:24 pm  _A_│
│ AIRPLANE.WPG   8484   4/27/88   2:24 pm  _A_│
│ ALTB.WPM         69   5/27/90   5:23 pm  _A_│
│ ALTC.WPM         75   1/23/90   3:43 pm  _A_│
│ ALTRNAT.WPK     919   6/02/88   2:12 pm  _A_│
│ ALTS.WPM         75  11/05/88   3:36 pm  _A_│
│ ALTT.WPM         86  12/04/88  11:23 am  _A_│
│ ALTU.WPM         69   3/10/89  11:34 am  _A_│
│ ALTW.WPM         83   8/06/90   2:47 pm  _A_│
│ ALTY.WPM         88  11/13/88  10:47 am  _A_│
│ AND.WPG        1978   4/27/88   2:24 pm   A │
└─────────────────────────────────────────────┘
```

Figure 16-4 You can also use the Dir (Directory) Tool to open a Directory window

it, Aporia opens a Directory window for whatever directory happens to be current at the time. Figure 16-4 shows an example Directory window that was displayed by running the Dir Tool. Notice that in addition to the name of each file, this Directory window shows the size of each file in bytes, its date and time of creation, and any attribute that is currently assigned to the file. You can have any Directory window display file information in this way, if you so desire. See "Using the View Menu" later in this chapter under "Managing Files with Directory Windows" for details on how you can do this.

Copying Tools

You can use Aporia's Copy Tool to create replicas of existing tools. This is an easy way to create a new tool without using either the Directory Tree window or using a Directory window. For example, imagine that you want to create a new desk to store a new set of tools you are creating. To do this, drag the tool labeled Desk (located in the upper-right corner of your screen) on top of the Copy Tool. (Remember to locate the hot spot for the Desk Tool—its upper-left corner—squarely on top of the Copy Tool.) Aporia creates a new Desk tool with the same icon and the same description. In a moment, you'll learn how to store other tools in this desk and to change the name of this desk so that you can differentiate it from other desks you create.

Creating Desk Tools

Desk Tools allow you to organize your User Tools and Directory Tools into meaningful groups. In addition, you can store one Desk Tool within another, allowing you to create multiple layers of desks and access all of them from a single Desk Tool. Aporia's Desk Tools are often referred to simply as "desks," for short.

616 *Windows 3 Power Tools*

Aporia's default set of tools are stored under a single Desk Tool, labeled simply Desk. By default, this tool is located in the upper-right corner when you first start Aporia. Any new User or Directory Tools you've created up to this point are also associated with this desk. To give you an idea of what this means, double-click on this Desk Tool. All the tools displayed on your screen except the Hide Tool disappear from your screen. In effect, you have just put away the tools for that desk. To make your tools reappear, double-click on this tool a second time. The tools associated with that Desk Tool are restored to the Windows desktop.

Creating New Desks

To create a new desk, you use the Copy Tool as described above to make a replica of Aporia's default Desk Tool. Once the new desk is created, you can later change its name so that you can differentiate it from your other desk tools. See "Customizing Tools" later for details on how you can change the name of a tool.

Storing Tools in Desks

To store a User or Directory Tool in a Desk Tool, simply drag that tool onto the appropriate Desk Tool. Aporia displays the dialog box shown in Figure 16-5, asking you to confirm the operation. Select OK to have Aporia store the tool in the desk. The next time that you double-click on that Desk Tool, Aporia will remove the User or Directory Tool from the desktop and store it in the Desk Tool.

You cannot store the same tool in two different desks. If a tool is already stored in one desk and you attempt to store it in another desk, Aporia takes the tool out of the old desk and puts it in the new one. You can, however, make a copy of a tool and store that copy in a different desk. That way, you can have the same tool in two different desks. See "Copying Tools," earlier, for a description of how you can make a copy of a tool.

You can also store one desk within another. To do this, simply drag the Desk Tool you want to store on top of its parent Desk Tool, then select OK to confirm the operation. The next time you double-click on the parent Desk Tool, Aporia will remove the child Desk Tool from the desktop and store it in the parent Desk Tool.

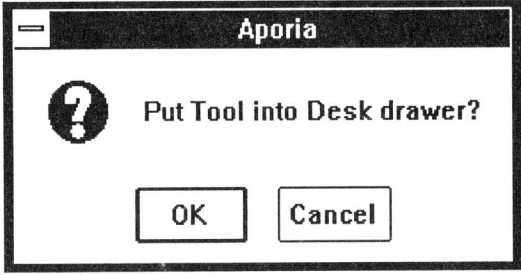

Figure 16-5 Aporia allows you to organize your tools by storing them in desks

As mentioned, you can double-click on a Desk Tool to have the tools it contains displayed on your desktop. However, when one desk is stored within another, opening the parent desk serves only to display the tools contained in that desk. This includes other desks it may contain. To see the contents of a "child desk," you must double-click on it separately.

Customizing Tools

Aporia provides an extensive system for customizing the appearance and operation of tools. To customize a tool, grab that tool with your mouse and drag it on top of Aporia's Opt (Options) Tool. Aporia displays the dialog box shown in Figure 16-6. By modifying the contents of this dialog box, you can set options for the current tool. Briefly, the following options are available:

- Displayed Name: Displays the name that is currently assigned to the tool. However, you can type a new name of up to 30 characters. You might use this feature to change the name of a Desk Tool so that you can differentiate it from other Desk Tools. You might also want to use this feature to assign more descriptive names to your data

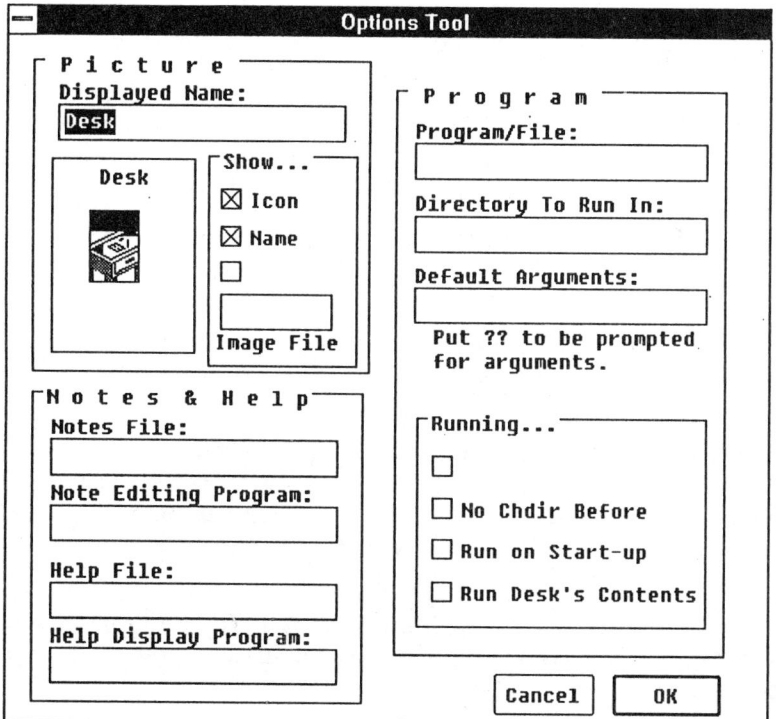

Figure 16-6 Aporia allows you to set options for its tools

file and application tools. For purposes of display, this feature, in effect, allows you to overcome the eight character limit that is imposed on you by DOS.

- Show: Lets you change the appearance of the current tool. The Icon, Name, and Dir check boxes control the display of the icon for the tool, its description, and its directory (Directory Tools only). For example, if you clear the Icon check box, only the name of the tool will be displayed.

- Image File: Allows you to specify the name of an image file (bitmap) you want to use in place of the current one. When you installed Aporia, it copied a series of Aporia Image Files (files with a .AIF extension) for different applications to an \APORIA\IMAGES directory. You can type the name of any one of these image files to have it displayed as the icon for the current tool. When you type the name if an image file, Aporia will search for that file in the \APORIA\IMAGES directory. If it finds the file, Aporia will display it in the Displayed Icon window to the left. Alternatively, you can create your own image file and specify its name in the Image File text box. See the next section, "Creating Image Files," for details on how you can create your own Aporia Image Files.

- Notes File: Later, under "Keeping Notes," you'll learn how you can use the Notes Tool to have Aporia start a text editor—for example, Notepad—and load a file into that editor that displays notes for the current tool. This text box allows you to specify the name of the file that will be loaded. If you are changing options for a user tool, you must prepare this file yourself before actually using it.

- Note Editing Program: Lets you specify the file name of the text editor that will be used to display note files for the current tool. This editor will be used when you drag the current tool onto the Notes Tool. A common choice for a text editor is NOTEPAD.EXE.

- Help File: This box is only used for User Tools. Nevertheless, you can use this box to specify the name of a help file you want Aporia to load when you drag this icon onto the Help Tool. You must prepare this file yourself in advance.

- Help Display Program: The executable filename of a text editor that will be used for help files. A common choice here is NOTEPAD.EXE.

- Program/File: If you are changing options for a User Tool that starts an application, this text box shows the path and name of that application's executable file. You can change the current entry to show the path and name of another application, if you so desire. This lets you completely change the character and function of the current tool without having to delete an old tool and create a new one.

- Directory To Run In: If you are changing options for a User Tool that starts an application, this text box shows the directory in which that application resides. However, you can change this entry to have a specific directory made current when you start the application.

- Default Arguments: If you are changing options for a User Tool that starts an application, this text lets you pass parameters to the application. For example, if you want a specific data file to be loaded each time you start the application, you enter the path and name of that data file in this box. If you place two question marks (??) in this box, Aporia will prompt you for the parameters when you start the application.

- Default: You can use this check box to select from one of three different modes for running an application: Default, Fullscreen, or Iconic. Clicking repeatedly will cycle you through each of these three options. If you select Default, Aporia will run the application in a window whose default size and position is set by Windows or by the Size Tool. If you select Fullscreen, the application will run in a maximized window. If you select Iconic, Aporia will start the application and immediately minimize it to an icon.

- No Chdir Before: Instructs Aporia to ignore any entry in the Directory To Run In text box. You might use this check box when you want an application to start up in its own directory.

- Run On Startup: Runs the current tool whenever you start Aporia. This check box allows you to run a specific application whenever you start Aporia.

- Run Desks Contents: If you are setting options for a Desk Tool, this check box allows you to specify that all the tools in a desk be run when you double-click on the Desk Tool. This check box provides a convenient way to set up a work session that requires the use of multiple applications.

Note: You can set general parameters that apply to all of Aporia's tools by double-clicking on the Opt (Options) tool. When you do this, Aporia displays a dialog box that lets you modify many of the default settings both for its tools and for its general operation. These include such features as the maximum tool size in pixels, the font, size and color used for the names of Directory and User Tools, the status of trash management, and the text editor used to display Help and Notes files.

Creating Aporia Image Files

Aporia comes with a utility called Image Maker that lets you capture screen elements and save them as Aporia Image Files (.AIF bitmap files). Once you have saved an .AIF file, you can display it as an icon for one of Aporia's Tools.

The Image Maker utility allows you to capture an icon, an area of the screen, or an entire window and save it as a .AIF file. Therefore, you can borrow an icon from another application and save it is as a .AIF file, or you can create your image with a draw package—for example, Paintbrush or Icondraw—and save it as an .AIF file.

To run the Image Maker utility, use the Tree Tool to open the Directory window and then double-click on the directory containing Aporia. Aporia opens up a Directory window showing the names of files in that directory. Find the file IMAGEMKR.EXE and double-click on it. Aporia opens the Image Maker utility window shown in Figure 16-7. Minimize this window to an icon for now.

Figure 16-7 The Image Maker window

To create an Aporia Image File, begin by deciding on an area of the screen you want to capture. It can be an icon from another Windows application or an image you have created in Paintbrush. When you are ready, restore the Image Maker window by double-clicking on its icon. Then, open the Capture menu. Aporia displays a pull-down menu with the following options:

- Area: Lets you capture an area of your screen. When you select this option, Aporia changes the shape of the mouse pointer to a crosshair. Click on the upper-left corner of the area you want to capture and hold your mouse button down. Then, drag to the lower-right corner of the area. As you drag, Aporia builds a box around the area of the screen you've selected. When you are ready, release your mouse button. Aporia copies the area of the screen you have selected to the Image Maker window. You might use this option to select an image that you have created in Paintbrush. However, try to keep the area you capture small—about one inch by one inch. When Aporia copies the image to the Image Maker window, it shrinks it to a 32 x 32 pixel size. If the copied image is larger than this, it may become distorted when its size is reduced.

- Icon: Lets you capture an icon from another application. When you select this option, Aporia changes the shape of the mouse pointer to a large vertical arrow. Click on any icon that is displayed on your screen. Aporia copies that icon to the Image Maker window.

- Window: Lets you capture an entire window. When you select this option, Aporia changes the shape of the mouse pointer to a large vertical arrow. Click on any window that is displayed on your screen. Aporia copies an image of the window you've selected to the Image Maker window. Aporia reduces the size of that image to make it small enough for use as an icon (approximately 32 x 32 pixels). This tends to distort the image of the window.

Once you have captured an icon, an area of the screen, or a window, you are ready to save that image to an .AIF file. To do this, select the File Save command from Image Maker's window. Aporia presents a dialog box that allows you to assign a name to the file. Type a name of eight characters or less and make sure you use the .AIF extension. When you select OK or press ENTER to confirm the filename, Aporia saves the file to the \APORIA\IMAGES directory.

To have your new image file displayed as an icon for one of your User or Directory Tools, drag that tool on top of the Opt (Options) Tool. Aporia displays the Options Tool dialog box shown earlier in Figure 16-6. This dialog box displays the settings for the current tool. Type the name of your new Aporia Image File in the Image File text box. Aporia displays the image in the Displayed Icon window to the left. Select OK to return to Aporia and have your new image file displayed as an icon for the current tool.

Note: As mentioned, your new image file may appear distorted because Aporia has reduced its size. You may be able to improve on its appearance, though, by increasing the displayed size of Aporia's tools. To do this, double-click on the Opt (Options) icon to have Aporia display the General Options dialog box and select the Set Tool Size push button. Aporia displays a second dialog box that displays the value 32, meaning 32 x 32 pixels. You can increase this value as high as 99 pixels, thereby tripling the displayed size of all of Aporia's tools.

The Image Maker window offers two other menu options that you may find useful. For example, you can use the File Load command to open an image file. This allows you to check what is in a specific image file when you cannot remember. The Options menu contains a single option, Displayed Size, that lets you set the displayed height and width of the current image in pixels.

Getting Information about a Tool

You can easily get information about any tool that is displayed on the desktop. To do this, simply double-click your *right-hand* mouse button on that tool. Aporia displays the dialog box in Figure 16-8. This dialog box contains information about the tool itself as well as the desk in which it is stored.

Hiding Tools

You can use Aporia's Hide Tool to hide individual tools temporarily. This allows you to avoid a cluttered desktop. To do this, drag any tool, except a Desk Tool, onto the Hide Tool. That tool then disappears from your screen. You can easily restore that tool to the desktop at a later time by double-clicking on its Desk Tool.

Keeping Notes

Aporia allows you to maintain a note file for any tool on the desktop, which provides a powerful method of documenting your applications and data files. To do this, drag any

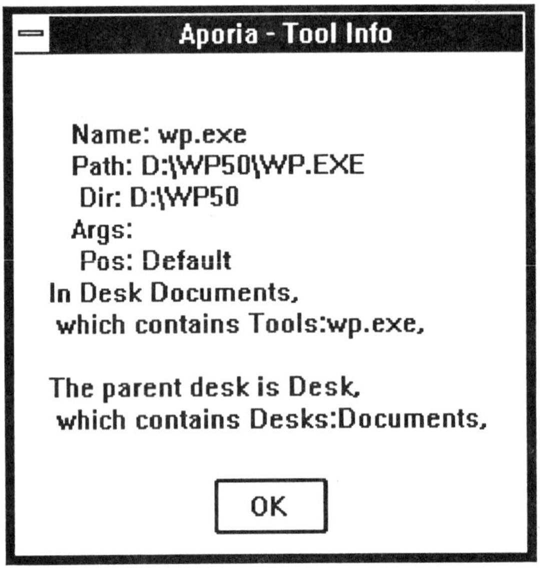

```
┌─────────────────────────────────────┐
│ ═           Aporia - Tool Info      │
├─────────────────────────────────────┤
│                                     │
│     Name: wp.exe                    │
│     Path: D:\WP50\WP.EXE            │
│     Dir: D:\WP50                    │
│     Args:                           │
│      Pos: Default                   │
│   In Desk Documents,                │
│     which contains Tools:wp.exe,    │
│                                     │
│   The parent desk is Desk,          │
│     which contains Desks:Documents, │
│                                     │
│              ┌──────┐               │
│              │  OK  │               │
│              └──────┘               │
└─────────────────────────────────────┘
```

Figure 16-8 You can double-click your right mouse button on a tool to get information about it

tool on top of the Notes Tool. If a notes file already exists for that tool, Aporia will open Notepad and load that file. If a notes file does not already exist, Aporia will inform you of this by displaying a message box. When you select OK to clear this message box, Notepad takes over and asks you if you want to create a file with the name that begins with the name of the current tool followed by a .TXT extension. Select OK to create the file. You can then type any notes you may feel are pertinent to the current tool. When you are done, use the File Save command to save the file, and close the Notepad window to return to Aporia.

Removing Tools

Suppose you've created a tool you no longer need and you want to permanently remove that tool from the desktop. To do this, simply grab that tool with your mouse and drag it on top of the Trash Tool. Aporia displays a Yes/No message asking you to confirm the deletion. If you select Yes, Aporia displays a second Yes/No/Cancel message box asking you if you also want the file associated with that tool deleted from your hard disk. If you select Yes, Aporia removes the tool from the desktop and deletes its associated file on disk. If you select No, Aporia simply removes the tool from the desk top and leaves the file on disk alone. Finally, if you select Cancel, Aporia cancels the delete operation altogether and neither the tool nor its associated file is affected.

When you use the Trash Tool to delete a file on your hard disk, and trash management is enabled (the default), Aporia doesn't delete it right away. Instead, it moves the file to a special directory (\APORIA\!TRASH). That way, you can recover the file if you need to. However, if you quit Aporia or leave Windows before recovering the trashed file, the \TRASH directory is cleared and the file is lost.

To reclaim files from the \!TRASH directory, double-click on the Trash Tool. Aporia displays a dialog box with two push buttons, Restore Files and Empty Trash. If you select Restore Files, Aporia opens a Directory Window displaying the files in the Trash directory. You can then copy the files you want to save to another directory. See "Copying Files" later under "Managing Files with Directory Windows" for details on how you can copy files from one directory to another. On the other hand, if you select the Empty Trash push button, Aporia will remove all files in the \!TRASH directory, deleting them permanently from your hard disk.

Using the Size Tool

The Size Tool lets you control the size and position of application windows. To use this tool, first use an existing tool to start a Windows application. Once that application is open, adjust the size of its window to meet your needs. When you are ready, drag the application tool of your choice onto the Size Tool. Aporia displays a Yes/No/Cancel message box. If you select Yes, the message box is cleared and an icon is displayed that follows the movement of your mouse pointer. Click on the title bar of the application window whose size you have just finished adjusting. Aporia assigns the sizing for the window you've selected to the current tool. The next time you use that tool to start an application, Aporia will adjust the size and position of the application's window to meet the specifications you've defined.

To remove sizing from a tool, simply drag that tool onto the Size Tool. Aporia displays the Yes/No/Cancel dialog box. Select No to clear the sizing settings for the current tool.

MANAGING FILES AND DIRECTORIES

Like the Windows File Manager, Aporia allows you to manage files and directories. For example, you can create new directories, delete old ones, or rename directories. You can also copy, move, rename, and delete files.

To manage files and directories with Aporia, you can use a combination of the Tree tool and Directory windows. The Tree tool allows you to manage directories, and Directory windows allow you to manage files.

Managing Directories with the Tree Tool

To manage directories with Aporia, you use the Tree Tool. When you double-click on this tool, Aporia opens the Directory Tree window, shown earlier in Figure 16-1. This window contains a graphical representation of the structure of the directories on the current drive. The root directory, usually C:\, appears highlighted. To make another directory current, simply click on the name of that directory in the directory tree.

The Directory Tree comes with its own menu that you can use to manage the directories on your hard disk and to create Directory Tools for the Aporia desktop. The sections that follow show you how to go about using these commands.

Changing Drives

You can use the Drives menu to select from the different drives on your system. When you select this menu option, Aporia displays a pull-down menu showing the letters of the drives that are available on your system. (If you are connected to network drives, those drives appear in the list as well.) When you select a drive, Aporia updates the Directory Tree window to show the directories on that drive. The root directory for the drive you've selected appears highlighted in the directory tree. You can, of course, click on the name of any directory in the directory tree to make that directory current.

Using the Directories Menu

The Directories menu lets you create a new directory, delete an old one, or rename a directory on the current drive. Before using this menu option, select the name of a directory from the directory tree below. Any operation you perform with the Directories menu will then apply to that directory.

To create a new subdirectory for the current directory, select the Create option from the Directories menu. Aporia displays the dialog box shown in Figure 16-9. Type the name for the new directory and select OK or press ENTER to create it.

To delete the directory that is currently on the directory tree, select the Delete option from the Directories menu. Aporia displays a dialog box asking you to confirm the deletion. Select OK to delete the directory.

Note: Aporia will not allow you to delete a directory that contains either files or subdirectories. Therefore, if you want to delete such a directory, you must first delete the files or subdirectories it contains. See "Deleting Files" later under "Managing Files with Directory Windows" for information on how you can use Aporia to delete the files in a directory.

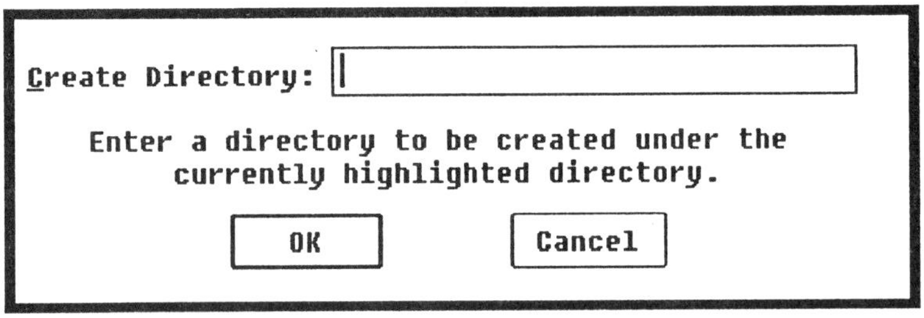

```
Create Directory: |
    Enter a directory to be created under the
         currently highlighted directory.
              [  OK  ]     [ Cancel ]
```

Figure 16-9 Aporia allows you to create new directories

To change the name of the directory that is currently selected on the tree, select the Rename option from the Directories menu. Aporia displays a dialog box with two text boxes entitled Rename and To, respectively. Only the To box is enabled, and the name of the current directory appears in the Rename box. Type the new name for the directory in the To box and press ENTER or select OK. Aporia renames the directory with the new name you've specified.

Using the Options Menu

The Options menu allows you to display a Directory window that is linked to the Directory Tree window. Whenever you click on a new directory in the Directory Tree window, the linked Directory Window is updated to display the files in that directory. To create a Directory window of this kind, open the Options menu in the Directory Tree window. This menu contains a single option, Directory Window. When you select this option, Aporia opens a Directory window that is linked to the currently displayed directory tree. When you open a Directory window that is linked to the directory tree, that window is displayed immediately to the right. Further, when you move the Directory Tree window, its associated Directory window moves along with it.

Using the Special Menu

The Special menu contains three options, Make Directory Window, Make Directory Tool, and Disk Information. These options allow you to perform the following functions:

- Make Directory Window: Lets you open a Directory window for the currently selected directory in the directory tree. However, that Directory window is not linked to the directory tree. As an alternative to this command, you can simply double-click your left mouse button on the name of a directory in the directory tree.

- Make Directory Tool: Lets you create a directory tool that represents the directory currently selected on the directory tree. Once that tool exists, you can use it to open a Directory window for that specific directory whenever you want. The use of this option is discussed in more detail above in the section on "Creating Directory Tools." As an alternative to this command, you can double-click your *right-hand* mouse button on the name of a directory in the directory tree.

- Disk Information: When you select this option, Aporia displays a dialog box that shows you the total capacity of the current drive, the total amount of free space on that drive, and number of directories it contains.

Managing Files with Directory Windows

To manage files with Aporia, you must use a Directory window. As you know, Directory windows are used to display the files in a specific directory. In addition to displaying a list of files, though, Directory windows include a menu system that allows you to manage the files in the current directory. This section familiarizes you with the available menu options and how you can use them to manage files from within Aporia.

Opening Directory Windows

Aporia allows you to open Directory windows in several ways. On the one hand, you can use the Tree tool as described earlier to open the Directory Tree window. Once that window is displayed, you can double-click on the name of any directory to open a Directory window for that directory.

As an alternative to using the Tree Tool, you can use Aporia's Dir (Directory) Tool. When you double-click on this tool, Aporia opens a Directory window, as shown earlier in Figure 16-4. Normally, Aporia only displays the names of files in a Directory window. However, when you use the Dir Tool to access a Directory window, additional information is displayed for each file including its size in bytes, its date and time of creation, and any attributes that may be assigned to the file. You can have any Directory display your files in this way by using the View Long command. See "Using the View Menu" later for more details on this command.

A Directory window accessed with the Dir Tool shows the contents of the current directory. When you start Aporia, the current directory is your root (C:\) directory. However, you can change the current directory for Aporia by using the Tree Tool to open the Directory Window and selecting the name of the directory from the directory tree. The contents of the directory you select will be displayed in the Directory window that you open with the Dir Tool.

Note: You can also create a directory tool for a specific directory. That way you can open a Directory window for a specific directory, other than the current directory, whenever you want to. See "Creating Directory Tools" earlier in this chapter for more details on this.

Selecting Files

Most of the commands offered in the Directory window menu require that you select one or more files to which the command will apply. You can select a single file from a Directory window by clicking on its name. When you click on the name of a file, Aporia moves the highlight to that file, indicating that it is selected. To select multiple files scattered throughout a Directory window, hold down the CTRL key and click on each of the files you want to select. To select a group of files, hold down the SHIFT and click on the first and last items in the group. To select all the files in a Directory window, choose the Special Select All command from the Directory window menu.

Running Applications

To run an application, you can select the File Run command from the directory-window menu. When you select this command, Aporia presents a dialog box prompting you for the name of the file you want to run. Type the name of an executable file and select OK or press ENTER to run the file. As an alternative to using the File Run command, you can simply double-click on the name of an executable file in a Directory window to have Aporia run that file.

Note: You can also create a User tool for an application and have it displayed on the Windows desktop. Once that tool is displayed, you can double-click on it to run the application. See "Creating User Tools" earlier in this chapter for details on how to do this.

Copying Files

In Aporia, you can copy files in one of two ways. On the one hand, you can use the File Copy command from the Directory window menu. On the other hand, you can use your mouse to copy a file from one Directory window to another.

To use the File Copy command to copy a file, first select the name of the file you want to copy from the current Directory window, then select File Copy. Aporia displays a dialog box with two text boxes entitled Copy and To, respectively. The name of the currently selected file appears in the Copy box. In the To text box, type the path and name of the directory that you want to copy the file to. (You can also specify a new name for the file if you want.) To execute the copy, select OK.

As an alternative to the File Copy command, you can use your mouse to simply drag the name of a file from one Directory window to another. To do this, both the source and destination Directory windows must be open on the desktop. Click your left mouse button on the name of the file in the source Directory window and drag it to the destination Directory window. (When you begin to drag, Aporia transforms the shape of the mouse pointer to an icon.) When you are ready, release your mouse button. Aporia displays a dialog box asking you to confirm the copy. Select OK to complete the copy operation.

Note: You can also copy a file to a directory by dragging the tool for a data file onto a Directory Tool.

Moving Files

You can also move files from one directory to another by using the File Move command or by dragging with your mouse. To use the File Move command, begin by selecting the name of the file you want to move from the current Directory window. When you are ready, select the File Move command. Aporia displays a dialog box that contains two text boxes entitled Move and To, respectively. The name of the currently selected file appears in the Move box. In the To text box, type the name of the directory to which you want to move the file. To execute the move, select OK.

You can also move a file by dragging it from one Directory window to another with your mouse. Obviously, both the source and destination Directory windows must be open before you attempt this operation. Once both windows are open, click your *right-hand* mouse button on the file you want to move in the source window, then drag that file to the destination window and release the mouse button. (As you begin to drag, Aporia transforms the shape of the mouse pointer to an icon.) Aporia then displays a dialog box asking you to confirm the move. Select OK to complete the move operation.

Renaming Files

You can also change the name of a file by using the File Rename command from the Directory window menu. First, however, select the file whose name you want to change from the list of files in the current Directory window. When you are ready, select the File Rename command. Aporia displays a dialog box that contains two text boxes labeled Rename and To, respectively. The name of the currently selected file appears in the Rename box. Type the new name for the file in the To text box and press ENTER to rename the file.

Deleting Files

To delete a file from your hard disk, you can either use the File Delete command from the Directory window menu or use your mouse to drag the file to the Trash Tool. To use the File Delete command, begin by selecting the file from an open Directory window. Once you have made your selection, select the File Delete command from the Directory window menu. Aporia displays a dialog box asking you to confirm the deletion. Select OK to delete the file.

To delete a file by using your mouse, click on the name of that file in an open Directory window and drag it to the Trash Tool. Aporia displays a dialog box asking you to confirm the deletion. Select OK to delete the file. Aporia copies the file to its \APORIA\!TRASH directory located on the drive on which you've installed Aporia. That way, you can recover the file if you later change your mind. See "Removing Tools" earlier on this chapter for details on how you can recover files from the \!TRASH directory.

Using the View Menu

You can use the View option from the Directory window menu to control how the contents of a Directory window are displayed. For example, you can change the order of the files in the current Directory window. You can also limit the list of files displayed to a specific group that you select. When you open the View menu, the following options are available:

- Long: Causes the current Directory window to show all information that is available for each file, including the file's name, size in bytes, date and time of creation, and the attributes that are currently assigned to the file.

- Short: Causes only the names of files to be displayed in the current Directory window. All other information about the files is suppressed. (This is the default setting.)

- All: Causes all the files in a directory to be displayed in the current Directory window.

- Partial: Displays a dialog box that lets you specify one or more groups of files to be displayed in the current Directory window. In the text box provided, enter one or more file specifications that describe the group(s) of files you want to display. Separate each file specification with a space. For example, to display only those files with a .BMP or .WRI extension, enter ***.BMP   *.WRI**. Select OK to implement the change.

- Programs: Displays only those files in the current directory that have a .EXE, .COM, or .BAT extension.
- By Name: Sorts all displayed files alphabetically by name (the default).
- By Size: Sorts all displayed files by their relative size, working from smallest to largest.
- By Date: Sorts all displayed files by date and time of creation, working from newest to oldest.
- By Kind: Sorts all displayed files alphabetically by file extension.
- Update: Causes Aporia to reread the directory that is currently displayed in a Directory window. You might want to use this option if you are working on a network. For example, imagine another user has added a file to the current directory without your knowledge. To make sure you are using the most up-to-date information, you can have Aporia reread the current directory and refresh the files list for the current Directory window.

Using the Special Menu

The Special menu contains commands that let you create user tools, select files, and get information about the size of a group of files. The following options are available on this menu:

- Make User Tool: Creates User Tools for the files that are selected in the current Directory window. See "Creating User Tools" earlier in the chapter for more details on how to use this option.
- Make Directory Tool: Lets you create a directory tool for the directory that is displayed in the current Directory window. See "Creating Directory Tools" earlier in this chapter for more details on how to use this option.
- Select All: Selects all the files in the current Directory window. You can then issue a command that affects all the files in the directory.
- Disk Space Used: When you select this option, Aporia displays a dialog box that shows you the total size in bytes of all the files that are selected in the current Directory window.

SUMMARY

This chapter provides a brief overview of the commands and options that are available from Aporia. You now know enough about Aporia to get you started. For example, you now know how to create User Tools and Directory Tools that represent the applications, data files, and directories on your hard disk. You can use these tools to start applications as well as view the files in a given directory whenever you want.

You also know how to use Aporia to manage directories and files on your hard disk. For example, you now know how to copy, rename, or delete directories and files. If you want, you can now begin using Aporia as your gateway to Windows.

17
Icondraw

Icondraw is a drawing program written by Philip B. Eskelin, Jr. that lets you create your own custom icons to use with any application. With Icondraw, you can create 16-color 32x32 pixel icons that are stored in icon (.ICO) files. After creating an .ICO file, you can use it to replace an application's icon in Program Manager.

Figure 17-1 shows the Icondraw window with a finished icon. Notice that there are two areas where the icon appears. On the left is the area where you actually draw the icon. On the right is the viewing area, which shows how the icon will appear on the screen. As you draw your icon on the left, Icondraw instantly updates the viewing area on the right.

Because Icondraw is so easy to work with, many power users don't need any guidance whatsoever on its commands or options. However, almost everyone needs to know how to use an .ICO file in Program Manager, so that topic is covered first.

Note: Icondraw is *not* public domain or free software—it is being distributed as "shareware." See Appendix A for information on how to install Icondraw and a summary of the registration procedure for the program.

632   *Windows 3 Power Tools*

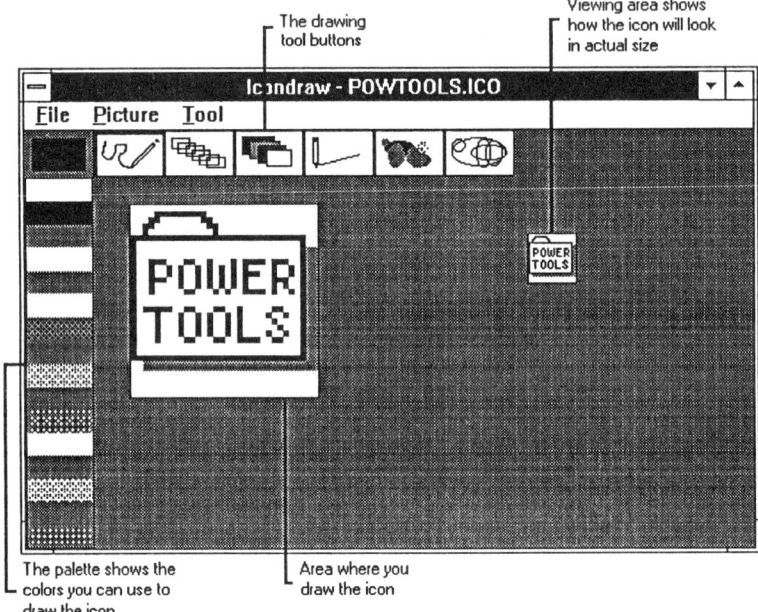

Figure 17-1 The Icondraw window

USING AN .ICO FILE IN PROGRAM MANAGER

After creating an icon in Icondraw, it's easy to substitute it for an application's icon in Program Manager. Here are the steps:

1. After saving an .ICO file in Icondraw, switch to Program Manager and highlight the program whose icon you want to change.
2. Select File Properties and choose the Change Icon button.
3. Type the name of the .ICO file, including the path and file extension.
4. Select OK twice.

THE DRAWING TOOLS

Whether you are editing an existing icon or creating a new icon from scratch, you use the tools at the top of the Icondraw window to draw your icon. You can choose a tool by clicking on its button or selecting its name from the Tool menu. Table 17-1 describes Icondraw's tools.

Button	Tool	Description
	Pencil	Fills the drawing area with the current drawing color on a pixel-by-pixel basis.
	Box	Draws a hollow rectangle using the current drawing color.
	Filled Rectangle	Draws a rectangle and fills it with the current drawing color.
	Line Draw	Draws a straight line between two selected points using the current drawing color.
	Ellipse	Draws a circle or ellipse and fills it with the current drawing color.
	Hollow Ellipse	Draws a hollow circle or ellipse using the current drawing color.

Table 17-1 Icondraw's Drawing Tools

THE COLOR PALETTE

A palette of 16 colors appears at the left of the Icondraw window, while the selected color appears at the upper-left corner above the palette. You can change colors at any time while drawing an icon. To choose a color from the color palette, simply click on it. You can also select a color by using the Color option from the Picture menu.

Here are some things to keep in mind as you use colors in Icondraw:

- If you use any colors other than black and white, your icon may not be as recognizable on a monochrome system as it is on an EGA or VGA system. In other words, colors that appear on an EGA or VGA system may not show up at all on a monochrome screen.
- The icons you create with Icondraw are opaque. That is, the desktop's background color will not show through any part of the icon. If you want to create an icon whose "background" appears to be transparent, you should match that background color

634 *Windows 3 Power Tools*

with the group window's background color (usually white), as was done with the area around the file folder in Figure 17-1.

USING THE CLIPBOARD

Icondraw lets you paste bitmap information from the Clipboard using the Paste Bitmap command from the Picture menu. You can paste bitmaps that you've created using either of the following methods:

- An image you've created using Paintbrush or another paint program and cut or copied to the Clipboard.
- A window or full-screen image you copied to the Clipboard using ALT+PRINTSCREEN or PRINTSCREEN.

When you load a bitmap from the Clipboard into Icondraw, only the first 32x32 pixels of the bitmap will appear. If you want to paste another portion of the Clipboard's bitmap, you must first paste the entire bitmap into Paintbrush, then cut or copy that portion of the bitmap you want back to the Clipboard. You can then return to Icondraw and paste the image you want.

NOTES ON ICONDRAW

Here are notes you may find useful when using Icondraw:

- Icondraw comes with nine sample icons that you can use right away. Figure 17-2 shows them.
- Icondraw has trouble reading certain icon files created with SDKPaint, the application that Windows programmers use to create .ICO files. In particular, if an icon file created with SDKPaint contains multiple icons or two-color icons for mono-

Figure 17-2 Sample icons that come with Icondraw

chrome screens, you will not be able to open the file with Icondraw. However, if the .ICO file contains only one 16-color icon, you will have no trouble using it with Icondraw.

- Icondraw is not the most robust Windows program you will ever use. In particular, if you are creating a new icon from scratch, you may have trouble clearing the current image with the Picture Clear command, and maximizing or minimizing the Icondraw window may destroy its contents. However, rather than creating a new icon, if you've loaded an existing icon from disk, none of these problems manifest themselves. Therefore, if you are creating an icon from scratch, you'll have the best luck with Icondraw if you save your icon to a file early on and then load the icon file back in from disk. From that point on, you should have no trouble at all with the program.

Appendix A: The Windows 3 Power Tools Software

The accompanying Windows 3 Power Tools diskette contains an impressive suite of software for Windows 3. It also contains a special setup program (SETUP.EXE) that allows you to install the software. This appendix tells you more about the software on the accompanying diskette and how you can install it on your system.

ABOUT THE SOFTWARE

The Windows 3 Power Tools diskette comes with four software applications for Windows 3. The featured application is Oriel for Windows, a graphics-based batch language composed of 33 commands that lets you customize the Windows environment. There are also three shareware programs on the accompanying diskette, including: Command Post, a character-based program that is capable of serving as an alternate shell or a replacement for File Manager; Aporia, a completely graphical object-oriented shell for Windows; and Icondraw, an icon-drawing program that lets you design your own icons for applications or major data files. An additional application, WinEdit, a programmer's ASCII text editor, has been included as a convenience to programmers; documentation for WinEdit can be found in the file WINEDIT.TXT.

Only one of the applications on the Windows 3 Power Tools diskette—Oriel for Windows from the LeBlond Group—is a fully licensed version of the software. The other applications on the disk are shareware. If you like one of these applications, and you decide to use it, you should register it by paying a license fee to the appropriate developer.

Paying the software licensing fee for a shareware product may entitle you to certain privileges. For example, in most cases, you'll get a fully illustrated manual giving you detailed instructions on how to use the software. In addition, some of the shareware applications on the accompanying disk display a "nag" screen when you start the application. These screens are purposefully rather annoying in order to encourage you to register the software. However, once you register the software, these screens are disabled. Finally, once you register the software, you will usually be notified when new releases of the product become available.

The following developers have provided shareware products for the Windows 3 Power Tools diskette:

Command Post and *WinEdit*

Morrie Wilson
Wilson WindowWare
2701 California Ave. SW
Suite 212W
Seattle, WA 98116
(800) 762-8383

Aporia™

Michael Davis and Jeffrey Greenberg
NewTools
P.O. Box 3269
Church St. Station
New York, NY 10008-3269
(718) 789-5980

Icondraw

Philip B. Eskelin, Jr.
10814 Orchid Place NW.
Silverdale, WA 98383

You can, of course, use the information above to contact the appropriate developer and pay your license fee. As an alternative, however, you'll find special ordering coupons at the back of this book for Command Post and Aporia that give you a 20 percent discount on the software simply because you bought this book.

INSTALLING THE SOFTWARE

To install the Windows 3 Power Tools software on your system, you use the SETUP.EXE program. You'll find this program located on the root directory of Windows 3 Power

Tools diskette. We strongly recommend that you use this program to install the software. Virtually all of the files on the Power Tools diskette are in compressed format, which means they are unusable in their current form. Therefore, simply copying them to your hard disk with the DOS COPY command will not get the job done. The SETUP.EXE program, however, will not only decompress these files for you, but it will copy them to the appropriate directories on your hard disk.

When you run the SETUP.EXE program, it will automatically create a special Power Tools software directory for you. Attached to this directory, it will create a subdirectory for each of the applications you elect to install. It will then copy the needed files for each application to the appropriate directory. As a final step, SETUP.EXE will create a separate Program Manager group window containing one or more icons for each of the applications you have elected to install.

Note: The SETUP.EXE program was designed and written by Dave Edson. The Windows 3 Power Tools master diskette was prepared by Morrie Wilson of Wilson WindowWare. The authors of the Windows 3 Power Tools would like to extend our thanks to both Dave and Morrie. We think you'll find that SETUP.EXE provides a flexible and elegant way to install the Windows 3 Power Tools software on your system.

Running SETUP.EXE

To run the SETUP.EXE program, start File Manager by double-clicking on its icon located in Program Manager's Main group window. After a short time, File Manager's Directory Tree window appears on your screen. Insert the Windows 3 Power Tools diskette into your 3.5" diskette drive (let us assume this is drive A) and close the door. When you are ready, click on the disk-drive icon for drive A located at the top of File Manager's Directory Tree window. If you are using the keyboard, press TAB to jump to the disk-drive icon section, move the highlight to drive A, and press ENTER. Either way, File Manager updates the Directory Tree window to show the directories on the Windows 3 Power Tools diskette in drive A. The root directory of that disk, A:\, appears highlighted.

Double-click on the A:\ directory icon in the directory tree, or simply press ENTER. File Manager opens a directory window showing you the files and directories on the disk in drive A. Locate the SETUP.EXE file and either double-click on it or highlight it and press ENTER. Windows runs the SETUP.EXE program.

When you start the SETUP.EXE program, a small window appears on your screen informing you that the SETUP.EXE program is loading. A short time later, the Power Tools Setup dialog box shown in Figure A-1 is displayed. This dialog box contains a text box that suggests a directory in which the Power Tools software will be installed. By default, the suggested directory is called PWR-TOOL. It will be created as a subdirectory of your Windows program directory, usually C:\WINDOWS\PWR-TOOL. You can of course change this directory by typing the name of the directory you want to use in the text box provided. If the directory does not already exist, SETUP.EXE will create it. To accept the directory you've specified and continue with the SETUP procedure, select the Continue push button. Alternatively, you can cancel the SETUP procedure by selecting the Cancel push button.

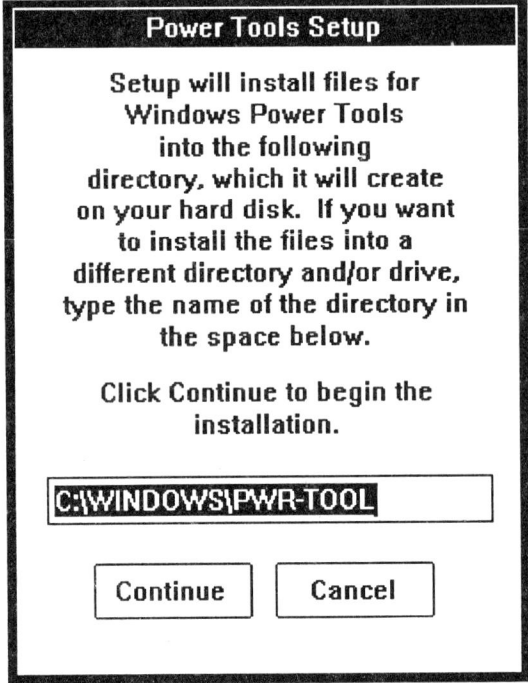

Figure A-1 Power Tools Setup dialog box

When you select the Continue push button to continue with the SETUP procedure, the dialog box shown in Figure A-2 appears on your screen. The list box on the left-hand side of this dialog box contains the names of the applications included with the Windows 3 Power Tools software. Next to each name, the amount of disk space required to install the program files is shown. From this list box, select the name of each application you want to install. You can do this by simply clicking on the name of each application you want to install. Alternatively, you can use the UPARROW or DOWNARROW keys to move to the name of an application and press the SPACEBAR to select it. To unselect a product, simply click on it again or move to it and press the SPACEBAR a second time.

You can select just a few of the applications from the left-hand list box or you can select all of them. Each time you make a selection, information about the application you've selected appears in the information box located at the lower-left corner of the dialog box. In addition, three entries—Disk Space Req'd, Available, and Remaining—are displayed in the lower right corner of the dialog box shown in Figure A-2. These entries indicate whether the disk space needed to install the products you've selected is available.

If adequate space is available, the Disk Space Req'd entry is followed by OK. In addition, the total amount of free space available on the current drive is shown next to the Available entry. Finally, the Remaining entry indicates the total amount of disk space that will be available after the products you've selected are installed.

Appendix A: The Windows 3 Power Tools Software 641

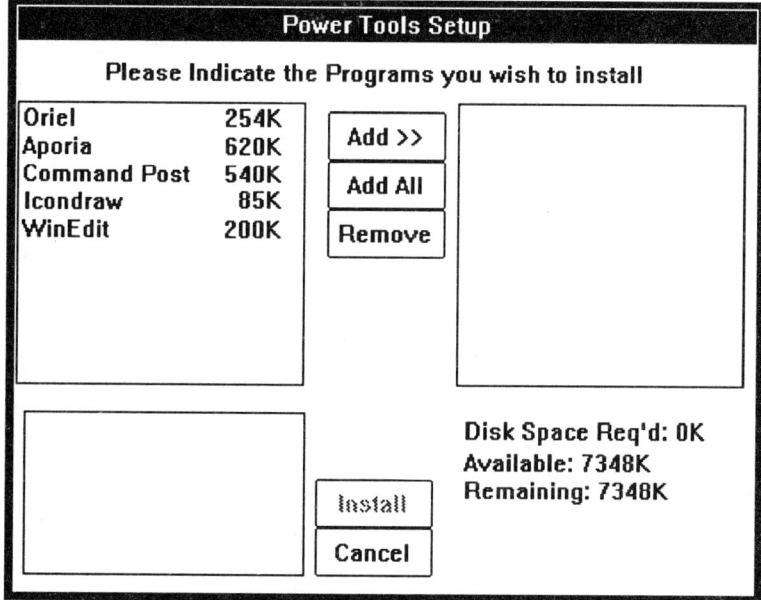

Figure A-2 Choosing the applications to install

Once you've selected the products you want to install, you are ready to add them to the list box on the right side of the dialog box shown in Figure A-2. To do this, select the Add>> push button. You can select this button by clicking on it with your mouse or by pressing TAB to move to it and pressing ENTER. When you select the ADD>> button, SETUP adds the products you've selected from the left-hand list box to the list box on the right. If you change your mind about a product, simply highlight it in the right-hand list box, either by clicking on it or by using the SPACEBAR, and then select the Remove button. When you select this button, SETUP removes the currently selected product(s) from the right-hand list box.

Note: A quick way to add all the products in the Power Tools software to the list box on the right of Figure A-2 is to select the Add All button. You can select this button either by clicking on it with your mouse or by pressing TAB to move to it and then pressing ENTER.

To install the products displayed in the right-hand list box, select the Install push button located near the bottom of the dialog box shown in Figure A-2. SETUP copies the appropriate files from the Power Tools diskette to your hard disk. As a prelude to this process, however, SETUP creates a directory for each of the products you've elected to install. These directories are actually subdirectories of the main Power Tools directory you specified earlier by using the dialog box shown in Figure A-1.

Note: SETUP will create a separate subdirectory for each application on the Windows 3 Power Tools Diskette, whether or not that application is actually installed. If you definitely do not want to install a particular application, that subdirectory can be deleted.

To inform you of its progress, SETUP displays an information box that catalogs the percentage of completion for the copy operation. Once all the files have been copied, SETUP goes about the process of creating a Program Manager group window for each product you have elected to install. Once this is accomplished, SETUP displays a message box informing you that the install procedure has been completed.

Note: In addition to the SETUP program, Aporia also has its own installation program. This is run automatically once the SETUP program has completed if you elect to install Aporia.

See "Aporia" later for details on the Aporia installation program.

Installing a Product at a Later Time

If you elected to install only a few of the applications included in the Windows 3 Power Tools software, don't worry about it. You can always install the rest of the applications at a later time. To do this, simply use the procedure described above to run the SETUP.EXE program a second time. When the dialog box in Figure A-1 is displayed, make sure you specify the same master Power Tools directory you specified the first time. Then, select Continue to access the dialog box in Figure A-2. Select the names of the products you have not as yet installed from the left-hand list box and then select the Add>> button to add them to the right-hand list box. Finally, select the Install button. Setup installs the applications you've selected and creates Program Manager group windows for them.

Note: If you reinstall a product, SETUP will simply overwrite the files for the appropriate application. No real damage is done. However, in addition, SETUP will replace the current Program Manager group window for an application with a new default group window. If you've set up any custom icons in the group window, those icons are either lost or replaced by the default set of icons. You'll have to set up your custom icons all over again.

If Things Go Wrong

The Windows Power Tools SETUP program usually works without a hitch. However, occasionally you might encounter problems when you are installing applications. The following is a list of the most common trouble areas and what to do about them:

- Unrecoverable Application Error: If you get this error message after completing the Aporia installation program, do not be concerned. If you exit Windows then restart it, you will find that the Windows 3 Power Tools applications are all properly installed.

- Command Post Readme icon doesn't work: Occasionally the Notepad icon assigned to the Command Post Readme isn't properly installed. You can correct this problem by highlighting the icon in Program Manager, selecting the File Properties command, and entering the following command line:

```
C:\WINDOWS\PWR-TOOL\CMDPOST\CP-DOCS\README.TXT
```

Of course, the command line will be slightly different if you have installed Command Post in a directory other than the one suggested by the SETUP program.

- Cannot leave Aporia installation program: Because the Aporia installation program does not support keyboard input, you may have trouble leaving it if you do not have a mouse. To leave the program using the keyboard, press CTRL+ESC to access the Task Manager and select End Task.

TRYING OUT THE SOFTWARE

Once the Windows 3 Power Tools software has been installed on your system, you are ready to test run each of the applications. The sections that follow should get you started.

Oriel for Windows

To give you an idea of some potential applications for Oriel for Windows, the LeBlond Group has included a sample demonstration program (DEMO.ORL) that you can experiment with. An icon for this demo has been set up in Oriel's group window. To run the demo, simply open the Oriel group window and double click on the icon.

To learn more about how you can use Oriel for Windows to customize the Windows environment, see Chapter 14, "Oriel for Windows." This chapter gives you a blow-by-blow description of how to use Oriel. It also provides a complete reference to Oriel commands and a quick-reference section for your convenience. In addition, you find a README.TXT file in the \ORIEL directory that gives you late-breaking information about the Oriel for Windows software.

Command Post

Command Post can be used as an alternate shell for launching your Windows programs and managing your files. It comes with a sample menu file that is automatically loaded the first time you run the application. This lets you get started with Command Post right away.

When you install Command Post, the SETUP.EXE program creates a Program Manager group window that contains the icons associated with Command Post. Therefore, to test Command Post, you need only open this group window and double-click on the Command Post icon. After a short time, the Command Post Window will appear on your screen. For detailed instructions on how to use Command Post, as well as how you can customize the menus in the Command Post window, see Chapter 15, "Command Post."

Note: In order to assure that Command Post works properly, the directory in which you installed Command Post, usually C:\WINDOWS\PWR-TOOL\CMDPOST, must be included in the PATH statement in your AUTOEXEC.BAT file.

Aporia

Aporia provides an object-oriented graphical user interface for Windows. When you install this application, the SETUP.EXE program will decompress and copy Aporia's files from the Windows 3 Power Tools diskette into the directory you choose (by default C:\WINDOWS\PWR-TOOL\AP-SETUP). Once SETUP has finished installing the programs you have selected, it will launch Aporia's own installation routine.

Aporia's installation procedure opens the window shown in Figure A-3. If you are either installing a new version of Aporia or installing Aporia for the first time, the Install or update Aporia Files and Images check box should be checked (the default); if you are merely modifying an existing copy of Aporia, click on this check box to deselect it. The two option buttons in the lower portion of the window offer you the choice of continuing to use Program Manager as your Windows shell (the default) or substituting Aporia as your shell. If you wish to use Aporia as the default shell for Microsoft Windows, click on the first option button. Finally, click on OK to continue with the installation procedure.

Note: If at any time you decide to stop Aporia's own installation procedure, you can run the program at a later time by double-clicking on the file SETUPAP.EXE located in the Aporia setup directory (C:\WINDOWS\PWR-TOOL\AP-SETUP).

Aporia will then open a series of windows that prompt you for the names of the subdirectories into which it should place specific files. Although Aporia will suggest possible subdirectories, we recommend that, if necessary, you override Aporia's default preferences with the following:

Aporia system files	C:\WINDOWS\PWR-TOOL\APORIA
Icon image (.AIF) files	C:\WINDOWS\PWR-TOOL\APORIA\IMAGES
Deleted files	C:\WINDOWS\PWR-TOOL\APORIA\!TRASH
Help files	C:\WINDOWS\PWR-TOOL\APORIA\HELP
Note files	C:\WINDOWS\PWR-TOOL\APORIA\NOTES
Tool files	C:\WINDOWS\PWR-TOOL\APORIA\TOOLS
The Aporia program	C:\WINDOWS\PWR-TOOL\APORIA

You can, of course, designate any other directory or subdirectory into which you want the program to install Aporia.

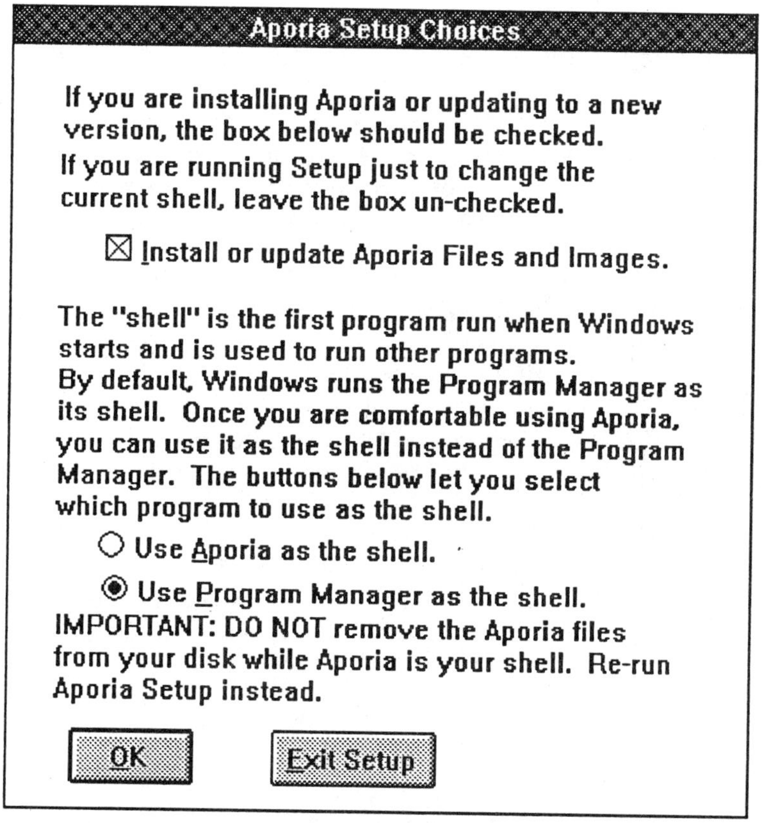

Figure A-3 The initial Aporia installation window

If you have decided to place the Aporia program (APORIA.EXE) into a directory other than Windows' home directory or a directory listed in the PATH statement in your AUTOEXEC.BAT file, Aporia's installation program will produce a Yes/No warning screen informing you of this. If you select Yes, Aporia's setup will return you to the previous dialog box and allow you to change the directory in which APORIA.EXE is to be installed, if you so desire. On the other hand, if you select the No button, Aporia's setup will display a verification dialog box with Yes and No buttons. This dialog box is asking you to verify the directories you have just selected. If you select Yes, the Aporia install program will continue. If you select No, Aporia's install program will cycle you through the earlier prompts to modify the names of the directories in which Aporia will be installed.

Note: If you decide to install the APORIA.EXE file in a directory other than your Windows directory, or in a directory that is not in your PATH, we recommend that you update the PATH statement to include that directory. In fact, if you intend to use Aporia as your default shell for Windows, the directory containing APORIA.EXE must be included in your PATH statement.

After asking you to verify the directories for its files, the Aporia setup program proceeds with the installation. As a final step, the setup program creates an Aporia group window for Program Manager, and opens the Aporia Setup: Summary Window to inform you that the installation procedure has been completed.

Note: SETUP.EXE creates a special Aporia setup directory, usually C:\WINDOWS\PWR-TOOL\AP-SETUP. Once Aporia's own installation program has installed Aporia, however, you no longer need the files in this subdirectory—they can be deleted and the subdirectory removed. If you wish to run Aporia's setup program again, double-click on the icon in Aporia's group window or use File Manager to run SETUPAP.EXE found in the subdirectory that you designated as Aporia's program directory during installation.

Since the installation procedure creates a separate group window containing Aporia's icon, you need only open the Aporia group window and double-click on the Aporia icon to run the application. After a short time, Aporia's graphical objects will begin to appear on your screen. For a detailed description of how you can use Aporia's objects to launch programs and manage your files, see Chapter 16, "Aporia."

Icondraw

Icondraw allows you to create custom icons for your applications and major data files. Like the other applications in the Windows 3 Power Tools set, the SETUP.EXE program sets up a separate Program Manager group window for the Icondraw icon. Therefore, you can test-fly this product by simply opening the Icondraw group window and double-clicking on the Icondraw icon. For a complete description of how to use Icondraw to create custom icons, see Chapter 17, "Icondraw."

Index

%COMPSEC% (DOS), 81
%PROMPT% (DOS), 81
/2 switch, 11
/3 switch, 12, 250
/C switch, used in entering DOS commands, 80
/E switch, 248
/F switch, 393
/L switch, 247
/N switch, 248
/R switch, 8, 247
/S switch, 11, 249
?, in the Optional Parameters text box of a PIF file, 320
@ECHO OFF command (DOS), 81
~GRB files, 257-258, 381, 393
~WOA files, 257, 380-381, 393
1024K VGA. See Extended (1K) VGA
1-2-3
   PIF settings for, 326
   Release 1A, 232
   Release 3, 240
   Release 3.1, in 386 enhanced mode, 343
286 standard mode, 10
286grabber= (SYSTEM.INI), 256, 427-428
386 enhanced mode. See also Operating modes
   changing a running application, 352-353

   DOS translation buffers in, 260-261
   performance check list, 409-410
   virtual addressing in, 259
386grabber= (SYSTEM.INI), 256, 427-428
386Max, 228, 236
386SPART.PAR, 373
386|DOS Extender, 240
3Com 3+Open, 438, 442-445
3Com 3+Share, 438, 442
   connecting to server directories, 443-444
   connecting to shared printers, 445
   creating sharenames, 442-443
   sharing network printers, 444
8086 and 8088 processors, 8
82C441 VGA card, 299
8514FIX.FON, 308, 309
8514OEM.FON, 308, 309
8514SYS.FON, 308, 309
8514/a display, 299-300

A

A20 line, defined, 238
Above Disk, 235
Access time (hard disk), 390
Accessories group window, 33
Adapter memory, including and excluding, 432-433

648 *Windows 3 Power Tools*

Adobe Type Manager, 153
Advanced PIF settings. *See* PIFs (Program Information Files)
.AIF files. *See* Aporia
Aldus, Pagemaker, 5
AllVMsExclusive= (SYSTEM.INI), 431
ALT+BACKSPACE, used in undoing a text entry, 71
ALT+↓, in opening a drop-down list box, 36
ALT+ENTER, used in running DOS applications in a window, 66, 352
ALT+ESC, used in switching between applications, 68-69
ALT+F4, using in closing a window, 73
ALT+PRINTSCREEN
  used in copying a window to the Clipboard, 211
  when not working, 368
ALT+SPACEBAR, in opening the Control menu for DOS applications, 73
ALT+TAB, used in switching between applications, 69
ALT+HYPHEN, used in opening the window Control menu, 87
ALT,
  used in opening menus, 68-69
  used in producing ANSI characters, 148
  used in running Recorder macros, 173
  used in selecting dialog box options, 69
ANSI characters, 563-564
Aporia, 607-630
  Aporia Image Files (.AIF bitmap files), 619
  capturing a window, 620
  capturing an area of the screen, 620
  capturing an icon, 620
  changing a tool's executable file, 618
  changing a tool's help file, 618
  changing a tool's icon, 618
  changing a tool's name, 617
  changing a tool's notes file editor, 618
  changing a tool's notes file, 618
  changing drives with the Drives menu, 624
  changing the directory for an application tool, 618
  Control menu options described, 610
  controlling the contents of a directory window, 628-629
  Copy tool described, 609, 615
  copying files in a directory window, 627
  creating a new directory, 624
  creating Aporia image files, 619-621
  creating Desk Tools, 615-616
  creating desks with tools for Program Manager icons, 608
  creating Directory Tools, 614-615
  creating Help files for individual tools, 611-612
  creating User Tools, 612-614
  customizing tools, 617-619
  default tools described, 608-609
  deleting an existing directory, 624
  deleting files from a directory window, 627

desk defined, 607
Desk Tool described, 608, 616-617
Dir Tool described, 609, 614-615, 626
Directory Tree window, 612, 624
Directory window, 612
getting disk information, 625
getting information about a tool, 621
getting information about files, 629
Help Tool described, 609, 611-612
Hide Tool described, 609
hiding tools, 621
Image Maker (IMAGEMKR.EXE), 619-621
installing. *See* Power Tools Software, installing
linking a Directory window to a directory tree, 625
maintaining notes for tools, 621-622
making a directory tool, 625, 629
making a directory window for a selected directory, 625
making user tools, 629
managing directories with the Directories menu, 624-625
managing files and directories, 623-625
managing files with directory windows, 625-629
modifying Aporia's default settings, 619
moving files in a directory window, 627
moving tools, 610-611
Notes Tool described, 609
opening directory windows, 626
Opt Tool described, 610, 617-619
Options menu, 625
overview of, 643
passing parameters to applications, 618
recovering files from the \!TRASH directory, 623
removing tools, 622-623
renaming a directory, 624-625
renaming files in a directory window, 627
running all the tools in a disk, 619
running an application on startup, 619
running applications as icons, 619
running applications from a directory window, 626
running applications full screen, 619
running tools, 611
saving an image in an .AIF file, 621
selecting files in a directory window, 626
SETUPAP.EXE installation program, 644
Size Tool described, 610, 623
sizing and positioning application windows, 623
Special menu, 625, 629
starting an application in its own directory, 619
starting an application with a specific data file, 613
storing tools in Desks, 616-617
tools defined, 607
Trash Tool described, 608
Tree Tool described, 608, 623-625
using the Trash Tool, 622-623

Index 649

viewing file information in a directory window, 628-629
View Menu, 628-629
Apple LaserWriter II NTX, 128
Application shortcut key, 351
Application swap files, 257-258, 372
　changing the location of, 430
　improving Windows' use of, 380-382
Application windows
　closing, 73
　controlling tiling and stacking of, 64
　maximizing, 72
　restoring a maximized window, 72-73
Applications
　adding to Windows, 302-303
　copying screens to the Clipboard, 210-211
　included with Windows (Table), 39
　installing with Windows Setup, 26
　positioning application windows on a grid, 285-286
　running from File Manager, 105-106
　running from Program Manager, 33
　running multiple instances of, 78
　running older applications, 8
　running shared network applications, 460-462
　setting up icons for, 37-42
　shrinking to an icon when starting, 65, 414
　starting as windows, 414
　starting in a specific directory, 45-46
　switching away when a process is running, 76-77
　switching between, 66-69
　tiling and stacking application windows, 62-64
Ashton-Tate, 232
Associations, creating between data files and applications, 48, 104-105
AST, 232
AST Rampage board, 382
ATI VIP VGA card, 299
ATTRIB command (DOS), 108, 464
AutoCAD 386, 240
AUTOEXEC.BAT, 144, 147
　editing with SysEdit, 27, 46
　slimming down, 386-388

B

Backfilling, 233
Backward compatibility with older applications, 8
Bad applications, 255
Bank line. *See* EMS bank line
Bank switching, 232
Batch files. *See* DOS batch files
Beep (Oriel), 487
Beep (Windows), 289
　setting in WIN.INI, 415
BIOS tables, place in memory, 228-229
BIOS, place in memory, 228-229
Bitmap files. *See* .BMP files
Bitmaps
　device dependent bitmaps, 20
　device independent bitmaps, 20

Bitstream FaceLift, 149-152
.BMP files, 210
　converting to .PCX format, 210-211
　in Oriel for Windows, 480-481, 490-491
　used as wallpaper, 282
Border width, changing in WIN.INI, 416
BorderWidth= (WIN.INI), 416
Browser, 550, 562-567. *See also* Command Post
　browsing nontext files, 566-567
　browsing text files, 563
　changing the display format, 563-564
　copying to the clipboard with, 566
　hiding and seeking with, 564-565
　viewing nontext files in hexadecimal mode, 567
Buffers, place in memory, 229
BUFFERS= (CONFIG.SYS), 383

C

CALC.EXE, 39
CALENDAR.EXE, 39
CARDFILE.EXE, 39
CEMM, 236
CGA display, 299-300
CGA40WOA.FON= (SYSTEM.INI), 307-308, 431
CGA80WOA.FON= (SYSTEM.INI), 307-308, 431
CHKDSK, using the /F switch with, 393-394
Clipboard, 25, 203. *See also* Sharing data and DOS applications, 212-218. *See also* Window Control menu
　capturing screens, 210-211
　capturing the currently active window, 211
　Clipboard Viewer application, 25, 203
　copying from DOS applications in 386 enhanced mode, 214-216
　copying graphics from DOS applications, 212, 216
　copying to DOS applications in standard or real mode, 212-213
　defined, 203
　deleting the contents of, 210
　difficulty pasting to DOS applications, 217
　file formats, 210, 218-219
　lines of text appear cut off, 206
　memory used by, 211-212
　overview of using, 204-205
　pasting data (Windows applications), 207-208
　pasting to DOS applications in 386 enhanced mode, 216-217
　pasting to DOS applications in standard or real mode, 213-214
　pasting to spreadsheet applications, 214
　regaining memory used by, 209
　saving the contents of, 208-209
　selecting data to copy to (Windows applications), 205
　using in 386 enhanced mode, 11
　using with applications in different modes, 209
　viewing contents of, 206
　viewing file formats on, 218-219
CLIPBRD.EXE, 39, 203, 206

CLOCK.EXE, 39
.CLP files, 208
Clusters, 391
CMDPOST.CPM (Command Post), 550
CMDUSER.CPM (Command Post), 550
CMOS setup, 388, 391
Colors. *See also* Control Panel
    changing a predefined color scheme, 273
    changing for Windows, 272-276
    choosing from predefined color schemes, 273
    defining custom colors, 274-276
    understanding Windows' color values, 276
    settings in WIN.INI, 425-426
COM Ports
    baud rate setting, 117, 277
    configuring for both a printer and a modem, 278
    copying settings between ports, 278
    data bits setting, 117, 278
    flow control setting, 117, 278
    parity setting, 117, 278
    stop bits setting, 117, 278
COM1-COM4, 117, 121, 275
Command Post Menu Language (CPML), 548. *See also* Command Post
    pushing the limits of, 591-595
    syntax, 572-574
    table of statements, 595-605
Command Post, 547-605
    accessory programs, 562-568
    arranging windows in, 557-559
    asking for information, 575
    Browser. *See* Browser
    browsing files, 550. *See also* Browser
    browsing text files, 563
    building your own menus, 569-590
    changing the size and position of other windows, 585
    choosing from a list, 575-577
    clock, 567-568
    CMDPOST.CPM, 550
    CMDUSER.CPM, 550
    conditional branching (IF-THEN, GOTO), 579-580
    controlling other windows, 584-586
    CPML syntax, 572-574
    creating a trashcan, 583-584
    debugging your programs, 590
    Dir menu, 555-556
    Directory Tree, 555
    displaying messages, 579
    editing selected files, 571-572
    Execute statement, 593-594
    faking arrays, 592-593
    file and directory handling, 582-584
    File menu, 550-554
    getting help, 560
    getting information about windows, 585
    hiding windows, 584
    iconizing windows, 585
    initialization section in menu files, 586-587
    installing. *See* Power Tools Software, installing
    launching programs in, 569-571
    linking menu files together, 587-588
    looping, 580-582
    Main menu, 560-561
    menus, 550-562
    modifying WIN.INI, 588
    overview of, 643-644
    password protecting Windows, 588-590
    pushing CPML's limits, 591-595
    running a macro from a menu, 594-595
    selecting files, 549-550
    setting up a menu file, 569-586
    stopping a menu, 577-579
    System menu, 561-562
    using as a file manager, 549-562
    using as your shell, 568-569
    using substitution to build statements, 591-592
    View menu, 556-559
    viewing files in, 556-559
    WinInfo, 585
Communications errors, 367
Communications ports, controlling in WIN.INI, 423-424
Compaq Portable Plasma display, 299-300
CompuServe, 135
ComxAutoAssign= (SYSTEM.INI), 433-434
COMx:= (WIN.INI), 423-424
CONFIG.SYS
    BUFFERS= setting, 383
    DEVICE=HIMEM.SYS statement, 13
    editing with SysEdit, 27
    Files= setting, 383
    on 80286-based systems, 384-385
    on 80386- and 80486-based systems, 382-384
    on 8088-based systems, 385-386
    slimming down, 386-387
Control Panel
    386 Enhanced icon, 160, 290
    386 Enhanced options, 290-295. *See also* Multitasking
    adjusting your mouse, 279-280. *See also* Mouse
    changing colors of Windows, 272-276. *See also* Colors
    Color icon, 272
    date and time options, 288-289
    Date/Time icon, 288
    Desktop icon, 280
    desktop options, 280-286. *See also* Desktop
    features of, 23-25
    Fonts icon, 139
    International icon, 286
    International options, 286-287
    Keyboard icon, 288
    keyboard options, 288
    modifying WIN.INI settings with, 272
    Network icon, 456
    opening, 269
    overview of, 269-272
    Ports icon, 117

Index   651

Sound icon, 289
Sound options, 289-290
used in installing printers, 116
Controller (hard disk), 392
CONTROL.EXE, 36, 269
CONTROL.INI, 27
Conventional memory, defined, 288-289
COPY command (DOS), used in printing, 127
Copying data. *See* Clipboard
COURE.FON, 309
COURF.FON, 309-310
CP_TREE.EXE (Command Post), 556. *See also* Command Post
CTRL+BREAK, used in stopping a Recorder macro, 182-183
CTRL+ESC, used in opening the Task List window, 67
CTRL+F6, 32
in moving between File Manager directory windows, 87
CTRL+INS, used in copying data to the Clipboard, 71, 204
CTRL+TAB, 32
in moving between File Manager directory windows, 87
CTRL+*, used in expanding File Manager's directory tree, 86
CTRL, used in running Recorder macros, 173
Currency format, 286
CursorBlinkRate= (WIN.INI), 417
Cursor
changing blink rate in WIN.INI, 417
setting blink rate, 286
Cutting data. *See* Clipboard
Cylinders, 389

D

Data files, linking to icons, 47
Date
changing, 288
format, 286
DDE (Dynamic Data Exchange), 4, 25, 203-204, 220-224
an example, 221-222
client application defined, 220
"conversation", 220
server application defined, 220
types of links, 221
DEFAULT.CLP, 208
_DEFAULT.PIF, 317. *See also* PIFs
Desktop
adjusting cursor blink rate, 286
controlling pattern in WIN.INI, 420
displaying patterns on, 281-282
displaying wallpaper on, 282-284
granularity setting, 285-286
modifying patterns for, 281
setting distance between icons, 285
window border width setting, 286

DESQview, 233
Device contention, 290-293
Device contention settings, in SYSTEM.INI, 433-434
Device driver, installing, 25
Device independence, 20-21
for applications, 3
DeviceNotSelectedTimeout= (WIN.INI), 419
Device= (WIN.INI), 415-416
Directly Modifies Memory option, in Windows/286, 255
Directories
copying, 95-993
creating, 92-93
deleting, 101-102
moving, 99-100
Disk Connect Net Drive command (File Manager), 447
Disk Copy Diskette command (File Manager), 111
Disk Disconnect Net Drive command (File Manager), 450
Disk Format Diskette command (File Manager), 111
Disk Label Disk command (File Manager), 112
Disk Make System Diskette command (File Manager), 111
Disk Manager, 374, 392, 435
Disks
changing volume labels for, 112
copying data between, 111
creating a boot disk, 111
formatting, 111
Disk-caching, 399. *See also* SMARTDrive
Display command (Clipboard Viewer), 219
Display driver, changing to a lower-resolution driver, 410
Display fonts, changing manually, 306-310
Display standards, list of, 300
Display, changing drivers, 299-301
Display.drv= (SYSTEM.INI), 428
DMDRIVER.BIN, 435
DMDRVR.BIN, 392
Document files, defining in WIN.INI, 418-419
Documents, associating with applications in WIN.INI, 422-423
Documents= (WIN.INI), 418-419
DOS 5.0, 268
and the HMA, 345
DOS application font, changing manually, 307-308
DOS applications. *See also* Non-Windows applications
changing a running application, 352-353
compatibility with Windows 3, 17-18
displaying the window Control menu, 73
expanded memory with, 259
forcing to run full screen, 431
full screen versus windowed display, 11, 17
high resolution graphics and Windows, 18
identifying a second instance of, 78
if all else fails, 360
in 386 enhanced mode, 259-261

652 Windows 3 Power Tools

in real and standard mode, 255-259
limitations imposed by Windows, 18
Program Information Files. *See* PIFs
running in the background, 333-337, 338-339
running in a window, 66
when a DOS application won't start, 360
when a key doesn't work, 367-368
when running too slowly, 365-367
when the display is lost, 363
when things go wrong, 357-369
when you cannot exit, 369
when you cannot switch away, 361-362
when you cannot switch to full screen, 362-363
when you run out of memory, 357-358
when your system hangs, 369
screen grabber, 256
DOS batch files, running from within Windows, 318-319
DOS extenders, 239-240
DOS Prompt icon, disfunctional, 80
customizing, 80-81
DOS Protected Mode Interface (DPMI), 241-242
DOS translation buffers, 260-261, 431-432
DOS, tips on running under Windows, 79-81
Dot matrix printers
using fonts with, 148
dip-switch settings, 134
installing, 133-134
setting options for, 133
DoubleClickSpeed= (WIN.INI), 418
DPMI, 343. *See also* DOS Protected Mode Interface
DrawArc (Oriel), 480, 487-489
DrawBackground (Oriel), 490
DrawBitmap (Oriel), 480-481, 490-491
DrawChord (Oriel), 480, 491-493
DrawEllipse (Oriel), 480, 491-493
DrawFlood (Oriel), 480, 495-496
DrawLine (Oriel), 480, 496-497
DrawNumber (Oriel), 479, 497-499
DrawPie (Oriel), 480, 499-501
DrawRectangle (Oriel), 480, 501-502
DrawRoundRectangle (Oriel), 480, 503
DrawSizedBitmap (Oriel), 480-481, 504
DrawText (Oriel), 479, 504-506
Drivers. *See also* Setup program
changing, 298-302
.DRV, 127

E

Edit Copy command (general use), 204
Edit Cut command (general use), 204
Edit Delete command (Clipboard Viewer), 210, 212
Edit Paste command (general use), 204
EEMS 3.2, 232
EGA display, 299-300
EGA palettes, 409
EGA80WOA.FON= (SYSTEM.INI), 307-308, 431

EGA40WOA.FON= (SYSTEM.INI), 307-308, 431
EGA.SYS, 409
EMBs, 237
EMM386, 407-409
installing, 408
EMM386.SYS, 10, 236, 340
changes in DOS 5.0, 268
in standard mode, 258
EMMExclude= (SYSTEM.INI), 432-433
EMMInclude= (SYSTEM.INI), 432-433
EMMPageFrame= (SYSTEM.INI), 433
EMS 4.0 memory, 245-248
moving the EMS bank line, 247-248
EMS Emulators, 235-236
EMS Memory, in DOS applications, 340-342
End (Oriel), 507
Enhanced Small Device Interface. *See* ESDI
.EPS (Encapsulated PostScript), 128
Epson LQ2500, 133
EPT, 122
EPT:= (WIN.INI), 423-424
ESDI, 391
.EXE files included with Windows (Table), 39
EXIT, in returning from DOS to windows, 79
Exiting Windows, 57
when DOS applications are active, 59
EXPAND utility, 355
Expanded memory emulator (EMM), 407. *See also* EMM386
Expanded Memory Manager (EMM), 232
Expanded memory (EMS), 229-236
allocating the page frame, 432
backfilling with, 233
controlling EMS page frame position, 432-433
disabling support of, 433
EMS emulators, 235-236
EMS simulator, 235-236
in 386 enhanced mode, 261
large-frame EMS, 234
LIM-EMS 3.2, 232
LIM-EMS 4.0, 233
page frame, 232
pages, 232
small-frame EMS, 234
EXPAND.EXE utility, 308
Extended memory blocks. *See* EMBs
Extended memory manager. *See* HIMEM.SYS
eXtended Memory Specification (XMS), 13, 237. *See also* XMS memory
Extended memory, 236-242
in PIFs, 325-326
in real mode, 245
Extended (1K) VGA, 300

F

F1 (Help), 28, 29
F4, in opening a drop-down list box, 36
F7, used in moving files in File Manager, 100
F8, used in copying files in File Manager, 98

Index 653

FAT, 393
  scrambling of, 392
FDISK, 374, 392
File Allocation Table. *See* FAT
File Association command (File Manager), 48, 104
File associations
  controlling in WIN.INI, 422-423
  creating, 48
File Attributes, 91
File Attributes command (File Manager), 107
File Control Block (FCB), 350
File Copy command
  (File Manager), 98-99
  (Program Manager), 35
File Create Directory command (File Manager), 92-93
File Delete command
  File Manager, 101
  Program Manager, 37
File Deselect All command (File Manager), 95
File Manager, 7, 16
  calculating the size of a group of files, 94
  changing disk volume labels with, 112
  changing file attributes with, 107-108
  changing the display of directory windows, 88-92
  controlling window updates, 433
  copying data between disks with, 111
  copying files and directory, 95-99
  creating a boot disk with, 111
  creating directories with, 92-93
  defining File Manager as a primary shell, 85
  deleting files and directories with, 101-102
  Directory Tree window, 84
  displaying a different directory tree, 84
  displaying names in lower case, 110
  formatting disks with, 111
  identifying network drives in, 447
  limiting directory window contents, 89
  managing directory trees in, 86
  managing directory windows in, 86-87
  managing files and directories with, 92-103
  moving files and directories with, 99-100
  opening a directory window, 85
  printing ASCII files from, 108-109
  renaming files with, 101
  replacing one directory window with another, 88
  saving settings for, 92
  searching for files and directories with, 102-103
  selecting files in, 93-95
  starting an application with specific file, 105-106
  tiling and stacking directory windows, 88
  turning off confirmation messages for, 109
  turning off status bar display, 110-111
  using, 83-112
  viewing file details, 90-91
  viewing hidden system files, 89-90
  sorting files in directory windows, 88-89
File Merge command (Recorder), 178
File Move command

File Manager, 100
Program Manager, 36
File New command (Program Manager), 37, 45
  used in creating new group windows, 52
File Open command
  File Manager, 106
  Recorder, 169, 178
File Printer Setup command, 126, 148
File Properties command (Program Manager), 42, 45
File Rename command (File Manager), 101
File Run command (File Manager), 106
  used in Recorder macros, 186, 193
File Save As command
  Clipboard Viewer, 208
  Recorder, 169
File Search command (File Manager), 103
File Select All command (File Manager), 95
FileSysChange= (SYSTEM.INI), 433
Files
  calculating the size of a group of files, 94
  changing attributes for, 107-108
  copying, 95-99
  creating associations for data files, 104-105
  defining document files in WIN.INI, 418-419
  defining program files in WIN.INI, 418
  deleting, 101-102, 392-393
  moving, 99-100
  printing to (WIN.INI), 423-424
  renaming, 101
  searching for, 102-103
FILES= (CONFIG.SYS), 383
FILE:= (WIN.INI), 423-424
fixedfon.fon= (SYSTEM.INI), 308-309
Focus, 67
.FON files, 139, 307-310
Fonts, 21-22, 136-156. *See also* Screen fonts; Printer fonts
  Adobe Font Foundry, 153
  Adobe Type Manager, 153
  attributes (bold, italic, and so on), 140
  Bitstream FaceLift, 149-152
  Bitstream Hewlett Packard LaserJet III Companion Pack, 152
  Bitstream PostScript Companion Pack, 152
  cartridge-based printer fonts, 21
  changing display fonts manually. *See* Display fonts
  controlling DOS application fonts, 431
  disparity between displayed and printed output, 138
  downloading defined, 141
  downloading permanently, 21
  downloading temporarily, 21
  families, 140
  fixed pitch, 140
  formatting text with, 148
  Hewlett Packard Intellifont, 155
  Hewlett Packard Type Director 2.0, 155
  kerning, 140

654 Windows 3 Power Tools

point size defined, 140
PostScript, 141
printer fonts, 21-22
proportional, 140
Publishers Type Foundry, 154
resident printer fonts, 21
scalable outline fonts, 141
screen fonts, 22
soft fonts, 21
sources of, 136
technology, 141-142
terminology, 139-140
third party soft font packages for Windows, 149
TrueType and TrueImage, 156
typeface defined, 139
using with dot-matrix printers, 148
Windows system font, 22, 138
ZSoft SoftType, 153-154
fonts.fon= (SYSTEM.INI), 309
FORMAT (DOS), 392
Fragmentation (hard disk), 390-391
Free Memory setting, 261
Free System Resources settings, 261-262
Full-screen display, switching to, 352

G

Games group window, 33
GDI (Graphics Device Interface), 20, 469
GDI.EXE, 262
Global heap, 242
Good applications, 255
Gosub (Oriel), 481, 507-508
Goto (Oriel), 481, 508-509
Grabber files, 257-258, 427-428
Graphics Device Interface. *See* GDI
Grid granularity, 285-286
    controlling in WIN.INI, 422
GridGranularity= (WIN.INI), 422
Group windows. *See* Program Manager
.GRP files, 52
GUI (Graphical User Interface), refinements to, 15-16

H

Handshake, 119, 278
    hardware, 119, 278
    software, 119
Hard disk controller, terminating interrupts from, 435
Hard disk
    access time, 390
    clusters, 391
    compacting, 394-395
    cylinders, 389
    ESDI, 391
    fragmentation, 390-391
    fundamentals, 388-392
    head, 388

improving performance of, 388-397
MFM encoding, 389
optimizing the interleave of, 395-397
platters, 388
RLL encoding, 389
sector ID header, 390
sectors, 389
sides, 388
smart controllers, 392
space allocation by DOS, 390-392
tracks, 389
Help
    annotating Help text, 30
    bookmarks in, 30
    copying text to the Clipboard, 30
    navigating the standard Windows Help window, 28-29
    printing Help text, 30
Help About box settings, 261-262
Help About... command, 8, 28
    File Manager, 75
    Program Manager, 75
Help command, 28-29
Help Commands command, 28
Help Keyboard command, 28
Help Procedures command, 28

HELVE.FON, 309
HELVF.FON, 309-310
Hercules display, 300
Hewlett Packard Intellifont, 155
High memory area (HMA), 237-239
    in 386 enhanced mode, 344-345
High memory. *See* Reserved I/O memory
HIMEM.SYS, 13, 237, 239, 243
    adjusting, 397-399
.HLP files, 29
HMA. *See* High memory area
HP LaserJet
    adding fonts, 142-143
    choosing a download method for fonts, 144
    configuring, 121-122
    copying fonts between ports for, 147
    Editing fonts for, 145-146
    getting Help for the HP LaserJet driver, 124
    IID and duplex printing, 124
    III, 141
    installing fonts for, 142-148. *See also* Printer fonts
    installing, 119-124
    removing fonts from, 146
    selecting the PCL/HP driver, 119-124
    setting options for, 123-124
    using PostScript cartridges with, 132

I

IBM PC LAN Program, 438
IBM Personal Communications/3270 utility, 313
IBMBIO.COM, 228

Index 655

IBMDOS.COM, 288
IBM, 4
　Pageprinter Adapter Program, 122
　Personal Pageprinter, 122
.ICO files, 43, 631
Icondraw, 631-635
　color palette, 633-634
　drawing tools, 632-633
　installing. *See* Power Tools Software, installing
　overview of, 646
　using an .ICO file in Program Manager, 632
　using the clipboard with, 634
IconSpacing= (WIN.INI), 422
Icons
　applications, 33
　arranging automatically, 50
　arranging for running applications, 50-51
　arranging in group windows, 49-50
　assigning macros to, 197-198
　associated with CONTROL.EXE, 41
　associated with PROGMAN.EXE, 41
　available for use with DOS applications, 40
　borrowing from other applications, 42
　browsing for executable files, 38
　changing properties for, 42
　changing the command line, 42
　changing the description, 42
　changing the icon displayed, 42
　controlling spacing between (WIN.INI), 422
　copying between group windows with the keyboard, 35
　copying between group windows with the mouse, 34
　copying to a minimized group window, 35
　defining a command line for an application icon, 37
　defining descriptions for application icons, 37
　defining for applications, 40
　deleting, 37
　drawing your own with Icondraw, 631-635
　group windows icons, 32
　in consuming memory, 36
　.ICO files, 43
　linking to data files, 47
　managing, 34-51
　moving between group windows with the keyboard, 36
　moving between group windows with the mouse, 36
　setting the distance between, 285
　setting up new icons, 37-42
　setting up with the aid of File Manager, 44-45
　types of icons in message boxes, 77
　using an .ICO file in Program Manager, 632
If (Oriel), 481, 509-511
Image Maker (Aporia), 619-621. *See also* Aporia
.INI files, 26-27. *See also* WINFILE.INI, CONTROL.INI, WIN.INI, SYSTEM.INI, PROGMAN.INI
　editing, 26-27

　overview of, 411
InnerSpace, 392
Installing Windows 3 Power Tools. *See* Power Tools Software
Intel Aboveboard, 382
Interleave (hard disk), 395-397
　changing, 396-397
　when to change, 398
International settings, 286-287
Interrupt vector table, place in memory, 228-229

K

KERNEL.EXE, 262
Keyboard
　changing drivers, 301
　changing speed of in WIN.INI, 416
　repeat rate, 288

L

LAN Manager, 438
Language, 286
Large-frame EMS, defined, 234, 245-248
LASTDRIVE= (CONFIG.SYS), 387
List boxes, key sequences used in, 70
Load= (WIN.INI), 414
Local heap, 244
Logitech Mouse, 318, 355
Lost chains, 393
Lotus Development, 232, 241
Lotus-Intel-Microsoft (LIM) Expanded Memory Specification (EMS). *See* Expanded memory
LPT1-LPT3, 117, 121, 275
LPTxAutoAssign= (SYSTEM.INI), 433-434
LPTx.OS2= (WIN.INI), 423-424
LPTx:= (WIN.INI), 423-424

M

Macro
　Delete command (Recorder), 169, 171, 177
　Properties command (Recorder), 177, 178, 184
　Record command (Recorder), 164, 170
　Run command (Recorder), 168
Macros, 163. *See* also Recorder
Main group window, 33
MaxPagingFileSize= (SYSTEM.INI), 379
MaxUserDiskSpace= (SYSTEM.INI), 379
Memory configurations, 242
Memory management, 7-8, 227-267
　discarding program code, 3
　DOS applications, 254-261
　in real mode, 243-245
Memory requirements
　386 enhanced mode, 250-251
　real mode, 242
　standard mode, 248-249
Memory

656 Windows 3 Power Tools

checking available memory, 74
checking expanded memory claimed by
 SMARTDrive, 76
checking free expanded memory, 76
checking free memory, 75
checking free system resources, 76
configuring expanded memory as extended
 memory, 13
configuring, 382-388
effect of wallpaper on, 284
paging defined, 12
reclaiming through PIF settings, 358-359
running out of, 74
running out of with DOS applications, 357-358
virtual (disk-based) memory, 11
Memory-resident utilities, 312-314
 loading after starting Windows, 312-314
 loading before Windows, 312-313
 loading by itself, 313
 loading with a batch file, 313-314
 overview of, 312
Menus, clicking and dragging to select items, 69
MessageBox (Oriel), 481-482, 511-513
Messages, from background applications, 77-78
 sending and receiving on a network, 460
Messaging system, 3
MFM encoding, 389
Microsoft Excel, 5
Microsoft Mouse, 355-357
Minimize on Use command (Program Manager), 64
MinUserDiskSpace= (SYSTEM.INI), 434
Mode. *See* Operating modes
MODE command (DOS), 279
Modem, 277
Modified Frequency Modulation encoding (MFM),
 389
Monitor Ports options, 410
MouseSpeed= (WIN.INI), 417-418
MouseThreshold1= (WIN.INI), 417-418
MouseThreshold2= (WIN.INI), 417-418
Mouse
 adjusting double-click rate of, 280
 adjusting the speed of, 279
 changing drivers, 301
 changing sensitivity of in WIN.INI, 417-418
 configuring, 279-280. *See also* Control Panel
 controlling double-click speed in WIN.INI, 418
 hit-testing regions in Oriel, 483, 527
 Logitech Mouse, 355
 Microsoft Bus Mouse problems, 356
 Microsoft Mouse, 355-357
 Microsoft Serial Mouse problems, 356
 MOUSE.COM, 354
 MOUSE.SYS, 354
 swapping left and right buttons on, 280
 using with DOS applications, 353-357
MOUSE.COM, 318, 354
 problems with, 356-357
 using the latest version of, 355
MOUSE.DRV, 353
MOUSE.SYS, 354

using the latest version of, 355
MSDOS.EXE, 39
MS-DOS Executive, 2, 16, 457
 Windows 3 version, 79
MS-DOS, place in memory, 228-229
MSNet Redirector module, 380
Multitaskers, 241
Multitasking
 adjusting the duration of a time slice, 294
 device contention with DOS applications,
  290-293
 DOS applications, 15
 DOS applications in 386 enhanced mode, 11
 foreground versus background applications,
  294-295
 giving priority to DOS applications, 294-295
 giving priority to Windows applications,
  294-295
 nonpreemptive multitasking, 15
 preemptive multitasking, 15, 259
 setting options for a running application, 353
 setting options for DOS applications, 294-295
 Time slice defined, 16
 Windows applications, 15
 Windows as compared to OS/2, 15

N

NEC Multisync, 304
NETWARE.HLP, 467
NETWARE.INI, 467
NetWarn= (WIN.INI), 419-420
Network
 changing drivers, 301
 controlling warning message (WIN.INI),
  419-420
Network drive, using for a temporary swap file, 380
Networking, 27, 437-467. *See also* 3Com 3+Share,
  Novell NetWare
 accessing network features from Windows,
  456-460
 accessing network-specific features, 28
 administration, 462-467
 browsing for a network printer connection, 452
 browsing network directories for a connection,
  448-449
 changing a password, 459
 checking status of network print queues, 27
 configuring a local copy of Windows, 439
 configuring shared copies of Windows, 464-465
 configuring user workstations, 465-466
 connecting to a network printer, 27, 451-452
 connecting to network drives, 27, 447-450
 disconnecting a network drive, 27, 450
 disconnecting a network printer, 452
 enabling Print Manager for network printing,
  455-456
 file server, 437
 fundamentals, 440-447
 installing a shared copy on a workstation,
  439-440

Index 657

installing Windows on a workstation, 438-439
installing Windows on the server, 462-464
logging on and off the network, 441
logging on and off the network server, 457-459
logical drive defined, 441
network driver, 439
network log-in script, 441
networks supported, 438
password, 448, 452
personal Windows directory, 439
print queues, 453
printing from Windows applications, 453
printing on a network, 450-456. *See also* Printing
reusing previous link commands, 448
running a shared versus local copy of Windows, 440-441
running shared applications, 460
selecting a printer, 440
sending and receiving messages, 460
viewing network print queues, 453-456
viewing the contents of network print queues, 454-455
workstation, 437
NETWORKS.TXT, 467
NewTools, 638
NoEMMDriver= (SYSTEM.INI), 433
Non-Windows applications, 311-370. *See also* DOS applications
Non-Windows Applications group window, 33
Norton Utilities, 393, 394
NOTEPAD.EXE, 39
Novell NetWare, 438, 445-447
  connecting to network printers, 445-446
  connecting to server directories, 445-446
  System Console (SYSCON.EXE) utility, 445
  trustee rights, 445
Nullport= (WIN.INI), 415
Number format, 286

O

OBJECT Linking and Embedding (OLE), 224
oemfonts.fon= (SYSTEM.INI), 308-309
OEMSETUP.INF, 310
Olivetti/AT&T Monochrome display, 299
Ontrack Systems, 374, 392
Operating modes
  386 enhanced mode defined, 11-12
  checking the mode in which Windows is running, 8
  defined, 8-12
  real mode defined, 8-10
  real mode with EMS 4.0 memory, 245-248
  real mode, 242-245
  running DOS applications in 386 mode, 11, 17
  running DOS applications in real mode, 8, 17
  running DOS applications in standard mode, 10, 17
  standard mode, 10-11, 248-250
  starting Windows in 386 enhanced mode, 12
  starting Windows in real mode, 8

starting Windows in standard mode, 10
use of expanded memory in real mode, 10
Options
  Alert Always command (Print Manager), 159
  Auto Arrange command (Program Manager), 50
  Change System Settings command (Setup), 439
  Confirmation command (File Manager), 109
  Exit command (Print Manager), 158
  Flash if Inactive command (Print Manager), 159
  High Priority command (Print Manager), 159
  Ignore if Inactive command (Print Manager), 159
  Low Priority command (Print Manager), 159
  Lower Case command (File Manager), 110
  Medium Priority command (Print Manager), 159
  Minimize on Use command (Recorder), 191
  Shortcut Keys command (Recorder), 191
  Status Bar command (File Manager), 110
Oriel for Windows, 469-545
  { }, 473-474
  arc, 487-489
  background color in, 490, 531-533
  basic rules and syntax, 471-474
  Beep, 487
  .BMP files in, 480-481, 490-491, 504
  brushes, 478, 533-535
  cannot find the language file error, 475
  character cells, 531-532
  chord, 491-493
  command reference, 487-543
  command syntax, 471-472
  comments, 473-474
  coordinate system, 477, 536-537
  CTRL+BREAK in, 476
  default brush, 478
  default font, 479
  default pen, 478
  DrawArc, 480, 487-489
  DrawBackground, 490
  DrawBitmap, 480-481, 490-491
  DrawChord, 480, 491-493
  DrawEllipse, 480, 491-493
  DrawFlood, 480, 495-496
  drawing lines and shapes, 480
  drawing numbers, 479
  drawing text, 479
  DrawLine, 480, 496-497
  DrawNumber, 479, 497-499
  DrawPie, 480, 499-501
  DrawRectangle, 480, 501-502
  DrawRoundRectangle, 480, 503
  DrawSizedBitmap, 480-481, 504
  DrawText, 479, 504-506
  ellipse or circle, 491-493
  End, 507
  flooding an area, 495-496
  font mapping by the GDI, 538
  fonts, 479, 537-541
  Gosub, 481, 507-508
  Goto, 481, 508-509
  how it works, 470-471
  If, 481, 509-511

installing. *See* Power Tools Software, installing
keyboard input in, 485-486, 517-523
labels, 473
line, 496-497
mathematical calculations, 515-517
maximizing the window, 530-531
memory requirements for, 471
menus in, 483, 523-526
message boxes in, 481-482, 511-513
MessageBox, 481-482, 511-513
minimizing the window, 530-531
mouse input in, 483-485, 526-528
numbers, 497-499
overview of, 643
pausing a program, 482-483, 542-543
pens, 478, 541-542
pie wedge, 499-501
quick reference, 543-545
rectangle with rounded edges, 503
rectangle, 501-502
restoring the window, 530-531
Return, 507
running other programs within, 486, 514-515
Run, 486, 514-515
selecting drawing tools, 477-479
SetKeyboard, 485-486, 517-523
SetMenu, 483, 523-526
SetMouse, 483-485, 526-528
SetWaitMode, 486, 528-530
SetWindow, 482, 530-531
Set, 472, 515-517
sizing a bitmap, 504
sounding the bell, 487
starting a program, 474-476
stopping a program, 476
subroutines, 481, 507-508
terminating a program, 507
text, 504-506
tokens, 473
UseBackground, 531-533
UseBrush, 533-535
UseCaption, 535-536
UseCoordinates, 536-537
UseFont, 479, 537-541
UsePen, 541-542
variables, 472-473, 515-517
virtual keys, 518, 520-523
waiting for input, 528-530
WaitInput, 482-483, 542-543
white space, 474
window caption, 535-536
window size in, 482, 530-531
OS/2, 239
 Presentation Manager, 4
Output port. *See* Ports

P

Page fault, 253
Page frame, 232
PagingDrive= (SYSTEM.INI), 378-379, 434

Paging, 252, 259-260
 changing the paging drive, 434
 preventing, 434
Paging= (SYSTEM.INI), 378, 434
Paradox, 240, 386
Parallel ports, controlling in WIN.INI, 423-424
Partitioning software, 374
 problems with, 391-392, 435
Pasting. *See also* Clipboard
 when not working, 368-369
Pattern, changing in WIN.INI, 420
Pattern= (WIN.INI), 420
PBRUSH.EXE, 39
PBRUSH.HLP, 30
PCL/HP LaserJet= (WIN.INI), 424-425
PCL/HP driver, 119. *See also* HP LaserJet
PCTools, 393, 394
Performance checklist, 386 enhanced mode, 409-410
Performance, improving, 13, 371-410
Permanent swap file, 372, 373-378
 changing the size of, 377
 deleting, 378
 effect in 386 enhanced mode, 253
 setting the size of, 375-376
 setting up, 374-377
Phar Lap, 240
Philip B. Eskelin, Jr., 638
PIF Editor, 18, 317. *See also* PIFs
 changing the mode, 318
 duplicate options between modes, 318
PIFEDIT.EXE, 39
PIFs (Program Information Files), 11, 255, 314
 386 enhanced mode options, 330-337
 advanced 386 enhanced mode PIF options, 19-21, 337-351
 allocating processor time to DOS applications, 336
 Allow Close When Active, 349-351
 Allow Fast Paste, 349
 Application Shortcut Key, 351
 Background, 336-337
 Background Priority, 338-339
 being prompted for optional parameters, 320
 changing the standard settings, 317
 Close Window on Exit, 330
 controlling the pasting rate, 349
 defined, 19-21
 Detect Idle Time, 339-340
 Directly Modifies, 326-328
 Display Options, 346-349
 Display Usage, 335-336
 EMS Memory, 340-342
 EMS Memory: Locked check box, 342
 Emulate Text Mode, 348
 Exclusive, 337
 Execution, 336-337
 Foreground Priority, 339
 giving a DOS application all processor time, 337
 Graphics/Multiple Text button, 323
 how Windows allocates EMS memory, 340-342

Index 659

limiting conventional memory in 386 enhanced mode, 333-335
list of Microsoft-supplied PIFs, 315-316
locking an application in memory, 345
Memory Options, 340-345
Memory Requirements (386 enhanced mode), 332-335
Memory Requirements: KB Desired (386 enhanced mode), 334-335
Memory Requirements: KB Required (386 enhanced mode), 333-334
Memory Requirements: KB Required (standard mode), 324-325
Monitor Ports, 347-348
Multitasking Options, 338-340
naming the program to be executed from, 320
No Screen Exchange, 328-329
Optional Parameters, 320
PIF Editor, 317
predefined, 314-317
Prevent Program Switch, 329
Program Filename, 320
recovering settings, 316-317
Reserve Shortcut Keys, 330, 351
Retain Video Memory, 348-349
running a DOS application in the background, 336-337
running a DOS application within a window, 335-336
settings that reclaim memory, 358-359
specifying command line parameters in, 320
standard and real mode options, 320-330
standard settings in, 317
Start Up Directory, 321-323
Uses High Memory Area, 344-345
Video Memory check boxes, 346
Video Mode, 323-324
Windowed radio button, 335-336
Windows Title, 320
XMS memory (standard mode), 325-326
XMS Memory (386 enhanced mode), 342-344
Platters, 388
Pop-ups. *See* Memory-resident utilities
Ports
communications port, 117-118, 276-279. *See also* COM ports
controlling settings in WIN.INI, 423-424
supported by Windows, 117
PostScript printers
creating a header file for, 130
downloading a header file for, 131
installing an unlisted printer, 131-132
installing, 128-132
selecting a driver for, 128
setting handshake for, 131-132
setting options for, 129
specifying a timeout setting for, 129
Power Tools Software, 637-646
if things go wrong when installing, 642-643
installing a product at a later time, 642
installing, 637-643
SETUP.EXE, 637-643
WinEdit, 637
Preemptive multitasking, 259. *See also* Multitasking
Print Manager, 22, 156-160
cancelling all print jobs, 158
changing the display in, 159-160
controlling messages displayed by, 159
disabling, 160
getting information about print jobs, 157
in causing applications to slow down, 158-159
pausing and resuming printing, 158
removing a print job from, 158
rescheduling print jobs with, 157-158
using to view network print queues, 453-456
viewing the print queue of, 156-157
Printer driver, defined, 21
Printer fonts
defined, 136
installing, 142-148. *See also* HP LaserJet
Printers
activating, 125
assigning to a port, 121-122
changing default printer from an application, 126
device not selected timeout setting (WIN.INI), 419
drivers defined, 116
establishing the default printer, 125, 415-416
installing an unlisted printer driver, 120, 135-136
installing dot-matrix printers, 133-134. *See* Dot-matrix
installing HP LaserJet II, 119-124. *See also* HP LaserJet
installing two printers on the same parallel port, 123
installing, 21-22, 116-136
PostScript, 128-132. *See also* PostScript printers
removing an installed printer, 126-127
setting in WIN.INI, 424-425
specifying a time out setting for, 121, 122
specifying a transmission retry setting, 122
transmission retry timeout setting (WIN.INI), 419
Printing
ANSI characters, 148
device contention with DOS applications, 160
on a network, 23, 450-456
sending a file to the printer, 127
to a file, 122, 127
to a print queue, 23
with Print Manager, 156-160, 415. *See also* Print Manager
PRINTMAN.EXE, 39
PRINTSCREEN
screen dumps from DOS applications, 329
using in copying screens to the Clipboard, 210
when not working, 368
Processor, 80386 "virtual 8086 mode", 5
PROGMAN.EXE, 39
PROGMAN.HLP, 30

PROGMAN.INI, 27
Program files, defining in WIN.INI, 418
Program Information Files. *See* PIFs
Program Manager, 6, 15, 31-65
  arranging group window icons, 56
  changing group window properties, 52
  controlling stacking and tiling order, 55-56
  creating new group windows in, 52
  default group window arrangement, 32-33
  deleting group windows, 53
  group window icons, 32
  group windows 16, 32
  managing group windows in, 51-62
  minimizing on use, 64-65
  moving between group windows, 32
  organizing group windows, 59-62
  setting up icons for network applications, 461
  starting applications, 32
  tiling and stacking group windows in, 54-56
  undoing stacking and tiling of group windows, 55
Programs= (WIN.INI), 418
PROMPT command (DOS), 71
Protected mode, 10, 231, 236
PVC display, 299

Q

QEMM-386, 228, 236, 262-267
  fine-tuning, 266
  in standard mode, 258
  installing, 263-266
  special considerations for Windows, 266-267
Quadram, 232
QuadVGA card, 299
Quarterdeck, 233, 240
Q&A 386, 240

R

RAM disk, 236, 258. *See also* RAMDrive
  assigning temporary swap file to, 379-380
  setting TEMP environment variable to, 406-407
  setting up, 404-406
RAMDrive, 14, 237, 404-406
RAMDRIVE.SYS, 381
Raster fonts, changing manually, 309-310
Rational Systems, 241
Real mode, 231, 236
Real mode (Windows operating mode). *See* Operating modes
.REC files, 169
Recorder, 10, 163-202
  any-application macros, 183-188
  application-specific macros, 183
  assigning a macro to an icon, 197-198
  assigning names to macros, 176
  assigning nonalphanumeric shortcut keys to macros, 174
  assigning shortcut keys to macros, 173-176
  basics, 164
  changing combined macros, 189
  changing the playback speed for a macro, 177-178
  choosing where a macro is played back, 183
  choosing where mouse actions are recorded, 182-182
  choosing which mouse actions are recorded, 180-181
  closing with a macro, 198-200
  combining macros, 188-189
  conflicts with DOS applications, 175-176
  conflicts with Windows applications, 175
  continuous loop macros, 193-195
  correcting mistakes in a macro, 169
  dealing with errors in macros, 177
  deleting macros, 177
  disabling, 191
  incorporating File Manager into macros, 185
  incorporating Task List into macros, 184
  limitations, 163
  loading a macro file on Windows startup, 196-197
  loading applications with, 172-173
  managing macros, 178
  merging macro files, 178
  minimizing on use, 191
  modifying macro properties, 189-191
  nonstop macros for demonstrations, 195
  pausing during recording, 182
  recording a macro that uses menus, 170-171
  recording a text-input macro, 165-168
  recording mouse actions, 179-182
  running a macro, 168
  running a macro on Windows startup, 195-196
  saving macros to disk, 169
  setting defaults for, 191-192
  setting up for recording, 165-166
  shortcut key defined, 164
  starting, 165
  starting an application in specific directory, 192-193
  stopping a macro, 182
  stopping recording, 167
  supplementing with DOS.BAT files, 200-202
RECORDER.EXE, 39
Replace on Open command (File Manager), 88
Reserved I/O memory, defined, 288-289
ReservePageFrame= (SYSTEM.INI), 261, 410, 431-432
Resource-intensive applications, 255
REVERSI.EXE, 39
Rich Text Format (RTF), 208
RLL encoding, 389
ROM BIOS. *See* BIOS
Run command, in starting applications, 65
Run (Oriel), 486, 514-515
Run= (WIN.INI), 414

S

SAA (Systems Application Architecture), 204
Sans serif, 140

Index 661

Screen dumps, from DOS applications, 329
Screen fonts, 136-139
    defined, 136
    installing, 139
    raster, 136, 141
    vector, 136, 141
Screen grabber, 256
SDK (Software Development Kit), 4, 42
SDKPaint, 42, 634
SDL. *See* Windows 3 Supplemental Driver Library (SDL)
Sector ID header, 390
Sectors, 389
    how a hard disk locates, 389-390
Segments
    discardable, 244
    fixed, 244
    in memory management, 243-245
    movable, 244
Selection, extending, 72, 93
Serial ports. *See* COM ports
Serif, 140
Set (Oriel), 472, 515-517
SetKeyboard (Oriel), 485-486, 517-523
SetMenu (Oriel), 483, 523-526
SetMouse (Oriel), 483-485, 526-528
Settings command (Control Panel), 270
Setup, saving on exiting windows, 57-58
Setup program, 26, 116, 297-306, 314-315
    adding applications with, 302-303
    /i switch with, 306, 307
    running from DOS, 303-306
    running within Windows, 297-303
    when system hangs with, 306, 307
SETUP.EXE, 39
SETUP.EXE (Power Tools Software), 637-643
SETUP.INF, 256, 310
    PIF settings stored in, 315-316
    used in networking, 464, 466
SetWaitMode (Oriel), 486, 528-530
SetWindow (Oriel), 482, 530-531
SFLPT1.BAT, 144
Shadow RAM, 398
Sharing data between applications, 25, 203-225. *See also* Clipboard
Shell program, 547
    changing the default, 429
SHELL= (CONFIG.SYS), 387
Shell= (SYSTEM.INI), 85, 429
SHIFT, used in running Recorder macros, 173
SHIFT+DEL, used in cutting data to the Clipboard, 71, 204
SHIFT+F4
    used in stacking File Manager directory windows, 88
    used in stacking group windows in Program Manager, 54
SHIFT+F5
    used in stacking group windows in Program Manager, 54

used in tiling File Manager directory windows, 88
SHIFT+F8, used in selecting files in File Manager, 94
SHIFT+INS, used in pasting data from the Clipboard, 71, 204
SHIFT+PRINTSCREEN, screen dumps from DOS applications, 329
Shortcut keys. *See also* Application shortcut key
    for DOS applications, 11
    assigning in Recorder, 173-176
Shortcuts
    key sequences used in list boxes (Table), 70
    key sequences used in text boxes, 71
Sides (hard disk), 388
Small-frame EMS, defined, 234, 245-248
SMARTDrive, 14, 399-404
    effect in 386 enhanced mode, 253
    how it works, 400-401
    how to set, 401-403
    improving performance of, 403-404
    reducing to make more memory available, 344
Software Development Kit (SDK), 4
Software Driver Library, 135
SOL.EXE, 39
SPACEBAR, used in selecting files in File Manager, 94
SPART.PAR, 373
Special Make Directory Tool command (Aporia), 614
Special Make User Tool command (Aporia), 612
Speedstor, 392
Spinrite II, 398-399
Spooler= (WIN.INI), 415
STACKS= (CONFIG.SYS), 387
Standard mode. *See* Operating modes
Starting applications as icons, load= setting (WIN.INI), 414
Starting applications as windows, run= setting (WIN.INI), 414
Super VGA, 300
Swap file, 11, 12, 253, 372-382
    application, 372. *See also* Application swap file
    permanent, 14, 372. *See also* Permanent swap file
    temporary, 14, 372. *See also* Temporary swap file
Swapdisk= (SYSTEM.INI), 258, 380-381
Swapdisk= (WIN.INI), 258, 419, 430
SWAPFILE.EXE, 39, 373-378
Swapping. *See* Paging
Switching
    between applications, 66-69
    between DOS applications in 386 enhanced mode, 10
    between DOS applications in real mode, 9
    between DOS applications in standard mode, 10
SYMBOLE.FON, 309
SYMBOLF.FON, 309-310
SysEdit, 27, 412
SYSEDIT.EXE, 27, 39

662 Windows 3 Power Tools

System Configuration Editor. *See* SysEdit
System font, changing manually, 308-309
SYSTEM.INI, 27, 411-413, 427-435
    [386Enh] section, 431-435
    AllVMsExclusive=, 431
    [Boot] section, 427-429
    [Boot.description] section, 430
    changing the default shell, 429
    ComxAutoAssign=, 433-434
    device contention settings in, 433-434
    disabling EMS memory support, 433
    display.drv=, 428
    editing, 412
    EMMExclude, 432-433
    EMMInclude, 432-433
    EMMPageFrame=, 433
    EMS page frame position, 432-433
    FileSysChange=, 433
    [Keyboard] section, 430
    LPTxAutoAssign, 433-434
    MinUserDiskSpace=, 434
    NoEMMDriver=, 433
    [NonWindowsApp] section, 430
    organization of, 427
    Paging=, 434
    PagingDrive=, 434
    preventing paging, 434
    shell=, 429
    [Standard] section, 430
    SwapDisk=, 430
    temporary swap file drive, 434
    VirtualHDIrq=, 435
Systems Application Architecture (SAA), 4, 204

T

Task database, 247
Task List
    Arrange Icons button in, 51
    used in closing an application, 68
    in tiling and stacking application windows, 62-64
    used in switching between applications, 67-68
TASKMAN.EXE, 39
TEMP directory, 393
TEMP environment variable, 258, 280, 406-407
Temporary application swap file, 9, 10
Temporary swap file, 372, 378-380
    changing the location of, 378-379
    effect in 386 enhanced mode, 253
    leaving disk space free, 434
    restricting the size of, 379
    using a network drive for, 380
    using a RAM disk for, 379, 381
TERMINAL.EXE, 39
Terminate-and-stay-resident programs. *See* TSRs
Terminating, a DOS application, 353
Text boxes, key sequences used in, 71

TileWallpaper= (WIN.INI), 420-421
Time
    changing, 286
    format, 286
Time slice, 16
    adjusting duration of, 294
TMSRE.FON, 309
TMSRF.FON, 309-310
ToolBook, 469
Tracks, 389
TransmissionRetryTimeout= (WIN.INI), 419
Tree
    Collapse Directory command (File Manager), 86
    Expand All command (File Manager), 86
    Expand Branch command (File Manager), 86
    Expand One Level command (File Manager), 86
TrueType and TrueImage, 156
TSRs, 232. *See also* Memory-resident utilities
Turbo EMS, 235

U

Upper memory blocks (UMBs), 237
Use High Memory Area check box, 239
UseBackground (Oriel), 531-533
UseBrush (Oriel), 478, 533-535
UseCaption (Oriel), 535-536
UseCoordinates (Oriel), 536-537
UseFont (Oriel), 479, 537-541
UsePen (Oriel), 478, 541-542
USER.EXE, 262

V

VCPI. *See* Virtual Control Program Interface
VDISK, 236
Vfeatures Deluxe, 392
VGA display, 299-300, 301-302
    a common error, 363-365
    changing drivers for, 299-300, 303-306
    problem VGA cards, 365
View
    By Name command (File Manager), 88
    By Type command (File Manager), 88
    File Details command (File Manager), 90-91
    Include command (File Manager), 89
    Other command (File Manager), 91-92
    Other Net Queue command (Print Manager), 454
    Selected Net Queue command (Print Manager), 454
    Sort By command (File Manager), 88
    Time/Date Sent command (Print Manager), 160
Virtual 8086 mode, 5, 15, 17, 236, 259. *See also* Virtual machine
Virtual addressing, 259
Virtual Control Program Interface (VCPI), 240-241, 343
Virtual key (Oriel), 518, 520-523
Virtual machine, 15, 17
    DOS environment in, 260

Index 663

Virtual memory, 250, 252, 251-254, 259-260
VirtualHDIrq= (SYSTEM.INI), 392, 435

W

WaitInput (Oriel), 482-483, 542-543
Wallpaper, 282-284
   changing in WIN.INI, 420
   effect on available memory, 282-284
   positioning settings in WIN.INI, 421-422
WallpaperOriginX= (WIN.INI), 421-422
WallpaperOriginY= (WIN.INI), 421-422
Wallpaper= (WIN.INI), 420-421
Wilson WindowWare, 547, 638
WIN386.SWP, 378
Window Arrange Icons command, in arranging group window icons, 56
Window command (Program Manager), 32
Window Control menu
   Paste option, 213
   Switch To option, 67
Window Control menu (DOS application)
   Edit Copy option, 215
   Edit Mark option, 215
   Edit Paste option, 215
   Edit Scroll option, 215
Window Tile command (Program Manager), 54
Windowed display, switching a DOS application to, 352, 335-336
Windows
   Applications group window, 33
   applications, starting from the DOS prompt, 73-74
   Arrange Icons command (Program Manager), 50
   Cascade command (Program Manager), 54
   adjusting width of window borders, 286
   aligning according to a grid, 422
   compatibility with DOS applications, 17-18
   enhancements to Windows applications, 20
   global heap, 242
   history of, 1-7
   improving performance of, 371-410
   memory configurations, 242
   Power Tools Software. *See* Power Tools Software
   real mode, 242
   Setup program. *See* Setup program
   Version 1, 2
   Version 2, 4
   Version 3, 6
   /286, 5
   /386, 5
Windows 3
   features, 7-30
   Software Development Kit (SDK), 469
Windows 3 Supplemental Driver Library (SDL), 303-304
Windows/286, DOS applications in, 254-255
WINDOWS\SYSTEM directory, 121
WinEdit, 637

WINFILE.EXE, 39
WINFILE.INI, 27
WINHELP.EXE, 28, 39
WinInfo (Command Post), 585 *See also* Command Post
WINOA286.MOD, 256
WINOA386.MOD, 256
WINOLDAP.GRB, 256
WINOLDAP.MOD, 256
WinPopup (NWPOPUP.EXE) utility, 453, 460
WINSTART.BAT, 313
WINVER.HLP, 39
WIN.INI, 27, 411-426
   ActiveBorder=, 425-426
   ActiveTitle=, 425-426
   AppWorkspace=, 425-426
   Background=, 425-426
   beep=, 414
   blink rate setting, 417
   BorderWidth=, 416
   border width setting, 416
   ButtonFace=, 425-426
   ButtonShadow=, 425-426
   ButtonText=, 425-426
   color-related settings, 425-426
   [Colors] section, 425-426
   COMx:=, 423-424
   CursorBlinkRate=, 417
   default printer setting, 415-416
   desktop pattern setting, 420
   [Desktop] section, 420-422
   device=, 415-416
   DeviceNotSelectedTimeout=, 419
   [Devices] section, 425
   Documents=, 418-419
   DoubleClickSpeed=, 418
   editing, 412
   EPT:=, 423-424
   [Extensions] section, 422-423
   FILE:=, 423-424
   file association settings, 422-423
   [Fonts] section, 424
   GrayText=, 425-426
   GridGranularity=, 422
   Hilight=, 425-426
   HilightText=, 425-426
   IconSpacing=, 422
   InactiveBorder=, 425-426
   InactiveTitle=, 425-426
   [Intl] section, 423
   KeyboardSpeed=, 416
   load=, 414
   LPTx:=, 423-424
   LPTx.OS2=, 423-424
   Menu=, 425-426
   MenuText=, 425-426
   mouse settings, 417-418
   MouseSpeed=, 417-418
   MouseThreshold1=, 417-418
   MouseThreshold2=, 417-418

NetWarn=, 419-420
network warning message setting, 419-420
nullport=, 415
organization of, 413-414
Pattern=, 420
[Ports] section, 424
[PrinterPorts] section, 424-425
Programs=, 418
run=, 414
Scrollbar=, 425-426
spooler=, 415
starting applications as icons, 414
starting applications as windows, 414
TileWallpaper=, 420-421
TitleText=, 425-426
TransmissionRetryTimeout=, 419
updating [Extensions] section for file associations, 49, 105
using load to open a macro file, 196-197
Wallpaper=, 420-421
wallpaper settings, 420-422
WallpaperOriginX=, 421-422
WallpaperOriginY=, 421-422
warning beep setting, 414
Window=, 425-426
WindowFrame= 425-426
[Windows] section, 414-420
WindowText= 425-426
.WPD (Windows PostScript Description) file, 132, 141
WRITE.EXE, 39

X

XMS (eXtended Memory Specification) memory, 13, 237
  in DOS applications, 342-344
  setting PIFs, 325-326
Xon/Xoff, setting for a serial port, 118, 278.
  See also Ports

Z

ZSoft SoftType, 153-154

Announcing....

The Windows Power Letter

*From Geoffrey T. LeBlond and William B. LeBlond,
authors of* **Windows 3 Power Tools**

During our months of work on *Windows 3 Power Tools,* we accumulated more information about Windows$_{TM}$ than we could possibly fit in a single book. As a result, we've decided to publish *The Windows Power Letter,* a monthly journal for those users who want an ongoing source of fresh ideas for Microsoft Windows.

Each issue of *The Windows Power Letter* contains 16 information-packed pages of in-depth articles that are sure to increase your knowledge of Windows. What's more, there's no advertising, just page after page of practical, useful information.

We've spent countless hours carefully researching every aspect of Windows. Let us save you time by showing you practical solutions to difficult Windows problems. You find all the topics in *The Windows Power Letter* are covered thoroughly in an easy-to-read style.

To get your first 12 issues of *The Windows Power Letter*, just fill out the order form below and send it to: The LeBlond Group, P.O. Box 247, Soquel, CA 95073-0247. Or, you can order direct by calling us at (408) 479-9055. Have your VISA or MasterCard ready.

```
┌─────────────────────────────────────────────────────────────────────────┐
      Yes, send me The Windows Power Letter for only $79.00 per year.
     Name: _____
     Company: _____ Title: _____
     Address: _____
     City: _____ State: _____ Zip: _____
     Country: _____ Phone ( ) _____
          □ Check/Money Order Enclosed  □ VISA  □ MasterCard  □ Bill Me Later
     Name on Card: _____
     Charge Card Acct #: _____ Exp: _____
└─────────────────────────────────────────────────────────────────────────┘
```

California residents add 6.5% sales tax. All international orders must be paid in US funds or by VISA or MasterCard; Canada 1 Yr/$91.00; other international 1 Yr/$115.00.

Announcing....

The Oriel for Windows™ Runtime

From The LeBlond Group, co-authors of Oriel for Windows™

Distribute your Oriel for Windows applications royalty free with the **Oriel for Windows Runtime**. The Runtime lets you combine the Oriel command interpreter and your Oriel script file into a single executable (.EXE) file and name it anything you want. That way, you can freely distribute your application to other users who don't have a copy of Oriel.

The **Oriel for Windows Runtime** is a snap to use and it comes with a 30 day no-risk guarantee. If you're not happy with the Runtime, send it back within 30 days, and we'll refund your money, no questions asked.

To get your copy of the Oriel for Windows Runtime, just fill out the order form below and send it to us at the following address:

The LeBlond Group

P.O. Box 247

Soquel, CA 95073-0247

Or, you can order direct by calling us at (408) 479-9055. Have your VISA or MasterCard ready.

Yes, send me **The Oriel for Windows Runtime** for only $99.00.

Name: _____

Company: _____ Title: _____

Address: _____

City: _____ State: _____ Zip: _____

Country: _____ Phone ( ) _____

☐ Check/Money Order Enclosed ☐ VISA ☐ MasterCard

Name on Card: _____

Charge Card Acct #: _____ Exp: _____

California residents add 6.5% sales tax.

SPECIAL DISCOUNT OFFER FOR APORIA

THE POWERFUL OBJECT-ORIENTED APPLICATION AND FILE MANAGER FOR WINDOWS

NewTools, Inc. is offering a special discount to purchasers of *Windows 3 Power Tools*!

Now that you've given Aporia a try, you will want to become a registered user. Registered users receive a printed, bound manual, a disk containing the latest version of the software, technical support, and are entitled to future upgrades. Aporia is shareware. If you continue to use it, you must purchase a registration.

A discount registration costs only $39.95, more than 20% off the normal registration price of $50. To take advantage of this offer, just fill out and send in this form along with your check, money order, or credit card information. Be sure to send in this page as photocopies will not be accepted for this offer.

YES....please send me _____ copies of Aporia 1.4 at $39.95 each (U.S. funds only) _____

                        Sales Tax: New York Residents add 8 1/4% sales tax _____

                        Postage and Handling Charges: $5 (US, Canada, Mexico) _____
                        $10 (outside North America)
                                                                         TOTAL _____

Name   **Date**

Address

                                                                                  Daytime Phone Number

City   **State**   **Zip**

Payment: Check/Money Order [ ] Visa [ ] Master Card [ ] American Express [ ] .

Card Number: **Card Expiration Date**

Cardholder Signature

Mail To: NewTools, Inc. - POB 3269 Church Street Station, New York, N.Y. 10008-3269
(800) 395-1532

Wilson WindowWare
Money-Saving Discount Coupon
Save about 20% on these Wilson WindowWare products

Name: _____

Address: _____

City: _____ State: _____ Zip _____

Phone: _____ Disk Size Required: ___ 5.25" ___ 3.5"

___ Command Post(s)	@	~~$49.95~~	$40.00	_____
___ WinEdit(s)	@	~~$59.95~~	$48.00	_____
___ WinBatch(s)	@	~~$69.95~~	$56.00	_____
Foreign air shipping (except Canada):			$9.50	_____
			Total:	_____

Please enclose coupon and a check payable to Wilson WindowWare.
Mail to: 2701 California Ave SW, Suite 212, Seattle WA 98116
Original coupon only. No photocopies accepted.
Please allow 2 to 3 weeks for delivery.

50% OFF COUPON!

NEW ICONDRAW ENHANCED VERSION 3.0

REGULAR PRICE $50.00

INCLUDES: 150 PRE-DRAWN ICONS
DRAWING GRID & UNDO FEATURES
BOTH 5.25" & 3.5" DISKS
REGISTRATION CARD-FULL COLOR BOX

NAME _____

ADDRESS _____

CITY _____ STATE ____ ZIP CODE _____

PHONE NO. (____) - _____

VISA ☐
MC ☐   NO. _____ EXP. DATE _____
AMERX ☐

ICONDRAW ENHANCED VERSION 3.0	$25.00
Shipping & Handling Add For Each Item	$3.00
Wash. State Residents Add Sales Tax	8.2%
Total Amount Enclosed	

WinSoft™   18732 142nd Ave NE Woodinville, WA 98072
Phone (206)-485-7329   Fax (206)-485-7488